THE TRUE LIFE OF THE WORLD'S GREATEST SHOWMAN

Creative Texts Publishers products are available at special discounts for bulk purchase for sale promotions, premiums, fund-raising, and educational needs. For details, write Creative Texts Publishers, PO Box 50, Barto, PA 19504, or visit www.creativetexts.com

THE TRUE LIFE OF THE WORLD'S GREATEST SHOWMAN
by PT Barnum
Published by Creative Texts Publishers
PO Box 50
Barto, PA 19504
www.creativetexts.com

The following is a work of fiction. Any resemblance to actual names, persons, businesses, and incidents is strictly coincidental. Locations are used only in the general sense and do not represent the real place in actuality.

ISBN: 9780692101742

THE TRUE LIFE OF THE WORLD'S GREATEST SHOWMAN

Previously published as *"The Life of PT Barnum"*

by

PT BARNUM

Creative Texts Publishers, LLC

Barto, Pa

The noblest art
Is that of making others happy.

—P. T. Barnum.

PREFACE TO THE 1888 EDITION.

Written originally in 1869, this book is my recollections of more than fifty busy years. Few men in civil life have had a career more crowded with incident, enterprise, and various intercourse with the world than mine. With the alternations of success and defeat, extensive travel in this and foreign lands; a large acquaintance with the humble and honored; having held the preeminent place among all who have sought to furnish healthful entertainment to the American people, and, therefore, having had opportunities for garnering an ample storehouse of incident and anecdote, while, at the same time, needing a sagacity, energy, foresight and fortitude rarely required or exhibited in financial affairs, my struggles and experiences (it is not altogether vanity in me to think) cannot be without interest to my fellow-countrymen.

Various leading publishers have solicited me to place at their disposal my recollections of what I have been, and seen, and done. These proposals, together with the partiality of friends and kindred, have constrained me to put in a permanent form what, it seems to me, may be instructive, entertaining and profitable.

Thirty years since, for the purpose, principally, of advancing my interests as proprietor of the American Museum, I gave to the press some personal reminiscences and sketches. They were, however, very hastily, and therefore imperfectly, prepared. Though including, necessarily, in common with them, some of the facts of my early life, in order to make this autobiography a complete and continuous narrative, yet, as the latter part of my life has been the more eventful, and my recollections so various and abundant, this book is new and independent of the former. It is the matured and leisurely reviewing of more than half a century of work and struggle, and final success, in spite of fraud and fire — the story of which is blended with amusing anecdotes, funny passages, felicitous jokes, captivating narratives, novel experiences, and remarkable interviews — the sunny and somber so intermingled as not only to entertain but convey useful lessons to all classes of readers.

And above and beyond this personal satisfaction, I have thought that the review of a life, with the wide contrasts of humble origin and high and honorable success; of most formidable obstacles overcome by courage and constancy; of affluence that had been patiently won, suddenly wrenched away, and triumphantly regained — would be a help and incentive to the young man, struggling, it may be, with adverse fortune, or, at the start, looking into the future with doubt or despair.

All autobiographies are necessarily egotistical. If my pages are as plentifully sprinkled with "I's," as was the chief ornament of Hood's peacock, "who thought he had the eyes of Europe on his tail," I can only say, that the "I's " are essential to the story I have told. It has been my purpose to narrate, not the life of another, but that career in which I was the principal actor.

There is an almost universal, and not unworthy curiosity to learn the methods and measures, the ups and downs, the strifes and victories, the mental and moral *personnel* of those who have taken an active and prominent part in human affairs. But an autobiography has attractions and merits superior to those of a "life" written by another, who, however intimate with its subject, cannot know all that helps to give interest and accuracy to the narrative, or completeness to the character. The story from the actor's own lips has always a charm it can never have when told by another.

That my narrative is interspersed with amusing incidents, and even the recital of some very practical jokes, is simply because my natural disposition impels me to look upon the brighter side of life, and I hope my humorous experiences will entertain my readers as much as they were enjoyed by myself. And if this record of trials and triumphs, struggles and successes, shall stimulate any to the exercise of that integrity, energy, industry, and courage in their callings, which will surely lead to happiness and prosperity, one main object I have in yielding to the solicitations of my friends and my publishers will have been accomplished.

P. T. BARNUM
Waldemere, Bridgeport, Conn., 1888

CONTENTS

LIST OF ILLUSTRATIONS.

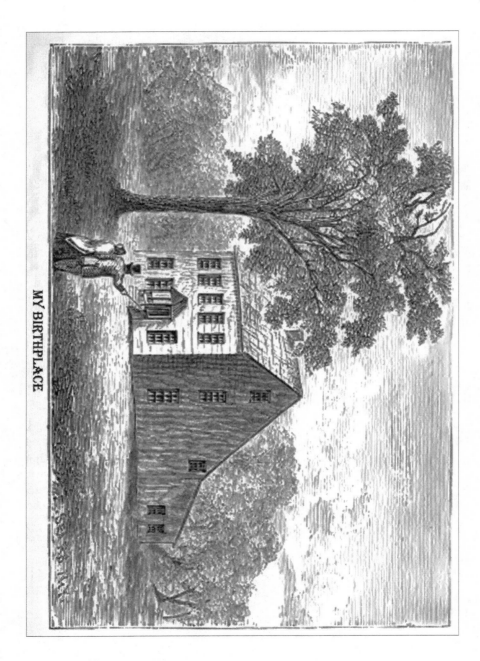

MY BIRTHPLACE

CHAPTER I.

EARLY LIFE.

I was born in the town of Bethel, in the State of Connecticut, July 5, 1810. My name, Phineas Taylor, is derived from my maternal grandfather, who was a great wag in his way, and who, as I was his first grandchild, handed over to his daughter Irena, my mother, at my christening, a gift-deed, in my behalf, of five acres of land, called "Ivy Island," situated in that part of the parish of Bethel known as the "Plum Trees."

My father, Philo Barnum, was the son of Ephraim Barnum, of Bethel, who was a captain in the revolutionary war. My father was a tailor, a farmer, and sometimes a tavern-keeper, and my advantages and disadvantages were such as fall to the general run of farmers' boys. I drove cows to and from the pasture, shelled corn, weeded the garden; as I grew larger I rode horse for ploughing, turned and raked hay; in due time I handled the shovel and the hoe, and when I could do so I went to school.

I was six years old when I began to go to school, and the first date I remember inscribing upon my writing-book was 1818. The ferule, in those days, was the assistant school-master. I was a willing, and, I think, a pretty apt scholar. In arithmetic I was unusually ready and accurate, and I remember, at the age of ten years, being called out of bed one night by my teacher, who had wagered with a neighbor that I could calculate the correct number of feet in a load of wood in five minutes. The dimensions given, I figured out the result in less than two minutes, to the great delight of my teacher and to the equal astonishment of his neighbor.

My organ of "acquisitiveness" was manifest at an early age. Before I was five years of age I began to accumulate pennies and "four-pence," and when I was six years old my capital amounted to a sum sufficient to exchange for a silver dollar, the possession of which made me feel far richer than I have ever since felt in the world.

Nor did my dollar long remain alone. As I grew older I earned ten cents a day for riding the horse which led the ox-team in ploughing, and on holidays and "training days," instead of spending money, I earned it. I was a small peddler of molasses candy (of home make), ginger-bread, cookies and cherry rum, and I generally found myself a dollar or two richer at the end of a holiday than I was at the beginning. By the time I was twelve years old, besides other property, I was the owner of a sheep and a calf, and should soon, no doubt, have become a small Croesus, had not my father kindly permitted me to purchase my own clothing, which somewhat reduced my little store.

When I was nearly twelve years old I made my first visit to the metropolis. It happened in this wise: Late one afternoon in January, 1822, Mr. Daniel Brown, of Southbury, Connecticut, arrived at my father's tavern, in Bethel with some fat cattle he was driving to New York to sell, and put up for the night. After supper hearing Mr. Brown say to my father that he intended to buy more cattle, and that he would be glad to hire a boy to assist in driving them, I immediately besought my father to secure the situation for me, and he did so. My mother's consent was gained, and at daylight next morning, I started on foot in the midst of a heavy snow storm to help drive the cattle. Before reaching Ridgefield, I was sent on horseback after a stray ox, and, in galloping, the horse fell and my ankle was sprained. I suffered severely but did not complain lest my employer should send me back. We arrived at New York, in three or four days, and put up at the Bull's Head Tavern, where we were to stay a week while the drover disposed of his cattle. It was an eventful week for me. Before I left home my mother had given me a dollar which I supposed would supply every want that heart could wish.

My first outlay was for oranges which I was told were four pence apiece, and as "four pence" in Connecticut was six cents, I offered ten cents for two oranges, which was of course readily taken; and thus, instead of saving two cents, as I thought, I actually paid two cents more than the price demanded. I then bought two more oranges, reducing my capital to eighty cents. Thirty-one cents was the "charge" for a small gun which would "go off" and send a stick some little distance, and this gun I bought. Amusing myself with this toy in the bar-room of the Bull's Head, the arrow happened to hit the bar-keeper, who forthwith came from behind the counter and shook me, and soundly boxed my ears, telling me to put that gun out of the way or he would put it into the fire. I sneaked to my room, put my treasure under the pillow, and went out for another visit to the toy shop.

There I invested six cents in "torpedoes," with which I intended to astonish my schoolmates in Bethel. I could not refrain, however, from experimenting upon the guests of the hotel, which I did when they were going in to dinner. I threw two of the torpedoes against the wall of the hall through which the guests were passing, and the immediate results were as follows: two loud reports, — astonished guests, — irate landlord, — discovery of the culprit, and summary punishment — for the landlord immediately floored me with a single blow with his open hand, and said:

"There, you little greenhorn, see if that will teach you better than to explode your infernal fire-crackers in my house again."

The lesson was sufficient if not entirely satisfactory. I deposited the balance of the torpedoes with my gun, and as a solace for my wounded feelings I again visited the toy shop, where I bought a watch, breastpin and top, leaving but eleven cents of my original dollar.

The following morning found me again at the fascinating toy shop, where I saw a beautiful knife with two blades, a gimlet, and a corkscrew, — a whole carpenter shop in miniature, and all for thirty-one cents. But, alas! I had only eleven cents. Have that knife I must, however, and so I proposed to the shop-woman to take back the top and breastpin at a slight deduction, and with my eleven cents to let me have the knife. The kind creature consented, and this makes memorable my first "swap." Some fine and nearly white molasses candy then caught my eye, and I proposed to trade the watch for its equivalent in candy. The transaction was made and the candy was so delicious that before night my gun was absorbed in the same way. The next morning the torpedoes "went off " in the same direction, and before night even my beloved knife was similarly exchanged. My money and my goods all gone, I traded two pocket handkerchiefs and an extra pair of stockings I was sure I should not want for nine more rolls of molasses candy, and then wandered about the city disconsolate, sighing because there was no more molasses candy to conquer.

I doubt not that in these first wanderings about the city I often passed the corner of Broadway and Ann street — never dreaming of the stir I was destined at a future day to make in that locality as proprietor and manager of the American Museum.

After wandering, gazing and wondering for a week, Mr. Brown took me in his sleigh and on the evening of the following day we arrived in Bethel. I had a thousand questions to answer, and for a long time I was quite a lion among my mates because I had seen the great metropolis. My brothers and sisters, however, were much disappointed at my not bringing them something from my dollar, and when my mother examined my wardrobe and found two pocket handkerchiefs and one pair of stockings missing she whipped me and sent me to bed. Thus, ingloriously terminated my first visit to New York.

Previous to my visit to New York, I think it was in 1820, when I was ten years of age, I made my first expedition to my landed property, "Ivy Island." From the time when I was four years old I was continually hearing of this "property." My grandfather always spoke of me (in my presence) to the neighbors and to strangers as the richest child in town, since I owned the whole of "Ivy Island," one of the most valuable farms in the State. My father and mother frequently reminded me of my wealth and hoped I would do something for the family when I attained my majority. The neighbors professed to fear that I might refuse to play with their children because I had inherited so large a property.

These constant allusions, for several years, to "Ivy Island" excited at once my pride and my curiosity and stimulated me to implore my father's permission to visit my property. At last, he promised I should do so in a few days, as we should be getting some hay near "Ivy Island." The wished-for day arrived and my father told me that as we were to mow an adjoining meadow, I might visit my property in company with the hired man during the "nooning." My grandfather reminded me that it was to his bounty I was indebted for this wealth, and that had not my name been Phineas I might never have been proprietor of "Ivy Island." To this my mother added:

"Now, Taylor, don't become so excited when you see your property as to let your joy make you sick, for remember, rich as you are, that it will be eleven years before you can come into possession of your fortune."

She added much more good advice, to all of which I promised to be calm and reasonable and not to allow my pride to prevent me from speaking to my brothers and sisters when I returned home.

When we arrived at the meadow, which was in that part of the "Plum Trees" known as "East Swamp," I asked my father where "Ivy Island " was. "Yonder, at the north end of this meadow, where you see those beautiful trees rising in the distance."

All the forenoon I turned grass as fast as two men could cut it, and after a hasty repast at noon, one of our hired men, a good-natured Irishman, named Edmund, took an axe on his shoulder and announced that he was ready to accompany me to "Ivy Island." We started, and as we approached the north end of the meadow we found the ground swampy and wet and were soon obliged to leap from bog to bog on our route. A misstep brought me up to my middle in water, and to add to the dilemma a swarm of hornets attacked me. Attaining the altitude of another bog I was cheered by the assurance that there was only a quarter of a mile of this kind of travel to the edge of my property. I waded on. In about fifteen minutes more, after floundering through the morass, I found myself half-drowned, hornet-stung, mud-covered, and out of breath, on comparatively dry land.

"Never mind, my boy," said Edmund, "we have only to cross this little creek, and ye'll be upon your own valuable property."

We were on the margin of a stream, the banks of which were thickly covered with alders. I now discovered the use of Edmund's axe, for he felled a small oak to form a temporary bridge to my "Island" property. Crossing over, I proceeded to the center of my domain. I saw nothing but a few stunted ivies and straggling trees. The truth flashed upon me. I had been the laughing-stock of the family and neighborhood for years. My valuable "Ivy Island" was an almost inaccessible, worthless bit of barren land, and while I stood deploring my sudden downfall, huge black snake (one of my tenants) approached me with upraised head. I gave one shriek and rushed for the bridge. This was my first and last visit to "Ivy Island." My father asked me "how I liked my property?" and I responded that I would sell it pretty cheap.

As I grew older my settled aversion to manual labor, farm or other kind, was manifest in various ways, which were set down to the general score of laziness. In despair of doing better with me, my father concluded to make a merchant of me. He erected a building in Bethel, and with Mr. Hiram Weed as a partner, purchased a stock of dry goods, hardware, groceries, and general notions and installed me as clerk in this country store.

We kept a cash, credit and barter store, and I drove sharp bargains with women who brought butter, eggs, beeswax and feathers to exchange for dry goods, and with men who wanted to trade oats, corn, buckwheat, axe-helves, hats, and other commodities for tenpenny nails, molasses, or New England rum. It was a drawback upon my dignity that I was obliged to take down the shutters, sweep the store, and make the fire. I received a small salary for my services and the perquisites of what profit I could derive from purchasing candies on my own account to sell to our younger customers, and, as usual, my father stipulated that I should clothe myself.

There is a great deal to be learned in a country store, and principally this—that sharp trades, tricks, dishonesty and deception are by no means confined to the city. More than once, in cutting open bundles of rags, brought to be exchanged for goods, and warranted to be all linen and cotton, I have discovered in the interior worthless woolen trash and sometimes stones, gravel or ashes. Sometimes, too, when measuring loads of oats, corn or rye, declared to contain a specified number of bushels, say sixty, I have found them four or five bushels short. In the evenings and on wet days trade was always dull and at such times the story-telling and joke-playing wits and wags of the village used to assemble in our store, and from them I derived considerable amusement, if not profit. After the store was closed at night, I frequently joined some of the village boys at the houses of their parents, where, with story-telling and play, a couple of hours would soon pass by, and then as late, perhaps, as eleven o'clock, I went home and slyly crept up stairs so as not to awaken my brother with whom I slept, and who would be sure to report my late hours. He made every attempt and laid all sorts of plans to catch me on my return, but as sleep always overtook him, I managed easily to elude his efforts.

Like most people in Connecticut in those days, I was brought up to attend church regularly on Sunday, and long before I could read I was a prominent scholar in the Sunday school. My good mother taught me my lessons in the New Testament and the Catechism, and my every effort was directed to win one of those "Rewards of Merit," which promised to pay the bearer one mill, so that ten of these prizes amounted to one cent, and one hundred of them, which might be won by faithful assiduity every Sunday for two years, would buy a Sunday school book worth ten cents. Such were the magnificent rewards held out to the religious ambition of youth in those days.

There was but one church or "meeting-house" in Bethel, which all attended, sinking all differences of creed in the Presbyterian faith. The old meeting-house had neither steeple nor bell and was a plain edifice, comfortable enough in summer, but my teeth chatter even now when I think of the dreary, cold, freezing hours we passed in that place in winter. A stove in a meeting-house in those days would have been a sacrilegious innovation. The sermons were from an hour and one-half to two hours long, and through these the congregation would sit and shiver till they really merited the title the profane gave them of "blue skins." Some of the women carried a "foot-stove" consisting of a small square tin box in a wooden frame, the sides perforated, and in the interior, there was a small square iron dish, which contained a few five coals covered with ashes. These stoves were usually replenished just before meeting time at some neighbors near the meeting-house.

After many years of shivering and suffering, one of the brethren had the temerity to propose that the church should be warmed with a stove. His impious proposition was voted down by an overwhelming majority. Another year came around, and in November the stove question was again brought up. The excitement was immense. The subject was discussed in the village stores and in the juvenile debating club; it was prayed over in conference; and finally, in a general "society's meeting," in December, the stove was carried by a majority of one and was introduced into the meeting-house. On the first Sunday thereafter, two ancient maiden ladies were so oppressed by the dry and heated atmosphere occasioned by the wicked innovation, that they fainted away and were carried out into the cool air where they speedily returned to consciousness, especially when they were informed that owing to the lack of two lengths of pipe, no fire bad yet been made in the stove. The next Sunday was a bitter cold day, and the stove, filled with well-seasoned hickory, was a great gratification to the many, and displeased only a few.

During the Rev. Mr. Lowe's ministrations at Bethel, he formed a Bible class, of which I was a member. We used to draw promiscuously from a hat a text of scripture and write a composition on the text, which compositions were read after service in the afternoon, to such of the congregation as remained to hear the exercises of the class. Once, I remember, I drew the text, Luke 10:42: *"But one thing is needful; and Mary hath chosen that good part which shall not be taken away from her."* Question, "What is the one thing needful?" My answer was nearly as follows:

"This question 'what is the one thing needful? ' is capable of receiving various answers, depending much upon the persons to whom it is addressed. The merchant might answer that 'the one thing needful is plenty of customers, who buy liberally, without beating down and pay cash for all their purchases.' The farmer might reply, that 'the one thing needful is large harvests and high prices.' The physician might answer that 'it is plenty of patients.' The lawyer might be of opinion that 'it is an unruly community, always engaging in bickerings and litigations.' The clergyman might reply, 'It is a fat salary with multitudes of sinners seeking salvation and paying large pew rents.' The bachelor might exclaim, 'It is a pretty wife who loves her husband, and who knows how to sew on buttons.' The maiden might answer, 'It is a good husband, who will lore, cherish and protect me while life shall last.' But the most proper answer, and doubtless that which applied to the case of Mary, would be, 'The one thing needful is to believe on the Lord Jesus Christ, follow in his footsteps, love God and obey His commandments, love our fellow-man, and embrace every opportunity of administering to his necessities. In short, 'the one thing needful' is to live a life that we can always look back upon with satisfaction and be enabled ever to contemplate its termination with trust in Him who has so kindly vouchsafed it to us, surrounding us with innumerable blessings, if we have but the heart and wisdom to receive them in a proper manner."

The reading of a portion of this answer occasioned some amusement in the congregation, in which the clergyman himself joined, and the name of "Taylor Barnum" was whispered in connection with the composition; but at the close of the reading I had the satisfaction of hearing Mr. Lowe say that it was a well-written answer to the question, "What is the one thing needful?"

P. T. BARNUM'S MOTHER, IRENA,
AT THE AGE OF 78.

CHAPTER II.

INCIDENTS AND ANECDOTES.

In the month of August, 1825, my maternal grandmother met with an accident in stepping on the point of a rusty nail, and, though the incident was at first considered trivial, it resulted in her death. Alarming symptoms soon made her sensible that she was on her death-bed; and while she was in full possession of her faculties, the day before she died she sent for her grandchildren to take final leave of them. I shall never forget the sensations I experienced when she took me by the hand and besought me to lead a religious life, and especially to remember that I could in no way so effectually prove my love to God as by loving all my fellow-beings. The impressions of that death-bed scene have ever been among my most vivid recollections, and I trust they have proved in some degree salutary.

My father, for his time and locality, was a man of much enterprise. He could, and actually did, "keep a hotel;" he had a livery stable and ran, in a small way, what in our day would be called a Norwalk Express; and he also kept a country store. With greater opportunities and a larger field for his efforts and energies, he might have been a man of mark and means. Not that he was successful, for he never did a profitable business; but I, who saw him in his various pursuits, and acted as his clerk, caught something of his enterprising spirit, and, perhaps without egotism, I may say I inherited that characteristic. My business education was as good as the limited field afforded, and I soon put it to account and service.

On the 7th of September, 1825, my father, who had been sick since the month of March, died at the age of forty-eight years. My mother was left with five children, of whom I, at fifteen years of age, was the eldest, while the youngest was but seven. It was soon apparent that my father had provided nothing for the support of his family; his estate was insolvent and did not pay fifty cents on the dollar. My mother, by economy, industry, and perseverance, succeeded in a few years afterwards in redeeming the homestead and becoming its sole possessor; but, at the date of the death of my father, the world looked gloomy indeed; the few dollars I had accumulated and loaned to my father, holding his note therefore, were decided to be the property of a minor, belonging to the father and so to the estate, and my small claim was ruled out. I was obliged to get trusted for the pair of shoes I wore to my father's funeral I literally began the world with nothing and was barefooted at that.

I went to Grassy Plain, a mile northwest of Bethel, and secured a situation as clerk in the store of James S. Keeler & Lewis Whitlock at six dollars a month and my board. I lived with Mrs. Jerusha Wheeler and her daughters, Jerusha and Mary, and found an excellent home. I chose my uncle, Alanson Taylor, as my guardian. I soon gained the confidence and esteem of my employers; they afforded me many faculties for making money on my own account, and I soon entered upon sundry speculations and succeeded in getting a small sum of money ahead.

I made a very remarkable trade at one time for my employers by purchasing, in their absence, a whole wagon-load of green glass bottles of various sizes, for which I paid in unsalable goods at very profitable prices. How to dispose of the bottles was then the problem, and as it was also desirable to get rid of a large quantity of tin-ware which had been in the shop for years and was considerably 'shop-worn,' I conceived the idea of a lottery in which the highest prize should be twenty-five dollars, payable in any goods the winner desired, while there were to be fifty prizes of five dollars each, payable in goods, to be designated in the scheme. Then there were one hundred prizes of one dollar each, one hundred prizes of fifty cents each, and three hundred prizes of twenty-five cents each. It is unnecessary to state that the minor prizes consisted mainly of glass and tin-ware; the tickets sold like wildfire, and the worn tin and glass bottles were speedily turned into cash.

As my mother continued to keep the village tavern at Bethel, I usually went home on Saturday night and stayed till Monday morning, going to church with my mother on Sunday. This habit was the occasion of an adventure of momentous consequence to me. One Saturday evening, during a violent thunder shower, Miss Mary Wheeler, a milliner, sent me word that there was a girl from Bethel at her house, who had come up on horseback to get a new bonnet; that she was afraid to go back alone; and if I was going to Bethel that evening she wished me to escort her customer. I assented and went over to "Aunt Rushia's" where I was introduced to "Chairy" (Charity) Hallett, a fair, rosy-cheeked, buxom girl, with beautiful white teeth. I assisted her to her saddle, and, mounting my own horse, we trotted towards Bethel.

My first impressions of this girl as I saw her at the house were exceedingly favorable. As soon as we started I began a conversation with her, and, finding her very affable, I regretted that the distance to Bethel was not five miles instead of one. A flash of lightning gave me a distinct view of the face of my fair companion, and then I wished the distance was twenty miles. During our ride I learned that she was a tailoress, working with Mr. Zerah Benedict, of Bethel. The next day I saw her at church, and, indeed, many Sundays afterwards, but I had no opportunity to renew the acquaintance that season.

Mrs. Jerusha Wheeler, with whom I boarded, and her daughter Jerusha were familiarly known, the one as "Aunt Rushia," and the other as "Rushia," Many of our store customers were hatters, and among the many kinds of furs we sold for the nap of hats was one known to the trade as "Russia," One day a hatter, Walter Dibble, called to buy some furs. I sold him several kinds, including "beaver" and "cony," and he then asked for some "Russia." We had none, and, as I wanted to play a joke upon him, I told him that Mrs. Wheeler had several hundred pounds of "Rushia."

"What on earth is a woman doing with 'Russia?'" said he.

I could not answer, but I assured him that there were one hundred and thirty pounds of old Rushia and one hundred and fifty pounds of young Rushia in Mrs. Wheeler's house, and under her charge, but whether or not it was for sale I could not say. Off he started to make the purchase and knocked at the door. Mrs. Wheeler, the elder, made her appearance.

"I want to get your Russia," said the hatter.

Mrs. Wheeler asked him to walk in and be seated. She, of course, supposed that he had come for her daughter "Rushia."

"What do you want of Rushia?" asked the old lady.

"To make hats," was the reply.

"To trim hats, I suppose you mean."' responded Mi's. Wheeler.

"No, for the outside of hats," replied the hatter.

"Well, I don't know much about hats," said the old lady, "but I will call my daughter."

Passing into another room where "Rushia" the younger was at work, she informed her that a man wanted her to make hats.

"Oh, he means sister Mary, probably. I suppose he wants some ladies hats." replied Rushia, as she went into the parlor.

"This is my daughter," said the old lady.

"I want to get your Russia," said he, addressing the young lady.

"I suppose you wish to see my sister Mary; she is our milliner," said young Russia.

"I wish to see whoever owns the property," said the hatter.

Sister Mary was sent for, and, as she was introduced, the hatter informed her that he wished to buy her "Russia."

"Buy Rushia! " exclaimed Mary in surprise; "I don't understand you."

"Your name is Miss Wheeler, I believe," said the hatter, who was annoyed by the difficulty he met with in being understood.

"It is, sir."

"Ah: very well. Is there old and young Russia in the house?"

"I believe there is," said Mary, surprised at the familiar manner in which he spoke of her mother and sister, who were present.

"What is the price of old Russia per pound?" asked the hatter.

"I believe, sir, that old Rushia is not for sale," replied Mary indignantly.

"Well, what do you ask for young Russia?" pursued the hatter.

"Sir," said Miss Rushia the younger, springing to her feet, "do you come here to insult defenseless females? If you do, sir, our brother, who is in the garden, will punish you as you deserve."

"Ladies!" exclaimed the hatter, in astonishment, "what on earth have I done to offend you? I came here on a business matter. I want to buy some Russia I was told you had old and young Russia in the house. Indeed, this young lad just stated such to be the fact, but she says the old Russia is not for sale. Now if I can buy the young Russia I want to do so — but if that can't be done, please just say so and I will trouble you no further."

"Mother, open the door and let this man go out, he is undoubtedly crazy." said Miss Mary.

"By thunder! I believe I shall be if I remain here long," exclaimed the hatter considerably excited. "I wonder if folks never do business in these parts, that you think a man is crazy if he attempts such a thing?"

"Business! poor man!" said Mary soothingly, approaching the door.

"I am not a poor man, madam," replied the hatter. "My name is Walter Dibble; I carry on hatting extensively in Danbury; I came to Grassy Plain to buy fur and have purchased some 'beaver' and 'cony,' and now it seems I am to be called 'crazy ' and a 'poor man,' because I want to buy a little 'Russia' to make up my assortment."

The ladies began to open their eyes; they saw that Mr. Dibble was quite in earnest, and his explanation threw considerable light upon the subject.

"Who sent you here?" asked sister Maty.

"The clerk at the opposite store," was the reply.

"He is a wicked young fellow for making all this trouble," said the old lady "he has been doing this for a joke."

"A joke!" exclaimed Dibble, in surprise. "Have you no Russia, then?"

"My name is Jerusha, and so is my daughter's," said Mrs. Wheeler, "and that, I suppose, is what he meant by telling you about old and young Russia."

Mr. Dibble bolted through the door without another word and made directly for our store. "You young scamp! " said he, as he entered; "what did you mean by sending me over there to buy Russia? "

"I did not send you to *buy* Rushia; I supposed you were either a bachelor or widower and wanted to *marry* Rushia," I replied, with a serious countenance.

"You lie, you young dog, and you know it; but never mind, I'll pay you off some day;" and taking his furs, he departed with less ill-humor than could have been expected under the circumstances.

Among our customers were three or four old Revolutionary pensioners, who traded out the amounts of their pensions before they were due, leaving their papers as security. One of these pensioners was old Bevans, commonly known as "Uncle Bibbins," a man who loved his glass and was very prone to relate romantic Revolutionary anecdotes and adventures, in which he, of course, was conspicuous. At one time he was in our debt, and though we held his pension papers, it would be three months before the money could be drawn. It was desirable to get him away for that length of time, and we hinted to him that it would be pleasant to make a visit to Guilford, where he had relations, but he would not go. Finally, I hit upon a plan which "moved" him.

A journeyman hatter, named Benton, who was fond of a practical joke, was let into the secret, and was persuaded to call "Uncle Bibbins" a coward, to tell him that he had been wounded in the back, and thus to provoke a duel, which he did, and at my suggestion "Uncle Bibbins" challenged Benton to fight him with musket and ball at a distance of twenty yards. The challenge was accepted, I was chosen second by "Uncle Bibbins," and the duel was to come off immediately. My principal, taking me aside, begged me to put nothing in the guns but blank cartridges. I assured him it should be so, and therefore that he might feel perfectly safe.

The ground was measured in the lot at the rear of our store, and the principals and seconds took their places. At the word given both parties fired. "Uncle Bibbins" of course, escaped unhurt, but Benton leaped several feet into the air, and fell upon the ground with a dreadful yell, as if he had been really shot. "Uncle Bibbins" was frightened. I ran to him, told him I had neglected to extract the bullet from his gun (which was literally true, as there was no bullet in it to extract), and he supposed, of course, he had killed his adversary. I then whispered to him to go immediately to Guilford, to keep quiet, and he should hear from me as soon as it would be safe to do so. He started up the street on a run, and immediately quit the town for Guilford, where he kept himself quiet until it was time for him to return and sign his papers. I then wrote him that "he could return in safety; that his adversary had recovered from his wound, and now forgave him all, as he felt himself much to blame for having insulted a man of his known courage."

"Uncle Bibbins" returned, signed the papers, and we obtained the pension money. A few days thereafter he met Benton.

"My brave old friend," said Benton, "I forgive you my terrible wound and long confinement on the brink of the grave, and I beg you to forgive me also. I insulted you without a cause."

"I forgive you freely," said "Uncle Bibbins;" "but," he added, "you must be careful next time how you insult a dead shot."

CHAPTER III.

IN BUSINESS FOR MYSELF.

Mr. Oliver Taylor removed from Danbury to Brooklyn, Long Island, where he kept a grocery store and also had a large comb factory and a comb store in New York. In the fall of 1826, he offered me a situation as clerk in his Brooklyn store, which I accepted, and before long was entrusted with the purchasing of all goods for his store. I bought cash entirely, going into the lower part of New York city in search of the cheapest market for groceries, often attending auctions of teas, sugars, molasses, etc., watching the sales, noting prices and buyers, and frequently combining with other grocers to bid off large lots, which we subsequently divided, giving each of us the quantity wanted at a lower rate than if the goods had passed into other hands, compelling us to pay another profit. Well treated as I was by my employer, who manifested great interest in me, still I was dissatisfied. A salary was not sufficient for me. My disposition was of that speculative character which refused to be satisfied unless I was engaged in some business where my profits might be enhanced, or, at least, made to depend upon my energy, perseverance, attention to business, tact, and "calculation."

In the following summer, 1827, I was taken down with the small-pox and was confined to the house for several months. This sickness made a sad inroad upon my means. When I was sufficiently recovered, I went home to replenish.

During my convalescence at my mother's house, I visited my old friends and neighbors and had the opportunity to renew my acquaintance with the attractive tailoress, "Chairy" Hallett. A month afterwards, I returned to Brooklyn, where I gave Mr. Taylor notice of my desire to leave his employment; and I then opened a porter-house on my own account. In a few months I sold out to good advantage and accepted a favorable offer to engage as clerk in a similar establishment, kept by Mr. David Thorp, 29 Peck Slip, New York. It was a great resort for Danbury and Bethel comb makers and hatters, and I thus had frequent opportunities of seeing and hearing from my fellow-townsmen. I lived with Mr. Thorp's family and was kindly treated. I was often permitted to visit the theater with friends who came to New York, and, as I had considerable taste for the drama, I soon became, in my own opinion, a discriminating critic — nor did I fail to exhibit my powers to my Connecticut friends who accompanied me to the play.

Let me gratefully add that my habits were not bad. Though I sold liquors to others, I do not think I ever drank a pint of liquor, wine, or cordials before I was twenty-two years of age. I always had a Bible, which I frequently read, and I attended church regularly. These habits, so far as they go, are in the right direction, and I am thankful today that they characterized my early youth. However worthy or unworthy may have been my later years, I know that I owe much of the better part of my nature to my youthful regard for Sunday and its institutions — a regard, I trust. still strong in my character.

In February, 1828, I returned to Bethel and opened a retail fruit and confectionery store in a part of my grandfather's carriage-house, which was situated on the main street, and which was offered to me rent free if I would return to my native village and establish some sort of business. This beginning of business on my own account was an eventful era in my life. My total capital was one hundred and twenty dollars, fifty of which I had expended in fitting up the store, and the remaining seventy dollars purchased my stock in trade. I had arranged with fruit dealers whom I knew in New York, to receive my orders, and I decided to open my establishment on the first Monday in May — our "general training" day.

It was a "red letter" day for me. The village was crowded with people from the surrounding region and the novelty of my little shop attracted attention. Long before noon I was obliged to call in one of my old schoolmates to assist in waiting upon my numerous customers and when I closed at night I had the satisfaction of reckoning up sixty-three dollars as my day's receipts. Nor, although I had received the entire cost of my goods, less seven dollars, did the stock seem seriously diminished; showing that my profits had been large. I need not say how much gratified I was with the result of this first day's experiment. The store was a fixed fact. I went to New York and expended all my money in a stock of fancy goods, such as pocket-books, combs, beads, rings, pocket-knives, and a few toys. These, with fruit, nuts, etc., made the business good through the summer, and in the fall, I added stewed oysters to the inducements.

My grandfather, who was much interested in my success, advised me to take an agency for the sale of lottery tickets, on commission. In those days, the lottery was not deemed objectionable on the score of morality. Very worthy people invested in such schemes without a thought of evil and then, as now, churches even got up lotteries, with this difference— that then they were called lotteries, and now they go under some other name. While I am very glad that an improved public sentiment denounces the lottery in general as an illegitimate means of getting money, and while I do not see how anyone, especially in or near a New England State, can engage in a lottery without feeling a reproach which no pecuniary return can compensate, yet I cannot now accuse myself for having been lured into a business which was then sanctioned by good Christian people, who now join with me in reprobating enterprises they once encouraged. But as public sentiment was forty-five years ago, I obtained an agency to sell lottery tickets on a commission of ten percent, and this business, in connection with my little store, made my profits quite satisfactory.

I used to have some curious customers. On one occasion a young man called on me and selected a pocket-book which pleased him, asking me to give him credit for a few weeks. I told him that if he wanted any article of necessity in my line, I should not object to trust him for a short time, but it struck me that a pocket-book was a decided superfluity for a man who had no money.

PHINEAS TAYLOR.

My store had much to do in giving shape to my future character as well as career, in that it became a favorite resort; the theater of village talk, and the scene of many practical jokes. For any excess of the jocose element in my character, part of the blame must attach to my early surroundings as a village clerk and merchant. In that true resort of village wits and wags, the country store, fun, pure and simple, will be sure to find the surface. My Bethel store was the scene of many most amusing incidents, in some of which I was an immediate participant, though in many, I was only a listener or spectator.

The following scene makes a chapter in the history of Connecticut, as the State was when "blue laws" were something more than a dead letter. To swear in those days was according to custom, but contrary to law. A person from New York State, whom I will call Crofut, who was a frequent visitor at my store, was equally noted for his self-will and his really terrible profanity. One day he was in my little establishment engaged in conversation, when Nathan Seelye, Esq. one of our village justices of the peace, and a man of strict religious principles, came in, and hearing Crofut's profane language he told him he considered it his duty to fine him one dollar for swearing.

Crofut responded immediately with an oath, that he did not care a d---n for the Connecticut blue laws.

"That will make two dollars," said Mr. Seelye.

This brought forth another oath.

"Three dollars," said the sturdy justice.

Nothing but oaths were given in reply, until Esquire Seelye declared the damage to the Connecticut laws to amount to fifteen dollars.

Crofut took out a twenty-dollar bill, and handed it to the justice of the peace, with an oath.

"Sixteen dollars," said Mr. Seelye, counting out four dollars to hand to Mr. Crofut, as his change.

"Oh, keep it, keep it," said Crofut, "I don't want any change, I'll d----d soon swear out the balance." He did so, after which he was more circumspect in his conversation, remarking that twenty dollars a day for swearing was about as much as he could stand.

On another occasion, a man arrested for assault and battery was to be tried before my grandfather, who was a justice of the peace. A young medical student named Newton, volunteered to defend the prisoner, and Mr. Couch, the grand juryman, came to me and said that as the prisoner had engaged a pettifogger, the State ought to have someone to represent its interests and he would give me a dollar to present the case. I accepted the fee and proposition. The fame of the "eminent counsel" on both sides drew quite a crowd to hear the case. As for the case itself, it was useless to argue it, for the guilt of the prisoner was established by evidence of half a dozen witnesses. However, Newton was bound to display himself, and so, rising with much dignity, he addressed my grandfather with, "May it please the honorable court," etc., proceeding with a mixture of poetry and invective against Couch, the grand juryman whom he assumed to be the vindictive plaintiff in this case. After alluding to him as such for the twentieth time, my grandfather stopped Newton in the midst of his splendid peroration and informed him that Mr. Couch was not the plaintiff in the case.

"Not the plaintiff! Then may it please your honor I should like to know who is the plaintiff?" inquired Newton.

He was quietly informed that the State of Connecticut was the plaintiff, whereupon Newton dropped into his seat as if he had been shot. Thereupon, I rose with great confidence, and speaking from my notes, proceeded to show the guilt of the prisoner from the evidence; that there was no discrepancy in the testimony; that none of the witnesses had been impeached; that no defense had been offered; that I was astonished at the audacity of both counsel and prisoner in not pleading guilty at once; and then, soaring aloft on general principles, I began to look about for a safe place to alight, when my grandfather interrupted me with— "Young man, will you have the kindness to inform the court which side you are pleading for — the plaintiff or the defendant ?"

It was my turn to drop, which I did amid a shout of laughter from every corner of the court-room. Newton, who had been very downcast, looked up with a broad grin and the two "eminent counsels" sneaked out of the room in company, while the prisoner was bound over to the next County Court for trial.

While my business in Bethel continued to increase beyond my expectations, I was also happy in believing that my suit with the fair tailoress, Charity Hallett, was duly progressing.

How I managed one of our sleigh rides may be worth narrating. My grandfather would, at any time, let me have a horse and sleigh, always excepting his new sleigh, the finest in the village, and a favorite horse called "Arabian." I especially coveted this turnout for one of our parties, knowing that I could eclipse all my comrades, and so I asked grandfather if I could have "Arabian " and the new sleigh.

"Yes, if you have twenty dollars in your pocket," was the reply.

I immediately showed the money, and, putting it back in my pocket, said with a laugh: "You see I have the money. I am much obliged to you; I suppose I can have 'Arab' and the new sleigh?"

Of course, he meant to deny me by making what he thought to be an impossible condition, to wit: that I should hire the team, at a good round price, if I had it at all, but I had caught him so suddenly that he was compelled to consent, and "Chairy" and I had the crack team of the party.

There was a young apprentice to the tailoring trade in Bethel, whom I will call John Mallett, whose education had been much neglected, and who had been paying his addresses to a certain "Lucretia" for some six months, with a strong probability of being jilted at last. On a Sunday evening she had declined to take his arm, accepting instead the arm of the next man who offered, and Mallett determined to demand an explanation. He accordingly came to me the Saturday evening following, asking me, when I had closed my store, to write a strong and remonstratory "love-letter" for him. I asked "Bill Shepard," who was present, to remain and assist, and, in due time, the joint efforts of Shepard, Mallett and myself resulted in the following production. I give the letter as an illustrative chapter in real life. It is certainly not after the manner of Chesterfield, but it is such a letter as a disappointed lover, spurred by frequent proclamations.

The green-eyed monster, which doth mock
The meat it feeds on,

With a demand from Mallett that we should begin in strong terms, and Shepard acting as scribe, we concocted the following:

Bethel_____. 18_____.

Miss Lucretia: I write this to ask an explanation of your conduct in giving me the mitten on Sunday night last. If you think, madam, that you can trifle with my affections, and turn me off for every little whipper-snapper that you can pick up, you will find yourself considerably mistaken. [We read thus far to Mallett, and it met his approval. He said he liked the idea of calling her "madam," for he thought it sounded so "distant."' it would hurt her feelings very much. The term "little whipper-snapper" also delighted him. He said he guessed that would make her feel cheap. Shepard and myself were not quite so sure of its aptitude, since the chap who succeeded in capturing Lucretia. on the occasion alluded to, was a head and shoulders taller than Mallett. However, we did not intimate our thoughts to Mallett, and he desired us to "go ahead and give her another dose."]
You don't know me, madam, if you think you can snap me up in this way. I wish you to understand that I can have the company of girls as much above you as the sun is above the earth, and I won't stand any of your impudent nonsense no how. [This was duly read and approved. "Now," said Mallett, "try to touch her feelings. Remind her of the pleasant hours we have spent together;" and we continued as follows:]
My dear Lucretia, when I think of the many pleasant hours we have spent together— of the delightful walks which we have had on moonlight evenings to Fenner's Rocks, Chestnut Ridge, Grassy Plain, Wildcat, and Puppy-town— of the strolls which we have taken upon Shelter Rocks. Cedar Hill— the visits we have made co Old Lane, Wolfpits, Toad-hole and Plum-trees*— when all these things come rushing on my mind, and when, my dear girl, I remember how often you have told me that you loved me better than anybody else, and I assured you my feelings were the same as yours, it almost breaks my heart to think of last Sunday night. ["Can't you stick in some affecting poetry here?" said Mallett. Shepard could not recollect any to the point, nor could I, but as the exigency of the case seemed to require it, we concluded to manufacture a verse or two, which we did, as follows:]

Lucretia, dear, what have I done,
That you should use me thus and so,
To take the arm of Tom Beers' son,
And let your dearest true love go?

Miserable fate, to lose you now,
And tear this bleeding heart asunder!
Will you forget your tender vow?
I can't believe it— no, by thunder

*These were the euphonious names of localities in the vicinity of Bethel.

[Mallett did not like the word " thunder," but being informed that no other word could be substituted without destroying both rhyme and reason, he consented that it should remain, provided we added two more stanzas of a softer nature; something, he said, that would make the tears come, if possible. We then ground out the following:]

Lucretia, dear, do write to Jack,
And say with Beers you are not smitten;
And thus, to me in love come back.
And give all other boys the mitten.

Do this, Lucretia, and till death
I'll love you to intense distraction;
I'll spend for you my every breath,
And we will live in satisfaction.

["That will do very well," said Mallett. "Now I guess you had better blow her up a little more." We obeyed orders as follows:]

It makes me mad to think what a fool I was to give you that finger-ring and bosom-pin, and spend so much time in your company, just to be flirted and bamboozled as I was on Sunday night last. If you continue this course of conduct, we part forever, and I will thank you to send back that jewelry. I would sooner see it crushed under my feet than worn by a person who abused me as you have done. I shall despise you forever if you don't change your conduct towards me, and send me a letter of apology on Monday next. I shall not go to meeting tomorrow, for I would scorn to sit in the same meeting-house with you until I have an explanation of your conduct. If you allow any young man to go home with you tomorrow night, I shall know it, for you will be watched."

["There," said Mallett. "that is pretty strong. Now I guess you had better touch her feelings once more, and wind up the letter." We proceeded as follows:]

My sweet girl, if you only knew the sleepless nights which I have spent during the present week, the torments and sufferings which I endure on your account; if you could but realize that I regard the world as less than nothing without you. I am certain you would pity me. A homely cot and a crust of bread with my adorable Lucretia would be a paradise, where a palace without you would be a hades. ["What in thunder is hades?" inquired Jack. We explained. He considered the figure rather bold, and requested us to close as soon as possible.] Now, dearest, in bidding you adieu. I implore you to reflect on our past enjoyments, look forward with pleasure to our future happy meetings, and rely upon your affectionate Jack in storm or calm, in sickness, distress, or want, for all these will be powerless to change my love. I hope to hear from you on Monday next, and, if favorable, I shall be happy to call on you the same evening, when in ecstatic joy we will laugh at the past, hope for the future, and draw consolation from the fact that "the course of true love never did run smooth." This from your disconsolate but still hoping lover and admirer,

Jack Mallett.

P. S. — On reflection I have concluded to go to meeting tomorrow. If all is well, hold your pocket handkerchief in your left hand as you stand up to sing with the choir— in which case I shall expect the pleasure of giving you my arm tomorrow night.   J. M.

The effect of this letter upon Lucretia, I regret to say, was not as favorable as could have been desired. She declined to remove her handkerchief from her right hand, and she returned the "ring and bosom-pin" to her disconsolate admirer, while, not many months after, Mallett's rival led Lucretia to the altar. As for Mallett's agreement to pay Shepard and myself five pounds of carpet rags and twelve yards of broadcloth "lists," for our services, owing to his ill success, we compromised for one-half the amount.

MY PROPERTY AND MY TENANT

CHAPTER IV.

STRUGGLES FOR A LIVELIHOOD.

During this season I made arrangements with Mr. Samuel Sherwood, of Bridgeport, to go on an exploring expedition to Pittsburg, Pennsylvania, where we understood there was a fine opening for a lottery office, and where we meant to try our fortunes, provided the prospects should equal our expectations. We went to New York, where I had an interview with Mr. Dudley S. Gregory, the principal business man of Messrs. Yates and McIntyre, who dissuaded me from going to Pittsburg, and offered me the entire lottery agency for the State of Tennessee, if I would go to Nashville and open an office. The offer was tempting, but the distance was too far from a certain tailoress in Bethel.

The Pittsburg trip given up, Sherwood and I went to Philadelphia for a pleasure excursion and put up at Congress Hall in Chestnut street where we lived in much grander style than we had been accustomed to, and for a week we were in clover. At the end of that time, however, when we concluded to start for home, the amount of our hotel bill astounded us. After paying it and securing tickets for New York, our combined purses showed a balance of but twenty-seven cents.

Twenty-five cents of this sum went to the boot-black. Fortunately, our breakfast was included in our bilk and we secured from the table a few biscuits for our dinner on the way to New York.

On arriving, we carried our own baggage to Holt's Hotel. The next morning Sherwood obtained a couple of dollars from a friend and went to Newark and borrowed fifty dollars from his cousin, Dr. Sherwood, loaning me one-half the sum. After a few days' sojourn in the city we returned home.

During our stay in New York, I derived considerable information from the city managers with regard to the lottery business, and thereafter I bought my tickets directly from the Connecticut lottery managers at what was termed "the scheme price," and also established agencies throughout the country, selling considerable quantities of tickets at handsome profits. My uncle, Alanson Taylor, joined me in the business, and, as we sold several prizes, my office came to be considered "lucky," and I received orders from all parts of the country.

During this time, I kept a close eye upon the attractive tailoress, Charity Hallett, and in the summer of 1829, I asked her hand in marriage. My suit was accepted, and the wedding day was appointed; I, meanwhile, applying myself closely to business, and no one but the parties immediately interested suspecting that the event was so near at hand. Miss Hallett went to New York in October, ostensibly to visit her uncle, Nathan Beers, who resided at No. 3 Allen Street. I followed in November, pressed by the necessity of purchasing goods for my store; and the evening after my arrival, November 8, 1829, the Rev. Dr. McAuley married us in the presence of sundry friends and relatives of my wife, and I became the husband of one of the best women in the world. In the course of the week we went back to Bethel and took board in the family where Charity Barnum as "Chairy " Hallett had previously resided.

I do not approve or recommend early marriages. The minds of men and women taking so important a step in life should be matured, but although I was only little more than nineteen years old when I was married, I have always felt assured that if I had waited twenty years longer I could not have found another woman so well suited to my disposition and so admirable and valuable in every character as a wife, a mother, and a friend.

In the winter of 1829-30, my lottery business had so extended that I had branch offices in Danbury, Norwalk, Stamford and Middletown, as well as agencies in the small villages for thirty miles around Bethel. I had also purchased from my grandfather three acres of land on which I built a house and went to housekeeping. My lottery business, which was with a few large customers, was so arranged that I could safely entrust it to an agent, making it necessary for me to find some other field for my individual enterprise.

So, I tried my hand as an auctioneer in the book trade, traveling about the country, but at Newburgh, New York, several of my best books were stolen, and I quit the business in disgust.

In July, 1831, my uncle, Alanson Taylor, and myself opened a country store in a building, which I had put up in Bethel in the previous spring, and we stocked the "yellow store," as it was called, with a full assortment of groceries, hardware, crockery, and "notions;" but we were not successful in the enterprise, and in October following, I bought out my uncle's interest and we dissolved partnership.

About this time, circumstances, partly religious and partly political in their character, led me into still another field of enterprise which honorably opened to me that notoriety of when in later life I surely have had a surfeit. Considering my youth, this new enterprise reflected credit upon my ability, as well as energy, and so I may be excused if I now recur to it with something like pride. In a period of strong political excitement, I wrote several communications for the Danbury weekly paper, setting forth what I conceived to be the dangers of a sectarian interference which was then apparent in political affairs. The publication of these communications was refused, and I accordingly purchased a press and types, and October 19, 1831, I Issued the first number of my own paper, *The Herald of Freedom*.

I entered upon the editorship of this journal with all the vigor and vehemence of youth. The boldness with which the paper was conducted soon excited widespread attention and commanded a circulation which extended beyond the immediate locality into nearly every State in the Union. But lacking that experience which induces caution, and without the dread of consequences, I frequently laid myself open to the charge of libel, and three times in three years I was prosecuted. A Danbury butcher, a zealous politician, brought a civil suit against me for accusing him of being a spy in a Democratic caucus. On the first trial the jury did not agree, but after a second trial I was fined several hundred dollars. Another libel suit against me was withdrawn. The third was sufficiently important to warrant the following detail:

A criminal prosecution was brought against me for stating in my paper that a man in Bethel, prominent in church, had "been guilty of taking *usury* of an orphan boy," and for severely commenting on the fact in my editorial columns. When the case came to trial the truth of my statement way substantially proved by several witnesses and even by the prosecuting party. But "the greater the truth, the greater the libel" and then I had used the term "usury," instead of extortion, or note-shaving, or some other expression which might have softened the verdict. The result was that I was sentenced to pay a fine of one hundred dollars and to be imprisoned in the common jail for sixty days.

The most comfortable provision was made for me in Danbury jail. My room was papered and carpeted; I lived well; I was overwhelmed with the constant visits of my friends; I edited my paper as usual and received large accessions to my subscription list; and at the end of my sixty days' term the event was celebrated, by a large concourse of people from the surrounding country. The court room in which I was convicted was the scene of the celebration. An ode, written for the occasion, was sung; an eloquent oration on the freedom of the press was delivered; and several hundred gentlemen afterwards partook of a sumptuous dinner followed by appropriate toasts and speeches. Then came the triumphant part of the ceremonial, which was reported in my paper of December 12, 1832, is follows:

"P. T. Barnum and the band of music took their seats in a coach drawn by six horses, which had been prepared for the occasion. The coach was preceded by forty horsemen. and a marshal, bearing the national standard. Immediately in the rear of the coach was the carriage of the orator and the President of the day, followed by the committee of arrangements and sixty carnages of citizens, which joined in escorting the editor to his home in Bethel.

"When the procession commenced its march amidst the roar of cannon, three cheers were given by several hundred citizens who did not join in the procession. The band of music continued to play a variety of national airs until their arrival in Bethel (a distance of three miles), when they struck up the beautiful and appropriate tune of 'Home, Sweet Home!' After giving three hearty cheers, the procession returned to Danbury. The utmost harmony and unanimity of feeling prevailed throughout the day, and we are happy to add that no accident occurred to mar the festivities of the occasion."

My editorial career was one of continual contest. I, however, published the 160th number of *The Herald of Freedom* in Danbury, November 5, 1834, after which my brother-in-law, John W. Amerman, issued the paper for me at Norwalk till the following year, when the *Herald* was sold to Mr. George Taylor.

Meanwhile, I had taken Horace Fairchild into partnership in my mercantile business in 1831, and I had sold out to him and to a Mr. Toucey, in 1833, they forming a partnership under the firm of Fairchild & Co. So far as I was concerned, my store was not a success. Ordinary trade was too slow for me. I bought largely and in order to sell I was obliged to give extensive credits. Hence, I had an accumulation of bad debts; and my old ledger presents a long series of accounts balanced by "death," by "running away," by "failing," and by other similarly remunerative returns.

There was nothing more for me to do in Bethel; and in the winter of 1834—5, I removed my family to New York, where I hired a house in Hudson street. I had no pecuniary resources, excepting such as might be derived from debts left for collection with my agent at Bethel, and I went to the metropolis literally to seek my fortune. I hoped to secure a situation in some mercantile house, not at a fixed salary, but so as to derive such portion of the profits as might be due to my individual tact, energy, and perseverance in the interests of the business. But I could find no such position; my resources began to fail; my family were in ill health; I must do something for a living; and so, I acted as "drummer " to several stores which allowed me a small commission on sales to customers of my introduction.

Nor did all my efforts secure a situation for me during the whole winter; but in the spring, I received several hundred dollars from my agent in Bethel, and finding no better business, May 1, 1835, I opened a small private boarding-house at No. 52 Frankfort street. We soon had a very good run of customers from our Connecticut acquaintances who had occasion to visit New York, and as this business did not sufficiently occupy my time, I bought an interest with Mr. John Moody in a grocery store, No. 156 South street.

Although the years of manhood brought cares, anxieties, and struggles for a livelihood, they did not change my nature and the jocose element was still an essential ingredient of my being. I loved fun, practical fun, for itself and for the enjoyment which it brought. During the year, I occasionally visited Bridgeport where I almost always found at the hotel a noted joker, named Darrow, who spared neither friend nor foe in his tricks. He was the life of the bar-room and would always try to entrap some stranger in a bet and so win a treat for the company. He made several ineffectual attempts upon me, and at last, one evening, Darrow, who stuttered, made a final trial as follows: "Come, Barnum, I'll make you another proposition; I'll bet you hain't got a whole shirt on your back." The catch consists in the fact that generally only one-half of that convenient garment is on the back; but I had anticipated the proposition — in fact I had induced a friend, Mr. Hough, to put Darrow up to the trick — and had folded a shirt nicely upon my back, securing it there with my suspenders. The bar-room was crowded with customers who thought that if I made the bet I should be nicely caught, and I made pretense of playing off and at the same time stimulated Darrow to press the bet by saying:

"That is a foolish bet to make; I am sure my shirt is whole because it is nearly new; but I don't like to bet on such a subject."

"A good reason why," said Darrow, in great glee; "it's ragged. Come, I'll bet you a treat for the whole company you hain't got a whole shirt on your b-b-b-back!"

"I'll bet my shirt is cleaner than yours," I replied.

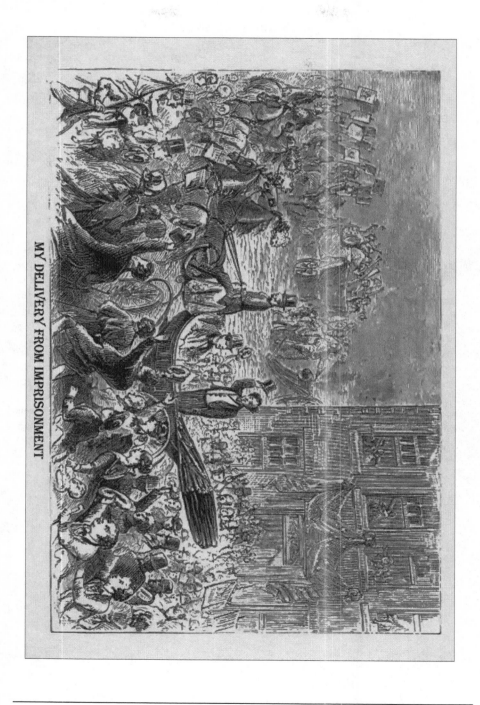

MY DELIVERY FROM IMPRISONMENT

"That's nothing to do w-w-with the case; it's ragged, and y-y-you know it."

"I know it is not," I replied, with pretended anger, which caused the crowd to laugh heartily.

"You poor ragged f-f -fellow, come down here from D-D-Danbury, I'm sorry for you," said Darrow tantalizingly.

"You would not pay if you lost," I remarked.

"Here's f-f -five dollars I'll put in Captain Hinman's (the landlord's) hands. Now b-b-bet if you dare, you ragged c-c-creature, you."

I put five dollars in Captain Hinman's hands and told him to treat the company from it if I lost the bet.

"Remember," said Darrow, "I b-b-bet you hain't got a whole shirt on your b-b-back!"

"All right," said I, taking off my coat and commencing to unbutton my vest.

The whole company, feeling sure that I was caught, began to laugh heartily.

Old Darrow fairly danced with delight, and as I laid my coat on a chair he came running up in front of me, and slapping his hands together, exclaimed:

"You needn't t-t-take off any more c-c-clothes, for if it ain't all on your b-b-back, you've lost it."

"If it is, I suppose you have!" I replied, pulling the whole shirt from off my back!

Such a shriek of laughter as burst forth from the crowd I scarcely ever heard, and certainly such a blank countenance as old Darrow exhibited it would be hard to conceive. Seeing that he was most incontinently "done for," and perceiving that his neighbor Hough had helped to do it, he ran up to him in great anger and shaking his fist in his face exclaimed:

"H-H-Hough, you infernal r-r-rascal to go against your own neighbor in favor of a D-D-Danbury man. I'll pay you for that some time, you see if I d-d-don't."

All hands went up to the bar and drank with a hearty good will for it was seldom that Darrow got taken in, and he was such an inveterate joker they liked to see him paid in his own coin. Never till the day of his death did he hear the last of the "whole shirt".

CHAPTER V.

MY START AS A SHOWMAN.

By this time, it was clear to my mind that my proper position in this big world was not yet reached. The business for which I was destined, and, I believe, made, had not yet come to me. I had not found that I was to cater for that insatiate want of human nature— the love of amusement; that I was to make a sensation on two continents; and that fame and fortune awaited me so soon as I should appear before the public- in the character of a showman. The show business has all phases and grades of dignity, from the exhibition of a monkey to the exposition of that highest art in music or the drama, which entrances empires and secures for the gifted artist a world-wide fame which princes well might envy. Men, women and children, who cannot live on gravity alone, need something to satisfy their gayer, lighter moods and hours, and he who ministers to this want is in a business established by the Author of our nature. If he worthily fulfills his mission, and amuses without corrupting, he need never feel that he has lived in vain.

The least deserving of all my efforts in the show line was the one which introduced me to the business: a scheme in no sense of my own devising; one which had been sometime before the public and which had so many vouchers for its genuineness that at the time of taking possession of it that I honestly believed it to be genuine.

In the summer of 1835, Mr. Coley Bartram, of Reading, Connecticut, informed me that he had owned an interest in a remarkable negro woman whom he believed to be one hundred and sixty-one years old, and whom he also believed to have been the nurse of General Washington. He then showed me a copy of the following advertisement in the *Pennsylvania Inquirer*, of July 15, 1835:

Curiosity. — The citizens of Philadelphia and its vicinity have an opportunity of witnessing at the Masonic Hall, one of the greatest natural curiosities ever witnessed, viz.: Joice Heth, a negress, aged 161 years, who formerly belonged to the father of General Washington. She has been a member of the Baptist Church one hundred and sixteen years, and can rehearse many hymns, and sing them according to former custom. She was born near the old Potomac River in Virginia and has for ninety or one hundred years lived in Paris, Kentucky, with the Bowling family.

All who have seen this extraordinary woman are satisfied of the truth of the account of her age. The evidence of the Bowling family, which is respectable, is strong, had the original bill of sale of Augustine Washington, in his own hand-writing, and other evidences which the proprietor has in his possession, will satisfy even the most incredulous.

A lady will attend at the hall during the afternoon and evening for the accommodation of those ladies who may call.

Mr. Bartram further stated that he had sold out his interest to his partner, R. W. Lindsay, of Jefferson county, Kentucky, who was then exhibiting Joice Heth in

Philadelphia, but was anxious to sell out and go home — the alleged reason being that he had very little tact as a showman. As the New York papers had also contained some account of Joice Heth, I went on to Philadelphia to see Mr. Lindsay and his exhibition Joice Heth was certainly a remarkable curiosity, and she looked as if she might have been far older than her age as advertised. She was apparently in good health and spirits, but from age or disease, or both, was unable to change her position; she could move one arm at will, but her lower limbs could not be straightened; her left arm lay across her breast and she could not remove it; the fingers of her left hand were drawn down so as nearly to close it, and were fixed ; the nails on that hand were almost four inches long and extended above her wrist; the nails on her large toes had grown to the thickness of a quarter of an inch; her head was covered with a thick bush of grey hair; but she was toothless and totally blind, and her eyes had sunk so deeply in the sockets as to have disappeared altogether.

Nevertheless, she was pert and sociable and would talk as long as people would converse with her. She was quite garrulous about her *protege* "dear little George," at whose birth she declared she was present, having been at the time a slave of Elizabeth Atwood, a half-sister of Augustine Washington, the father of George Washington. As nurse she put the first clothes on the infant, and she claimed to have "raised him." She professed to be a member of the Baptist church, talking much in her way on religious subjects, and she sang a variety of ancient hymns.

In proof of her extraordinary age and pretensions, Mr. Lindsay exhibited a bill of sale, dated February 5, 1727, from Augustine Washington, county of Westmoreland, Virginia, to Elizabeth Atwood, a half-sister and neighbor of Mr. Washington, conveying "one negro woman named Joice Heth, aged fifty-four years, for and in consideration of the sum of thirty-three pounds lawful money of Virginia." It was further claimed that she had long been a nurse in the Washington family; she was called in at the birth of George and clothed the newborn infant. The evidence seemed authentic, and in answer to the inquiry why so remarkable a discovery had not been made before, a satisfactory explanation was given in the statement that she had been carried from Virginia to Kentucky, had been on the plantation of John S. Bowling so long that no one knew or cared how old she was, and only recently the accidental discovery by Mr. Bowling's son of the old bill of sale in the Record Office in Virginia had led to the identification of this negro woman as "the nurse of Washington."

Everything seemed so straightforward that I was anxious to become proprietor of this novel exhibition, which was offered to me at one thousand dollars, though the price first demanded was three thousand. I had five hundred dollars, borrowed five hundred dollars more, sold out my interest in the grocery business to my partner, and began life as a showman. At the outset of my career I saw that everything depended upon getting the people to think, and talk, and become curious and excited over and about the "rare spectacle." Accordingly, posters, transparencies, advertisements, newspaper paragraphs — all calculated to extort attention — were employed, regardless of expense. My exhibition rooms in New York, Boston, Philadelphia, Albany, and in other large and small cities, were continually thronged and much money was made. In the following February, Joice Heth died, literally of old age, and her remains received a respectable burial in the town of Bethel.

At a post-mortem examination of Joice Heth by Dr. David L. Rogers, in the presence of some medical students, it was thought that the absence of ossification indicated considerably less age than had been assumed for her; but the doctors disagreed, and this "dark subject" will probably always continue to be shrouded in mystery.

I had at last found my true vocation. My next venture, whatever it may have been in other respects, had the merit of being, in every essential, unmistakably genuine. I engaged from the Albany Museum an Italian who called himself "Signor Antonio" and who performed certain remarkable feats of balancing, stilt-walking, plate-spinning, etc. I made terms with him for one year to exhibit anywhere in the United States at twelve dollars a week and expenses and induced him to change his stage name to "Signor Vivalla." I then wrote a notice of his wonderful qualities and performances, printed it in one of the Albany papers as news, sent copies to the theatrical managers in New York and in other cities, and went with Vivalla to the metropolis. Manager William Dinneford, of the Franklin Theatre, had seen so many performances of the kind that he declined to engage my "eminent Italian artist;" but I persuaded him to try Vivalla one night for nothing, and by the potent aid of printer's ink the house was crammed. I appeared as a supernumerary to assist Vivalla in arranging his plates and other "properties;" and to hand him his gun to fire while he was hopping on one stilt ten feet high. This was "my first appearance on any stage." The applause which followed Vivalla's feats was tremendous, and Manager Dinneford was so delighted that he engaged him for the remainder of the week at fifty dollars. At the close of the performance, in response to a call from the house, I made a speech for Vivalla, thanking the audience for their appreciation and announcing a repetition of the exhibition every evening during the week.

Vivalla remained a second week at the Franklin Theatre, for which I received $150. I realized the same sum for a week in Boston. We then went to Washington to fulfill an engagement which was far from successful, since my remuneration depended upon the receipts, and it snowed continually during the week. I was a loser to such an extent that I had not funds enough to return to Philadelphia. I pawned my watch and chain for thirty-five dollars, when, fortunately, Manager Wemyss arrived on Saturday morning and loaned me the money to redeem my property.

As this was my first visit to Washington, I was much interested in visiting the capitol and other public buildings. I also satisfied my curiosity in seeing Clay, Calhoun, Benton, John Quincy Adams, Richard M. Johnson, Polk, and other leading statesmen of the time. I was also greatly gratified in calling upon Anne Royall, author of the Black Book, publisher of a little paper called *"Paul Pry,"* and quite a celebrated personage in her day. I had exchanged *The Herald of Freedom* with her journal, and she strongly sympathized with me in my persecutions. She was delighted to see me, and although she was the most garrulous old woman I ever saw, I passed a very amusing and pleasant time with her. Before leaving her, I manifested my showman propensity by trying to hire her to give a dozen or more lectures on "Government," in the Atlantic cities, but I could not engage her at any price, although I am sure the speculation would have been a very profitable one. I never saw this eccentric woman again; she died at a very advanced age, October 1, 1854, at her residence in Washington.

I went with Vivalla to Philadelphia and opened at the Walnut Street Theatre. Though his performances were very meritorious and were well received, theatricals were dull and houses were slim, it was evident that something must be done to stimulate the public.

And now that instinct — I think it must be — which can arouse a community and make it patronize, provided the article offered is worthy of patronage — an instinct which served me strangely in later years, astonishing the public and surprising me, came to my relief, and the help, curiously enough, appeared in the shape of an emphatic hiss from the pit!

This hiss, I discovered, came from one Roberts, a circus performer, and I had an interview with him. He was a professional balancer and juggler, who boasted that he could do all Vivalla had done and something more. I at once published a card in Vivalla's name, offering $1,000 to anyone who would publicly perform Vivalla's feats at such place as should be designated, and Roberts issued a counter card, accepting the offer. I then contracted with Mr. Warren, treasurer of the Walnut Street Theatre, for one-third of the proceeds, if I should bring the receipts up to $400 a night — an agreement he could well afford to make as his receipts the night before had been but seventy-five dollars. From him I went to Roberts, who seemed disposed to "back down," but I told him I should not insist upon the terms of his published card, and ask him if he was under any engagement? Learning that he was not, I offered him thirty dollars to perform under my direction one night at the Walnut, and he accepted. A great trial of skill between Roberts and Vivalla was duly announced by posters and through the press. Meanwhile, they rehearsed privately to see what tricks each could perform, and the "business" was completely arranged.

Public excitement was at fever heat, and on the night of the trial the pit and upper boxes were crowded to the full. The "contest" between the performers was eager, and each had his party in the house. So far as I could learn, no one complained that he did not get all he paid for on that occasion. I engaged Roberts for a month and his subsequent "contests" with Vivalla amused the public and put money in my purse.

In April, 1836, I connected myself with Aaron Turner's traveling circus company as ticket-seller, secretary and treasurer, at thirty dollars a month and one-fifth of the entire profits, while Vivalla was to receive a salary of fifty dollars. As I was already paying him eighty dollars a month, our joint salaries reimbursed me and left me the chance of twenty per cent, of the net receipts. We started from Danbury for West Springfield, Massachusetts, April 26th, and on the first day, instead of halting to dine, as I expected, Mr. Turner regaled the whole company with three loaves of rye bread and a pound of butter, bought at a farm house at a cost of fifty cents, and after watering the horses, we went on our way.

We began our performances at West Springfield, April 28th, and as our expected band of music had not arrived from Providence, I made a prefatory speech announcing our disappointment, and our intention to please our patrons, nevertheless. The two Turner boys, sons of the proprietor, rode finely. Joe Pentland, one of the wittiest, best, and most original of clowns, with Vivalla's tricks and other performances in the ring, more than made up for the lack of music. In a day or two our band arrived and our "houses" improved. My diary is full of incidents of our summer tour through numerous villages, towns, and cities in New England, New York, New Jersey,

Pennsylvania, Delaware, Maryland, District of Columbia, Virginia, and North Carolina.

While we were at Cabotville, Massachusetts, on going to bed one night one of my room-mates threw a lighted stump of a cigar into a spit-box filled with saw-dust, and the result was that about one o'clock T. V. Turner, who slept in the room, awoke in the midst of a dense smoke, and barely managed to crawl to the window to open it, and to awaken us in time to save us from suffocation.

At Lenox, Massachusetts, one Sunday I attended church as usual and the preacher denounced our circus and all connected with it as immoral, and was very abusive; whereupon, when he had read the closing hymn, I walked up the pulpit stairs and handed him a written request, signed "P.T. Barnum, connected with the circus, June 5th, 1836," to be permitted to reply to him. He declined to notice it, and after the benediction I lectured him for not giving me an opportunity to vindicate myself and those with whom I was connected. The affair created considerable excitement, and some of the members of the church apologized to me for their clergyman's ill-behavior. A similar affair happened afterwards at Port Deposit, on the lower Susquehanna, and in this instance, I addressed the audience for half an hour, defending the circus company against the attacks of the clergyman, and the people listened, though their pastor repeatedly implored them to go home. Often have I collected our company on Sunday and read to them the Bible or a printed sermon, and one or more of the men frequently accompanied me to church. We made no pretense of religion, but we were not the worst people in the world, and we thought ourselves entitled to at least decent treatment when we went to hear the preaching of the Gospel.

The proprietor of the circus, Aaron Turner, was a self-made man, who had acquired a large fortune by his industry. He believed that any man with health and common sense could become rich if he only resolved to be so, and he was very proud of the fact that he began the world with no advantages, no education, and without a shilling. Withal, he was a practical joker, as I more than once discovered to my cost. While we were at Annapolis, Maryland, he played a trick upon me which was fun to him but was very nearly death to me.

We arrived on Saturday night, and as I felt quite "flush" I bought a fine suit of black clothes. On Sunday morning I dressed myself in my new suit and started out for a stroll. While passing through the bar-room Turner called the attention of the company present to me and said: "I think it very singular you permit that rascal to march your streets in open day. It wouldn't be allowed in Rhode Island, and I suppose that is the reason the black-coated scoundrel has come down this way."

"Why, who is he? " asked half a dozen at once.

"Don't you know? Why that is the Rev. E. K. Avery, the murderer of Miss Cornell!"

"Is it possible!" they exclaimed, all starting for the door, eager to get a look at me, and swearing vengeance. It was only recently that the Rev. Ephraim K. Avery had been tried in Rhode Island for the murder of Miss Cornell, whose body was discovered in a stack-yard, and though Avery was acquitted in court, the general sentiment of the country condemned him. It was this Avery whom Turner made me represent. I had not walked far in my fine clothes, before I was overtaken by a mob of a dozen, which rapidly increased to at least a hundred, and my ears were suddenly t saluted with such observations as, "the lecherous old hypocrite," "the sanctified murderer," "the black-coated villain," "lynch the scoundrel," "let's tar and feather him," and like remarks which I had no idea applied to me till one man seized me by the collar, while five or six more appeared on the scene with a rail. "Come," said the man who collared me, "old chap, you can't walk any further: we know you, and as we always make gentlemen ride in these parts, you may just prepare to straddle that rail!"

My surprise may be imagined. "Good heavens!" I exclaimed, as they all pressed around me, "gentlemen, what have I done?"

"Oh, we know you," exclaimed half a dozen voices; "you needn't roll your sanctimonious eyes; that game don't take in this country! Come, straddle the rail, and remember the stock-yard."

I grew more and more bewildered; I could not imagine what possible offence I was to suffer for, and I continued to exclaim, "Gentlemen, what have I done?" Don't kill me, gentlemen, but tell me what I have done."

"Come, make him straddle the rail; we'll show him how to hang poor factory girls," shouted a man in the crowd.

The man who had me by the collar then remarked, "Come, Mr. Avery, it's no use, you see, we know you, and we'll give you a touch of Lynch law, and start you for home again."

"My name is not Avery, gentlemen; you are mistaken in your man," I exclaimed.

"Come, come, none of your gammon; straddle the rail, Ephraim."

The rail was brought and I was about to be placed on it, when the truth flashed upon me.

"Gentlemen," I exclaimed, " I am not Avery; I despise that villain as much as you can; my name is Barnum; I belong to the circus which arrived here last night, and I am sure Old Turner, my partner, has hoaxed you with this ridiculous story."

"If he has, we'll lynch him," said one of the mob.

"Well, he has, I'll assure you, and if you will walk to the hotel with me. I'll convince you of the fact."

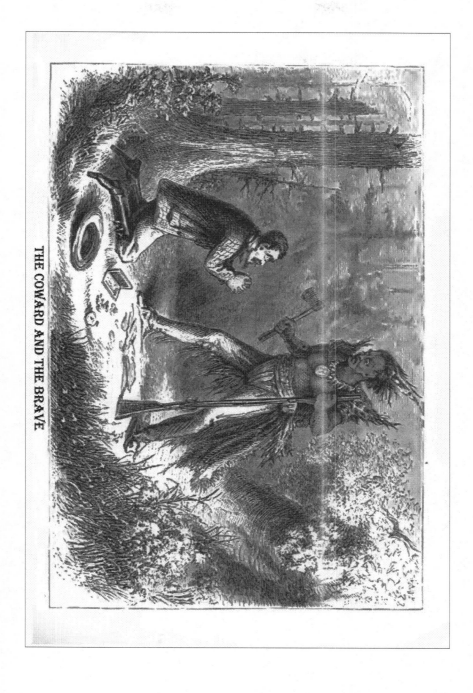

THE COWARD AND THE BRAVE

This they reluctantly assented to, keeping, however, a close hand upon me. As we walked up the main street, the mob received a re-enforcement of some fifty or sixty, and I was marched like a malefactor up to the hotel. Old Turner stood on the piazza, ready to explode with laughter. I appealed to him for heaven's sake to explain this matter, that I might be liberated. He continued to laugh, but finally told them he believed there was some mistake about it. "The fact is," said he, "my friend Barnum has a new suit of black clothes on and he looks so much like a priest that I thought he must be Avery."

The crowd saw the joke and seemed satisfied. My new coat had been half torn from my back, and I had been very roughly handled. But some of the crowd apologized for the outrage, declaring that Turner ought to be served in the same way, while others advised me to "get even with him." I was very much offended, and when the mob dispersed I asked Turner what could have induced him to play such a trick upon me.

"My dear Mr. Barnum," he replied, "it was all for our good. Remember, all we need to insure success is notoriety. You will see that this will be noised all about town as a trick played by one of the circus managers upon the other, and our pavilion will be crammed tomorrow night."

It was even so; the trick was told all over town and every one came to see the circus managers who were in a habit of playing practical jokes upon each other.

We had fine audiences while we remained at Annapolis, but it was a long time before I forgave Turner for his rascally "joke."

CHAPTER VI.

MY FIRST TRAVELING COMPANY.

An amusing incident occurred when we were at Hanover Court House, in Virginia. It rained so heavily that we could not perform there, and Turner decided to start for Richmond immediately after dinner, when he was informed by the landlord that as our agent had engaged three meals and lodging for the whole company, the entire bill must be paid whether we went then, or next morning. No compromise could be effected with the stubborn landlord, and so Turner proceeded to get the worth of his money as follows: He ordered dinner at twelve o'clock, which was duly prepared and eaten. The table was cleared and reset for supper at half-past twelve. At one o'clock we all went to bed, every man carrying a lighted candle to his room. There were thirty-six of us and we all undressed and tumbled into bed as if we were going to stay all night. In half an hour we rose and went down to the hot breakfast which Turner had demanded and which we found smoking on the table. Turner was very grave, the landlord was exceedingly angry, and the rest of us were convulsed with laughter at the absurdity of the whole proceeding. We disposed of our breakfast as if we had eaten nothing for ten hours, and then started for Richmond with the satisfaction that we fairly settled with our unreasonable landlord.

At Richmond, after performances were over one night, I managed to partially pay Turner for his Avery trick. A dozen or more of us were enjoying ourselves in the sitting-room of the hotel, telling stories and singing songs, when some of the company proposed sundry amusing arithmetical questions, followed by one from Turner which was readily solved. Hoping to catch Turner, I then proposed the following problem: "Suppose a man is thirty years of age, and he has a child one year of age; he is thirty times older than his child. When the child is thirty years old, the father, being sixty, is only twice as old as his child. When the child is sixty the father is ninety, and therefore only one-third older than the child. When the child is ninety the father is one hundred and twenty, and therefore only one-fourth older than the child. Thus, you see, the child is gradually but surely gaining on the parent, and as he certainly continues to come nearer and nearer, in time he must overtake him, the question therefore is, suppose it was possible for them to live long enough, how old would the father be when the child overtook him and became of the same age?"

The company generally saw the catch; but Turner was very much interested in the problem, and although he admitted he knew nothing about arithmetic, he was convinced that as the son was gradually gaining on the father he must reach him if there was time enough — say, a thousand years, or so — for the race. But an old gentleman gravely remarked that the idea of a son becoming as old as his father while both were living, was simply nonsense, and he offered to bet a dozen of champagne that the thing was impossible, even "in figures." Turner, who was a betting man, and who thought the problem might be proved, accepted the wager; but he was soon convinced that however much the boy might relatively gain upon his father, there would always be thirty years difference in their ages. The champagne cost him £25, and he railed to see the fun of my arithmetic, though at last he acknowledged that it was a fair offset to the Avery trick.

We went from Richmond to Petersburg, and from that place to Warrenton, North Carolina, where, October 30th, my engagement expired with a profit to myself of $1,200. I now separated from the circus company, taking Vivalla, James Sandford (a negro singer and dancer), several musicians, horses, wagons, and a small canvas tent with which I intended to begin a traveling exhibition of my own. My company started and Turner took me on the way in his own carriage some twenty miles. We parted reluctantly, and my friend wished me every success in my new venture.

On Saturday, November 12, 1836, we halted at Rocky Mount Falls, North Carolina, and on my way to the Baptist Church, Sunday morning, I noticed a stand and benches in a grove nearby and determined to speak to the people if I was permitted. The landlord who was with me said that the congregation, coming from a distance to attend a single service, would be very glad to hear a stranger, and I accordingly asked the venerable clergyman to announce that after service I would speak for half an hour in the grove. Learning that I was not a clergy-man, he declined to give the notice, but said that he had no objection to my making the announcement, which I did, and the congregation, numbering about three hundred, promptly came to hear me.

I told them I was not a preacher and had very little experience in public speaking; but I felt a deep interest in matters of morality and religion, and would attempt, in a plain way, to set before them the duties and privileges of man. I appealed to every man's experience, observation and reason, to confirm the Bible doctrine of wretchedness in vice and happiness in virtue. We cannot violate the laws of God with impunity, and He will not keep back the wages of well-doing. The outside show of things is of very small account. We must look to realities and not to appearances. "Diamonds may glitter on a vicious breast," but "the soul's calm sunshine and the heart-felt joy is virtue's prize." The rogue, the passionate man, the drunkard, are not to be envied even at the best, and a conscience hardened by sin is the most sorrowful possession we can think of. I went on in this way, with some scriptural quotations and familial illustrations, for three-quarters of an hour. At the close of my address several persons took me by the hand, expressing themselves as greatly pleased and desiring to know my name; and I went away with the feeling that possibly I might have done some good in the beautiful grove on that charming Sunday morning. When we were at Camden, South Carolina, Sandford suddenly left me, and as I had advertised negro songs and none of my company was competent to fill Sandford's place, not to disappoint my audience, I blacked myself and sung the advertised songs "Zip Coon," etc., and to my surprise was much applauded, while two of the songs were encored. One evening, after singing my songs, I heard a disturbance outside the tent, and going to the spot found a person disputing with my men. I took part on the side of the men, when the person who was quarreling with them drew a pistol and exclaiming, "You black scoundrel! how dare you use such language to a white man," he proceeded to cock it. I saw that he thought I was a negro and meant to blow my brains out. Quick as thought, I rolled my sleeve up, showed my skin, and said, "I am as white as you are, sir." He dropped his pistol in positive fright and begged my pardon. My presence of mind had saved me.

On four different occasions in my life I have had a loaded pistol pointed at my head and each time I have escaped death by what seemed a miracle. I have also often been in deadly peril by accidents, and when I think of these things I realize my indebtedness to an all-protecting Providence. Reviewing my career, too, and considering the kind of company I kept for years and the associations with which I was surrounded and connected, I am surprised as well as grateful that I was not ruined. I honestly believe that I owe my preservation from the degradation of living and dying a loafer and a vagabond, to the single fact that I was never addicted to strong drink. To be sure, I have in times past drank liquor, but I have generally wholly abstained from intoxicating beverages, and for more than twenty years past, I am glad to say, I have been a strict "teetotaler."

At Camden, I lost one of my musicians, a Scotchman named Cochran, who was arrested for advising the negro barber who was shaving him to run away to the Free States or to Canada. I made every effort to effect Cochran's release, but he was imprisoned more than six months.

I bought four horses and two wagons and hired Joe Pentland and Robert White to join my company. White, as a negro singer, would relieve me from that roll, and Pentland, besides being a capital clown, was celebrated as a ventriloquist, comic singer, balancer, and legerdemain performer. My reinforced exhibition was called "Barnum's Grand Scientific and Musical Theatre."

Sometime previously, in Raleigh, North Carolina, I had sold one-half of my establishment to a man, whom I will call Henry, who now acted as treasurer and ticket-taker. At Augusta, Georgia, the sheriff served a writ upon this Henry for a debt of $500. As Henry had $600 of the company's money in his possession, I immediately procured a bill of sale of all his property in the exhibition and returned to the theatre where Henry's creditor and the creditor's lawyer were waiting for me. They demanded the key of the stable so as to levy on the horses and wagons. I begged delay till I could see Henry, and they consented. Henry was anxious to cheat his creditor and he at once signed the bill of sale. I returned and informed the creditor that Henry refused to pay or compromise the claim. The sheriff then demanded the keys of the stable door to attach Henry's interest in the property. "Not yet," said I, showing a bill of sale, "you see I am in full possession of the property as entire owner. You confess that you have not yet levied on it, and if you touch my property, you do it at your peril."

They were very much taken aback, and the sheriff immediately conveyed Henry to prison. The next day I learned that Henry owed his creditors thirteen hundred dollars, and that he had agreed when the Saturday evening performance was ended to hand over five hundred dollars (company money) and a bill of sale of his interest, in consideration of which one of the horses was to be ready for him to run away with, leaving me in the lurch! Learning this, I had very little sympathy for Henry, and my next step was to secure the five hundred dollars he had secreted. Vivalla had obtained it from him to keep it from the sheriff; I received it from Vivalla, on Henry's order, as a supposed means of procuring bail for him on Monday morning. I then paid the creditor the full amount obtained from Henry as the price of his half interest in the exhibition and received in return an assignment of five hundred dollars of the creditor's claims and a guaranty that I should not be troubled by my late partner on that score.

Thus, promptness of action and good luck relieved me from one of the most unpleasant positions in which I had ever been placed.

While traveling with our teams and show through a desolate part of Georgia, our advertiser, who was in advance of the party finding the route, on one occasion, when it took too long for us to reach a town at night, arranged with a poor widow woman named Hayes, to furnish us with meals and let us lodge in her hut and out-houses. It was a beggarly place, belonging to one of the poorest of "poor whites." Our horses were to stand out all night, and a farmer, six miles distant, was to bring a load of provender on the day of our arrival. Bills were then posted announcing a performance under a canvas tent near Widow Hayes's, for, as a show was a rarity in that region, it was conjectured that a hundred or more small farmers and "poor whites" might be assembled and that the receipts would cover the expenses.

Meanwhile, our advertiser, who was quite a wag, wrote back informing us of the difficulties of reaching a town on that part of our route, and stating that he had made arrangements for us to stay overnight on the plantation of "Lady Hayes," and that although the country was sparsely settled, we could doubtless give a profitable performance to a fair audience.

Anticipating a fine time on this noble "plantation," we started at four o'clock in the morning so as to arrive at one o'clock, thus avoiding the heat of the afternoon. Towards noon we came to a small river where some men, whom we afterwards discovered to be down-east Yankees, from Maine, were repairing a bridge. Every flooring plank had been taken up, and it was impossible for our teams to cross. "Could the bridge be fixed so that we could go over?" I inquired. "No; it would take half a day, and meantime, if we must cross, there was a place about sixteen miles down the river where we could get over. "But we can't go so far as that; we are under engagement to perform on Lady Hayes's place tonight, and we must cross here. Fix the bridge and we will pay you handsomely."

They wanted no money, but if we would give them some tickets to our show they thought they might do something for us. I gladly consented, and in fifteen minutes we crossed that bridge. The cunning rascals had seen our posters and knew we were coming; so, they had taken up the planks of the bridge and had hidden them till they had levied upon us for tickets, when the floor was re-laid in a quarter of an hour.

Towards dinner-time we began to look out for the grand mansion of "lady Hayes," and seeing nothing but little huts we quietly pursued our journey. At one o'clock — the time when we should have arrived at our destination — I became impatient, and riding up to a poverty-stricken hovel and seeing a ragged, barefooted old woman, with her sleeves rolled up to her shoulders, who was washing clothes in front of the door, I inquired—

"Hallo! Can you tell me where Lady Hayes lives?"

The old woman raised her head, which was covered with tangled locks and matted hair, and exclaimed —

"Hey?"

"No, Hayes, Lady Hayes; where is her plantation?"

This is the place,"she answered; " I'm Widder Hayes, and you are all to stay here tonight."

We could not believe our ears or eyes; but after putting the dirty old woman through a severe cross-examination she finally produced a contract, signed by our advertiser, agreeing for board and lodging for the company, and we found ourselves booked for the night. It appeared that our advertiser could find no better quarters in that forlorn section, and he had indulged in a joke at our expense by exciting our appetites and imaginations in anticipation of the Luxuries we should find in the magnificent mansion of "Lady Hayes."

Joe Pentland grumbled, Bob White indulged in some very strong language, and Signor Vivalla laughed. He had traveled with his monkey and organ in Italy and could put up with any fare that offered. I took the disappointment philosophically, simply remarking that we must make the best of it and compensate ourselves when we reached a town next day.

The next forenoon we arrived at Macon and congratulated ourselves that we had again reached the regions of civilization.

In going from Columbus, Georgia, to Montgomery, Alabama, we were obliged to cross a thinly-settled, desolate tract, known as the "Indian Nation," and as several persons had been murdered by hostile Indians in that region, it was deemed dangerous to travel the road without an escort. Only the day before we started, the mail stage had been stopped and the passengers murdered, the driver alone escaping. We were well armed, however, and trusted that our numbers would present too formidable a force to be attacked, though we dreaded to incur the risk. Vivalla alone was fearless and was ready to encounter fifty Indians and drive them into the swamp.

Accordingly, when we had safely passed over the entire route to within fourteen miles of Montgomery, and were beyond the reach of danger, Joe Pentland determined to test Vivalla's bravery. He had secretly purchased at Mount Megs, on the way, an old Indian dress with a fringed hunting shirt and moccasins and these he put on, after coloring his face with Spanish brown. Then, shouldering his musket he followed Vivalla and the party and, approaching stealthily, leaped into their midst with a tremendous whoop.

Vivalla's companions were in the secret, and they instantly fled in all directions. Vivalla himself ran like a deer and Pentland after him, gun in hand and yelling horribly. After running a full mile, the poor little Italian, out of breath and frightened nearly to death, dropped on his knees and begged for his life. The "Indian" leveled his gun at his victim, but soon seemed to relent, and signified that Vivalla should turn his pockets inside out — which he did, producing and handing over a purse containing eleven dollars. The savage then marched Vivalla to an oak, and with a handkerchief tied him in the most approved Indian manner to the tree, leaving him half dead with fright.

Pentland then joined us, and washing his face and changing his dress, we all went to the relief of Vivalla. He was overjoyed to see us, and when he was released his courage returned; he swore that after his companions left him, the Indian had been re-enforced by six more, to whom, in default of a gun or other means to defend himself, Vivalla had been compelled to surrender. We pretended to believe his story for a week, and then told him the joke, which he refused to credit, and also declined to take the money which Pentland offered to return, as it could not possibly be his since seven Indians had taken his money.

We had a great deal of fun over Vivalla's courage, but the matter made him so cross and surly that we were finally obliged to drop it altogether. From that time forward, however, Vivalla never again boasted of his prowess.

We arrived at Montgomery, February 27th, 1837. Here I met Henry Hawley, a legerdemain performer, and I sold him one-half of my exhibition. He had a ready wit, a happy way of localizing his tricks, was very popular in that part of the country, where he had been performing for several years, and I never saw him nonplussed but once. This was when he was performing on one occasion the well-known egg and bag trick, which he did with his usual success, producing egg after egg from the bag, and finally breaking one to show that they were genuine.

"Now," said Hawley, "I will show you the old hen that laid them." It happened, however, that the negro boy to whom had been entrusted the duty of supplying the bag had made a slight mistake, which was manifest when Hawley triumphantly produced, not "the old hen that laid the eggs," but a rooster! The whole audience was convulsed with laughter, and the abashed Hawley retreated to the dressing-room, cursing the stupidity of the black boy who had been paid to put a hen in the bag.

After performing in different places in Alabama, Kentucky, and Tennessee, we disbanded at Nashville in May, 1837, Vivalla going to New York, where he performed on his own account for a while previous to sailing for Cuba, Hawley staying in Tennessee to look after our horses which had been turned out to grass, and I returning home to spend a few weeks with my family.

VICTORY OVER VESTRYMEN

Early in July, returning west with a new company of performers, I rejoined Hawley, and we began our campaign in Kentucky. We were not successful; one of our small company was incompetent; another was intemperate — both were dismissed; and our negro-singer was drowned in the river at Frankfort. Funds were low, and I was obliged to leave pledges here and there, in payment for bills, which I afterwards redeemed. Hawley and I dissolved in August, and making a new partnership with Z. Graves, I left him in charge of the establishment and went to Tiffin, Ohio, where I re-engaged Joe Pentland, buying his horses and wagons, and taking him, with several musicians, to Kentucky.

During my short stay at Tiffin, a religious conversation at the hotel introduced me to several gentlemen who requested me to lecture on the subjects we had discussed, and I did so to a crowded audience in the school-house Sunday afternoon and evening. At the solicitation of a gentleman from Republic, I also delivered two lectures in that town, on the evenings of September 4th and 5th.

On our way to Kentucky, just before we reached Cincinnati, we met a drove of hogs, and one of the drivers making an insolent remark because our wagons interfered with his swine, I replied in the same vein, when he dismounted and, pointing a pistol at my breast, swore he would shoot me if I did not apologize. I begged him to permit me to consult a friend in the next wagon, and the misunderstanding should be satisfactorily settled. My friend was a loaded double-barreled gun, which I pointed at him and said:

"Now, sir, you must apologize, for your brains are in danger. You directed a weapon upon me for a trivial remark. You seem to hold human life at a cheap price; and now, sir, you have the choice between a load of shot and an apology."

This led to an apology and a friendly conversation, in which we both agreed that many a life is sacrificed in sudden anger, because one or both of the contending parties carry deadly weapons.

In our subsequent southern tour, we exhibited at Nashville (where I visited General Jackson, at the Hermitage), Huntsville, Tuscaloosa, Vicksburg and intermediate places, doing tolerably well. At Vicksburg, we sold all our land conveyances, excepting the band wagon and our horses, bought the steamboat "Ceres," for six thousand dollars, hired the captain and crew, and started down the river to exhibit at places on the way. At Natchez our cook left us, and in the search for another I found a white widow who would go, only she expected to marry a painter. I called on the painter who had not made up his mind whether to marry the widow or not, but I told him if he would marry her the next morning, I would lure her at twenty-five dollars a month as cook, employ him at the same wages as painter, with board for both, and a cash bonus of fifty dollars. There was a wedding on board the next day, and we had a good cook and a good dinner.

Dining one of our evening performances at Francisville, Louisiana, a man tried to pass me at the door of the tent, claiming that he had paid for admittance. I refused him entrance; and as he was slightly intoxicated, he struck me with a slung shot, mashing my hat and grazing what phrenologists call "the organ of caution." He went away and soon returned with a gang of armed and half-drunken companions, who ordered us to pack up our "traps and plunder" and to get on board our steamboat within an hour. The big tent speedily came down. No one was permitted to help us, but the company worked with a will, and within five minutes of the expiration of the hour we were on board and ready to leave. The scamps who had caused our departure escorted us and our last load, waving pine torches, and saluted us with a hurrah as we swung into the stream.

The New Orleans papers of March 19, 1838, announced the arrival of the "Steamer Ceres, Captain Barnum, with a theatrical company." After a week's performances, we started for the Attakapas country. At Opelousas we exchanged the steamer for sugar and molasses; our company was disbanded, and I started for home, arriving in New York, June 4, 1838.

CHAPTER VII.

AT THE FOOT OF THE LADDER.

Longing now for some permanent, respectable business, I advertised for a partner, stating that I had $82,500 to invest, and would add my unremitting personal attention to the capital and the business. This advertisement gave me an altogether new insight into human nature. Whoever wishes to know how some people live, or want to live, let him advertise for a partner, at the same time stating that he has a large or small capital to invest. I was flooded with answers to my advertisements and received no less than ninety-three different propositions for the use of my capital. Of these, at least one-third were from porter-house keepers. Brokers, pawnbrokers, lottery-policy dealers, patent medicine men, inventors, and others also made application. Some of my correspondents declined to specifically state the nature of their business, but they promised to open the door to untold wealth.

I had interviews with some of these mysterious million-makers. One of them was a counterfeiter, who, after much hesitation and pledges of secrecy, showed me some counterfeit coin and bank notes; he wanted $2,500 to purchase paper and ink and to prepare new dies, and he actually proposed that I should join him in the business which promised, he declared, a safe and rich harvest. Another sedate individual, dressed in Quaker costume, wanted me to join him in an oat speculation. By buying a horse and wagon, and by selling oats, bought at wholesale, in bags, he thought a good business could be done, especially as people would not be particular to measure after a Quaker.

"Do you mean to cheat in measuring your oats?" I asked.

"O, I should probably make them hold out," he answered, with a leer.

One application came from a Pearl street wool merchant, who failed a month afterwards. Then came a "perpetual motion" man who had a fortune-making machine, in which I discovered a main-spring slyly hid in a hollow post, the spring making perpetual motion — till it ran down. Finally, I went into partnership with a German, named Proler, who was a manufacturer of paste-blacking, water-proof paste for leather, Cologne water and bear's grease. We took the store No. 101 Bowery, at a rent (including the dwelling) of $600 per annum and opened a large manufactory of the above articles. Proler manufactured and sold the goods at wholesale in Boston, Charleston, Cleveland, and various other parts of the country. I kept the accounts, and attended to sales in the store, wholesale and retail. For a while the business seemed to prosper— at least till my capital was absorbed and notes for stock began to fall due, with nothing to meet them, since we had sold our goods on long credits. In January, 1840, I dissolved partnership with Proler, he buying the entire interest for $2,600 on credit, and then running away to Rotterdam without paying his note and leaving me nothing but a few receipts. Proler was a good-looking, plausible, promising — scamp.

During my connection with Proler, I became acquainted with a remarkable young dancer named John Diamond, one of the first and best of the numerous negro and "break-down" dancers who have since surprised and amused the public, and I entered into an engagement with his father for his services, putting Diamond in the hands of an agent, as I did not wish to appear in the transaction. In the spring of 1840, I hired and opened the Vauxhall Garden saloon, in New York, and gave a variety of performances, including singing, dancing, Yankee stories, etc. In this saloon Miss Mary Taylor, afterwards so celebrated as an actress and singer, made her first appearance on the stage. The enterprise, however, did not meet my expectation, and I relinquished it in August.

What was to be done next? I dreaded resuming the life of an itinerant showman, but funds were low, I had a family to care for, and as nothing better presented, I made up my mind to endure the vexations and uncertainties of a tour in the "West and South". I collected a company, consisting of Mr. C. D. Jenkins, an excellent singer and delineator of Yankee and other characters; Master John Diamond, the dancer; Francis Lynch, an orphan vagabond, fourteen years old, whom I picked up at Troy, and a fiddler. My brother-in-law, Mr. John Hallett, preceded us as agent and advertiser, and our route passed through Buffalo, Toronto, Detroit, Chicago, Ottawa, Springfield, the intermediate places, and St. Louis, where I took the steamboat for New Orleans with a company reduced by desertions to Master Diamond and the fiddler.

Arriving in New Orleans, January 2d, 1841, I had but $100 in my purse, and I had started from New York four months before with quite as much in my pocket. Excepting some small remittances to my family, I had made nothing more than current expenses: and, when I had been in New Orleans a fortnight, funds were so low that I was obliged to pledge my watch as security for my board. But on the 16th, I received from the St. Charles Theatre $500 as my half share of Diamond's benefit; the next night I had $50; and the third night $479 was my share of the proceeds of a grand dancing match at the theatre between Diamond and a negro dancer from Kentucky. Subsequent engagements at Vicksburg and Jackson were not so successful, but returning to New Orleans we again succeeded admirably, and afterwards at Mobile. Diamond, however, after extorting considerable sums of money from me, finally ran away, and, March 12th, I started homeward by way of the Mississippi and the Ohio.

At Pittsburg, where I arrived March 30th, I learned that Jenkins, who had enticed Francis Lynch away from me at St. Louis, was exhibiting him at the Museum under the name of "Master Diamond," and visiting the performance, the next day I wrote Jenkins an ironical review, for which he threatened suit, and he actually instigated R. W. Lindsay, from whom I hired Joice Heth in Philadelphia in 1835, and whom I had not seen since, though he was then residing in Pittsburg, to sue me for a pipe of brandy which, it was pretended, was promised in addition to the money paid him. I was required to give bonds of $500, which, as I was among strangers, I could not immediately procure, and I was accordingly thrown into jail till four o'clock in the afternoon, when I was liberated. The next day I caused the arrest of Jenkins for trespass in assuming Master Diamond's name and reputation for Master Lynch, and he was sent to jail till four o'clock in the afternoon. Each having had his turn at this amusement, we adjourned our controversy to New York where I beat him. As for Lindsay, I heard nothing more of his claim or him till twelve years afterwards, when he called on me in Boston with an apology. He was very poor and I was highly prosperous, and I may add that Lindsay did not lack a friend.

I arrived in New York, April 23d, 1841, after an absence of eight months, resolved once more that I would never again be an itinerant showman. Three days afterwards I contracted with Hubert Sears, the publisher, for five hundred copies of "Sears' Pictorial Illustrations of the Bible," at $500, and accepting the United States agency, I opened an office, May 10th, at the corner of Beekman and Nassau streets, the site of the present Nassau Bank. I had had a limited experience with that book in this way: When I was in Pittsburg, an acquaintance, Mr. C. D. Harker, was complaining that he had nothing to do, when I picked up a New York paper and saw the advertisement of "Sears' Pictorial Illustrations of the Bible, price $2 a copy." Mr. Harker thought he could get subscribers, and I bought him a specimen copy, agreeing to furnish him with as many as he wanted at $1.37½ a copy, though I had never before seen the work, and did not know the wholesale price. The result was that he obtained eighty subscribers in two days and made $50. My own venture in the work was not so successful; I advertised largely, had plenty of agents, and in six months, sold thousands of copies; but irresponsible agents used up all my profits and my capital

While engaged in this business I once more leased Vauxhall saloon, opening it June 14th, 1841, employing Mr. John Hallett, my brother-in-law, as manager under my direction, and at the close of the season, September 25th, we had cleared about two hundred dollars. This sum was soon exhausted, and, with my family on my hands and no employment, I was glad to do anything that would keep the wolf from the door. I wrote advertisements and notices for the Bowery Amphitheatre, receiving for the service four dollars a week, which I was very glad to get, and I also wrote articles for the Sunday papers, deriving a fair remuneration and managing to get a living. But I was at the bottom round of fortune's ladder, and it was necessary to make an effort which would raise me above want.

I was specially stimulated to this effort by a letter which I received, about this time, from my esteemed friend, Hon. Thomas T. Whittlesey, of Danbury. He held a mortgage of five hundred dollars on a piece of property I owned in that place, and, as he was convinced that I would never lay up anything, he wrote me that I might as well pay him then as ever. This letter made me resolve to live no longer from hand to mouth, but to concentrate my energies upon laying up something for the future.

While I was forming this practical determination, I was much nearer to its realization than my most sanguine hopes could have predicted. The road to fortune was close by.

As outside clerk for the Bowery Amphitheatre, I had casually learned that the collection of curiosities comprising Scudder's American Museum, at the corner of Broadway and Ann streets, was for sale. It belonged to the daughters of Mr. Scudder, and was conducted for their benefit by John Furzman, under the authority of Mr. John Heath, administrator. The price asked for the entire collection was fifteen thousand dollars. It had cost its founder, Mr. Scudder, probably fifty thousand dollars, and from the profits of the establishment he had been able to leave a large competency to his children. The Museum, however, had been for several years a losing concern, and the heirs were anxious to sell it. Looking at this property, I thought I saw that energy, tact and liberality, were only needed to make it a paying institution, and I determined to purchase it if possible.

"You buy the American Museum!" said a friend, who knew the state of my funds, "what do you intend buying it with?"

"Brass," I replied, "for silver and gold have I none."

The Museum building belonged to Mr. Francis W. Olmsted, a retired merchant, to whom I wrote stating my desire to buy the collection, and that although I had no means, if it could be purchased upon reasonable credit, I was confident that my tact and experience, added to a determined devotion to business, would enable me to make the payments when due. I therefore asked him to purchase the collection in his own name; to give me a writing securing it to me, provided I made the payments punctually, including the rent of his building; to allow me twelve dollars and a half a week on which to support my family; and if at any time I failed to meet the installment due, I would vacate the premises, and forsake all that might have been paid to that date. "In fact, Mr. Olmsted," I continued in my earnestness, "you may bind me in any way, and as tightly as you please — only give me a chance to dig out, or scratch out, and I will do so or forfeit all the labor and trouble I may have incurred."

In reply to this letter, which I took to his house myself, he named an hour when I could call on him, and as I was there at the exact moment, he expressed his pleasure with my punctuality. He inquired closely as to my habits and antecedents, and I frankly narrated my experiences as a caterer for the public, mentioning my amusement ventures in Vauxhall Garden, the circus, and in the exhibitions that I had managed at the South and West.

"Who are your references?" he inquired.

"Any man in my line," I replied, "from Edmund Simpson, manager of the Park Theatre, or William Niblo, to Messrs. Welch, June, Titus, Turner, Angevine, or other circus or menagerie proprietors; also Moses Y. Beach, of the *New York Sun*."

"Can you get any of them to call on me?" he continued.

I told him that I could, and the next day my friend Niblo rode down and had an interview with Mr. Olmsted, while Mr. Beach and several other gentlemen also called, and the following morning I waited upon him for his decision.

"I don't like your references, Mr. Barnum," said Mr. Olmsted, abruptly, as soon as I entered the room.

I was confused and said "I regretted to hear it."

"They all speak too well of you," he added, laughing; "in fact they all talk as if they were partners of yours, and intended to share the profits."

Nothing could have pleased me better. He then asked me what security I could offer in case he concluded to make the purchase for me, and it was finally agreed that, if he should do so, he should retain the property till it was entirely paid for and should also appoint a ticket-taker and accountant (at my expense), who should render him a weekly statement. I was further to take an apartment hitherto used as a billiard room in his adjoining building, allowing therefore $500 a year, making a total rental of $3,000 per annum, on a lease of ten years. He then told me to see the administrator and heirs of the estate, to get their best terms, and to meet him on his return to town a week from that time.

I at once saw Mr. John Heath, the administrator, and his price was $15,000. I offered $10,000, payable in seven annual installments, with good security. After several interviews, it was finally agreed that I should have it for $12,000, payable as above — possession to be given on the 15th of November. Mr. Olmsted assented to this, and a morning was appointed to draw and sign the writings. Mr. Heath appeared, but said he must decline proceeding any further in my case, as he had sold the collection to the directors of Peale's Museum (an incorporated institution) for $15,000 and had received $1,000 in advance.

I was shocked and appealed to Mr. Heath's honor. He said that he had signed no writing with me; was in no way legally bound, and that it was his duty to do the best he could for the heirs. Mr. Olmsted was sorry but could not help me; the new tenants would not require him to incur any risk, and my matter was at an end. Of course, I immediately informed myself as to the character of Peale's Museum company. It proved to be a band of speculators who had bought Peale's collection for a few thousand dollars, expecting to unite the American Museum with it, issue and sell stock to the amount of $50,000, pocket $30,000 profits, and permit the stockholders to look out for themselves.

I went immediately to several of the editors, including Major M.M. Noah, M.Y. Beach, my good friends "West, Herrick and Ropes, of the *Atlas*, and others, and stated my grievances. "Now," said I, "if you will grant me the use of your columns, I'll blow that speculation sky-high." They all consented, and I wrote a large number of squibs, cautioning the public against buying the Museum stock, ridiculing the idea of a board of broken-down bank directors engaging in the exhibition of stuffed monkeys and gander-skins; appealing to the case of the Zoological Institute, which had failed by adopting such a plan as the one now proposed; and finally, I told the public that such a speculation would be infinitely more ridiculous than Dickens' "Grand United Metropolitan Hot Muffin and Crumpet-baking and Punctual Delivery Company."

The stock was as "dead as a herring!" I then went to Mr. Heath and asked him when the directors were to pay the other $14,000. "On the 26th day of December, or forfeit the $1,000 already paid," was the reply. I assured him that they would never pay it, that they could not raise it, and that he would ultimately find himself with the Museum collection on his hands, and if once I started off with an exhibition for the South, I would not touch the Museum at any price. "Now," said I, "if you will agree with me confidentially, that in case these gentlemen do not pay you on the 26th of December, I may have it on the 27th for $12,000, I will run the risk, and wait in this city until that date." He readily agreed to the proposition, but said he was sure they would not forfeit their $1,000.

"Very well" said I; "all I ask of you is, that this arrangement shall not be mentioned." He assented. "On the 27th day of December, at ten o'clock a.m., I wish you to meet me in Mr. Olmsted's apartments, prepared to sign the writings, provided this incorporated company do not pay you $14,000 on the 26th." He agreed to this, and by my request put it in writing.

From that moment I felt that the Museum was mine. I saw Mr. Olmsted and told him so. He promised secrecy and agreed to sign the document if the other parties did not meet their engagement. This was about November 10th, and I continued my shower of newspaper squibs at the new company, which could not sell a dollar's worth of its stock. Meanwhile, if any one spoke to me about the Museum, I simply replied that I had lost it.

CHAPTER VIII.

THE AMERICAN MUSEUM.

My newspaper squib war against the Peale combination was vigorously kept up; when one morning, about the first of December, I received a letter from the secretary of that company (now calling itself the "New York Museum Company"), requesting me to meet the directors at the Museum on the following Monday morning. I went and found the directors in session. The venerable president of the board, who was also the ex-president of a broken bank, blandly proposed to hire me to manage the united museums, and though I saw that he merely meant to buy my silence, I professed to entertain the proposition, and in reply to an inquiry as to what salary I should expect, I specified the sum of $3,000 a year. This was at once acceded to, the salary to begin January 1, 1842, and after complimenting me on my ability, the president remarked: "Of course, Mr. Barnum, we shall have no more of your squibs through the newspapers" — to which I replied that I should "ever try to serve the interests of my employers," and I took my leave.

It was as clear to me as noonday, that after buying my silence so as to appreciate their stock, these directors meant to sell out to whom they could, leaving me to look to future stockholders for my salary. They thought, no doubt, that they had nicely entrapped me, but I knew I had caught them.

For, supposing me to be out of the way, and having no other rival purchaser, these directors postponed the advertisement of their stock to give people time to forget the attacks I had made on it, and they also took their own time for paying the money promised to Mr. Heath, December 26th — indeed, they did not even call on him at the appointed time. But on the following morning, as agreed, I was promptly and hopefully at Mr. Olmsted's apartments with my legal adviser, at half-past nine o'clock; Mr. Heath came with his lawyer at ten, and before two o'clock that day I was in formal possession of the American Museum. My first managerial act was to write and dispatch the following complimentary note:

American Museum, New York, Dec. 27, 1841.

To the President and Directors of the New York Museum:

Gentlemen: It gives me great pleasure to Inform you that you are placed upon the Free List of this establishment until further notice.

P. T. Barnum, Proprietor.

It is unnecessary to say that the "President of the New York Museum" was astounded, and when he called upon Mr. Heath, and learned that I had bought and was really in possession of the American Museum, he was indignant. He talked of prosecution, and demanded the $1,000 paid on his agreement, but he did not prosecute, and he justly forfeited his deposit money. And now that I was proprietor and manager of the American Museum, I had reached a new epoch in my career, which I felt was the beginning of better days, though the full significance of this important step I did not see. I was still in the show business, but in a settled, substantial phase of it, that invited industry and enterprise, and called for ever earnest and ever heroic endeavor. Whether 1 should sink or swim, depended wholly upon my own energy. I must pay for the establishment within a stipulated time or forfeit it with whatever I had paid on account. I meant to make it my own, and brains, hands and every effort were devoted to the interests of the Museum.

The nucleus of this establishment, Scudder's Museum, was formed in 1810, the year in which I was born. It was begun in Chatham street, and was afterwards transferred to the old City Hall, and from small beginnings, by purchases, and to a considerable degree by presents, it had grown to be a large and valuable collection. People, in all parts of the country, had sent in relics and rare curiosities; sea captains, for years, had brought and deposited strange things from foreign lands; and besides all these gifts, I have no doubt that the previous proprietor had actually expended, as was stated, $50,000, in making the collection. No one could go through the halls, as they were when they came under my proprietorship, and see one-half there was worth seeing in a single day; and then, as I always justly boasted afterwards, no one could visit my Museum and go away without feeling that he had received the full worth of his money. In looking over the immense collection, the accumulation of so many years, I saw that it was only necessary to properly present its merits to the public, to make it the most attractive and popular place of resort and entertainment in the United States.

Valuable as the collection was when I bought it, it was only the beginning of the American Museum as I made it. In my long proprietorship, I considerably more than doubled the permanent attractions and curiosities of the establishment. In 1842, I bought and added to my collection the entire contents of Peale's Museum; in 1850, I purchased the large Peale collection in Philadelphia; and year after year, I bought genuine curiosities, regardless of cost, wherever I could find them, in Europe or America.

At the very outset, I was determined to deserve success. My plan of economy included the intention to support my family in New York on $600 a year, and my treasure of a wife, not only gladly assented, but was willing to reduce the sum to $400, if necessary. Some six months after I had bought the Museum, Mr. Olmsted happened in at my ticket-office at noon and found me eating a frugal dinner of cold corned beef and bread, which I had brought from home.

"Is this the way you eat your dinner? " he asked.

"I have not eaten a warm dinner, except on Sundays," I replied, "since I bought the Museum, and I never intend to, on a week day, till I am out of debt."

"Ah!" said he, clapping me on the shoulder, "you are safe, and will pay for the Museum before the year is out."

And he was right, for within twelve months I was in full possession of the property as my own, and it was entirely paid for from the profits of the business.

In 1865, the space occupied for my Museum purposes was more than double what it was in 1842. The Lecture Room, originally narrow, ill-contrived and inconvenient, was so enlarged and improved that it became one of the most commodious and beautiful amusement halls in the city of New York. At first, my attractions and inducements were merely the collection of curiosities by day, and an evening entertainment, consisting of such variety performances as were current in ordinary shows. Then Saturday afternoons, and, soon afterwards, Wednesday afternoons were devoted to entertainments, and the popularity of the Museum grew so rapidly that I presently found it expedient and profitable to open the great Lecture Room every afternoon, as well as every evening, on every weekday in the year. The first experiments in this direction, more than justified my expectations, for the day exhibitions were always more thronged than those of the evening. Of course, I made the most of the holidays, advertising extensively and presenting extra inducements; nor did attractions elsewhere seem to keep the crowd from coming to the Museum. On great holidays, I gave as many as twelve performances to as many different audiences.

By degrees the character of the stage performances was changed. The transient attractions of the Museum were constantly diversified, and educated dogs, industrious fleas, automatons, jugglers, ventriloquists, living statuary, tableaux, gypsies, Albinos, fat boys, giants, dwarfs, rope-dancers, live "Yankees," pantomime, instrumental music, singing and dancing in great variety, dioramas, panoramas, models of Niagara, Dublin, Paris, and Jerusalem; Hannington's dioramas of the Creation, the Deluge, Fairy Grotto, Storm at Sea; the first English Punch and Judy in this country, Italian Fantoccini, mechanical figures, fancy glass-blowing, knitting machines and other triumphs in the mechanical arts; dissolving views, American Indians, who enacted their warlike and religious ceremonies on the stage, — these, among others, were all exceedingly successful.

I thoroughly understood the art of advertising, not merely by means of printer's ink, which I have always used freely, and to which I confess myself so much indebted for my success, but by morning every possible circumstance to my account. It was my monomania to make the Museum the town wonder and town talk. I often seized upon an opportunity by instinct, even before I had a very definite conception as to how it should be used, and it seemed, somehow, to mature itself and serve my purpose. As an illustration, one morning a stout, hearty-looking man came into my ticket-office and begged some money. I asked him why he did not work and earn his living? He replied that he could get nothing to do, and that he would be glad of any job at a dollar a day. I handed him a quarter of a dollar, told him to go and get his breakfast and return, and I would employ him, at light labor, at a dollar and a half a day. When he returned I gave him five common bricks.

"Now," said I, "go and lay a brick on the sidewalk, at the corner of Broadway and Ann street; another close by the Museum; a third diagonally across the way, at the corner of Broadway and Vesey street, by the Astor House; put down the fourth on the sidewalk, in front of St. Paul's Church, opposite; then, with the fifth brick in hand, take up a rapid march from one point to the other, making the circuit, exchanging your brick at every point, and say nothing to anyone.

"What is the object of this?" inquired the man.

"No matter," I replied; "all you need to know is that it brings you fifteen cents wages per hour. It is a bit of my fun, and to assist me properly you must seem to be as deaf as a post; wear a serious countenance; answer no questions; pay no attention to any one; but attend faithfully to the work, and at the end of every hour, by St. Paul's clock, show this ticket at the Museum door; enter, walking solemnly through every hall in the building; pass out, and resume your work."

With the remark that it was "all one to him, so long as he could earn his living," the man placed his bricks, and began his round. Half an hour afterwards, at least five hundred people were watching his mysterious movements. He had assumed a military step and bearing, and, looking as sober as a judge, he made no response whatever to the constant inquiries as to the object of his singular conduct. At the end of the first hour, the sidewalks in the vicinity were packed with people, all anxious to solve the mystery. The man, as directed, then went into the Museum, devoting fifteen minutes to a solemn survey of the halls, and afterwards returning to his round. This was repeated every hour till sundown, and whenever the man went into the Museum a dozen or more persons would buy tickets and follow him, hoping to gratify their curiosity in regard to the purpose of his movements. This was continued for several days — the curious people who followed the man into the Museum considerably more than paying his wages — till finally the policeman, to whom I had imparted my object, complained that the obstruction of the sidewalk by crowds, had become so serious that I must call in my "brick man." This trivial incident excited considerable talk and amusement; it advertised me; and it materially advanced my purpose of making a lively corner near the Museum.

The stories illustrating merely my introduction of novelties would more than fill this book, but I must make room for a few of them.

An actor, named La Rue, presented himself as an imitator of celebrated histrionic personages, including Macready, Forrest, Kemble, the elder Booth, Kean, Hamblin and others. Taking him into the green-room for a private rehearsal, and finding his imitations excellent, I engaged him. For three nights he gave great satisfaction, but early in the fourth evening he staggered into the Museum so drunk that he could hardly stand, and in half an hour he must be on the stage!

Calling an assistant, we took La Rue between us, and marched him up Broadway as far as Chambers street, and back to the lower end of the Park, hoping to sober him. At this point we put his head under a pump, and gave him a good ducking, with visible beneficial effect — then a walk around the Park, and another ducking, — when he assured me that he should be able to give his imitations "to a charm." "You drunken brute," said I, "if you fail, and disappoint my audience, I will throw you out of the window."

He declared that he was "all right," and I led him behind the scenes, where I waited with considerable trepidation to watch his movements on the stage. He began by saying:

"Ladies and gentlemen: I will now give you an imitation of Mr. Booth, the eminent tragedian."

His tongue was thick, his language somewhat incoherent, and I had great misgivings as he proceeded; but as no token of disapprobation came from the audience, I began to hope he would go through with his parts without exciting suspicion of his condition. But before he had half finished his representation of Booth, in the soliloquy in the opening act of Richard III., the house discovered that he was very drunk, and began to hiss. This only seemed to stimulate him to make an effort to appear sober, which, as is usual in such cases, only made matters worse, and the hissing increased. I lost all patience, and going on the stage and taking the drunken fellow by the collar, I apologized to the audience, assuring them that he should not appear before them again. I was about to march him off, when he stepped to the front, and said:

"Ladies and gentlemen: Mr. Booth often appeared on the stage in a state of inebriety, and I was simply giving you a truthful representation of him on such occasions. I beg to be permitted to proceed with my imitations."

The audience at once supposed it was all right, and cried out, 'go on, go on'; which he did, and at every imitation of Booth, whether as Richard, Shylock, or Sir Giles Overreach, he received a hearty round of applause. I was quite delighted with his success; but when he came to imitate Forrest and Hamblin, necessarily representing them as drunk also, the audience could be no longer deluded; the hissing was almost deafening, and I was forced to lead the actor off. It was his last appearance on my stage.

I determined to make people talk about my Museum; to exclaim over its wonders; to have men and women all over the country say: "There is not another place in the United States where so much can be seen for twenty-five cents as in Barnum's American Museum." It was the best advertisement I could possibly have, and one for which I could afford to pay. I knew, too, that it was an honorable advertisement, because it was as deserved as it was spontaneous. And so, in addition to the permanent collection and the ordinary attractions of the stage, I labored to keep the Museum well supplied with transient novelties; I exhibited such living curiosities as a rhinoceros, giraffes, grizzly bears, orangutans, great serpents, and whatever else of the kind money would buy or enterprise secure.

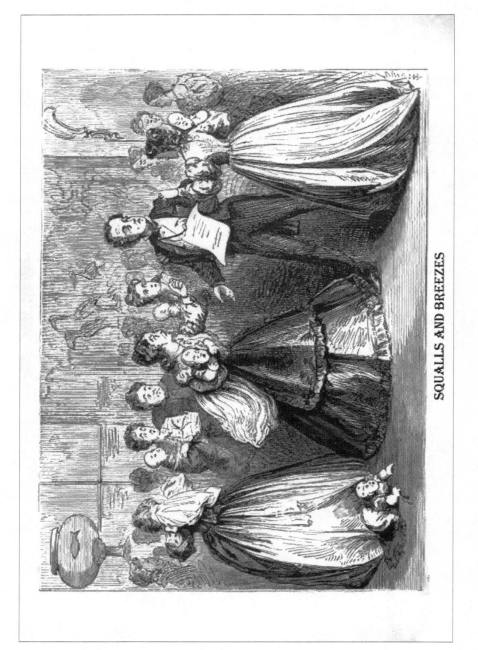

SQUALLS AND BREEZES

It was the world's way then, as it is now, to excite the community with flaming posters, promising almost everything for next to nothing. I confess that I took no pains to set my enterprising fellow-citizens a better example. I fell in with the world's way; and if my "puffing" was more persistent, my advertising more audacious, my posters more glaring, my pictures more exaggerated, my flags more patriotic and my transparencies more brilliant than they would have been under the management of my neighbors, it was not because I had less scruple than they, but more energy, far more ingenuity, and a better foundation for such promises. In all this, if I cannot be justified, I at least find palliation in the fact that I presented a wilderness of wonderful, instructive and amusing realities of such evident and marked merit that I have yet to learn of a single instance where a visitor went away from the Museum complaining that he had been defrauded of his money. Surely this is an offset to any eccentricities to which I may have resorted to make my establishment widely known.

Very soon after introducing my extra exhibitions, I purchased for $200, a curiosity which had much merit and some absurdity. It was a model of Niagara Falls, in which the merit was that the proportions of the great cataract, the trees, rocks, and buildings in the vicinity were mathematically given, while the absurdity was in introducing "real water" to represent the falls. Yet the model served a purpose in making "a good line in the bill" — an end in view which was never neglected — and it helped to give the Museum notoriety. One day I was summoned to appear before the Board of Croton Water Commissioners and was informed that as I paid only $25 per annum for water at the Museum, I must pay a large extra compensation for the supply for my Niagara Falls. I begged the board not to believe all that appeared in the papers, nor to interpret my show-bills too literally, and assured them that a single barrel of water, if my pump was in good order, would furnish my falls for a month.

It was even so, for the water flowed into a reservoir behind the scenes and was forced back with a pump over the falls. On one occasion, Mr. Louis Gaylord Clark, the editor of the *Knickerbocker*, came to view my Museum, and introduced himself to me. As I was quite anxious that my establishment should receive a first-rate notice at his hands, I took pains to show him everything of interest, except the Niagara Falls, which I feared would prejudice him against my entire show. But as we passed the room, the pump was at work, warning me that the great cataract was in full operation, and Clark, to my dismay, insisted upon seeing it.

"Well, Barnum, I declare, this is quite a new idea; I never saw the like before."

"No?" I faintly inquired, with something like reviving hope.

"No," said Clark, "and I hope, with all my heart, I never shall again."

But the *Knickerbocker* spoke kindly of me and refrained from all allusions to "the Cataract of Niagara, with real water." Some months after, Clark came in breathless one day, and asked me if I had the club with which Captain Cook was killed. As I had a lot of Indian war clubs in the collection of aboriginal curiosities and owing Clark something on the old Niagara Falls account, I told him I had the veritable club, with documents which placed its identity beyond question, and I showed him the warlike weapon.

"Poor Cook! Poor Cook!" said Clark, musingly. "Well, Mr. Barnum," he continued, with great gravity, at the same time extending his hand and giving mine a hearty shake, "I am really very much obliged to you for your kindness. I had an irrepressible desire to see the club that killed Captain Cook, and I felt quite confident you could accommodate me. I have been in half a dozen smaller museums, and as they all had it, I was sure a large establishment like yours would not be without it."

A few weeks afterwards, I wrote to Clark that if he would come to my office I was anxious to consult him on a matter of great importance. He came, and I said: "Now, I don't want any of your nonsense, but I want your sober advice."

He assured me that he would serve me in any way in his power, and I proceeded to tell him about a wonderful fish from the Nile, offered to me for exhibition at $100 a week, the owner of which was willing to forfeit $5,000, if, within six weeks, this fish did not pass through a transformation in which the tail would disappear and the fish would then have legs.

"Is it possible!" asked the astonished Clark.

I assured him that there was no doubt of it.

Thereupon he advised me to engage the wonder at any price; that it would startle the naturalists, wake up the whole scientific world, draw in the masses, and make $20,000 for the Museum. I told him that I thought well of the speculation, only I did not like the name of the fish.

"That makes no difference whatever," said Clark; "what is the name of the fish?"

"Tadpole," I replied, with becoming gravity, "but it is vulgarly called 'pollywog.'"

"Sold, by thunder!" exclaimed Clark, and he left.

A curiosity, which in an extraordinary degree served my ever-present object of extending the notoriety of the Museum, was the so-called "Feejee Mermaid." It has been supposed that this mermaid was manufactured by my order, but such is not the fact. I was known as a successful showman, and strange things of every sort were brought to me from all quarters, for sale or exhibition. In the summer of 1842, Mr. Moses Kimball, of the Boston Museum, came to New York and showed me what purported to be a mermaid. He had bought it from a sailor, whose father, a sea captain, had purchased it in Calcutta, in 1822, from some Japanese sailors. I may mention here that this identical preserved specimen was exhibited in London in 1822, as I fully verified in my visit to that city in 1858, for I found an advertisement of it in an old file of the *London Times*, and a friend gave me a copy of the *Mirror*, published by J. Limbird, 335 Strand, November 9, 1822, containing a cut of this same creature and two pages of letterpress describing it, together with an account of other mermaids said to have been captured in different parts of the world. The *Mirror* stated that this specimen was "the great source of attraction in the British metropolis, and three to four hundred people every day paid their shilling to see it."

This was the curiosity which had fallen into Mr. Kimball's hands. I requested my naturalist's opinion of the genuineness of the animal, and he said he could not conceive how it could have been manufactured, for he never saw a monkey with such peculiar teeth, arms, hands, etc., and he never saw a fish with such peculiar fins; but he did not believe in mermaids. Nevertheless, I concluded to hire this curiosity and to modify the general incredulity as to the possibility of the existence of mermaids, and to awaken curiosity to see and examine the specimen, I invoked the potent power of printer's ink.

Since Japan has been opened to the outer world, it has been discovered that certain "artists" in that country manufacture a great variety of fabulous animals, with an ingenuity and mechanical perfection well calculated to deceive. No doubt my mermaid was a specimen of this curious manufacture. I used it mainly to advertise the regular business of the Museum, and this effective indirect advertising is the only feature I can commend, in a special show of which, I confess, I am not proud. Newspapers throughout the country copied the mermaid notices, for they were novel and caught the attention of readers. Thus was the fame of the Museum, as well as the mermaid, wafted from one end of the land to the other. I was careful to keep up the excitement, for I knew that every dollar sown in advertising would return in tens, and perhaps hundreds, in a future harvest, and after obtaining all the notoriety possible by advertising and by exhibiting the mermaid at the Museum, I sent the curiosity throughout the country, directing my agent to everywhere advertise it as "From Barnum's Great American Museum, New York." The effect was immediately felt; money flowed in rapidly, and was readily expended in more advertising.

When I became proprietor of the establishment, there were only the words: "American Museum," to indicate the character of the concern; there was no bustle or activity about the place; no posters to announce what was to be seen. the whole exterior was as dead as the skeletons and stuffed skins within. My experiences had taught me the advantages of advertising. I printed whole columns in the papers, setting forth the wonders of my establishment. Old "fogies" opened their eyes in amazement at a man who could expend hundreds of dollars in announcing a show of "stuffed monkey skins;" but these same old fogies paid their quarters, nevertheless, and when they saw the curiosities and novelties in the Museum halls, they, like all other visitors, were astonished as well as pleased, and went home and told their friends and neighbors, and thus assisted in advertising my business.

Other and not less effective advertising, — flags and banners, — began to adorn the exterior of the building. I kept a band of music on the front balcony and announced "Free Music for the Million." People said, "Well, that Barnum is a liberal fellow to give us music for nothing," and they flocked down to hear my outdoor free concerts. But I took pains to select and maintain the poorest band I could find— one whose discordant notes would drive the crowd into the Museum, out of earshot of my outside orchestra. Of course, the music was poor. When people expect to get "something for nothing " they are sure to be cheated. Powerful Drummond lights were placed at the top of the Museum, which, in the darkest night, threw a flood of light up and down Broadway, from the Battery to Niblo's, that would enable one to read a newspaper in the street. These were the first Drummond lights ever seen in New York, and they made people talk, and so advertised my Museum.

CHAPTER IX.

THE ROAD TO RICHES.

The American Museum was the ladder by which I rose to fortune. Whenever I cross Broadway at the head of Vesey street, and see the *Herald* building and that gorgeous pile, the Park Bank, my mind's eye recalls that less solid, more showy edifice which once occupied the site, and was covered with pictures of all manner of beasts, birds and creeping things, and in which were treasures that brought treasures and notoriety and pleasant hours to me. The Jenny Lind enterprise was more audacious, more immediately remunerative, and I remember it with a pride which I do not attempt to conceal; but instinctively I often go back and live over again the old days of my struggles and triumphs in the American Museum.

The Museum was always open at sunrise, and this was so well known throughout the country that strangers coming to the city would often take a tour through my halls before going to breakfast or to their hotels. I do not believe there was ever a more truly popular place of amusement. I frequently compared the annual number of visitors with the number officially reported as visiting (free of charge) the British Museum in London, and my fist was invariably the larger. Nor do I believe that any man or manager ever labored more industriously to please his patrons. I furnished the most attractive exhibitions which money could procure; I abolished all vulgarity and profanity from the stage, and I prided myself upon the fact, that parents and children could attend the dramatic performances in the so-called Lecture Room, and not be shocked or offended by anything they might see or hear; I introduced the "Moral Drama," producing such plays as "The Drunkard," "Uncle Tom's Cabin," "Moses in Egypt," "Joseph and his Brethren," and occasional spectacular melodramas produced with great care at considerable outlay.

Mr. Sothern, who has since attained such wide-spread celebrity at home and abroad as a character actor, was a member of my dramatic company for one or two seasons. Mr. Barney Williams also began his theatrical career at the Museum, occupying, at first, quite a subordinate position, at a salary of ten dollars a week. During his last twelve or fifteen years, I presume his weekly receipts, when he acted, must have been nearly $3,000. The late Miss Mary Gannon also commenced at the Museum, and many more actors and actresses of celebrity have been, from time to time, engaged there. What was once the small Lecture Room was converted into a spacious and beautiful theater, extending over the lots adjoining the Museum, and capable of holding about three thousand persons. The saloons were greatly multiplied and enlarged, and the "egress" having been made to work to perfection, on holidays I advertised Lecture Room performances every hour through the afternoon and evening, and consequently the actors and actresses were dressed for the stage as early as eleven o'clock in the morning, and did not resume their ordinary clothes till ten o'clock at night. In these busy days the meals for the company were brought in and served in the dressing-rooms and green-rooms, and the company always received extra pay.

I confess that I liked the Museum mainly for the opportunities it afforded for rapidly making money. Before I bought it, I weighed the matter well in my mind, and was convinced that I could present to the American public such a variety, quantity and quality of amusement, blended with instruction, "all for twenty-five cents, children half price," that my attractions would be irresistible, and my fortune certain. I myself relished a higher grade of amusement, and I was a frequent attendant at the opera, first-class concerts, lectures, and the like; but I worked for the million, and I knew the only way to make a million from my patrons was to give them abundant and wholesome attractions for a small sum of money.

About the first of July, 1842, I began to make arrangements for extra novelties, additional performances, a large amount of extra advertising, and an outdoor display for the "Glorious Fourth." Large parti-colored bills were ordered, transparencies were prepared, the free band of music was augmented by a trumpeter, and columns of advertisements, headed with large capitals, were written and put on file.

I wanted to run out a string of American flags across the street on that day, for I knew there would be thousands of people passing the Museum with leisure and pocket-money, and I felt confident that an unusual display of national flags would arrest their patriotic attention and bring many of them within my walls.

Unfortunately for my purpose, St. Paul's Church stood directly opposite, and there was nothing to which I could attach my flag-rope, unless it might be one of the trees in the church-yard. I went to the vestrymen for permission to so attach my flag-rope on the Fourth of July, and they were indignant at what they called my "insulting proposition;" such a concession would be "sacrilege." I plied them with arguments, and appealed to their patriotism, but in vain.

Returning to the Museum, I gave orders to have the string of flags made ready, with directions at daylight on the Fourth of July to attach one end of the rope to one of the third-story windows of the Museum, and the other end to a tree in St. Paul's churchyard. The great day arrived, and my orders were strictly followed. The flags attracted great attention. By half-past nine Broadway was thronged, and about that time two gentlemen, in a high state of excitement, rushed into my office, announcing themselves as injured and insulted vestrymen of St. Paul's Church.

"Keep cool, gentlemen," said I; "I guess it is all right."

"Right!" indignantly exclaimed one of them, "do you think it is right to attach your Museum to our Church? "We will show you what is 'right ' and what is law, if we live till tomorrow; those flags must come down instantly."

"Thank you," I said, "but let us not be in a hurry. I will go out with you and look at them, and I guess we can make it all right."

Going into the street, I remarked: "Really, gentlemen, these flags look very beautiful; they do not injure your tree; I always stop my balcony music for your accommodation whenever you hold week-day services, and it is but fair that you should return the favor."

"We could indict your 'music,' as you call it, as a nuisance, if we chose," answered one vestryman, "and now I tell you that if these flags are not taken down in ten minutes, *I* will cut them down. "

His indignation was at boiling point. The crowd in the street was dense, and the angry gesticulation of the vestryman attracted their attention. I saw there was no use in trying to parley with him or coax him, and so, assuming an angry air, I rolled up my sleeves, and exclaimed, in a loud tone,

"Well, Mister, I should just like to see you dare to cut down the American flag on the Fourth of July; you must be a 'Britisher' to make such a threat as that; but I'll show you a thousand pairs of Yankee hands in two minutes, if you dare to attempt to take down the stars and stripes on this great birth-day of American freedom!"

"What's that John Bull a-saying?" asked a brawny fellow, placing himself in front of the irate vestryman. "Look here, old fellow," he continued, "if you want to save a whole bone in your body, you had better slope, and never dare to talk again about hauling down the American flag in the city of New York."

Throngs of excited, exasperated men crowded around, and the vestryman, seeing the effect of my ruse, smiled faintly and said, "Oh, of course it is all right," and he and his companion quietly edged out of the crowd.

On that Fourth of July, at one o'clock p.m., my Museum was so densely crowded that we could admit no more visitors, and we were compelled to stop the sale of tickets. Looking down into the street it was a sad sight to see the thousands of people who stood ready with their money to enter the Museum, but who were actually turned away. It was exceedingly harrowing to my feelings. Rushing down stairs, I told my carpenter and his assistants to cut through the partition and floor in the rear and to put in a temporary flight of stairs so as to let out people by that egress into Ann street. By three o'clock the egress was opened, and a few people were passed down the new stalls, while a corresponding number came in at the front. But I lost a large amount of money that day by not having sufficiently estimated the value of my own advertising, and consequently not having provided for the thousands who had read my announcements and seen my outside show and had taken the first leisure day to visit the Museum. I had learned one lesson, however, and that was to have the egress ready on future holidays.

Early in the following March, I received notice from some of the Irish population that they meant to visit me in great numbers on "St. Patrick's Day in the morning." "All right," said I to my carpenter, "get your egress ready for March 17;" and I added, to my assistant manager: "If there is much of a crowd, don't let a single person pass out at the front, even if it were St. Patrick himself; put every man out through the egress in the rear." The day came, and before noon we were caught in the same dilemma as we were on the Fourth of July; the Museum was jammed, and the sale of tickets was stopped. I went to the egress and asked the sentinel how many hundreds had passed out?

"Hundreds," he replied, "why only three persons have gone out by this way and they came back, saying that it was a mistake and begging to be let in again."

"What does this mean?" I inquired; "surely thousands of people have been all over the Museum since they came in."

"Certainly," was the reply, "but after they have gone from one saloon to another, and have been on every floor, even to the roof, they come down and travel the same route over again."

At this time, I espied a tall Irish woman with two good-sized children whom I had happened to notice when they came early in the morning."

"Step this way, madam," said I, politely, "you will never be able to get into the street by the front door without crushing these dear children. We have opened a large egress here, and you can pass by these rear stairs into Ann street and thus avoid all danger."

"Sure," replied the woman, indignantly, "an' I'm not going out at all, at all, nor the children aither, for we've brought our dinners and we are going to stay all day."

Further investigation showed that pretty much all of my visitors had brought their dinners with the evident intention of literally "making a day of it." No one expected to go home till night; the building was overcrowded, and meanwhile hundreds were waiting at the front entrance to get in when they could.

In despair I sauntered upon the stage behind the scenes, biting my lips with vexation, when I happened to see the scene-painter at work and a happy thought struck me: "Here," I exclaimed, "take a piece of canvas four feet square, and paint on it, as soon as you can, in large letters,

☞ TO THE EGRESS"

Seizing his brush, he finished the sign in fifteen minutes, and I directed the carpenter to nail it over the door leading to the back stairs. He did so, and as the crowd, after making the entire tour of the establishment, came pouring down the main stairs from the third story, they stopped and looked at the new sign, while some of them read audibly: "To the Aigress."

"The Aigress," said others, "sure that's an animal we haven't seen," and the throng began to pour down the back stairs only to find that the "Aigress" was the elephant, and that the elephant was all out o' doors, or so much of it as began with Ann street. Meanwhile, I began to accommodate those who had long been waiting with their money at the Broadway entrance.

Money poured in upon me so rapidly that I was sometimes actually embarrassed to devise means to carry out my original plan for laying out the entire profits of the first year in advertising. I meant to sow first and reap afterwards. I finally hit upon a plan which cost a large sum, and that was to prepare large oval oil paintings to be placed between the windows of the entire building, representing nearly every important animal known in zoology. These paintings were put on the building in a single night, and so complete a transformation in the appearance of an edifice is seldom witnessed. When the living stream rolled down Broadway the next morning and reached the Astor House corner, opposite the Museum, it seemed to meet with a sudden check. I never before saw so many open mouths and astonished eyes. Some people were puzzled to know what it all meant; some looked as if they thought it was an enchanted palace that had suddenly sprung up; others exclaimed, "Well, the animals all seem to have 'broken out' last night," and hundreds came in to see how the establishment survived the sudden eruption.

From that morning the Museum receipts took a jump forward of nearly a hundred dollars a day, and they never fell back again.

The Museum had become an established institution in the land. Now and then someone would cry out "humbug" and "charlatan," but so much the better for me; it helped to advertise me, and I was willing to bear the reputation.

On several occasions I got up "Baby shows," at which I paid liberal prizes for the finest baby, the fattest baby, the handsomest twins, for triplets, and so on. These shows were as popular as they were unique, and while they paid, in a financial point of view, my chief object in getting them up was to set the newspapers to talking about me, thus giving another blast on the trumpet which I always tried to keep blowing for the Museum. Flower shows, dog shows, poultry shows and bird shows, were held at intervals in my establishment and in each instance the same end was attained as by the baby shows. I gave prizes in the shape of medals, money and diplomas, and the whole came back to me four-fold in the shape of advertising.

There was great difficulty, however, in awarding the principal prize of $100 at the baby shows. Every mother thought her own baby the brightest and best, and confidently expected the capital prize.

For where was ever seen the mother
Would give her baby for another?

Not foreseeing this when I first stepped into the expectant circle and announced in a matter of fact way that a committee of ladies had decided upon the baby of Mrs. So and So as entitled to the leading prize, I was ill-prepared for the storm of indignation that arose on every side. Ninety-nine disappointed and, as they thought, deeply injured mothers made common cause and pronounced the successful little one the meanest, homeliest baby in the lot, and roundly abused me and my committee for our stupidity and partiality. "Very well, ladies," said I in the first instance, "select a committee of your own and I will give another $100 prize to the baby you shall pronounce to be the best specimen."

This was only throwing oil upon flame; the ninety-nine confederates were deadly enemies from the moment, and no new babies were presented in competition for the second prize. Thereafter, I took good care to send in a written report and did not attempt to announce the prize in person.

In June, 1843, a herd of yearling buffaloes was on exhibition in Boston. I bought the lot, brought them to New Jersey, hired the race-course at Hoboken, chartered the ferry-boats for one day, and advertised that a hunter had arrived with a herd of buffaloes — I was careful not to state their age — and that August 31st there would be a "Grand Buffalo Hunt" on the Hoboken race-course— all persons to be admitted free of charge.

The appointed day was warm and delightful, and no less than twenty-four thousand people crossed the North River in the ferry-boats to enjoy the cooling breeze and to see the "Grand Buffalo Hunt." The hunter was dressed as an Indian and mounted on horseback; he proceeded to show how the wild buffalo is captured with a lasso, but unfortunately the yearlings would not run till the crowd gave a great shout, expressive at once of derision and delight at the harmless humbug. This shout started the young animals into a weak gallop and the lasso was duly thrown over the head of the largest calf. The crowd roared with laughter, listened to my balcony band, which I also furnished "free," and then started for New York, little dreaming who was the author of this sensation, or what was its object.

Mr. N.P. Willis, then editor of the *Home Journal,* wrote an article illustrating the perfect good nature with which the American public submit to a clever humbug. He said that he went to Hoboken to witness the buffalo hunt. It was nearly four o'clock when the boat left the foot of Barclay street, and it was so densely crowded that many persons were obliged to stand on the railings and hold on to the awning-posts. When they reached the Hoboken side a boat equally crowded was coming out of the slip. The passengers just arriving cried out to those who were coming away, "Is the buffalo hunt over?" To which came the reply, " Yes, and it was the biggest humbug you ever heard of!" Willis added that passengers on the boat with him instantly gave three cheers for the author of the humbug, whoever he might be.

After the public had enjoyed a laugh for several days over the Hoboken "Free Grand Buffalo Hunt," I permitted it to be announced that the proprietor of the American Museum was responsible for the joke, thus using the buffalo hunt as a sky-rocket to attract public attention to my Museum. The object was accomplished, and although some people cried out "humbug", I had added to the notoriety which I so much wanted, and I was satisfied. As for the cry of "humbug," it never harmed me, and I was in the position of the actor who had much rather be roundly abused than not to be noticed at all. I ought to add, that the forty-eight thousand sixpences — the usual fare — received for ferry fares, less what I paid for the charter of the boats on that one day, more than remunerated me for the cost of the buffaloes and the expenses of the "hunt;" and the enormous gratuitous advertising of the Museum must also be placed to my credit.

With the same object — that is, advertising my Museum, I purchased for $500, in Cincinnati, Ohio, a "Woolly Horse" I found on exhibition in that city. It was a well-formed, small-sized horse, with no mane, and not a particle of hair on his tail, while his entire body and legs were covered with thick, fine hair or wool, which curled tight to his skin. This horse was foaled in Indiana, and was a remarkable freak of nature, and certainly a very curious-looking animal.

I had not the remotest idea, when I bought this horse, what I should do with him: but when the news came that Colonel John C. Fremont (who was supposed to have been lost in the snows of the Rocky Mountains) was in safety, the "Woolly Horse" was exhibited in New York and was widely advertised as a most remarkable animal that had been captured by the great explorer's party in the passes of the Rocky Mountains. The exhibition met with only moderate success in New York, and in several Northern provincial towns, and the show would have fallen flat in Washington, had it not been for the over-zeal of Colonel Thomas H. Benton, then a United States Senator from Missouri. He went to the show, and then caused the arrest of my agent for obtaining twenty-five cents from him under "false pretenses." No mention had been made of this curious animal in any letter he had received from his son-in-law, Colonel John C. Fremont, and therefore the Woolly Horse had not been captured by any of Fremont's party. The reasoning was hardly as sound as were most of the arguments of "Old Bullion," and the case was dismissed.

After a few days of merriment, public curiosity no longer turned in that direction, and the old horse was permitted to retire to private life. My object in the exhibition, however, was fully attained. When it was generally known that the proprietor of the American Museum was also the owner of the famous "Woolly Horse," it caused yet more talk about me and my establishment, and visitors began to say that they would give more to see the proprietor of the Museum than to view the entire collection of curiosities. As for my ruse in advertising the "Woolly Horse" as having been captured by Fremont's exploring party, of course the announcement neither added to nor took from the interest of the exhibition; but it arrested public attention, and it was the only feature of the show that I now care to forget.

It will be seen that very much of the success which attended my many years proprietorship of the American Museum was due to advertising, and especially to my odd methods of advertising. Always determined to have curiosities worth showing and worth seeing, at "twenty-five cents admission, children half price," I studied ways to arrest public attention; to startle, to make people talk and wonder; in short, to let the world know that I had a Museum.

About this time, I engaged a band of Indians from Iowa. They had never seen a railroad or steamboat until they saw them on the route from Iowa to New York. The party comprised large and noble specimens of the untutored savage, as well as several very beautiful squaws, with two or three interesting "papooses." They lived and lodged in a large room on the top floor of the Museum, and cooked their own victuals in their own way. They gave their war-dances on the stage in the Lecture Room with great vigor and enthusiasm, much to the satisfaction of the audiences. But these wild Indians seemed to consider their dances as realities. Hence, when they gave a real war dance, it was dangerous for any parties, except their manager and interpreter, to be on the stage, for the moment they had finished their war dance, they began to leap and peer about behind the scenes in search of victims for their tomahawks and scalping knives! Indeed, lest in these frenzied moments they might make a dash at the orchestra or the audience, we had a high rope barrier placed between them and the savages on the front of the stage.

After they had been a week in the Museum, I proposed a change of performance for the week following, by introducing new dances. Among these was the Indian wedding dance. At that time, I printed but one set of posters (large bills) per week, so that whatever was announced for Monday, was repeated every day and evening during that week. Before the wedding dance came off on Monday afternoon, I was informed that I was to provide a large new red woolen blanket, at a cost of ten dollars, for the bridegroom to present to the father of the bride. I ordered the purchase to be made; but was considerably taken aback, when I was informed that I must have another new blanket for the evening, inasmuch as the savage old Indian Chief, father-in-law to the bridegroom, would not consent to his daughter's being approached with the wedding dance unless he had his blanket present.

I undertook to explain to the chief, through the interpreter, that this was only a "make believe" wedding; but the old savage shrugged his shoulders and gave such a terrific "Ugh!" that I was glad to make my peace by ordering another blanket. As we gave two performances per day, I was out of pocket $120 for twelve "wedding blankets," that week.

One of the beautiful squaws named Do-humme died in the Museum. She had been a great favorite with many ladies, among whom I can especially name Mrs. C. M. Sawyer, wife of the Rev. Dr. T. J. Sawyer. Do-humme was buried on the border of Sylvan Water, at Greenwood Cemetery, where a small monument erected by her friends, designates her last resting-place.

The poor Indians were very sorrowful for many days, and desired to get back again to their western wilds. The father and the betrothed of Do-humme cooked various dishes of food and placed them upon the roof of the Museum, where they believed the spirit of their departed friend came daily for its supply; and these dishes were renewed every morning during the stay of the Indians at the Museum.

It was sometimes very amusing to hear the remarks of strangers who came to visit my Museum. One afternoon a prim maiden lady from Portland, Maine, walked into my private office, where I was busily engaged in writing, and, taking a seat on the sofa, she asked:

"Is this Mr. Barnum?"

"It is," I replied.

"Is this Mr. P. T. Barnum, the proprietor of the Museum?" she asked.

"The same," was my answer.

"Why, really, Mr. Barnum," she continued, "you look much like other common folks, after all."

"Dear me! Mr. Barnum," said she, "I never went to any Museum before, nor to any place of amusement or public entertainment, excepting our school exhibitions; and I have sometimes felt that they even may be wicked, for some parts of the dialogues seemed frivolous; but I have heard so much of your 'moral drama,' and the great good you are doing for the rising generation that I thought I must come here and see for myself."

At this moment the gong sounded to announce the opening of the Lecture Room, and the crowd passed on in haste to secure seats. My spinster visitor sprang to her feet and anxiously inquired:

"Are the services about to commence?"

"Yes," I replied, "the congregation is now going up."

CHAPTER X.

ANOTHER SUCCESSFUL SPECULATION.

By some arrangement, the particulars of which I do not remember, if, indeed, I ever cared to know them, Mr. Peale was conducting Peale's Museum, which he claimed was a more "scientific" establishment than mine, and he pretended to appeal to a higher class of patrons. Mesmerism was one of his scientific attractions, and he had a subject upon whom he operated at times with the greatest seeming success, and fairly astonished his audiences. But there were times when the subject was wholly unimpressible and then those who had paid their money to see the woman put into the mesmeric state cried out "humbug," and the reputation of the establishment seriously suffered.

It devolved upon me to open a rival mesmeric performance, and accordingly I engaged a bright little girl who was exceedingly susceptible to such mesmeric influences as I could induce. That is, she learned her lesson thoroughly, and when I had apparently put her to sleep with a few passes and stood behind her, she seemed to be duly "impressed" as I desired; raised her hands as I willed, fell from her chair to the floor; and if I put candy or tobacco into my mouth, she was duly delighted or disgusted. She never failed in these routine performances. Strange to say, believers in mesmerism used to witness her performances with the greatest pleasure and adduce them as positive proofs that there was something in mesmerism, and they applauded tremendously — up to a certain point.

That point was reached when, leaving the girl "asleep," I called up someone in the audience, promising to put him "in the same state" within five minutes, or forfeit fifty dollars. Of course, all my "passes" would not put a man in the mesmeric state; at the end of three minutes he was as wide awake as ever. "Never mind," I would say, looking at my watch; "I have two minutes more, and meantime, to show that a person in this state is utterly insensible to pain, I propose to cut off one of the fingers of the little girl who is still asleep." I would then take out my knife and feel of the edge, and when I turned around to the girl whom I left on the chair, she had fled behind the scenes, to the intense amusement of the greater part of the audience, and to the amazement of the mesmerists who were present.

"Why! where's my little girl?" I asked with feigned astonishment.

"Oh! she ran away when you began to talk about cutting off fingers."

"Then she was wide awake, was she?"

"Of course, she was, all the time."

"I suppose so; and, my dear sir, I promised that you should be 'in the same state' at the end of five minutes, and as I believe you are so, I do not forfeit fifty dollars."

I kept up this performance for several weeks, till I quite killed Peale's "genuine" mesmerism in the rival establishment. At the end of six months I bought Peale's Museum, and the whole, including the splendid gallery of American portraits, was removed to the American Museum, and I immediately advertised the great card of a "Double attraction" and "Two Museums in One," without extra charge.

The Museum became a mania with me, and I made everything possible subservient to it. On the eve of elections, rival politicians would ask me for whom I was going to vote, and my answer invariably was, "I vote for the American Museum." In fact, at that time, I cared very little about politics, and a great deal about my business. Meanwhile the Museum prospered wonderfully, and everything I attempted or engaged in, seemed at the outset an assured success.

The giants whom I exhibited from time to time, were always literally great features in my establishment, and they oftentimes afforded me, as well as my patrons, food for much amusement as well as wonder. The Quaker giant, Hales, was quite a wag in his way. He went once to see the new house of an acquaintance who had suddenly become rich, but who was a very ignorant man. When he came back he described the wonders of the mansion, and said that the proud proprietor showed him everything from basement to attic: parlors, bed-rooms, dining-room, and," said Hales, "what he calls his 'study'—meaning, I suppose, the place where he intends to study his spelling-book!"

I had at one time two famous men, the French giant, M. Bihin, a very slim man, and the Arabian giant, Colonel Goshen. These men generally got on together very well, though, of course, each was jealous of the other, and of the attention the rival received, or the notice he attracted. One day they quarreled, and a lively interchange of compliments ensued, the Arabian calling the Frenchman a "Shanghai," and received in return the epithet of "Nigger." From words both were eager to proceed to blows, and both ran to my collection of arms, one seizing the club with which Captain Cook, or any other man, might have been killed, if it were judiciously wielded, and the other laying hands on a sword of the terrific size, which is supposed to have been conventional in the days of the Crusades. The preparations for a deadly encounter, and the high words of the contending parties, brought a dozen of the Museum *attaches* to the spot, and these men threw themselves between the gigantic combatants. Hearing the disturbance, I ran from my private office to the dueling ground, and said: "Look here! This is all right; if you want to fight each other, maiming and perhaps killing one or both of you, that is your affair; but my interest lies here: you are both under engagement to me, and if this duel is to come off, I and the public have a right to participate. It must be duly advertised, and must take place on the stage of the Lecture Room. No performance of yours would be a greater attraction, and if you kill each other, our engagement can end with your duel."

THE AUTHOR TRAINING TOM THUMB

This proposition, made in apparent earnest, so delighted the giants that they at once burst into a laugh, shook hands, and quarreled no more. In November, 1842, I was at Bridgeport, Connecticut, where I heard of a remarkably small child, and, at my request, my brother, Philo F. Barnum, brought him to the hotel. He was not two feet high; he weighed less than sixteen pounds and was the smallest child I ever saw that could walk alone; he was a perfectly formed, bright-eyed little fellow, with fight hair and ruddy cheeks, and he enjoyed the best of health. He was exceedingly bashful, but after some coaxing, he was induced to talk with me, and he told me that he was the son of Sherwood E. Stratton, and that his own name was Charles S. Stratton After seeing him and talking with him, I at once determined to secure his services from his parents and to exhibit him in public. I engaged him for four weeks, at three dollars a week, with all traveling and boarding charges for himself and his mother at my expense. They came to New York Thanksgiving Day, December 8, 1842, and I announced the dwarf on my Museum bills as "General Tom Thumb."

I took the greatest pains to educate and train my diminutive prodigy, devoting many hours to the task by day and by night, and I was very successful, Cor he was an apt pupil, with a great deal of native talent, and a keen sense of the ludicrous.

I afterwards re-engaged him for one year, at seven dollars a week, with a gratuity of fifty dollars at the end of the engagement, and the privilege of exhibiting him anywhere in the United States, in which event his parents were to accompany him and I was to pay all traveling expenses. He speedily became a public favorite, and long before the year was out, I voluntarily increased his weekly salary to twenty-five dollars, and he fairly earned it.

Two years had now elapsed since I bought the Museum, and I had long since paid for the entire establishment from the profits; I had bought out my only rival; I was free from debt and had a handsome surplus in the treasury. The business had long ceased to be an experiment; it was an established success, and was in such perfect running order, that it could safely be committed to the management of trustworthy and tried agents.

Accordingly, looking for a new field for my individual efforts, I entered into an agreement for General Tom Thumb's services for another year, at fifty dollars a week and all expenses, with the privilege of exhibiting him in Europe. I proposed to test the curiosity of men and women on the other side of the Atlantic.

After arranging my business affairs for a long absence, and making every preparation for an extended foreign tour, on Thursday, January 18, 1844, I went on board the new and fine sailing ship "Yorkshire," Captain D. G. Bailey, bound for Liverpool. Our party included General Tom Thumb, his parents, his tutor, and Professor Guillaudeu, the French naturalist. We were accompanied by several personal friends, and the City Brass Band kindly volunteered to escort us to Sandy Hook.

A voyage to Liverpool is now an old, familiar story, and I abstain from entering into details, though I have abundant material respecting my own experiences of my first sea voyage in the first two of a series of one hundred letters which I wrote in Europe, as correspondent of the New York *Atlas*.

On our arrival at Liverpool, quite a crowd had assembled at the dock to see Tom Thumb, for it had been previously announced that he would arrive in the

"Yorkshire," but his mother managed to smuggle him ashore unnoticed, for she carried him, as if he was an infant, in her arms.

My letters of introduction speedily brought me into friendly relations with many excellent families, and I was induced to hire a hall and present the General to the public, for a short season in Liverpool. I had intended to proceed directly to London, and begin operations at "headquarters," that is, in Buckingham Palace, if possible; but I had been advised that the royal family was in mourning for the death of Prince Albert's father, and would not permit the approach of any entertainments.

Meanwhile, confidential letters from London, informed me that Mr. Maddox, Manager of Princess's Theater, was coming down to witness my exhibition, with a view to making an engagement. He came privately, but I was fully informed as to his presence and object. A friend pointed him out to me hi the hall, and when I stepped up to him, and called him by name, he was "taken all aback," and avowed his purpose in visiting Liverpool. An interview resulted in an engagement of the General for three nights at Princess's Theater. I was unwilling to contract for a longer period, and even this short engagement, though on liberal terms, was acceded to only as a means of advertisement. So soon, therefore, as I could bring my short, but highly successful season in Liverpool to a close, we went to London.

CHAPTER XI.

GENERAL TOM THUMB IN ENGLAND,

Immediately after our arrival in London, the General came out at the Princess's Theater, and made so decided a "hit" that it was difficult to decide" who was best pleased, the spectators, the manager, or myself. I was offered far higher terms for a re-engagement, but my purpose had been already answered; the news was spread everywhere that General Tom Thumb, an unparalleled curiosity, was in the city; and it only remained for me to bring him before the public, on my own account, and in my own time and way.

I took a furnished mansion in Grafton street, Bond street, West End, in the very center of the most fashionable locality. The house had previously been occupied for several years by Lord Talbot, and Lord Brougham and half a dozen families of the aristocracy and many of the gentry were my neighbors. From this magnificent mansion, I sent letters of invitation to the editors and several of the nobility, to visit the General. Most of them called, and were highly gratified. The word of approval was indeed so passed around in high circles, that uninvited parties drove to my door in crested carriages, and were not admitted.

This procedure, though in some measure a stroke of policy, was neither singular nor hazardous, under the circumstances. I had not yet announced a public exhibition, and as a private American gentleman, it became me to maintain the dignity of my position. I therefore instructed my liveried servant to deny admission to see my "ward," excepting to persons who brought cards of invitation. He did it in a proper manner, and no offence could be taken, though I was always particular to send an invitation immediately to such as had not been admitted.

During our first week in London, the Hon. Edward Everett, the American Minister, to whom I had letters of introduction, called and was highly pleased with his diminutive though renowned countryman. We dined with him the next day, by invitation, and his family loaded the young American with presents. Mr. Everett kindly promised to use influence at the Palace in person, with a view to having Tom Thumb introduced to Her Majesty Queen Victoria.

A few evenings afterwards the Baroness Rothschild sent her carriage for us. We were received by a half a dozen servants, and were ushered up a broad flight of marble stairs to the drawing-room, where we met the Baroness and a party of twenty or more ladies and gentlemen. In this sumptuous mansion of the richest banker in the world, we spent about two hours, and when we took our leave a well-filled purse was quietly slipped into my hand. The golden shower had begun to fall.

I now engaged the "Egyptian Hall," in Piccadilly, and the announcement of my unique exhibition was promptly answered by a rush of visitors, in which the wealth and fashion of London were liberally represented. I made these arrangements because I had little hope of being soon brought to the Queen's presence (for the reason before mentioned), but Mr. Everett's generous influence secured my object. I breakfasted at his house one morning, by invitation, in company with Mr. Charles Murray, an author of creditable repute, who held the office of Master of the Queen's Household. In the course of conversation, Mr. Murray inquired as to my plans, and I informed him that I intended going to the Continent shortly, though I should be glad to remain if the General could have an interview with the Queen, adding that such an event would be of great consequence to me.

Mr. Murray kindly offered his good offices in the case, and the next day one of the Life Guards, a tall, noble-looking fellow, bedecked as became his station, brought me a note, conveying the Queen's invitation to General Tom Thumb and his guardian, Mr. Barnum, to appear at Buckingham Palace on an evening specified. Special instructions were the same day orally given me by Mr. Murray, by Her Majesty's command, to suffer the General to appear before her, as he would appear anywhere else, without any training in the use of the titles of royalty, as the Queen desired to see him act naturally and without restraint.

Determined to make the most of the occasion, I put a placard on the door of the Egyptian Hall: "Closed this evening, General Tom Thumb being at Buckingham Palace by command of Her Majesty."

On arriving at the Palace, the Lord in Waiting put me "under drill" as to the manner and form in which I should conduct myself in the presence of royalty. I was to answer all questions by Her Majesty through him, and, in no event, to speak directly to the Queen. In leaving the royal presence I was to "back out," keeping my face always towards Her Majesty, and the illustrious lord, kindly gave me a specimen of that sort of backward locomotion. How far I profited by his instructions and example, will presently appear.

We were conducted through a long corridor to a broad flight of marble steps, which led to the Queen's magnificent picture gallery, where Her Majesty and Prince Albert, the Duchess of Kent, the Duke of Wellington, and others were awaiting our arrival. They were standing at the farther end of the room when the doors were thrown open, and the General walked in, looking like a wax doll gifted with the power of locomotion. Surprise and pleasure were depicted on the countenances of the royal circle at beholding this remarkable specimen of humanity so much smaller than they had evidently expected to find him.

The General advanced with a firm step, and, as he came within hailing distance, made a very graceful bow, and exclaimed, "Good evening, ladies and gentlemen!"

A burst of laughter followed this salutation. The Queen then took him by the hand, led him about the gallery, and asked him many questions, the answers to which kept the party in an uninterrupted strain of merriment. The General familiarly informed the Queen that her picture gallery was "first-rate," and told her he should like to see the Prince of Wales. The Queen replied that the Prince had retired to rest, but that he should see him on some future occasion. The General then gave his songs, dances, and imitations, and, after a conversation with Prince Albert and all present, which continued for more than an hour, we were permitted to depart.

Before describing the process and incidents of "backing out," I must acknowledge how sadly I broke through the counsel of the Lord in Waiting. While Prince Albert and others were engaged with the General, the Queen was gathering information from me in regard to his history, etc. Two or three questions were put and answered through the process indicated in my drill. It was a round-about way of doing business, not at all to my liking, and I suppose the Lord in waiting was seriously shocked, if not outraged, when I entered directly into conversation with Her Majesty. She, however, seemed not disposed to check my boldness, for she immediately spoke directly to me in obtaining the information which she sought. I felt entirely at ease in her presence, and could not avoid contrasting her sensible and amiable manners with the stiffness and formality of upstart gentility at home or abroad.

The Queen was modestly attired in plain black, and wore no ornaments. Indeed, surrounded as she was by ladies arrayed in the highest style of magnificence, their dresses sparkling with diamonds, she was the last person whom a stranger would have pointed out in that circle as the Queen of England.

The Lord in waiting was perhaps mollified toward me when he saw me following his illustrious example in retiring from the royal presence. He was accustomed to the process, and therefore was able to keep somewhat ahead (or rather aback) of me, but even *I* stepped rather fast for the other member of the retiring party. We had a considerable distance to travel in that long gallery before reaching the door, and whenever the General found he was losing ground, he turned around and ran a few steps, then resumed the position of "backing out," then turned around and ran, and so continued to alternate his methods of getting to the door, until the gallery fairly rang with the merriment of the royal spectators. It was really one of the richest scenes I ever saw; running, under the circumstances, was an offence sufficiently heinous to excite the indignation of the Queen's favorite poodle dog, and he vented his displeasure by barking so sharply as to startle the General from his propriety. He, however, recovered immediately, and, with his little cane, commenced an attack on the poodle, and a funny fight ensued, which renewed and increased the merriment of the royal party.

This was near the door of exit. We had scarcely passed into the ante-room, when one of the Queen's attendants came to us with the expressed hope of Her Majesty that the General had sustained no damage; to which the Lord in Waiting playfully added, that in case of injury to so renowned a personage, he should fear a declaration of war by the United States!

The courtesies of the Palace were not yet exhausted, for we were escorted to an apartment in which refreshments had been provided for us. I was anxious that the "Court Journal" of the ensuing day should contain more than a mere line in relation to the General's interview with the Queen, and, on inquiry, I learned that the gentleman who had charge of that feature in the daily papers was then in the Palace. He was sent for by my solicitation, and promptly acceded to my request for such a notice as would attract attention. He even generously desired me to give him an outline of what I sought, and I was pleased to see afterwards, that he had inserted my notice verbatim.

This notice of my visit to the Queen wonderfully increased the attraction of "Gen. Tom Thumb," and compelled me to obtain a more commodious hall for my exhibition. I accordingly removed to the larger room in the same building.

On our second visit to the Queen, we were received in what is called the "Yellow Drawing-Room," a magnificent apartment, surpassing in splendor and gorgeousness anything of the kind I had ever seen. It is on the north side of the gallery, and is entered from that apartment. It was hung with drapery of rich yellow satin damask, the couches, sofas and chairs being covered with the same material. The vases, urns and ornaments were all of modern patterns, and the most exquisite workmanship. The room was paneled in gold, and the heavy cornices beautifully carved and gilt. The tables, pianos, etc., were mounted with gold, inlaid with pearl of various hues, and of the most elegant designs.

We were ushered into this gorgeous drawing-room before the Queen and royal circle had left the dining-room, and, as they approached, the General bowed respectfully, and remarked to Her Majesty "that he had seen her before," adding, "I think this is a prettier room than the picture gallery; that chandelier is very fine."

The Queen smilingly took him by the hand, and said she hoped he was very well.

"Yes, ma'am," he replied, "I am first rate."

"General," continued the Queen, "this is the Prince of Wales."

"How are you, Prince?" said the General, shaking him by the hand; and then standing beside the Prince, he remarked, "the Prince is taller than I am, but I feel as big as anybody," upon which he strutted up and down the room as proud as a peacock, amid shouts of laughter from all present.

The Queen then introduced the Princess Royal, and the General immediately led her to his elegant little sofa, which we took with us, and with much politeness sat himself down beside her. Then, rising from his seat, he went through his various performances, and the Queen handed him an elegant and costly souvenir, which had been expressly made for him by her order, for which, he told her, "he was very much obliged, and would keep it as long as he lived." The Queen of the Belgians (daughter of Louis Philippe) was present on this occasion. She asked the General where he was going when he left London?

"To Paris," he replied."

"Whom do you expect to see there?" she continued.

Of course, all expected he would answer, "the King of the French," but the little fellow replied, "Monsieur Guillaudeu." The two Queens looked inquiringly to me, and when I informed them that M. Gillaudeu was my French naturalist, who had preceded me to Paris, they laughed most heartily.

On our third visit to Buckingham Palace, Leopold, King of the Belgians, was also present. He was highly pleased, and asked a multitude of questions. Queen Victoria desired the General to sing a song, and asked him what song he preferred to sing.

"Yankee Doodle," was the prompt reply.

This answer was as unexpected to me as it was to the royal party. When the merriment it occasioned had somewhat subsided, the Queen good-humoredly remarked, "That is a very pretty song, General, sing it, if you please." The General complied, and soon afterwards we retired. I ought to add, that after each of our three visits to Buckingham Palace, a very handsome sum was sent to me, of course by the Queen's command. This, however, was the smallest part of the advantage derived from these interviews, as will be at once apparent to all who consider the force of Court example in England.

The British public were now fairly excited. Not to have seen General Tom Thumb was decidedly unfashionable, and from March 30th until July 20th, the levees of the little General, at Egyptian Hall, were continually crowded, the receipts averaging during the whole period about five hundred dollars per day, and sometimes going considerably beyond that sum. At the fashionable hour, sixty carriages of the nobility have been counted at one time standing in front of our exhibition rooms in Piccadilly.

Portraits of the little General were published in all the pictorial papers of the time. Polkas and quadrilles were named after him, and songs were sung in high praise. He was an almost constant theme for the London *Punch*, which served up the General and myself so daintily that it no doubt added vastly to our receipts.

Besides his three public performances per day, the little General attended three or four private parties per week, for which we were paid eight to ten guineas each.

Frequently we would visit two parties in the same evening, and the demand in that line was much greater than the supply. The Queen Dowager Adelaide requested the General's attendance at Marlborough House one afternoon. He went in his court dress, consisting of a richly embroidered brown silk-velvet coat and short breeches, white satin vest with fancy colored embroidery, white silk stockings and pumps, wig, bagwig, cocked hat, and a dress sword.

"Why, General," said the Queen Dowager, "I think you look very smart today."

"I guess I do," said the General complacently.

A large party of the nobility were present. The old Duke of Cambridge offered the little General a pinch of snuff, which he declined. The General sang his songs, performed his dances, and cracked his jokes, to the great amusement and delight of the distinguished circle of visitors.

"Dear little General," said the kind-hearted Queen, taking him upon her lap, "I see you have got no watch. Will you permit me to present you with a watch and chain?"

"I would like them very much," replied the General, his eyes glistening with joy as he spoke.

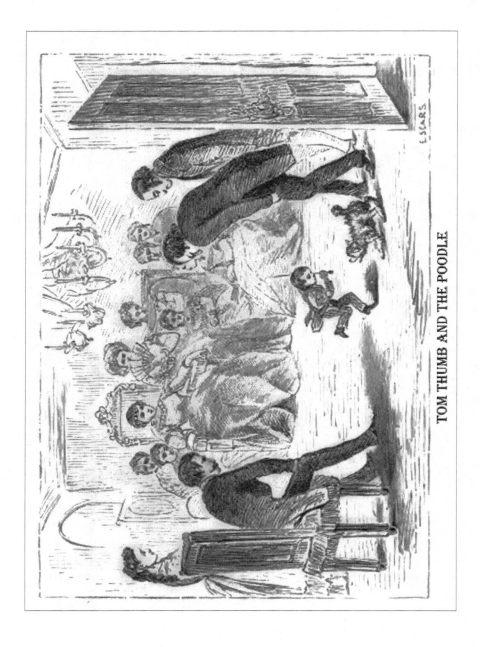

TOM THUMB AND THE POODLE.

"I will have them made expressly for you," responded the Queen Dowager; and at the same moment she called a friend and desired him to see that the proper order was executed. A few weeks thereafter we were called again to Marlborough House. A number of the children of the nobility were present, as well as some of their parents. After passing a few compliments with the General, Queen Adelaide presented him with a beautiful little gold watch, placing the chain around his neck with her own hands.

After giving his performances, we withdrew from the royal presence, and the elegant little watch presented by the hands of Her Majesty the Queen Dowager was not only duly *Herald*ed, but was also placed upon a pedestal in the hall of exhibition, together with the presents from Queen Victoria, and covered with a glass vase. These presents, to which were soon added an elegant gold snuff-box mounted with turquois, presented by his Grace the Duke of Devonshire, and many other costly gifts of the nobility and gentry, added to the attractions of the exhibition. The Duke of Wellington called frequently to see the little General at his public levees. The first time he called, the General was impersonating Napoleon Bonaparte, marching up and down the platform, and apparently taking snuff in deep meditation. He was dressed in the well-known uniform of the Emperor. I introduced him to the "Iron Duke," who inquired the subject of his meditations. "I was thinking of the loss of the battle of Waterloo," was the little General's immediate reply. This display of wit was chronicled throughout the country and was of itself worth thousands of pounds to the exhibition.

General Tom Thumb had visited the King of Saxony and also Ibrahim Pacha who was then in London. At the different parties we attended, we met, in the course of the season, nearly all of the nobility. Scarcely a nobleman in England failed to see General Tom Thumb at his own house, at the house of a friend, or at the public levees at Egyptian Hall. The General was a decided pet with some of the first personages in the land, among whom may be mentioned Sir Robert and Lady Peel the Duke and Duchess of Buckingham, Duke of Bedford, Duke of Devonshire, Count d'Orsay, Lady Blessington, Daniel O'Connell, Lord Adolphus Fitzclarence, Lord Chesterfield. Mr. and Mrs. Joshua Bates, of the firm of Baring Brothers & Co., and many other persons of distinction. We had the free entree to all the theaters, public gardens, and places of entertainment, and frequently met the principal artists, editors, poets, and authors of the country. Albert Smith wrote a play for the General entitled "Hop o' my Thumb," which was presented with great success at the Lyceum Theater, London, and in several of the provincial theaters. Our visit in London and tour through the provinces were enormously successful, and after a brilliant season in Great Britain I made preparations to take the General to Paris.

CHAPTER XII.

IN FRANCE.

Before taking the little General and party to Paris, I went over alone to arrange the preliminaries for our campaign in that city.

I was very fortunate in making the acquaintance of Mr. Dion Boueieault, who was then temporarily sojourning in that city, and who at once kindly volunteered to advise and assist me in regard to numerous matters of importance relating to the approaching visit of the General. He spent a day with me in the search for suitable accommodations for my company, and by giving me the benefit of his experience, he saved me much trouble and expense. I have never forgotten the courtesy extended to me by this gentleman.

I hired, at a large rent, the Salle Musard, Rue Vivienne. I made the most complete arrangements, even to starting the preliminary paragraphs in the Paris papers; and after calling on the Honorable William Rufus King, the United States Minister at the Court of France, who assured me that, after my success in London, there would be no difficulty whatever in my presentation to King Louis Philippe, I returned to England.

I went back to Paris with General Tom Thumb and party some time before I intended to begin my exhibitions, and on the very day after my arrival I received a special command to appear at the Tuileries on the following Sunday evening.

At the appointed hour the General and I, arrayed in the conventional court costume, were ushered into a grand saloon of the palace, where we were introduced to the King, the Queen, Princess Adelaide, the Duchess d'Orleans and her son, the Count de Paris, Prince de Joinville, Duke and Duchess de Nemours, the Duchess d'Aumale, and a dozen or more distinguished persons, among whom was the editor of the official *Journal des Debats*. General Tom Thumb went through his various performances to the manifest pleasure of all who were present, and at the close the King presented to him a large emerald brooch set with diamonds. The General expressed his gratitude, and the King, turning to me, said: "You may put it on the General, if you please," which I did, to the evident gratification of the King as well as the General.

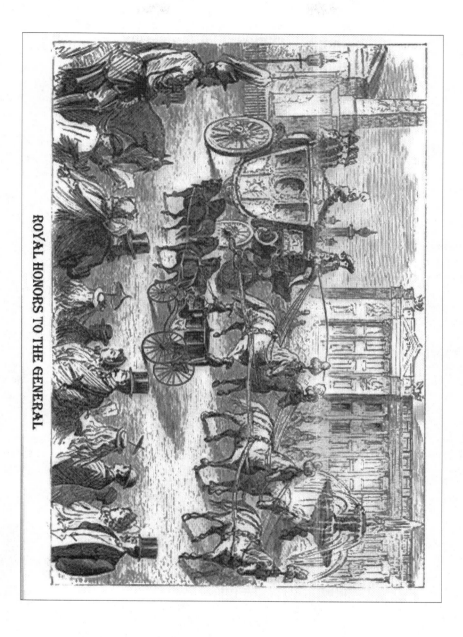

ROYAL HONORS TO THE GENERAL

King Louis Philippe was so condescending and courteous, that I felt quite at home in the royal presence and ventured upon a bit of diplomacy. The Longchamps celebration was coming — a day once devoted to religious ceremony, but now conspicuous for the display of court and fashionable equipages in the Champs Elysees and the Bois des Boulogne, and, as the King was familiarly conversing with me, I ventured to say that I had hurried over to Paris to take part in the Longchamps display, and I asked him if the General's carriage could not be permitted to appear in the avenue reserved for the court and the diplomatic corps, representing that the General's small, but elegant establishment, with its ponies and little coachman and footman, would be in danger of damage in the general throng, unless the special privilege I asked was accorded.

The King smilingly turned to one of the officers of his household, and, after conversing with him for a few moments, he said to me:

"Call on the Prefect of Police tomorrow afternoon, and you will find a permit ready for you."

Our visit occupied two hours, and when we went away the General was loaded with fine presents. The next morning all the newspapers noticed the visit, and the *Journal des Debuts*, gave a minute account of the interview and of the General's performances, taking occasion to say, in speaking of the character parts, that "there was one costume which the General wisely kept at the bottom of his box." That costume, however — the uniform of Bonaparte — was once exhibited, by particular request, as will be seen anon.

Longchamps day arrived, and among the many splendid equipages on the grand avenue, none attracted more attention than the superb little carriage with four ponies and liveried and powdered coachman and footman, belonging to the General, and conspicuous in the line of carriages containing the Ambassadors to the Court of France. Thousands upon thousands rent the air with cheers for "General Tom *Pouce*."

Thus, before I opened the exhibition, all Paris knew that General Tom Thumb was in the city. The elite of the city came to the exhibition; the first day's receipts were 5,500 francs, which would have been doubled if I could have made room for more patrons. There were afternoon and evening performances, and from that day secured seats, at an extra price, were engaged in advance for the entire two months. The season was more than a success; it was a triumph.

It seemed, too. as if the whole city was advertising me. The papers were profuse in their praises of the General and his performances. *Figaro*, the *Punch* of Paris, gave a picture of an immense mastiff running away with the General's carriage and horses in his mouth. Statuettes of "Tom Pouce" appeared in all the windows, in plaster, Parian, sugar and chocolate; songs were written about him, and his lithograph was seen everywhere. A fine cafe on one of the boulevards, took the name of "Tom Pouce." and displayed over the door a life-size statue of the General. In Paris, as in London, several eminent painters expressed their desire to paint his portrait, but the General's engagements were so pressing that he found little time to sit for artists. All the leading actors and actresses came to the General's levees, and petted him and made him many presents. Meanwhile, the daily receipts continued to swell, and I was compelled to take a cab to carry my bag of silver home at night.

We were commanded to appear twice more at the Tuileries, and we were also invited to the palace on the King's birthday, to witness the display of fireworks in honor of the anniversary. Our fourth and last visit to the royal family was, by special invitation, at St. Cloud. On this one occasion, and by the special request of the King, the General impersonated Napoleon Bonaparte in full costume. Louis Philippe had heard of the General in this character, and particularly desired to see him; but the affair was quite "on the sly," and no mention was made of it in the papers. We remained an hour, and, at parting, each of the royal company gave the General a splendid present, almost smothered him with kisses, wished him a safe journey through France, and a long and happy life. After bidding them *adieu*, we retired to another portion of the palace to make a change of the General's costume, and to partake of some refreshments which were prepared for us. Half an hour afterwards, as we were about leaving the palace, we went through a hall leading to the front door, and in doing so, passed the sitting- room in which the royal family were spending the evening. The door was open, and some of them happening to espy the General, called out for him to come in and shake hands with them once more. We entered the apartment, and there found the ladies sitting around a square table, each provided with two candles, and every one of them, including the Queen, was engaged in working at embroidery, while a young lady was reading aloud for their edification. I am sorry to say, I believe this is a sight seldom seen in families of the aristocracy on either side of the water. At the church fairs in Paris, I had frequently seen pieces of embroidery for sale, which were labelled as having been presented and worked by the Duchess d'Orleans, Princess Adelaide, Duchess de Nemours, and other titled ladies.

During my stay in Paris, a Russian Prince, who had been living in great splendor in that city, suddenly died, and his household and personal effects were sold at auction. I attended the sale for several days in succession, buying many articles of vertu, and, among others, a magnificent gold tea-set, and a silver dining-service, and many rare specimens of Sevres china. These articles bore the initials of the family name of the Prince, and his own, "P. T." thus damaging the articles, so that the silver and gold were sold for their weight value only. I bought them, and adding "B." to the "P. T.," had a very fine table service, still in my possession, and bearing my own initials, "P. T. B."

After a protracted and most profitable season we started on a tour through France. We went first to Rouen, and from thence to Toulon, visiting all the intermediate towns, including Orleans, Nantes, Brest, Bordeaux, where I witnessed a review by the Dukes de Nemours and d'Aumale, of 20,000 soldiers who were encamped near the city. From Bordeaux we went to Toulouse, Montpellier, Nismes, Marseilles, and many other less important places, holding levees for a longer or shorter time. While at Nantes, Bordeaux and Marseilles, the General also appeared in the theaters in his French part of "Petit Poucet," a French play written expressly for him in Paris, and performed with great éclat in the theater Vaudeville in that city.

CHAPTER XIII.

IN BELGIUM.

In crossing the border from France into Belgium, Professor Pinte, our interpreter and General Tom Thumb's preceptor, discovered that he had left his passport behind him — at Lille, at Marseilles, or elsewhere in France, he could not tell where, for it was a long time since he had been called upon to present it.

When we came to Courtrai on the Belgian frontier, I managed to procure a permit for him which enabled him to proceed with the party.

Brussels is Paris' in miniature and is one of the most charming cities I ever visited. We found elegant quarters, and the day after our arrival by command we visited King Leopold and the Queen at their palace. The King and Queen had already seen the General in London, but they wished to present him to their children and to the distinguished persons whom we found assembled. After a most agreeable hour we came away, the General, as usual, receiving many fine presents.

The following day I opened the exhibition in a beautiful hall which on that day and on every afternoon and evening while we remained there, was crowded by throngs of the first people in the city. On the second or third day, in the midst of the exhibition, I suddenly missed the case containing the valuable presents the General had received from kings, queens, noblemen and gentlemen, and instantly gave the alarm; some thief had intruded for the express purpose of stealing these jewels, and, in the crowd, had been entirely successful in his object.

The police were notified, and I offered 2,000 francs reward for the recovery of the property. A day or two afterwards a man went into a jeweler's shop and offered for sale, among other things, a gold snuff-box, mounted with turquoises, and presented by the Duke of Devonshire to the General. The jeweler, seeing the General's initials on the box, sharply questioned the man, who became alarmed and ran out of the shop. An alarm was raised, and the man was caught. He made a clean breast of it, and in the course of a few hours the entire property was returned, to the great delight of the General and myself. Wherever we exhibited afterwards, no matter how respectable the audience, the case of presents was always carefully watched.

While I was in Brussels I could do no less than visit the battlefield of Waterloo, and I proposed that our party should be composed of Professor Pinte, Mr. Stratton, father of General Tom Thumb, Mr. H.G. Sherman and myself.

We engaged a coach and horses the night previous, and started punctually at the hour appointed. We stopped at the neat little church in the village of Waterloo, for the purpose of examining the tablets erected to the memory of some of the English who fell in the contest. Thence we passed to the house in which the leg of Lord Uxbridge (Marquis of Anglesey) was amputated. A neat little monument in the garden designates the spot where the shattered member had been interred. In the house is shown a part of the boot which is said to have once covered the unlucky leg. I expressed a desire to have a small piece of the boot to exhibit in my Museum; the lady cut off, without hesitation, a slip three inches long by one in width. I could not help thinking that if the lady was thus liberal in dispensing pieces of the "identical boot" to all visitors, this must have been about the ninety-nine thousandth boot that had been cut as the "Simon pure " since 1815.

Arriving at Mont Saint Jean, a quarter of a mile from the ground, we were beset by some eighteen or twenty persons, who offered their services as guides, to indicate the most important localities. Each applicant professed to know the exact spot where every man had been placed who had taken part in the battle, and each, of course, claimed to have been engaged in that sanguinary contest, although it had occurred thirty years before, and some of these fellows were only, it seemed, from twenty-five to twenty-eight years of age! We accepted an old man, who, at first declared that he was killed in the battle, but, perceiving our looks of incredulity, consented to modify his statement so far as to assert that he was horribly wounded, and lay upon the ground three days before receiving assistance.

Once upon the ground, our guide, with much gravity, pointed out the place where the Duke of Wellington took his station during a great part of the action; the locality where the reserve of the British army was stationed; the spot where Napoleon placed his favorite guard; the little mound on which was erected a temporary observatory for his use during the battle; the portion of the field at which Blucher entered with the Prussian army; the precise location of the Scotch Greys; the spot where fell Sir Alexander Gordon, Lieut. Col. Canning, and many others of celebrity. I asked him if he could tell me where Captain Tippitiwichet, of the Connecticut Fusileers, was killed. "*Oui, Monsieur*," he replied, with perfect confidence, for he felt bound to know, or to pretend to know, every particular. He then proceeded to point out exactly the spot where my unfortunate Connecticut friend had breathed his last. After indicating the locations where some twenty more fictitious friends from Coney Island, New Jersey, Cape Cod and Saratoga Springs, had given up the ghost, we handed him his commission and declined to give him further trouble.

Upon quitting the battlefield, we were accosted by a dozen persons of both sexes with baskets on their arms or bags in their hands, containing relics of the battle for sale. These consisted of a great variety of implements of war, pistols, bullets, etc., besides brass French eagles, buttons, etc. I purchased a number of them for the Museum, and Stratton was equally liberal in obtaining a supply for his friends in "Old Bridgeport." We also purchased maps of the battleground, pictures of the triumphal mound surmounted by the colossal Belgic Lion in bronze, etc., etc. These frequent and renewed taxations annoyed Stratton very much, and, as he handed out a five-franc piece for a "complete guide-book," he remarked, Chat "he guessed the battle of Waterloo had cost a darned sight more since it was fought than it did before!"

MANURE CART EXPRESS

But his misfortunes did not terminate here. When we had proceeded four or five miles upon our road home, crash went the carriage. We alighted, and found that the axle-tree was broken. It was now a quarter past one o'clock. The little General's exhibition was advertised to commence in Brussels at two o'clock, and could not take place without us. We were unable to walk the distance in double the time at our disposal, and, as no carriage was to be got in that part of the country, I concluded to take the matter easy, and forego all idea of exhibiting before evening. Stratton, however, could not bear the thought of losing the chance of taking in six or eight hundred francs, and he determined to take matters in hand, in order, if possible, to get our party into Brussels in time to save the afternoon exhibition. He hastened to a farmhouse, accompanied by the interpreter, Professor Pinte, Sherman and myself leisurely bringing up the rear. Stratton asked the old farmer if he had a carriage. He had not. "Have you no vehicle? " he inquired.

"Yes, I have that vehicle," he replied, pointing to an old cart filled with manure, and standing in his barnyard.

"Thunder! is that all the conveyance you have got?" asked Stratton, being assured that it was, Stratton concluded that it was better to ride in a manure-cart than not to get to Brussels in time.

"What will you ask to drive us to Brussels in three-quarters of an hour?" demanded Stratton.

"It is impossible," replied the fanner; "I should want two hours for my horse to do it in."

"But ours is a very pressing case, and if we are not there in time we lose more than five hundred francs," said Stratton.

The old farmer pricked up his ears at this, and agreed to get us to Brussels in an hour, for eighty francs. Stratton tried to beat him down, but it was of no use.

"Oh, go it, Stratton," said Sherman; "eighty francs you know is only sixteen dollars, and you will probably save a hundred by it, for I expect a full house at our afternoon exhibition today."

"But I have already spent about ten dollars for nonsense," said Stratton, " and we shall have to pay for the broken carriage besides."

"But what can you do better?" chimed in Professor Pinte. "It is an outrageous extortion to charge sixteen dollars for an old horse and cart to go ten miles. Why, in old Bridgeport I could get it done for three dollars," replied Stratton, in a tone of vexation

"It is the custom of the country," said Professor Pinte, "and we must submit to it."

"Well, it's a thundering mean custom, anyhow," said Stratton, "and I won't stand such imposition."

"But what shall we do?" earnestly inquired Mr. Pinte. "It may be a high price, but it is better to pay that than to lose our afternoon performance and five or six hundred francs."

This appeal to the pocket touched Stratton's feelings; so, submitting to the extortion, he replied to our interpreter, "Well tell the old robber to dump his dung-cart as soon as possible, or we shall lose half an hour in starting."

The cart was "dumped" and a large, lazy-looking Flemish horse was attached to it with a rope harness. Some boards were laid across the cart for seats, the party tumbled into the rustic vehicle, a red-haired boy, son of the old fanner, mounted the horse, and Stratton gave orders to "get along."

"Wait a moment," said the farmer, " you have not paid me yet."

"I'll pay your boy when we get to Brussels, provided he gets there within the hour," replied Stratton.

"Oh, he is sure to get there in an hour," said the fanner, "but I can't let him go unless you pay in advance." The minutes were flying rapidly, the anticipated loss of the day exhibition of General Tom Thumb flitted before his eyes, and Stratton, in very desperation, thrust his hand into his pocket and drew forth sixteen five-franc pieces, which he dropped, one at a time, into the hand of the farmer, and then called out to the boy, "There now, do try to see if you can go ahead."

The boy did go ahead, but it was with such a snail's pace that it would have puzzled a man of tolerable eyesight to have determined whether the horse was moving or standing still. To make it still more interesting, it commenced raining furiously. As we had left Brussels in a coach, and the morning had promised us a pleasant day, we had omitted our umbrellas. We were soon soaked to the skin. We "grinned and bore it" awhile without grumbling. At length Stratton, who was almost too angry to speak, desired Mr. Pinte to ask the red-haired boy if he expected to walk his horse all the way to Brussels.

"Certainly," replied the boy; "he is too big and fat to do anything but walk. "We never trot him."

Stratton was terrified as he thought of the loss of the day exhibition; and he cursed the boy, the cart, the rain, the luck, and even the battle of Waterloo itself. But it was all of no use, the horse would not run, but the rain did — down our backs.

At two o'clock, the time appointed for our exhibition, we were yet some seven miles from Brussels. The horse walked slowly and philosophically through the pitiless storm, the steam majestically rising from the old manure-cart, to the no small disturbance of our unfortunate olfactories. "It will take two hours to get to Brussels at this rate," growled Stratton. "Oh, no," replied the boy, "it will only take about two hours from the time we started "

"But your father agreed to get us there in an hour," answered Stratton.

"I know it," responded the boy, "but he knew it would take more than two."

"I'll sue him for damage, by thunder! " said Stratton.

"Oh, there would be no use in that," chimed in Mr. Pinte, "for you could get no satisfaction in this country."

"But I shall lose more than a hundred dollars by being two hours instead of one," said Stratton.

"They care nothing about that; all they care for is your eighty francs," remarked Pinte.

"But they have lied and swindled me," replied Stratton.

"Oh, you must not mind that, it is the custom of the country."

All things will finally have an end, and our party did at length actually arrive in Brussels, cart and all, in precisely two hours and a half from the time we left the farmer's house. Of course, we were too late to exhibit the little General. Hundreds of visitors had gone away disappointed.

Several months subsequent to our visit to Waterloo, I was in Birmingham, and there made the acquaintance of a firm who manufactured to order, and sent to Waterloo, barrels of "relics" every year. At Waterloo these "relics" are planted, and in due time dug up, and sold at large prices as precious remembrances of the great battle. Our Waterloo purchases looked rather cheap after this discovery.

CHAPTER XIV.

IN ENGLAND AGAIN.

In London the General again opened his levees in Egyptian Hall with increased success. His unbounded popularity on the Continent, and his receptions by King Louis Philippe, of France, and King Leopold, of Belgium, had added greatly to his prestige and fame. Those who had seen him when he was in London months before, came to see him again, and new visitors crowded by thousands to the General's levees.

Besides giving these daily entertainments, the General appeared occasionally for an hour, during the intermissions, at some place in the suburbs; and for a long time, he appeared every day at the Surrey Zoological Gardens, under the direction of the proprietor, my particular friend, Mr. W. Tyler. This place subsequently became celebrated for its great music hall, in which Spurgeon, the sensational preacher, first attained his notoriety. The place was always crowded, and when the General had gone through with his performances on the little stage, in order that all might see him, he was put into a balloon, which, secured by ropes, was then passed around the ground, just above the people's heads. Some forty men managed the ropes and prevented the balloon from rising; but, one day, a sudden gust of wind took the balloon fairly out of the hands of half the men who had hold of the ropes, while others were lifted from the ground, and had not an alarm been instantly given, which called at least two hundred to the rescue, the little General would have been lost.

In October, 1844, I made my first return visit to the United States, leaving General Tom Thumb in England, in the hands of an accomplished and faithful agent. One of the principal reasons for my return at this time, was my anxiety to renew the Museum building lease, although my first lease of five years had still three years longer to run.

Having completed my business arrangements in New York, I returned to England with my wife and daughters, and hired a house in Loudon. My house was the scene of constant hospitality, which I extended to my numerous friends in return for the many attentions shown to me. It seemed then as if I had more and stronger friends in London than in New York, I had met and had been introduced to "almost everybody who was anybody," and among them all, some of the best soon became to me much more than mere acquaintances.

Among the distinguished people whom I met, I was introduced to the poet-banker, Samuel Rogers. I saw him at a dinner party at the residence of the American Minister, the Honorable Edward Everett. As we were going in to dinner, I stepped aside, so that Mr. Rogers who was tottering along leaning on the arm of a friend, could go in before me, when Mr. Rogers said:

"Pass in, Mr. Barnum, pass in; I always consider it an honor to follow an American."

PUT ME IN IRONS

When our three months' engagement at Egyptian Hall had expired, I arranged for a protracted provincial tour through Great Britain. I had made a flying visit to Scotland before we went to Paris — mainly to procure the beautiful Scotch costumes, daggers, etc., which were carefully made for the General at Edinburgh, and to teach the General the Scotch dances, with a bit of the Scotch dialect, which added so much to the interest of his exhibitions in Paris and elsewhere. My second visit to Scotland, for the purpose of giving exhibitions, extended as far as Aberdeen.

In England we went to Manchester, Birmingham, and to almost every city, town and even village of importance. We traveled by post much of the time — that is, I had a suitable carriage made for my party, and a van which conveyed the General's carriage, ponies, and such other "property" as was needed for our levees. This mode of traveling was not only very comfortable and independent, but it enabled us to visit many out of the way places, off from the great lines of travel, and in such places, we gave some of our most successful exhibitions. We also used the railway lines freely, leaving our carriages at any station, and taking them up again when we returned.

I remember once making an extraordinary effort to reach a branch-line station, where I meant to leave my teams and take the rail for Rugby. I had a time-table, and knew at what hour exactly I could hit the train; but unfortunately, the axle to my carriage broke, and, as an hour was lost in repairing it, I lost exactly an hour in reaching the station. The train had long been gone, and I must be in Rugby, where we had advertised a performance. I stormed around till I found the superintendent, and told him "I must instantly have an extra train to Rugby."

"Extra train?" said he, with surprise and a half sneer, "extra train?" why you can't have an extra train to Rugby for less than sixty pounds."

"Is that all?" I asked; "well, get up your train immediately and here are your sixty pounds. What in the world are sixty pounds to me, when I wish to go to Rugby, or elsewhere, in a hurry! "

The astonished superintendent took the money, bustled about, and the train was soon ready. He was greatly puzzled to know what distinguished person — he thought he must be dealing with some prince, or, at least, a duke — was willing to give so much money to save a few hours of time, and he hesitatingly asked whom he had the honor of serving.

"General Tom Thumb."

We reached Rugby in time to give our performance, as announced, and our receipts were £160, which quite covered the expense of our extra train and left a handsome margin for profit.

When we were in Oxford, a dozen or more of the students came to the conclusion that, as the General was a little fellow, the admission fee to his entertainments should be paid in the smallest kind of money. They accordingly provided themselves with farthings, and as each man entered, instead of handing in a shilling for his ticket, he laid down forty-eight farthings. The counting of these small coins was a great annoyance to Mr. Stratton, the General's father, who was ticket-seller, and after counting two or three handfuls, vexed at the delay which was preventing a crowd of ladies and gentlemen from buying tickets, Mr. Stratton lost his temper and cried out:

"Blast your quarter-pennies! I am not going to count them! You chaps who haven't bigger money can chuck your copper into my hat and walk in."

Mr. Stratton was a genuine Yankee, and thoroughly conversant with the Yankee vernacular, which he used freely. In exhibiting the General, I often said to visitors, that Tom Thumb's parents, and the rest of the family, were persons of the ordinary size, and that the gentleman who presided in the ticket office was the General's father. This made poor Stratton an object of no little curiosity, and he was pestered with all sorts of questions; on one occasion an old dowager said to him:

"Are you really the father of General Tom Thumb?"

"Wa'al," replied Stratton, "I have to support him!"

This evasive answer is common enough in New England, but the literal dowager had her doubts, and promptly rejoined:

"I rather think he supports you!"

It must not be supposed that during my protracted stay abroad I confined myself wholly to business, or limited my circle of observation with a golden rim. To be sure, I ever had "an eye to business," but I had also two eyes for observation, and these were busily employed in leisure hours. I made the most of my opportunities and saw, hurriedly, it is true, nearly everything worth seeing in the various places which I visited. All Europe was a great curiosity shop to me, and I willingly paid my money for the show.

"While in London, my friend Albert Smith, a jolly companion, as well as a witty and sensible author, promised that when I reached Birmingham he would come and spend a day with me in "sight-seeing," including a visit to the house in which Shakespeare was born.

Early one morning in the autumn of 1844, my friend Smith and myself took the box-seat of an English mail-coach and were soon whirling at the rate of twelve miles an hour over the magnificent road leading from Birmingham to Stratford. The distance is thirty miles. At little village four miles from Stratford, we found that the fame of the bard of Avon, had traveled thus far, for we noticed a sign over a miserable barber's shop, "Shakespeare hair-dressing — a good shave for a penny." In twenty minutes more, we were set down at the door of the Bed Horse Hotel, in Stratford. The coachman and guard were each paid half a crown as their perquisites.

"While breakfast was preparing, we called for a guide-book to the town, and the waiter brought in a book, saying that we should find in it the best description extant of the birth and burial place of Shakespeare. I was not a little proud to find this volume to be no other than the "Sketch-Book" of our illustrious countryman, Washington Irving; and, in glancing over his humorous description of the place, I discovered that he had stopped at the same hotel where we were then awaiting breakfast.

After examining the Shakespeare House, as well as the tomb and the church in which all that is mortal of the great poet rests, we ordered a post-chaise for Warwick Castle. While the horses were harnessing, a stage-coach stopped at the hotel, and two gentlemen alighted. One was a sedate, sensible-looking man; the other an addle-headed fop. The former was mild and unassuming in his manners; the latter was all talk, without sense or meaning — in fact, a regular Charles Chatterbox. He evidently had a high opinion of himself and was determined that all within hearing should understand that he was — somebody. Presently the sedate gentleman said:

"Edward, this is Stratford. Let us go and see the house where Shakespeare was born. "

"Who the devil is Shakespeare?" asked the sensible young gentleman.

Our post-chaise was at the door; we leaped into it, and were off, leaving the "nice young man " to enjoy a visit to the birth-place of an individual of whom he had never before heard. The distance to Warwick is fourteen miles. We went to the Castle, and, approaching the door of the Great Hall, were informed by a well-dressed porter that the Earl of Warwick and family were absent, and that he was permitted to show the apartments to visitors. He introduced us successively into "The Red Drawing-Room," "The Cedar Drawing-Room," "The Gilt Room," "The State Bed-Room" "Lady Warwick's Boudoir," "The Compass Room," "The Chapel" and "The Great Dining-Room." As we passed out of the Castle, the polite porter touched his head (he of course had no hat on it) in a style which spoke plainer than words, "Half a crown each, if you please, gentlemen." We responded to the call, and were then placed in charge of another guide, who took us to the top of "Guy's Tower," at the bottom of which he touched his hat a shilling's worth; and placing ourselves in charge of a third conductor, an old man of seventy, we proceeded to the Greenhouse to see the Warwick Vase — each guide announcing at the end of his short tour: "Gentlemen, I go no farther," and indicating that the bill for his services was to be paid. The old gentleman mounted a rostrum at the side of the vase, and commenced a set speech, which we began to fear was interminable; so, tossing him the usual fee, we left him in the middle of his oration.

Passing through the porter's lodge on our way out, under the impression that we had seen all that was interesting, the old porter informed us that the most curious things connected with the Castle were to be seen in his lodge. Feeling for our coin, we bade him produce his relics, and he showed us a lot of trumpery, which he gravely informed us, belonged to that hero of antiquity, Guy, Earl of Warwick. Among these were his sword, shield, helmet, breast-plate, walking-staff, and tilting-pole, each of enormous size — the horse armor, nearly large enough for an elephant, a large pot which would hold seventy gallons, called "Guy's Porridge Pot," his flesh-fork, the size of a fanner's hay-fork, his lady's stirrups, the rib of a mastodon, which the porter pretended belonged to the great "Dun Cow," which, according to tradition, haunted a ditch near Coventry, and, after doing injury to many persons, was slain by the valiant Guy. The sword weighed nearly 100 pounds, and the armor 200 pounds.

I told the old porter he was entitled to great credit for having concentrated more lies than I had ever before heard in so small a compass. He smiled, and evidently felt gratified by the compliment.

"I suppose," I continued, "that you have told these marvelous stories so often that you believe them yourself? "

"Almost!" replied the porter, with a grin of satisfaction that showed he was "up to snuff," and had really earned two shillings.

"Come now, old fellow," said I, " what will you take for the entire lot of those traps? I want them for my Museum in America."

"No money would buy these valuable historical mementoes of a bygone age," replied the old porter, with a leer.

"Never mind," I exclaimed, "I'll have them duplicated for my Museum, so that Americans can see them and avoid the necessity of coming here, and in that way, I'll burst up your show."

Albert Smith laughed immoderately at the astonishment of the porter when I made this threat, and I was greatly amused some years afterwards, when Albert Smith became a successful showman and was exhibiting his "Mont Blanc" to delighted audiences in London, to discover that he had introduced this very incident into his lecture, of course, changing the names and locality. He often confessed that he derived his very first idea of becoming a showman from my talk about the business and my doings, on this charming day when we visited Warwick.

We returned to the hotel, took a post-chaise, and drove through decidedly the most lovely country I ever beheld. Since taking that tour, I have heard that two gentlemen once made a bet, each that he could name the most delightful drive in England. Many persons were present, and each gentleman wrote on a separate slip of paper the scene which he most admired. One gentleman wrote, "The road from Warwick to Coventry;" the other had written, "The road from Coventry to Warwick."

In less than an hour we were set down at the outer walls of Kenilworth Castle. This once noble and magnificent castle is now a stupendous ruin, which has been so often described that I think it unnecessary to say anything about it here. We spent half an hour in examining the interesting ruins, and then proceeded by post-chaise to Coventry, a distance of six or eight miles. Here we visited St. Mary's Hall, which has attracted the notice of many antiquaries. We also took our own "peep" at the effigy of the celebrated "Peeping Tom," after which we visited an exhibition called the "Happy Family", consisting of about two hundred birds and animals of opposite natures and propensities, all living in harmony together in one cage. This exhibition was so remarkable that I bought it and hired the proprietor to accompany it to New York, and it became an attractive feature in my Museum.

We took the cars the same evening for Birmingham, where we arrived at ten o'clock, Albert Smith remarking, that never before in his life had he accomplished a day's journey on the Yankee go-ahead principle. He afterwards published a chapter in *Bentley's Magazine* entitled "A Day with Barnum." in which he said we accomplished business with such rapidity that, when he attempted to write out the accounts of the day, he found the whole thing so confused in his brain that he came near locating "Peeping Tom" in the house of Shakespeare, while Guy of Warwick would stick his head above the ruins of Kenilworth, and the Warwick Vase appeared in Coventry.

CHAPTER XV

RETURN TO AMERICA.

While I was at Aberdeen, in Scotland, I met Anderson, the "Wizard of the North." I had known him for a long time, and we were on familiar terms. He came to our exhibition, and, at the close, we went to the hotel together to get a little supper. After supper, we were having some fun and jokes together, when it occurred to Anderson to introduce me to several persons who were sitting in the room, as the "Wizard of the North," at the same time asking me about my tricks and my forthcoming exhibition. He kept this up so persistently that some of our friends who were present declared that Anderson was "too much for me," and, meanwhile, fresh introductions to strangers who came in, had made me pretty generally known in that circle as the "Wizard of the North," who was to astonish the town in the following week. I accepted the situation at last, and said:

"Well, gentlemen, as I perform here for the first time, on Monday evening, I like to be liberal, and I should be very happy to give orders of admission to those of you who will attend my exhibition."

The applications for orders were quite general, and I had written thirty or forty, when Anderson, who saw that I was in a fair way of filling his house with "deadheads," cried out:

"Hold on! I am the 'Wizard of the North.' I'll stand the orders already given, but not another one."

Our friends, including the "Wizard " himself, began to think that I had rather the best of the joke.

During our three years' stay abroad, I made a second hasty visit to America, leaving the General in England in the hands of my agents. I took passage from Liverpool on board a Cunard steamer, commanded by Captain Judkins. One of my fellow passengers was the celebrated divine, Robert Baird, who had been for some time a missionary in Sweden, and was now paying a visit to his native land.

On Sunday divine service was held as usual in the large after-cabin. Of course, it was the Episcopal form of worship.

Those who have witnessed this service, as conducted by Captain Judkins, need not be reminded that he does it much as he performs his duties on deck. He speaks as one having authority; and a listener could hardly help feeling that there would be some danger of a "row" if the petitions (made as a sort of command) were not speedily answered.

After dinner, I asked Dr. Baird if he would be willing to preach to the passengers in the forward cabin. He said he would cheerfully do so if it was desired. I mentioned it to the passengers, and there was a generally expressed wish among them that he should preach. I went into the forward cabin, and requested the steward to arrange the chairs and tables properly for religious service. He replied that I must first get the captain's consent. Of course, I thought this was a mere matter of form; so, I went to the captain's office, and said:

"Captain, the passengers desire to have Dr. Baird conduct a religious service in the forward cabin. I suppose there is no objection."

"Decidedly there is," replied the captain, gruffly; "and it will not be permitted."

"Why not?" I asked, in astonishment.

"It is against the rules of the ship."

"What! to have religious services on board?"

"There have been religious services once today, and that is enough. If the passengers do not think that is good enough, let them go without," was the captain's hasty and austere reply.

"Captain," I replied, "do you pretend to say you will not allow a respectable and well-known clergyman to offer a prayer and hold religious services on board your ship at the request of your passengers?"

"That, sir, is exactly what I say. So, now, let me hear no more about it."

By this time a dozen passengers were crowding around his door, and expressing their surprise at his conduct. I was indignant, and used sharp language.

"Well," said I, "this is the most contemptible thing I ever heard of on the part of the owners of a public passenger ship. Their meanness ought to be published far and wide.

"You had better 'shut up,' " said Captain Judkins, with great sternness.

"I will not 'shut up,' " I replied; "for this thing is perfectly outrageous. In that out-of-the-way forward cabin, you allow, on week days, gambling, swearing, smoking and singing, till late at night; and yet on Sunday you have the impudence to deny the privilege of a prayer-meeting, conducted by a gray-haired and respected minister of the gospel. It is simply infamous!"

Captain Judkins turned red in the face; and, no doubt feeling that he was "monarch of all he surveyed," exclaimed, in a loud voice:

"If you repeat such language, I will put you in irons."

"Do it, if you dare," said I, feeling my indignation rising rapidly. "I dare and defy you to put your finger on me. I would like to sail into New York Harbor in handcuffs, on board a British ship, for the terrible crime of asking that religious Worship may be permitted on board. So, you may try it as soon as you please; and, when we get to New York, I'll show you a touch of Yankee ideas of religious intolerance."

The captain made no reply; and, at the request of friends, I walked to another part of the ship. I told the doctor how the matter stood, and then, laughingly, said to him:

"Doctor, it may be dangerous for you to tell of this incident when you get on shore; for it would be a pretty strong draught upon the credulity of many of my countrymen if they were told that my zeal to hear an Orthodox minister preach was so great that it came near getting me into solitary confinement. But I am not prejudiced, and I like fair play."

The old Doctor replied: "Well, you have not lost much; and, if the rules of this ship are so stringent, I suppose we must submit."

The captain and myself had no further intercourse for five or six days: not until a few hours before our arrival in New York. Being at dinner, he sent his champagne bottle to me, and asked to "drink my health," at the same time stating that he hoped no ill feeling would be carried ashore. I was not then, as I am now, a teetotaler; so, I accepted the proffered truce, and I regret that I must add I "washed down" my wrath in a bottle of Heidsick — a poor example, which I hope never to repeat. We have frequently met since, and always with friendly greetings; but I have ever felt that his manners were unnecessarily coarse and offensive in carrying out an arbitrary and bigoted rule of the steamship company.

With the exception of the brief time passed in making two short visits to America, I had now passed three years with General Tom Thumb in Great Britain and on the Continent. The entire period had been a season of unbroken pleasure and profit. I had immensely enlarged my business experiences and had made money and many friends. Among those to whom I am indebted for special courtesies while I was abroad are Dr. C. S. Brewster, whose prosperous professional career in Russia and France is well known, and Henry Sumner, Esq., who occupied a high position in the social and literary circles of Paris, and who introduced me to George Sand and to many other distinguished persons. To both these gentlemen, as well as to Mr. John Nimmo, an English gentleman connected with *Galignani's Messenger*, Mr. Lorenzo Draper, the American Consul, and Mr. Dion Boucicault, I was largely indebted for attention. In London, two gentlemen especially merit my warm acknowledgments for many valuable favors. I refer to the late Thomas Brettell, publisher, Haymarket; and Mr. R. Fillingham, Jr., Fenchurch street. I was also indebted to Mr. G. P. Putnam, at that time a London publisher, for much useful information.

We had visited nearly every city and town in France and Belgium, all the principal places in England and Scotland, besides going to Belfast and Dublin, in Ireland. I had several times met Daniel O'Connell in private life, and in the Irish capital I heard him make an eloquent and powerful public Repeal speech in Conciliation Hall. In Dublin, after exhibiting a week in Rotunda Hall, our receipts on the last day were £261, or $1,305, and the General also received £50, or $250, for playing the same evening at the Theater Royal. Thus, closing a truly triumphant tour, we set sail for New York, arriving in February, 1847

Note. — This Autobiography was originally written fifteen years ago (1869). On now revising it in 1884, I am forcibly struck with the brevity and uncertainty of human life. Every person mentioned on this page, with the exception of Mr. Boucicault, has passed away. My assistant museum manager, John Greenwood, Jr., became a consul to Brunswick, Germany, and died there about 1872. Another valuable assistant manager, Fordyce Hitchcock, died the present year. General Tom Thumb died at Middleboro, Mass., July 15, 1883, aged 45½ years. His parents are also both deceased. Minnie Warren died July 23, 1878, aged 29 years. Commodore Nutt died May 25. 1881, aged 33 years.

CHAPTER XVI.

AT HOME.

One of my main objects in returning home at this time, was to obtain a longer lease of the premises occupied by the American Museum. My lease had still three years to run, but Mr. Olmsted, the proprietor of the building, was dead, and I was anxious to make provision in time for the perpetuity of my establishment, for I meant to make the Museum a permanent institution in the city, and if I could not renew my lease, I intended to build an appropriate edifice on Broadway. I finally succeeded, however, in getting the lease of the entire building, covering fifty-six feet by one hundred, for twenty-five years, at an annual rent of $10,000 and the ordinary taxes and assessments. I had already hired in addition the upper stories of three adjoining buildings. My Museum receipts were more in one day than they formerly were in an entire week, and the establishment had become so popular that it was thronged at all hours, from early morning to closing time at night.

On my return, I promptly made use of General Tom Thumb's European reputation. He immediately appeared in the American Museum, and for four weeks drew such crowds of visitors as had never been seen there before. He afterwards spent a month in Bridgeport with his kindred. To prevent being annoyed by the curious, who would be sure to throng the houses of his relatives, he exhibited two days at Bridgeport, and the receipts, amounting to several hundred dollars, were presented to the Bridgeport Charitable Society.

On January 1, 1845, while in England, my engagement with the General at a salary ceased, and we made a new arrangement by which we were equal partners, the General or his father for him, taking one-half of the profits. A reservation, however, was made of the first four weeks after our arrival in New York, during which he was to exhibit at my Museum for two hundred dollars. When we returned to America, the General's father had acquired a handsome fortune, and settling a large sum upon the little General personally, he placed the balance at interest, secured by bond and mortgage, excepting thirty thousand dollars, with which he purchased land near the city limits of Bridgeport, and erected a large and substantial mansion, where he resided till the day of his death.

After spending a month in visiting his friends, it was determined that the General and his parents should travel through the United States. I agreed to accompany them, with occasional intervals of rest at home, for one year, sharing the profits equally. We proceeded to Washington city, where the General held his levees in April, 1847, visiting President Polk and lady at the White House — thence to Richmond, returning to Baltimore and Philadelphia. Our receipts in Philadelphia in twelve days were $5,594.01. The tour for the entire year realized about the same average. The expenses were from twenty-five dollars to thirty dollars per day. From Philadelphia we went to Boston, Lowell, and Providence. Our receipts on one day in the latter city were $976.97. We then visited New Bedford, Fall River, Salem, Worcester,

Springfield, Albany, Troy, Niagara Falls, Buffalo, and intermediate places, and in returning to New York we stopped at the principal towns on the Hudson River. After this we visited New Haven, Hartford, Portland, Me., and intermediate towns.

I was surprised to find that, during my long absence abroad, I had become very much of a curiosity to my patrons. If I showed myself about the Museum or wherever else I was known, I found eyes peering and fingers pointing at me, and could frequently overhear the remark, "There's Barnum." On one occasion soon after my return, I was sitting in the ticket-office reading a newspaper. A man came and purchased a ticket of admission. "Is Mr. Barnum in the Museum?" he asked. The ticket-seller, pointing to me, answered, "This is Mr. Barnum," supposing the gentleman had business with me, I looked up from the paper. "Is this Mr. Barnum?" he asked. "It is," I replied. He stared at me for a moment, and then, throwing down his ticket, exclaimed, "It's all right; I have got the worth of my money;" and away he went, without going into the Museum at all!

In November, 1847, we started for Havana taking the steamer from New York to Charleston, where the General exhibited, as well as at Columbia, Augusta, Savannah, Milledgeville, Macon, Columbus, Montgomery, Mobile and New Orleans. At this latter city we remained three weeks, including Christmas and New Year's. We arrived in Havana by the schooner Adams Gray, in January, 1848, and were introduced to the Captain-General and the Spanish nobility. We remained a month in Havana and Matanzas, the General proving an immense favorite. In Havana he was the especial pet of Count Santovania. In Matanzas, we were very much indebted to the kindness of a princely American merchant, Mr. Brinckerhoff. Mr. J.S. Thrasher, the American patriot and gentleman, was also of great assistance to us, and placed me under deep obligations.

The hotels in Havana are not good. An American who is accustomed to substantial living finds it difficult to get enough to eat. We stopped at the Washington House, which at that time was "first-rate bad."

From Havana we went to New Orleans, where we remained several days, and from New Orleans we proceeded to St. Louis, stopping at the principal towns on the Mississippi river, and returning via Louisville, Cincinnati, and Pittsburgh. We reached the latter city early in May, 1848. From this point it was agreed between Mr. Stratton and myself, that I should go home and henceforth travel no more with the little General. I had competent agents who could exhibit him without my personal assistance, and I preferred to relinquish a portion of the profits, rather than continue to be a traveling showman. I had now been a straggler from home most of the tune for thirteen years, and I cannot describe the feelings of gratitude with which I reflected, that having by the most arduous toil and deprivations succeeded in securing a satisfactory competence, I should henceforth spend my days in the bosom of my family.

My new home, at Bridgeport, Connecticut, which was then nearly ready for occupancy, was the well-known *Iranistan*. More than two years had been employed in building this beautiful residence.

I wished to reside within a few hours of New York. I had never seen more delightful locations than there are upon the borders of Long Island Sound, between New Rochelle, New York, and New Haven, Connecticut: and my attention was therefore turned in that direction. Bridgeport seemed to be about the proper distance from the great metropolis. It is pleasantly situated at the terminus of two railroads, which traverse the fertile valleys of the Naugatuck and Housatonic rivers. The New York and New Haven Railroad runs through the city, and there is also daily steamboat communication with New York. The enterprise which characterized the city, seemed to mark it as destined to become the first in the State in size and opulence; and I was not long in deciding, with the concurrence of my wife, to fix our future residence in that vicinity.

I accordingly purchased seventeen acres of land, less than a mile west of the city, and fronting with a good view upon the Sound.

In visiting Brighton, in England, I had been greatly pleased with the Pavilion erected by George IV. It was the only specimen of Oriental architecture in England, and the style had not been introduced into America. I concluded to adopt it, and engaged a London architect to furnish me a set of drawings after the general plan of the Pavilion, differing sufficiently to be adapted to the spot of ground selected for my homestead. On my second return visit to the United States, I brought these drawings with me and engaged a competent architect and builder, giving him instructions to proceed with the work, not "by the job" but "by the day," and to spare neither time nor expense in erecting a comfortable, convenient, and tasteful residence. The work was thus begun and continued while I was still abroad, and during the time when I was making my tour with General Tom Thumb through the United States and Cuba. Elegant and appropriate furniture was made expressly for every room in the house. I erected expensive water works to supply the premises. The stables, conservatories and out-buildings were perfect in their kind. There was a profusion of trees set out on the grounds. The whole was built and established literally "regardless of expense," for I had no desire even to ascertain the entire cost.

The whole was finally completed to my satisfaction. My family removed into the premises and, on the fourteenth of November, 1818, nearly one thousand invited guests, including the poor and the rich, helped us in the old-fashioned custom of "house-warming."

When the name "*Iranistan*" was announced, a waggish New York editor syllabled it, I-ran-i-stan, and gave as the interpretation, that "I ran a long time before I could stand! "Literally, however, the name signifies, "Eastern Country Place," or, more poetically, "Oriental Villa."

The years 1848 and 1849 were mainly spent with my family, though I went every week to New York to look after the interests of the American Museum. While I was in Europe, in 1845, my agent, Mr. Fordyce Hitchcock, had bought out for me the Baltimore Museum, a fully-supplied establishment, in full operation, and I placed it under the charge of my uncle, Alanson Taylor.

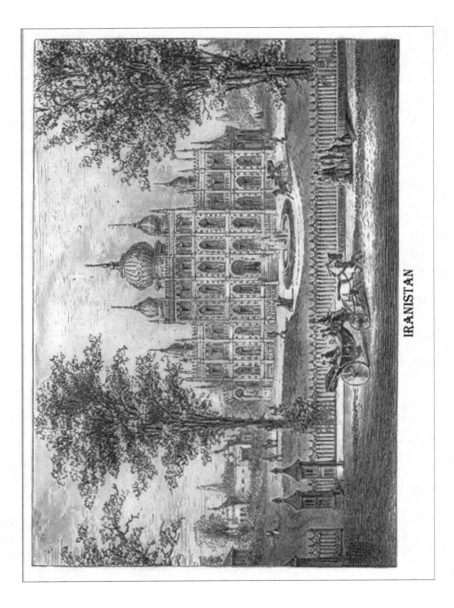

IRANISTAN

He died in 1846, and I then sold the Baltimore Museum to the "Orphean Family," by whom it was subsequently transferred to Mr. John E. Owens, the celebrated comedian. After my return from Europe, I opened, in 1849, a Museum in Dr. Swain's fine building, at the comer of Chestnut and Seventh streets, in Philadelphia.

I stayed in Philadelphia long enough to identify myself with this Museum and to successfully start the enterprise, and then left it in the hands of different managers who profitably conducted it till 1851, when, finding that it occupied too much of my time and attention, I sold it to Mr. Clapp Spooner for $40,000. At the end of that year, the building and contents were destroyed by fire.

While my Philadelphia Museum was in full operation, Peale's Philadelphia Museum ran me a strong opposition at the Masonic Hall. Peale's enterprise proved disastrous, and I purchased the collection at sheriff 's sale, for five or six thousand dollars, on joint account of my friend Moses Kimball and myself. The curiosities were equally divided, one-half going to his Boston Museum and the other half to my American Museum in New York. In 1848, I was elected President of the Fairfield County Agricultural Society in Connecticut. Although not practically a farmer, I had purchased about one hundred acres of land in the vicinity of my residence and felt and still feel a deep interest in the cause of agriculture. I had begun by importing some blood stock for *Iranistan*, and, as I was at one time attacked by the "hen fever," I erected several splendid poultry-houses on my grounds.

In 1849 it was determined by the Society that I should deliver the annual address. I begged to be excused on the ground of incompetency, but my excuses were of no avail, and, as I could not instruct my auditors in farming, I gave them the benefit of several mistakes which I had committed. Among other things, I told them that in the fall of 1848 my head-gardener reported that I had fifty bushels of potatoes to spare. I thereupon directed him to barrel them up and ship them to New York for sale. He did so, and received two dollars per barrel, or about sixty-seven cents per bushel. But, unfortunately, after the potatoes had been shipped, I found that my gardener had selected all the largest for market and left my family nothing but "small potatoes" to live on during the winter. But the worst is still to come. My potatoes were all gone before March, and I was obliged to buy, during the spring, over fifty bushels of potatoes, at $1.25 per bushel! I also related my first experiment in the arboricultural line, when I cut from two thrifty rows of young cherry-trees any quantity of what I supposed to be "suckers," or "sprouts," and was thereafter informed by my gardener that I had cut off all his grafts!

A friend of mine, Mr. James D. Johnson, lived in a fine house a quarter of a mile west of *Iranistan*, and, as I owned several acres of land at the corner of two streets, directly adjoining his homestead, I surrounded the ground with high pickets, and, introducing a number of Rocky Mountain elk, reindeer, and American deer, I converted it into a deer park. Strangers passing by would naturally suppose that it belonged to Johnson's estate, and to render the illusion more complete, his son-in-law, Mr. S. H. Wales, of the Scientific American, placed a sign in the park, fronting on the street, and reading:

"ALL PERSONS ARE FORBID TRESPASSING ON THESE GROUNDS, OR DISTURBING THE DEER. J. D. Johnson."

I "acknowledged the corn," and was much pleased with the joke. Johnson was delighted, and bragged considerably of having got ahead of Barnum, and the sign remained undisturbed for several days. It happened at length that a party of friends came to visit him from New York, arriving in the evening. Johnson told them he had got a capital joke on Barnum; he would not explain, but said they should see it for themselves the next morning. Bright and early he led them into the street, and, after conducting them a proper distance, wheeled them around in front of the sign. To his dismay he discovered that I had added directly under his name the words

"Game-keeper to P. T. Barnum."

Thereafter, Mr. Johnson was known among his friends and acquaintances as "Barnum's game-keeper." Sometime afterwards, when I was President of the Pequonnock Bank, it was my custom every year to give a grand dinner at *Iranistan*, to the directors, and in making preparations I used to send to certain friends in the West for prairie chickens and other game. On one occasion, a large box, marked "P. T. Barnum, Bridgeport; Game," was lying in the express office, when Johnson, seeing it and espying the word "game," said:

"Look here! I am 'Barnum's game-keeper,' and I'll take charge of this box." And "take charge" of it he did, carrying it home and notifying me that it was in his possession, and that, as he was my game-keeper, he would "keep" this, unless I sent him an order for a new hat. He knew very well, that I would give fifty dollars rather than be deprived of the box, and as he also threatened to give a game dinner at his own house, I speedily sent the order for the hat, acknowledged the good joke, and my own guests enjoyed the double "game." During the year 1848, Mr. Frank Leslie, since so widely known as the publisher of several illustrated journals, came to me with letters of introduction from London, and I employed him to get up for me an illustrated catalogue of my Museum. This he did in a splendid manner, and hundreds of thousands of copies were sold and distributed far and near, thus adding greatly to the renown of the establishment.

CHAPTER XVII.

THE JENNY LIND ENTERPRISE.

And now I come to speak of an undertaking which all will admit was bold in its conception, complete in its development, and astounding in its success. That I am proud of it, I freely confess. It placed me before the world in a new light; it gained me many warm friends in new circles; it was in itself a fortune to me — I risked much, but I made more.

It was in October, 1849, that I conceived the idea of bringing Jenny Lind to this country. I had never heard her sing, inasmuch as she arrived in London a few weeks after I left that city with General Tom Thumb. Her reputation, however, was sufficient for me.

I found in Mr. John Hall Wilton, an Englishman who had visited this country with the Sax-Horn Players, the best man whom I knew for that purpose. A few minutes sufficed to make the arrangement with him, by which I was to pay but little more than his expenses if he failed in his mission, but by which, also, he was to be paid a large sum if he succeeded in bringing Jenny Lind to our shores on any terms within a liberal schedule which I set forth to him in writing.

The sum of all my instructions, public and private, to Wilton, amounted to this: He was to engage her on shares, if possible. I, however, authorized him to engage her at any rate, not exceeding one thousand dollars a night, for any number of nights up to one hundred and fifty, with all her expenses, including servants, carriages, secretary, etc., besides also engaging such musical assistants, not exceeding three in number, as she should select, let the terms be what they might. If necessary, I should place the entire amount of money named in the engagement, in the hands of London bankers before she sailed. Wilton's compensation was arranged on a kind of sliding scale, to be governed by the terms which he made for me. He proceeded to London, and opened a correspondence with Miss Lind, who was then on the Continent. He learned from the tenor of her letters, that if she could be induced to visit America at all, she must be accompanied by Mr. Julius Benedict, the accomplished composer, pianist, and musical director, and also, she was impressed with the belief that Signor Belletti, the fine baritone, would be of essential service. Wilton, therefore, at once called upon Mr. Benedict and also Signor Belletti, who were both then in London, and in numerous interviews, was enabled to learn the terms on which they would consent to engage to visit this country with Miss Lind. Having obtained the information desired, he proceeded to Lubeck, in Germany, to seek an interview with Miss Lind herself.

In the course of the first conversation, she frankly told him that during the time occupied by their correspondence, she had written to friends in London, including my friend Mr. Joshua Bates, of the house of Baling Brothers, and had informed herself respecting my character, capacity, and responsibility, which she assured him were quite satisfactory. She informed him, however, that at that time there were four persons anxious to negotiate with her for an American tour. One of these gentlemen was a well-known opera manager in London; another, a theatrical manager in Manchester; a third, a musical composer and conductor of the orchestra of Her Majesty's Opera in London; and the fourth, Chevalier Wyckoff, a person who had conducted a successful speculation some years previously, by visiting America in charge of the celebrated danseuse, Fanny Elisler.

Several interviews ensued, during which she learned from Wilton that he had settled with Messrs. Benedict and Belletti, in regard to the amount of their salaries, provided the engagement was concluded, and in the course of a week, Mr. Wilton and Miss Lind had arranged the terms and conditions on which she was ready to conclude the negotiations. As these terms were within the limits fixed in my private letter of instructions, the following agreement was duly drawn in triplicate, and signed by herself and Wilton at Lubeck, January 9, 1850; and the signatures of Messrs. Benedict and Belletti were affixed in London a few days afterwards:

Memorandum of an agreement entered into this ninth day of January, in the year of our Lord one thousand eight hundred and fifty, between John Hall Wilton, as agent for Phineas T. Barnum. of New York, in the United States of North America, of the one part, and Mademoiselle Jenny Lind, Vocalist, of Stockholm, in Sweden, of the other part wherein the said Jenny Lind doth agree:

First. To sing for the said Phineas T. Barnum in one hundred and fifty concerts, including oratorios, within (if possible; one year or eighteen months from the date of her arrival in the city of New York— the said concerts to be given in the United States of North America and Havana. She, the said Jenny Lind, having full control as to the number of nights or concerts in each week, and the number of pieces in which she will sing in each concert, to be regulated conditionally with her health and safety of voice, but the former never less than one or two, nor the latter less than four; but in no case to appear in operas.

Second. In consideration of said services, the said John Hall Wilton, as agent for the said Phineas T. Barnum, of New York, agrees to furnish the said Jenny Lind with a servant as waiting-maid, and a male servant to and for the sole service of her and her party; to pay the traveling and hotel expenses of a friend to accompany her as a companion; to pay also a secretary to superintend her finances; to pay all her and her party's traveling expenses from Europe, and during the tour in the United States of North America and Havana; to pay all hotel expenses' for board and lodging during the same period; to place at her disposal in each city, a carriage and horses with their necessary attendants, and to give her in addition, the sum of two hundred pounds sterling, or one thousand dollars, for each concert or oratorio in which the said Jenny Lind shall sing.

Third. And the said John Hall Wilton, as agent for the said Phineas T. Barnum, doth further agree to give the said Jenny Lind the most satisfactory security and assurance for the full amount of her engagement, which will be placed in the hands of Messrs. Baring Brothers, of London, previous to the departure, and subject to the order of the said Jenny Lind, with its interest due on its current reduction, by her services in the concerts or oratorios.

Fourth. And the said John Hall Wilton, on the part of the said Phineas T. Barnum, further agrees, that should the said Phineas T. Barnum, after seventy-five concerts, have realized so much as shall, after paying all current expenses, have returned to him all the sums disbursed, either as deposits at interest, for securities of salaries, preliminary outlay, or moneys in any way expended consequent on this engagement, and in addition, have gained a clear profit of at least fifteen thousand pounds sterling, then the said Phineas T. Barnum will give the said Jenny Lind, in addition to the former sum of one thousand dollars current money of the United States of

North America, nightly, one-fifth part of the profits arising from the remaining seventy-five concerts or oratorios, after deducting every expense current and appertaining thereto; or the said Jenny Lind agrees to try, with the said Phineas T. Barnum, fifty concerts or oratorios on the aforesaid and first-named terms, and if then found to fall short of the expectations of the said Phineas T. Barnum, then the said Jenny Lind agrees to re-organize this agreement, on terms quoted in his first proposal, as set forth in the annexed copy of his letter; but should such be found unnecessary, then the engagement continues up to seventy-five concerts or oratorios, at the end of which, should the aforesaid profit of fifteen thousand pounds sterling have not been realized, then the engagement shall continue as at first — the sums herein, after expenses for Julius Benedict and Giovanni Belletti, to remain unaltered, except for advancement.

Fifth. And the said John Hall Wilton, agent for the said Phineas T. Barnum, at the request of the said Jenny Lind, agrees to pay to Julius Benedict, of London, to accompany the said Jenny Lind as musical director, pianist, and superintendent of the musical department, also to assist the said Jenny Lind in one hundred and fifty concerts or oratorios, to be given in the United States of North America and Havana, the sum of five thousand pounds (£5,000) sterling, to be satisfactorily secured to him with Messrs. Baring Brothers, of London, previous to his departure from Europe; and the said John Hall Wilton agrees further, for the said Phineas T. Barnum to pay all his traveling expenses from Europe, together with his hotel and traveling expenses during the time occupied in giving the aforesaid one hundred and fifty concerts or oratorios— he, the said Julius Benedict to superintend the organization of oratorios, if required.

Sixth. And the said John Hall Wilton, at the request, selection, and for the aid of the said Jenny Lind, agrees to pay to Giovanni Belletti, baritone vocalist, to accompany the said Jenny Lind during her tour and in one hundred and fifty concerts or oratorios in the United States of North America and Havana, and in conjunction with the aforesaid Julius Benedict, the sum of two thousand five hundred pounds (£2,500) sterling, to be satisfactorily secured to him previous to his departure from Europe, in addition to all his hotel and traveling expenses.

Seventh. And it is further agreed that the said Jenny Lind shall be at full liberty to sing at any time she may think fit for charitable institutions, or purposes independent of the engagement with the said Phineas T. Barnum, she, the said Jenny Lind, consulting with the said Phineas T. Barnum with a view to mutually agreeing as to the time and its propriety, it being understood that in no case shall the first or second concert in any city selected for the tour be for such purpose, or wherever it shall appear against the interests of the said Phineas T. Barnum.

Eighth. It is further agreed that should the said Jenny Lind by any act of God, be incapacitated to fulfil the entire engagement before mentioned, that an equal proportion of the terms agreed upon shall be given to the said Jenny Lind, Julius Benedict, and Giovanni Belletti, for services rendered to that time.

Ninth. It is further agreed and understood, that the said Phineas T. Barnum shall pay every expense appertaining to the concerts or oratorios before mentioned, excepting those for charitable purposes, and that all accounts shall be settled and rendered by all parties weekly.

Tenth. And the said Jenny Lind furthers agrees that she will not engage to sing for any other person during the progress of this said engagement with the said Phineas T. Barnum, of New York, for one hundred and fifty concerts or oratorios, excepting for charitable purposes as before mentioned; and all traveling to be first and best class.

In witness hereof to the within written memorandum of agreement we set hereunto om hand and seal.

[L.S.]   John Hall Wilton, Agent for Phineas T. Barnum, of New York.
[L.S.]   Jenny Lind.
[L.S.]   Julius Benedict.
[L.S]   Giovanni Belletti.

In the presence of C. Achilling, Consul of His Majesty the King of Sweden and Norway.

Extract from a letter addressed to John Hall Wilton by Phineas T. Barnum, and referred to in paragraph No 4 of the annexed agreement:

New York, November 6, 1849. Mr. J. Hall Wilton:
Sir: In reply to your proposal to attempt a negotiation with Mlle. Jenny Lind to visit the United States professionally, I propose to enter into an arrangement with her to the following effect: I will engage to pay all her expenses from Europe, provide for and pay for one principal tenor, and one pianist, their salaries not exceeding together, one hundred and fifty dollars per night; to support for her a carriage, two servants, and a friend to accompany her and superintend her finances. I will furthermore pay all and every expense appertaining to her appearance before the public, and give her half of the gross receipts arising from concerts or operas. I will engage to travel with her personally, and attend to the arrangements, provided she will undertake to give not less than eighty, nor more than one hundred and fifty concerts, or nights' performances.

Phineas T. Barnum.

I certify the above to be a true extract from the letter.   -J. H. Wilton

I was at my Museum in Philadelphia when Wilton arrived in New York, February 19, 1850. He immediately telegraphed to me, in the cipher we had agreed upon, that he had signed an engagement with Jenny Lind, by which she was to commence her concerts in America in the following September. I was somewhat startled by this sudden announcement; and feeling that the time to elapse before her arrival was so long that it would be policy to keep the engagement private for a few months, I immediately telegraphed him not to mention it to any person, and that I would meet him the next day in New York.

This portrait of Jenny Lind is taken from "OUR FIRST CENTURY," and for the privilege of using it I am indebted to the courtesy of Messrs. C. A. Nichols & Co., Springfield, Mass., the publishers of that work. Jenny Lind was 28 years old in 1851.
P. T. B.

1851.

WELCOME TO JENNY LIND

When we reflect how thoroughly Jenny Lind, her musical powers, her character, and wonderful successes, were subsequently known by all classes in the country as well as throughout the civilized world, it is difficult to realize that, at the time this engagement was made, she was comparatively unknown on this side of the water. We can hardly credit the fact that millions of persons in America had never heard of her, that other millions had merely read her name, but had no distinct idea of who or what she was. Only a small portion of the public were really aware of her great musical triumphs in the Old World, and this portion was confined almost entirely to musical people, travelers who had visited the Old World, and the conductors of the press.

The next morning, I started for New York. On arriving at Princeton, we met the New York cars, and, purchasing the morning papers, I was surprised to find in them a full account of my engagement with Jenny Lind. This premature announcement could not be recalled, and I put the best face on the matter. Anxious to learn how this communication would strike the public mind, I informed the conductor, whom I well knew, that I had made an engagement with Jenny Lind, and that she would surely visit this country in the following August.

"Jenny Lind! Is she a dancer?" asked the conductor.

I informed him who and what she was, but his question had chilled me as if his words were ice. Really, thought I, if this is all that a man in the capacity of a railroad conductor between Philadelphia and New York knows of the greatest songstress in the world, I am not sure that six months will be too long a time for me to occupy in enlightening the public in regard to her merits.

I had an interview with Wilton, and learned from him that, in accordance with the agreement, it would be requisite for me to place the entire amount stipulated, $187,500, in the hands of the London bankers. I at once resolved to ratify the agreement, and immediately sent the necessary documents to Miss Lind and Messrs. Benedict and Belletti.

I then began to prepare the public mind, through the newspapers, for the reception of the great songstress. How effectually this was done, is still within the remembrance of the American public. As a sample of the manner in which I accomplished my purpose, I present the following extract from my first letter, which appeared in the New York papers of February 22, 1850:

"Perhaps I may not make any money by this enterprise; but I assure you that if I knew I should not make a farthing profit, I would ratify the engagement, so anxious am I that the United States should be visited by a lady whose vocal powers have never been approached by any other human being, and whose character is charity, simplicity, and goodness personified.

"Miss Lind has great anxiety to visit America. She speaks of this country and its institutions in the highest terms of praise. In her engagement with me (which includes Havana), she expressly reserves the right to give charitable concerts whenever she thinks proper.

"Since her debut in England, she has given to the poor from her own private purse more than the whole amount which I have engaged to pay her, and the proceeds of concerts for charitable purposes in Great Britain, where she has sung gratuitously, have realized more than ten times that amount."

After getting together all my available funds for the purpose of transmitting them to London in the shape of United States bonds, I found a considerable sum still lacking to make up the amount. I had some second mortgages which were perfectly good, but I could not negotiate them in Wall street. Nothing would answer there, short of first mortgages on New York or Brooklyn city property.

I went to the president of the bank where I had done all my business for eight years. I offered him, as security for a loan, my second mortgages, and as an additional inducement, I proposed to make over to him my contract with Jenny Land, with a written guaranty that he should appoint a receiver, who, at my expense, should take charge of all the receipts over and above three thousand dollars per night, and appropriate them towards the payment of my loan. He laughed in my face, and said: "Mr. Barnum, it is generally believed in Wall street, that your engagement with Jenny Lind will ruin you. I do not think you will ever receive so much as three thousand dollars at a single concert." I was indignant at his want of appreciation, and answered him that I would not at that moment take $150,000 for my contract; nor would I. I found, upon further inquiry, that it was useless in Wall street to offer the "Nightingale" in exchange for Goldfinches. I finally was introduced to Mr. John L. Aspinwall, of the firm of Messrs. Howland & Aspinwall, and he gave me a letter of credit from his firm on Baring Brothers, for a large sum on collateral securities, which a spirit of genuine respect for my enterprise induced him to accept.

After disposing of several pieces of property for cash, I footed up the various amounts, and still discovered myself five thousand dollars short. I felt that it was indeed "the last feather that breaks the camel's back." Happening casually to state my desperate case to the Rev. Abel C. Thomas, of Philadelphia, for many years a friend of mine, he promptly placed the requisite amount at my disposal. I gladly accepted his proffered friendship and felt that he had removed a mountain-weight from my shoulders.

CHAPTER XVIII.

THE NIGHTINGALE IN NEW YORK.

On Wednesday morning, August 21, 1850, Jenny Lind and Messrs. Benedict and Belletti, set sail from Liverpool in the steamship Atlantic, in which I had long before engaged the necessary accommodations, and on board of which I had shipped a piano for their use. They were accompanied by my agent, Mr. Wilton, and also by Miss Ahmansen and Mr. Max Hjortzberg, cousins of Miss Lind, the latter being her secretary; also, by her two servants, and the valet of Messrs. Benedict and Belletti.

It was expected that the steamer would arrive on Sunday, September 1 but, determined to meet the songstress on her arrival whenever it might be, I went to Staten Island on Saturday, and slept at the hospitable residence of my friend Dr. A. Sidney Doane, who was at that time the Health Officer of the Port of New York. A few minutes before twelve o'clock, on Sunday morning, the Atlantic hove in sight, and immediately afterwards, through the kindness of my friend Doane, I was on board the ship, and had taken Jenny Lind by the hand.

After a few moments' conversation, she asked me when and where I had heard her sing.

"I never had the pleasure of seeing you before in my life," I replied

"How is it possible that you dared risk so much money on a person whom you never heard sing? " she asked in surprise.

"I risked it on your reputation, which in musical matters I would much rather trust than my own judgment," I replied

I may as well state, that although I relied prominently upon Jenny Lind's reputation as a great musical *artiste*, I also took largely into my estimate of her success with all classes of the American public, her character for extraordinary benevolence and generosity. Without this peculiarity in her disposition, I never would have dared make the engagement which I did, as I felt sure that I were multitudes of individuals in America who would be prompted to attend her concerts by this feeling alone.

Thousands of persons covered the shipping and piers, and other thousands had congregated on the wharf at Canal street to see her. The wildest enthusiasm prevailed as the steamer approached the dock. So great was the rush on a sloop near the steamer's berth, that one man, in his zeal to obtain a good view, accidentally tumbled overboard, amid the shouts of those near him, Miss Lind witnessed this incident, and was much alarmed. He was, however, soon rescued, after taking to himself a cold duck instead of securing a view of the Nightingale. A bower of green trees, decorated with beautiful flags, was discovered on the wharf, together with two triumphal arches, on one of which was inscribed, "Welcome, Jenny Lind!"

The second was surmounted by the American eagle, and bore the inscription, "Welcome to America!" These decorations were not produced by magic, and I do not know that I can reasonably find fault with those who suspected I had a hand in their erection. My private carriage was in waiting, and Jenny Land was escorted to it by

Captain West. The rest of the musical party entered the carriage, and, mounting the box at the driver's side, I directed him to the Irving House. I took that seat as a legitimate advertisement, and my presence on the outside of the carriage aided those who filled the windows and sidewalks along the whole route, in coming to the conclusion that Jenny Lind had arrived.

A reference to the journals of that day will show that never before had there been such enthusiasm in the city of New York, or indeed in America. Within ten minutes after our arrival at the Irving House, not less than twenty thousand persons had congregated around the entrance in Broadway, nor was the number diminished before nine o'clock in the evening. At her request, I dined with her that afternoon, and when, according to European custom, she prepared to pledge me in a glass of wine, she was somewhat surprised at my saying, "Miss Lind, I do not think you can ask any other favor on earth which I would not gladly grant; but I am a teetotaler, and must beg to be permitted to drink your health and happiness in a glass of cold water."

At twelve o'clock that night, she was serenaded by the New York Musical Fund Society, numbering, on that occasion, two hundred musicians. They were escorted to the Irving House by about three hundred firemen, in their red shirts, bearing torches. There was a far greater throng in the streets than there was even during the day. The calls for Jenny Lind were so vehement that I led her through a window to the balcony. The loud cheers from the crowds lasted for several minutes, before the serenade was permitted to proceed again.

I have given the merest sketch of but a portion of the incidents of Jenny Lind's first day in America. For weeks afterwards, the excitement was unabated. Her rooms were thronged by visitors, including the magnates of the land in both Church and State. The carriages of the wealthiest citizens could be seen in front of her hotel, at nearly all hours of the day, and it was with some difficulty that I prevented the "fashionables " from monopolizing her altogether, and thus, as I believed, sadly marring my interests by cutting her off from the warm sympathies she had awakened among the masses. Presents of all sorts were showered upon her. Milliners, mantua-makers, and shopkeepers vied with each other in calling her attention to their wares, of which they sent her many valuable specimens, delighted if, in return, they could receive her autograph acknowledgment. Songs, quadrilles and polkas were dedicated to her, and poets sung in her praise. We had Jenny Lind gloves, Jenny Lind bonnets, Jenny Lind riding hats, Jenny Lind shawls, mantillas, robes, chairs, sofas, pianos — in fact, everything was Jenny Lind. Her movements were constantly watched, and the moment her carriage appeared at the door, it was surrounded by multitudes, eager to catch a glimpse of the Swedish Nightingale.

In looking over my "scrap-books" of extracts from the New York papers of that day, in which all accessible details concerning her were duly chronicled, it seems almost incredible that such a degree of enthusiasm should have existed. An abstract of the "sayings and doings" in regard to the Jenny Lind mania for the first ten days after her arrival, appeared in the *London Times* of Sept. 23, 1850, and, although it was an ironical "showing up" of the American enthusiasm, filling several columns, it was nevertheless a faithful condensation of facts which at this late day seem, even to myself, more like a dream than reality.

Before her arrival, I had offered $200 for a prize ode, "Greeting to America," to be sung by Jenny Lind at her first concert. Several hundred "poems" were sent in from all parts of the United States and the Canadas. The duties of the Prize Committee, in reading these effusions and making choice of the one mod worthy the prize, were truly arduous. The "offerings," with perhaps dozen exceptions, were the merest doggerel trash. The prize was awarded to Bayard Taylor for the following ode:

GREETING TO AMERICA.
WORDS BT BAYARD TAYLOR— MUSIC BY JULIUS BENEDICT.

I greet with a full heart the Land of the West,
Whose Banner of Stars o'er a world is unrolled;
Whose empire o'ershadows Atlantic's wide breast,
And opens to sunset its gateway of gold!
The land of the mountain, the land of the lake,
And rivers that roll in magnificent tide —
Where the souls of the mighty from slumber awake,
And hallow the soil for whose freedom they died!

Thou Cradle of empire! though wide be the foam
That severs the land of my fathers and thee,
I hear, from thy bosom, the welcome of home,
For song has a home in the hearts of the Free!
And long as thy waters shall gleam in the sun,
And Long as thy heroes remember their scars,
Be the hands of thy children united as one,
And Peace shed her light on thy Banner of Stars!

This award, although it gave general satisfaction, yet was met with disfavor by several disappointed poets, who, notwithstanding the decision of the committee, persisted in believing and declaring their own productions to be the best. This state of feeling was doubtless, in part, the cause which led to the publication, about this time, of a witty pamphlet entitled "Barnum's Parnassus; being Confidential Disclosures of the Prize Committee on the Jenny Lind song."

It gave some capital hits in which the committee, the enthusiastic public, the Nightingale, and myself, were roundly ridiculed. The following is a fair specimen from the work in question:

BARNUMOPSIS.
A RECITATIVE.

When to the common rest that crowns his days,
Dusty and worn the tired pedestrian goes,
What light is that whose wide o'erlooking blaze
A sudden glory on his pathway throws?

'Tis not the setting sun, whose drooping lid
Closed on the weary world at half-past six;
'Tis not the rising moon, whose rays are hid
Behind the city's sombre piles of bricks.

It is the Drummond Light, that from the top
Of Barnum's massive pile, sky-mingling there,
Darts its quick gleam o'er every shadowed -hop.
And gilds Broadway with unaccustomed glare.

There o'er the sordid gloom, whose deepening track*
Furrow the city's brow, the front of ages,
Thy loftier light descends on cabs and hacks,
And on two dozen different lines of stages!

O twilight Sun. with thy far darting ray,
Thou art a type of him whose tireless hands
Hung thee on high to guide the stranger's way,
Where, in its pride, his vast Museum stands.

Him, who in search of wonder? new and strange,
Grasps the wide skirts oi Nature's mystic robe
Explores the circles of eternal change,
And the dark chambers of the central globe.

He, from the reedy shores of fabled Nile.
Has brought, thick-ribbed and ancient as old iron,
That venerable beast, the crocodile,
And many a skin of many a famous lion.

Go lose thyself in those continuous halls,
Where strays the fond papa with son and daughter:
And all that charms or startles or appals,
Thou shalt behold, and for a single quarter.

Far from the Barcan deserts now withdrawn,
There huge constrictors coil their scaly backs;
There, cased in glass, malignant and unshorn,
Old murderers glare in sullenness and wax.

There many a varied form the sight beguiles,
In rusty broadcloth decked and shocking hat,
And there the unwieldy Lambert sits and smiles,
In the majestic plenitude of fat.

Or for thy gayer hours, the orang-outang

Or ape salutes thee with his strange grimace,
And in their shapes, stuffed as on earth they sprang,
Thine individual being thou canst trace!

And joys the youth in life's green spring, who goes
With the sweet babe and the gray-headed nurse,
To see those Cosmoramic orbs disclose
The varied beauties of the universe.

And last, not least, the marvelous Ethiope,
Changing his skin by preternatural skill,
Whom every setting sun's diurnal slope
Leaves whiter than the last, and whitening still.

All that of monstrous, scaly, strange and queer.
Has come from out the womb of earliest time,
Thou hast, O Barnum, in thy keeping here,
Nor is this all— for triumphs more sublime

Await thee yet! I, Jenny Lind, who reigned
Sublimely throned, the imperial queen of song.
Wooed by thy golden harmonies, have deigned
Captive to join the heterogeneous throng.

Sustained by an unfaltering trust in coin,
Dealt from thy hand, O thou illustrious man,
Gladly I heard the summons come to join
Myself the innumerable caravan.

Besides the foregoing, this pamphlet contained eleven poems, most of which abounded in wit. I have room but for a single stanza. The poet speaks of the various curiosities in the Museum, and, representing me as still searching for further novelties, makes me address the Swedish Nightingale as follows:

"So, Jenny, come along! you're just the card for me.
And quit these kings and queens, for the country of the free:
They'll welcome you with speeches, and serenades, and rockets,
and you will touch their hearts, and I will tap their pockets;
And if between us both the public isn't skinned,
Why, my name isn't Barnum, nor your name Jenny Lind!"

Among the many complimentary poems sent in, was the following, by Mrs. L. H. Sigourney, which that distinguished writer enclosed in a letter to me, with the request that I should hand it to Miss Lind:

THE SWEDISH SONGSTRESS AND HER CHARITIES.
BY MRS. L. H. SIGOURNET.

Blest must their vocation be
Who, with tones of melody,
Charm the discord and the strife
And the railroad rash of life,
And with Orphean magic move
Souls inert to life and love.
But there's one who doth inherit
Angel gift and angel spirit,
Bidding tides of gladness flow
Through the realms of want and woe;
'Mid lone age and misery's lot.
Kindling pleasures long forgot,
Seeking minds oppressed with night,
And on darkness shedding light,
She the seraph's speech doth know,
She hath done their deeds below;
So, when o'er this misty strand
She shall clasp their waiting hand,
They will fold her to their breast,
More a sister than a guest.

Jenny Lind's first concert was fixed to come off at Castle Garden, on Wednesday evening, September 11th, and most of the tickets were sold at auction on the Saturday and Monday previous to the concert. John N. Genin, the hatter, laid the foundation of his fortune by purchasing the first ticket at $225. It has been extensively reported that Mr. Genin and I are brothers-in-law, but our only relations are those of business and friendship. The proprietors of the Garden saw fit to make the usual charge of one shilling to all persons who entered the premises, yet three thousand people were present at the auction. One thousand tickets were sold at auction on the first morning for an aggregate sum of $10,141.

On the Tuesday after her arrival, I informed Miss Lind that I wished to make a slight alteration in our agreement. "What is it?" she asked in surprise.

"I am convinced," I replied, "that our enterprise will be much more successful than either of us anticipated. I wish, therefore, to stipulate that you shall receive not only $1,000 for each concert, besides all the expenses, as heretofore agreed on, but after taking $5,500 per night for expenses and my services, the balance shall be equally divided between us.

Jenny looked at me with astonishment. She could not comprehend my proposition. After I had repeated it, and she fully understood its import, she cordially grasped me by the hand, and exclaimed, "Mr. Barnum, you are a gentleman of honor; you are generous; it is just as Mr. Bates told me; I will sing for you as long as you please; I will sing for you in America — in Europe — anywhere!"

On Tuesday, September 10th, I informed Miss Lind that, judging by present appearances, her portion of the proceeds of the first concert would amount to $10,000. She immediately resolved to devote every dollar of it to charity; and, sending for Mayor Woodhull, she acted under his and my advice in selecting the various institutions among which she wished the amount to be distributed.

My arrangements of the concert-room were very complete. The great *parterre* and gallery of Castle Garden were divided by imaginary lines into four compartments, each of which was designated by a lamp of a different color. The tickets were printed in colors corresponding with the location which the holders were to occupy, and one hundred ushers, with rosettes and bearing wands ripped with ribbons of the several hues, enabled every individual to find his or her seat without the slightest difficulty. Every seat was of course numbered in color to correspond with the check, which each person retained after giving up an entrance ticket at the door. Thus, tickets, checks, lamps, rosettes, wands, and even the seat numbers were all in the appropriate colors to designate the different departments. These arrangements were duly advertised, and every particular was also printed upon each ticket. In order to prevent confusion, the doors were opened at five o'clock, while the concert did not commence until eight. The consequence was, that although about five thousand persons were present at the first concert, their entrance was marked with as much order and quiet as was ever witnessed in the assembling of a congregation at church. These precautions were observed at all the concerts given throughout the country under my administration, and the good order which always prevailed was the subject of numberless encomiums from the public and the press.

The reception of Jenny Lind on her first appearance, in point of enthusiasm, was probably never before equaled. As Mr. Benedict led her towards the foot-lights, the entire audience rose to their feet and welcomed her with three cheers, accompanied by the waving of thousands of hats and handkerchiefs. This was perhaps the largest audience to which Jenny Lind had ever sung. She was evidently much agitated, but the orchestra commenced, and before she had sung a dozen notes of "Casta Diva," she began to recover her self-possession, and long before the scene was concluded, she was as calm as if she was in her own drawing-room. Towards the last portion of the cavatina, the audience were so completely carried away by their feelings, that the remainder of the air was drowned in a perfect tempest of acclamation. Enthusiasm had been wrought to its highest pitch, but the musical powers of Jenny Lind exceeded all the brilliant anticipations which had been formed, and her triumph was complete. At the conclusion of the concert Jenny Lind was loudly called for, and was obliged to appear three times before the audience could be satisfied. Then they called vociferously for "Barnum," and I reluctantly responded to their demand.

On this first night, Mr. Julius Benedict firmly established with the American people his European reputation, as a most accomplished conductor and musical composer; while Signor Belletti inspired an admiration, which grew warmer and deeper in the minds of the public, to the end of his career in this country.

The Rubicon was passed. The successful issue of the Jenny Lind enterprise was established. I think there were a hundred men in New York, the day after her first concert, who would have willingly paid me $200,000 for my contract. I received repeated offers for an eighth, a tenth, or a sixteenth, equivalent to that price. But mine had been the risk, and I was determined mine should be the triumph.

The amount of money received for tickets to the first concert was $17,864.05, As this made Miss Lind's portion too small to realize the $10,000 which had been announced as devoted to charity, I proposed to divide equally with her the proceeds of the first two concerts, and not count them at all in our regular engagement. Accordingly, the second concert was given September 13th, and the receipts, amounting to $14,203.03, were, like those of the first concert, equally divided. Our third concert, but which, as between ourselves, we called the " first regular concert," was given Tuesday, September 17, 1850.

CHAPTER XIX.

SUCCESSFUL MANAGEMENT.

The first great assembly at Castle Garden was not gathered by Jenny Lind's musical genius and powers alone. She was effectually introduced to the public before they had seen or heard her. She appeared in the presence of a jury already excited to enthusiasm in her behalf. She more than met their expert actions, and all the means I had adopted to prepare the way were thus abundantly justified.

As a manager, I worked by setting others to work. Biographies of the Swedish Nightingale were largely circulated; "Foreign Correspondence" glorified her talents and triumphs by narratives of her benevolence; and "printer's ink" was invoked in every possible form, to put and keep Jenny Lind before the people. I am happy to say that the press generally echoed the voice of her praise from first to last. I could fill many volumes with the printed extracts which are nearly all of a similar tenor to the following unbought, unsolicited editorial article, which appeared in the *New York Herald* of Sept. 10, 1850 (the day before the first concert given by Miss Lind in the United States):

"Jenny Lind and the American People. — What ancient monarch was he, either in history or in fable, who offered half his kingdom (the price of box-tickets and choice seats in those days) for the invention of an original sensation, or the discovery of a fresh pleasure? That sensation — that pleasure which royal power in the Old World failed to discover — has been called into existence at a less price, by Mr. Barnum, a plain republican, and is now about to be enjoyed by the sovereigns of the New World.

"Jenny Lind, the most remarkable phenomenon in the musical art which has for the last century flashed across the horizon of the Old World, is now among us, and will make her debut tomorrow night to a house of nearly ten thousand listeners, yielding in proceeds by auction, a sum of forty or fifty thousand dollars. For the last ten days our musical reporters have furnished our readers with every matter connected with her arrival in this metropolis, and the steps adopted by Mr. Barnum in preparation for her first appearance. The proceedings of yesterday, consisting of the sale of the remainder of the tickets, and the astonishing, the wonderful sensation produced at her first rehearsal on the few persons, critics in musical art, who were admitted on the occasion, will be found elsewhere in our columns.

"'We concur in everything that has been said by our musical reporter, describing her extraordinary genius — her unrivalled combination of power and art. Nothing has been exaggerated, not an iota. Three years ago, more or less, we heard Jenny Lind on many occasions, when she made the first great sensation in Europe, by her debut, at the London Opera House. Then she was great in power — in art — in genius; now she is greater in all. We speak from experience and conviction. Then she astonished, and pleased, and fascinated the thousands of the British aristocracy, now she will fascinate, and please, and delight, and almost make mad with musical excitement, the millions of the American democracy. Tomorrow night, this new sensation— this fresh movement— this excitement excelling all former excitements— will be called into existence, when she pours out the notes of Casta Diva, and exhibits her astonishing powers — her wonderful peculiarities, that seem more of heaven than of earth — more of a voice from eternity, than from the lips of a human being.

"We speak soberly — seriously — calmly. The public expectation has run very high for the last week— higher than at any former period of our past musical annals. But high as it has risen, the reality — the fact — the concert — the voice and power of Jenny Lind — will far surpass all past expectations. Jenny Lind is a wonder, and a prodigy in song— and no mistake."

After the first month the business became thoroughly systematized, and by the help of such agents as my faithful treasurer, L.C. Stewart, and the indefatigable Le Grand Smith, my personal labors were materially relieved; but from the first concert on the 11th of September, 1850, until the ninety-third concert on the 9th of June 1851, a space of nine months, I did not know a waking moment that was entirely free from anxiety.

I could not hope to be exempted from trouble and perplexity in managing an enterprise which depended altogether on popular favor, and which involved great consequences to myself. Miss Lind did not dream, nor did anyone else, of the unparalleled enthusiasm that would greet her; and the first immense assembly at Castle Garden somewhat prepared her, I suspect, to listen to evil advisers. It would seem that the terms of our revised contract were sufficiently liberal to her and sufficiently hazardous to myself, to justify the expectation of perfectly honorable treatment; but certain envious intermeddlers appeared to think differently. "Do you not see, Miss Lind, that Mr. Barnum is coining money out of your genius?" said they; of course, she saw it, but the high-minded Swede despised and spumed the advisers who recommended her to repudiate her contract with me at all hazards, and take the enterprise into her own hands — possibly to put it into theirs. I, however, suffered much from the unreasonable interference of her lawyer, Mr. John Jay. Benedict and Belletti behaved like men, and Jenny afterwards expressed to me her regret that she had for a moment listened to the vexatious exactions of her legal counselor.

To show the difficulties with which I had to contend thus early in my enterprise, I copy a letter which I wrote, a little more than one month after Miss Lind commenced her engagement with me, to my friend Mr. Joshua Bates, of Messrs. Baring, Brothers & Co., London:

New York, Oct. 23, 1850.

Joshua Bates, Esq.:

Dear Sir; I take the liberty to write you a few lines, merely to say that we are getting along as well as could reasonably be expected. In this country you are aware that the rapid accumulation of wealth always creates much envy, and envy soon augments to malice. Such are the elements at work to a limited degree against myself, and although Miss Lind, Benedict and myself have never, as yet, had the slightest feelings between us, to my knowledge, except those of friendship, yet I cannot well see how this can long continue in the face of the fact that, nearly every day they allow persons (some moving in the first classes of society) to approach them, and spend hours in traducing me: even her attorney, Mr. John Jay, has been so blind to her interests, as to aid in poisoning her mind against me, by pouring into her ears the most silly twaddle, all of which amounts to nothing and less than nothing— such as the regret that I was a showman, exhibitor of Tom Thumb, etc. etc.

Without the elements which I possess for business, as well as my knowledge of human nature, acquired in catering for the public, the result of her concerts here would not have been pecuniarily one-half as much as the present— and such men as the Hon. Edward Everett. G. G. Howland. and others, will tell you that there is no charlatanism or lack of dignity in my management of these concerts. I know as well as any person, that the merits of Jenny Lind are the best capital to depend upon to secure public favor, and I have thus far acted on this knowledge. Everything which money and attention can procure for their comfort, they have, and I am glad to know that they are satisfied on this score. All I fear is, that these continual backbitings, if listened to by her, will, by and by, produce a feeling of distrust or regret, which will lead to unpleasant results.

The fact is. her mind ought to be as free as air, and she herself as free as a bird, and being satisfied of my probity and ability, she should turn a deaf ear to all envious and malevolent attacks on me. I have hoped that by thus briefly stating to you the facts in the case, you might be induced for her interests as well as mine to drop a line of advice to Mr. Benedict and another to Mr. Jay on this subject. If I am asking or expecting too much, I pray you to not give it a thought, for I feel myself fully able to carry through my rights alone, although I should deplore nothing so much as to be obliged to do so in a feeling of unfriendliness. I have risked much money on the issue of this speculation— it has proved successful, I am full of perplexity and anxiety, and labor continually for success, and I cannot allow ignorance or envy to rob me of the fruits of my enterprise.

Sincerely and gratefully, yours,   P. T. Barnum.

Jenny Lind's character for benevolence became so generally known, that her door was beset by persons asking charity, and she was in the receipt, while in the principal cities, of numerous letters, all on the same subject. I knew of many instances in which she gave sums of money to applicants, varying in amount from $20, $50, $500, to $1,000, and in one instance she gave $5,000 to a Swedish friend.

The night after Jenny's arrival in Boston, a display of fireworks was given in her honor, in front of the Revere House, after which followed a beautiful torchlight procession by the Germans of that city.

On her return from Boston to New York, Jenny, her companion, and Messrs. Benedict and Belletti, stopped at *Iranistan*, my residence in Bridgeport, where they remained until the following day. The morning after her arrival, she took my arm and proposed a promenade through the grounds. She seemed much pleased, and said, "I am astonished that you should have left such a beautiful place for the sake of traveling through the country with me."

THE PRINCE IN THE MUSEUM

The same day she told me in a playful mood, that she had heard a most extraordinary report. "I have heard that you and I are about to be married," said she; "now how could such an absurd report ever have originated?"

"Probably from the fact that we are 'engaged,' " I replied. She enjoyed a joke and laughed heartily.

"Do you know, Mr. Barnum," said she, "that if you had not built *Iranistan*, I should never have come to America for you?"

I expressed my surprise and asked her to explain.

"I had received several applications to visit the United States," she continued, "but I did not much like the appearance of the applicants, nor did I relish the idea of crossing 3,000 miles of ocean; so, I declined them all. But the first letter which Mr. Wilton, your agent, addressed me, was written upon a sheet headed with a beautiful engraving of *Iranistan*. It attracted my attention. I said to myself, a gentleman who has been so successful in his business as to be able to build and reside in such a palace cannot be a mere 'adventurer.' So, I wrote to your agent, and consented to an interview, which I should have declined, if I had not seen the picture of *Iranistan*!"

"That, then, fully pays me for building it," I replied.

Jenny Lind always desired to reach a place in which she was to sing, without having the time of her arrival known, thus avoiding the excitement of promiscuous crowds. As a manager, however, I knew that the interests of the enterprise depended in a great degree upon these excitements.

On reaching Philadelphia, a large concourse of persons awaited the approach of the steamer which conveyed her. With difficulty, we pressed through the crowd, and were followed by many thousands to Jones's Hotel. The street in front of the building was densely packed by the populace, and poor Jenny, who was suffering from a severe headache, retired to her apartments. I tried to induce the crowd to disperse, but they declared they would not do so until Jenny Lind should appear on the balcony. I would not disturb her, and, knowing that the tumult might prove an annoyance to her, I placed her bonnet and shawl upon her companion, Miss Ahmansen, and led her out on the balcony. She bowed gracefully to the multitude, who gave her three hearty cheers and quietly dispersed. Miss Lind was so utterly averse to anything like deception, that we never ventured to tell her the part which her bonnet and shawl had played in the absence of their owner.

Jenny was in the habit of attending church whenever she could do so without attracting notice. She always preserved her nationality, also, by inquiring out and attending Swedish churches wherever they could be found. She gave $1,000 to a Swedish church in Chicago.

My eldest daughter, Caroline, and her friend, Mrs. Lyman, of Bridgeport, accompanied me on the tour from New York to Havana, and thence home, via New Orleans and the Mississippi.

We were at Baltimore on the Sabbath, and my daughter, accompanying a friend, who resided in the city, to church, took a seat with her in the choir, and joined in the singing. A number of the congregation, who had seen Caroline with me the day previous, and supposed her to be Jenny Lind, were yet laboring under the same mistake, and it was soon whispered through the church that Jenny Lind was in the choir! The excitement was worked to its highest pitch when my daughter rose as one of the musical group. Every ear was on the alert to catch the first notes of her voice, and when she sang, glances of satisfaction passed through the assembly. Caroline, quite unconscious of the attention she attracted, continued to sing to the end of the hymn. Not a note was lost upon the ears of the attentive congregation. "What an exquisite singer!", "Heavenly sounds!", "I never heard the like!" and similar expressions were whispered through the church.

At the conclusion of the services, my daughter and her friend found the passageway to their carriage blocked by a crowd who were anxious to obtain a nearer view of the "Swedish Nightingale." The pith of the joke is that we have never discovered that my daughter has any extraordinary claims as a vocalist.

Our orchestra in New York consisted of sixty. When we started on our southern tour, we took with us permanently as the orchestra, twelve of the best musicians we could select, and in New Orleans augmented the force to sixteen. We increased the number to thirty-five, forty or fifty, as the case might be, by choice of musicians residing where the concerts were given. On our return to New York from Havana, we enlarged the orchestra to one hundred performers.

The morning after our arrival in Washington, President Fillmore called, and left his card, Jenny being out. When she returned and found the token of his attention, she was in something of a flurry. "Come," said she, "we must call on the President immediately."

"Why so?" I inquired.

"Because he has called on me, and of course that is equivalent to a command for me to go to his house."

I assured her that she might make her mind at ease, for whatever might be the custom with crowned heads, our Presidents were not wont to "command" the movements of strangers, and that she would be quite in time if she returned his call the next day. She was accompanied to the "White House" by Messrs. Benedict, Belletti and myself, and several happy hours were spent in the private circle of the President's family.

Both concerts in Washington were attended by the President and his family, and every member of the Cabinet. I noticed, also, among the audience, Henry Clay, Benton, Foote, Cass and General Scott, and nearly every member of Congress. On the following morning, Miss Lind was called upon by Mr. Webster, Mr. Clay, General Cass, and Colonel Benton, and all parties were evidently gratified. I had introduced Mr. Webster to her in Boston. Upon hearing one of her wild mountain songs in New York, and also in Washington, Mr. Webster signified his approval by rising, drawing himself up to his full height, and making a profound bow. Jenny was delighted by this expression of praise from the great statesman. When I first introduced Miss Lind to Mr. Webster, at the Revere House, in Boston she was greatly impressed with his manners and conversation, and after his departure, walked up and down excitement, exclaiming: "Ah! Mr. Barnum, that is a man; I have never before seen such a man!"

We visited the Capitol while both Houses were in session. Miss Lind took the arm of Hon C. F. Cleveland, representative from Connecticut, and was by him escorted into various parts of the Capitol and the grounds, with all of which she was much pleased. During the week I was invited with Miss Lind and her immediate friends, to visit Mount Vernon, with Colonel Washington, the then proprietor, and Mr. Seaton, ex-Mayor of Washington, and editor of the *Intelligencer*. Colonel Washington chartered a steamboat for the purpose. We were landed a short distance from the tomb, which we first visited. Proceeding to the house, we were introduced to Mrs. Washington, and several other ladies. Much interest was manifested by Miss Lind in examining the mementoes of the great man whose home it had been. A beautiful collation was spread out and arranged in fine taste. Before leaving, Miss Washington presented Jenny with a book from the library, with the name of Washington written by his own hand. She was much overcome at receiving this present, called me aside, and expressed her desire to give something in return. "I have nothing with me," she said, "excepting this watch and chain, and I will give that if you think it will be acceptable." I knew the watch was very valuable, and told her that so costly a present would not be expected, nor would it be proper. "The expense is nothing, compared to the value of that book," she replied, with deep emotion; "but as the watch was a present from a near friend, perhaps I should not give it away." Jenny Lind, I am sure, never forgot the pleasurable emotions of that day.

The voyage from Wilmington to Charleston was an exceedingly rough and perilous one. We were about thirty-six hours in making the passage, the usual time being seventeen. We arrived safely at last, and I was grieved to learn that for twelve hours the loss of the steamer had been considered certain, and had even been announced by telegraph in the Northern cities. We remained at Charleston about ten days, to take the steamer "Isabella" on her regular trip to Havana. Jenny had been through so much excitement at the North, that she determined to have quiet here, and therefore declined receiving any calls. One young lady, the daughter of a wealthy planter near Augusta, was so determined upon seeing her in private, that she paid one of the servants to allow her to put on a cap and white apron, and carry in the tray for Jenny's tea. I afterwards told Miss Lind of the joke, and suggested that after such an evidence of admiration, she should receive a call from the young lady.

"It is not admiration — it is only curiosity," replied Jenny, "and I will not encourage such folly."

Christmas was at hand, and Jenny Lind determined to honor it in the way she had often done in Sweden. She had a beautiful Christmas tree privately prepared, and from its boughs depended a variety of presents for members of the company. These gifts were encased in paper, with the names of the recipients written on each.

After spending a pleasant evening in her drawing-room, she invited us into the parlor, where the "surprise" awaited us. Each person commenced opening the packages bearing his or her address, and although every individual had one or more pretty presents, she had prepared a joke for each. Mr. Benedict, for instance, took off wrapper after wrapper from one of his packages, which at first was as large as his head, but after having removed some forty coverings of paper, it was reduced to a size smaller than his hand, and the removal of the last envelope exposed to view a piece of cavendish tobacco. One of my presents, choicely wrapped in a dozen coverings, was a jolly young Bacchus in Parian marble, inter tied as a pleasant hit at my temperance principles!

The night before New Year's Day was spent in her apartment with great hilarity. Enlivened by music, singing, dancing and story-telling, the hours glided swiftly away. Miss Lind asked me if I would dance with her. I told her my education had been neglected in that line, and that I had never danced in my life. "That is all the better," said she; "now dance with me in a cotillion. I am sure you can do it." She was a beautiful dancer, and I never saw her laugh more heartily than she did at my awkwardness. She said she would give me the credit of being the poorest dancer she ever saw!

I had arranged with a man in New York to transport furniture to Havana, provide a house, and board Jenny Lind and our immediate party during our stay.

When we arrived, we found the building converted into a semi-hotel and the apartments were anything but comfortable. Jenny was vexed. Soon after dinner, she took a volante and an interpreter, and drove into the suburbs. She was absent four hours. Whither or why she had gone, none of us knew. At length she returned and informed us that she had hired a commodious furnished house in a delightful location outside the walls of the city, and invited us all to go and live with her during our stay in Havana, and we accepted the invitation. She was now freed from all annoyances; her time was her own, she received no calls, went and came when she pleased, had no meddlesome advisers about her, legal or otherwise, and was as merry as a cricket. We had a large courtyard in the rear of the house, and here she would come and romp and run, sing and laugh, like a young school-girl. "Now, Mr. Barnum, for another game of ball," she would say half a dozen times a day; whereupon, she would take an India-rubber ball, (of which she had two or three), and commence a game of throwing and catching, which would be kept up until, being completely tired out, I would say, "I give it up." Then her rich, musical laugh would be heard ringing through the house, as she exclaimed, "Oh, Mr. Barnum, you are too fat and too lazy; you cannot stand it to play ball with me!"

Her celebrated countrywoman, Miss Frederika Bremer, spent a few days with us very pleasantly, and it is difficult to conceive of a more delightful month than was passed by the entire party at Jenny Lind's house in the outskirts of Havana.

CHAPTER XX.

INCIDENTS OF THE TOUR.

Soon after arriving in Havana, I discovered that a strong prejudice existed against our musical enterprise. I might rather say that the Habaneros, not accustomed to the high figure which tickets had commanded in the Status, were determined on forcing me to adopt their opera prices; whereas I paid one thousand dollars per night for the Tacon Opera House, and other expenses being in proportion, I was determined to receive remunerating prices or give no concerts. They attended the concert, but were determined to show the great songstress no favor. I perfectly understood this feeling in advance, but studiously kept all knowledge of it from Miss Lind. I went to the first concert, therefore, with some misgivings in regard to her reception. The following, which I copy from the Havana correspondence of the New York Tribune, gives a correct account of it:

*   *   *   *   *   *   *   *   *   *   *

"Jenny Lind soon appeared, led on by Signor Belletti. Some three or four hundred persons clapped their hands at her appearance, but this token of approbation was instantly silenced by at least two thousand five hundred decided hisses. Thus, having settled the matter that there should be no forestalling of public opinion, and that if applause was given to Jenny Lind in that house it should first be incontestably earned, the most solemn silence prevailed. I have heard the Swedish Nightingale often in Europe as well as in America, and have ever noticed a distinct tremulousness attending her first appearance in any city. Indeed, this feeling was plainly manifested in her countenance as she neared the foot-lights; but when she witnessed the kind of reception in store for her — so different from anything she had reason to expect — her countenance changed in an instant to a haughty self-possession, her eyes flashed defiance, and, becoming immovable as a statue. she stood there perfectly calm and beautiful. She was satisfied that she now had an ordeal to pass and a victory to gain worthy of her powers. In a moment her eye scanned the immense audience, the music began and then followed — how can I describe it? — such heavenly strains as I verily believe mortal never breathed except Jenny Lind, and mortal never heard except from her lips. Some of the oldest Castilians kept a frown upon their brow and a curling sneer upon their lips; their ladies, however, and most of the audience began to look surprised. The gushing melody flowed on, increasing in beauty and glory. The *caballeros*, the *senoras* and *senoritas* began to look at each other; nearly all, however, kept their teeth clenched and their lips closed, evidently determined to resist to the last. The torrent flowed deeper and faster, the lark flew higher and higher, the melody grew richer and grander; still every lip was compressed. By and by, as the rich notes came dashing in rivers upon our enraptured ears, one poor critic involuntarily whispered a 'brava.' This outbursting of the soul was instantly hissed down. The stream of harmony roll on till, at the close, it made a clean sweep of every obstacle, and carried all before it. Not a vestige of opposition remained, but such a tremendous shout of applause as went up I never before heard.

The triumph was most complete. And how was Jenny Lind affected? She who stood a few moments previous like adamant, now trembled like a reed in the wind before the storm of enthusiasm which her own simple notes had produced. Tremblingly, slowly, and almost bowing her face to the ground, she withdrew. The roar and applause of victory increased. *"Encore! Encore! Encore!"* came from every lip. She again appeared, and curtsying low, again withdrew; but again, again and again did they call her out and at every appearance the thunders of applause rang louder and louder. Thus, five times was Jenny Lind called out to receive their unanimous and deafening plaudits."

I cannot express what my feelings were as I watched this scene from the dress circle. Poor Jenny! I deeply sympathized with her when I heard that first hiss. I indeed observed the resolute bearing which she assumed but was apprehensive of the result. When I witnessed her triumph, I could not restrain the tears of joy that rolled down my cheeks; and rushing through a private box, I reached the stage just as she was withdrawing after the fifth encore. "God bless you, Jenny, you have settled them!" I exclaimed.

"Are you satisfied?" said she, throwing her arms around my neck. She, too, was crying with joy, and never before did she look so beautiful in my eyes as on that evening.

One of the Havana papers, notwithstanding the great triumph, continued to cry out for low prices. This induced many to absent themselves, expecting soon to see a reduction. It had been understood that we would give twelve concerts in Havana; but when they saw after the fourth concert, which was devoted to charity, that no more were announced, they became uneasy. Committees waited upon us requesting more concerts, but we peremptorily declined. Some of the leading Dons, among whom was Count Penalver, then offered to guarantee us $25,000 for three concerts. My reply was, that there was not money enough on the island of Cuba to induce me to consent to it.

I found my little Italian plate-dancer, Vivalla, in Havana. He called on me frequently. He was in great distress, having lost the use of his limbs on the left side of his body by paralysis. He was thus unable to earn a livelihood, although he still kept a performing dog, which turned a spinning-wheel and performed some curious tricks. One day as I was passing him out of the front gate, Miss Lind inquired who he was. I briefly recounted to her his history. She expressed deep interest in his case, and said something should be set apart for him in the benefit which she was about to give for charity. Accordingly, when the benefit came off, Miss Land appropriated $500 to him and I made the necessary arrangements for his return to his friends in Italy. At the same benefit $4,000 were distributed between two hospitals and a convent.

A few mornings after the benefit our bell was rung, and the servant announced that I was wanted. I went to the door and found a large procession of children, neatly dressed and bearing banners, attended by ten or twelve priests, arrayed in their rich and flowing robes. I inquired their business, and was informed that they had come to see Miss Lind, to thank her in person for her benevolence. I took their message, and informed Miss Lind that the leading priests of the convent had come in great state to see and thank her. "I will not see them," she replied; "they have nothing to thank me for. If I have done good, it is no more than my duty, and it is my pleasure. I do not deserve their thanks, and I will not see them." I returned her answer, and the leaders of the grand procession went away in disappointment.

The same day Vivalla called and brought her a basket of the most luscious fruit that he could procure. The little fellow was very happy and extremely grateful. Miss Lind had gone out for a ride.

"God bless her! I am so happy; she is such a good lady. I shall see my brothers and sisters again. Oh, she is a very good lady," said poor Vivalla, overcome by his feelings. He begged me to thank her for him and give her the fruit. As he was passing out of the door, he hesitated a moment, and then said, "Mr. Barnum I should like so much to have the good lady see my dog turn a wheel; it is very nice; he can spin very good. Shall I bring the dog and wheel for her? She is such a good lady, I wish to please her very much." I smiled and told him she would not care for the dog: that he was quite welcome to the money, and that she refused to see the priests from the convent that morning, because she never received thanks for favors.

When Jenny came in I gave her the fruit, and laughingly told her that Vivalla wished to show her how his performing dog could turn a spinning-wheel "Poor man, poor man, do let him come; it is all the good creature can do for me," exclaimed Jenny, and the tears flowed thick and fast down her cheeks. "I like that, I like that," she continued, "do let the poor creature come and bring his dog. It will make him so happy."

I confess it made me happy, and I exclaimed, for my heart was full, "God bless you, it will make him cry for joy; he shall come tomorrow."

I saw Vivalla the same evening, and delighted him with the intelligence that Jenny would see his dog perform the next day, at four o'clock precisely.

"I will be punctual," said Vivalla, in a voice trembling with emotion; but I was sure she would like to see my dog perform."

For full half an hour before the time appointed did Jenny Lind sit in her window on the second floor and watch for Vivalla and his dog. A few minutes before the appointed hour, she saw him coming. "Ah, here he comes! here he comes!" she exclaimed in delight, as she ran down stairs and opened the door to admit him. A negro boy was bringing the small spinning-wheel, while Vivalla led the dog. Handing the boy a silver coin, she motioned him away, and taking the wheel in her arms, she said, "This is very kind of you to come with your dog. Follow me. I will carry the wheel upstairs." Her servant offered to take the wheel, but no, she would let no one carry it but herself. She called us all up to her parlor, and for one full hour did she devote herself to the happy Italian. She went down on her knees to pet the dog and to ask Vivalla all sorts of questions about his performances, his former course of life, his friends in Italy, and his present hopes and determinations. Then she sang and played for him, gave him some refreshments, finally insisted on carrying his wheel to the door, and her servant accompanied Vivalla to his boarding-house.

Poor Vivalla! He was probably never so happy before, but his enjoyment did not exceed that of Miss Lind. That scene alone would have paid me for all my labors during the entire musical campaign. A few months later, however, the Havana correspondent of the *New York Herald* announced the death of Vivalla and stated that the poor Italian's last words were about Jenny Lind and Mr. Barnum.

In the party which accompanied me to Havana, was Mr. Henry Bennett, who formerly kept Peale's Museum in New York, afterwards managing the same establishment for me when I purchased it, and he was now with me in the capacity of a ticket-taker. He was as honest a man as ever lived, and a good deal of a wag. I remember his going through the market once and running across a decayed actor who was reduced to tending a market stand; Bennett hailed him with "Hallo! what are you doing here; what are you keeping that old turkey for?"

"O! for a profit," replied the actor.

"Prophet, prophet!" exclaimed Bennett, "patriarch, you mean!"

With all his waggery he was subject at times to moods of the deepest despondency, bordering on insanity. Madness ran in his family. His brother, in a fit of frenzy, had blown his brains out. Henry himself had twice attempted his own Life while in my employ in New York. Sometime after our present journey to Havana, I sent him to London. He conducted my business precisely as I directed, writing up his account with me correctly to a penny. Then handing it to a mutual friend with directions to give it to me when I arrived in London the following week, he went to his lodgings and committed suicide.

While we were in Havana, Bennett was so despondent at times that we were obliged to watch him carefully, lest he should do some damage to himself or others. When we left Havana for New Orleans, on board the steamer "Falcon," Mr. James Gordon Bennett, editor of the *New York Herald*, and his wife, were also passengers. After permitting one favorable notice in his paper, Bennett had turned around, as usual, and had abused Jenny Lind and bitterly attacked me. I was always glad to get such notices, for they served as inexpensive advertisements to my Museum.

Ticket-taker Bennett, however, took much to heart the attacks of Editor Bennett upon Jenny Lind. When Editor Bennett came on board the "Falcon," his violent name-sake said to a by-stander:

"I would willingly be drowned if I could see that old scoundrel go to the bottom of the sea."

Several of our party overheard the remark and I turned laughingly to Bennett and said: "Nonsense; he can't harm anyone, and there is an old proverb about the impossibility of drowning those who are born to another fate."

That very night, however, as I stood near the cabin door, conversing with my treasurer and other members of my company, Henry Bennett came up to me with a wild air, and hoarsely whispered:

"Old Bennett has gone forward alone in the dark — and I am going to throw him overboard!"

We were all startled, for we knew the man and he seemed terribly in earnest.

Knowing how most effectively to address him at such times, I exclaimed:

"Ridiculous! you would not do such a thing."

"I swear I will," was his savage reply. I expostulated with him, and several of our party joined me.

"Nobody will know it," muttered the maniac, "and I shall be doing the world a favor."

I endeavored to awaken him to a sense of the crime he contemplated, assuring him that it could not possibly benefit anyone, and that from the fact of the relations existing between the editor and myself, I should be the first to be accused of his murder. I implored him to go to his state-room, and he finally did so, accompanied by some of the gentlemen of our party. I took pains to see that he was carefully watched that night, and, indeed, for several days, till he became calm again. He was a large, athletic man, quite able to pick up his namesake and drop him overboard. The matter was too serious for a joke, and we made little mention of it; but more than one of our party said then, and has said since, what I really believe to be true, that "James Gordon Bennett would have been drowned that night had it not been for P. T. Barnum."

In New Orleans the wharf was crowded by a great concourse of persons, as the steamer "Falcon" approached. Jenny Lind had enjoyed a month of quiet, and dreaded the excitement which she must now again encounter.

"Mr. Barnum, I am sure I can never get through that crowd," said she, in despair.

"Leave that to me. Remain quiet for ten minutes, and there shall be no crowd here," I replied.

Taking my daughter on my arm, she threw her veil over her face, and we descended the gangway to the dock. The crowd pressed around. I had beckoned for a carriage before leaving the ship.

"That's Barnum, I know him," called out several persons at the top of their voices.

"Open the way, if you please, for Mr. Barnum and Miss Lind! " cried Le Grand Smith over the railing of the ship, the deck of which he had just reached from the wharf.

"Don't crowd her, if you please, gentlemen," I exclaimed, and by dint of pushing, squeezing and coaxing, we reached the carriage, and drove for the Montalba buildings, where Miss Land's apartments had been prepared, and the whole crowd came following at our heels. In a few minutes afterwards, Jenny and her companion came quietly in a carriage, and were in the house before the ruse was discovered. In answer to incessant calls, she appeared a moment upon the balcony, waved her handkerchief, received three hearty cheers, and the crowd dispersed.

A funny incident occurred at New Orleans. Our concerts were given in the St. Charles Theater, then managed by my good friend, the late Sol Smith. In the open lots near the theater were exhibitions of mammoth hogs, five-footed horses, grizzly bears, and other animals.

A gentleman had a son about twelve years old, who had a wonderful ear for music. He could whistle or sing any tune after hearing it once. His father did not know nor care for a single note, but so anxious was he to please his son, that he paid thirty dollars for two tickets to the concert.

"I liked the music better than I expected," said he to me the next day, "but my son was in raptures. He was so perfectly enchanted that he scarcely spoke the whole evening, and I would on no account disturb his delightful reveries."

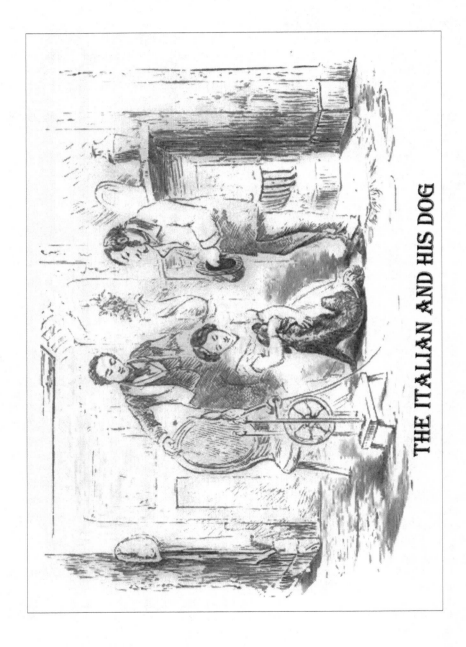

THE ITALIAN AND HIS DOG

"When the concert was finished we came out of the theater. Not a word was spoken. I knew that my musical prodigy was happy among the clouds, and I said nothing. I could not help envying him his love of music, and considered my thirty dollars as nothing, compared to the bliss which it secured to him. Indeed, I was seriously thinking of taking him to the next concert, when he spoke. We were just passing the numerous shows upon the vacant lots. One of the signs attracted him, and he said, 'Father, let us go in and see the big hog!' The little scamp! I could have horsewhipped him!" said the father, who, loving a joke, could not help laughing at the ludicrous incident.

Some months afterwards, I was relating this story at my own table to several guests, among whom was a very matter-of-fact man who had not the faintest conception of humor. After the whole party had laughed heartily at the anecdote, my matter-of-fact friend gravely asked: And was it a very large hog, Mr. Barnum?"

I made arrangements with the captain of the splendid steamer "Magnolia," of Louisville, to take our party as far as Cairo, the junction of the Mississippi and Ohio rivers, stipulating for sufficient delay in Natchez, Mississippi, and in Memphis, Tennessee, to give a concert in each place. It was no unusual thing for me to charter a steamboat or a special train of cars for our party. With such an enterprise as that, time and comfort were paramount to money.

The time on board the steamer was whiled away in reading, viewing the scenery of the Mississippi, and other diversions. One day we had a pleasant musical festival in the ladies' saloon for the gratification of the passengers, at which Jenny volunteered to sing without ceremony. It seemed to us she never sang so sweetly before. I also did my best to amuse my fellow passengers with anecdotes and the exhibition of sundry legerdemain tricks which I had been obliged to learn and use in the South years before, and under far different circumstances than those which attended the performance now. Among other tricks, I caused a quarter of a dollar to disappear so mysteriously from beneath a card, that the mulatto barber on board came to the conclusion that I was in league with the devil.

The next morning, I seated myself for the operation of shaving, and the colored gentleman ventured to dip into the mystery. "Beg pardon, Mr. Barnum, but I have heard a great deal about you, and I saw more than I wanted to see last night. Is it true that you have sold yourself to the devil so that you can do what you've a mind to?"

"Oh, yes," was my reply, "that is the bargain between us."

"How long did you agree for?" was the question next in order.

"Only nine years," said I. "I have had three of them already. Before the other six are out, I shall find a way to nonplus the old gentleman, and I have told him so to his face."

At this avowal, a larger space of white than usual was seen in the darkey's eyes, and he inquired, "Is it by this bargain that you get so much money?"

"Certainly, No matter who has money, nor where he keeps it, in his box or till, or anywhere about him, I have only to speak the words, and it comes."

The shaving was completed in silence, but thought had been busy in the barber's mind, and he embraced the speediest opportunity to transfer his bag of coin to the iron safe in charge of the clerk.

The movement did not escape me, and immediately a joke was afoot. I had barely time to make two or three details of arrangement with the clerk, and resume my seat in the cabin, ere the barber sought a second interview, bent on testing the alleged powers of Beelzebub's colleague.

"Beg pardon, Mr. Barnum, but where is my money? Can you get it?"

"I do not want your money," was the quiet answer. "It is safe."

"Yes, I know it is safe — ha! ha! — it is in the iron safe in the clerk's office — safe enough from you! "

"It is not in the iron safe!" said I. This was said so quietly, yet positively, that the colored gentleman ran to the office, and inquired if all was safe. "All right," said the clerk. "Open, and let me see," replied the barber. The safe was unlocked and lo! the money was gone!

In mystified terror the loser applied to me for relief. "You will find the bag in your drawer," said I, and there it was found!

His curiosity was still great. "Please do another trick," said he.

"Very well," I replied, "stand perfectly still."

He did so, and I commenced muttering some mysterious words, as if performing an incantation.

"What are you doing?" asked the barber.

"I am changing you into a black cat," I replied, "but don't be afraid; I will change you back again, if I don't forget the words to do it with."

This was too much for the terrified darkey; with an awful screech he rushed to the side of the boat resolved to drown rather than undergo such a transformation.

He was captured and brought back to me, when I dispelled his fright by explaining the way in which I had tricked him. Relieved and reassured, he clapped his hands and executed an impromptu jig, exclaiming, "Ha! ha! when I get back to New Orleans won't I come de Barnum ober dem niggers!"

CHAPTER XXI.

JENNY LIND.

According to agreement, the "Magnolia " waited for us at Natchez and Memphis, and we gave profitable concerts at both places. The concert at Memphis was the sixtieth in the list since Miss Land's arrival in America, and the first concert in St. Louis would be the sixty-first. When we reached that city, on the morning of the day when our first concert was to be given, Miss Lind's secretary came to me, commissioned, he said, by her, and announced that as sixty concerts had already taken place, she proposed to avail herself of one of the conditions of our contract, and cancel the engagement next morning. As this was the first intimation of the kind I had received, I was somewhat startled, though I assumed an entirely placid demeanor, and asked:

"Does Miss Lind authorize you to give me this notice?"

"I so understand it," was the reply.

I immediately reflected that if our contract was thus suddenly canceled, Miss Land was bound to repay to me all I had paid her over the stipulated $1,000 for each concert, and a little calculation showed that the sum thus to be paid back was $77,000, since she had already received from me $137,000 for sixty concerts. In this view, I could not but think that this was a ruse of some of her advisers, and, possibly, that she might know nothing of the matter. So, I told her secretary that I would see him again in an hour, and meanwhile I went to my old friend Mr. Sol. Smith for his legal and friendly advice.

I showed him my contract and told him how much I had been annoyed by the selfish and greedy hangers-on and advisers, legal and otherwise, of Jenny Lind. I talked to him about the "wheels within wheels" which moved this great musical enterprise, and asked and gladly accepted his advice, which mainly coincided with my own views of the situation. I then went back to the secretary and quietly told him that I was ready to settle with Miss Lind and to close the engagement.

"But," said he, manifestly "taken aback," "you have already advertised concerts in Louisville and Cincinnati, I believe."

"Yes," I replied; "but you may take my contracts for halls and printing off my hands at cost." I further said that he was welcome to the assistance of my agent who had made these arrangements, and, moreover, that I would cheerfully give my own services to help them through with these concerts, thus giving them a good start "on their own hook."

My liberality, which he acknowledged, emboldened him to make an extraordinary proposition:

"Now suppose," he asked, "Miss Lind should wish to give some fifty concerts in this country, what would you charge as manager, per concert?"

"A million dollars each, not one cent less," I replied. I was now thoroughly aroused; the whole thing was as clear as daylight, and I continued: "Now we might as well understand each other; I don't believe Miss Lind has authorized you to propose to me to cancel our contract; but if she has, just bring me a line to that effect over her signature and her check for the amount due me by the terms of that contract, some $77,000, and we will close our business connections at once."

"But, why not make a new arrangement," persisted the secretary, "for fifty concerts more, by which Miss Land shall pay you liberally, say $1,000 per concert?"

"Simply because I hired Miss Lind, and not she me," I replied, "and because I never ought to take a farthing less for my risk and trouble than the contract gives me. I have voluntarily paid Miss Lind more than twice as much as I originally contracted to pay her, or as she expected to receive when she first engaged with me. Now, if she is not satisfied, I wish to settle instantly and finally. If you do not bring me her decision today, I shall go to her for it tomorrow morning."

I met the secretary soon after breakfast next morning and asked him if he had a written communication for me from Miss Lind? He said he had not, and that the whole thing was a "joke." He merely wanted, he added, to see what I would say to the proposition. I asked him if Miss Lind was in the "joke," as he called it? He hoped I would not inquire but would let the matter drop. I went on, as usual, and gave four more concerts in St. Louis, and followed out my program as arranged in other cities for many weeks following; nor at that time, nor at any time afterwards, did Miss Lind give me the slightest intimation that she had any knowledge of the proposition of her secretary to cancel our agreement or to employ me as her manager.

During our stay at St. Louis, I delivered a temperance lecture in the theater, and, at the close, among other signers of the pledge, was my friend and adviser, Sol. Smith. "Uncle Sol.", as every one called him, was a famous character in his time. He was an excellent comedian, an author, a manager and a lawyer.

In 1854, he published an autobiographical work, preceded by a dedication which I venture to copy:

"TO PHINEAS T. BARNUM, PROPRIETOR OF
THE AMERICAN MUSEUM, ETC.

"Great Impresario: Whilst you were engaged in your grand Jenny Lind speculation, the following conundrum went the rounds of the American newspapers:

"'Why is it that Jenny Lind and Barnum will never fall out?' Answer: 'Because he is always for-getting, and she is always for-giving.' " I have never asked you the question directly, whether you, Mr. Barnum, started that conundrum, or not; but I strongly suspect that you did. At all events, I noticed that your whole policy was concentrated into one idea — to make an angel of Jenny and depreciate yourself in contrast.

"You may remember that in this city (St. Louis), I acted in one instance as your 'legal adviser,' and, as such, necessarily became acquainted with all the particulars of your contract with the so-called Swedish Nightingale, as well as the various modifications claimed by that charitable lady, and submitted to by you after her arrival in this country; which modifications (I suppose it need no longer be a secret) secured

138

to her — besides the original stipulation of one thousand dollars for every concert, attendants, carriages, assistant artists, and a pompous and extravagant retinue, fit (only) for a European princess — one-half of the profits of each performance. You may also remember the legal advice I gave you on the occasion referred to, and the salutary effect of your following it. You must remember the extravagant joy you felt afterwards, in Philadelphia, when the 'Angel' made up her mind to avail herself of one of the stipulations in her contract, to break off at the end of a hundred nights, and even bought out seven of that hundred — supposing that she could go on without your aid as well as with it. And you cannot but remember, how, like a rocket-stick she dropped, when your business connection with her ended, and how she 'fizzed out' the remainder of her concert nights in this part of the world, and soon afterwards retired to her domestic blissitude in Sweden.

"You know, Mr. Barnum, if you would only tell, which of the two it was that was 'for-getting,' and which 'for-giving;' and you also know who actually gave the larger portion of those sums which you *Herald*ed to the world as the sole gifts of the 'divine Jenny.'

"Of all your speculations— from the negro centenarian, who didn't nurse General Washington, down to the Bearded Woman of Genoa — there was not one which required the exercise of so much humbuggery as the Jenny Lind concerts; and I verily believe there is no man living, other than yourself, who could, or would, have risked the enormous expenditure of money necessary to carry them through successfully— traveling, with sixty artists, four thousand miles, and giving ninety-three concerts, at an actual cost of forty-five hundred dollars each, is what no other man would have undertaken — you accomplished this, and pocketed by the operation but little less than two hundred thousand dollars! Mr. Barnum, you are yourself, alone!

"I honor you, oh! Great Impresario, as the most successful manager in America or any other country. Democrat, as you are, you can give a practical lesson to the aristocrats of Europe how to live. At your beautiful and tasteful residence, '*Iranistan*' (I don't like the name, though), you can and do entertain your friends with a warmth of hospitality, only equaled by that of the great landed proprietors of the old country, or of our own 'sunny South.' Whilst riches are pouring into your coffers from your various 'ventures' in all parts of the world, you do not hoard your immense means, but continually 'cast them forth upon the waters,' rewarding labor, encouraging the arts, and lending a helping hand to industry in all its branches. Not content with doing all this, you deal telling blows, whenever opportunity offers, upon the monster Intemperance. Your labors in this great cause alone should entitle you to the thanks of all good men, women and children in the land. Mr. Barnum, you deserve all your good fortune, and I hope you may long five to enjoy your wealth and honor.

"As a small installment towards the debt, I, as one of the community, owe you, and with the hope of affording you an hour's amusement (if you can spare that amount of time from your numerous avocations to read it), I present you with this little volume, containing a very brief account of some of my 'journey-work' in the south and west; and remain, very respectfully,"

Your friend, and affectionate uncle,
"Sol. Smith." Chouteau Avenue, St. Louis, "Nov. 1, 1854."

"Uncle" Sol. Smith must be held solely responsible for his extravagant estimate of P. T. Barnum, and for his somewhat deprecatory view of the attributes of the "divine Jenny."

Whenever Miss Lind sang for a public or private charity, she gave her voice, which was worth a thousand dollars to her every evening. At such times, I always insisted upon paying for the hall, orchestra, printing, and other expenses, because I felt able and willing to contribute my full share towards the worthy objects which prompted these benefits.

We were in Havana when I showed to Miss Lind a paper containing the conundrum on "for-getting " and "for-giving," at which she laughed heartily, but immediately checked herself and said:

"O! Mr. Barnum, this is not fair; you know that you really give more than I do from the proceeds of every one of these charity concerts." And it is but just to her to say that she frequently remonstrated with me, and declared that the actual expenses should be deducted, and the thus lessened sum devoted to the charity for which the concert might be given; but I always laughingly told her that I must do my part, give my share, and that if it was purely a business operation, "bread cast upon the waters," it would return, perhaps, buttered; for the larger her reputation for liberality, the more liberal the public would surely be to us and to our enterprise.

I have no wish to conceal these facts, and I certainly have no desire to receive a larger need of praise than my qualified generosity merits. Justice to myself and to my management, as well as to Miss Lind, seems to permit, if not to demand, this explanation.

CHAPTER XXII.

CLOSE OF THE CAMPAIGN.

After five concerts in St. Louis, we went to Nashville, Tennessee, where we gave our sixty-sixth and sixty-seventh concerts in this country. While there, Jenny Lind, accompanied by my daughter, Mrs. Lyman, and myself, visited the "Hermitage," the late residence of General Jackson. On that occasion, for the first time that season, we heard the wild mocking-birds singing in the trees. This gave Jenny Lind great delight, as she had never before heard them sing except in their wire-bound cages.

The first of April occurred while we were in Nashville. I was considerably annoyed during the forenoon by the calls of members of the company, who came to me under the belief that I had sent for them. After dinner, I concluded to give them all a touch of "April fool." The following article, which appeared the next morning in the *Nashville Daily American*, my amanuensis having imparted the secret to the editor, will show how it was done:

"A series of laughable jokes came off yesterday at the Veranda in honor of All Fools' Day. Mr. Barnum was at the bottom of the mischief. He managed, in some mysterious manner, to obtain a lot of blank telegraphic dispatches and envelopes from one of the offices in this city, and then went to work and manufactured 'astounding intelligence' for most of the parties composing the Jenny Lind suite. Almost every person in the company received a telegraphic dispatch, written under the direction of Barnum. Mr. Barnum's daughter was informed that her mother, her cousin, and several other relatives, were waiting for her in Louisville, and various other important and extraordinary items of domestic intelligence were communicated to her. Mr. Le Grand Smith was told by a dispatch from his father that his native village, in Connecticut, was in ashes, including his own homestead, etc. Several of Barnum's employees had most liberal offers of engagements from banks and other institutions at the North. Burke, and others of the musical professors, were offered princely salaries by opera managers, and many of them received most tempting inducements to proceed immediately to the World's Fair in London.

"One married gentleman in Mr. Barnum's suit received the gratifying intelligence that he had for two days been the father of a pair of bouncing boys (mother and children doing well), an event which he had been anxiously looking for during the week, though on a somewhat more limited scale. In fact, nearly every person in the party engaged by Barnum received some extraordinary telegraphic intelligence; and, as the great impresario managed to have the dispatches delivered simultaneously, each recipient was for some time busily occupied with his own personal news.

"By and by each began to tell his neighbor his good or bad tidings; and each was, of course, rejoiced or grieved, according to circumstances. Several gave Mr. Barnum notice of their intention to leave him, in consequence of better offers; and a number of them sent off telegraphic dispatches and letters by mail, in answer to those received.

"The man who had so suddenly become the father of twins, telegraphed to his wife to 'be of good cheer,' and that he would 'start for home tomorrow'. At a late hour last night, the secret had not got out, and we presume that many of the victims will first learn from our columns that they have been taken in by Barnum and All Fools' Day!"

From Nashville, Jenny Lind and a few friends went by way of the Mammoth Cave to Louisville, while the rest of the party proceeded by steamboat.

While in Havana, I engaged Signor Salvi for a few months, to begin about the tenth of April. He joined us at Louisville, and sang in the three concerts there with great satisfaction to the public. Mr. George D. Prentice, of the *Louisville Journal*, and his beautiful and accomplished lady, who had contributed much to the pleasure of Miss Lind and our party, accompanied us to Cincinnati. As the steamer from Louisville to Cincinnati would arrive at Madison about sundown, and would wait long enough for us to give a concert, we did so, and at ten o'clock we were again on board the fine steamer "Ben Franklin" bound for Cincinnati.

The next morning the crowd upon the wharf was immense. I was fearful that an attempt to repeat the New Orleans ruse with my daughter would be of no avail as the joke had been published in the Cincinnati papers. So, I gave my arm to Miss Lind, and begged her to have no fears for I had hit upon an expedient which would save her from annoyance. We then descended the plank to the shore, and as soon as we had touched it, Le Grand Smith called out from the boat, as if he had been one of the passengers, "That's no go, Mr. Barnum; you can't pass your daughter off for Jenny Lind this time."

The remark elicited a peal of merriment from the crowd, several persons calling out, "That won't do, Barnum! You may fool the New Orleans folks, but you can't come it over the 'Buckeyes.' We intend to stay here until you bring out Jenny Lind!" They readily allowed me to pass with the lady whom they supposed to be my daughter, and in five minutes afterwards the Nightingale was complimenting Mr. Coleman upon the beautiful and commodious apartments which were devoted to her in the Burnett House.

In passing up the river to Pittsburg, the boat waited four hours to enable us to give a concert at Wheeling.

At Pittsburg, we gave one concert.

We reached New York early in May, 1851 and gave fourteen concerts in Castle Garden and Metropolitan Hall. The last of these made the ninety-second regular concert under our engagement. Jenny Lind had now again reached the atmosphere of her legal and other "advisers," and I soon discovered the effects of their influence. I, however, cared little what course they advised her to pursue. I, indeed, wished they would prevail upon her to close with her hundredth concert, for I had become weary with constant excitement and unremitting exertions. I felt it would be well for her to try some concerts on her own account, if she saw fit to credit her advisers' assurance that I had not managed the enterprise as successfully as it might have been done.

At about the eighty-fifth concert, therefore, I was most happy to learn from her lips that she had concluded to pay the forfeiture of twenty-five thousand dollars and terminate the concerts with the one hundredth.

We went to Philadelphia, where I had advertised the ninety-third and ninety-fourth concerts. Not caring enough for the profits of the remaining seven concerts to continue the engagement at the risk of disturbing the friendly feelings which had hitherto uninterruptedly existed between that lady and myself, I wrote her a letter offering to relinquish the engagement, if she desired it, at the termination of the concert which was to take place that evening, upon her simply allowing me a thousand dollars per concert for the seven which would yet remain to make up the hundred, besides paying me the sum stipulated as a forfeiture for closing the engagement at the one hundredth concert. This offer she accepted, and our engagement terminated.

Jenny Lind gave several concerts, with varied success, and then retired to Niagara Falls, and afterwards to Northampton, Massachusetts. While sojourning at the latter place, she visited Boston and was married to Mr. Otto Goldschmidt, a German composer and pianist, to whom she was much attached, and who had studied music with her in Germany. He played several times in our concerts. He was a very quiet, inoffensive gentleman, and an accomplished musician.

I met her several times after our engagement terminated. She was always affable. On one occasion, while passing through Bridgeport, she told me that she had been sadly harassed in giving her concerts. "People cheat me and swindle me very much," said she, "and I find it very annoying to give concerts on my own account."

I was always supplied with complimentary tickets when she gave concerts in New York, and on the occasion of her last appearance in America, I visited her in her room back of the stage, and bade her and her husband *adieu*, with my best wishes. She expressed the same feeling to me in return. She told me she should never sing much, if any more, in public; but I reminded her that a good Providence had endowed her with a voice which enabled her to contribute in an eminent degree to the enjoyment of her fellow beings, and if she no longer needed the large sums of money which they were willing to pay for this elevating and delightful entertainment, she knew by experience what a genuine pleasure she would receive by devoting the money to the alleviation of the wants and sorrows of those who needed it.

"Ah! Mr. Barnum," she replied, "that is very true; and it would be ungrateful in me to not continue to use, for the benefit of the poor and lowly, that gift which our kind Heavenly Father has so graciously bestowed upon me. Yes, I will continue to sing so long as my voice lasts, but it will be mostly for charitable objects, for I am thankful to say that I have all the money which I shall ever need." Pursuant to this resolution, the larger portion of the concerts which this noble lady has given since her return to Europe have been for objects of benevolence.

If she consents to sing for a charitable object in London, for instance, the fact is not advertised at all, but the tickets are readily disposed of in a private, quiet way, at a guinea and half a guinea each.

After so many months of anxiety, labor and excitement, in the Jenny Lind enterprise, it will readily be believed that I desired tranquility. I spent a week at Cape May, and then came home to *Iranistan*, where I remained during the entire summer.

JENNY LIND CONCERTS.

TOTAL RECEIPTS, EXCEPTING OF CONCERTS DEVOTED TO CHARITY.

NEW YORK	$17,864.05	No. 39. WASH CITY	6,878.55
....	14,203.03	40.	8,507.05
		41. RICHMOND	12,385.21
No. 1	12,519.59	42. CHARLESTON	6,775.00
2............	14,266.09	43.	3,658.75
3............	12,174.74	44. HAVANA	4,666.17
4............	16,028.39	45.	2,837.92
5 BOSTON	16,479.50	46.	2,931.95
6............	11,848.62	47. NEW ORLEANS	12,599.85
7............	8,639.92	48.	10,210.42
8............	10,169.25	49.	8,131.15
9 PROVIDENCE	6,325.54	50.	6,019.85
10 BOSTON	10,524.87	51.	6,644.00
11............	5,240.00	52.	9,720.80
12............	7,586.00	53.	7,545.50
13 PHIL	9,291.25	54.	6,058.50
14............	7,547.00	55.	4,850.25
15............	8,458.65	56.	4,495.85
16 NEW YORK	6,415.90	57.	6,689.85
17............	4,009.70	58.	4,745.10
18............	5,982.00	59. NATCHEZ	5,000.00
19............	8,007.10	60. MEMPHIS	4,539.56
20............	6,334.20	61. ST. LOUIS	7,811.85
21............	9,429.15	62.	7,961.92
22............	9,912.17	63.	7,708.70
23............	5,773.40	64.	4,086.50
24............	4,993.50	65.	3,044.70
25............	6,670.15	66. NASHVILLE	7,786.30
26............	9,840.33	67.	4,218.00
27............	7,097.15	68. LOUISVILLE	7,833.90
28............	8,263.30	69.	6,595.60
29............	10,570.25	70.	5,000.00
30............	10,646.43	71. MADISON	8,693.25
31. PHIL.	5,480.75	72. CINCINATTI	9,339.75
32..........	5,728.65	73.	11,001.50
33..........	8,709.88	74	8,446.30
34..........	4,813.48	75.	8,954.18
35. BALTIMORE	7,117.00	76.	6,540.00
36..........	8,357.03	77. WHEELING	5,000.00
37..........	8,406.50	78. PITTSBURGH	7,210.58
38..........	8,121.33	79. NEW YORK	6,858.42

Charity Concerts. — Of Miss Lind's half receipts of the first two Concerts she devoted $10,000 to charity in New York. She afterwards gave Charity Concerts in Boston, Baltimore. Charleston, Havana, New Orleans, New York and Philadelphia, and donated large sums for the like purposes in Richmond, Cincinnati and elsewhere. There were also several Benefit Concerts, for the Orchestra, Le Grand Smith, and other persons and objects.

No. 80..........	$5,453.00	87.	3,738.75
81..........	5,463.70	88.	4,335.28
82..........	7,378.35	89.	5,339.23
83..........	7,179.27	90.	4,087.03
84..........	6,641.00	91.	5,717.00
85..........	6,917.13	92.	9,529.80
86..........	6,642.04	93. PHILADELPHIA	3,852.75

RECAPITULATION.

New York	Concerts, 35	Receipts, $286,216.64	Avg. 8,177.50
Philadelphia	8	......48.884.41	...... 6,110.55
Boston	7	...... 70.3S8.16	......10,055.45
Providence	1	...... 6.525.54	......6,525.54
Baltimore	4	...... 32,101.88	......8000.47
Washington	2	...... 15,385.60	......7,692.80
Richmond	1	......12.3S5.21	......12,385.21
Charleston	2	......10.42S.75	......5,214.37
Havana	3	......10,436.04	......3,478.68
New Orleans	12	......87,646.12	......7,303.84
Natchez	 1	...... 5.000.00	......5000.00
Memphis	1	...... 4.539.56	......4,530.56
St. Louis	5	........30,613.67	......6,152.73
Nashville	2	......12.034.30	......6017.15
Louisville	3	......19,429.50	......6,476.50

Madison	1	...... 3,693.25	......3,693.25
Cincinnati	5	......44,242.13	......8,848.43
Wheeling	1	...... 5,000.00	......5,000.00
Pittsburg	1	...... 7,210.58	......7,210.58

Total 95 Concerts.   Receipts, $712,161.34   Average, $7,496.43

JENNY LIND'S RECEIPTS.

From the Total Receipts of Ninety-Five Concerts $712,161.34

Deduct the receipts of the first two, which, as between
P. T. Barnum and Jenny Lind. were aside from the contract,
and are not numbered in the Table...................................... 82,067.08

Total Receipts of Concerts from No. 1 to No. 93................... $680,094.26

Deduct the Receipts of the 28 Concerts, each of
which fell short of $5,500........................$123.311 .15

Also deduct $5,500 for each of the remaining
65 Concerts.................................... $357,500.00 $480,811.15

Leaving the total excess, as above $199,283.11

Being equally divided, Miss Lind's portion was $99,641.55

I paid her $1,000 for each of the 93 Concerts $93,000.00

Also, one-half the receipts of the first two Concerts $16,033.54

Amount paid to Jenny Lind $208,675.09

She refunded to me as forfeit ore, per contract,
in case she withdrew after the 100th Concert. $ 25,000.00

She also paid me $1,000 each for the seven
concerts relinquished, ... $ 7,000.00 $ 32,000.00

Jenny Lind's net avails of 95 concerts............................. $176,675. 00
P.T. Barnum's gross receipts, after paying Miss Lind............. $535,486.25
Total Receipts of 95 Concerts...................................... $712,161.31

Price of Tickets. — The highest prices paid for tickets were at auction, as follows: John N. Genin, In New York, $225; Ossian E. Dodge, in Boston, $625; Col. William C. Ross in Providence, $650; M. A. Root, in Philadelphia, $625; Mr. D'Arcy, in New Orleans, - a keeper of a refreshment saloon in St. Louis, $150: A Daguerreotypist, in Baltimore: $100. I cannot now recall the names of the last two. Alter the sale of the first ticket the premium usually fell to $20, and downward in the scale of figures. The fixed price of tickets ranged from $7 to $3. Promenade tickets were from $2 to $1 each.

CHAPTER XXIII.

OTHER ENTERPRISES.

In 1849, I had projected a great traveling museum and menagerie, and, as I had neither time nor inclination to manage such a concern, I induced Mr. Seth B. Howes, justly celebrated as a "showman," to join me, and take the sole charge. Mr. Sherwood E. Stratton, father of General Tom Thumb, was also admitted to partnership, the interest being in thirds.

In carrying out a portion of the plan, we chartered the ship "Regatta," Captain Pratt, and dispatched her, together with our agents, Messrs. June and Nutter, to Ceylon. The ship left New York in May, 1850 and was absent one year. Their mission was to procure, either by capture or purchase, twelve or more living elephants, besides such other wild animals as they could secure. In order to provide sufficient drink and provender for a cargo of these huge animals, we purchased a large quantity of hay in New York. Five hundred tons were left at the Island of St. Helena, to be taken on the return trip of the ship, and staves and hoops of water-casks were also left at the same place.

They arrived in New York in 1851, with ten elephants, and these harnessed it pairs to a chariot, paraded up Broadway past the Irving House, while Jenny Lind was staying at that hotel, on the occasion of her second visit to New York. We added a caravan of wild animals and many museum curiosities, the entire outfit, including horses, vans, carriages, tent, etc., costing $109,000, and commenced operations, with the presence and under the "patronage" of General Tom Thumb, who traveled nearly four years as one of the attractions of "Barnum's Great Asiatic Caravan, Museum and Menagerie," returning us immense profits.

At the end of that time, after exhibiting in all sections of the country, we sold out the entire establishment — animals, cages, chariots and paraphernalia, excepting one elephant, which I retained in my own possession two months for agricultural purposes. It occurred to me that if I could put an elephant to plowing for a while on my farm at Bridgeport, it would be a capital advertisement for the American Museum, which was then, and always during my proprietorship of that establishment, foremost in my thoughts.

So, I sent him to Connecticut in charge of his keeper, whom I dressed in Oriental costume, and keeper and elephant were stationed on a six-acre lot which lay close beside the track of the New York and New Haven railroad. The keeper was furnished with a time-table of the road, with special instructions to be busily engaged in his work whenever passenger trains from either way were passing through. Of course, the matter soon appeared in the papers and went the entire rounds of the press in this country and even in Europe. Hundreds of people came many miles to witness the novel spectacle. Letters poured in upon me from the secretaries of hundreds of State and county agricultural societies throughout the Union, stating that the presidents and directors of such societies had requested them to propound to me a series of questions in regard to the new power I had put in operation on my farm. These questions were greatly diversified, but the "general run" of them were something like the following:

1. "Is the elephant a profitable agricultural animal?"
2. "How much can an elephant plow in a day?"
3. "How much can he draw?"
4. "How much does he eat?" — this question was invariably asked and was very important one.
5. "Will elephants make themselves generally useful on a farm?"
6. "What is the price of an elephant?"
7. "Where can elephants be purchased?"

Then would follow a score of other inquiries, such as, whether elephants were easily managed; if they would quarrel with cattle; if it was possible to breed them; how old calf elephants must be before they would earn their own living: and so on, indefinitely. I began to be alarmed lest someone should buy an elephant, and so share the fate of the man who drew one in a lottery and did not know what to do with him. I accordingly had a general letter printed, which I mailed to all my anxious inquirers. It was headed "strictly confidential," and I then stated, begging my correspondents "not to mention it," that to me the elephant was a valuable agricultural animal, because he was an excellent advertisement to my Museum; but that to other farmers he would prove very unprofitable for many reasons. In the first place, such an animal would cost from $3,000 to $10,000; in cold weather he could not work at all; in any weather he could not earn even half his living; he would eat up the value of his own head, trunk, and body every year; and I begged my correspondents not to do so foolish a thing as to undertake elephant farming.

Newspaper reporters came from far and near and wrote glowing accounts of the elephantine performances. Pictures of Barnum's plowing elephant appeared in illustrated papers at home and abroad.

The six acres were plowed over at least sixty times before I thought the advertisement sufficiently circulated, and I then sold the elephant to Van Amburgh's Menagerie.

In 1851, I became a part owner of the steamship "North America," Our intention in buying it was to run it to Ireland as a passenger and freight ship. The project was, however, abandoned, and Commodore Cornelius Vanderbilt bought one-half of the steamer, while the other half was owned by three persons, of whom I was one. The steamer was sent around Cape Horn to San Francisco and was put into the Vanderbilt line. After she had made several trips I called upon Mr. Vanderbilt, at his office, and introduced myself, as this was the first time we had met.

"Is it possible you are Barnum?" exclaimed the Commodore, in surprise, "why, I expected to see a monster, part lion, part elephant, and a mixture of rhinoceros and tiger! Is it possible," he continued, "that you are the showman who has made so much noise in the world?"

ELEPHANTINE AGRICULTURE

I laughingly replied that I was and added that if I too had been governed in my anticipation of his personal appearance by the fame he had achieved in his line, I should have expected to have been saluted by a steam whistle, and to have seen him dressed in a pea jacket, blowing off steam, and crying out "all aboard that's going."

"Instead of which," replied Mr. Vanderbilt, "I suppose you have come to ask me 'to walk up to the Captain's office and settle.'"

After this interchange of civilities, we talked about the success of the "North America" in having got safely around the Horn, and of the acceptable manner in which she was doing her duty on the Pacific side.

"We have received no statement of her earnings yet," said the Commodore, "but if you want money, give your receipt to our treasurer, and take some."

A few months subsequent to this, I sold out my share in the steamship to Mr. Daniel Drew.

Some references to the various enterprises and "side shows" connected with and disconnected from my Museum, is necessary to show how industriously I have catered for the public's amusement, not only in America but abroad. When I was in Paris in 1844, in addition to the purchase of Robert Houdini's ingenious automaton writer, and many other costly curiosities for the Museum, I ordered, at an expense of $3,000, a panoramic diorama of the obsequies of Napoleon. Every event of that grand pageant, from the embarkation of the body at St. Helena, to its entombment at the Hotel des Invalides, amid the most gorgeous parade ever witnessed in France, was wonderfully depicted. This exhibition, after having had its day at the American Museum, was sold, and extensively and profitably exhibited elsewhere. While I was in London, during the same year, I engaged a company of "Campanalogians", or "Lancashire Bell Ringers," then performing in Ireland, to make an American tour. They were really admirable performers, and by means of their numerous bells, of various sizes, they produced the most delightful music. They attracted much attention hi various parts of the United States, in Canada, and in Cuba.

As a compensation to England for the loss of the Bell Ringers, I dispatched an agent to America for a party of Indians, including squaws. He proceeded to Iowa and returned to London with a company of sixteen. They were exhibited by Mr. Catlin on our joint account and were finally left in his sole charge.

On my first return visit to America from Europe, I engaged Mr. Faber, an elderly and ingenious German, who had constructed an automaton speaker. It was of life-size, and when worked with keys similar to those of a piano, it really articulated words and sentences with surprising distinctness. My agent exhibited it for several months in Egyptian Hall, London, and also in the provinces. This was a marvelous piece of mechanism, though for some unaccountable reason it did not prove a success.

The Duke of Wellington visited it several times, and at first, he thought that the "voice" proceeded from the exhibitor, whom he assumed to be a skillful ventriloquist. He was asked to touch the keys with his own fingers, and, after some instruction in the method of operating, he was able to make the machine speak, not only in English but also in German, with which language the Duke seemed familiar. Thereafter, he entered his name on the exhibitor's autograph book, and certified that the "Automaton Speaker" was an extraordinary production of mechanical genius.

The models of machinery exhibited in the Royal Polytechnic Institution in London, pleased me so well that I procured a duplicate; also duplicates of the "Dissolving Views," the Chromatrope and Physioscope, including many American scenes painted expressly to my order, at an aggregate cost of $7,000. After they had been exhibited in my Museum, they were sold to itinerant showmen, and some of them were afterwards on exhibition in various parts of the United States.

In June, 1850, I added the celebrated Chinese Collection to the attractions of the American Museum. I also engaged the Chinese Family, consisting of two men, two "small-footed" women and two children.

The giants whom I sent to America were not the greatest of my curiosities, though the dwarfs might have been the least. The "Scotch Boys" were interesting, not so much on account of their weight, as for the mysterious method by which one of them, though blindfolded, answered questions put by the other respecting objects presented by persons who attended the surprising exhibition. The mystery, which was merely the result of patient practice, consisted wholly in the manner in which the question was propounded; in fact, the question invariably carried its own answer; for instance:

"What is this?" meant gold; "Now what is this? " silver; "Say what is this?" copper; "Tell me what this is?" iron; "What is the shape?" long; "Now what shape?" round; "Say what shape," square; "Please say what this is," a watch; "Can you tell what is in this lady's hand?" a purse; "Now please say what this is?" a key; "Come now, what is this?" money; "How much?" a penny "Now how much?" sixpence; "Say how much," a quarter of a dollar; " What color is this?" black; "Now what color is this?" red; "Say what color," green; and so on, *ad infinitum*. To such perfection was this brought that it was almost impossible to present any object that could not be quite closely described by the blindfolded boy. This is the key to all exhibitions of what is called "second sight."

In 1850, the celebrated Bateman children acted for several weeks at the American Museum, and in June of that year I sent them to London with their father and Mr. Le Grand Smith, where they played in the St. James Theater, and afterwards in the principal provincial theaters. The elder of these children, Miss Kate Bateman, subsequently attained the highest histrionic distinction in America and abroad, and reached the very head of her profession.

In October, 1852, having stipulated with Mr. George A. Wells and Mr. Bushnell that they should share in the enterprise and take the entire charge, I engaged Miss Catherine Hayes and Herr Begnis, to give a series of sixty concerts in California, and the engagement was fulfilled to our entire satisfaction. Mr. Bushnell afterwards went to Australia with Miss Hayes, and they were subsequently married. Both of them are now dead.

Before setting out for California, Miss Catherine Hayes, her mother and sister, spent several days at *Iranistan* and were present at the marriage of my eldest daughter, Caroline, to Mr. David W. Thompson. The wedding was to take place in the evening, and in the afternoon, I was getting shaved in a barber-shop in Bridgeport, when. Mr. Thompson drove up to the door in great haste and exclaimed:

"Mr. Barnum, *Iranistan* is in flames!"

I ran out half-shaved, with the lather on my face, jumped into his wagon and bade him drive home with all speed. I was greatly alarmed, for the house was full of visitors who had come from a distance to attend the wedding, and all the costly presents, dresses, refreshments, and everything prepared for a marriage celebration to which nearly a thousand guests had been invited, were already in my house. Mr. Thompson told me that he had seen the flames bursting from the roof, and it seemed to me that there was little hope of saving the building.

My mind was distressed, not so much at the great pecuniary loss which the destruction of *Iranistan* would involve, as at the possibility that some of my family or visitors would be killed or seriously injured in attempting to save something from the fire. Then I thought of the sore disappointment this calamity would cause to the young couple, as well as to those who were invited to the wedding. I saw that Mr. Thompson looked pale and anxious.

"Never mind!" said I; "we can't help these things; the house will probably be burned; but if no one is killed or injured, you shall be married tonight, if we are obliged to perform the ceremony in the coach-house."

On our way, we overtook a fire-company, and I implored them to "hurry up their machine." Arriving in sight of *Iranistan*, we saw huge volumes of smoke rolling out from the roof and many men on the top of the house were passing buckets of water to pour upon the fire. Fortunately, several men had been engaged during the day in repairing the roof, and their ladders were against the house. By these means and with the assistance of the men employed upon my grounds, water was passed very rapidly, and the flames were soon subdued without serious damage. The inmates of *Iranistan* were thoroughly frightened; Catherine Hayes and other visitors, packed their trunks and had them carried out on the lawn; and the house came as near destruction as it well could, and escape.

While Miss Hayes was in Bridgeport, I induced her to give a concert for the benefit of the "Mountain Grove Cemetery," and the large proceeds were devoted to the erection of the beautiful stone tower and gateway at the entrance of that charming ground. The land for this cemetery, about eighty acres, had been bought by me, years before, from several farmers. I had often shot over the ground while hunting a year or two before, and had then seen its admirable capabilities for the purpose to which it was eventually devoted. After deeds for the property were secured, it was offered for a cemetery, and at a meeting of citizens several lots were subscribed for, enough, indeed, to cover the amount of the purchase money. Thus was begun the "Mountain Grove Cemetery," which is now beautifully laid out and adorned with many tasteful and costly monuments. Among these are my own substantial granite monument, the family monuments of Harral, Bishop, Hubbell, Lyon, Wood, Loomis, Wordin, Hyde, and others, and General Tom Thumb has erected a tall marble shaft which is surmounted by a life-size statue of himself. There is no more charming burial-ground in the whole country; yet when the project was suggested, many persons preferred an intermural cemetery to this rural resting-place for their departed friends; though now all concur in considering it fortunate that this adjunct was secured to Bridgeport before the land could be permanently devoted to other purposes.

Sometime afterwards, when Mr. Dion Boucicault visited me at Bridgeport, at my solicitation, he gave a lecture for the benefit of this cemetery. I may add that on several occasions I have secured the services of General Tom Thumb, and others, for this and equally worthy objects in Bridgeport. When the General first returned with me from England, he gave exhibitions for the benefit of the Bridgeport Charitable Society. September 28, 1867, I induced him and his wife, with Commodore Nutt and Minnie Warren, to give their entertainment for the benefit of the Bridgeport Library, thus adding $475 to the funds of that institution; and on one occasion, I lectured to a full house in the Methodist Church, and the entire receipts were given to the library, of which I was already a life member, on account of previous subscriptions and contributions.

CHAPTER XXIV.

WORK AND PLAY.

In the summer, I think, of 1853, I saw it announced in the newspapers that Mr. Alfred Bunn, the great ex-manager of Drury Lane Theater, in London, had arrived in Boston. I knew Mr. Bunn by reputation, not only from his managerial career, but from the fact that he made the first engagement with Jenny Lind to appear in London. This engagement, however, Mr. Lumley, of Her Majesty's Theater, induced her to break, he standing a lawsuit with Mr. Bunn, and paying heavy damages. I had never met Mr. Bunn, but he took it for granted that I had seen him, for one day after his arrival in this country, a burly Englishman abruptly stepped into my private office in the Museum, and, assuming a theatrical attitude, addressed me:

"Barnum, do you remember me?"

I was confident I had never seen the man before, but it struck me at once that no Englishman I ever heard of would be likely to exhibit more presumption or assumption than the ex-manager of Drury Lane, and I jumped at the conclusion:

"Is not this Mr. Bunn?"

"Ah! Ah! my boy!" he exclaimed, slapping me familiarly on the back, "I thought you would remember me. "Well Barnum, how have you been since I last saw you!"

I replied in a manner that would humor his impression that we were old acquaintances, and during his two hours' visit we had much gossip about men and things in London. He called upon me several times, and it probably never entered into his mind that I could possibly have been in London two or three years without having made the personal acquaintance of so great a lion as Alfred Bunn.

I met Mr. Bunn again in 1858, in London, at a dinner party of a mutual friend, Mr. Levy, proprietor of the London Daily Telegraph. Of course, Bunn and I were great chums and very old and intimate acquaintances. At the same dinner, I met several literary and dramatic gentlemen.

In 1851, 1852, and 1853, I spent much of my time at my beautiful home in Bridgeport, going very frequently to New York, to attend to matters in the Museum, but remaining in the city only a day or two at a time. I resigned the office of President of the Fairfield County Agricultural Society in 1853, but the members accepted my resignation, only on condition that it should not go into effect until after the fair of 1851. During my administration, the society held six fairs and cattle-shows — four in Bridgeport and two in Stamford— and the interest in these gatherings increased from year to year.

Pickpockets are always present at these country fairs, and every year there were loud complaints of the depredations of these operators. In 1853 a man was caught in the act of taking a pocket-book from a country farmer, nor was this farmer the only one who had suffered in the same way. The scamp was arrested and proved to be a celebrated English pickpocket. As the fair would close the next day, and as most persons had already visited it, we expected our receipts would be light.

Early in the morning the detected party was legally examined, plead guilty, and was bound over for trial. I obtained consent from the sheriff that the culprit should be put in the fair room for the purpose of giving those who had been robbed an opportunity to identify him. For this purpose, he was handcuffed, and placed in a conspicuous position, where, of course, he was "the observed of all observers." I then issued handbills, stating that as it was the last day of the Fair, the managers were happy to announce that they had secured extra attractions for the occasion, and would accordingly exhibit, safely handcuffed, and without extra charge, a live pickpocket, who had been caught in the act of robbing an honest farmer the day previous. Crowds of people rushed in "to see the show." Some good mothers brought their children ten miles for that purpose, and our treasury was materially benefited by the operation.

At the close of my presidency in 1854, I was requested to deliver the opening speech at our county fair, which was held at Stamford. As I was not able to give agricultural advice, I delivered a portion of my lecture on the "Philosophy of Humbug." The next morning, as I was being shaved in the village barber's shop, which was at the time crowded with customers, the ticket-seller to the fair came in.

"What kind of a house did you have last night?" asked one of the gentlemen in waiting.

"Oh, first-rate, of course. Barnum always draws a crowd," was the reply of the ticket-seller, to whom I was not known.

Most of the gentlemen present, however, knew me, and they found much difficulty in restraining their laughter.

"Did Barnum make a good speech?" I asked.

"I did not hear it. I was out in the ticket-office. I guess it was pretty good, for I never heard so much laughing as there was all through his speech. But it makes no difference whether it was good or not," continued the ticket-seller, "the people will go to see Barnum."

"Barnum must be a curious chap," I remarked.

"Well, I guess he is up to all the dodges."

"Do you know him?" I asked.

"Not personally," he replied; "but I always get into the Museum for nothing. I know the doorkeeper, and he slips me in free."

"Barnum would not like that, probably, if he knew it," I remarked

"But it happens he don't know it," replied the ticket-seller, in great glee.

"Barnum was on the cars the other day, on his way to Bridgeport," said I, "and I heard one of the passengers blowing him up terribly as a humbug. He was addressing Barnum at the time, but did not know him. Barnum joined in lustily, and endorsed everything the man said. When the passenger learned whom he had been addressing, I should think he must have felt rather flat."

"I should think so, too," said the ticket-seller.

This was too much, and we all indulged in a burst of laughter; still the ticket-seller suspected nothing. After I had left the shop, the barber told him who I was. I called into the ticket-office on business several times during the day, but the poor ticket-seller kept his face turned from me and appeared so chap-fallen that I did not pretend to recognize him as the hero of the joke in the barber's shop.

This incident reminds me of numerous similar ones which have occurred at various times. On one occasion — it was in 1847 — I was on board the steamboat from New York to Bridgeport. As we approached the harbor of the latter city, a stranger desired me to point out "Barnum's house" from the upper deck. I did so, whereupon a bystander remarked, "I know all about that house, for I was engaged in painting there for several months while Barnum was in Europe." He then proceeded to say that it was the meanest and most ill-contrived house he ever saw. "It will cost old Barnum a mint of money and not be worth two cents after it is finished," he added.

"I suppose old Barnum don't pay very punctually," I remarked. Oh, yes, he pays punctually every Saturday night — there's no trouble about that; he has made half a million by exhibiting a little boy whom he took from Bridgeport, and whom we never considered any great shakes till Barnum took him and trained him."

Soon afterwards one of the passengers told him who I was, whereupon he secreted himself, and was not seen again while I remained on the boat.

On another occasion, I went to Boston by the Fall River route. Arriving before sunrise, I found but one carriage at the depot. I immediately engaged it, and, giving the driver the check for my baggage, told him to take me directly to the Revere House, as I was in great haste, and enjoined him to take in no other passengers, and I would pay his demands. He promised compliance with my wishes, but soon afterwards appeared with a gentleman, two ladies, and several children, whom he crowded into the carriage with me, and, placing their trunks on the baggage rack, started off. I thought there was no use in grumbling, and consoled myself with the reflection that the Revere House was not far away. He drove up one street and down another, for what seemed to me a very long time, but I was wedged in so closely that I could not see what route he was taking.

After half an hour's drive he halted, and I found we were at the Lowell Railway depot. Here my fellow-passengers alighted, and, after a long delay, the driver delivered their baggage, received his fare, and was about closing the carriage door preparatory to starting again. I was so thoroughly vexed at the shameful manner in which he had treated me, that I remarked:

"Perhaps you had better wait till the Lowell train arrives; you may possibly get another load of passengers. Of course, my convenience is of no consequence. I suppose if you land me at the Revere House any time this week, it will be as much as I have a right to expect."

"I beg your pardon," he replied, "but that was Barnum and his family. He was very anxious to get here in time for the first train, so I stuck him for $2, and now I'll carry you to the Revere House free."

"What Barnum is it?" I asked.

"The Museum and Jenny Lind man," he replied.

The compliment and the shave both having been intended for me, I was of course mollified, and replied, "You are mistaken, my friend, *I* am Barnum."

"Coachee" was thunderstruck, and offered all sorts of apologies.

"A friend at the other depot told me that I had Mr. Barnum on board," said he," and I really supposed he meant the other man. When I come to notice you, I perceive my mistake, but I hope you will forgive me. I have carried you frequently before and hope you will give me your custom while you are in Boston. I never will make such a mistake again."

In the spring of 1851, the Connecticut legislature chartered the Pequonnock Bank of Bridgeport, with a capital of two hundred thousand dollars. I had no interest whatever in the charter and did not even know that an application was to be made for it. More banking capital was needed in Bridgeport in consequence of the great increase of trade and manufactures in that growing and prosperous city, and this fact appearing in evidence, the charter was granted as a public benefit. The stock-books were opened under the direction of State commissioners, according to the laws of the Commonwealth, and nearly double the amount of capital was subscribed on the first day. The stock was distributed by the commissioners among several hundred applicants. Circumstances unexpectedly occurred which induced me to accept the presidency of the bank, in compliance with the unanimous vote of its directors. Feeling that I could not, from my many avocations, devote the requisite personal attention to the duties of the office, C. B. Hubbell, Esq., then mayor of Bridgeport, was at my request appointed vice-president of the institution.

In the fall of 1852 a proposition was made by certain parties to commence the publication of an illustrated weekly newspaper in the city of New York. The field seemed to be open for such an enterprise, and I invested twenty thousand dollars in the concern, as special partner, in connection with two other gentlemen who each contributed twenty thousand dollars, as general partners. Within a month after the publication of the first number of the *Illustrated News*, which was issued on the first day of January, 1853, our weekly circulation had reached seventy thousand. Numerous and almost insurmountable difficulties, for novices in the business, continued however to arise, and my partners, becoming weary and disheartened with constant over-exertion, were anxious to wind up the enterprise at the end of the first year. The goodwill and the engravings were sold to *Gleason's Pictorial*, in Boston, and the concern was closed without loss.

In February, 1854, numerous stockholders applied to me to accept the presidency of the Crystal Palace, or, as it was termed, "The Association for the Exhibition of the Industry of all Nations." I utterly declined listening to such a project, as I felt confident that the novelty had passed away, and that it would be difficult to revive public interest in the affair.

Shortly afterwards, however, I was waited upon by numerous influential gentlemen, and strongly urged to allow my name to be used. I repeatedly objected to this, and at last consented, much against my own judgment. Having been elected one of the directors, I was by that body chosen president. I accepted the office conditionally, reserving the right to decline if I thought, upon investigation, that there was no vitality left in the institution. Upon examining the accounts said to exist against the association, many were pronounced indefensible by those who I supposed knew the facts in the case, while various debts existing against the concern were not exhibited when called for, and I knew nothing of their existence until after I accepted the office of president. I finally accepted it, only because no suitable person could be found who was willing to devote his entire time and services to the enterprise, and because I was frequently urged by directors and stockholders to take hold of it for the benefit of the city at large, inasmuch as it was well settled that the Palace would be permanently closed early in April, 1854, if I did not take the helm.

These considerations moved me, and I entered upon my duties with all the vigor which I could command. To save it from bankruptcy, I advanced large sums of money for the payment of debts and tried by every legitimate means to create an excitement and bring it into life. By extraneous efforts, such as the Re-inauguration, the Monster Concerts of Jullien, the Celebration of Independence, etc., it was temporarily revived, but it was up-hill work, and I resigned the presidency.

The following trifling incident, which occurred at *Iranistan* in the winter of 1852, has been called to my mind by a lady friend from Philadelphia, who was visiting us at the time. The poem was sent to me soon after the occurrence, but was lost and the subject forgotten until my Philadelphia friend recently sent it to me with the wish that I should insert it in the present volume:

WINTER BOUQUETS.

AN INCIDENT IN THE LITE OF AN AMERICAN CITIZEN.

The poor man's garden lifeless lay
Beneath a fall of snow;
But Art in costly greenhouses,
Keeps Summer in full glow.
And Taste paid gold for bright bouquets.
The parlor vase that drest,
That scented Fashion's gray boudoir.
Or bloomed on Beauty's breast.

A rich man sat beside the fire,
Within his sculptured halls;
Brave heart, clear head, and busy hand
Had reared those stately walls.
He to his gardener spake, and said
In tone of quiet glee—
"I want a hundred fine bouquets-
Canst make them, John, for me?"

John's eyes became exceeding round,
This question when he heard;
He gazed upon his master,
And he answered not a word.
"Well, John," the rich man laughing said,
"If these too many be, What sayest to half the number, man?
Canst fifty make for me?"

Now John prized every flower, as 'twere
A daughter or a son;

And thought, like Regan—"what the need
Of fifty, or of one?"
But, keeping back the thought, he said,
"I think, sir. that I might;
But it would leave my lady's flowers
In very ragged plight."

"Well, John, thy vegetable pets
Must needs respected be;
We'll halve the number once again —
Make twenty-five for me.
And hark ye, John, when they are made
Come up and let me know;
And I'll give thee a list of those
To whom the flowers must go."

The twenty-five bouquets were made.
And round the village sent;
And to whom thinkest thou, my friend,
These floral jewels went?
Not to the beautiful and proud—
Not to the rich and gay—
Who, Dives-like, at Luxury's feast
Are seated every day.

An aged Pastor, on his desk.
Saw those fair preachers stand;
A Widow wept upon the gift,
And blessed the giver's baud.
Where Poverty bent o'er her task,
They cheered the lonely room;
And round the bed where sickness lay,
They breathed Health's Irish perfume.

Oh! kindly heart and open hand—
Those flowers in dust are trod,
But they bloom to weave a wreath for thee,
In the Paradise of God.
Sweet is the Minstrel's task, whose song
Of deeds like these may tell;
And long may he have power to give,
Who wields that power so well!

Mrs. Anna Bach.   Philadelphia.

CHAPTER XXV.

THE JEROME CLOCK COMPANY ENTANGLEMENT.

I now come to a series of events which, all things considered, constitute one of the most remarkable experiences of my life — an experience which brought me much pain and many trials; which humbled my pride and threatened me with hopeless financial ruin; and yet, nevertheless, put new blood in my veins, fresh vigor in my action, warding off all temptation to rust in the repose which affluence induces, and developed, I trust, new and better elements of manliness in my character.

When the blow fell upon me, I thought I could never recover; the event has shown, however, that I have gained both in character and fortune, and what threatened, for years, to be my ruin, has proved one of the most fortunate happenings of my career. The "Bull Run" of my life's battle was a crushing defeat, which, unknown to me at the time, only presaged the victories which were to follow.

It is vital to the narrative that I should give some account of the new city, East Bridgeport, and my interests therein, which led directly to my subsequent complications with the Jerome Clock Company.

In 1851, I purchased from Mr. William H. Noble, of Bridgeport, the undivided half of his late father's homestead, consisting of fifty acres of land, lying on the eastside of the river, opposite the city of Bridgeport. We intended this as the nucleus of a new city, which we concluded could soon be built up, in consequence of many natural advantages that it possesses.

Before giving publicity to our plans, however, we purchased one hundred and seventy-four acres contiguous to that which we already owned, and laid out the entire property in regular streets, and lined them with trees, reserving a beautiful grove of six or eight acres, which we enclosed, and converted into a public park. We named this "Washington Park" and subsequently presented it to the city.

We then commenced selling alternate lots, at about the same price which the land cost us by the acre, always on condition that a suitable dwelling-house, store, or manufactory should be erected upon the land, within one year from the date of purchase; that every building should be placed at a certain distance from the street, in a style of architecture approved by us; that the grounds should be enclosed with acceptable fences, and kept clean and neat, with other conditions which would render the locality a desirable one for respectable residents, and operate for the mutual benefit of all persons who should become settlers in the new city.

This entire property consists of a beautiful plateau of ground, lying within than half a mile of the center of Bridgeport city. Considering the superiority of the situation, it is a wonder that the city of Bridgeport was not originally founded upon that side of the river. The late Dr. Timothy Dwight, for a long time President of Yale College, in his "Travels in New England in 1815" says of the locality:

"There is not in the State a prettier village than the borough of Bridgeport. In the year 1783, there were scarcely half a dozen houses in this place. It now contains probably more than one hundred, built on both sides of Pughquonnuck (Pequonnock) river, a beautiful mill-stream, forming at its mouth the harbor of Bridgeport. The situation of this village is very handsome, particularly on the eastern side of the river. A more cheerful and elegant piece of ground can scarcely be imagined than the point which stretches between the Pughquonnuck and the old mill-brook; and the prospects presented by the harbors at the mouths of these streams, the Sound, and the surrounding country, are, in a fine season, gay and brilliant, perhaps without a parallel."

This "cheerful and elegant piece of ground," as Dr. Dwight so truly describes it, had only been kept from market by the want of means of access. A new footbridge was built, connecting this place with the city of Bridgeport, and a public toll-bridge which belonged to us, was thrown open to the public free. We also obtained from the State Legislature a charter for erecting a toll-bridge between the two bridges already existing, and under that charter we put up a fine covered draw-bridge at a cost of $16,000, which also we made free to the public for several years. We built and leased to a union company of young coach-makers a large and elegant coach manufactory, which was one of the first buildings erected there, and which went into operation on the first of January, 1852, and was the beginning of the extensive manufactories which were subsequently built in East Bridgeport.

Besides the inducement which we held out to purchasers to obtain their lots at a merely nominal price, we advanced one-half, two-thirds, and frequently all the funds necessary to erect their buildings, permitting them to repay us in sums as small as five dollars, at their own convenience. This arrangement enabled many persons to secure and ultimately pay for homes which they could not otherwise have obtained. We looked for our profits solely to the rise in the value of the reserved lots, which we were confident must ensue. These extraordinary inducements led many persons to build in the new city, and it began to develop and increase with a rapidity rarely witnessed in this section of the country.

It will thus be seen that, in 1851, my pet scheme was to build up a city in East Bridgeport.

I can truly say that mere money-making was a secondary consideration in my scheme. I wanted to build a city on the beautiful plateau across the river; in the expressive phrase of the day, I "had East Bridgeport on the brain." Whoever approached me with a project which looked to the advancement of my new city, touched my weak side and found me an eager listener, and it was in this way that the coming city connected me with that source of so many annoyances and woes, the Jerome Clock Company.

There was a small clock manufactory in the town of Litchfield, Connecticut, in which I became a stockholder to the amount of six or seven thousand dollars, and my duties as a director in the company called me occasionally to Litchfield and made me somewhat acquainted with the clock business. Thinking of plans to forward my pet East Bridgeport enterprise, it occurred to me that if the Litchfield clock concern could be transferred to my prospective new city, it would necessarily bring many families, thus increasing the growth of the place and the value of the property.

MOUNTAIN GROVE CEMETERY

Negotiations were at once commenced and the desired transfer of the business was the result. A new stock company was formed under the name of the "Terry & Barnum Manufacturing Company" and in 1852 a factory was built in East Bridgeport.

In 1855, I received a suggestion from a citizen of New Haven, that the Jerome Clock Company, then reputed to be a wealthy concern, should be removed to East Bridgeport, and shortly afterwards I was visited at *Iranistan* by Mr. Chauncey Jerome, the President of that company. The result of this visit was a proposition from the agent of the company, who also held power of attorney for the president, that I should lend my name as security for $110,000 in aid of the Jerome Clock Company, and the proffered compensation was the transfer of this great manufacturing concern, with its seven hundred to one thousand operatives, to my beloved East Bridgeport. It was just the bait for the fish; I was all attention; yet I must do my judgment the justice to say that I called for proofs, strong and ample, that the great company deserved its reputation as a substantial enterprise that might safely be trusted.

Accordingly, I was shown an official report of the directors of the company: exhibiting a capital of $400,000, and a surplus of $187,000, in all, $587,000. The need for $110,000 more, was on account of a dull season, and the market glutted with the goods, and immediate money demands which must be met. I was also impressed with the pathetic tale that the company was exceedingly loth to dismiss any of the operatives, who would suffer greatly if their only dependence for their daily food was taken away.

The official statement seemed satisfactory, and I cordially sympathized with the philanthropic purpose of keeping the workmen employed, even in the dull season. The company was reputed to be rich; the President, Mr. Chauncey Jerome, had built a church in New Haven, at a cost of $40,000, and proposed to present it to a congregation; he had given a clock to a church in Bridgeport, and these things showed that he, at least, thought he was wealthy. The Jerome clocks were for sale all over the world, even in China, where the Celestials were said to take out the "movements," and use the cases for little temples for their idols, thus proving that faith was possible without "works." So wealthy and so widely-known a company would surely be a grand acquisition to my city.

Further testimony came in the form of a letter from the cashier of one of the New Haven banks, expressing the highest confidence in the financial strength of the concern, and much satisfaction that I contemplated giving temporary aid which would keep so many workmen and their families from suffering, and perhaps starvation. I had not, at the time, the slightest suspicion that my voluntary correspondent had any interest in the transfer of the Jerome Company from New Haven to East Bridgeport, though I was subsequently informed that the bank, of which my correspondent was the cashier, was almost the largest, if not the largest, creditor of the clock company.

Under all the circumstances, and influenced by the rose-colored representations made to me, not less than by my mania to push the growth of my new city, I finally accepted the proposition and consented to an agreement that I would lend the clock company my notes for a sum not to exceed $50,000 and accept drafts to an amount not to exceed $60,000. It was thoroughly understood that I was in no case to be responsible for one cent in excess of $110,000. I also received the written guaranty of Chauncey Jerome that in no event should I lose by the loan, as he would become personally responsible for the repayment. I was willing that my notes, when taken up, should be renewed, I cared not how often, provided the stipulated maximum of $110,000 should never be exceeded. I was weak enough, however, under the representation that it was impossible to say exactly when it would be necessary to use the notes, to put my name to several notes for $3,000, $5,000, and $10,000, leaving the date of payment blank, but it was agreed that the blanks should be filled to make the notes payable in five, ten, or even sixty days from date, according to the exigencies of the case, and I was I was careful to keep a memorandum of the several amounts of the notes.

On the other side, it was agreed that the Jerome Company should exchange its stock with the Terry & Barnum stockholders and thus absorb that company and unite the entire business in East Bridgeport. It was scarcely a month, before the secretary wrote me that the company would soon be in a condition to "snap its fingers at the banks."

Nevertheless, three months after the consolidation of the companies, a reference to my memoranda showed that I had already become responsible for the stipulated sum of $110,000. I was then called upon in New York by the agent, who wanted five notes of $5,000 each, and I declined to furnish them, unless I should receive in return an equal amount of my own canceled notes, since he assured me they were canceling these "every week." The canceled notes were brought to me next day, and I renewed them. This I did frequently, always receiving canceled notes, till finally my confidence in the company became so established, that I did not ask to see the notes that had been taken up but furnished new accommodation paper as it was called for.

By and by I heard that the banks began to hesitate about discounting my paper and knowing that I was good for $110,000 several times over, I wondered what was the matter, till the discovery came at last that my notes had not been taken up as was represented, and that some of the blank date notes had been made payable in twelve, eighteen, and twenty-four months. Further investigation revealed the frightful fact that I had endorsed for the clock company to the extent of more than half a million dollars, and most of the notes had been exchanged for old Jerome Company notes due to the banks and other creditors. My agent who made these startling discoveries came back to me with the refreshing intelligence that I was a ruined man!

Not quite; I had the mountain of Jerome debts on my back, but I found means to pay every claim against me at my bank, all my store and shop debts, notes to the amount of $40,000, which banks in my neighborhood, relying upon my personal integrity, had discounted for the clock company, and then I — failed!

What a dupe had I been! Here was a great company pretending to be worth $587,000, asking temporary assistance to the amount of $110,000, coming down with a crash, so soon as my helping hand was removed, and sweeping me down with it. It failed; and, even after absorbing my fortune, it paid but from twelve to fifteen per cent, of its obligations, while, to cap the climax, it never removed to East Bridgeport at all, notwithstanding this was the only condition which ever prompted me to advance one dollar to the rotten concern!

If at any time my vanity had been chilled by the fear that after my retirement from the Jenny Lind enterprise the world would forget me, this affair speedily reassured me; I had notice enough to satisfy the most inordinate craving for notoriety. All over the country, and even across the ocean, "Barnum and the Jerome Clock Bubble," was the great newspaper theme. I was taken to pieces, analyzed, put together again, kicked, "pitched into," tumbled about, preached to, preached about, and made to serve every purpose to which a sensation-loving world could put me. Well! I was now in training, in a new school, and was learning new and strange lessons.

Yet these new lessons conveyed the old, old story. There were those who had fawned upon me in my prosperity, who now jeered at my adversity; people whom I had specially favored, made special efforts to show their ingratitude; papers, which, when I had the means to make it an object for them to be on good terms with me, overloaded me with adulation, now attempted to overwhelm me with abuse: and then the immense amount of moralizing over the "instability of human fortunes," and especially the retributive justice that is sure to follow "ill-gotten gains," which my censors assumed to be the sum and substance of my honorably acquired and industriously worked for property. I have no doubt that much of this kind of twaddle was believed by the twaddlers to be sincere; and thus, my case was actual capital to certain preachers and religious editors who were in want of fresh illustrations wherewith to point their morals.

I was in the depths, but did not despond. I was confident that with energetic purpose and divine assistance, I should, if my health and life were spared, get on my feet again; and events have since fully justified and verified the expectation and the effort.

CHAPTER XXVI.

CLOUDS AND SUNSHINE.

Happily, there is always more wheat than there is chaff. While my enemies and a few envious persons and misguided moralists were abusing and traducing me, my very misfortunes revealed to me hosts of hitherto unknown friends who tendered to me something more than mere sympathy. Funds were offered to me in unbounded quantity for the support of my family and to re-establish me in business. I declined these tenders because, on principle, I never accepted a money favor, unless I except the single receipt of a small sum which came to me by mail at this time, and anonymously so that I could not return it. Even this small sum I at once devoted to charity towards one who needed the money far more than I did.

The generosity of my friends urged me to accept "benefits" by the score, the returns of which would have made me quite independent. There was a proposition among leading citizens in New York to give a series of benefits which I felt obliged to decline, though the movement in my favor deeply touched me. To show the class of men who sympathized with me in my misfortunes, and also the ground which I took in the matter, I venture to copy the following correspondence which appeared in the New York papers of the day:

New York, June 2, 1856.

Mr. P. T. Barnum:

Dear Sir: The financial ruin of a man of acknowledged energy and enterprise is a public calamity. The sudden blow, therefore, that has swept away, from a man like yourself, the accumulated wealth of years, justifies, we think, the public sympathy. The better to manifest our sincere respect for your liberal example in prosperity, as well as exhibit our honest admiration of your fortitude under overwhelming reverses, we propose to give that sympathy a tangible expression by soliciting your acceptance of a series of benefits for your family, the result of which may possibly secure for your wife and children a future home, or at. least rescue them from the more immediate consequences of your misfortune.

Freeman Hunt, E. K. Collins, Isaac V. Fowler, James Phalen, Cornelius Vanderbilt, P. B. Cutting, James W. Gerard, Simeon Draper, Thomas McElrath, Park Godwin. R. F. Carman, Gen. C. W. Sanford, Philo Hurd, President H. R. R.; Wm. Ellsworth, President Brooklyn Ins. Co.; George S. Doughty, President Excelsior Ins. Co.; Chas. T. Cromwell, Robert Stuyvesant, E. L. Livingston, R. Busteed, Wm. P. Fettridge. E. N. Haughwout, Geo. F. Nesbitt, Osborne. Boardman & Townsend, Charles H. Delavan, I. & C. Berrien, Fisher & Bird, Solomon & Hart, B. Young, M. D., Treadwell, Acker & Co., St. Nicholas Hotel, John Wheeler, Union Square Hotel, S. Leland & Co., Metropolitan Hotel, Albert Clark, Brevoort House, H. D. Clapp, Everett House. John Taylor, International Hotel, Sydney Hopman, Smithsonian Hotel, Messrs. Delmonico, Delmonico's, Geo. W. Sherman, Florence's Hotel, Kingsley &

Ainslee, Howard Hotel, Libby & Whitney, Lovejoy's Hotel, Howard & Brown, Tammany Hall. Jonas Bartlett, Washington Hotel, Patten & Lynde, Pacific Hotel, J. Johnson, Johnson's Hotel, and over 1,000 others.

To this gratifying communication I replied as follows:

Long Island, Tuesday, June 3, 1856.
To Messrs. Freeman Hunt, E. K. Collins, and others.

Gentlemen: I can hardly find words to express my gratitude for your very kind proposition. The popular sympathy is to me far more precious than gold, and that sympathy seems in my case to extend from my immediate neighbors, in Bridgeport, to all parts of our Union.

Proffers of pecuniary assistance have reached me from every quarter, not only from friends, but from entire strangers. Mr. Wm. E. Burton, Miss Laura Keene and Mr. Wm. Niblo have in the kindest manner tendered me the receipts of their theaters for one evening.

Mr. Gough volunteered the proceeds of one of his attractive lectures; Mr. James Phalon generously offered me the free use of the Academy of Music; many professional ladies and gentlemen have urged me to accept their gratuitous services. I have, on principle, respectfully declined them all, as I beg, with the most grateful acknowledgments (at least for the present), to decline yours — not because a benefit, in itself, is an objectionable thing, but because I have ever made it a point to ask nothing of the public on personal grounds, and should prefer, while I can possibly avoid that contingency, to accept nothing from it without the honest conviction that I had individually given it in return a full equivalent.

While favored with health, I feel competent to earn an honest livelihood for myself and family. More than this, I shall certainly never attempt with such a load of debt suspended *in terrorem* over me. While I earnestly thank you, therefore, for your generous consideration, gentlemen I trust you will appreciate my desire to live unhumiliated by a sense of dependence, and believe me, sincerely yours,

P. T. Barnum.

And with other offers of assistance from far and near, came the following from a little gentleman who did not forget his old friend and benefactor in the time of trial:

Jones' Hotel, Philadelphia, May 12, 1856.
My Dear Mr. Barnum: I understand your friends, and that means "all creation," intend to get up some benefits for your family. Now, my dear sir, just be good enough to remember that I belong to that mighty crowd, and I must have a finger (or at least a "thumb") in that pie! I am bound to appear on all such occasions in some shape, from "Jack the Giant Killer," upstairs, to the door-keeper down, whichever may serve you best; and there are some feats that I can perform as well as any other man of my inches. I have just started out on my western tour, and have my carriage, ponies and assistants

all here, but I am ready to go on to New York, bag and baggage, and remain at Mrs. Barnum's service as long as I, in my small way, can be useful. Put me into any "heavy" work, if you like. Perhaps I cannot lift as much as some other folks, but just take your pencil in hand and you will see I can draw a tremendous load. I drew two hundred tons at a single pull today, embracing two thousand persons, whom I hauled up safely and satisfactorily to all parties, at one exhibition. Hoping that you will be able to fix up a lot of magnets that will attract all New York, and volunteering to sit on any part of the loadstone, I am, as ever, your little but sympathizing friend,

Gen. Tom Thumb

Even this generous offer from my little friend I felt compelled to refuse. But kind words were written and spoken which I could not prevent, nor did I desire to do so, and which were worth more to me than money. I should fail to find space, if I wished it, to copy one-tenth part of the cordial and kind articles and paragraphs that appeared about me in newspapers throughout the country. The following sentence from an editorial article in a prominent New York journal was the key-note to many similar kind notices in all parts of the Union: "It is a fact beyond dispute that Mr. Barnum's financial difficulties have accumulated from the goodness of his nature; kind-hearted and generous to a fault, it has ever been his custom to lend a helping hand to the struggling; and honest industry and enterprise have found his friendship prompt and faithful." The *Boston Journal* dwelt especially upon the use I had made of my money in my days of prosperity in assisting deserving laboring men and in giving an impulse to business in the town where I resided. It seems only just that I should make this very brief allusion to these things, if only as an offset to the unbounded abuse of those who believed in kicking me merely because I was down; nor can I refrain from copying the following from the *Boston Saturday Evening Gazette*, of May 3, 1856:

BARNUM REDIVIVUS.

A WORD FOR BARNUM.

Barnum, your hand! Though you are "down,"
And see full many a frigid shoulder,
Be brave, my brick, and though they frown,
Prove that misfortune makes you bolder.
There's many a man that sneers, my hero,
And former praise converts to scorning,
Would worship— when he fears— a Nero,
And bend "where thrift may follow fawning "

You humbugged us— that we have seen,
We got our money's worth, old fellow,
And though you thought our *minds* were *green*,
We never thought your *heart* was *yellow*.
We knew you liberal, generous, warm,
Quick to assist a falling brother,

And, with such virtues, what's the harm
All memories of your faults to smother?
We had not heard the peerless Lind,
But for your spirit enterprising,
You were the man to raise the wind,
And make a *coup* confessed surprising.
You're reckoned in your native town
A friend in need, a friend in danger,
You ever keep the latchstring down,
And greet with open hand the stranger.
Stiffen your upper lip. You know
Who are your friends and who your foes now;
We pay for knowledge as we go;
And though you get some sturdy blows now,
You've a fair field — no favors crave —
The storm once passed will find you braver—
In virtue's cause long may you wave,
And on the right side, never waver.

Desirous of knowing who was the author of this kindly effusion, I wrote, while preparing this autobiography, to Mr. B. P. Shillaber, one of the editors of the journal, and well known to the public as "Mrs. Partington." In reply, I received the following letter in which it will be seen that he makes sympathetic allusion to the burning of my last Museum, only a few weeks before the date of ins letter:

Chelsea, April 25, 1868.
My Dear Mr. Barnum: The poem in question was written by A. Wallace Thaxter, associate editor with Mr. Clapp and myself, on the Gazette— since deceased, a glorious fellow — who wrote the poem from a sincere feeling of admiration for yourself. Mr. Clapp, (Hon. W. W. Clapp,) published it with his full approbation. I heard of your new trouble, in my sick chamber, where I have been all winter, with regret, and wish you as ready a release from attending difficulty as your genius has hitherto achieved under like circumstances.

Yours, very truly,
B. P. Shillaber.

But the manifestations of sympathy which came to me from Bridgeport, where my home had been for more than ten years, were the most gratifying of all, because they showed unmistakably that my best friends, those who were most constant in their friendship and most emphatic in their esteem, were my neighbors and associates who, of all people, knew me best. With such support I could easily endure the attacks of traducers elsewhere. *The New York Times*, April 25, 1856, under the head of "Sympathy for Barnum," published a full report of the meeting of my fellow-citizens of Bridgeport, the previous evening, to take my case into consideration.

In response to a call headed by the mayor of the city, and signed by several hundred citizens, this meeting was held in Washington Hall "for the purpose of

THE TRUE LIFE OF THE WORLD'S GREATEST SHOWMAN

sympathizing with P. T. Barnum, Esq., in his recent pecuniary embarrassments, and of giving some public expression to their views in reference to his financial misfortunes." It was the largest public meeting which, up to that time, had ever been held in Bridgeport. Several prominent citizens made addresses, and resolutions were adopted, declaring "that respect and sympathy were due to P. T. Barnum in return for his many acts of liberality, philanthropy and public spirit," expressing unshaken confidence in his integrity, admiration for the "fortitude and composure with which he has met reverses into which he has been dragged through no fault of his own except a too generous confidence in pretended friends," and hoping that he would "yet return to that wealth which he has so nobly employed, and to the community he has so signally benefited." During the evening the following letter was read:

New York, Thursday, April 24, 1856.
Wm. H. Noble, Esq.,
Dear Sir: I have just received a slip containing; a call for a public meeting of the citizens of Bridgeport to sympathize with me in my troubles. It is headed by His Honor the Mayor, and is signed by most of your prominent citizens, as well as by many men who by hard labor earn their daily bread, and who appreciate a calamity which at a single blow strips a man of his fortune, his dear home, and all the worldly comforts which years of diligent labor had acquired. It is due to truth to say that I knew nothing of this movement until your letter informed me of it.

In misfortune the true sympathy of neighbors is more consoling and precious than anything which money can purchase. This voluntary offering of my fellow-citizens, though it thrills me with painful emotions and causes tears of gratitude, yet imparts to me renewed strength, and tills my heart with thankfulness to Providence for raising up to my sight, above all this wreck, kind hearts which soar above the sordid atmosphere of "dirty dollars." I can never forget this unexpected kindness from my old friends and neighbors.

I trust I am not blind to my many faults and shortcomings. I, however, do feel great consolation in believing that I never used money or position to oppress the poor or wrong my fellow-men, and that I never turned empty away those whom I had the power to aid.

My poor sick wife, who needs the bracing air which our own dear home (made beautiful by her willing hands) would now have afforded her, is driven by the orders of her physician to a secluded spot on Long Island where the sea-wind lends its healthful influence, and where I have also retired for the double purpose of consoling her and of recruiting my own constitution, which, through the excitements of the last few months, has most seriously failed me.

In our quiet and humble retreat, that which I most sincerely pray for is tranquility and contentment. I am sure that the remembrance of the kindness of my Bridgeport neighbors will aid me in securing these cherished blessings. No man who has not passed through similar scenes can fully comprehend the misery which has been crowded into the last few months of my life; but I have endeavored to preserve my integrity, and I humbly hope and believe that I am being taught humility and reliance upon Providence, which will yet afford a thousand times more peace and true happiness than can be acquired in the din, strife and turmoil, excitements and struggles of this money-worshipping age. The man who coins his brains and blood into gold, who wastes all of his time and thought upon the almighty dollar, who looks no higher than blocks of houses, and tracts of land, and whose iron chest is crammed with stocks and mortgages tied up with his own heart-strings, may console himself with the idea of safe investments, but he misses a pleasure which I firmly believe this lesson was intended to secure to me, and which it will secure if I can fully bring my mind to realize its wisdom. I think I hear you say—

> "When the devil was sick,
> The devil a saint would be,
> But when the devil got well.
> The devil a saint was he."

Granted, but, after all, the man who looks upon the loss of money as anything compared to the loss of honor, or health, or self-respect, or friends— a man who can find no source of happiness except in riches— is to be pitied for his blindness. I certainly feel that the loss of money, of home and my home comforts, is dreadful— that to be driven again to find a resting-place away from those I love, and from where I had fondly supposed I was to end my days, and where I had lavished time, money, everything, to make my descent to the grave placid and pleasant — is, indeed, a severe lesson; but, after all. I firmly believe it is for the best, and though my heart may break, I will not repine.

I regret, beyond expression, that any man should be a loser for having trusted to my name; it would not have been so, if I had not myself been deceived. As it is, I am gratified in knowing that all my individual obligations will be met. It would have been much better if clock creditors had accepted the best offer that it was in my power to make them; but it was not so to be. It is now too late, and, as I willingly give up all I possess, I can do no more.

Wherever my future lot may be cast, I shall ever fondly cherish the kindness which I have always received from the citizens of Bridgeport.

I am, my dear sir, truly yours,
P. T. BARNUM.

Shortly after this sympathetic meeting, a number of gentlemen in Bridgeport offered me a loan of $50,000 if that sum would be instrumental in extricating me from my entanglement. I could not say that this amount would meet the exigency; I could only say, "wait, wait, and hope."

Meanwhile, my eyes were fully open to the entire magnitude of the deception that had been practiced upon my too confiding nature. I not only discovered that my notes had been used to five times the amount I stipulated or expected, but that they had been applied, not to relieving the company from temporary embarrassment after my connection with it, but almost wholly to the redemption of old and rotten claims of years and months gone by. To show the extent to which the fresh victim was deliberately bled, it may be stated that I was induced to become surety to one of the New Haven banks in the sum of $30,000 to indemnify the bank against future losses it might incur from the Jerome Company after my connection with it, and by some legerdemain this bond was made to cover past obligations which were older even than my knowledge of the existence of the company. In every way it seemed as if I had been cruelly swindled and deliberately defrauded.

As the clock company had gone to pieces and was paying but from twelve to fifteen per cent for its paper, I sent two of my friends to New Haven to ask for a meeting of the creditors, and I instructed them to say in substance for me as follows:

"Gentlemen: This is a capital, practical joke! Before I negotiated with your clock company at all, I was assured by several of you, and particularly by a representative of the bank, which was the largest creditor of the concern, that the Jerome Company was eminently responsible, and that the head of the same was uncommonly pious. On the strength of such representations solely, I was induced to agree to endorse and accept paper for that company to the extent of $110,000 — no more. That sum I am now willing to pay for my own verdancy, with an additional sum of $40,000 for your 'cuteness', making a total of $150,000, which you can have if you cry 'quits' with the fleeced showman and let him off."

Many of the old creditors favored this proposition; but it was found that the indebtedness was so scattered it would be impracticable to attempt a settlement by a unanimous compromise of the creditors. It was necessary to liquidation that my property should go into the hands of assignees; I therefore at once turned over my Bridgeport property to Connecticut assignees, and I removed my family to New York, where I also made an assignment of all my real and personal estate, excepting what had already been transferred in Connecticut.

About this time, I received a letter from Philadelphia proffering $500 in case my circumstances were such that I really stood in need of help. The very wording of the letter awakened the suspicion in my mind, that it was a trick to ascertain whether I really had any property, for I knew that banks and brokers in that city held some of my Jerome paper which they refused to compound or compromise. So, I at once wrote that I did need $500, and, as I expected, the money did not come, nor was my letter answered; but, as a natural consequence, the Philadelphia bankers who were holding the Jerome paper for a higher percentage, at once acceded to the terms which I had announced myself able and willing to pay.

Every dollar which I honestly owed on my own account, I had already paid in full or had satisfactorily arranged. For the liabilities incurred by the deliberate deception which had involved me, I offered such a percentage as I thought my estate, when sold, would eventually pay; and my wife, from her own property, advanced from time to time money to take up such notes as could be secured upon these terms. It was, however, a slow process.

We were now living in a very frugal manner in a hired furnished house in Eighth street, near Sixth avenue, in New York, and our landlady and her family boarded with us. At the age of forty-six, after the acquisition and the loss of a handsome fortune, I was once more nearly at the bottom of the ladder, and was about to begin the world again. The situation was disheartening, but I had energy, experience, health and Lope.

CHAPTER XXVII.

REST, BUT NOT RUST.

In the summer of 1855, previous to my financial troubles, feeling that I was independent and could retire from active business, I sold the American Museum collection and good-will to Messrs. John Greenwood, Junior, and Henry D. Butler. They paid me double the amount the collection had originally cost, giving me notes for nearly the entire amount, secured by a chattel mortgage, and hired the premises from my wife, who owned the Museum property lease, and on which, by the agreement of Messrs. Greenwood and Butler, she realized a profit of $19,000 a year. The chattel mortgage of Messrs. Greenwood and Butler, was, of course, turned over to the New York assignee with the other property.

And now there came to me a new sensation, which was, at times, terribly depressing and annoying. My wide-spread reputation for shrewdness as a showman, had induced the general belief that my means were still ample, and certain outside creditors who had bought my clock notes at a tremendous discount, and entirely on speculation, made up their minds that they must be paid at once without waiting for the slow process of the sale of my property by the assignees.

They therefore took what are termed "supplementary proceedings," which enabled them to haul me any day before a judge, for the purpose, as they phrased it, of "putting Barnum through a course of sprouts," and which meant an examination of the debtor under oath, compelling him to disclose everything with regard to his property, his present means of living, and so on.

I repeatedly answered all questions on these points; and reports of the daily examinations were published. Still another and another, and yet another creditor would haul me up; and his attorney would ask me the same questions which had already been answered and published half a dozen times. This persistent and unnecessary annoyance, created considerable sympathy for me, which was not only expressed by letters I received daily from various parts of the country, but the public press, with now and then an exception, took my part, and even the judges, before whom I appeared, said to me on more than one occasion, that as men they sincerely pitied me, but as judges, of course they must administer the law. After a while, however, the judges ruled that I need not answer any questions propounded to me by an attorney, if I had already answered the same question to some other attorney in a previous examination in behalf of other creditors. In fact, one of the judges, on one occasion, said pretty sharply to an examining attorney:

"This, sir, has become simply a case of persecution. Mr. Barnum has many times answered every question that can properly be put to him, to elicit the desired information; and I think it is time to stop these examinations, I advise him to not answer one interrogatory which he has replied to under any previous inquiries."

These things gave me some heart, so that at last, I went up to the "sprouts" with less reluctance, and began to try to pay off my persecutors in their own coin.

On one occasion, a dwarfish little lawyer, who reminded me of "Quilp," commenced his examination in behalf of a note-shaver, who held a thousand-dollar note, which it seemed he had bought for seven hundred dollars. After the oath had been administered, the "limb of the law" arranged his pen, ink and paper, and in a loud voice, and with a most peremptory and supercilious air, asked:

"What is your name, sir? "

I answered him; and his next question, given in a louder and more peremptory tone, was:

"What is your business?"

"Attending bar," I meekly replied.

"Attending bar!" he echoed, with an appearance of much surprise; "attending bar! Why, don't you profess to be a temperance man— a teetotaler?"

"I do," I replied.

"And yet, sir, do you have the audacity to assert that you peddle rum all day, and drink none yourself?"

"I doubt whether that is a relevant question," I said in a low tone of voice.

"I will appeal to his honor, the judge, if you don't answer it instantly," said Quilp in great glee.

"I attend bar, and yet never drink intoxicating liquors," I replied.

"Where do you attend bar, and for whom?" was the next question.

"I attend the bar of this court, nearly every day, for the benefit of two-penny, would-be lawyers and their greedy clients," I answered.

A loud tittering in the vicinity only added to the vexation which was already visible on the countenance of my interrogator, and he soon brought his examination to a close.

On another occasion, a young lawyer was pushing his inquiries to a great length, when, in a half-laughing, apologetic tone, he said:

"You see, Mr. Barnum, I am searching after the small things; I am willing to take even the crumbs which fall from the rich man's table!"

"Which are you? Lazarus, or one of his dogs?" I asked.

"I guess a blood-hound would not smell out much on this trail," he said good naturedly, adding that he had no more questions to ask.

Just after my failure, and on account of the ill-health of my wife, I spent a portion of the summer with my family in the farmhouse of Mr. Charles Howell, at Westhampton, on Long Island. The place is a mile west of Quogue, and was then called "Ketchebonneck." The thrifty and intelligent farmers of the neighborhood were in the habit of taking summer boarders, and the place had become a favorite resort. Mr. Howell's farm lay close upon the ocean, and I found the residence a cool and delightful one. Surf bathing, fishing, shooting and fine roads for driving made the season pass pleasantly, and the respite from active life and immediate annoyance from my financial troubles was a very great benefit to me.

One morning we discovered that the waves had thrown upon the beach a young black whale some twelve feet long. It was dead, but the fish was hard and fresh and I bought it for a few dollars from the men who had taken possession of it. I sent it at once to the Museum, where it was exhibited in a huge refrigerator for a few days, creating considerable excitement, the general public considering it "a big thing on ice," and the managers gave me a share of the profits, which amounted to a sufficient sum to pay the entire board bill of my family for the season.

This incident both amused and amazed my Long Island landlord. "Well, I declare," said he, "that beats all; you are the luckiest man I ever heard of. Here you come and board for four months, with your family, and when your time is nearly up, and you are getting ready to leave, out rolls a black whale on our beach, a thing never heard of before in this vicinity, and you take that whale and pay your whole bill with it."

Soon after my return to New York, something occurred which I foresaw at the time, was likely indirectly to lead me out of the wilderness into a clear field again. Strange to say, my new city, which had been my ruin was to be my redemption.

The now gigantic Wheeler & Wilson Sewing Machine Company was then doing a comparatively small, yet rapidly growing business at Watertown, Connecticut. The Terry & Barnum clock factory was standing idle, almost worthless, in East Bridgeport, and Wheeler & Wilson saw in the empty building, the situation, the ease of communication with New York, and other advantages, precisely what they wanted, provided they could procure the premises at a rate which would compensate them for the expense and trouble of removing their establishment from Watertown. The clock factory was sold for a trifle and the Wheeler & Wilson Company moved into it and speedily enlarged it. It was a fresh impulse towards the building up of a new city and the consequent increase of the value of the land belonging to my estate.

This important movement of the Wheeler & Wilson Company gave me the greatest hope, and, moreover, Mr. Wheeler kindly offered me a loan of $5,000, without security, and, as I was anxious to have it used in purchasing the East Bridgeport property, when sold at public auction by my assignees, and also in taking up such clock notes as could be bought at a reasonable percentage, I accepted the offer and borrowed the $5,000. This sum, with many thousand dollars more belonging to my wife, was devoted to these purposes.

Though the new plan promised relief, and actually did succeed, even beyond my most sanguine expectations, eventually putting more money into my pocket than the Jerome complication had taken out — yet I also foresaw that the process would necessarily be very slow. In fact, two years afterwards I had made very little progress. But I concluded to let the new venture work out itself and it would go on as well without my personal presence and attention, perhaps even better. Growing trees, money at interest, and rapidly rising real estate, work for their owners all night as well as all day, Sundays included, and when the proprietors are asleep or away, and with the design of co-operating in the new accumulation and of saving something to add to the amount, I made up my mind to go to Europe again. I was anxious for a change of scene and for active employment, and equally desirous of getting away from the immediate pressure of troubles which no effort on my part could then remove. While my affairs were working out themselves in their own way and in the speediest manner possible, I might be doing something for myself and for my family.

Accordingly, leaving all my business affairs at home in the hands of my friends, early in 1857 I set sail once more for England, taking with me General Tom Thumb, and also little Cordelia Howard and her parents. This young girl had attained an extended reputation for her artistic personation of "Little Eva," in the play of "Uncle

Tom," and she displayed a precocious talent in her rendering of other juvenile characters. With these attractions, and with what else I might be able to do myself, I determined to make as much money as I could, intending to remit the same to my wife's friends, for the purpose of re-purchasing a portion of my estate, when it was offered at auction, and of redeeming such of the clock notes as could be obtained at reasonable rates.

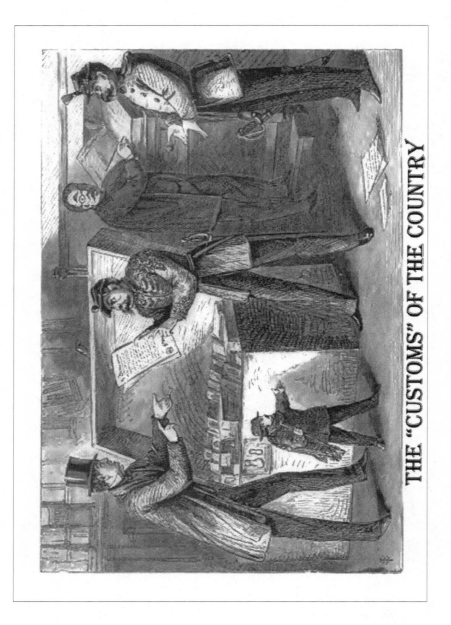

THE "CUSTOMS" OF THE COUNTRY

CHAPTER XXVIII.

ABROAD AGAIN.

When I reached London, I found Mr. Albert Smith, who, when I first knew him, was a dentist, a literary hack, a contributor to Punch, and a writer for the magazines, now transformed to a first-class showman in the full tide of success, in my own old exhibition quarters in Egyptian Hall, Piccadilly. He was exhibiting a panorama of his ascent of Mont Blanc. His lecture was full of amusing and interesting incidents, illustrative of his remarkable experiences in accomplishing the difficult feat.

Calling upon Albert Smith, I found him the same kind, cordial friend as ever, and he at once put me on the free list at his entertainment and insisted upon my dining frequently with him at his favorite club, the Garrick.

The first time I witnessed his exhibition, he gave me a sly wink from the stage at the moment of his describing a scene in the golden chamber of St. Ursula's church in Cologne, where the old sexton was narrating the story of the ashes and bones of the eleven thousand innocent virgins, who, according to tradition, were sacrificed on a certain occasion. One of the characters whom he pretended to have met several times on his trip to Mont Blanc, was a Yankee, whom he named "Phineas Cutecraft." The wink came at the time he introduced Phineas in the Cologne Church, and made him say at the end of the sexton's story about the Virgins' bones:

"Old fellow, what will you take for that whole lot of bones? I want them for my Museum in America! "

When the question had been interpreted to the old German, he exclaimed in horror, according to Albert Smith:

"Mine Gott! it is impossible! We will never sell the Virgins' bones! "

"Never mind," replied Phineas Cutecraft, "I'll send another lot of bones to my Museum, swear mine are the real bones of the Virgins of Cologne, and burst up your show!"

This always excited the heartiest laughter; but Mr. Smith knew very well that I would at once recognize it as a pharaphrase of the scene wherein he had figured with me, in 1844, at the porter's lodge of Warwick Castle. In the course of the entertainment, I found he had woven in numerous anecdotes I had told him at that time, and many incidents of our excursion were also travestied and made to contribute to the interest of his description of the ascent of Mont Blanc.

When we went to the Garrick club that day, Albert Smith introduced me to several of his acquaintances as his "teacher in the show business." As we were quietly dining together, he remarked that I must have recognized several old acquaintances in the anecdotes at his entertainment. Upon my answering that I did, "indeed," he remarked, "you are too old a showman not to know that in order to be popular, we must snap up and localize all the good things which we come across." By thus engrafting his various experiences upon this Mont Blanc entertainment, Albert Smith succeeded in serving up a salmagundi feast which was relished alike by royal and less distinguished palates.

When the late William M. Thackeray made his first visit to the United States, I think in 1852, he called on me at the Museum with a letter of introduction from our mutual friend, Albert Smith. He spent an hour with me, mainly for the purpose of asking advice in regard to the management of the course of lectures on "The English Humorists of the Eighteenth Century," which he proposed to deliver, as he did afterwards, with very great success, in the principal cities of the Union. I gave him the best advice I could as to management, and the cities he ought to visit, for which he was very grateful and he called on me whenever he was in New York. I also saw him repeatedly when he came to America the second time with his admirable lectures on "The Four Georges," which, it will be remembered, he delivered in the United States in the season of 1855-56, before he read them to audiences in Great Britain. My relations with this great novelist, I am proud to say, were cordial and intimate; and now, when I called upon him, in 1857, at his own house, he grasped me heartily by the hand and said:

"Mr. Barnum, I admire you more than ever. I have read the accounts in the papers of the examinations you underwent in the New York courts; and the positive pluck you exhibit under your pecuniary embarrassments is worthy of all praise. You would never have received credit for the philosophy you manifest, if these financial misfortunes had not overtaken you."

I thanked him for his compliment, and he continued:

"But tell me, Barnum, are you really in need of present assistance? for if you are, you must be helped."

"Not in the least," I replied, laughing; "I need more money in order to get out of bankruptcy, and I intend to earn it; but so far as daily bread is concerned, I am quite at ease, for my wife is worth £30,000 or £40,000."

"Is it possible?" he exclaimed, with evident delight; "well, now, you have lost all my sympathy; why, that is more than I ever expect to be worth; I shall be sorry for you no more."

During my stay in London, I met Thackeray several times, and on one occasion dined with him. He repeatedly expressed his obligations to me for the advice and assistance I had given him on the occasion of his first lecturing visit to the United States.

Otto Goldschmidt, the husband of Jenny Lind, also called on me in London. He and his wife were then living in Dresden, and he said the first thing his wife desired him to ask me was, whether I was in want! I assured him that I was not, although I was managing to live in an economical way, and my family would soon come over to reside in London. He then advised me to take them to Dresden, saying that living was very cheap there; and, he added, "my wife will gladly look up a proper house for you to live in." I thankfully declined his proffered kindness, as Dresden was too far away from my business.

My old friends, Julius Benedict and Giovanni Belletti, called on me and we had some very pleasant dinners together, when we talked over incidents of their travels in America, Among the gentlemen whom I met in London, some of them quite frequently at dinners, were Mr. George Augustus Sala, Mr. Edmund Yates, Mr. Horace

Mayhew, Mr. Alfred Bunn, Mr. Lumley, of Her Majesty's Theater, Mr. Buckstone, of the Haymarket, Mr. Charles Kean, our princely countrymen Mr. George Peabody, Mr. J. M. Morris, the manager, Mr. Bates, of Baring, Brothers & Co., Mr. Oxenford, dramatic critic of the London Times, Dr. Ballard, the American dentist, and many other eminent persons.

I had numerous offers from professional friends, on both sides of the Atlantic, who supposed me to be in need of employment. Mr. Barney Williams, who had not then acted in England, proposed, in the kindest manner, to make me his agent for a tour through Great Britain, and to give me one-third of the profits which he and Mrs. "Williams might make by their acting. Mr. S. M. Pettengill, of New York, the newspaper advertising agent, offered me the fine salary of $10,000 a year to transact business for him in Great Britain. He wrote to me: "When you failed in consequence of the Jerome clock notes, I felt that your creditors were dealing hard with you; that they should have let you up and give you a chance, and they would have fared better, and I wish I was a creditor so as to show what I would do." These offers, both from Mr. Williams and Mr. Pettengill, I felt obliged to decline.

Mr. Lumley, manager of Her Majesty's Theater, used to send me an order for a private box for every opera night, and I frequently availed myself of his courtesy.

Meanwhile, I was by no means idle. Cordelia Howard as "Little Eva," with her mother as the inimitable "Topsy," were highly successful in London and other large cities, while General Tom Thumb, returning after so long an absence, drew crowded houses wherever he went. These were strong spokes in the wheel that was moving slowly but surely in the effort to get me out of debt, and, if possible, to save some portion of my real estate. Of course, it was not generally known that I had any interest whatever in either of these exhibitions; if it had been, possibly some of the clock creditors would have annoyed me; but I busied myself in these and in other ways, working industriously and making much money, which I constantly remitted to my trusty agent at home.

CHAPTER XXIX.

IN GERMANY.

After a pleasant and successful season of several weeks in London and in the provinces, I took the little General into Germany, going from London to Paris, and from thence to Strasbourg and Baden-Baden.

I dreaded to pass the custom-house at Kebl nearly opposite Strasbourg, and the first town on the German border at that point. I knew that I had no baggage which was rightfully subject to duty, as I had nothing but my necessary clothing, and the package of placards and lithographs, illustrating the General's exhibitions. As the official was examining my trunks, I assured him in French, that I had nothing subject to duty; but he made no reply and deliberately handled every article in my luggage. He then cut the strings to the large packages of show-bills. I asked him in French, whether he understood that language. He gave a grunt, which was the only audible sound I could get out of him, and then laid my show-bills and lithographs on his scales as if to weigh them. I was much excited. An English gentleman, who spoke German, kindly offered to act as my interpreter.

"Please do tell him," said I, "that those bills and lithographs are not articles of commerce; that they are simply advertisements."

My English friend did as I requested; but it was of no use; the custom-house officer kept piling them upon his scales. I grew more excited.

"Please tell him I give them away," I said. The translation of my assertion into German did not help me; a double grunt from the functionary, was the only response. Tom Thumb, meanwhile, jumped about like a little monkey, for he was fairly delighted at my worry and perplexity. Finally, I said to my new found English friend: "Be good enough to tell the officer to keep the bills if he wants them, and that I will not pay duty on them, anyhow."

He was duly informed of my determination, but he was immovable. He lighted his huge Dutch pipe, got the exact weight, and, marking it down, handed it to a clerk, who copied it on his book, and solemnly passed it over to another clerk, who copied it on still another book; a third clerk then took it, and copied it on to a printed bill, the size of a half letter sheet, which was duly stamped in red ink with several official devices. By this time, I was in a profuse perspiration; and, as the document passed from clerk to clerk, I told them they need not trouble themselves to make out a bill, for I would not pay it; they would get no duty and they might keep the property.

To be sure, I could not spare the placards for any length of time, for they were exceedingly valuable to me as advertisements, and I could not easily have duplicated them in Germany; but I was determined that I would not pay duties on articles which were not merchandise. Every transfer, therefore, of the bill to a new clerk, gave me a fresh twinge, for I imagined that every clerk added more charges, and that every charge was a tighter turn to the vise which held my fingers. Finally, the last clerk defiantly thrust in my face the terrible official document, on which were scrawled certain cabalistic characters, signifying the amount of money I should be forced to pay to the German government before I could have my property. I would not touch it; but resolved I would really leave my packages until I could communicate with one of our consuls in Germany, and I said as much to the English gentleman who had kindly interpreted for me.

He took the bill, and, examining it, burst into a loud laugh. "Why, it is but fifteen kreutzers!" he said.

"How much is that?" I asked, feeling for the golden sovereigns in my pocket. "Sixpence!" was the reply.

I was astonished and delighted, and, as I handed out the money, I begged him to tell the officials that the custom-house charge would not pay the cost of the paper on which it was written. But this was a very fair illustration of sundry red-tape dealings in other countries as well as in Germany.

I found Baden a delightful little town, cleaner and neater than any city I had ever visited.

When our preliminary arrangements were completed, the General's attendants, carriage, ponies and liveried coachmen and footmen arrived at Baden-Baden, and were soon seen in the streets. The excitement was intense and increased from day to day. Several crowned heads, princes, lords and ladies, who were spending the season at Baden-Baden, with a vast number of wealthy pleasure-seekers and travelers, crowded the saloon in which the General exhibited, during the entire time we remained in the place. The charges for admission were much higher than had been demanded in any other city.

From Baden-Baden we went to other celebrated German Spas, including Ems, Homburg and Weisbaden. These were all fashionable gambling as well as watering places, and during our visits they were crowded with visitors from all parts of Europe. Our exhibitions were attended by thousands who paid the same high prices that were charged for admission at Baden-Baden, and at Wiesbaden, among many distinguished persons, the King of Holland came to see the little General. These exhibitions were among the most profitable that had ever been given, and I was able to remit thousands of dollars to my agents in the United States, to aid in re-purchasing my real estate, and to assist in taking up such clock notes as were offered for sale. A short but very remunerative season at Frankfort-on-the-Maine, the home and starting-place of the great house of the Rothschilds, assisted me largely in carrying out these purposes.

We exhibited at Mayence, and several other places in the vicinity, reaping golden harvests everywhere, and then went down the Rhine to Cologne.

We remained at Cologne only long enough to visit the famous cathedral and to see other curiosities and works of art, and then pushed on to Rotterdam and Amsterdam.

CHAPTER XXX.

IN HOLLAND.

Holland gave me more genuine satisfaction than any other foreign country I have ever visited, if I except Great Britain. Redeemed as a large portion of the whole surface of the land has been from the bottom of the sea, by the wonderful dykes, which are monuments of the industry of whole generations of human beavers, Holland seems to me the most curious, as well as interesting country in the world. The people, too, with their quaint costumes, their extraordinary cleanliness, their thrift, industry and frugality, pleased me very much. It is the universal testimony of all travelers, that the Hollanders are the neatest and most economical people among all nations. So far as cleanliness is concerned, in Holland it is evidently not next to, but far ahead of godliness. It is rare, indeed, to meet a ragged, dirty, or drunken person. The people are very temperate and economical in their habits; and even the very rich — and there is a vast amount of wealth in the country — live with great frugality, though all of the people live well.

As for the scenery, I cannot say much for it, since it is only diversified by thousands of windmills, which are made to do all kinds of work, from grinding grain to pumping water from the inside of the dykes back to the sea again. As I exhibited the General only in Rotterdam and Amsterdam, and to no great profit in either city, we spent most of our time in rambling: about to see what was to be seen. In the country villages it seemed as if every house was scrubbed twice and whitewashed once every day in the week, excepting Sunday. Some places were almost painfully pure, and I was in one village where horses and cattle were not allowed to go through the streets, and no one was permitted to wear their boots or shoes in the houses. There is a general and constant exercise of brooms, pails, floor-brushes and mops all over Holland, and in some places, even, this kind of thing is carried so far, I am told, that the only trees set out are scrub-oaks.

The reason, I think, why our exhibitions were not more successful in Rotterdam and Amsterdam, is that the people are too frugal to spend much money for amusements, but they and their habits and ways afforded us so much amusement, that we were quite willing they should give our entertainment the "go by," as they generally did. We were in Amsterdam at the season of "Kremis," or the annual fair which is held in all the principal towns, and where shows of all descriptions are open, at prices for admission ranging from one to five pennies, and are attended by nearly the whole population. For the people generally, this one great holiday seems all-sufficient for the whole year. I went through scores of booths, where curiosities and monstrosities of all kinds were exhibited, and was able to make some purchases and engagements for the American Museum. Among these, was the Albino family consisting of a man, his wife, and son, who were by far the most interesting and attractive specimens of their class I had ever seen.

We visited The Hague, the capital and the finest city in Holland. It is handsomely and regularly laid out, and contains a beautiful theater, a public picture gallery, which contains some of the best works of Vandyke, Paul Potter, and other Dutch masters, while the museum is especially rich in rarities from China and Japan. When we arrived at The Hague, Mr. August Belmont, who had been the United States Minister at that court, had just gone home; but I heard many encomiums passed upon him and his family, and I was told some pretty good stories of his familiarity with the king, and of the "jolly times" these two personages frequently enjoyed together. I did not miss visiting the great government museum, as I wished particularly to see the rich collection of Japan ware and arms, made during the many years when the Dutch carried on almost exclusively the entire foreign trade with the Japanese. I spent several days in minutely examining these curious manufactures of a people who were then almost as little known to nations generally as are the inhabitants of the planet Jupiter.

On the first day of my visit to this museum, I stood for an hour before a large case containing a most unique and extraordinary collection of fabulous animals, made from paper and other materials, and looking as natural and genuine as the stuffed skins of any animals in the American Museum. There were serpents two yards long, with a head and pair of feet at each end; frogs as large as a man, with human hands and feet; turtles with three heads; monkeys with two heads and six legs; scores of equally curious monstrosities; and at least two dozen mermaids, of all sorts and sizes. Looking at these "sirens", I easily divined from whence the Feejee mermaid originated.

After a truly delightful visit in Holland, we went back to England; and, proceeding to Manchester, opened our exhibition. For several days the hall was crowded to overflowing at each of the three, and sometimes four, entertainments we gave every day. By this time, my wife and two youngest daughters had come over to London, and I hired furnished lodgings in the suburbs where they could live within the strictest limits of economy. It was necessary now for me to return for a few weeks to America, to assist personally in forwarding a settlement of the clock difficulties. So, leaving the little General in the hands of trusty and competent agents to carry on the exhibitions in my absence, I set my face once more towards home and the west, and took steamer at Liverpool for New York.

The trip, like most of the passages which I have made across the Atlantic, was an exceedingly pleasant one. These frequent voyages were to me the rests, the reliefs from almost unremitting industry, anxiety, and care, and I always managed to have more or less fun on board ship every time I crossed the ocean. During the present trip, for amusement and to pass away the time, the passengers got up a number of mock trials, which afforded a vast deal of fun. A judge was selected, jurymen drawn, prisoners arraigned, counsel employed, and all the formalities of a court established. I have the vanity to think that if my good fortune had directed me to that profession, I should have made a very fair lawyer, for I have always had a great fondness for debate and especially for the cross-examination of witnesses, unless that witness was P.T. Barnum in examination under supplementary proceedings at the instance of some note-shaver, who had bought a clock note at a discount of thirty-six per cent. In this mock court, I was unanimously chosen as prosecuting attorney, and, as the court was established expressly to convict, I had no difficulty in carrying the jury and securing the punishment of the prisoner. A small fine was generally imposed, and the fund thus collected was given to a poor sailor boy who had fallen from the mast and broken his leg.

After several of these trials had been held, a dozen or more of the passengers secretly put their heads together and resolved to place the " showman " on trial for his life. An indictment, covering twenty pages, was drawn up by several legal gentlemen among the passengers, charging him with being the Prince of Humbugs, and enumerating a dozen special counts, containing charges of the most absurd and ridiculous description. Witnesses were then brought together, and privately instructed what to say and do. Two or three days were devoted to arranging this mighty prosecution. When everything was ready, I was arrested, and the formidable indictment read to me. I saw at a glance that time and talent had been brought into requisition, and that my trial was to be more elaborate than any that had preceded it. I asked for half an hour to prepare for my defense, which was granted. Meanwhile, seats were arranged to accommodate the court and spectators, and extra settees were placed for the ladies on the upper deck, where they could look down, see and hear all that transpired. Curiosity was on tip-toe, for it was evident that this was to be a long, exciting and laughable trial. At the end of half an hour the judge was on the bench, the jury had taken their places; the witnesses were ready; the counsel for the prosecution, four in number, with pens, ink, and paper in profusion, were seated, and everything seemed ready. I was brought in by a special constable, the indictment read, and I was asked to plead guilty, or not guilty. I rose, and in a most solemn manner, stated that I could not conscientiously plead guilty or not guilty; that I had, in fact, committed many of the acts charged in the indictment, but these acts, I was ready to show, were not criminal, but on the contrary, worthy of praise. My plea was received and the first witness called.

He testified to having visited the prisoner's Museum, and of being humbugged by the Feejee Mermaid; the nurse of Washington; and by other curiosities natural and unnatural. The questions and answers having been all arranged in advance, everything worked smoothly. Acting as my own counsel, I cross-examined the witness by simply asking whether he saw anything else in the Museum besides what he had mentioned.

"Oh! yes, I saw thousands of other things."

"Were they curious?"

"Certainly; many of them very astonishing."

"Did you witness a dramatic representation in the Museum?"

"Yes, sir, a very good one."

"What did you pay for all this?"

"Twenty-five cents."

"That will do, sir; you can step down."

A second, third and fourth witness were called, and the examination was similar to the foregoing. Another witness then appeared to testify in regard to another count in the indictment. He stated that for several weeks he was the guest of the prisoner, at his country residence, *Iranistan*, and he gave a most amusing description of the various schemes and contrivances which were there originated, for the purpose of being carried out at some future day in the Museum.

"How did you live there?" asked one of the counsel for the prosecution.

"Very well, indeed, in the daytime," was the reply; "plenty of the best to eat and drink, except liquors. In bed, however, it was impossible to sleep. I rose the first night, struck a light, and on examination found myself covered with myriads of little bugs, so small as to be almost imperceptible. By using my microscope, I discovered them to be infantile bedbugs. After the first night I was obliged to sleep in the coach-house in order to escape this annoyance."

Of course, this elicited much mirth. The first question put on the cross-examination was this:

"Are you a naturalist, sir?"

The witness hesitated. In all the drilling that had taken place before the trial, neither the counsel nor witnesses had thought of what questions might come up in the cross-examination, and now, not seeing the drift of the question, the witness seemed a little bewildered, and the counsel for the prosecution looked puzzled.

The question was repeated with some emphasis.

"No, sir! " replied the witness, hesitatingly, "I am not a naturalist."

"Then, sir, not being a naturalist, dare you affirm that those microscopic insects were not humbugs instead of bedbugs?" — (here the prisoner was interrupted by a universal shout of laughter, in which the solemn judge himself joined) — "and if they were humbugs, I suppose that even the learned counsel opposed to me, will not claim that they were out of place?"

"They may have been humbugs," replied the witness.

"That will do, sir; you may go," said I; and at the same time, turning to the array of counsel, I remarked, with a smile, " You had better have a naturalist for your next witness, gentlemen."

"Don't be alarmed, sir, we have got one, and we will now introduce him," replied the counsel.

The next witness testified that he was a planter from Georgia, that some years since the prisoner visited his plantation with a show, and that while there he discovered an old worthless donkey belonging to the planter, and bought him for five dollars. The next year the witness visited *Iranistan*, the country seat of the prisoner, and, while walking about the grounds, his old donkey, recognizing his former master, brayed; "whereupon," continued the witness, "I walked up to the animal and found that two men were engaged in sticking wool upon him, and this animal was afterwards exhibited by the prisoner as the woolly horse."

The whole court — spectators, and even the "prisoner" himself, were convulsed with laughter at the gravity with which the planter gave his very ludicrous testimony.

"What evidence have you," I inquired, "that this was the same donkey which you sold to me?"

"The fact that the animal recognized me, as was evident from his braying as soon as he saw me."

"Are you a naturalist, sir?"

"Yes, I am, replied the planter, with firm emphasis, as much as to say, you can't catch me as you did the other witness.

"Oh! you are a naturalist, are you? Then, sir, I ask you, as a naturalist, do you not know it to be a fact in natural history, that one jackass always brays as soon as he sees another?"

This question was received with shouts of laughter, in the midst of which the nonplussed witness backed out of court, and all the efforts of special constables, and even the high sheriff himself, were unavailing in getting him again on the witness stand.

This trial lasted two days, to the great delight of all on board. After my success with the "naturalist," not one-half of the witnesses would appear against me. In my final argument I sifted the testimony, analyzed its bearings, ruffled the learned counsel, disconcerted the witnesses, flattered the judge and jury, and when the judge had delivered his charge, the jury acquitted me without leaving their seats.

The judge received the verdict, and then announced that he should fine the naturalist for the mistake he made, as to the cause of the donkey's braying, and he should also fine the several witnesses, who, through fear of the cross-fire, had refused to testify.

The trial afforded a pleasant topic of conversation for the rest of the voyage; and the morning before arriving in port, a vote of thanks was passed to me, in consideration of the amusement I had intentionally and unintentionally furnished to the passengers during the voyage.

After my arrival in New York, oftentimes, in passing up and down Broadway, I saw old and prosperous friends coming, but before I came anywhere near them, if they espied me, they would dodge into a store, or across the street, or opportunely meet someone with whom they had pressing business, or they would be very much interested in something that was going on over the way, or on top of the City Hall. I was delighted at this, for it gave me at once a new sensation and a new experience.

"Ah, ha!" I said to myself; "my butterfly friends, I know you now; and, what is more to the point, if ever I get out of this bewilderment of broken clock-wheels, I shall not forget you;" and I heartily thanked the old clock concern for giving me the opportunity to learn this sad but most needful lesson. I had a very few of the same sort of experiences in Bridgeport, and they proved valuable to me.

Mr. James D. Johnson, of Bridgeport, one of my assignees, who had written to me that my personal presence might facilitate a settlement of my affairs, told me, soon after my arrival, that there was no probability of disposing of *Iranistan* at present, and that I might as well move my family into the house. I had arrived in August, and my family followed me from London in September, and October 20, 1857, my second daughter, Helen, was married in the house of her elder sister, Mrs. D. W. Thompson, in Bridgeport, to Mr. Samuel H. Hurd.

Meanwhile, *Iranistan*, which had been closed and unoccupied for more than two years, was once more opened to the carpenters and painters whom Mr. Johnson sent there to put the house in order. He agreed with me that it was best to keep the property as long as possible, and in the interval, till a purchaser for the estate appeared, or till it was forced to auction, to take up the clock notes whenever they were offered. The workmen who were employed in the house were specially instructed not to smoke there, but, nevertheless, it was subsequently discovered that some of the men were in the habit occasionally of going into the main dome to eat their dinners which they brought with them, and that they stayed there awhile after dinner to smoke their pipes. In all probability, one of these lighted pipes was left on the cushion which covered the circular seat in the dome and ignited the tow with which the cushion was stuffed. It may have been days and even weeks before this smoldering tow fire burst into flame.

I was staying at the Astor House, in New York, when, on the morning of December 18, 1857, I received a telegram from my brother Philo F. Barnum, dated at Bridgeport, and informing me that *Iranistan* was burned to the ground that morning. The alarm was given at eleven o'clock on the night of the 17th, and the fire burned till one o'clock on the morning of the 18th. My beautiful *Iranistan* was gone! This was not only a serious loss to my estate, for it had probably cost at least $150,000, but it was generally regarded as a public calamity. It was the only building in its peculiar style of architecture of any pretension in America, and many persons visited Bridgeport every year expressly to see *Iranistan*. The insurance on the mansion had usually been about $62,000, but I had let some of the policies expire without renewing them, so that at the time of the fire there was only $28,000 insurance on the property. Most of the furniture and pictures were saved, generally in a damaged state.

Subsequently, my assignees sold the grounds and outhouses of *Iranistan* to the late Elias Howe, Jr., the celebrated inventor of the needle for sewing-machines. The property brought $50,000, which, with the $28,000 insurance, went into my assets to satisfy clock creditors. It was Mr. Howe's intention to erect a splendid mansion on the estate, but his untimely and lamented death prevented the fulfillment of the plan.

CHAPTER XXXI.

THE ART OF MONEY-GETTING.

Seeing the necessity of making more money to assist in extricating me from. my financial difficulties and leaving my affairs in the hands of Mr. James D. Johnson — my wife and youngest daughter, Pauline, boarding with my eldest daughter, Mrs. Thompson, in Bridgeport — early in 1858, I went back to England, and took Tom Thumb to all the principal places in Scotland and Wales, giving many exhibitions and making much money which was remitted, as heretofore, to my agents and assignees in America.

Finding, after a while, that my personal attention was not needed in the Tom Thumb exhibitions and confiding him almost wholly to agents who continued the tour through Great Britain, under my general advice and instruction, I turned my individual attention to a new field. At the suggestion of several American gentlemen, resident in London, I prepared a lecture on "The Art of Money-Getting." I told my friends that, considering my clock complications, I thought I was more competent to speak on "The Art of Money Losing;" but they encouraged me by reminding me that I could not have lost money, if I had not previously possessed the faculty of making it. They further assured me that my name having been intimately associated with the Jenny Lind concerts and other great money-making enterprises, the lecture would be sure to prove attractive and profitable.

The old clocks ticked in my ear the reminder that I should improve every opportunity to "turn an honest penny," and my lecture was duly announced for delivery in the great St. James' Hall, Regent street, Piccadilly. It was thoroughly advertised— a feature I never neglected— and, at the appointed time, the hall, which would hold three thousand people, was completely filled, at prices of three and two shillings (seventy-five and fifty cents), per seat, according to location. It was the evening of December 29, 1858. I could see in my audience all my American friends who had suggested this effort; all my theatrical and literary friends; and as I saw several gentlemen whom I knew to be connected with the leading London papers, I felt sure that my success or failure would be duly chronicled next morning. There was, moreover, a general audience that seemed eager to see the "showman" of whom they had heard so much, and to catch from his lips the "art" which, in times past, had contributed so largely to his success in life. Stimulated by these things, I tried to do my best, and I think I did it. The following is the lecture substantially as it was delivered, though it was interspersed with many anecdotes and illustrations which are necessarily omitted; and I should add, that the subjoined copy being adapted to the meridian in which it has been repeatedly delivered, contains numerous local allusions to men and matters in the United States, which, of course, did not appear in the original draft prepared for my English audiences:

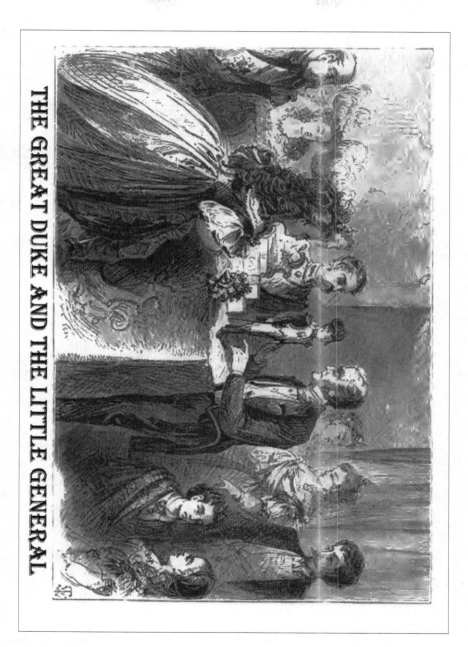

THE GREAT DUKE AND THE LITTLE GENERAL

THE ART OF MONEY-GETTING

In the United States, where we have more land than people, it is not at all difficult for persons in good health to make money. In this comparatively new field there are so many avenues of success open, so many vocations which are not crowded, that any person of either sex who is willing, at least for the time being, to engage in any respectable occupation that offers, may find lucrative employment.

Those who really desire to attain an independence, have only to set their minds upon it, and adopt the proper means, as they do in regard to any other object which they wish to accomplish, and the thing is easily done. But however easy it may be found to make money, I have no doubt many of my hearers will agree it is the most difficult thing in the world to keep it. The road to wealth is, as Dr. Franklin truly says, "as plain as the road to mill" It consists simply in expending less than we earn; that seems to be a very simple problem. Mr. Micawber, one of those happy creations of the genial Dickens, puts the case in a strong fight when he says that to have an income of twenty pounds, per annum, and spend twenty pounds and sixpence, is to be the most miserable of men; whereas, to have an income of only twenty pounds, and spend but nineteen pounds and sixpence, is to be the happiest of mortals. Many of my hearers may say, "we understand this; this is economy, and we know economy is wealth; we know we can't eat our cake and keep it also." Yet I beg to say that perhaps more cases of failure arise from mistakes on this point than almost any other. The fact is, many people think they understand economy when they really do not.

True economy is misapprehended, and people go through life without properly comprehending what that principle is. One bays, "I have an income of so much, and here is my neighbor who has the same; yet every year he gets something ahead and I fall short; why is it? I know all about economy." He thinks he does, but he does not. There are many who think that economy consists in saving cheese-parings and candle-ends, in cutting off two pence from the laundress' bill and doing all sorts of little, mean, dirty things. Economy is not meanness. The misfortune is, also, that this class of persons let their economy apply in only one direction. They fancy they are so wonderfully economical in saving a half-penny where they ought to spend two pence, that they think they can afford to squander in other directions.

A few years ago, before kerosene oil was discovered or thought of, one might stop overnight at almost any farmer's house in the agricultural districts and get a very good supper, but after supper he might attempt to read in the sitting-room, and would find it impossible with the inefficient light of one candle. The hostess, seeing his dilemma, would say: "It is rather difficult to read here evenings; the proverb says 'you must have a ship at sea in order to be able to burn two candles at once;' we never have an extra candle except on extra occasions." These extra occasions occur, perhaps, twice a year. In this way the good woman saves five, six, or ten dollars in that time; but the information which might be derived from having the extra light would, of course, far outweigh a ton of candles.

But the trouble does not end here. Feeling that she is so economical in tallow candles, she thinks she can afford to go frequently to the village and spend twenty or thirty dollars for ribbons and furbelows, many of which are not necessary. This false economy may frequently be seen in men of business, and in those instances, it often runs to writing-paper. You find good business men who save all the old envelopes, and scraps, and would not tear a new sheet of paper, if they could avoid it, for the world. This is all very well; they may in this way save five or ten dollars a year, but being so economical (only in note paper), they think they can afford to waste time to have expensive parties, and to drive their carriages. This is an illustration of Dr. Franklin's "saving at the spigot and wasting at the bung-hole;" "penny wise and pound foolish." Punch in speaking of this "one idea" class of people says "they are like the man who bought a penny herring for his family's dinner and then hired a coach and four to take it home." I never knew a man to succeed by practicing this kind of economy.

True economy consists in always making the income exceed the out-go. Wear the old clothes a little longer if necessary; dispense with the new pair of gloves; mend the old dress; live on plainer food if need be; so that, under all circumstances, unless some unforeseen accident occurs, there will be a margin in favor of the income. A penny here, and a dollar there, placed at interest, goes on accumulating, and in this way the desired result is attained. It requires some training, perhaps, to accomplish this economy, but when once used to it, you will find there is more satisfaction in rational saving, than in irrational spending. Here is a recipe which I recommend; I have found it to work an excellent cure for extravagance, and especially for mistaken economy: When you find that you have no surplus at the end of the year, and yet have a good income, I advise you to take a few sheets of paper and form them into a book and mark down every item of expenditure. Post it every day or week in two columns, one headed "necessaries " or even "comforts," and the other headed "luxuries," and you will find that the latter column will be double, triple, and frequently ten times greater than the former. The real comforts of life cost but a small portion of what most of us can earn. Dr. Franklin says "it is the eyes of others and not our own eyes which ruin us. If all the world were blind except myself I should not care for fine clothes or furniture." It is the fear of what Mrs. Grundy may say that keeps the noses of many worthy families to the grindstone. In America many persons like to repeat "we are all free and equal" but it is a great mistake in more senses than one.

That we are born "free and equal" is a glorious truth in one sense, yet we are not all born equally rich, and we never shall be. One may say, "there is a man who has an income of fifty thousand dollars per annum, while I have but one thousand dollars; I knew that fellow when he was poor like myself, now he is rich and thinks he is better than I am; I will show him that I am as good as he is; I will go and buy a horse and buggy; no, I cannot do that, but I will go and hire one and ride this afternoon on the same road that he does, and thus prove to him that I am as good as he is."

My friend, you need not take that trouble; you can easily prove that you are "as good as he is;" you have only to behave as well as he does; but you cannot make anybody believe that you are rich as he is. Besides, if you put on these "airs," and waste your time and spend your money, your poor wife will be obliged to scrub her fingers off at home, and buy her tea two ounces at a time, and everything else in proportion, in order that you may keep up "appearances," and, after all, deceive nobody. On the other hand, Mrs. Smith may say that her next-door neighbor married Johnson for his money, and "everybody says so." She has a nice one-thousand-dollar camel's hair shawl, and she will make Smith get her an imitation one, and she will sit in a pew right next to her neighbor in church, in order to prove that she is her equal.

My good woman, you will not get ahead in the world, if your vanity and envy thus take the lead. In this country, where we believe the majority ought to rule, we ignore that principle in regard to fashion, and let a handful of people, railing themselves the aristocracy, run up a false standard of perfection, and in endeavoring to rise to that standard, we constantly keep ourselves poor: all the time digging away for the sake of outside appearances. How much wiser to be a "law unto ourselves" and say, "we will regulate our out-go by our income, and lay up something for a rainy day." People ought to be as sensible on the subject of money-getting as on any other subject Like causes produces like effects. You cannot accumulate a fortune by liking the road that leads to poverty. It needs no prophet to tell us that those who live fully up to their means, without any thought of a reverse in this life, can never attain a pecuniary independence.

Men and women accustomed to gratify every whim and caprice, will find it hard, at first, to cut down their various unnecessarily expenses, and will feel it a great self-denial to live in a smaller house than they have been accustomed to, with less expensive furniture, less company, less costly clothing, fewer servants, a less number of balls, parties, theater-goings, carriage-ridings, pleasure excursions, cigar-smokings, liquor-drinkings, and other extravagances; but, after all, if they will try the plan of laying by a "nest-egg," or, in other words, a small sum of money, at interest or judiciously invested in land, they will be surprised at the pleasure to be derived from constantly adding to their little "pile," as well as from all the economical habits which are engendered by this course.

The old suit of clothes, and the old bonnet and dress, will answer for another season; the Croton or spring water will taste better than champagne; a cold bath and a brisk walk will prove more exhilarating than a ride in the finest coach; a social chat, an evening's reading in the family circle, or an hour's play of "hunt the slipper" and "blind man's buff," will be far more pleasant than a fifty or five hundred dollar party, when the reflection on the difference in cost is indulged in by those who begin to know the pleasures of saving. Thousands of men are kept poor, and tens of thousands are made so after they have acquired quite sufficient to support them well through life, in consequence of laying their plans of living on too broad a platform. Some families expend twenty thousand dollars per annum, and some much more, and would scarcely know how to live on less, while others secure more solid enjoyment frequently on a twentieth part of that amount. Prosperity is a more severe ordeal than adversity, especially sudden prosperity. "Easy come, easy go," is an old and true proverb. A spirit of pride and vanity, when permitted to have full sway, is the undying canker-worm which gnaws the very vitals of a man's worldly possessions, let them be small or great, hundreds or millions. Many persons, as they begin to prosper, immediately expand their ideas and commence expending for luxuries, until in a short time their expenses swallow up their income, and they become ruined in their ridiculous attempts to keep up appearances, and make a "sensation."

I know a gentleman of fortune who says, that when he first began to prosper, his wife would have a new and elegant sofa. "That sofa," he says, "cost me thirty thousand dollars! " When the sofa reached the house, it was found necessary to get chairs to match; then side-boards, carpets and tables "to correspond" with them, and so on through the entire stock of furniture ; when at last it was found that the house itself was quite too small and old-fashioned for the furniture, and a new one was built to correspond with the new purchases; "thus," added my friend, "summing up an outlay of thirty thousand dollars, caused by that single sofa, and saddling on me, in the shape of servants, equipage, and the necessary expenses attendant upon keeping up a fine 'establishment,' a yearly outlay of eleven thousand dollars, and a tight pinch at that; whereas, ten years ago, we lived with much more real comfort, because with much less care, on as many hundreds. "The truth is," he continued, "that sofa would have brought me to inevitable bankruptcy, had not a most unexampled tide of prosperity kept me above it, and had I not checked the natural desire to 'cut a dash.'"

The foundation of success in life is good health; that is the substratum of fortune; it is also the basis of happiness. A person cannot accumulate a fortune very well when he is sick. He has no ambition; no incentive; no force. Of course, there are those who have bad health and cannot help it; you cannot expect that such persons can accumulate wealth; but there are a great many in poor health who need not be so.

If, then, sound health is the foundation of success and happiness in life, how important it is that we should study the laws of health, which is but another expression for the laws of nature! The closer we keep to the laws of nature, the nearer we are to good health, and yet how many persons there are who pay no attention to natural laws, but absolutely transgress them, even against their own natural inclination. We ought to know that the "sin of ignorance" is never winked at in regard to the violation of nature's laws: their infraction always brings the penalty. A child may thrust its finger into the flames without knowing it will burn, and so suffers, repentance, even, will not stop the smart.

Many of our ancestors knew very little about the principle of ventilation. They did not know much about oxygen, whatever other "gin" they might have been acquainted with; and consequently, they built their houses with little seven-by-nine feet bedrooms, and these good old pious Puritans would lock themselves up in one of these cells, say their prayers and go to bed. In the morning they would devoutly return thanks for the "preservation of their lives," during the night, and nobody had better reason to be thankful. Probably some big crack in the window, or in the door, let in a little fresh air, and thus saved them.

Many persons knowingly violate the laws of nature against their better impulses, for the sake of fashion. For instance, there is one thing that nothing living except a vile worm ever naturally loved, and that is tobacco; yet how many persons there are who deliberately train an unnatural appetite, and overcome this implanted aversion for tobacco, to such a degree that they get to love it. They have got hold of a poisonous, filthy weed, or rather that takes a firm hold of them. Here are married men who run about spitting tobacco juice on the carpet and floors, and sometimes even upon their wives besides. They do not kick their wives out of doors like drunken men, but their wives, I have no doubt, often wish they were outside of the house.

Another perilous feature is that this artificial appetite, like jealousy, "grows by what it feeds on;" when you love that which is unnatural, a stronger appetite is created for the hurtful thing than the natural desire for what is harmless. There is an old proverb which says that "habit is second nature," but an artificial habit is stronger than nature. Take for instance, an old tobacco-chewer; his love for the "quid' is stronger than his love for any particular kind of food. He can give up roast beef easier than give up the weed.

Young lads regret that they are not men; they would like to go to bed boys and wake up men; and to accomplish this they copy the bad habits of their seniors. Little Tommy and Johnny see their fathers or uncles smoke a pipe, and they say, "If I could only do that, I would be a man too; uncle John has gone out and left his pipe of tobacco, let us try it." They take a match and fight it, and then puff away. "We will learn to smoke; do you like it Johnny?" That lad dolefully replies: "Not very much; it tastes bitter;" by and by he grows pale, but he persists and he soon offers up a sacrifice on the altar of fashion; but the boys stick to it and persevere until at last they conquer their natural appetites and become the victims of acquired tastes.

I speak "by the book," for I have noticed its effects on myself, having gone so far as to smoke ten or fifteen cigars a day, although I have not used the during the last fourteen years, and never shall again. The more a man smokes, the more he craves smoking; the last cigar smoked simply excites the desire for another, and so on incessantly.

Take the tobacco-chewer. In the morning, when he gets up, he puts a quid in his mouth and keeps it there all day, never taking it out except to exchange it for a fresh one, or when he is going to eat; oh! yes, at intervals during the day and evening, many a chewer takes out the quid and holds it in his hand long enough to take a drink, and then pop it goes back again. This simply proves that the appetite for rum is even stronger than that for tobacco. When the tobacco-chewer goes to your country seat and you show him your grapery and fruit house, and the beauties of your garden, when you offer him some fresh, ripe fruit, and say, "My friend, I have got here the most delicious apples, and pears, and peaches, and apricots ; I have imported them from Spain, France and Italy — just see those luscious grapes; there is nothing more delicious nor more healthy than ripe fruit, so help yourself; I want to see you delight yourself with these things;" he will roll the dear quid under his tongue and answer, "No, I thank you, I have got tobacco in my mouth." His palate has become narcotized by the noxious weed, and he has lost, in a great measure, the delicate and enviable taste for fruits. This shows what expensive, useless and injurious habits men will get into. I speak from experience. I have smoked until I trembled like an aspen leaf, the blood rushed to my head, and I had a palpitation of the heart which I thought was heart disease, till I was almost killed with fright. When I consulted my physician, he said "break off tobacco using." I was not only injuring my health and spending a great deal of money, but I was setting a bad example. I obeyed his counsel. No young man in the world ever looked so beautiful, as he thought he did, behind a fifteen-cent cigar or a meerschaum!

These remarks apply with tenfold force to the use of intoxicating drinks. To make money requires a clear brain. A man has got to see that two and two make four; he must lay all his plans with reflection and forethought, and closely examine all the details and the ins and outs of business. As no man can succeed in business unless he has a brain to enable him to lay his plans, and reason to guide him in their execution, so, no matter how bountifully a man may be blessed with intelligence, if the brain is muddled, and his judgment warped by intoxicating drinks, it is impossible for him to carry on business successfully. How many good opportunities have passed, never to return, while a man was sipping a "social glass," with his friend! How many foolish bargains have been made under the influence of the "nervine," which temporarily makes its victim think he is rich. How many important chances have been put off until tomorrow, and then forever, because the wine cup has thrown the system into a state of lassitude, neutralizing the energies so essential to success in business. Verily, "wine is a mocker." The use of intoxicating drinks as a beverage, is as much an infatuation, as is the smoking of opium by the Chinese, and the former is quite as destructive to the success of the business man as the latter. It is an unmitigated evil, utterly indefensible in the light of philosophy, religion or good sense. It is the parent of nearly every other evil in our country.

Don't Mistake your Vocation. — The safest plan, and the one most sure of success for the young man starting in life, is to select the vocation which is most congenial to his tastes. Parents and guardians are often quite too negligent in regard to this. It is very common for a father to say, for example: "I have five boys. I will make Billy a clergyman; John a lawyer; Tom a doctor, and Dick a farmer." He then goes into town and looks about to see what he will do with Sammy. He returns home and says "Sammy, I see watch-making is a nice, genteel business; I think I will make you a goldsmith." He does this, regardless of Sam's natural inclinations, or genius.

We are all, no doubt, born for a wise purpose. There is as much diversity in our brains as in our countenances. Some are born natural mechanics, while some have great aversion to machinery. Let a dozen boys of ten years get together, and you will soon observe two or three are "whittling" out some ingenious device; working with locks or complicated machinery. When they were but five years old, their father could find no toy to please them like a puzzle. They are natural mechanics; but the other eight or nine boys have different aptitudes. I belong to the latter class; I never had the slightest love for mechanism; on the contrary, I have a sort of abhorrence for complicated machinery. I never had ingenuity enough to whittle a cider tap so it would not leak. I never could make a pen that I could write with, or understand the principle of a steam engine. If a man was to take such a boy as I was, and attempt to make a watchmaker of him, the boy might, after an apprenticeship of five or seven years, be able to take apart and put together a watch; but all through life he would be working up hill and seizing every excuse for leaving his work and idling away his time. Watch-making is repulsive to him.

Unless a man enters upon the vocation intended for him by nature, and best suited to his peculiar genius, he cannot succeed. I am glad to believe that the majority of persons do find their right vocation. Yet we see many who have mistaken their calling, from the blacksmith up (or down) to the clergyman. You will see, for instance, that extraordinary linguist the "learned blacksmith," who ought to have been a teacher of languages; and you may have seen lawyers, doctors and clergymen who were better fitted by nature for the anvil or the lapstone.

Select the Right Location. — After securing the right vocation, you must be careful to select the proper location. You may have been cut out for a hotel keeper, and they say it requires a genius to "know how to keep a hotel." You might conduct a hotel like clock-work, and provide satisfactorily for five hundred guests every day; yet, if you should locate your house in a small village where there is no railroad communication or public travel, the location would be your ruin. It is equally important that you do not commence business where there are already enough to meet all demands in the same occupation. I remember a case which illustrates this subject. When I was in London in 1858, I was passing down Holborn with an English friend and came to the "penny shows." They had immense cartoons outside, portraying the wonderful curiosities to be seen "all for a penny." Being a little in the "show line" myself, I said "let us go in here." We soon found ourselves in the presence of the illustrious showman, and he proved to be the sharpest man in that line I had ever met. He told us some extraordinary stories in reference to his bearded ladies, his Albinos, and his Armadillos, which we could hardly believe, but thought it "better to believe it than look after the proof." He finally begged to call our attention to some wax statuary and showed us a lot of the dirtiest and filthiest wax figures imaginable. They looked as if they had not seen water since the Deluge.

"What is there so wonderful about your statuary?" I asked.

"I beg you not to speak so satirically, he replied, "Sir, these are not Madam Tussaud's wax figures, all covered with gilt and tinsel and imitation diamonds, and copied from engravings and photographs. Mine, sir, were taken from life. "Whenever you look upon one of those figures, you may consider that you are looking upon the living individual."

Glancing casually at them, I saw one labelled "Henry VIII.," and feeling a little curious upon seeing that it looked like Calvin Edson, the living skeleton, I said:

"Do you call that Henry the Eighth?"'

He replied, "Certainly, sir; it was taken from life at Hampton Court, by special order of his majesty, on such a day."

He would have given the hour of the day if I had insisted; I said, "Everybody knows that 'Henry VIII.' was a great stout old king, and that figure is lean and lank; what do you say to that?"

"Why," he replied, "you would be lean and lank yourself, if you sat there as long as he has."

There was no resisting such arguments. I said to my English friend, "Let us go out; do not tell him who I am; I show the white feather; he beats me."

He followed us to the door, and seeing the rabble in the street, he called out, "ladies and gentlemen, I beg to draw your attention to the respectable character of my visitors," pointing to us as we walked away. I called upon him a couple of days afterwards; told him who I was, and said:

"My friend, you are an excellent showman, but you have selected a bad location."

He replied, "This is true, sir; I feel that all my talents are thrown away; but what can I do? "

"You can go to America," I replied. " You can give full play to your faculties over there; you will find plenty of elbow-room in America; I will engage you for two years; after that you will be able to go on your own account."

He accepted my offer and remained two years in my New York Museum. He then went to New Orleans and carried on a traveling show business during the summer. Today he is worth sixty thousand dollars, simply because he selected the right vocation and also secured the proper location. The old proverb says, "Three removes are as bad as a fire," but when a man is in the fire, it matters but little how soon or how often he removes.

Avoid Debt. — Young men starting in Life should avoid running into debt. There is scarcely anything that drags a person down like debt. It is a slavish position to get in, yet we find many a young man, hardly out of his "teens," running in debt. He meets a chum and says, "Look at this: I have got trusted for a new suit of clothes." He seems to look upon the clothes as so much given to him; well, it frequently is so, but, if he succeeds in paying and then gets trusted again. he is adopting a habit which will keep him in poverty through Life. Debt robs a man of his self-respect, and makes him almost despise himself. Granting and groaning and working for what he has eaten up or worn out, and now when he is called upon to pay up, he has nothing to show for his money; this is properly termed "working for a dead horse." I do not speak of merchants buying and selling on credit, or of those who buy on credit in order to turn the purchase to a profit. The old Quaker said to his farmer son, "John, never get trusted; but if thee gets trusted for anything, let it be for 'manure,' because that will help thee pay it back again,"

Mr. Beecher advised young men to get in debt if they could to a small amount in the purchase of land, in the country districts. "If a young man," he says, "will only get in debt for some land and then get married, these two things will keep him straight, or nothing will." This may be safe to a limited extent, but getting in debt for what you eat and drink and wear is to be avoided. Some families have a foolish habit of getting credit at "the stores," and thus frequently purchase many things which might have been dispensed with.

It is all very well to say, "I have got trusted for sixty days, and if I don't have the money the creditor will think nothing about it." There is no class of people in the world, who have such good memories as creditors. When the sixty days run out, you will have to pay. If you do not pay, you will break your promise, and probably resort to a falsehood. You may make some excuse or get in debt elsewhere to pay it, but that only involves you the deeper.

A good-looking, lazy young fellow, was the apprentice boy, Horatio. His employer said, "Horatio, did you ever see a snail?" "I — think — I — have," he drawled out. "You must have met him then, for I am sure you never overtook one," said the "boss." Your creditor will meet you or overtake you and say, " Now, my young friend, you agreed to pay me; you have not done it, you must give me your note." You give the note on interest and it commences working against you; "it is a dead horse." The creditor goes to bed at night and wakes up in the morning better off than when he retired to bed, because his interest has increased during the night, but you grow poorer while you are sleeping, for the interest is accumulating against you.

Money is in some respects like fire; it is a very excellent servant but a terrible master. When you have it mastering you; when interest is constantly piling up against you, it will keep you down in the worst kind of slavery. But let money work for you, and you have the most devoted servant in the world. It is no "eye- servant." There is nothing animate or inanimate that will work so faithfully as money when placed at interest, well secured. It works night and day, and in wet or dry weather.

I was born in the blue-law State of Connecticut, where the old Puritans had laws so rigid that it was said, "they fined a man for kissing his wife on Sunday." Yet these rich old Puritans would have thousands of dollars at interest, and on Saturday night would be worth a certain amount; on Sunday they would go to church and perform all the duties of a Christian. On waking up on Monday morning, they would find themselves considerably richer than the Saturday night previous, simply because their money placed at interest had worked faithfully for them all day Sunday, according to law!

Do not let it work against you; if you do there is no chance for success in life so far as money is concerned. John Randolph, the eccentric Virginian, once exclaimed in Congress, "Mr. Speaker, I have discovered the philosopher's stone: pay as you go." This is, indeed, nearer to the philosopher's stone than any alchemist has ever yet arrived.

Persevere. — When a man is in the right path, he must persevere. I speak of this because there are some persons who are "born tired;" naturally lazy and possessing no self-reliance and no perseverance. But they can cultivate these qualities, as Davy Crockett said:

> "This thing remember, when I am dead,
> Be sure you are right, then go ahead."

It is this go-aheaditiveness, this determination not to let the "horrors" or the "blues" take possession of you, so as to make you relax your energies in the struggle for independence, which you must cultivate.

How many have almost reached the goal of their ambition, but, losing faith in themselves, have relaxed their energies, and the golden prize has been lost forever.

It is, no doubt, often true, as Shakespeare says:

> "There is a tide in the affairs of men,
> Which, taken at the flood, leads on to fortune."

If you hesitate, some bolder hand will stretch out before you and get the prize. Remember the proverb of Solomon: "He becometh poor that dealeth with a slack hand; but the hand of the diligent maketh rich."

Perseverance is sometimes but another word for self-reliance. Many persons naturally look on the dark side of life, and borrow trouble. They are born so. Then they ask for advice, and they will be governed by one wind and blown by another, and cannot rely upon themselves. Until you can get so that you can rely upon yourself, you need not expect to succeed I have known men, personally, who have met with pecuniary reverses, and absolutely committed suicide, because they thought they could never overcome their misfortune. But I have known others who have met more serious financial difficulties, and have bridged them over by simple perseverance, aided by a firm belief that they were doing justly, and that Providence would "overcome evil with good." You will see this illustrated in any sphere of life.

Take two generals; both understand military tactics, both educated at West Point, if you please, both equally gifted; yet one, having this principle of perseverance, and the other lacking it, the former will succeed in his profession, while the latter will fail One may hear the cry, "the enemy are coming, and they have got cannon."

"Got cannon? " says the hesitating general.

"Yes."

"Then halt every man."

He wants time to reflect; his hesitation is his ruin; the enemy passes unmolested, or overwhelms him; while on the other hand, the general of pluck, perseverance and self-reliance, goes into battle with a will, and, amid the clash of arms, the booming of cannon, the shrieks of the wounded, and the moans of the dying, you will see this man persevering, going on, cutting and slashing his way through with unwavering determination, inspiring his soldiers to deeds of fortitude, valor and triumph.

"Whatever you do, do it with all your might. — Work at it, if necessary, early and late, in season and out of season, not leaving a stone unturned, and never deferring for a single hour that which can be done just as well now. The old proverb is full of truth and meaning, "Whatever is worth doing at all, is worth doing well." Many a man acquires a fortune by doing his business thoroughly, while his neighbor remains poor for life, because he only half does it. Ambition, energy, industry, perseverance, are indispensable requisites for success in business.

Fortune always favors the brave, and never helps a man who does not help himself. It won't do to spend your time like Mr. Micawber, in waiting for some- thing to "turn up." To such men one of two things usually "turns up:" the poor-house or the jail; for idleness breeds bad habits, and clothes a man in rags. The poor spendthrift vagabond said to a rich man:

"I have discovered there is money enough in the world for all of us, if it was equally divided; this must be done, and we shall all be happy together."

"But." was the response, "if everybody was like you, it would be spent in two months, and what would you do then? "

"Oh! divide again; keep dividing, of course!"

I was recently reading in a London paper an account of a like philosophic pauper who was kicked out of a cheap boarding-house because he could not pay his bill, but he had a roll of papers sticking out of his coat pocket, which, upon examination, proved to be his plan for paying off the national debt of England without the aid of a penny. People have got to do as Cromwell said: "not only trust in Providence, but keep the powder dry." Do your part of the work, or you cannot succeed. Mahomet, one night, while encamping in the desert, overheard one of his fatigued followers remark: "I will loose my camel, and trust it to God." "No, no, not so," said the prophet, "tie thy camel, and trust it to God!" Do all you can for yourselves, and then trust to Providence, or luck, or whatever you please to call it, for the rest.

Depend upon your own personal exertions. — The eye of the employer is often worth more than the hands of a dozen employees. In the nature of things, an agent cannot be so faithful to his employer as to himself. Many who are employers will call to mind instances where the best employees have overlooked important points which could not have escaped their own observation as a proprietor. No man has a right to expect to succeed in life unless he understands his business, and nobody can understand his business thoroughly unless he learns it by personal application and experience. A man may be a manufacturer; he has got to learn the many details of his business personally; he will learn something every day, and he will find he will make mistakes nearly every day. And these very mistakes are helps to him in the way of experiences if he but heeds them. He will be like the Yankee tin-peddler, who, having been cheated as to quality in the purchase of his merchandise, said: "All right, there's a little information to be gained every day; I will never be cheated in that way again." Thus, a man buys his experience, and it is the best kind if not purchased at too dear a rate.

I hold that every man should, like Cuvier, the French naturalist, thoroughly know his business. So proficient was he in the study of natural history, that you might bring to him the bone, or even a section of a bone of an animal which he had never seen described, and, reasoning from analogy, he would be able to draw a picture of the object from which the bone had been taken. On one occasion his students attempted to deceive him. They rolled one of their number in a cow skin and put him under the professor's table as a new specimen. When the philosopher came into the room, some of the students asked him what animal it was. Suddenly the animal said "I am the devil and I am going to eat you." It was but natural that Cuvier should desire to classify this creature, and, examining it intently, he said:

"Divided hoof; graminivorous! it cannot be done."

He knew that an animal with a split hoof must live upon grass and grain, or other kind of vegetation, and would not be inclined to eat flesh, dead or alive, so he considered himself perfectly safe. The possession of a perfect knowledge of your business is an absolute necessity in order to insure success.

Among the maxims of the elder Rothschild was one, an apparent paradox: "Be cautious and bold." This seems to be a contradiction in terms, but it is not, and there is great wisdom in the maxim. It is, in fact, a condensed statement of what I have already said. It is to say, "you must exercise your caution in laying your plans, but be bold in carrying them out." A man who is all caution, will never dare to take hold and be successful, and a man who is all boldness, is merely reckless, and must eventually fail. A man may go on "'change" and make fifty or one hundred thousand dollars in speculating in stocks, at a single operation. But if he has simple boldness without caution, it is mere chance, and what he gains today he will lose tomorrow. You must have both the caution and the boldness, to insure success.

The Rothschilds have another maxim: "Never have anything to do with an unlucky man or place." That is to say, never have anything to do with a man or place which never succeeds, because, although a man may appear to be honed; and intelligent, yet if he tries this or that thing and always fails, it is on account of some fault or infirmity that you may not be able to discover, but nevertheless which must exist.

There is no such thing in the world as luck. There never was a man who could go out in the morning and find a purse full of gold in the street today, and another tomorrow, and so on, day after day. He may do so once in his life; but so far as mere luck is concerned, he is as liable to lose it as to find it. "Like causes produce like effects." If a man adopts the proper methods to be successful, "luck" will not prevent him. If he does not succeed, there are reasons for it, although, perhaps, he may not be able to see them.

Use the best tools. — Men in engaging employees should be careful to get the best. Understand, you cannot have too good tools to work with, and there is no tool you should be so particular about as living tools. If you get a good one, it is better to keep him, than keep changing. He learns something today, and you are benefited by the experience he acquires. He is worth more to you this year than last, and he is the last man to part with, provided his habits are good, and he continues faithful. If, as he gets more valuable, he demands an exorbitant increase of salary, on the supposition that you can't do without him, let him go. Whenever I have such an employee, I always discharge him; first, to convince him that his place may be supplied, and second, because he is good for nothing if he thinks he is invaluable and cannot be spared.

But I would keep him, if possible, in order to profit from the result of his experience. An important element in an employee is the brain. You can see bills up, "Hands Wanted," but "hands" are not worth a great deal without "heads." Mr. Beecher illustrates this, in this wise:

An employee offers his services by saying, "I have a pair of hands and one of my fingers thinks." "That is very good," says the employer. Another man comes along, and says "he has two fingers that think." "Ah! that is better." But a third calls in and says that "all his fingers and thumbs think." That is better still. Finally, another steps in, and says, "I have a brain that thinks; I think all over; I am a thinking as well as a working man!" "You are the man I want," says the delighted employer.

Those men who have brains and experience are therefore the most valuable and not to be readily parted with; it is better for them, as well as yourself, to keep them, at reasonable advances in their salaries from time to time.

Don't get above your business. — Young men after they get through their business training, or apprenticeship, instead of pursuing their avocation and rising in their business, will often he about doing nothing. They say, "I have learned my business, but I am not going to be a hireling; what is the object of learning my trade or profession, unless I establish myself?"

"Have you capital to start with?"

" No, but I am going to have it."

"How are you going to get it?"

"I will tell you confidentially; I have a wealthy old aunt, and she will die pretty soon; but if she does not, I expect to find some rich old man who will lend me a few thousands to give me a start. If I only get the money to start with I will do well."

There is no greater mistake than when a young man believes he will succeed with borrowed money. Why? Because every man's experience coincides with that of Mr. Astor, who said, "it was more difficult for him to accumulate his first thousand dollars, than all the succeeding millions that made up his colossal fortune." Money is good for nothing unless you know the value of it by experience. Give a boy twenty thousand dollars and put him in business, and the chances are that he will lose every dollar of it before he is a year older. Like buying a ticket in the lottery, and drawing a prize, it is "easy come, easy go." He does not know the value of it; nothing is worth anything, unless it costs effort Without self-denial and economy, patience and perseverance, and commencing with capital which you have not earned, you are not sure to succeed in accumulating. Young men, instead of "waiting for dead men's shoes," should be up and doing, for there is no class of persons who are so unaccommodating in regard to dying as these rich old people, and it is fortunate for the expectant heirs that it is so. Nine out of ten of the rich men of our country today, started out in life as poor boys, with determined wills, industry, perseverance, economy and good habits. They went on gradually, made their own money and saved it; and this is the best way to acquire a fortune.

Stephen Girard started life as a poor cabin boy, and died worth nine million dollars, A.T. Stewart was a poor Irish boy; now he pays taxes on a million and a half dollars of income, per year. John Jacob Astor was a poor farmer boy, and died worth twenty millions. Cornelius Vanderbilt began life rowing a boat from Staten Island to New York; now he presents our government with a steamship worth a million of dollars, and he is worth fifty millions. "There is no royal road to learning," says the proverb, and I may say it is equally time, "there is no royal road to wealth." But I think there is a royal road to both. The road to learning is a royal one; the road that enables the student to expand his intellect and add every day to his stock of knowledge, until in the pleasant process of intellectual growth, he is able to solve the most profound problems, to count the stars, to analyze every atom of the globe, and to measure the firmament — this is a regal highway, and it is the only road worth traveling.

So, in regard to wealth. Go on in confidence, study the rules, and above all things, study human nature; for "the proper study of mankind is man," and you will find that while expanding the intellect and the muscles, your enlarged experience will enable you every day to accumulate more and more principal, which will increase itself by interest and otherwise, until you arrive at a state of independence. You will find, as a general thing, that the poor boys get rich and the rich boys get poor. For instance, a rich man at his decease, leaves a large estate to his family. His eldest sons, who have helped him earn his fortune, know by experience the value of money, and they take their inheritance and add to it. The separate portions of the young children are placed at interest, and the little fellows are patted on the head, and told a dozen times a day, "you are rich; you will never have to work, you can always have whatever you wish, for you were born with a golden spoon in your mouth." The young heir soon finds out what that means; he has the finest dresses and playthings; he is crammed with sugar candies and almost "killed with kindness," and he passes from school to school, petted and flattered. He becomes arrogant and self-conceited, abuses his teachers, and carries everything with a high hand. He knows nothing of the real value of money, having never earned any; but he knows all about the "golden spoon" business. At college, he invites his poor fellow-students to his room, where he "wines and dines " them. He is cajoled and caressed, and called a glorious good fellow, because he is so lavish of his money. He gives his game suppers, drives his fast horses, invites his chums to fetes and parties, determined to have lots of "good times." He spends the night in frolics and debauchery, and leads off his companions with the familiar song, "we won't go home till morning." He gets them to join him in pulling down signs, taking gates from their hinges and throwing them into back yards and horse-ponds. If the police arrest them, he knocks them down, is taken to the lock-up, and joyfully foots the bills.

THE MUSEUM BUILDING

"Ah! my boys," he cries, "what is the use of being rich, if you can't enjoy yourself?"

He might more truly say, "if you can't make a fool of yourself;" but he is "fast," hates slow things, and don't "see it." Young men loaded down with other people's money are almost sure to lose all they inherit, and they acquire all sorts of bad habits which, in the majority of cases, ruin them in health, purse and character. In this country, one generation follows another, and the poor of today are rich in the next generation, or the third. Their experience leads them on, and they become rich, and they leave vast riches to their young children. These children, having been reared in luxury, are inexperienced and get poor; and after long experience another generation comes on and gathers up riches again in turn. And thus "history repeats itself," and happy is he who by listening to the experience of others avoids the rocks and shoals on which so many have been wrecked.

"In England, the business makes the man." If a man in that country is a mechanic or working-man, he is not recognized as a gentleman. On the occasion of my first appearance before Queen Victoria, the Duke of Wellington asked me what sphere in life General Tom Thumb's parents were in.

"His father is a carpenter," I replied.

"Oh! I had heard he was a gentleman," was the response of His Grace.

In this Republican country, the man makes the business. No matter whether he is a blacksmith, a shoemaker, a farmer, banker or lawyer, so long as his business is legitimate, he may be a gentleman. So, any "legitimate" business is a double blessing — it helps the man engaged in it, and also helps others. The farmer supports his own family, but he also benefits the merchant or mechanic who needs the products of his farm. The tailor not only makes a living by his trade, but he also benefits the farmer, the clergyman and others who cannot make their own clothing. But all these classes of men may be gentlemen.

The great ambition should be to excel all others engaged in the same occupation.

The college-student who was about graduating, said to an old lawyer:

"I have not yet decided which profession I will follow. Is your profession full?"

"The basement is much crowded, but there is plenty of room upstairs," was the witty and truthful reply.

No profession, trade, or calling, is overcrowded in the upper story. Wherever you find the most honest and intelligent merchant or banker, or the best lawyer, the best doctor, the best clergyman, the best shoemaker, carpenter, or anything else, that man is most sought for, and has always enough to do. As a nation, Americans are too superficial — they are striving to get rich quickly, and do not generally do their business as substantially and thoroughly as they should, but whoever excels all others in his own line, if his habits are good and his integrity undoubted, cannot fail to secure abundant patronage, and the wealth that naturally follows. Let your motto then always be "Excelsior," for by living up to it there is no such word as fail.

Learn something useful. — Every man should make his son or daughter learn some trade or profession, so that in these days of changing fortunes — of being rich today and poor tomorrow — they may have something tangible to fall back upon. This provision might save many persons from misery, who by some unexpected turn of fortune have lost all their means.

Let hope predominate but be not too visionary. — Many persons are always kept poor, because they are too visionary. Every project looks to them like certain success, and therefore they keep changing from one business to another, always in hot water, always "under the harrow." The plan of "counting the chickens before they are hatched" is an error of ancient date, but it does not seem to improve by age.

Do not scatter your powers. — Engage in one kind of business only, and stick to it faithfully until you succeed, or until your experience shows that you should abandon it. A constant hammering on one nail will generally drive it home at last, so that it can be clinched. When a man's undivided attention is centered on one object, his mind will constantly be suggesting improvements of value, which would escape him if his brain was occupied by a dozen different subjects at once. Many a fortune has slipped through a man's fingers because he was engaged in too many occupations at a time. There is good sense in the old caution against having too many irons in the fire at once.

Be systematic. — Men should be systematic in their business. A person who does business by rule, having a time and place for everything, doing his work promptly, will accomplish twice as much and with half the trouble of him who does it carelessly and slipshod. By introducing system into all your transactions, doing one thing at a time, always meeting appointments with punctuality, you find leisure for pastime and recreation; whereas the man who only half does one thing, and then turns to something else, and half does that, will have his business at loose ends, and will never know when his day's work is done, for it never will be done. Of course, there is a limit to all these rules. We must try to preserve the happy medium, for there is such a thing as being too systematic. There are men and women, for instance, who put away things so carefully that they can never find them again. It is too much like the "red tape" formality at Washington, and Mr. Dickens' "Circumlocution Office," — all theory and no result.

When the "Astor House" was first started in New York city, it was undoubtedly the best hotel in the country. The proprietors had learned a good deal in Europe regarding hotels, and the landlords were proud of the rigid system which pervaded every department of their great establishment. When twelve o'clock at night had arrived, and there were a number of guests around, one of the proprietors would say, "Touch that bell, John;" and in two minutes sixty servants, with a water-bucket in each hand, would present themselves in the hall. "This," said the landlord, addressing his guests, "is our fire-bell; it will show you we are quite safe here; we do everything systematically." This was before the Croton water was introduced into the city. But they sometimes carried their system too far. On one occasion, when the hotel was thronged with guests, one of the waiters was suddenly indisposed, and although there were fifty waiters in the hotel, the landlord thought he must have his full complement, or his "system" would be interfered with. Just before dinner-time, he rushed down stairs and said. "There must be another waiter, I am one waiter abort; what can I do?" He happened to see "Boots," the Irishman. "Pat," said he, "wash your hands and face: take that white apron and come into the dining-room in five minutes." Presently Pat appeared as required, and the proprietor said: "Now Pat, you must stand behind these two chairs, and wait on the gentlemen who will occupy them; did you ever act as a waiter?

"I know all about it, sure, but I never did it."

Like the Irish pilot, on one occasion when the captain, thinking he was considerably out of his course, asked, "Are you certain you understand what you are doing?" Pat replied, "Sure, and I knows every rock in the channel." That moment, "bang" thumped the vessel against a rock. "Ah! be jabers, and that is one of 'em," continued the pilot. But to return to the dining-room. "Pat," said the landlord, "'here we do everything systematically. You must first give the gentlemen each a plate of soup, and when they finish that, ask them what they will have next." Pat replied, "Ah! an' I understand parfectly the vartues of shystem." Very soon in came the guests. The plates of soup were placed before them. One of Pat's two gentlemen ate his soup; the other did not care for it. He said: "Waiter, take this plate away and bring me some fish." Pat looked at the untasted plate of soup, and remembering the injunctions of the landlord in regard to "system," replied: "Not till ye have ate yer supe!"

Of course, that was carrying "system" entirely too far.

READ the newspapers. — Always take a trustworthy newspaper, and thus keep thoroughly posted in regard to the transactions of the world. He who is without a newspaper is cut off from his species. In these days of telegraphs and steam, many important inventions and improvements in every branch of trade, are being made, and he who don't consult the newspapers will soon find himself and his business left out in the cold.

Beware of "outside operations." — We sometimes see men who have obtained fortunes, suddenly become poor. In many cases, this arises from intemperance, and often from gaming, and other bad habits. Frequently it occurs because a man has been engaged in "outside operations," of some sort. When he gets rich in his legitimate business, he is told of a grand speculation where he can make a score of thousands. He is constantly flattered by his friends, who tell him that he is born lucky, that everything he touches turns into gold. Now, if he forgets that his economical habits, his rectitude of conduct and a personal attention to a business which he understood, caused his success in life, he will listen to the siren voices. He says:

"I will put in twenty thousand dollars. I have been lucky, and my good luck will soon bring me back sixty thousand dollars:

A few days elapse and it is discovered he must put in ten thousand dollars more; soon after he is told "it is all right," but certain matters not foreseen, require an advance of twenty thousand dollars more, which will bring him a rich harvest; but before the time comes around to realize, the bubble bursts, he loses all he is possessed of, and then he learns what he ought to have known at the first, that however successful a man may be in his own business, if he turns from that and engages in a business which he don't understand, he is like Samson when shorn of his locks— his strength has departed, and he becomes like other men.

If a man has plenty of money, he ought to invest something in everything that appears to promise success, and that will probably benefit mankind; but let the sums thus invested be moderate in amount, and never let a man foolishly jeopardize a fortune that he has earned in a legitimate way, by investing it in things in which he has had no experience.

Don't endorse without security. — I hold that no man ought ever to endorse a note or become security for any man, be it his father or brother, to a greater extent than he can afford to lose and care nothing about, without taking good security. Here is a man that is worth twenty thousand dollars; he is doing a thriving manufacturing or mercantile trade; you are retired and living on your money; he comes to you and says:

"You are aware that I am worth twenty thousand dollars, and don't owe a dollar; if I had five thousand dollars in cash, I could purchase a particular lot of goods and double my money in a couple of months; will you endorse my note for that amount?"

You reflect that he is worth twenty thousand dollars, and you incur no risk by endorsing his note; you like to accommodate him, and you lend your name without taking the precaution of getting security. Shortly after, he shows you the note with your endorsement canceled, and tells you, probably truly, "that he made the profit that he expected by the operation," you reflect that you have done a good action, and the thought makes you feel happy. By and by, the same thing occurs again and you do it again; you have already fixed the impression in your mind that it is perfectly safe to endorse his notes without security.

But the trouble is, this man is getting money too easily. He has only to take your note to the bank, get it discounted and take the cash. He gets money for the time being without effort; without inconvenience to himself. Now mark the result. He sees a chance for speculation outside of his business. A temporary investment of only $10,000 is required. It is sure to come back before a note at the bank would be due. He places a note for that amount before you. You sign it almost mechanically. Being firmly convinced that your friend is responsible and trustworthy, you endorse his notes as a "matter of course."

Unfortunately, the speculation does not come to a head quite so soon as was expected, and another $10,000 note must be discounted to take up the last one when due. Before this note matures the speculation has proved an utter failure and all the money is lost. Does the loser tell his friend, the endorser, that he has lost half of his fortune? Not at all. He don't even mention that he has speculated at all. But he has got excited; the spirit of speculation has seized him; he sees others making large sums in this way (we seldom hear of the losers), and, like other speculators, he "looks for his money where he loses it." He tries again. Endorsing notes has become chronic with you, and at every loss he gets your signature for whatever amount he wants. Finally, you discover your friend has lost all of his property and all of yours. You are overwhelmed with astonishment and grief, and you say "it is a hard thing; my friend here has ruined me," but, you should add, "I have also ruined him." If you had said in the first place, "I will accommodate you, but I never endorse without taking ample security," he could not have gone beyond the length of his tether, and he would never have been tempted away from his legitimate business. It is a very dangerous thing, therefore, at any time, to let people get possession of money too easily; it tempts them to hazardous speculations, if nothing more. Solomon truly said "he that hateth suretiship is sure."

So, with the young man starting in business; let him understand the value of money by earning it. When he does understand its value, then grease the wheels a little in helping him to start business, but remember, men who get money with too great facility, cannot usually succeed. You must get the first dollars by hard knocks, and at some sacrifice, in order to appreciate the value of those dollars.

Advertise your BUSINESS. — We all depend, more or less, upon the public for our support. We all trade with the public — lawyers, doctors, shoemakers, artists, blacksmiths, showmen, opera singers, railroad presidents, and college professors. Those who deal with the public must be careful that their goods are valuable; that they are genuine, and will give satisfaction. When you get an article which you know is going to please your customers, and that when they have tried it, they will feel they have got their money's worth, then let the fact be known that you have got it. Be careful to advertise it in some shape or other, because it is evident that if a man has ever so good an article for sale, and nobody knows it, it will bring him no return.

In a country like this, where nearly everybody reads, and where newspapers are issued and circulated in editions of five thousand to two hundred thousand, it would be very unwise if this channel was not taken advantage of to reach the public in advertising. A newspaper goes into the family, and is read by wife and children, as well as the head of the house; hence hundreds and thousands of people may read your advertisement, while you are attending to your routine business. Many, perhaps, read it while you are asleep. The whole philosophy of life is, first "sow," then "reap." That is the way the farmer does; he plants his potatoes and corn, and sows his grain, and then goes about something else, and the time comes when he reaps. But he never reaps first and sows afterwards. This principle applies to all kinds of business, and to nothing more eminently than to advertising. If a man has a genuine article, there is no way in which he can reap more advantageously than by "sowing" to the public in this way.

He must, of course, have a really good article, and one which will please his customers; anything spurious will not succeed permanently, because the public is wiser than many imagine. Men and women are selfish, and we all prefer purchasing where we can get the most for our money; and we try to find out where we can most surely do so.

You may advertise a spurious article, and induce many people to call and buy it once, but they will denounce you as an imposter and swindler, and your business will gradually die out and leave you poor. This is right. Few people can safely depend upon chance custom. You all need to have your customers return and purchase again. A man said to me, "I have tried advertising and did not succeed; yet I have a good article."

I replied, " My friend, there may be exceptions to a general rule. But how do you advertise?"

"I put it in a weekly newspaper three times, and paid a dollar and a half for it."

I replied: "Sir, advertising is like learning — 'a little is a dangerous thing!'"

A French writer says that "The reader of a newspaper does not see the first insertion of an ordinary advertisement; the second insertion he sees, but does not read; the third insertion he reads; the fourth insertion, he looks at the price; the fifth insertion, he speaks of it to his wife; the sixth insertion, he is ready to purchase, and the seventh insertion, he purchases." Your object in advertising is to make the public understand what you have got to sell, and if you have not the pluck to keep advertising, until you have imparted that information, all the money you have spent is lost. You are like the fellow who told the gentleman if he would give him ten cents it would save him a dollar. "How can I help you so much with so small a sum?" asked the gentleman in surprise. "I started out this morning (hiccupped the fellow) with the full determination to get drunk, and I have spent my only dollar to accomplish the object, and it has not quite done it. Ten cents worth more of whisky would just do it, and in this manner, I should save the dollar already expended."

So, a man who advertises at all must keep it up until the public know who and what he is, and what his business is, or else the money invested in advertising is lost.

Some men have a peculiar genius for writing a striking advertisement, one that will arrest the attention of the reader at first sight. This tact, of course, gives the advertiser a great advantage. Sometimes a man makes himself popular by a unique sign or a curious display in his window. Recently I observed a swing sign extending over the sidewalk in front of a store, on which was the inscription in plain letters,

"DON'T READ THE OTHER SIDE"

Of course, I did, and so did everybody else, and I learned that the man had made an independence by first attracting the public to his business in that way and then using his customers well afterwards.

Genin, the hatter, bought the first Jenny Lind ticket at auction for two hundred and twenty-five dollars, because he knew it would be a good advertisement for him "Who is the bidder?" said the auctioneer, as he knocked down that ticket at Castle Garden. "Genin, the hatter," was the response. Here were thousands of people from the Fifth avenue, and from distant cities in the highest stations in life. "Who is 'Genin,' the hatter?" they exclaimed. They had never heard of him before. The next morning the newspapers and telegraph had circulated the facts from Maine to Texas, and from five to ten millions of people had read that the tickets sold at auction for Jenny Lind's first concert amounted to about twenty thousand dollars, and that a single ticket was sold at two hundred and twenty-five dollars, to "Genin, the hatter." Men throughout the country involuntarily took off their hats to see if they had a "Genin" hat on their heads. At a town in Iowa it was found that in the crowd around the post-office, there was one man who had a "Genin" hat, and he showed it in triumph, although it was worn out and not worth two cents. "Why." one man exclaimed, "you have a real 'Genin' hat; what a lucky fellow you are." Another man said, "Hang on to that hat, it will be a valuable heirloom in your family." Still another man in the crowd, who seemed to envy the possessor of this good fortune, said, "Come, give us all a chance; put it up at auction!" He did so, and it was sold as a keepsake for nine dollars and fifty cents? What was the consequence to Mr. Genin? He sold ten thousand extra hats per annum, the first six years. Nine-tenths of the purchasers bought of him, probably, out of curiosity, and many of them, finding that he gave them an equivalent for their money, became his regular customers. This novel advertisement first struck their attention, and then, as he made a good article, they came again.

Now, I don't say that everybody should advertise as Mr. Genin did. But I say if a man has got goods for sale, and he don't advertise them in some way, the chances are that someday the sheriff will do it for him. Nor do I say that everybody must advertise in a newspaper, or indeed use "printers' ink" at all. On the contrary, although that article is indispensable in the majority of cases, yet doctors and clergymen, and sometimes lawyers and some others, can more effectually reach the public in some other manner. But it is obvious, they must be known in some way, else how could they be supported?

Be polite and kind to your customers. — Politeness and civility are the best capital ever invested in business. Large stores, gilt signs, flaming advertisements, "will all prove unavailing if you or your employees treat your patrons abruptly. The truth is, the more kind and liberal a man is, the more generous will be the patronage bestowed upon him. "Like begets like." The man who gives the greatest amount of goods of a corresponding quality for the least sum (still reserving to himself a profit) will generally succeed best in the long run. This brings us to the golden rule, "As ye would that men should do to you, do ye also to them," and they will do better by you than if you always treated them as if you wanted to get the most you could out of them for the least return. Men who drive sharp bargains with their customers, acting as if they never expected to see them again, will not be mistaken. They never will see them again as customers. People don't like to pay and get kicked also.

One of the ushers in my Museum once told me he intended to whip a man who was in the lecture-room as soon as he came out. "What for?" I inquired.

"Because he said I was no gentleman," replied the usher.

"Never mind," I replied, "he pays for that, and you will not convince him you are a gentleman by whipping him. I cannot afford to lose a customer. If you whip him, he will never visit the Museum again, and he will induce friends to go with him to other places of amusement instead of this, and thus, you see, I should be a serious loser."

"But he insulted me," muttered the usher.

"Exactly," I replied, "and if he owned the Museum, and you had paid him for the privilege of visiting it, and he had then insulted you, there might be some reason in your resenting it. but in this instance, he is the man who pays, while we receive, and you must, therefore, put up with his bad manners."

My usher laughingly remarked, that this was undoubtedly the true policy, but he added that he should not object to an increase of salary if he was expected to be abused in order to promote my interests.

Be charitable. — Of course, men should be charitable, because it is a duty and a pleasure. But even as a matter of policy, if you possess no higher incentive, you will find that the liberal man will command patronage, while the sordid, uncharitable miser will be avoided.

Solomon says: "There is that scattereth and yet increaseth; and there is that withholdeth more than meet, but it tendeth to poverty." Of course, the only true charity is that which is from the heart.

The best kind of charity is to help those who are willing to help themselves. Promiscuous almsgiving, without inquiring into the worthiness of the applicant, is bad in every sense. But to search out and quietly assist those who are struggling for themselves, is the kind that "scattereth and yet increaseth." But don't fall into the idea that some persons practice, of giving a prayer instead of a potato, and a benediction instead of bread, to the hungry. It is easier to make Christians with full stomachs than empty.

Don't blab. — Some men have a foolish habit of telling their business secrets. If they make money they like to tell their neighbors how it was done. Nothing is gained by this, and ofttimes much is lost. Say nothing about your profits, your hopes, your expectations, your intentions. And this should apply to letters as well as to conversation. Goethe makes Mephistophiles say: "never write a letter nor destroy one." Business men must write letters, but they should be careful what they put in them. If you are losing money, be especially cautious and not tell of it, or you will lose your reputation.

Preserve your integrity. — It is more precious than diamonds or rubies. The old miser said to his sons: "Get money; get it honestly, if you can, but get money." This advice was not only atrociously wicked, but it was the very essence of stupidity. It was as much as to say, "if you find it difficult to obtain money honestly, you can easily get it dishonestly. Get it in that way." Poor fool! Not to know that the most difficult thing in life is to make money dishonestly! Not to know that our prisons are full of men who attempted to follow this advice; not to understand that no man can be dishonest, without soon being found out, and that when his lack of principle is discovered, nearly every avenue to success is closed against him forever. The public very properly shun all whose integrity is doubted. No matter how polite and pleasant and accommodating a man may be, none of us dare to deal with him if we suspect "false weights and measures." Strict honesty, not only lies at the foundation of all success in life (financially), but in every other respect. Uncompromising integrity of character in invaluable. It secures to its possessor a peace and joy which cannot be attained without it — which no amount of money, or houses and lands can purchase.

A man who is known to be strictly honest, may be ever so poor, but he has the purses of all the community at his disposal — for all know that if he promises to return what he borrows, he will never disappoint them. As a mere matter of selfishness, therefore, if a man had no higher motive for being honest, all will find that the maxim of Dr. Franklin can never fail to be true, that "honesty is the best policy."

To get rich, is not always equivalent to being successful. "There are many rich poor men," while there are many others, honest and devout men and women, who have never possessed so much money as some rich persons squander in a week, but who are nevertheless really richer and happier than any man can ever be while he is a transgressor of the higher laws of his being.

The inordinate love of money, no doubt, may be and is "the root of all evil," but money itself, when properly used, is not only a "handy thing to have in the house," but affords the gratification of blessing our race by enabling its possessor to enlarge the scope of human happiness and human influence. The desire for wealth is nearly universal, and none can say it is not laudable, provided the possessor of it accepts its responsibilities, and uses it as a friend to humanity.

The history of money-getting, which is commerce, is a history of civilization, and wherever trade has flourished most, there, too, have art and science produced the noblest fruits. In fact, as a general thing, money-getters are the benefactors of our race. To them, in a great measure, are we indebted for our institutions of learning and of art, our academies, colleges and churches. It is no argument against the desire for, or the possession of, wealth, to say that there are sometimes misers who hoard money only for the sake of hoarding, and who have no higher aspiration than to grasp everything which comes within their reach. As we have sometimes hypocrites in religion, and demagogues in politics, so there are occasionally misers among money-getters. These, however, are only exceptions to the general rule. But when, in this country, we find such a nuisance and stumbling block as a miser, we remember with gratitude that in America we have no laws of primogeniture, and that in the due course of nature the time will come when the hoarded dust will be scattered for the benefit of mankind. To all men and women, therefore, do I conscientiously say, make money honestly, and not otherwise, for Shakespeare has truly said, "He that wants money, means and content, is without three good friends."

Nearly every paper in London had something to say about my lecture, and in almost every instance the matter and manner of the lecturer were unqualifiedly approved. Indeed, the profusion of praise quite overwhelmed me. The *London Times,* December 30, 1858, concluded a half -column criticism with the following paragraph:

"We are bound to admit that Mr. Barnum is one of the most entertaining lecturers that ever addressed an audience on a theme universally intelligible. The appearance of Mr. Barnum, it should be added, has nothing of the 'charlatan' about it, but is that of the thoroughly respectable man of business; and he has at command a fund of dry humor that convulses everybody with laughter, while he himself remains perfectly serious. A sonorous voice and an admirably clear delivery complete his qualifications as a lecturer, in which capacity he is no 'humbug,' either in a higher or lower sense of the word."

The London Morning Post, the Advertiser, the Chronicle, the Telegraph, the Herald, the News, the Globe, the Sun, and other lesser journals of the same date, all contained lengthy and favorable notices and criticisms of my lecture. My own lavish advertisements were as nothing to the notoriety with which the London newspapers voluntarily and editorially gave to my new enterprise. The weekly and literary papers followed in the train; and even Punch, which had already done so much to keep Tom Thumb before the public, gave me a half-page notice, with an illustration, and thereafter favored me with frequent paragraphs. The city thus prepared the provinces to give me a cordial reception.

During the year 1859, I delivered this lecture nearly one hundred times in different parts of England, returning occasionally to London to repeat it to fresh audiences, and always with pecuniary success. Every provincial paper had something to say about Barnum and "The Art of Money-Getting," and I was never more pleasantly or profusely advertised. The tour, too, made me acquainted with many new people and added fresh and fast friends to my continually increasing list. My lecturing season is among my most grateful memories of England.

Remembering my experiences, some years before, with General Tom Thumb at Oxford and Cambridge, and the fondness of the under-graduates for practical joking, I was quite prepared when I made up my mind to visit those two cities, to take any quantity of "chaff" and lampooning which the University boys might choose to bring.

I was sure of a full house in each city, and as I was anxious to earn all the money I could, so as to hasten my deliverance from financial difficulties, I fully resolved to put up with whatever offered — indeed I rather liked the idea of an episode in the steady run of praise which had followed my lecture everywhere, and I felt too, in the coming encounter, that I might give quite as much as I was compelled to take.

I commenced at Cambridge, and, as I expected, to an overflowing house, largely composed of under-graduates. Soon after I began to speak, one of the young men called out: "Where is Joice Heth?" to which I very coolly replied:

"Young gentleman, please to restrain yourself till the conclusion of the lecture, when I shall take great delight in affording you, or any others of her posterity, all the information I possess concerning your deceased relative."

This reply turned the laugh against the youthful and anxious inquirer and had the effect of keeping other students quiet for a half hour. Thereafter, questions of a similar character were occasionally propounded, but as each inquirer generally received a prompt Roland for his Oliver, there was far less interruption than I had anticipated. The proceeds of the evening were more than one hundred pounds sterling, an important addition to my treasury at that time. At the close of the lecture, several students invited me to a sumptuous supper where I met, among other under-graduates, a nephew of Lord Macaulay, the historian. This young gentleman insisted upon my breakfasting with him at his rooms next morning, but as I was anxious to take an early train for London, I only called to leave my card, and after his "gyp" had given me a strong cup of coffee, I hastened away, leaving the young Macaulay, whom I did not wish to disturb, fast asleep in bed.

At Oxford the large hall was filled half an hour before the time announced for the lecture to begin, and the sale of tickets was stopped. I then stepped upon the platform, and said: "Ladies and gentlemen: As every seat is occupied and the ticket-office is closed, I propose to proceed with my lecture now, and not keep you waiting till the advertised hour."

"Good for you, old Barnum," said one; "Time is money," said another; "Nothing like economy," came from a third, and other remarks and exclamations followed, which excited much laughter in the audience. Holding up my hand as a signal that I was anxious to say something so soon as silence should be restored, I thus addressed my audience:

"Young gentlemen, I have a word or two to say, in order that we may have a thorough understanding between ourselves at the outset. I see symptoms of a pretty jolly time here this evening, and you have paid me liberally for the single hour of my time which is at your service. I am an old traveler and an old showman, and I like to please my patrons. Now, it is quite immaterial to me; you may furnish the entertainment for the hour, or I will endeavor to do so, or we will take portions of the time by turns — you supplying a part of the amusement, and I a part — as we say sometimes in America, "you pays your money, and you takes your choice.'"

My auditors were in the best of humor from the beginning, and my frankness pleased them. "Good for you, old Barnum," cried their leader; and I went on with my lecture for some fifteen minutes, when a voice called out:

"Come, old chap! you must be tired by this time; hold up now till we sing 'Yankee Doodle,' " whereupon they all joined in that pleasing air with a vigor which showed that they had thoroughly prepared themselves for the occasion, and meanwhile I took a chair and sat down to show them that I was quite satisfied with their manner of passing the time. When the song was concluded, the leader of the party said: "Now, Mr. Barnum, you may go ahead again."

I looked at my watch and quietly remarked, "Oh! there is time for lots of fun yet; we have nearly forty minutes of the hour remaining," and I proceeded with my lecture, or rather a lecture, for I began to adapt my remarks to the audience and the occasion. At intervals of ten minutes, or so, came interruptions which I, as my audience saw, fully enjoyed as much as the house did. When this miscellaneous entertainment was concluded, and I stopped short at the end of the hour, crowds of the young men pressed forward to shake hands with me, declaring that they had had a "jolly good time," while the leader said: "Stay with us a week, Barnum, and we will dine you, wine you, and give you full houses every night." But I was announced to lecture in London the next evening, and I could not accept the pressing invitation, though I would gladly have stayed through the week. They asked me all sorts of questions about America, the Museum, my various shows and successes, and expressed the hope that I would come out of my clock troubles all right.

At least a score of them pressed me to breakfast with them next morning, but I declined, till one young gentleman put it on this purely personal ground:

"My dear sir, you must breakfast with me; I have almost split my throat in screaming here tonight, and it is only fair that you should repay me by coming to see me in the morning." This appeal was irresistible, and at the appointed time I met him and half a dozen of his friends at his table, and we spent a very pleasant hour together. They complimented me on the tact and equanimity I had exhibited the previous evening, but I replied: "Oh! I was quite inclined to have you enjoy your fun and came fully prepared for it."

But they liked better, they said, to get the party angry. A fortnight before, they told me, my friend Howard Paul had left them in disgust, because they insisted upon smoking while his wife was on the stage, adding that the entertainment was excellent, and that Howard Paul could have made a thousand pounds if he had not let his anger drive him away. My new-found friends parted with me at the railway station, heartily urging me to come again, and my ticket-seller returned £169 as the immediate result of an evening's good-natured fun with the Oxford boys.

After delivering my lecture many times in different places, a prominent publishing house in London, offered me £1,200 ($6,000), for the copyright. This offer I declined, not that I thought the lecture worth more money, but because I had engaged to deliver it in several towns and cities, and I thought the publication would be detrimental to the public delivery of my lecture. It was a source of very considerable emolument to me, bringing in much money, which went towards the redemption of my pecuniary obligations, so that the lecture itself was an admirable illustration of "The Art of Money-Getting."

CHAPTER XXXII.

AN ENTERPRISING ENGLISHMAN.

While visiting Manchester, in 1858, I was invited by Mr. Peacock, the lessee, to deliver a lecture in "Free Trade Hall" I gave a lecture, the title of which I now forget; but I well remember it contained numerous personal reminiscences. The next day a gentleman named John Fish sent his card to my room at the hotel where I was stopping. I requested the servant to show him up at once, and he soon appeared and introduced himself. At first, he seemed somewhat embarrassed, but gradually broke the ice by saying he had been pleased in listening to my lecture the previous evening, and added that he knew my history pretty well, as he had read my autobiography. As his embarrassment at first meeting with a stranger wore away, he informed me that he was joint proprietor with another gentleman in a "cotton-mill " in Bury, near Manchester, "although," he modestly added, "only a few years ago I was working as a journeyman, and probably should have been at this tune, had it not been for your book." Observing my surprise at this announcement, he continued:

"The fact is, Mr. Barnum, upon reading your autobiography, I thought I perceived you tried to make yourself out something worse than you really were; for I discovered a pleasant spirit and a good heart under the rougher exterior in which you chose to present yourself to the public; but," he added, "after reading your life I found myself in possession of renewed strength, and awakened energies and aspirations, and I said to myself, "Why can't I go ahead and make money as Barnum did? He commenced without money and succeeded; why may not I? In this train of thought," he continued, "I went to a newspaper office and advertised for a partner with money to join me in establishing a cotton-mill. I had no applications, and, remembering your experiences when you had money and wanted a partner, I spent half a crown in a similar experiment. I advertised for a partner to join a man who had plenty of capital.

Then I had lots of applicants ready to introduce me into all sorts of occupations, from that of a banker to that of a horse-jockey or gambler, if I would only furnish the money to start with. After a while, I advertised again for a partner, and obtained one with money. We have a good mill, I devote myself closely to business, and have been very successful I know every line in your book; so, indeed, do several members of my family; and I have conducted my business on the principles laid down in your published 'Rules for Money-making.' I find them correct principles; and, sir, I have sought this interview in order to thank you for publishing your autobiography, and to tell you that to that act of yours I attribute my present position in life."

Of course, I was pleased and surprised at this revelation, and, feeling that my new friend had somewhat exaggerated the results of my labors as influencing his own, I said:

"Your statement is certainly very flattering, and I am glad if I have been able in any manner, through my experiences, to aid you in starting in life; but I presume your genius would have found vent in good time if I had never written a book."

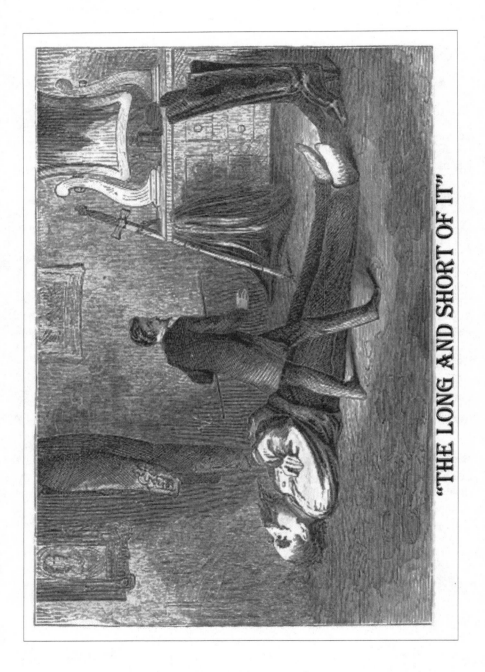

"THE LONG AND SHORT OF IT"

"No, indeed it would not," he replied, in an earnest tone; "I am sure I should have worked as a mill-hand all my life if it had not been for you. Oh, I have made no secret of it," he continued; "the commercial men with whom I deal know all about it; indeed, they call me 'Barnum' on 'change here in Manchester." On one occasion, when General Tom Thumb exhibited in Bury, Mr. Fish closed his mill, and gave each of his employees a ticket to the exhibition; out of respect, as he said, to Barnum. On a subsequent occasion, when the little General visited England the last time, Mr. Fish invited him, his wife, Commodore Nutt, Minnie Warren, and the managers of "the show," to a splendid and sumptuous dinner at his house, which the distinguished little party enjoyed exceedingly.

My friend Fish expressed himself extremely anxious to do any service for me which might at any time be in his power. Soon after I arrived in America, I read an account of a French giant, then exhibiting in Paris, and said to be over eight feet in height. As this was a considerably greater altitude than any specimen of the genus homo within my knowledge had attained, I wrote to my friend Fish to take a trip to Paris for me, secure an interview with this modern Anak, and by actual measurement obtain for me his exact height. I enclosed an offer for this giant's services, arranging the price on a sliding scale, according to what his height should actually prove to be — commencing at eight feet, and descending to seven feet two inches: and, if he was not taller than the latter figure, I did not want him at all.

Mr. Fish, placing an English two-foot rule in his pocket, started for Paris; and, after much difficulty and several days' delay in trying to speak with the giant, who was closely watched by his exhibitor, succeeded in appointing an interview at the giant's lodgings. And now came a trouble which required all the patience and diplomacy which my agent could command. Mr. Fish, arriving at the place of rendezvous, told the giant who he was, and the object of his visit. In fact, he showed him my letter, and read the tempting offers which I made for his services, provided he measured eight feet, or even came within six inches of that height. "Oh, I measure over eight feet in height," said the giant. "Very likely," replied my faithful agent, "but you see my orders are to measure you." "There's no need of that, you can see for yourself," stretching himself up a few inches, by aid of that peculiar muscular knack which giants and dwarfs exercise when they desire to extend or diminish their apparent stature.

"No doubt you are right," persisted the agent; "but you see that is not according to orders." "Well, stand alongside of me; see, the top of your hat don't come to my shoulder," said the giant, as he swung his arm completely over Mr. Fish's head, hat and all.

But my wary agent happened just then to be watching the giant's feet and knees, and he thought he saw a movement around the "understandings" that materially helped the elevation of the "upperworks," "It is all very well," said Mr. Fish; "but I tell you, if I am not permitted to measure your height, I shall not engage you." My offer had been very liberal; in fact, provided he was eight feet high, it was more than four times the amount the giant was then receiving; it was evidently a great temptation to his "highness," and quite as evidently, he did not want to be fairly measured. "Well," said the giant, " if you can't take my word for it, look at that door; you see my head is more than two feet above the top" (giving his neck and every muscle in his body a severe stretch); "just measure the height of that door." My English friend plainly saw that the giant felt that he could not come up to the mark, and he laughed at this last ruse. "Oh, I don't want to measure the door; I prefer to measure you," said Mr. Fish, coolly. The giant was now desperate, and, stretching himself up to the highest point, he exclaimed: "Well, be quick! put your rule down to my feet and measure me; no delay, if you please."

The giant knew he could not hold himself up many seconds to the few extra inches he had imparted to his extended muscles; but his remark had drawn Mr. Fish's attention to his feet, and from the feet to the boots, and he began to open his eyes. "Look here, Monsieur, " he exclaimed with much earnestness, "this sort of thing won't do, you know. I don't understand this contrivance around the soles of your boots, but it seems to me you have got a set of springs in there which materially aids your altitude a few inches when you desire it. Now, I shall stand no more nonsense. If I engage you at all, you must first take off your boots, and lie flat upon your back in the middle of the floor. The giant grumbled and talked about his word being doubted and his honor assailed, but Mr. Fish calmly persisted, until at length he slowly took off his coat and gradually got down on the floor. Stretched upon his back, he made several vain efforts to extend his natural height. Mr. Fish carefully applied his English two-foot rule, the result of the measurement causing him much astonishment, and the giant more indignation, the giant measuring exactly seven feet one and one-half inches. So, he was not engaged, and the agent returned to England and wrote me a most amusing letter, giving the particulars of the gigantic interview.

On the occasion of the erection of a new engine in his mill, Mr. Fish proposed naming it after his daughter, but she insisted it should be christened "Barnum," and it was so done, with considerable ceremony. Subsequently he introduced a second engine into his enlarged mill, and named this, after my wife, "Charity."

A short time since, I wrote informing him that I desired to give some of the foregoing facts in my book, and asked him to give me his consent, and also to furnish me some particulars in regard to the engines, and the capacity of his mill. He wrote in return a modest letter, which is so characteristic of my whole-souled friend that I cannot forbear making the following extracts from it:

"Had I made a fortune of £100,000 I should have been proud of a place in your Autobiography; but as I have only been able to make (here he named a sum which in this country would be considered almost a fortune), I feel I should be out of place in your pages; at all events, if you mention me at all, draw it mildly, if you please.

The American war has made sad havoc in our trade, and it is only by close attention to business that I have lately been at all successful. I have built a place for one thousand looms, and have, as you know, put in a pair of engines, which I have named "Barnum" and "Charity." Each engine has its name engraved on two large brass plates at either end of the cylinder, which has often caused much mirth when I have explained the circumstances to visitors, I started and christened "Charity" on the fourteenth of January last, and she has saved me £12 per month in coals ever since. The steam from the boiler goes first to "Charity" (she is high pressure), and "Barnum" only gets the steam after she has done with it. tie has to work at low pressure (a condensing engine), and the result is a saving. Barnum was extravagant when he took steam direct, but since I fixed Charity betwixt him and the boiler, he can only get what she gives him. This reminds me that you state in your "Life", you could always make money, but formerly did not save it. Perhaps you never took care of it till Charity became Chancellor of Exchequer. When I visited you at the Hull Hotel, in Blackburn, you pointed to General Tom Thumb, and said: "That is my piece of goods; I have sold it hundreds of thousands of times and have never yet delivered it!" That was ten years ago. In 1858. If I had been doing the same with my pieces of calico, I must have been wealthy by this time; but I have been hammering at one (cotton) nail several months, and, as it did not offer to clinch, I was almost tempted to doubt one of your "rules" and thought I would drive at some other nail; but, on reflection. I knew I understood cotton better than anything else, and so I back up your rule and stick to cotton, not doubting it will be all right and successful."

Mr. Fish was one of the large class of English manufacturers who suffered seriously from the effects of the rebellion in the United States, As an Englishman be could not have a patriot's interest in the progress of that terrible struggle; but he made a practical exhibition of sympathy for the suffering soldiers, in a pleasant and characteristic manner.

The great fair of the Sanitary Commission, held in New York during the war, affords one of the most interesting chapters in American history. None of those who visited the fair will forget, in the multiplicity of offerings to put money into the treasury of the commission, two monster cakes, which were as strange in shape and ornament as they were mammoth in their proportions. One of these great cakes was covered with miniature forts, ships of war, cannon, armies, arms of the whole "panoply of war," and it excited the attention of all visitors. This strange cake is what is called in Bury, England, where name, cake and custom originated, a "Simnel cake." It was sent to me expressly for this fair, by my friend Fish, and, while it was in itself a generous gift, it was doubly so as coming from an English manufacturer who had suffered by the war. The second great Simnel cake which stood beside it in the fair, was sent to me personally by Mr. Fish; but, with his permission, I took much pleasure in contributing it, with his own offering, for the benefit of our suffering soldiers.

CHAPTER XXXIII.

RICHARD'S HIMSELF AGAIN.

In 1859 I returned to the United States. During my last visit abroad, I had secured many novelties for the Museum, including the Albino Family, which I engaged at Amsterdam, and Thiodon's mechanical theater, which I found at Southampton, besides purchasing many curiosities. These things all afforded me a liberal commission, and thus, by constant and earnest effort, I made much money, besides what I derived from the Tom Thumb exhibitions, my lectures, and other enterprises. All of this money, as well as my wife's income, and a considerable sum raised by selling a portion of her property, was faithfully devoted to the one great object of my life at that period— my extrication from those crushing clock debts. I worked and I saved. When my wife and youngest daughter were not boarding in Bridgeport, they lived frugally in the suburbs, in a small one-story house which was hired at the rate of $150 a year. I had now been struggling about four years, with the difficulties of my one great financial mistake, and the end still seemed to be far off. I felt that the land, purchased by my wife in East Bridgeport at the assignees' sale, would, after a while, increase rapidly in value; and on the strength of this expectation more money was borrowed for the sake of taking up the clock notes, and some of the East Bridgeport property was sold in single lots, the proceeds going to the same object.

At last, in March, 1860, all the clock indebtedness was satisfactorily extinguished, excepting some $20,000, which I had bound myself to take up within a certain number of months, my friend, James D. Johnson, guaranteeing my bond to that effect. Mr. Johnson was by far my most effective agent in working me through these clock troubles, and in aiding to bring them to a successful conclusion.

On the seventeenth day of March, 1860, Messrs. Butler & Greenwood signed an agreement to sell and deliver to me on the following Saturday, March 24th, their good will and entire interest in the Museum collection. This fact was thoroughly circulated, and it was everywhere announced in blazing posters, placards and advertisements, which were headed, "Barnum on his feet again." It was furthermore stated that the Museum would be closed, March 24th, for one week for repairs and general renovation, to be re-opened, March 31st, under the management and proprietorship of its original owner. It was also announced that on the night of closing, I would address the audience from the stage.

The American Museum, decorated on that occasion as on holidays, with a brilliant display of flags and banners, was filled to its utmost capacity, and I experienced profound delight at seeing hundreds of old friends of both sexes in the audience. I lacked but four months of being fifty years of age; but I felt all the vigor and ambition that fired me when I first took possession of the premises twenty years before; and I was confident that the various experiences of that score of years would be valuable to me in my second effort to secure an independence.

At the rising of the curtain, and before the play commenced, I stepped on the stage and was received by the large and brilliant audience with an enthusiasm far surpassing anything of the kind I had ever experienced or witnessed in a public career of a quarter of a century. Indeed, this tremendous demonstration nearly broke me down, and my voice faltered and tears came to my eyes as I thought of this magnificent conclusion to the trials and struggles of the past four years. Recovering myself, however, I bowed my grateful acknowledgments for the reception, and addressed the audience as follows:

"LADIES AND GENTLEMEN: I should be more or less than human, if I could meet this unexpected and overwhelming testimonial at your hands, without the deepest emotion. My own personal connection with the Museum is now resumed, and I avail myself of the circumstance to say why it is so. Never did I feel stronger in my worldly prosperity than in September, 1855. Three months later I was so deeply embarrassed that I felt certain of nothing, except the uncertainty of everything. A combination of singular efforts and circumstances tempted me to put faith in a certain clock manufacturing company, and I placed my signature to papers which ultimately broke me down. After nearly five years of hard struggle to keep my head above water, I have touched bottom at last, and here tonight, I am happy to announce that I have waded ashore. Every clock debt of which I have any knowledge has been provided for. Perhaps, after the troubles and turmoils I have experienced, I should feel no desire to re-engage in the excitements of business, but a man like myself, less than fifty years of age, and enjoying robust health, is scarcely old enough to be embalmed and put in a glass case in the Museum as one of its millions of curiosities. 'It is better to wear out than rust out.' Besides, if a man of active temperament is not busy, he is apt to get into mischief.

To avoid evil therefore, and since business activity is a necessity of my nature, here I am, once more, in the Museum, and among those with whom I have been so long and so pleasantly identified. I am confident of a cordial welcome, and hence feel some claim to your indulgence while I briefly allude to the means of my present deliverance from utter financial ruin. Need I say, in the first place, that I am somewhat indebted to the forbearance of generous creditors. In the next place, permit me to speak of sympathizing friends, whose volunteered loans and exertions vastly aided my rescue. When my day of sorrow came, I first paid or secured every debt I owed of a personal nature. This done, I felt bound in honor to give up all of my property that remained towards liquidating my "clock debts." I placed it in the hands of trustees and receivers for the benefit of all the "clock" creditors. But at the forced sale of my Connecticut real estate, there was a purchaser behind the screen, of whom the world had little knowledge. In the day of my prosperity I was worth hundreds of thousands of dollars when, as a matter of love, I transferred a portion to my wife, little dreaming it would be needed during my lifetime. I made over to my wife much valuable property, including the lease of this Museum building — a lease then having about twenty-two years to run, and enhanced in value to more than double its original worth. I sold the Museum collection to Messrs. Greenwood and Butler, subject to my wife's separate interest in the lease, and she has received more than eighty thousand dollars over and above the sums paid to the owners of the building. Instead of selfishly applying this amount to private purposes, my family lived with a due regard to economy, and the savings (strictly belonging to my wife), were devoted to buying in portions of my estate at the assignees' sales, and to purchasing 'clock notes' bearing my endorsements. The Christian name of my wife is Charity. I may well acknowledge, therefore, that lam not only a proper 'subject of charity,' but that 'without Charity, I am nothing.'

"But, ladies and gentlemen, while Charity thus labored in my behalf, Faith and Hope were not idle. I have been anything but indolent during the last four years. Driven from pillar to post, and annoyed beyond description by all sorts of legal claims and writs, I was perusing protests and summonses by day, and dreaming of clocks run down by night. My head was ever whizzing with dislocated cog-wheels and broken main-springs; my whole mind (and my credit) was running upon tick, and everything pressing on me like a dead weight.

"In this state of affairs, I felt that I was of no use on this side of the Atlantic, so, giving the pendulum a swing, and seizing time by the forelock, I went to Europe. There I furtively pulled the wires of several exhibitions, among which that of Tom Thumb may be mentioned for example. I managed a variety of musical and commercial speculations in Great Britain, Germany, and Holland. These enterprises, together with the net profits of my public lectures, enabled me to remit large sums to confidential agents for the purchase of my obligations. In this manner, I quietly extinguished, little by little, every dollar of my clock liabilities. I could not have achieved this difficult feat, however, without the able assistance of enthusiastic friends — and among the chief of them let me gratefully acknowledge the invaluable services of Mr. James D. Johnson, a gentleman of wealth, in Bridgeport, Connecticut. Other gentlemen have been generous with me. Some have loaned me large sums without security, and have placed me under obligations which must ever command my honest gratitude; but Mr. Johnson has been a 'friend indeed,' for he has been truly a 'friend in need.'

"You must not infer, from what I have said, that I have completely recovered from the stunning blow to which I was subjected four years ago. I have lost more in the way of tens of thousands, yes, hundreds of thousands, than I care to remember. A valuable portion of my real estate in Connecticut, however, has been preserved, and as I feel all the ardor of twenty years ago, and the prospect here is so flattering, my heart is animated with the hope of ultimately, by enterprise and activity, obliterating unpleasant reminiscences, and retrieving the losses of the past. Experience, too, has taught me not only that, even in the matter of money, 'enough is as good as a feast,' but that there are, in this world, some things vastly better than the Almighty Dollar! Possibly I may contemplate, at times, the painful day when I said 'Othello's occupation's gone;' but I shall more frequently cherish the memory of this moment, when I am permitted to announce that 'Richard's himself again.'

"Many people have wondered that a man considered so acute as myself should have been deluded into embarrassments like mine, and not a few have declared, in short meter, that 'Barnum was a fool.' I can only reply that I never made pretensions to the sharpness of a pawnbroker, and I hope I shall never so entirely lose confidence in human nature as to consider every man a scamp by instinct, or a rogue by necessity. 'It is better to be deceived sometimes, than to distrust always,' says Lord Bacon, and I agree with him.

"Experience is said to be a hard schoolmaster, but I should be sorry to feel that this great lesson in adversity has not brought forth fruits of some value. I needed the discipline this tribulation has given me, and I really feel, after all, that this, like many other apparent evils, was only a blessing in disguise. Indeed, I may mention that the very clock factory which I built in Bridgeport, for the purpose of bringing hundreds of workmen to that city, has been purchased and quadrupled in size by the Wheeler and Wilson Sewing Machine Company, and is now filled with intelligent New England mechanics, whose families add two thousand to the population, and who are doing a great work in building up and beautifying that flourishing city. So that the same concern which prostrated me seems destined as a most important agent towards my recuperation. I am certain that the popular sympathy has been with me from the beginning; and this, together with a consciousness of rectitude, is more than an offset to all the vicissitudes to which I have been subjected.

"In conclusion, I beg to assure you and the public. that my chief pleasure, while health and strength are spared me, will be to cater for your and their healthy amusement and instruction. In future, such capabilities as I possess will be devoted to the maintenance of this Museum as a popular place of family resort, in which all that is novel and interesting shall be gathered from the four quarters of the globe, and which ladies and children may visit at all times unattended, without danger of encountering anything of an objectionable nature. The dramas introduced in the Lecture Room will never contain a profane expression or a vulgar allusion; on the contrary, their tendency will always be to encourage virtue, and frown upon vice.

"I have established connections in Europe, which will enable me to produce here a succession of interesting novelties otherwise inaccessible. Although I shall be personally present much of the time, and hope to meet many of my old acquaintances, as well as to form many new ones, I am sure you will be glad to learn that I have re-secured the services of one of the late proprietors, and the active manager of this Museum, Mr. John Greenwood, Jr. As he is a modest gentleman, who would be the last to praise himself, allow me to add that he is one to whose successful qualities as a caterer for the popular entertainments, the crowds that have often filled this building may well bear testimony. But, more than this, he is the unobtrusive one to whose integrity, diligence and devotion. I owe much of my present position of self-congratulation. Mr. Greenwood will hereafter act as assistant manager, while his late co-partner, Mr. Butler, has engaged in another branch of business. Once more, thanking you all for your kind welcome, I bid you, till the re-opening, an affectionate *adieu.*"

This off-hand speech was received with almost tumultuous applause. At nearly fifty years of age, I was now once more before the public with the promise to put on a full head of steam, to "rush things," to give double or treble the amount of attractions ever before offered at the Museum, and to devote all my own time and services to the enterprise. In return, I asked that the public should give my efforts the patronage they merited, and the public took me at my word. The daily number of visitors at once more than doubled, and my exertions to gratify them with rapid changes and novelties never tired.

The announcement that I was at last out of the financial entanglement was variously received. That portion of the press which had followed me with abuse when

I was down, under the belief that my case was past recovery, were cautious in allusions to the new state of things, or passed them over without comment. The sycophants always knew I would get up again, "and said so at the time;" the many and noble journals which had stood by me and upheld me in my misfortunes, were of course rejoiced, and their words of sincere congratulation gave me a higher satisfaction than I have power of language to acknowledge. Letters of congratulation came in upon me from every quarter. Friendly hands that had never been withheld during the long period of my misfortune, were now extended with a still heartier grip. I never knew till now the warmth and number of my friends.

Nor must I neglect to state that a large number of my creditors who held the clock notes, proved very magnanimous in taking into consideration the gross deception which had put me in their power. Not a few of them said to me in substance: "You never supposed you had made yourself liable for this debt; you were deluded into it; it is not right that it should be held over you to keep you hopelessly down; take it, and pay me such percentage as, under the circumstances, it is possible for you to pay." But for such men and such consideration I fear I should never have got on my feet again; and of the many who rejoiced in my bettered fortune, not a few were of this class of my creditors.

My old friend, the *Boston Saturday Evening Gazette*, which printed a few cheering poetical lines of consolation and hope when I was down, now gave me the following from the same graceful pen, conveying glowing words of congratulation at my rise again:

ANOTHER WORD FOR BARNUM.

Barnum, your hand! The struggle o'er,
You face the world and ask no favor;
You stand where you have stood before,
The old salt hasn't lost its savor.
You now can laugh with friends, at foes,
Ne'er heeding Mrs. Grundy's tattle;
You've dealt and taken sturdy blows,
Regardless of the rabble's prattle.
Not yours the heart to harbor ill
'Gainst those who've dealt in trivial jesting;
You pass them with the same good will
Erst shown when they their wit were testing.
You're the same Barnum that we knew,
You're good for years, still fit for labor,
Be as of old, be bold and true,
Honest as man, as friend, as neighbor.

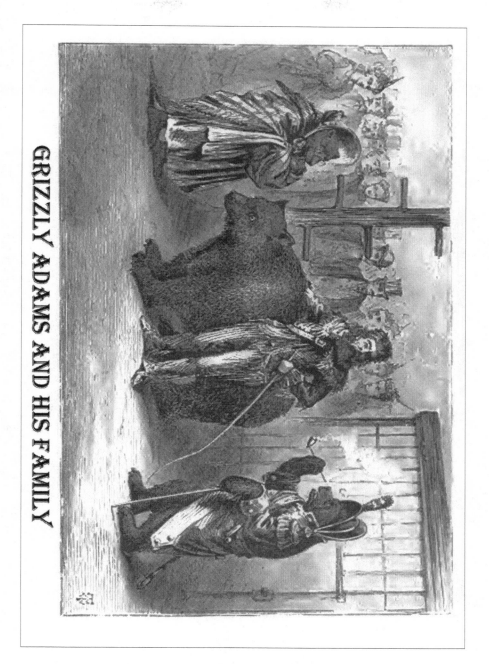

GRIZZLY ADAMS AND HIS FAMILY

At about this period, the following poem was published in a Pottsville, Pa. paper, and copied by many journals of the day:

A HEALTH TO BARNUM.

Companions! fill your glasses round,
And drink a health to one
Who has few coming after him,
To do as he has done;
Who made a fortune for himself,
Made fortunes, too, for many,
Yet wronged no bosom of a sigh,
No pocket of a penny.
Come! shout a gallant chorus,
And make the glasses ring,
Here's health and luck to Barnum!
The Exhibition King.
Who lured the Swedish Nightingale
To Western woods to come?
Who prosperous and happy made
The life of little Thumb?
Who opened Amusement's golden door
So cheaply to the crowd,
And taught Morality to smile
On all his stage allowed?
Come! shout a gallant chorus,
Until the glasses ring
Here's health and luck to Barnum!
The Exhibition King.
And when the sad reverses came,
As come they may to all,
Who stood a Hero, bold and true.
Amid his fortune's hill
Who to the utmost yielded up
What Honor could not keep,
Then took the field of life again
With courage calm and deep?
Cornel shout a gallant chorus,
Until the glasses dance-
Here's health and hick to Barnum,
The Napoleon of Finance.
Yet, no — our hero would not look
With smiles on such a cup;
Throw out the wine— with water clear,
Fill the pure crystal up.
Then rise, and greet with deep respect.

The courage he has shown.
And drink to him who well deserves
A seat on Fortune's throne.
Here's health and luck to Barnum!
An Elba he has seen,
And never may his map of life
Display a St. Helene?

Philadelphia.   Mrs. Anna Bache.

CHAPTER XXXIV.

MENAGERIE AND MUSEUM MEMORANDA.

I was now fairly embarked on board the good old ship American Museum, to try once more my skill as captain, and to see what fortune the voyage would bring me. Curiosities began to pour into the Museum Halls, and I was eager for enterprises in the show line, whether as part of the Museum itself, or as outside accessories or accompaniments. Among the first to give me a call, with attractions sure to prove a success, was James C. Adams, of hard-earned, grizzly-bear fame. This extraordinary man was eminently what is called "a character." He was universally known as "Grizzly Adams," from the fact that he had captured a great many grizzly bears, at the risk and cost of fearful encounters and perils. He was brave, and with his bravery there was enough of the romantic in his nature to make him a real hero. For many years a hunter and trapper in the Rocky and Sierra Nevada Mountains, he acquired a recklessness, which, added to his natural invincible courage, rendered him one of the most striking men of the age, and he was emphatically a man of pluck. A month after I had re-purchased the Museum, he arrived in New York with his famous collection of California animals, captured by himself, consisting of twenty or thirty immense grizzly bears, at the head of which stood "Old Samson," together with several wolves, half a dozen different species of California bears, California lions, tigers, buffalo, elk, and "Old Neptune," the great sea-lion from the Pacific.

Old Adams had trained all these monsters so that with him they were as docile as kittens, though many of the most ferocious among them would attack a stranger without hesitation, if he came within their grasp. In fact, the training of these animals was no fool's play, as Old Adams learned to his cost, for the terrific blows which he received from time to time, while teaching them "docility," finally cost him his life.

Adams called on me immediately on his arrival in New York. He was dressed in his hunter's suit of buckskin, trimmed with the skins and bordered with the hanging tails of small Rocky Mountain animals; his cap consisting of the skin of a wolf's head and shoulders, from which depended several tails, and under which appeared his stiff, bushy, gray hair and his long, white, grizzly beard; in fact, Old Adams was quite as much of a show as his beasts. They had come around Cape Horn on the clipper ship "Golden Fleece," and a sea voyage of three and a half months had probably not added much to the beauty or neat appearance of the old bear-hunter. During our conversation, Grizzly Adams took off his cap, and showed me the top of his head. His skull was literally broken in. It had, on various occasions, been struck by the fearful paws of his grizzly students; and the last blow, from the bear called "General Fremont," had laid open his brain so that its workings were plainly visible. I remarked that I thought it was a dangerous wound and might possibly prove fatal.

"Yes," replied Adams, "that will fix me out. It had nearly healed; but old Fremont opened it for me, for the third or fourth time, before I left California, and he did his business so thoroughly, I'm a used-up man. However, I reckon I may live six months or a year yet." This was spoken as coolly as it he had been talking about the life of a dog. The immediate object of "old Adams " in calling upon me was this; I had purchased, a week previously, one-half interest in his California menagerie, from a man who had come by way of the Isthmus from California, and who claimed to own an equal interest with Adams in the show. Adams declared that the man had only advanced him some money, and did not possess the right to sell half of the concern. However, the man held a bill of sale for half of the "California Menagerie," and old Adams finally consented to accept me as an equal partner in the speculation, saying that he guessed I could do the managing part, and he would show up the animals.

I obtained a canvas tent, and, erecting it on the present site of Wallack's theater. Adams there opened his novel California Menagerie. On the morning of opening, a band of music preceded a procession of animal cages down Broadway and up the Bowery, old Adams, dressed in his hunting costume, heading the line, with a platform wagon on which were placed three immense grizzly bears, two of which he held by chains, while he was mounted on the back of the largest grizzly, which stood in the center and was not secured in any manner whatever. This was the bear known as "General Fremont," and so docile had he become, that Adams said he had used him as a pack-bear, to carry his cooking and hunting apparatus through the mountains for six months, and had ridden him hundreds of miles. But apparently docile as were many of these animals, there was not one among them that would not occasionally give Adams a sly blow or a sly bite when a good chance offered; hence old Adams was but a wreck of his former self, and expressed pretty nearly the truth when he said:

"Mr. Barnum, I am not the man I was five years ago. Then I felt able to stand the hug of any grizzly living, and was always glad to encounter, single handed, any sort of an animal that dared present himself. But I have been beaten to a jelly, torn almost limb from limb, and nearly chawed up and spit out by these treacherous grizzly bears. However, I am good for a few months yet, and by that time I hope we shall gain enough to make my old woman comfortable, for I have been absent from her some years."

His wife came from Massachusetts to New York and nursed him. Dr. Johns dressed his wounds every day, and not only told Adams he could never recover, but assured his friends, that probably a very few weeks would lay him in his grave. But Adams was as firm as adamant and as resolute as a lion. Among the thousands who saw him dressed in his grotesque hunter's suit, and with the seeming vigor with which he "performed" the savage monsters, beating and whipping them into apparently the most perfect docility, probably not one suspected that this rough, fierce-looking, powerful demi-savage, as he appeared to be, was suffering intense pain from his broken skull and fevered system, and that nothing kept him from stretching himself on his death-bed but his most indomitable and extraordinary will.

Old Adams liked to astonish others, as he often did, with his astounding stories, but no one could astonish him; he had seen everything and knew everything, and I was anxious to get a chance of exposing this weak point to him. A fit occasion soon presented itself. One day, while engaged in my office at the Museum, a man with marked Teutonic features and accent approached the door and asked if I would like to buy a pair of living golden pigeons.

"Yes," I replied, "I would like a flock of golden pigeons, if I could buy them for their weight in silver; for there are no 'golden' pigeons in existence, unless they are made from the pure metal."

"You shall see some golden pigeons alive," he replied, at the same time entering my office, and closing the door after him. He then removed the lid from a small basket which he carried in his hand, and sure enough, there were snugly ensconced a pair of beautiful, living ruff-necked pigeons, as yellow as saffron, and as bright as a double-eagle fresh from the mint.

I confess I was somewhat staggered at this sight, and quickly asked the man where those birds came from. A dull, lazy smile crawled over the sober face of my German visitor, as he replied in a slow, guttural tone of voice:

"What you think yourself?"

Catching his meaning, I quickly replied:

"I think it is a humbug."

"Of course, I know you will say so; because you 'forstha' such things; so, I shall not try to humbug you; I have colored them myself."

On further inquiry, I learned that this German was a chemist, and that he possessed the art of coloring birds any hue desired, and yet retain a natural gloss on the feathers, which gave every shade the appearance of reality.

Thinking here was a good chance to catch "Grizzly Adams," I bought the pair of golden pigeons for ten dollars, and sent them up to the "Happy Family" (where I knew Adams would soon see them), marked, "Golden Pigeons, from California."

The next morning "Old Grizzly Adams," passed through the Museum when his eyes fell on the "Golden California Pigeons." He looked a moment and doubtless admired. He soon after came to my office.

"Mr. Barnum," said he, "you must let me have those California pigeons."

"I can't spare them," I replied.

"But you must spare them. All the birds and animals from California ought to be together. You own half of my California menagerie, and you must lend me those pigeons."

"Mr. Adams, they are too rare and valuable a bird to be hawked about in that manner."

"Oh, don't be a fool," replied Adams. "Rare bird, indeed! Why, they are just as common in California as any other pigeon I could have brought a hundred of them from San Francisco, if I had thought of it."

"But why did you not think of it?" I asked, with a suppressed smile.

"Because they are so common there," said Adams, "I did not think they would be any curiosity here."

I was ready to burst with laughter to see how readily Adams swallowed the bait, but, maintaining the most rigid gravity, I replied:

"Oh well, Mr. Adams, if they are really so common in California, you had probably better take them, and you may write over and have half a dozen pairs sent to me for the Museum."

Six or eight weeks after this incident, I was in the California Menagerie, and noticed that the "Golden Pigeons" had assumed a frightfully mottled appearance. Their feathers had grown out and they were half white. Adams had been so busy with his bears that he had not noticed the change. I called him up to the pigeon cage, and remarked-

"Mr. Adams, I fear you will lose your Golden Pigeons; they must be very sick; I observe they are turning quite pale."

Adams looked at them a moment with astonishment, then turning to me, and seeing that I could not suppress a smile, he indignantly exclaimed:

"Blast the Golden Pigeons! You had better take them back to the Museum. You can't humbug me with your painted pigeons!"

This was too much, and "I laughed till I cried," to witness the mixed look of astonishment and vexation which marked the grizzly features of old Adams.

After the exhibition on Thirteenth street and Broadway had been open six weeks, the doctor insisted that Adams should sell out his share in the animals and settle up his worldly affairs, for he assured him that he was growing weaker every day, and his earthly existence must soon terminate. "I shall live a good deal longer than you doctors think for," replied Adams, doggedly; and then, seeming after all to realize the truth of the doctor's assertion, he turned to me and said: "Well, Mr. Barnum, you must buy me out." He named his price for his half of the "show," and I accepted his offer. We had arranged to exhibit the bears in Connecticut and Massachusetts during the summer, in connection with a circus, and Adams insisted that I should hire him to travel for the season and exhibit the bears in their curious performances. He offered to go for $60 per week and traveling expenses of himself and wife. I replied that I would gladly engage him as long as he could stand it, but I advised him to give up business and go to his home in Massachusetts; "for," I remarked, "you are growing weaker every day, and at best cannot stand it more than a fortnight."

"What will you give me extra if I will travel and exhibit the bears every day for ten weeks?" added old Adams, eagerly.

"Five hundred dollars," I replied with a laugh.

"Done!" exclaimed Adams, "I will do it, so draw up an agreement to that effect at once. But, mind you, draw it payable to my wife, for I may be too weak to attend to business after the ten weeks are up, and if I perform my part of the contract, I want her to get the $500 without any trouble."

I drew up a contract to pay him $60 per week for his services, and if he continued to exhibit the bears for ten consecutive weeks I was then to hand him, or his wife, $500 extra.

"You have lost your $500!" exclaimed Adams on taking the contract; "for I am bound to live and earn it."

"I hope you may, with all my heart, and a hundred years more if you desire it," I replied.

"Call me a fool if I don't earn the $500!" exclaimed Adams, with a triumphant laugh.

The "show" started off in a few days, and at the end of a fortnight I met it at Hartford, Connecticut.

"Well," said I, "Adams, you seem to stand it pretty well. I hope you and your wife are comfortable."

"Yes," he replied with a laugh; "and you may as well try to be comfortable, too, for your $500 is a goner."

"All right," I replied, " I hope you will grow better every day."

But I saw by his pale face and other indications that he was rapidly failing. In three weeks more, I met him again at New Bedford, Massachusetts. It seemed to me, then, that he could not live a week, for his eyes were glassy and his hands trembled, but his pluck was as great ever.

"This hot weather is pretty bad for me," he said, "but my ten weeks are half expired, and I am good for your $500, and, probably, a month or two longer."

This was said with as much bravado as if he was offering to bet upon a horse-race. I offered to pay him half of the $500, if he would give up and go home; but he peremptorily declined making any compromise whatever. I met him the ninth week in Boston. He had failed considerably since I last saw him, but he still continued to exhibit the bears, although he was too weak to lead them in, and he chuckled over his almost certain triumph. I laughed in return, and sincerely congratulated him on his nerve and probable success. I remained with him until the tenth week was finished and handed him his $500. He took it with a leer of satisfaction, and remarked, that he was sorry I was a teetotaler, for he would like to stand treat!

Just before the menagerie left New York, I had paid $150 for a new hunting-suit, made of beaver skins, similar to the one which Adams had worn. This I intended for Herr Driesbach, the animal tamer, who was engaged by me to take the place of Adams, whenever he should be compelled to give up. Adams, on starting from New York, asked me to loan this new dress to him to perform in once in a while in a fair day, where he had a large audience, for his own costume was considerably soiled. I did so, and now when I handed him his $500, he remarked:

"Mr. Barnum, I suppose you are going to give me this new hunting-dress? "

"Oh, no," I replied, "I got that for your successor, who will exhibit the bears tomorrow; besides, you have no possible use for it."

"Now, don't be mean, but lend me the dress, if you won't give it to me, for I want to wear it home to my native village."

I could not refuse the poor old man anything, and I therefore replied:

"Well, Adams, I will lend you the dress; but you will send it back to me?"

"Yes, when I have done with it," he replied, with an evident chuckle of triumph.

I thought to myself, he will soon be done with it, and replied: "That's all right."

A new idea evidently struck him, for, with a brightening look of satisfaction, he said:

"Now, Barnum, you have made a good thing out of the California menagerie, and so have I; but you will make a heap more. So, if you won't give me this new hunter's dress, just draw a little writing, and sign it, saying that I may wear it until I have done with it."

I knew that in a few days, at longest, he would be "done" with this world altogether, and, to gratify him, I cheerfully drew and signed the paper.

"Come, old Yankee, I've got you this time — see if I hain't!" exclaimed Adams, with a broad grin, as he took the paper.

I smiled, and said:

"All right, my dear fellow; the longer you live, the better I shall like it."

We parted, and he went to Charlton, Worcester County, Mass., where his wife and daughter lived. He took at once to his bed, and never rose from it again. The excitement had passed away, and his vital energies could accomplish no more. The fifth day after arriving home, the physician told him he could not live until the next morning. He received the announcement in perfect calmness, and with the most apparent indifference; then, turning to his wife, with a smile he requested her to have him buried in the new hunting-suit. "For," said he, "Barnum agreed to let me have it until I have done with it, and I was determined to fix his flint this time. He shall never see that dress again." That dress was indeed the shroud in which he was entombed.

After the death of Adams, the grizzly bears and other animals, were added to the collection in my Museum, and I employed Herr Driesbach, the celebrated lion-tamer, as an exhibitor. Sometime afterwards, the bears were sold to a menagerie company, but I kept "Old Neptune," the sea-lion, for several years, Bending him occasionally for exhibitions in other cities, as far west as Chicago.

On the thirteenth of October, 1860, the Prince of Wales, then making a tour of the United States, in company with his suite, visited the American Museum. This was a very great compliment, since it was the only place of amusement the Prince attended in this country. Unfortunately, I was in Bridgeport at the time, and the Museum was in charge of my manager, Mr. Greenwood.

On leaving the Museum, the Prince asked to see Mr. Barnum, and when he was told that I was out of town, he remarked: "We have missed the most interesting feature of the establishment." A few days afterwards, when the Prince was in Boston, happening to be in that city, I sent my card to him at the Revere House, and was cordially received. He smiled when I reminded him that I had seen him when he was a little boy, on the occasion of one of my visits to Buckingham Palace with General Tom Thumb. The Prince told me that he was much pleased with his recent inspection of my Museum, and that he and his suite had left their autographs in the establishment, as mementoes of their visit.

Meanwhile the Museum nourished better than ever; and I began to make large holes in the mortgages which covered the property of my wife in New York and in Connecticut. Still, there was an immense amount of debts resting upon all her real estate, and nothing but time, economy, industry and diligence would remove the burdens.

CHAPTER XXXV.

EAST BRIDGEPORT.

For nearly five years my family had been knocked about, the sport of adverse fortune, without a settled home. Sometimes we boarded, and at other times we lived in a small hired house. Two of my daughters were married, and my youngest daughter, Pauline, was away at boarding-school. The health of my wife was much impaired, and she especially needed a fixed residence which she could call "home." Accordingly, in 1860, I built a pleasant house adjoining that of my daughter Caroline, in Bridgeport, one hundred rods west of the grounds of *Iranistan*.

Meanwhile, my pet city, East Bridgeport, was progressing with giant strides. The Wheeler and Wilson Sewing Machine manufactory had been quadrupled in size and employed about a thousand workmen. Numerous other large factories had been built, and scores of first-class houses were erected, besides many neat but smaller and cheaper houses for laborers and mechanics. That piece of property, which, but eight years before, had been farmland, with scarcely six houses upon the whole tract, was now a beautiful new city, teeming with busy life, and looking as neat as a new pin.

I copy from the files of the Bridgeport Standard, an offer which I made, and the editorial comment thereon. This offer was for the sake of helping those who were willing to help themselves, and, at the same time, contribute to my happiness, as well as their own, by forwarding the growth of the new city.

"NEW HOUSES IN EAST BRIDGEPORT."
"EVERY MAN TO OWN THE HOUSE HE LIVES IN."

"There is a demand at the present moment for two hundred more dwelling-houses In East Bridgeport. It is evident that if the money expended in rent can be paid towards the purchase of a house and lot, the person so paying will in a few years own the house he lives in, instead of always remaining a tenant. In view of this fact, I propose to loan money at six per cent, to any number, not exceeding fifty, industrious, temperate and respectable individuals, who desire to build their own houses.

"They may engage their own builders, and build according to any reasonable plan (which I may approve), or I will have it done for them at the lowest possible rate, without a farthing profit to myself or agent, I putting the lot at a fair price and advancing eighty per cent, of the entire cost; the other party to furnish twenty per cent, in labor, material or money, and they may pay me in small sums weekly, monthly or quarterly, any amount not less than three per cent, per quarter, all of which is to apply on the money advanced until it is paid.

"It has been ascertained that by purchasing building materials for cash, and in large quantities, nice dwellings, painted and furnished with green blinds, can be erected at a cost of $1,500 or $1,800, for house, lot, fences, etc., all complete, and if six or eight friends prefer to join in erecting a neat block of houses with verandas in front, the average cost need not exceed about $1,300 per house and lot. If, however, some parties would prefer a single or double house that would cost $2,500 to $3,000, I shall be glad to meet their views."

P. T. Barnum. February 16, 1864

The editor of the *Standard* printed the following upon my announcement:

"An Advantageous Offer. — We have read with great pleasure Mr. Barnum's advertisement, offering assistance to any number of persons, not exceeding fifty, in the erection of dwelling-houses. The plan combines all the advantages and none of the objections of Building Associations. Any individual who can furnish in cash, labor, or material, one-fifth only of the amount requisite for the erection of a dwelling-house, can receive the other four-fifths from Mr. Barnum, rent his house and by merely paying what may be considered as only a fair rent for a few years, find himself at last the owner, and all further payments cease. In the meantime, he can be making such inexpensive improvements in his property as would greatly Increase its market value, and besides have the advantage of any rise in the value of real estate. It is not often that such a generous offer is made to working men. It is a loan on what would be generally considered inadequate security, at six per cent., at a time when a much better use of money can be made by any capitalist. It is therefore generous. Mr. Barnum may make money by the operation. Very well, perhaps he will, but if he does, it will be by making others richer, not poorer; by helping those who need assistance, not by hindering them, and we can only wish that every rich man would follow such a noble example, and thus, without injury to themselves, give a helping hand to those who need it. Success to the enterprise. We hope that fifty men will be found before the weekends, each of whom desires in such a manner*to obtain a roof which he can call his own."

Quite a number of men at once availed themselves of my offer, and eventually succeeded in paying for their homes without much effort. I am sorry to add, that rent is still paid, month after month, by many men who would long ago have owned neat homesteads, free from all incumbrances, if they had accepted my proposals, and had signed and kept the temperance pledge, and given up the use of tobacco. The money they have since expended for whisky and tobacco, would have given them a house of their own, if the money had been devoted to that object, and their positions, socially and morally, would have been far better than they are today. How many infatuated men there are in all parts of the country, who could now be independent, and even owners of their own carriages, but for their slavery to these miserable habits!

The land in East Bridgeport was originally purchased by me at from $50 to $75, and from those sums to $300 per acre; and the average cost of all I bought on that side of the river was $200 per acre. Some portions of this land are now assessed in the Bridgeport tax-list at from $3,000 to $4,000 per acre. At the time I joined Mr. Noble in this enterprise, the site we purchased was not a part of the city of Bridgeport. It is now, however, a most important section of the city, and the three bridges connecting the two banks of the river, and originally chartered as toll-bridges, have been bought by the city and thrown open as free highways to the public. A horse railroad, in which I took one-tenth part of the stock, connects the two portions of the city, extending westerly beyond *Iranistan* and Lindencroft, while a branch road runs to the beautiful "Seaside Park" on the Sound shore.

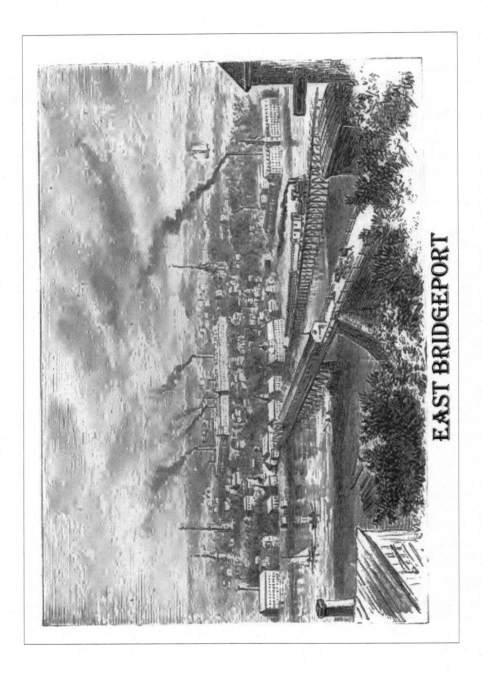

EAST BRIDGEPORT

General Noble, in laying out the first portion of our new city, named several streets after members of his own family, and also of mine. Hence, we have a "Noble" street — and a noble street it is; a "Barnum" street; while other streets are named "William," from Mr. Noble; "Harriet," the Christian name of Mrs. Noble; "Hallett," the maiden name of my wife; and "Caroline," "Helen," and " Pauline," the names of my three daughters. There is also the "Barnum School District " and schoolhouse; so that it seems as if, for a few scores of years at least, posterity would know who were the founders of the new, flourishing and beautiful city. We have yet another enduring and ever-growing monument in the many thousands of trees which we set out, and which now fine and gratefully shade the streets of East Bridgeport.

Three handsome churches, Methodist, Episcopal and Congregational, front on the beautiful Washington Park of seven acres, which Mr. Noble and myself presented to the city. Some of the largest and most prosperous manufactories in the United States are located in the new city.

The entire city of Bridgeport is advancing in population and prosperity with a rapidity far beyond that of any other city in Connecticut, and everything indicates that it will soon take its proper position as the second, if not the first, city in the State. Its situation as the terminus of the Naugatuck and the Housatonic railways, its accessibility to New York, with its two daily steamboats to and from the metropolis, and its dozen daily trains of the New York and Boston and Shore Line railways, are all elements of prosperity which are rapidly telling in favor of this busy, beautiful and charming city.

CHAPTER XXXVI.

MORE ABOUT THE MUSEUM.

In 1861, I learned that some fishermen at the mouth of the St. Lawrence had succeeded in capturing a living white whale, and I was also informed that a whale of this kind, if placed in a box lined with sea-weed and partially filled with salt water, could be transported by land to a considerable distance, and be kept alive. It was simply necessary that an attendant, supplied with a barrel of salt water and a sponge, should keep the mouth and blow-hole of the whale constantly moist.

Having made up my mind to capture and transport to my Museum at least two living whales, I prepared in the basement of the building a brick and cement tank, forty-feet long, and eighteen-feet wide, for their reception. This done, I started upon my whaling expedition. Going by rail to Quebec, and thence by the Grand Trunk Railroad, ninety miles, to Wells river, I chartered a sloop to Elbow island (*Isle au Coudres*), in the St. Lawrence river, populated by Canadian French people. I contracted with a party of twenty-four fishermen, to capture for me, alive and unharmed, a couple of white whales, scores of which could at all times be discovered by their "spouting" within sight of the island.

The plan decided upon was to plant in the river a "kraal," composed of stakes driven down in the form of a V, leaving the broad end open for the whales to enter. This was done in a shallow place, with the point of the *kraal* towards shore; and if by chance one or more whales should enter the trap at high water, my fishermen were to occupy the entrance with their boats, and keep up a tremendous splashing and noise till the tide receded, when the frightened whales would find themselves nearly "high and dry," or with too little water to enable them to swim, and their capture would be next thing in order. This was to be effected by securing a slip-noose of stout rope over their tails, and towing them to the sea-weed lined boxes in which they were to be transported to New York.

It was aggravating to see the whales glide so near the trap without going into it, and our patience was sorely tried. One day a whale actually went into the kraal, and the fishermen proposed to capture it; but I wanted another, and while we waited for number two to go in number one went out. After several days I was awakened at daylight by a great noise, and amid the clamor of many voices, I caught the cheering news that two whales were even then within the kraal. Leaving the details of capture and transportation to my trusty assistants, I started at once for New York, leaving at every station on the line instructions to telegraph operators to "take off" all whaling messages that passed over the wires to New York, and to inform their fellow-townsmen at what hour the whales would pass through each place.

The result of these arrangements may be imagined; at every station crowds of people came to the cars to see the whales which were traveling by land to Barnum's Museum, and those who did not see the monsters with their own eyes, at least saw someone who had seen them, and I thus secured a tremendous advertisement, seven hundred miles long, for the American Museum.

Arrived in New York, dispatches continued to come from the whaling expedition every few hours. These I bulletined in front of the Museum and sent copies to the papers. The excitement was intense, and, when at last, these marine monsters arrived and were swimming in the tank that had been prepared for them, anxious thousands literally rushed to see the strangest curiosities ever exhibited in New York.

Thus, was my first whaling expedition a great success; but I did not know how to feed or to take care of the monsters, and, moreover, they were in fresh water, and this, with the bad air in the basement, may have hastened their death, which occurred a few days after their arrival, but not before thousands of people had seen them. Not at all discouraged, I resolved to try again. My plan now was to connect the water of New York bay with the basement of the Museum by means of iron pipes under the street, and a steam engine on the dock to pump the water. This I actually did at a cost of several thousand dollars, with an extra thousand to the aldermanic "ring" for the privilege, and I constructed another tank in the second floor of the building. This tank was built of slate and French glass plates six feet long, five feet broad, and one inch thick, imported expressly for the purpose, and the tank, when completed, was twenty-four feet square, and cost $4,000. It was kept constantly supplied with what would be called, Hibernically, "fresh" salt water, and inside of it I soon had two white whales, caught, as the first had been, hundreds of miles below Quebec, to which city they were carried by a sailing vessel, and from thence were brought by railway to New York.

Of this whole enterprise, I confess I was very proud that I had originated it and brought it to such successful conclusion. It was a very great sensation, and it added thousands of dollars to my treasury. The whales, however, soon died — their sudden and immense popularity was too much for them — and I then dispatched agents to the coast of Labrador, and not many weeks thereafter I had two more live whales disporting themselves in my monster aquarium. Certain envious people started the report that my whales were only porpoises, but this petty malice was turned to good account, for Professor Agassiz, of Harvard University, came to see them, and gave me a certificate that they were genuine white whales, and this endorsement I published far and wide.

The tank which I had built in the basement served for a yet more interesting exhibition. On the twelfth of August, 1861, I began to exhibit the first and only genuine hippopotamus that had ever been seen in America, and for several weeks the Museum was thronged by the curious who came to see the monster. I advertised him extensively and ingeniously, as "the great behemoth of the Scriptures," giving a full description of the animal and his habits, and thousands of cultivated people, biblical students, and others, were attracted to this novel exhibition. There was quite as much excitement in the city over this wonder in the animal creation as there was in London when the first hippopotamus was placed in the zoological collection in Regent's Park.

Having a stream of salt water at my command at every high tide, I was enabled to make splendid additions to the beautiful aquarium, which I was the first to introduce into this country. I not only procured living sharks, porpoises, sea horses, and many rare fish from the sea in the vicinity of New York, but in the summer of

1861, and for several summers in succession, I dispatched a fishing smack and crew to the Islands of Bermuda and its neighborhood, whence they brought scores of specimens of the beautiful "angel fish," and numerous other tropical fish of brilliant colors and unique forms. In the same year, I bought out the Aquarial Gardens in Boston, and soon after removed the collection to the Museum.

In December, 1801, I made one of my most "palpable hits." I was visit. the Museum by a most remarkable dwarf, who was a sharp, intelligent little fellow, with a deal of drollery and wit. He had a splendid head, was perfectly formed, and was very attractive, and, in short, for a "showman," he is a perfect treasure. His name, he told me, was George Washington Morrison Nutt, and his father was Major Rodnia Nutt, a substantial farmer, of Manchester, New Hampshire. I was not long in dispatching an efficient agent to Manchester, and in overcoming the competition with other showmen who were equally eager to secure this extraordinary pigmy. The terms upon which I engaged him for three years were so large that he was christened the $30,000 Nutt; I, in the meantime, conferring upon him the title of Commodore. As soon as I engaged him, placards, posters and the columns of the newspapers proclaimed the presence of "Commodore Nutt," at the Museum. I also procured for the Commodore a pair of Shetland ponies, miniature coachman and footman, in livery, gold-mounted harness, and an elegant little carriage, which, when closed, represented a gigantic English walnut. The little Commodore attracted great attention, and grew rapidly in public favor. General Tom Thumb was then traveling in the South and West. For some years he had not been exhibited in New York, and during these years he had increased considerably in rotundity and had changed much in his general appearance. It was a singular fact, however, that Commodore Nutt was almost a facsimile of General Tom Thumb, as he looked half-a-dozen years before. Consequently, very many of my patrons, not making allowance for the time which had elapsed since they had last seen the General, declared that there was no such person as "Commodore Nutt;" but that I was exhibiting my old friend Tom Thumb under a new name.

Commodore Nutt enjoyed the joke very much. He would sometimes half admit the deception, simply to add to the bewilderment of the doubting portion of my visitors.

It was evident that here was an opportunity to turn all doubts into hard cash, by simply bringing the two dwarf Dromios together, and showing them on the same platform. I therefore induced Tom Thumb to bring his western engagements to a close, and to appear for four weeks, beginning with August 11, 1862, in my Museum. Announcements headed "The Two Dromios," and "Two Smallest Men, and Greatest Curiosities Living," as I expected, drew large crowds to see them, and many came specially to solve their doubts with regard to the genuineness of the "Nutt." But here I was considerably nonplussed, for astonishing as it may seem, the doubts of many of the visitors were confirmed! The sharp people who were determined "not to be humbugged, anyhow," still declared that Commodore Nutt was General Tom Thumb, and that the little fellow whom I was trying to pass off as Tom Thumb, was no more like the General than he was like the man in the moon. It is very amusing to see how people will sometimes deceive themselves by being too incredulous,

In 1862, I sent the Commodore to Washington, and, joining him there, I received an invitation from President Lincoln to call at the White House with my little friend. Arriving at the appointed hour, I was informed that the President was in a special cabinet meeting, but that he had left word if I called I was to be shown in to him with the Commodore. These were dark days in the rebellion and I felt that my visit, if not ill-timed, must at all events be brief. When we were admitted, Mr. Lincoln received us cordially, and introduced us to the members of the Cabinet. When Mr. Chase was introduced as the Secretary of the Treasury, the little Commodore remarked:

"I suppose you are the gentleman who is spending so much of Uncle Sam's money? "

"No, indeed," said Secretary of War Stanton, very promptly: " I am spending the money."

"Well" said Commodore Nutt, "it is in a good cause, anyhow, and I guess it will come out all right."

His apt remark created much amusement. Mr. Lincoln then bent down his long, lank body, and taking Nutt by the hand, he said:

"Commodore, permit me to give you a parting word of advice. When you are in command of your fleet, if you find yourself in danger of being taken prisoner, I advise you to wade ashore."

The Commodore found the laugh was against him, but placing himself at the side of the President, and gradually raising his eyes up the whole length of Mr. Lincoln's very long legs, he replied:

"I guess, Mr. President, you could do that better than I could."

Commodore Nutt and the Nova Scotia giantess, Anna Swan, illustrate the old proverb sufficiently to show how extremes occasionally met in my Museum. He was the shortest of men and she was the tallest of women. I first heard of her through a Quaker who came into my office one day and told me of a wonderful girl, seventeen years of age, who resided near him at Pictou, Nova Scotia, and who was probably the tallest girl in the world. I asked him to obtain her exact height, on his return home, which he did, and sent it to me, and I at once sent an agent who in due time came back with Anna Swan. She was an intelligent and by no means ill-looking girl, and during the long period while she was in my employ, she was visited by thousands of persons. After the burning of my second Museum, she went to England where she attracted great attention.

For many years I had been in the habit of engaging parties of American Indians from the far west, to exhibit at the Museum, and had sent two or more Indian companies to Europe, where they were regarded as very great "curiosities." In 1864, ten or twelve chiefs of as many different tribes, visited the President of the United States, at Washington. By a pretty liberal outlay of money, I succeeded in inducing the interpreter to bring them to New York, and to pass some days at my Museum. Of course, getting these Indians to dance, or to give any illustration of their games or pastimes, was out of the question. They were real chiefs of powerful tribes and would no more have consented to give an exhibition of themselves than the chief magistrate of our own nation would have done. Their interpreter could not therefore promise that they would remain at the Museum for any definite time; "for," said he, "you can only keep them just so long as they suppose all your patrons come to pay them visits of honor. If they suspected that your Museum was a place where people paid for entering," he continued, "you could not keep them a moment after the discovery."

On their arrival at the Museum, therefore, I took them upon the stage and personally introduced them to the public. The Indians liked this attention from me, as they had been informed that I was the proprietor of the great establishment in which they were invited and honored guests. My patrons were, of course, pleased to see these old chiefs, as they knew they were the "real thing," and several of them were known to the public, either as being friendly or cruel to the whites. After one or two appearances on the stage, I took them in carriages and visited the Mayor of New York in the Governor's room at the City Hall. Here the Mayor made them a speech of welcome, which being interpreted to the savages was responded to by a speech from one of the chiefs, in which he thanked the great "Father" of the city for his pleasant words, and for his kindness in pointing out the portraits of his predecessors hanging on the walls of the Governor's room.

On another occasion, I took them by special invitation to visit one of the large public schools uptown. The teachers were pleased to see them, and arranged an exhibition of special exercises by the scholars, which they thought would be most likely to gratify their barbaric visitors. At the close of these exercises, one old chief arose, and simply said, "This is all new to us. We are mere unlearned sons of the forest, and cannot understand what we have seen and heard."

On other occasions, I took them to ride in Central Park, and through different portions of the city. At every street corner which we passed, they would express their astonishment to each other, at seeing the long rows of houses which extended both ways on either side of each cross-street. Of course, between each of these outside visits I would return with them to the Museum, and secure two or three appearances upon the stage to receive the people who had there congregated "to do them honor."

As they regarded me as their host, they did not hesitate to trespass upon my hospitality. Whenever their eyes rested upon a glittering shell among my specimens of conchology, especially if it had several brilliant colors, one would take off his coat, another his shirt, and insist that I should exchange my shell for their garment. When I declined the exchange, but on the contrary presented them with the coveted article, I soon found I had established a dangerous precedent. Immediately, they all commenced to beg for everything in my vast collection, which they happened to take a liking to. This cost me many valuable specimens, and often "put me to my trumps" for an excuse to avoid giving them things which I could not part with.

The chief of one of the tribes one day discovered an ancient shirt of chain-mail which hung in one of my cases of antique armor. He was delighted with it, and declared he must have it. I tried all sorts of excuses to prevent his getting it, for it had cost me a hundred dollars, and was a great curiosity. But the old man's eyes glistened, and he would not take "no" for an answer. "The Utes have killed my little child," he told me through the interpreter; and now he must have this steel shirt to protect himself; and when he returned to the Rocky Mountains he would have his revenge. I remained inexorable until he finally brought me a new buckskin Indian suit, which he insisted upon exchanging. I felt compelled to accept his proposal; and never did I see a man more delighted than he seemed to be when he took the mailed shirt into his hands. He fairly jumped up and down with joy. He ran to his lodging-room, and soon appeared again with the coveted armor upon his body, and marched down one of the main halls of the Museum, with folded arms, and head erect, occasionally patting his breast with his right hand, as much as to say, "now, Mr. Ute, look sharp, for I will soon be on the war path!"

Among these Indians were War Bonnet, Lean Bear, and Hand-in-the-water, chiefs of the Cheyenne; Yellow Buffalo, of the Kiowas: Yellow Bear, of the same tribe; Jacob, of the Caddos; and White Bull, of the Apaches. The little wiry chief known as Yellow Bear had killed many whites as they had traveled through the "far west." He was a sly, treacherous, bloodthirsty savage, who would think no more of scalping a family of women and children, than a butcher would of wringing the neck of a chicken. But now, he was on a mission to the "Great Father" at Washington, seeking for presents and favors for his tribe, and he pretended to be exceedingly meek and humble, and continually urged the interpreter to announce him as a "great friend to the white man." He would fawn about me, and although not speaking or understanding a word of our language, would try to convince me that he loved me dearly.

In exhibiting these Indian warriors on the stage, I explained to the large audiences the names and characteristics of each. When I came to Yellow Bear, I would pat him familiarly upon the shoulder, which always caused him to look up to me with a pleasant smile, while he softly stroked down my arm with his right hand in the most loving manner. Knowing that he could not understand a word I said, I pretended to be complimenting him to the audience, while I was really saying something like the following:

"This little Indian, ladies and gentlemen, is Yellow Bear, chief of the Kiowas. He has killed, no doubt, scores of white persons, and he is probably the meanest, black-hearted rascal that lives in the far west." Here I patted him on the head, and he, supposing I was sounding his praises, would smile, fawn upon me, and stroke my arm, while I continued: "If the blood-thirsty little villain understood what I was saying, he would kill me in a moment; but as he thinks I am complimenting him, I can safely state the truth to you, that he is a lying, thieving, treacherous, murderous monster. He has tortured to death poor, unprotected women, murdered their husbands, brained their helpless little ones; and he would gladly do the same to you or to me, if he thought he could escape punishment. This is but a faint description of the character of Yellow Bear." Here I gave him another patronizing pat on the head, and he, with a pleasant smile, bowed to the audience, as much as to say that my words were quite true, and that he thanked me very much for the high encomiums I had so generously heaped upon him.

After they had been about a week at the Museum, one of the chiefs discovered that visitors paid money for entering. This information he soon communicated to the other chiefs, and I heard an immediate murmur of discontent. Their eyes were opened, and no power could induce them to appear again upon the stage. Their dignity had been offended, and their wild, flashing eyes were anything but agreeable. Indeed, I hardly felt safe in their presence, and it was with a feeling of relief that I witnessed their departure for Washington the next morning.

CAPTURING WHITE WHALES

CHAPTER XXXVII.

MR. AND MRS. GENERAL TOM THUMB.

In 1863, I heard of an extraordinary dwarf girl, named Lavinia Warren, who was residing with her parents at Middleboro, Massachusetts, and I sent an invitation to her and her parents to come and visit me at Bridgeport. They came, and I found her to be a most intelligent and refined young lady, well-educated, and an accomplished, beautiful and perfectly developed woman in miniature. I succeeded in making an engagement with her for several years, during which she contracted — as dwarfs are said to have the power to do — to visit Great Britain, France, and other foreign lands.

Having arranged the terms of her engagement, I took her to the house of one of my daughters in New York, where she remained quietly, while I was procuring her wardrobe and jewelry, and making arrangements for her debut.

I purchased a very splendid wardrobe for Mrs. Warren, including scores of the richest dresses that could be procured, costly jewels, and in fact everything that could add to the charms of her naturally charming little person. She was then placed on exhibition at the Museum, and from the day of her debut she was on extraordinary success. Commodore Nutt was on exhibition with her, and although he was several years her junior, he evidently took a great fancy to her. One day, I presented to Lavinia a diamond and emerald ring, and as it did not exactly fit her finger, I told her I would give her another one and that she might present this one to the Commodore in her own name. She did so, and an unlooked-for effect was speedily apparent; the little Commodore felt sure that this was a love-token, and poor Lavinia was in the greatest trouble, for she considered herself quite a woman, and regarded the Commodore only as a nice little boy. But she did not like to offend him, and while she did not encourage, she did not openly repel his attentions. Miss Lavinia Warren, however, was never destined to be Mrs. Commodore Nutt.

It was by no means an unnatural circumstance that I should be suspected of having instigated and brought about the marriage of Tom Thumb with Lavinia Warren. Had I done this, I should at this day have felt no regrets, for it has proved, in an eminent degree, one of the "happy marriages." I only say, what is known to all of their immediate friends, that from first to last their engagement was an affair of the heart— a case of "love at first sight"—that the attachment was mutual, and that it only grows with the lapse of time. But I had neither part nor lot in instigating or in occasioning the marriage. And as I am anxious to be put right before the public, I have procured the consent of all the parties to a sketch of the wooing, winning and nuptials. Of course, I should not lay these details before the public, except with the sanction of those most interested. In this they consent to pay the penalty of distinction. And if the wooings of kings and queens must be told, why not the courtship and marriage of General and Mrs. Tom Thumb? The story is an interesting one, and shall be told alike to exonerate me from the suspicion named, and to amuse those— and they count by scores of thousands — who are interested in the welfare of the distinguished couple.

In the autumn of 1802, when Lavinia Warren was on exhibition at the Museum, Tom Thumb had no business engagement with me; in fact, he was not on exhibition at the time at all; he was taking a "vacation" at his house in Bridgeport. Whenever he came to New York he naturally called upon me, his old friend, at the Museum. He happened to be in the city at the time referred to, and one day he called, quite unexpectedly to me, while Lavinia was holding one of her levees. Here he now saw her for the first time, and very naturally made her acquaintance He had a short interview with her, after which he came directly to my private office and desired to see me alone. Of course, I complied with his request, but without the remotest suspicion as to his object. I closed the door, and the General took a seat. His first question let in the light. He inquired about the family of Lavinia Warren. I gave him the facts, which I clearly perceived gave him satisfaction of a peculiar sort. He then said, with great frankness, and with no less earnestness:

"Mr. Barnum, that is the most charming little lady I ever saw, and I believe she was created on purpose to be my wife! Now," he continued, "you have always been a friend of mine, and I want you to say a good word for me to her. I have got plenty of money, and I want to marry and settle down in life, and I really feel as if I must marry that young lady."

The little General was highly excited, and his general manner betrayed the usual anxiety, which, I doubt not, most of my readers will understand without a description. I could not repress a smile, nor forget my joke, and I said:

"Lavinia is engaged already."

"To whom — Commodore Nutt?" asked Tom Thumb, with much earnestness, and some exhibition of the "green-eyed monster."

"No, General, to me," I replied

"Never mind," said the General, laughing, "you can exhibit her for a while, and then give up the engagement; but I do hope you will favor my suit with her."

"Well General," I replied, "I will not oppose you in your suit, but you must do your own courting. I tell you, however, the Commodore will be jealous of you, and more than that, Miss Warren is nobody's fool, and you will have to proceed very cautiously if you can succeed in winning her affections."

The General thanked me, and promised to be very discreet. A change now came suddenly over him in several particulars. He had been (much to his credit) very fond of his country home in Bridgeport, where he spent his intervals of rest with his horses, and especially with his yacht, for his fondness for the water was his great passion. But now he was constantly having occasion to visit the city, and horses and yachts were strangely neglected. He had a married sister in New York, and his visits to her multiplied, for, of course, he came to New York to see his sister! " His mother, who resided in Bridgeport, remarked that Charles had never before shown so much brotherly affection, nor so much fondness for city life.

His visits to the Museum were very frequent, and it was noticeable that new relations were being established between him and Commodore Nutt. The Commodore was not exactly jealous, yet he strutted around like a bantam rooster whenever the General approached Lavinia. One day he and the General got into a friendly scuffle in the dressing-room, and the Commodore threw the General upon his back in "double quick" time. The Commodore is lithe, wiry, and quick in his movements, but the

General is naturally slow, and although he was considerably heavier than the Commodore, he soon found that he could not stand before him in a personal encounter. Moreover, the Commodore is naturally quick-tempered, and, when excited, he brags about his knowledge of "the manly art of self-defense," and sometimes talks about pistols and bowie knives, etc. Tom Thumb, on the contrary, is by natural disposition decidedly a man of peace; hence, in this, agreeing with Falstaff as to what constituted the "better part of valor," he was strongly inclined to keep his distance, if the little Commodore showed any belligerent symptoms.

In the course of several weeks the General found numerous opportunities to talk with Lavinia, while the Commodore was performing on the stage, or was otherwise engaged; and, to a watchful discerner, it was evident he was making encouraging progress in the affair of the heart. He also managed to meet Lavinia on Sunday afternoons and evenings, without the knowledge of the Commodore; but he assured me he had not yet dared to suggest matrimony.

He finally returned to Bridgeport, and privately begged that on the following Saturday I would take Lavinia up to my house, and also invite him.

His immediate object in this was that his mother might get acquainted with Lavinia, for he feared opposition from that source whenever the idea of his marriage should be suggested. I could do no less than accede to his proposal and on the following Friday, while Lavinia and the Commodore were sitting in the green-room, I said:

"Lavinia, you may go up to Bridgeport with me tomorrow morning and remain until Monday."

"Thank you," she replied; "it will be quite a relief to get into the country for a couple of days."

The Commodore immediately pricked up his ears, and said:

"Mr. Barnum, I should like to go to Bridgeport tomorrow."

"What for?" I asked.

"I want to see my little ponies; I have not seen them for several months," he replied.

I whispered in his ear, "you little rogue, that is the pony you want to see," pointing to Lavinia.

He insisted I was mistaken. When I remarked that he could not well be spared from the Museum, he said:

"Oh! I can perform at half -past seven o'clock, and then jump on to the eight o'clock evening train, and go up by myself, reaching Bridgeport before eleven, and return early Monday morning."

I feared there would be a clashing of interests between the rival pigmies; but wishing to please him, I consented to his request, especially as Lavinia also favored it. I wished I could then fathom that little woman's heart, and see whether she (who must have discovered the secret of the General's frequent visits to the Museum) desired the Commodore's visit in order to stir up the General's ardor, or whether, as seemed to me the more likely, she was seeking in this to prevent a denouement which she was not inclined to favor. Certain it is, that though I was the General's confidant, and knew all his desires upon the subject, no person had discovered the slightest evidence that Lavinia Warren had ever entertained the remotest suspicion of his thoughts regarding marriage. If she had made the discovery, as I assume, she kept the secret well. In fact, I assured Tom Thumb that every indication, so far as any of us could observe, was to the effect that his suit would be rejected. The little General was fidgety, but determined; hence he was anxious to have Lavinia meet his mother, and also see his possessions in Bridgeport, for he owned considerable land and numerous houses there.

The General met us at the depot in Bridgeport, on Saturday morning, and drove us to my house in his own carriage — his coachman being tidily dressed, with a broad velvet ribbon and silver buckle placed upon his hat expressly for the occasion. Lavinia was duly informed that this was the General's "turn out;" and after resting half an hour at Lindencroft, he took her out to ride. He stopped a few moments at his mother's house, where she saw the apartments which his father had built expressly for him, and filled with the most gorgeous furniture— all corresponding to his own diminutive size. Then he took her to East Bridgeport, and undoubtedly took occasion to point out in great detail all of the houses which he owned, for he depended much upon having his wealth make some impression upon her. They returned, and the General stayed to lunch. I asked Lavinia how she liked her ride; she replied:

"It was very pleasant, but," she added, "it seems as if you and Tom Thumb owned about all of Bridgeport!"

The General took his leave and returned at five o'clock to dinner with his mother. Mrs. Stratton remained until seven o'clock. She expressed herself charmed with Lavinia Warren; but not a suspicion passed her mind that little Charlie was endeavoring to give her this accomplished young lady as a daughter-in-law. The General had privately asked me to invite him to stay overnight, "For," said he, "if I get a chance, I intend to 'pop the question' before the Commodore arrives." So, I told his mother I thought the General had better stop with us over night, as the Commodore would be up in the late train, adding that it would be more pleasant for the little folks to be together. She assented, and the General was happy.

After tea, Lavinia and the General sat down to play backgammon. As nine o'clock approached, I remarked that it was about time to retire, but somebody would have to sit up until nearly eleven o'clock, in order to let in the Commodore. The General replied:

"I will sit up with pleasure, if Miss Warren will remain also."

Lavinia carelessly replied, that she was accustomed to late hours, and she would wait and see the Commodore. A little supper was placed upon the table for the Commodore, and the family retired.

Now it happened that a couple of mischievous young ladies were visiting at my house, one of whom was to sleep with Lavinia, they were suspicious that the General was going to propose to Lavinia that evening, and, in a spirit of ungovernable curiosity, they determined, notwithstanding its manifest impropriety, to witness the operation, if they could possibly manage to do so on the sly. Of course, this was inexcusable, the more so as so few of my readers, had they been placed under the same temptation, would have been guilty of such an impropriety! Perhaps I should hesitate to use the testimony of such witnesses, or even to trust it. But a few weeks after, they told the little couple the whole story, were forgiven, and all had a hearty laugh over it.

It so happened that the door of the sitting-room, in which the General and Lavinia were left at the backgammon board, opened into the hall just at the side of the stairs, and these young misses, turning out the lights in the hall, seated themselves upon the stairs in the dark, where they had a full view of the cozy little couple, and were within easy ear-shot of all that was said.

The house was still The General soon acknowledged himself vanquished at backgammon, and gave it up. After sitting a few moments, he evidently thought it was best to put a clincher on the financial part of his abilities; so, he drew from his pocket a policy of insurance, and handing it to Lavinia, he asked her if she knew what it was.

Examining it, she replied, "It is an insurance policy. I see you keep your property insured."

"But the beauty of it is, it is not my property," replied the General, "and yet I get the benefit of the insurance in case of fire. You will see," he continued, unfolding the policy, "this is the property of Mr. Williams, but here, you will observe, it reads 'loss, if any, payable to Charles S. Stratton, as his interest may appear.' The fact is, I loaned Mr. Williams three thousand dollars, took a mortgage on his house, and made him insure it for my benefit. In this way, you perceive. I get my interest, and he has to pay the taxes."

"That is a very wise way, I should think," remarked Lavinia,

"That is the way I do all my business," replied the General, complacently, as he returned the huge insurance policy to his pocket. "You see," he continued, 'I never lend any of my money without taking bond and mortgage security, then I have no trouble with taxes; my principal is secure, and I receive my interest regularly."

The explanation seemed satisfactory to Lavinia, and the General's courage began to rise. Drawing his chair, a little nearer to hers, he said:

"So, you are going to Europe, soon?"

"Yes," replied Lavinia, "Mr. Barnum intends to take me over in a couple of months."

"You will find it very pleasant," remarked the General; "I have been there twice, in fact I have spent six years abroad, and I like the old countries very much."

"I hope I shall like the trip, and I expect I shall," responded Lavinia; "for Mr. Barnum says I shall visit all the principal cities, and he has no doubt I will be invited to appear before the Queen of England, the Emperor and Empress of France, the King of Prussia, the Emperor of Austria, and at the courts of any other countries which we may visit. Oh, I shall like that, it will be so new to me."

"Yes, it will be very interesting indeed. I have visited most of the crowned heads," remarked the General, with an evident feeling of self-congratulation. "But are you not afraid you will be lonesome in a strange country?" asked the General.

"No, I think there is no danger of that, for friends will accompany me," was the reply.

"I wish I was going over, for I know all about the different countries, and could explain them all to you," remarked Tom Thumb.

"That would be very nice," said Lavinia.

"Do you think so?" said the General, moving his chair still closer to Lavinia's.

"Of course," replied Lavinia, coolly, " for I, being a stranger to all the habits and customs of the people, as well as to the country, it would be pleasant to have some person along who could answer all my foolish questions."

"I should like it first rate, if Mr. Barnum would engage me," said the General.

"I thought you remarked the other day that you had money enough, and was tired of traveling," said Lavinia, with a slightly mischievous look from one corner of her eye.

"That depends upon my company while traveling," replied the General

"You might not find my company very agreeable."

"I would be glad to risk it."

"Well, perhaps Mr. Barnum would engage you, if you asked him," said Lavinia.

"Would you really like to have me go?" asked the General, quietly insinuating his arm around her waist, but hardly close enough to touch her.

"Of course, I would," was the reply.

The little General's arm clasped the waist closer as he turned his face nearer to hers, and said:

"Don't you think it would be pleasanter if we went as man and wife?"

The little fairy quickly disengaged his arm, and remarked that the General was a funny fellow to joke in that way.

"I am not joking at all," said the General, earnestly, "it is quite too serious a matter for that."

"I wonder why the Commodore don't come?" said Lavinia.

"I hope you are not anxious for his arrival, for I am sure I am not," responded the General "and what is more, I do hope you will say 'yes,' before he comes at all!"

"Really, Mr. Stratton," said Lavinia, with dignity, "if you are in earnest in your strange proposal, I must say I am surprised."

"Well, I hope you are not offended," replied the General, "for I was never more in earnest in my life, and I hope you will consent. The first moment I saw you I felt that you were created to be my wife."

"But this is so sudden."

"Not so very sudden; it is several months since we first met, and you know all about me and my family, and I hope you find nothing to object to in me."

"Not at all; on the contrary, I have found you very agreeable, in fact I like you very much as a Friend, but I have not thought of marrying, and — "

"And what, my dear?" said the General, giving her a kiss. "Now, I beg of you, don't have any 'buts' or 'ands' about it. You say you like me as a friend, why will you not like me as a husband? You ought to get married; I love you dearly, and I want you for a wife. Now, deary, the Commodore will be here in a few minutes, I may not have a chance to see you again alone; do say that we will be married, and I will get Mr. Barnum to give up your engagement."

Lavinia hesitated, and finally said:

"I think I love you well enough to consent, but I have always said I would never marry without my mother's consent."

"Oh! I'll ask your mother. May I ask your mother? Come, say yes to that, and I will go and see her next week. May I do that, pet?"

Then there was a sound of something very much like the popping of several corks from as many beer-bottles. The young eavesdroppers had no doubt as to the character of these reports, nor did they doubt that they sealed the betrothal, for immediately after they heard Lavinia say:

"Yes, Charles, you may ask my mother." Another volley of reports followed, and then Lavinia said, "Now, Charles, don't whisper this to a living soul; let us keep our own secrets for the present."

"All right," said the General, "I will say nothing; but next Tuesday I shall start to see your mother."

"Perhaps you may find it difficult to obtain her consent," said Lavinia,

At that moment a carriage drove up to the door, and immediately the bell was rung, and the little Commodore entered.

"You here, General?" said the Commodore, as he espied his rival.

"Yes," said Lavinia, "Mr. Barnum asked him to stay, and we were waiting for you; come, warm yourself."

"I am not cold," said the Commodore; "where is Mr. Barnum?"

"He has gone to bed," remarked the General, "but a nice supper has been prepared for you."

"I am not hungry, I thank you; I am going to bed. Which room does Mr. Barnum sleep in?" said the little bantam, in a petulant tone of voice.

His question was answered; the young eavesdroppers scampered to their sleeping apartments, and the Commodore soon came to my room, where he found me indulging in the foolish habit of reading in bed.

"Mr. Barnum, does Tom Thumb board here?" asked the Commodore, sarcastically.

"No," said I, "Tom Thumb does not board here. I invited him to stop overnight, so don't be foolish, but go to bed."

"Oh, it's no affair of mine. I don't care anything about it; but I thought he had taken up his board here," replied the Commodore, and off he went to bed, evidently in a bad humor.

Ten minutes afterwards, Tom Thumb came rushing into my room, and, closing the door, he caught hold of my hand in high state of excitement and whispered:

"We are engaged, Mr. Barnum! we are engaged! we are engaged!" and he jumped up and down in the greatest glee.

"Is that possible? " I asked.

"Yes, sir, indeed it is; but you must not mention it," he responded: "we agreed to tell nobody, so please don't say a word. I must tell you, of course, but 'mum is the word.' I am going, Tuesday, to get her mother's consent."

I promised secrecy, and the General retired in as happy a mood as I ever saw him. Lavinia also retired, but not a hint did she give to the young lady with whom she slept regarding the engagement. Indeed, our family plied her upon the subject the next day, but not a breath passed her lips that would give the slightest indication of what had transpired. She was quite sociable with the Commodore, and as the General concluded to go home the next morning, the Commodore's equanimity and good feelings were fully restored. The General made a call of half an hour Sunday evening, and managed to have an interview with Lavinia. The next morning, she and the Commodore returned to New York in good spirits, I remaining in Bridgeport.

The General called on me Monday, however, bringing a very nice letter which he had written to Lavinia's mother. He had concluded to send this letter by his trusty friend, Mr. George A. Wells, instead of going himself, and he had just seen Mr.

Wells, who had consented to go to Middleborough with the letter the following day, and to urge the General's suit, if it should be necessary.

The General went to New York on Wednesday, and was there to await Mr. Wells' arrival. On Wednesday morning the General and Lavinia walked into my office, and after closing the door, the little General said:

"Mr. Barnum, I want somebody to tell the Commodore that Lavinia and I are engaged, for I am afraid there will be a 'row' when he hears of it."

"Do it yourself, General" I replied.

"Oh," said the General, almost shuddering, "I would not dare to do it, he might knock me down."

"I will do it," said Lavinia; and it was at once arranged that I should call the Commodore and Lavinia into my office, and either she or myself would tell him. The General of course, "vamoosed."

When the Commodore joined us, and the door was closed, I said:

"Commodore, do you know what this little witch has been doing?"

"No, I don't," he answered.

"Well, she has been cutting up one of the greatest pranks you ever heard of," I replied. "She almost deserves to be shut up, for daring to do it. Can't you guess what she has done?"

He mused a moment, and then looking at me, said in a low voice, and with a serious-looking face, "Engaged?"

"Yes," said I, "absolutely engaged to be married to General Tom Thumb. Did you ever hear of such a thing? "

"Is that so, Lavinia?" asked the Commodore, looking her earnestly in the face.

"That is so," said Lavinia; "and Mr. Wells has gone to obtain my mother's consent."

The Commodore turned pale, and choked a little, as if he was trying to swallow something. Then, turning on his heel, he said, in a broken voice:

"I hope you may be happy."

As he passed out the door, a tear rolled down his cheek.

"That is pretty hard," I said to Lavinia.

"I am very sorry," she replied, "but I could not help it. That diamond and emerald ring which you bade me present in my name, has caused all this trouble."

Half an hour after this incident, the Commodore came to my office, and said:

"Mr. Barnum, do you think it would be right for Miss Warren to marry Charley Stratton if her mother should object?"

I saw that the little fellow had still a slight hope to hang on, and I said:

"No, indeed, it would not be right."

THE FAIRY WEDDING GROUP

"Well, she says she shall marry him anyway; that she gives her mother the chance to consent, but if she objects, she will have her own way and marry him," said the Commodore.

"On the contrary," I replied, "I will not permit it. She is engaged to go to Europe for me, and I will not release her, if her mother does not fully consent to her marrying Tom Thumb."

The Commodore's eyes glistened with pleasure, as he replied:

"Between you and me, Mr. Barnum, I don't believe she will give her consent."

But the next day dissipated his hopes. Mr. Wells returned, saying that Lavinia's mother at first objected, for she feared it was a contrivance to get them married for the promotion of some pecuniary advantage; but, upon reading the letter from the General, and one still more urgent from Lavinia, and also upon hearing from Mr. Wells that, in case of their marriage, I should cancel all claims I had upon Lavinia's services, she consented.

After the Commodore had heard the news, I said to him:

"Never mind, Commodore, Minnie Warren is a better match for you; she is a charming little creature, and two years younger than you, while Lavinia is several years your senior."

"I thank you, sir," replied the Commodore, pompously, "I would not marry the best woman living; I don't believe in women, anyway."

I then suggested that he should stand with little Minnie, as groom and bridesmaid, at the approaching wedding.

"No, sir!" replied the Commodore, emphatically; "I won't do it!"

That idea was therefore abandoned. A few weeks subsequently, when time had reconciled the Commodore, he told me that Tom Thumb had asked him to stand as groom with Minnie, at the wedding, and he was going to do so.

"When I asked you a few weeks ago, you refused," I said.

"It was not your business to ask me," replied the Commodore, pompously. "When the proper person invited me, I accepted."

The approaching wedding was announced. It created an immense excitement. Lavinia's levees at the Museum were crowded to suffocation, and her photographic pictures were in great demand. For several weeks she sold more than three hundred dollars' worth of her *cartes de visite* each day. And the daily receipts at the Museum were frequently over three thousand dollars. I engaged the General to exhibit, and to assist her in the sale of pictures, to which his own photograph, of course, was added. I could afford to give them a fine wedding, and I did so.

I did not hesitate to seek continued advantage from the notoriety of the prospective marriage. Accordingly, I offered the General and Lavinia fifteen thousand dollars if they would postpone the wedding for a month, and continue their exhibitions at the Museum.

"Not for fifty thousand dollars," said the General, excitedly.

"Good for you, Charley," said Lavinia, "only you ought to have said not for a *hundred thousand*, for I would not!"

They both laughed heartily at what they considered my discomfiture, and such, looked at from a business point of view, it certainly was. The wedding day approached and the public excitement grew. For several days, I might say weeks, the approaching marriage of Tom Thumb was the New York "sensation." For proof of this I did not need what, however, was ample, the newspaper paragraphs. A surer index was in the crowds that passed into the Museum, and the dollars that found their way into the ticket-office.

It was suggested to me that a small fortune in itself could be easily made out of the excitement. "Let the ceremony take place in the Academy of Music, charge a big price for admission, and the citizens will come in crowds." I have no manner of doubt that in this way twenty-five thousand dollars could easily have been obtained. But I had no such thought. I had promised to give the couple a genteel and graceful wedding, and I kept my word.

The day arrived, Tuesday, February 10, 1863. The ceremony was to take place in Grace Church, New York. The Rev. Junius Willey, Rector of St. John's Church in Bridgeport, assisted by the late Rev. Dr. Taylor, of Grace Church, was to officiate. The organ was played by Morgan. I know not what better I could have done, had the wedding of a prince been in contemplation. The church was comfortably filled by a highly select audience of ladies and gentlemen, none being admitted except those having cards of invitation. Among them were governors of several of the States, to whom I had sent cards, and such of those as could not be present in person were represented by friends, to whom they had given their cards. Members of Congress were present, also generals of the army, and many other prominent public men. Numerous applications were made from wealthy and distinguished persons, for tickets to witness the ceremony, as high as sixty dollars was offered for a single admission. But not a ticket was sold; and Tom Thumb and Lavinia Warren were pronounced "man and wife" before witnesses.

The following entirely authentic correspondence, the only suppression being the name of the person who wrote to Dr. Taylor, and to whom Dr. Taylor's reply is addressed, shows how a certain would-be "witness" was not a witness of the famous wedding. In other particulars the correspondence speaks itself.

To the Rev. Dr. Taylor,

Sir: The object of my unwillingly addressing you this note is to enquire what right you had to exclude myself and other owners of pews in Grace Church from entering it yesterday, enforced, too, by a cordon of police for that purpose. If my pew is not my property, I wish to know it; and if it is, I deny your right to prevent me from occupying it whenever the church is open, even at a marriage of mountebanks, which I would not take the trouble to cross the street to witness.

Respectfully, your obedient servant,
W*** S***

804 Broadway, New York, Feb. 16, 1863.

Mr. W * * * S * * *,

Dear Sir: I am sorry, my valued friend, that you should have written me the peppery letter that is now before me. If the matter of which you complain be so utterly insignificant and contemptible as "a marriage of mountebanks, which you would not take the trouble to cross the street to witness," it surprises me that you should have made such strenuous, but ill-directed efforts to secure a ticket of admission. And why, permit me to ask, in the name of reason and philosophy, do you still suffer it to disturb you so sadly? It would, perhaps, be a sufficient answer to your letter, to say that your cause of complaint exists only in your imagination. You have never been excluded from your pew. As rector, I am the only custodian of the church, and you will hardly venture to say that you have ever applied to me for permission to enter, and been refused.

Here I might safely rest, and leave you to the comfort of your own reflections in the case. But as you, in common with many other worthy persons, would seem to have very crude notions as to your rights of "property" in pews, you will pardon me for saying that a pew in a church is property only in a peculiar and restricted sense. It is not property, as your house or your horse is property. It vests you with no fee in the soil; you cannot use it in any way, and in every way, and at all times, as your pleasure or caprice may dictate; you cannot put it to any common or unhallowed uses; you cannot remove it, nor injure it, nor destroy it. In short, you hold by purchase, and may sell the right to the undisturbed possession of that little space within the church edifice which you call your pew during the hours of divine service. But even that right must be exercised decorously, and with a decent regard for time and place, or else you may at any moment be ignominiously ejected from it.

I regret to be obliged to add that, by the law of custom, you may, during those said hours of divine service (but at no other time) sleep in your pew; you must, however, do so noiselessly and never to the disturbance of your sleeping neighbors; your property in your pew has this extent and nothing more. Now, if Mr. W * * * S*** were at any time to come to me and say, "Sir, I would that you should grant me the use of Grace Church for a solemn service (a marriage, a baptism, or a funeral, as the case may be), and as it is desirable that the feelings of the parties should be protected as far as possible from the impertinent intrusion and disturbance of a crowd from the streets and lanes of the city, I beg that no one may be admitted within the doors of the church during the very few moments that we expect to be there, but our invited friends only,"— it would certainly, in such a case, be my pleasure to comply with your request, and to meet your wishes in every particular; and I think that even Mr. W * * * S * * * will agree that all this would be entirely reasonable and proper. Then, tell me, how would such a case differ from the instance of which you complain? Two young persons, whose only crimes would seem to be that they are neither so big, nor so stupid, nor so ill-mannered, nor so inordinately selfish as some other people, come to me and say, sir, we are about to be married, and we wish to throw around our marriage all the solemnities of religion. We are strangers in your city, and as there is no clergymen here standing in a pastoral relation to us, we have ventured to ask the favor of the bishop of New York to marry us, and he has kindly consented to do so; may we then venture a little further and request the use of your church in which the bishop may perform the marriage service? We assure you, sir, that we are no shams, no cheats, no mountebanks; we are neither monsters nor abortions; it is true we are little, but we are as God made us, perfect in our littleness. Sir, we are simply man and woman of like passions and infirmities with you and other mortals. The arrangements for our marriage are controlled by no "showman," and we are sincerely desirous that everything should be ordered with a most scrupulous regard to decorum. We hope to invite our relations and intimate friends, together with such persons as may in other years have extended civilities to either of us; but we pledge ourselves to you most sacredly that no invitation can be bought with money. Permit us to say further, that as we would most gladly escape from the insulting jeers, and ribald sneers and coarse ridicule of the unthinking multitude without, we pray you to allow us, at our own proper charges, so to guard the avenues of access from the street, as to prevent all unseemly tumult and disorder.

I tell you, sir, that whenever, and from whomsoever, such an appeal is made to my Christian courtesy, although it should come from the very humblest of the earth, I would go calmly and cheerfully forward to meet their wishes, although as many W*** S * * * 's as would reach from here to Kamchatka, clothed in furs and frowns, should rise up to oppose me.

In conclusion, I will say, that if the marriage of Charles S. Stratton and Lavinia Warren is to be regarded as a pageant, then it was the most beautiful pageant it has ever been my privilege to witness. If, on the contrary, it is rather to be thought of as a solemn ceremony, then it was as touchingly solemn as a wedding can possibly be rendered. It is true the bishop was not present, but Mr. Stratton's own pastor, the Rev. Mr. Willey, of Bridgeport, Connecticut, read the service with admirable taste and impressiveness, and the bride was given away by her mother's pastor and her own, "next friend." a venerable congregational clergyman from Massachusetts. Surely, there never was a gathering of so many hundreds of our best people, when everybody appeared so delighted with everything; surely it is no light thing to call forth so much innocent joy in so few moments of passing time; surely it is no light thing, thus to smooth the roughness and sweeten the acerbities which mar our happiness as we advance upon the wearing journey of life. Sir, it was most emphatically a high triumph of "Christian civilization!"

Respectfully submitted, by your obedient servant,
THOMAS HOUSE TAYLOR.

Several thousand persons attended the reception of Mr. and Mrs. Tom Thumb the same day at the Metropolitan Hotel. Alter this they started on a wedding tour, taking Washington in their way. They visited President Lincoln at the White House. After a couple of weeks, they returned, and, as they then supposed, retired to private life.

Habit, however, is indeed second nature. The General and his wife had been accustomed to excitement, and after a few months' retirement they again longed for the peculiar pleasures of a public life, and the public were eager to welcome them once more. They resumed their public career, and have since traveled around the world, holding public exhibitions more than half the time, Commodore Nutt and Minnie Warren accompanying them.

I met the little Commodore last summer, after his absence in Europe of three years, and said:

"Are you not married yet, Commodore?" "No, sir; my fruit is plucked," he replied.

"You don't mean to say you will never marry," I remarked.

"No, not exactly," replied the Commodore, complacently, "but I have concluded not to marry until I am thirty."

"I suppose you intend to marry one of your size?" I said.

"I am not particular in that respect," but seeing my jocose mood, he continued, with a comical leer, "I think I should prefer marrying a good, green, country girl, to anybody else."

This was said with a degree of nonchalance, which none can appreciate who do not know him.

To make sure that a lack of memory has not misled me as to any of the facts in regard to the courtship and wedding of Tom Thumb and Lavinia Warren, I will here say that, after writing out the story, I read it to the parties personally interested, and they give me leave to say that, in all particulars, it is a correct statement of the affair, except that Lavinia remarked:

"Well, Mr. Barnum, your story don't lose any by the telling;" and the Commodore denies the "rolling tear," when informed of the engagement of the little pair.

In June, 1869, the report was started, for the third or fourth time in the newspapers, that Commodore Nutt and Miss Minnie Warren were married, this time at West Haven, in Connecticut. The story was wholly untrue, nor do I think that such a wedding is likely to take place, for, on the principle that people like their opposites, Minnie and the Commodore are likely to marry persons whom they can literally "look up to," that is, if either of them marries at all it will be a tall partner.

Soon after the wedding of General Tom Thumb and Lavinia Warren, a lady came to my office and called my attention to a little six-paged pamphlet which she said she had written, entitled "Priests and Pigmies," and requested me to read it. I glanced at the title, and at once estimating the character of the publication, I promptly declined to devote any portion of my valuable time to its perusal.

"But you had better look at it, Mr. Barnum; it deeply interests you, and you may think it worth your while to buy it."

"Certainly, I will buy it, if you desire," said I, tendering her a sixpence, which I supposed to be the price of the little pamphlet.

"Oh! you quite misunderstand me; I mean buy the copyright and the entire edition, with the view of suppressing the work. It says some frightful things, I assure you," urged the author.

I lay back in my chair and fairly roared at this exceedingly feeble attempt at black-mail.

"But," persisted the lady, "suppose it says that your Museum and Grace Church are all one, what then?"

"My dear madam," I replied, " you may say what you please about me or about my Museum; you may print a hundred thousand copies of a pamphlet stating that I stole the communion service, after the wedding, from Grace Church altar, or anything else you choose to write; only have the kindness to say something about me, and then come to me and I will properly estimate the money value of your services to me as an advertising agent. Good morning, madam,"— and she departed.

MARRIAGE IN MINIATURE

CHAPTER XXXVIII.

POLITICAL AND PERSONAL.

I BEGAN my political life as a Democrat, and my newspaper, the *Herald of Freedom*, was a Jackson-Democratic journal. While always taking an active interest in political matters, I had no desire for personal preferment, and, up to a late period, steadily declined to run for office. Nevertheless, in 1852 or 1853, prominent members of the party with which I voted, urged the submission of my name to the State Convention, as a candidate for the office of Governor, and, although the party was then in the ascendancy, and a nomination would have been equivalent to an election, I peremptorily refused; in spite of this refusal, which was generally known, several votes were cast for me in the Convention. The Kansas strifes, in 1854, shook my faith in my party, though I continued to call myself a Democrat, often declaring that if I thought there was a drop of blood in me that was not democratic, I would let it out if I had to cut the jugular vein. When, however, secession threatened in 1860, I thought it was time for a "new departure," and I identified myself with the Republican party.

During the active and exciting political campaign of 1860, which resulted in Mr. Lincoln's first election to the presidency, it will be remembered that "Wide-Awake " associations, with their uniforms, torches and processions, were organized in nearly every city, town and village throughout the North. Arriving at Bridgeport from New York at five o'clock one afternoon, I was informed that the Wide-Awakes were to parade that evening and intended to march out to Lindencroft. So, I ordered two boxes of sperm candles, and prepared for a general illumination of every window in the front of my house. Many of my neighbors, including several Democrats, came to Lindencroft in the evening to witness the illumination and see the Wide-Awake procession. My nearest neighbor, Mr. T., was a strong Democrat, and before he came to my house, he ordered his servants to stay in the basement, and not to show a light above ground, thus intending to prove his Democratic convictions and conclusions by the darkness of his premises; and so, while Lindencroft was all ablaze with a flood of light, the next house was as black as a coal-hole.

My neighbor, Mr. James D. Johnson, was also a Democrat, but I knew he would not spoil a good joke for the sake of politics, and I asked him to engage the attention of Mr. and Mrs. T., and to keep their faces turned towards Bridgeport and the approaching procession, the light of whose torches could already be seen in the distance, while another Democratic friend, Mr. George A. Wells, and I, ran over and illuminated Mr. T.'s house. This we did with great success, completing our work five minutes before the procession arrived. As the Wide-Awakes turned into my grounds and saw that the house of Mr. T. was brilliantly illuminated, they concluded that he had become a sudden convert to Republicanism, and gave three rousing cheers for him. Hearing his name thus cheered and wondering at the cause, he happened to turn and see that his house was lighted up from basement to attic, and uttering a single profane ejaculation, he rushed for home. He was not able, however, to put out the lights till the Wide- Awakes had gone on their way rejoicing under the impression that one more Republican had been added to their ranks.

When the rebellion broke out in 1861, I was too old to go to the field, but I supplied four substitutes, and contributed liberally from my means for the cause of the Union. After the defeat at Bull Run, July 21, 1861, "peace meetings" began to be held in different parts of the Northern States, and especially in Fairfield and Litchfield counties, in Connecticut. It was usual in these assemblages to display a white flag, bearing the word "Peace " above the National flag, and to make and listen to harangues denunciatory of the war. One of these meetings was advertised to be held August 24th, at Stepney ten miles north of Bridgeport. On the morning of that day, I met Elias Howe, Jr., who proposed to me that we should drive up to Stepney, attend the peace meeting, and hear for ourselves whether the addresses were disloyal or not. We agreed to meet at the post-office, at twelve o'clock at noon, and I went home for my carriage. On the way I met several gentlemen to whom I communicated my intention, asking them to go also; and, as Mr. Howe invited several of his friends to accompany us, when we met at noon, at least twenty gentlemen were at the place of rendezvous with their carriages, ready to start for Stepney. I am quite confident that not one of us had any other intention in going to this meeting, than to quietly listen to the harangues, and if they were found to be in opposition to the government, and calculated to create disturbance or disaffection in the community, and deter enlistments, it would be best to represent the matter to the government at Washington, and ask that measures might be taken to suppress such gatherings.

As we turned into Main street, we discovered two large omnibuses filled with soldiers, who were at home on furlough, and who were going to Stepney. Our lighter carriages outran them, and so arrived at Stepney in time to see the white peace flag run up over the stars and stripes, when we quietly stood in the crowd while the meeting was organized. It was a very large gathering, and some fifty ladies were on the seats in front of the platform, on which were the officers and speakers of the meeting. A "preacher" — Mr. Charles Smith — was invited to open the proceedings with prayer, and "The Military and Civil History of Connecticut, during the War of 1861-65," by W. A Croffut and John M. Morris, thus continues the record of this extraordinary gathering:

"He (Smith) had not, however, progressed far in his supplication, when he slightly opened his eyes, and beheld, to his horror, the Bridgeport omnibuses coming over the hill, garnished with Union banners, and vocal with loyal cheers. This was the signal for a panic; Bull Run, on a small scale was re-enacted. The devout Smith, and the undelivered orators, it is alleged, took refuge in a field of corn. The procession drove straight to the pole unresisted, the hostile crowd parting to let them pass; and a tall man — John Platt — amid some mutterings, climbed the pole, reached the halliards, and the mongrel banners were on the ground. Some of the peacemen, rallying, drew weapons on 'the invaders,' and a musket and a revolver were taken from them by soldiers at the very instant of firing. Another of the defenders fired a revolver, and was chased into the fields. Still others, waxing belligerent, were disarmed, and a number of loaded muskets found stored in an adjacent shed were seized. The stars and stripes were hoisted upon the pole, and wildly cheered. P.T. Barnum was then taken on the shoulders of the boys in blue, and put on the platform, where he made a speech full of patriotism, spiced with the humor of the occasion. Captain James E. Dunham also said a few words to the point. 'The Star-Spangled Banner ' was then sung in chorus, and a series of resolutions passed, declaring that 'loyal men are the rightful custodians of the peace of Connecticut.' Elias Howe, Jr., chairman, made his speech, when the crowd threatened to shoot the speakers. 'If they fire a gun, boys, burn the whole town, and I'll pay for it!' After giving the citizens wholesome advice concerning the substituted flag, and their duty to the government, the procession returned to Bridgeport, with the white flag trailing in the mud behind an omnibus. They were received at Bridgeport by approving crowds, and were greeted with continuous cheers as they passed along."

On our way back to Bridgeport, the soldiers threatened a descent upon the *Farmer* office, but I strongly appealed to them to refrain from such a riotous proceeding, telling them that as law-abiding citizens they should refrain from acts of violence, and especially should make no appeal to the passions of a mob. So confident was I that the day's proceedings had ended with the reception of the soldiers on their return from Stepney, that, in telegraphing a full account of the facts to the New York papers, I added that there was no danger of an attack upon the *Farmer* office, since leading loyal citizens were opposed to such action as unnecessary and unwise. But the enthusiasm with which the soldiers had been received, and the excitement of the day, prompted them to break through their resolutions, and, half an hour after my telegram had been sent to New York, they rushed into the Farmer office, tumbled the type into the street, and broke the presses. I did not approve of this summary suppression of the paper and offered the proprietors a handsome subscription to assist in enabling them to renew the publication of the *Farmer*.

After the draft riots in New York and in other cities, in July, 1863, myself and other members of the "Prudential Committee" which had been formed in Bridgeport were frequently threatened with personal violence, and rumors were especially rife that Lindencroft would some night be mobbed and destroyed. On several occasions, soldiers volunteered as a guard and came and stayed at my house, sometimes for several nights in succession, and I was also provided with rockets, so that in case of an attempted attack I could signal to my friends in the city, and especially to the night watchman at the arsenal, who would see my rockets at Lindencroft and give the alarm. Happily, these signals were never needed, but the rockets came in play, long afterwards, in another way.

My house was provided with a magnetic burglar-alarm and one night the faithful bell sounded. I was instantly on my feet and summoning my servants, one ran and rung the large bell on the lawn which served in the day-time to call my coachman from the stable, another turned on the gas, while I fired a gun out of the window, and I then went to the top of the house and set off several rockets. The whole region round about was instantly aroused; dogs barked, neighbors half-dressed, but armed, flocked over to my grounds, every time a rocket went up, and I was by no means sparing of my supply; the whole place was as light as day, and in the general glare and confusion we caught sight of two retreating burglars, one running one way, the other another way, and both as fast as their legs could carry them; nor do I believe that the panic-stricken would-be plunderers stopped running till they reached New York!

In the spring of 1865, I accepted from the Republican party a nomination to the Connecticut legislature from the town of Fairfield, and I did this because I felt that it would be an honor to be permitted to vote for the then-proposed amendment to the Constitution of the United States, to abolish slavery for from the land.

I was elected, and, on arriving at Hartford the night before the session began, I found the wire-pullers at work laying their plans for the election of a Speaker of the House. Watching the movements closely, I saw that the railroad interests had combined in support of one of the candidates, and this naturally excited my suspicion. I never believed in making State legislation a mere power to support monopolies. I do not need to declare my full appreciation of the great blessings which railroad interests and enterprises have brought upon this country and the world. But the vaster the enterprise and its power for good, the greater its opportunity for mischief if its power is perverted. The time was when a whole community was tied to the track of one or two railway companies, and it was too truthful to be looked upon as satire to call New Jersey the "State of Camden and Amboy." A great railroad company, like fire, is a good servant, but a bad master; and when it is considered that such a company, with its vast number of men dependent upon it for their daily bread, can sometimes elect State officers and legislatures, the danger to our free institutions from such a force may well be feared.

Thinking of these things, and seeing in the combination of railroad interests to elect a speaker no promise of good to the community at large, I at once consulted with a few friends in the legislature, and we resolved to defeat the railroad "ring," if possible, in caucus. I had never seen either of the candidates for the speakership, nor had I a single selfish end in view to gratify by the election of one candidate or the other; but I felt that if the railroad favorite could be defeated, the public interest would be subserved. We succeeded; their candidate was not nominated, and the railroad men were taken by surprise. They had had their own way in every legislature since the first railroad was laid down in Connecticut, and to be beaten now fairly startled them.

Immediately after the caucus, I sought the successful nominee, Hon. E.K. Foster, of New Haven, and begged him not to appoint, as chairman of the railroad committee, the man who had held that office for several successive years, and who was, in fact, the great railroad factotum in the State. He complied with my request, and he soon found how important it was to check the strong and growing monopoly; for, as he said, the "outside pressure" from personal friends in both political parties, to secure the appointments of the person to whom I had objected, was terrible.

Though I had not foreseen nor thought of such a thing until I reached Hartford, I soon found that a battle with the railroad commissioners would be necessary, and my course was shaped accordingly. It was soon discovered that a majority of the railroad commissioners were mere tools in the hands of the railroad companies, and that one of them was actually a hired clerk in the office of the New York and New Haven Railroad Company. It was also shown that the chairman of the railroad commissioners permitted most of the accidents which occurred on that road to be taken charge of and reported upon by the paid lobby agent of that railroad. This was so manifestly destructive to the interests of all parties who might suffer from accidents on the road, or have any controversy therefor with the company, that I succeeded in enlisting the farmers and other true men on the side of right; and we defeated the chairman of the railroad commissioners, who was a candidate for re-election, and elected our own candidate in his place. I also carried through a law that no person who was in the employ of any railroad in the State, should serve as railroad commissioner.

But the great struggle which lasted nearly through the entire session, was upon the subject of railroad passenger commutations. Commodore Vanderbilt had secured control of the Hudson River and Harlem railroads, and had increased the price of commuters' tickets from two hundred to four hundred per cent. Many men living on the line of these roads, at distances of from ten to fifty miles from New York, had built fine residences in the country, on the strength of cheap transit to and from the city, and were compelled to submit to the extortion. Commodore Vanderbilt was a large shareholder in the New York and New Haven road; indeed, subsequent elections showed that he had a controlling interest, and it seemed evident to me that the same practice would be put in operation on the New Haven railroad, that commuters were groaning under on the two other roads. I enlisted as many as I could in an effort to strangle this outrage before it became too strong to grapple with. Several lawyers in the Assembly had promised me their aid, but, long before the final struggle came, every lawyer except one in that body, was enlisted in favor of the railroads! What potent influence had been at work with these legal gentlemen, could only be surmised. Certain it is, that all the railroad interests in the State were combined; and while they had plenty of money with which to carry out their designs and desires, the chances looked slim in favor of those members of the legislature who had no pecuniary interest in the matter, but were struggling simply for justice and the protection of the people. But "Yankee stick-to-it-iveness" was always a noted feature in my character. Every inch of the ground was fought over, day after day, before the legislative railroad committee. Examinations and cross-examinations of railroad commissioners and lobbyists were kept up. Scarcely more than one man, Senator Ballard, of Darien, aided me personally in the investigations which took place. But he was a host in himself, and left not a stone unturned; we succeeded by persistence, in letting in considerable light upon a dark subject. The man whom I had prevented from being made chairman, succeeded in becoming a member of the railroad committee; but, from the mouths of unwilling witnesses, I exhibited his connection with railroad reports, railroad laws, and railroad lobbyings, in such a light that he took to his bed some ten days before the end of the session, and actually remained there "sick," as he said, till the legislature adjourned

The speaker offered me the chairmanship of any one of several committees, and I selected that of the agricultural committee, because it would occupy but little of my time, and give me the opportunity I so much desired to devote my attention to the railway combinations. The Republicans had a majority in both branches of the legislature; the Democrats, however, were watchful and energetic. The amendment to the United States Constitution, abolishing slavery, met with but little open opposition; but the proposed amendment to the State Constitution, striking out the word "white" from that clause which defined the qualifications of voters, was violently opposed by the Democratic members. The report from the minority of the committee to whom the question was referred, gave certain reasons for opposing the contemplated amendment, and in reply to this, I spoke, May 26th, 1865, as follows:

SPEECH OF P.T. BARNUM.
ON THE CONSTITUTIONAL AMENDMENT.

MR. SPEAKER: I will not attempt to notice at any length the declamation of the honorable gentleman from Milford, for certainly I have heard nothing from his lips approaching to the dignity of argument. I agree with the gentleman that the right of suffrage is "dearly and sacredly cherished by the white man;" and it is because this right is so dear and sacred, that I wish to see it extended to every educated moral man within our State, without regard to color. He tells us that one race is a vessel to honor, and another to dishonor; and that he has seen on ancient Egyptian monuments the negro represented as "a hewer of wood and a drawer or water." This is doubtless true, and the gentleman seems determined always to keep the negro a "vessel of dishonor," and a "hewer of wood." We, on the other hand, propose to give him the opportunity of expanding his faculties and elevating himself to time manhood. He says he "hates and abhors, and despises demagogism." I am rejoiced to hear it, and I trust we shall see tangible evidence of the truth of what he professes in his abandonment of that slavery to party which is the mere trick and trap of the demagogue.

When, a few days since, this honorable body voted unanimously for the Amendment of the United States Constitution abolishing human slavery, I not only thanked God from my heart of hearts, but I felt like going down on my knees to the gentlemen of the opposition, for the wisdom they had exhibited in bowing to the logic of events by dropping that dead weight of slavery which had disrupted the Democratic party, with which I had been so long connected. And on this occasion, I wish again to appeal to the wisdom and loyalty of my Democratic friends. I say Democratic "friends," for I am and ever was, a thorough, out and out Democrat. I supported General Jackson, and voted for every Democratic president after him, up to and including Pierce; for I really thought Pierce was a Democrat until he proved the contrary, as I conceived, in the Kansas question. My democracy goes for the greatest good to the greatest number, for equal and exact justice to all men, and for a submission to the will of the majority. It was the repudiation by the southern democracy of this great democratic doctrine of majority rule which opened the rebellion.

And now, Mr. Speaker, let me remind our democratic friends that the present question simply asks that a majority of the legal voters, the white citizens of this State, may decide whether or not colored men of good moral character, *who are able to read*, and who possess all the qualifications of white voters, shall be entitled to the elective franchise. The opposition may have their own ideas, or may be in doubt upon this subject; but surely no true democrat will dare to refuse permission to our fellow-citizens to decide the question.

Negro slavery, and its legitimate outgrowths of ignorance, tyranny and oppression, have caused this gigantic rebellion which has cost our country thousands of millions of treasure, and hundreds of thousands of human lives in defending a principle. And where was this poor, down-trodden colored race in this rebellion? Did they seize the "opportunity" when their masters were engaged with a powerful foe, to break out in insurrection, and massacre those tyrants who had so long held them in the most cruel bondage? No, Mr. Speaker, they did not do this. My "democratic " friends would have done it. I would have done it. Irishmen, Chinamen, Portuguese, would have done it; any white man would have done it; put the poor black man is like a lamb in his nature compared with the white man. The black man possesses a confiding disposition, thoroughly tinctured with religious enthusiasm, and not characterized by a spirit of revenge. No, the only barbarous massacres we heard of, during the war, were those committed by their white masters on their poor, defenseless white prisoners, and to the eternal disgrace of southern white "democratic" rebels, be it said, these instances of barbarism were numerous all through the war. When this rebellion first broke out. the northern democracy raised a hue-and-cry against permitting the negroes to fight; but when such a measure seemed necessary, in order to put down traitors, these colored men took their muskets in hand and made their bodies a wall of defense for the loyal citizens of the north. And now, when our grateful white citizens ask from this assembly the privilege of deciding by their votes whether these colored men, who, at least, were partially our saviors in the war, may or may not, under proper restrictions, become participants in that great salvation, I am amazed that men calling themselves democrats dare refuse to grant this democratic measure. We wish to educate ignorant men, white or black. Ignorance is incompatible with the genius of our free institutions. In the very nature of things, it jeopardizes their stability, and it is always unsafe to transgress the laws of nature. We cannot safely shut ourselves up with ignorance and brutality; we must educate and Christianize those who are now by circumstances our social inferiors.

Years ago, I was afraid of foreign voters. I feared that when Europe poured her teeming millions of working people upon our shores, our extended laws of franchise would enable them to swamp our free institutions, and reduce us to anarchy. But much reflection has satisfied me that we have only to elevate these millions and their descendants to the standard of American citizenship, and we shall find sufficient of the leaven of liberty in our system of government to absorb all foreign elements and assimilate them to a truly democratic form of government.

Mr. Speaker: We cannot afford to carry passengers and have them live under our government with no real vital interest in its perpetuity. Every man must be a joint owner.

The only safe inhabitants of a free country are educated citizens who vote.

Nor in a free government can we afford to employ journeymen; they may be apprenticed until they learn to read, and study our institutions; and then let them become joint proprietors and feel a proportionate responsibility. The two learned and distinguished authors of the minority report have been studying the science of ethnology and have treated us with a dissertation on the races. And what have they attempted to show? Why, that a race which, simply on account of the color of the skin, has long been buried in slavery at the South, and even at the North has been tabooed and scarcely permitted to rise above the dignity of whitewashers and boot-blacks, does not exhibit the same polish and refinement that the white citizens do who have enjoyed the advantages of civilization, education, Christian culture and self-respect which can only be attained by those who share in making the laws under which they live.

Do our democratic friends assume that the negroes are not human? I have heard professed democrats claim even that; but do the authors of this minority report insist that the negro is a beast? Is his body not tenanted by an immortal spirit? If this is the position of the gentlemen, then I confess a beast cannot reason, and this minority committee are right in declaring that "the negro can develop no inventive faculties or genius for the arts." For although the elephant may be taught to plow, or the dog to carry your market-basket by his teeth, you cannot teach them to shave notes, to speculate in gold, or even to vote; whereas, the experience of all political parties shows that men may be taught to vote, even when they do not know what the ticket means.

But if the colored man is indeed a man, then his manhood with proper training can be developed. His soul may appear dormant, his brain inactive, but there is a vitality there; and Nature will assert herself if you will give her the opportunity.

Suppose an inhabitant of another planet should drop down upon this portion of our globe at mid-winter. He would find the earth covered with snow and ice and congealed almost to the consistency of granite. The trees are leafless, everything is cold and barren; no green thing is to be seen; the inhabitants are chilled, and stalk about shivering, from place to place; he would exclaim, "Surely this is not life; this means annihilation. No flesh and blood can long endure this; this frozen earth is bound in the everlasting embraces of adamantine frost, and can never develop vegetation for the sustenance of any living thing." He little dreams of the priceless myriads of germs which bountiful Nature has safely garnered in the warm bosom of our mother earth; he sees no evidence of that vitality which the beneficent sun will develop to grace and beautify the world. But let him remain until March or April, and as the snow begins to melt away, he discovers the beautiful crocus struggling through the half-frozen ground; the snow-drops appear in all their chaste beauty ; the buds of the swamp-maple shoot forth; the beautiful magnolia opens her splendid blossoms; the sassafras adds its evidence of life; the pearl-white blossoms of the dog-wood light up every forest; and while our stranger is rubbing his eyes in astonishment, the earth is covered with her emerald velvet carpet; rich foliage and brilliant colored blossoms adorn the trees; fragrant flowers are enwreathing every wayside; the swift-winged birds float through the air and send forth joyful notes of gratitude from every tree-top; the merry lambs skip joyfully around their verdant pasture grounds; and everywhere is our stranger surrounded with life, beauty, joy and gladness.

So, it is with the poor African. You may take a dozen specimens of both sexes from the lowest type of man found in Africa: their race has been buried for ages in ignorance and barbarism, and you can scarcely perceive that they have any more of manhood or womanhood than so many orangutans or gorillas. You look at their low foreheads, their thick skulls and lips, their woolly heads, their flat noses, their dull, lazy eyes, and you may be tempted to adopt the language of this minority committee, and exclaim: Surely these people have "no inventive faculties, no genius for the arts, or for any of those occupations requiring intellect and wisdom." But bring them out into the light of civilization; leathern and their children come into the genial sunshine of Christianity; teach them industry, self-reliance, and self-respect; let them learn what too few white Christians have yet understood, that cleanliness is akin to godliness, and a part of godliness; and the human soul will begin to develop itself. Each generation, blessed with churches and common schools, will gradually exhibit the result of such culture; the low foreheads will be raised and widened by an active and expanded brain; the vacant eye of barbarism, ignorance and idleness will light up with the fire of intelligence, education, ambition, activity and Christian civilization; and you will find the immortal soul asserting her dignity, by the development of a man who would startle, by his intelligence, the honorable gentleman from Wallingford, who has presumed to compare beings made in God's image with "oxen and asses." That honorable gentleman, if he is rightly reported in the papers (I did not have the happiness to hear his speech), has mistaken the nature of the colored man. The honorable gentleman reminds me of the young man who went abroad, and when he returned, there was nothing in America that could compare with what he had seen in foreign lands. Niagara Falls was nowhere; the White Mountains were "knocked higher than a kite" by Mont Blanc; our rivers were so large that they were vulgar, when contrasted with the beautiful little streams and rivulets of Europe; our New York Central Park was eclipsed by the *Bois de Bologne* and the *Champs Elysees* of Paris, or Hyde or Regent Park of London, to say nothing of the great Phoenix Park at Dublin.

"They have introduced a couple of Venetian gondolas on the large pond in Central Park," remarked a friend.

"All very well," replied the verdant traveler, "but, between you and me, these birds can't stand our cold climate more than one season." The gentleman from Wallingford evidently had as little idea of the true nature of the African as the young swell had of the pleasure-boats of Venice.

Mr. Johnson, of Wallingford: The gentleman misapprehends my remarks. The gentleman from Norwich had urged that the negro should vote because they have fought in our battles. I replied that oxen and asses can fight, and therefore should, on the same grounds, be entitled to vote.

Mr. Barnum: I accept the gentleman's explanation. Doubtless General Grant will feel himself highly complimented when he learns that it requires no great capacity to handle the musket, and meet armed battalions in the field, than "oxen and asses " possess.

Let the educated free negro feel that he is a man; let him be trained in New England churches, schools and workshops; let him support himself, pay his taxes, and cast his vote, like other men, and he will put to everlasting shame the champions of modern democracy, by the overwhelming evidence he will give in his own person of the great Scripture truth, that "God has made of one blood all the nations of men." A human soul, "that God has created and Christ died for," is not to be trifled with. It may tenant the body of a Chinaman, a Turk, an Arab or a Hottentot — it is still an immortal spirit; and, amid all assumptions of caste, it will in due time vindicate the great fact that, without regard to color or condition, all men are equally children of the common Father.

A few years since, an English lord and his family were riding in his carriage in Liverpool. It was an "elegant equipage; the servants were dressed in rich livery; the horses caparisoned in the most costly style; and everything betokened that the establishment belonged to a scion of England's proudest aristocracy. The carriage stopped in front of a palatial residence. At this moment a poor beggar woman rushed to the side of the carriage, and gently seizing the lady by the hand, exclaimed, "For the love of God give me something to save my poor sick children from starvation. You are rich; I am your poor sister, for God is our common Father."

"Wretch! " exclaimed the proud lady, casting the woman's hand away; "don't call me sister; I have nothing in common with such low brutes as you." And the great lady doubtless thought she was formed of finer clay than this suffering mendicant; but when a few days afterwards she was brought to a sick bed by the small-pox, contracted by touching the hand of that poor wretch, she felt the evidence that they belonged to the same great family, and were subject to the same pains and diseases.

The State of Connecticut, like New Jersey, is a border State of New York. New York has a great commercial city, where aldermen rob by the tens of thousands, and where principal is studied much more than principle. I can readily. understand how the negro has come to be debased at the North as well as at the South. The interests of the two sections in the product of negro labor were nearly identical. The North wanted Southern cotton and the South was ready in turn to buy from the North whatever was needed in the way of Northern supplies and manufactures. This community of commercial interests led to an identity in political principles, especially in matters pertaining to the negro race — the working race of the South — which produced the cotton and consumed so much of what Northern merchants and manufacturers sold for plantation use. The Southern planters were good customers and were worth conciliating. So, when Connecticut proposed in 1818 to continue to admit colored men to the franchise, the South protested against thus elevating the negroes, and Connecticut succumbed. No other New England State has ever so disgraced herself; and now Connecticut democrats are asked to permit the white citizens of this State to express their opinion in regard to re-instating the colored man where our Revolutionary sires placed him under the Constitution. Now, gentlemen, "democrats," as you call yourselves, you who speak so flippantly of your "loyalty," your "love for the Union" and your "love for the people;" you who are generally talking right and voting wrong, we ask you to come forward and act "democratically," by letting your masters, the people, speak.

The word "white" in the Constitution cannot be strictly and literally construed. The opposition express great love for white blood. "Will they let a mulatto vote half the time, a quadroon three-fourths, and an octoroon seven-eighths of the time? If not, why not? Will they enslave seven-eighths of a white man because one-eighth is not Caucasian? Is this democratic? Shall not the majority seven control the minority one? Out on such "democracy."

But a Democratic minority committee (of two) seem to have done something besides study ethnology. They have also paid great attention to fine arts, and are particularly anxious that all voters shall have a "genius for the arts." I would like to ask them if it has always been political practice to insist that every voter in the great "unwashed " and "unterrified" of any party should become a member of the Academy of Arts before he votes the "regular" ticket? I thought he was received into the full fellowship of a political party if he could exhibit sufficient "inventive faculties and genius for the arts," to enable him to paint a black eye. Can a man whose "genius for the arts "enables him to strike from the shoulder scientifically, be admitted to full fellowship in a political party? Is it evident that the political artist has studied the old masters, if he exhibits his genius by tapping an opponent's head with a shillelagh? The oldest master in this school of art was Cain; and so canes have been made to play their part in politics, at the polls and even in the United States Senate Chamber.

"Is genius for the arts and those occupations requiring intellect and wisdom" sufficiently exemplified in adroitly stuffing ballot-boxes, forging soldiers' votes, and copying a directory, as has been done, as the return list of votes? Is the "inventive faculty" of "voting early and often," a passport to political brotherhood? Is it satisfactory evidence of "artistic" genius, to head a mob? and a mob which is led and guided by political passion, as numerous instances in our history prove, is the worst of mobs. Is it evidence of "high art" to lynch a man by hanging him to the nearest tree or lamp-post? Is a "whisky scrimmage" one of the lost arts restored? We all know how certain "artists" are prone to embellish elections and to enhance the excitements of political campaigns by inciting riots, and the frequency with which these disgraceful outbreaks have occurred of late, especially in some of the populous cities, is cause for just alarm. It is dangerous "art."

Mr. Speaker: I repeat that I am a friend to the Irishman. I have traveled through his native country and have seen how he is oppressed. I have listened to the eloquent and patriotic appeals of Daniel O'Connell, in Conciliation Hall in Dublin, and I have gladly contributed to his fund for ameliorating the condition of his countrymen. I rejoice to see them rushing to this land of liberty and independence; and it is because I am their friend that I denounce the demagogues who attempt to blind and mislead them to vote in the interests of any party against the interests of humanity, and the principles of true democracy. My neighbors will testify that at mid-winter I employ Irishmen by the hundred to do work that is not absolutely necessary, in order to help them support their families.

After hearing the minority report last week, I began to feel that I might be disfranchised, for I have no great degree of "genius for the arts;" I felt, therefore, that I must get "posted" on that subject as soon as possible. I at once sauntered into the Senate Chamber to look at the paintings; there I saw portraits of great men, and I saw two empty frames from which the pictures had removed. These missing paintings, I was told, were portraits of two ex-Governors of the State, whose position on political affairs was obnoxious to dominant party in the Legislature; and especially obnoxious were the supposed sentiments of these governors on the war. Therefore, the Senate voted to remove the pictures, and thus proved as it would seem, that there is an intimate connection between politics and art.

I have repeatedly traveled through every State in the South, and I assert, what every intelligent officer and soldier who has resided there will corroborate, that the slaves, as a body, are more intelligent than the poor whites. No man who has not been there can conceive to what a low depth of ignorance the poor snuff-taking, clay-eating whites of some portion of the South have descended. I trust the day is not far distant when the "common school" shall throw its illuminating rays through this Egyptian pall.

I have known slave mechanics to be sold for $3,000, and even $5,000 each, and others could not be bought at all; and I have seen intelligent slaves acting as stewards for their masters, traveling every year to New Orleans, Nashville, and even to Cincinnati, to dispose of their master's crops. The free colored citizens of Opelousas, St Martinsville, and all the Attakapas country in Louisiana, are as respectable and intelligent as an ordinary community of whites. They speak the French and English languages, educate their children in music and "the arts," and they pay their taxes on more than fifteen millions of dollars.

Gentlemen of the opposition, I beseech you to remember that our State and our country ask from us something more than party tactics. It is absolutely necessary that the loyal blacks at the South should vote in order to save the loyal whites. Let Connecticut, without regard to party, set them an example that shall influence the action at the South, and prevent a new form of slavery from arising there, which shall make all our expenditure of blood and treasure fruitless.

But some persons have this color prejudice simply by the force of education, and they say, "Well, a nigger is a nigger, and he can't be anything else. I hate niggers, anyhow." Twenty years ago, I crossed the Atlantic, and among our passengers was an Irish judge, who was coming out to Newfoundland as chief justice. He was an exceedingly intelligent and polished gentleman, and extremely witty. The passengers from the New England States and those from the South got into a discussion on the subject of slavery, which lasted three days. The Southerners were finally worsted, and when their arguments were exhausted, they fell back on the old story, by saying: "Oh! curse a nigger, he ain't half human anyhow; he had no business to be a nigger, etc." One of the gentlemen then turned to the Irish judge and asked his opinion of the merits of the controversy. The judge replied:

"Gentlemen, I have listened with much edification to your arguments pro and con during three days. I was quite inclined to think the anti-slavery gentlemen had justice and right on their side, but the last argument from the South has changed my mind. I say a 'nigger has no business to be a nigger,' and we should kick him out of society and trample him under foot — always provided, gentlemen, you prove he was born black on his own particular request. If he had no word to say in the matter of course he is blameless for his color and is entitled to the same respect that other men are who properly behave themselves!"

Mr. Speaker: I am no politician; I came to this legislature simply because I wish to have the honor of voting for the two constitutional amendments — one for driving slavery entirely out of our country; the other to allow men of education and good moral character to vote, regardless of the color of then skins. To give my voice for these two philanthropic, just, and Christian measures is all the glory I ask legislative-wise. I care nothing whatever for any sect or party under heaven, as such. I have no axes to grind, no logs to roll, no favors to ask. All I desire is to do what is right and prevent what is wrong. I believe in no "expediency" that is not predicated of justice, for in all things — politics, as well as everything else — I know that "honesty is the best policy." A retributive Providence will unerringly and speedily search out all wrongdoing; hence, right is always the best in the long run. Certainly, in the light of the great American spirit of liberty and equal rights which is sweeping over this country and making the thrones of tyrants totter in the Old World, no party can afford to carry slavery, either of body or of mind. Knock off your manacles and let the man go free. Take down the blinds from his intellect and let in the light of education and Christian culture. When this is done you have developed a man. Give him the responsibility or a man and the self-respect of a man, by granting him the right of suffrage. Let universal education, and the universal franchise be the motto of free America, and the toiling millions of Europe, who are watching you with such intense interest, will hail us as then saviors. Let us loyally sink "party" on this question and go for "God and our Country." Let no man attach an eternal stigma to his name by shutting his eyes to the great lesson of the hour, and voting against permitting the people to express then opinion on this important subject. Let us unanimously grant this truly democratic boon. Then, when our laws of franchise are settled on a just basis, let future parties divide where they honestly differ on State or national questions which do not trench upon the claims of manhood or American citizenship.

ALARM AT LINDENCROFT

CHAPTER XXXIX.

THE AMERICAN MUSEUM IN RUINS.

On the thirteenth day of July, 1865, I was speaking in the Connecticut Legislature, in session at Hartford, against the railroad schemes, when a telegram was handed to me from my son-in-law, S.H. Hurd, my assistant manager in New York, stating that the American Museum was in flames, and that its total destruction was certain. I glanced over the dispatch, folded it, laid it on my desk, and calmly continued my speech as if nothing had happened. At the conclusion of my remarks, the bill I had been advocating was carried, and the House adjourned. I then handed the telegram, announcing my great loss in New York, to my friend and fellow-laborer, Mr. "William G. Coe, of Winsted, who immediately communicated the intelligence to several members. Warm sympathizers at once crowded around me, and Mr. Henry B. Harrison, of New Haven, my strongest railroad opponent, pushing forward, seized me by the hand, and said:

"Mr. Barnum, I am really very sorry to hear of your great misfortune."

"Sorry," I replied, "why, my dear sir, I shall not have time to be 'sorry' in a week! It will take me that length of time before I can get over laughing at having whipped you all so nicely in this attempted railroad imposition."

The Speaker of the House and many of my fellow-members testified that neither my face nor my manner betrayed the slightest intimation, when I read the telegram, that I had received unpleasant intelligence. One of the local journals, speaking of this incident, two days after the fire, said:

In the midst of Mr. Barnum's speech, a telegram was handed to him, announcing that his Museum was in flames, with no hope of saving any portion of his cherished establishment. Without the slightest evidence of agitation, he laid the telegram upon his desk and finished his speech. When he went next day to New York he saw only a pile of black, smoldering ruins.

Immediately after adjournment that afternoon, I took the cars for Bridgeport, spending the night quietly at home, and the following morning I went to New York to see the ruins of my Museum, and to learn the full extent of the disaster. When I arrived at the scene of the calamity and saw nothing but the smoldering debris of what a few hours before was the American Museum, the sight was sad indeed. Here were destroyed, almost in a breath, the accumulated results of many years of incessant toil, my own and my predecessors, in gathering from every quarter of the globe myriads of curious productions of nature and art — an assemblage of rarities which a half million of dollars could not restore, and a quarter of a century could not collect. In addition to these there were many Revolutionary relics and other links in our national history which never could be duplicated. Not a thousand dollars' worth of the entire property was saved; the destruction was complete; the loss was irreparable, and the total amount of insurance was but forty thousand dollars.

The fire probably originated in the engine room, where steam was constantly kept up to pump fresh air into the water of the aquaria and to propel the immense fans for cooling the: the halls.

All the New York newspapers made a great "sensation" of the fire, and the full particulars were copied in journals throughout the country. A facetious reporter, Mr. Nathan D. Urner, of the *Tribune*, wrote the following amusing account, which appeared in that journal, July 14, 1865, and was very generally quoted from and copied by provincial papers, many of whose readers accepted every line of the glowing narrative as "gospel truth:"

"Soon after the breaking out of the conflagration, a number of strange and terrible howls and moans proceeding from the large apartment in the third floor of the Museum, corner of Ann street and Broadway, startled the throngs who had collected in front of the burning building, and who were at first under the impression that the sounds must proceed from human beings unable to affect their escape. Their anxiety was somewhat relieved on this score, but their consternation was by no means decreased upon learning that the room in question was the principal chamber of the menagerie connected with the Museum, and that there was imminent danger of the release of the animals there confined, by the action of the flames. Our reporter fortunately occupied a room on the north corner of Ann street and Broadway, the windows of which looked immediately into this apartment; and no sooner was he apprised of the fire than he repaired there, confident of finding items in abundance. Luckily the windows of the Museum were unclosed, and he had a perfect view of almost the entire interior of the apartment. The following is his statement of what followed, in his own language:

"Protecting myself from the intense heat as well as I could, by taking the mattress from the bed and erecting it as a bulwark before the window, with only enough space reserved on the top so as to look out, I anxiously observed the animals in the opposite room. Immediately opposite the window through which I gazed, was a large cage containing a lion and lioness. To the right hand was the three-storied cage, containing monkeys at the top, two kangaroos in the second story, and a happy family of cats, rats, adders, rabbits, etc., in the lower apartment. To the left of the lion's cage was the tank containing the two vast alligators, and still further to the left, partially hidden from my sight, was the grand tank containing the great white whale, which has created such a furor in our sight-seeing midst for the past few weeks. Upon the floor were caged the boa-constrictor, anacondas and rattlesnakes, whose heads would now and then rise menacingly through the top of the cage. In the extreme right was the cage, entirely shut from my view at first, containing the Bengal tiger and the Polar bear, whose terrific growls could be distinctly heard from behind the partition. With a simultaneous bound, the lion and his mate sprang against the bars, which gave way and came down with a great crash, releasing the beasts, which for a moment, apparently amazed at their sudden liberty, stood in the middle of the floor lashing their sides with their tails and roaring dolefully.

Almost at the same moment the upper part of the three-storied cage, consumed by the flames, fell forward, letting the rods drop to the floor, and many other animals were set free. Just at this time the door fell through and the flames and smoke rolled in like a whirlwind from the Hadean river Cocytus. A horrible scene in the right-hand corner of the room, a yell of indescribable agony, and a crashing, grating sound, indicated that the tiger and Polar bear were stirred up to the highest pitch of excitement. Then there came a great crash, as of the giving way of the bars of their cage. The flames and smoke momentarily rolled back, and for a few seconds the interior of the room was visible in the lurid light of the flames, which revealed the tiger and the lion, locked together in close combat.

The monkeys were perched around the windows shivering with dread, and afraid to jump out. The snakes were writhing about, crippled and blistered by the heat, darting out their forked tongues, and expressing their rage and fear in the most sibilant of hisses. The "Happy Family" were experiencing an amount of beatitude which was evidently too cordial for philosophical enjoyment. A long tongue of flame had crept under the cage, completely singing every hair from the cat's body. The felicitous adder was slowly burning in two and busily engaged in impregnating his organic system with his own venom. The joyful rat had lost his tail by a falling bar of iron; and the beatific rabbit, perforated by a red-hot nail, looked as if nothing would be more grateful than a cool corner in some Esquimaux farmyard. The members of the delectated convocation were all huddled together in the bottom of their cage, which suddenly gave way, precipitating them out of view in the depths below, which by this time were also blazing like the fabled Tophet.

At this moment the flames rolled again into the room, and then again retired. The whale and alligators were by this time suffering dreadful torments. The water in which they swam was literally boiling. The alligators dashed fiercely about endeavoring to escape, and opening and shutting their great jaws in ferocious torture; but the poor whale, almost boiled, with great ulcers bursting from his blubbery sides, could only feebly swim about, though blowing excessively, and every now and then sending up great fountains of spray. At length, crack went the glass sides of the great cases, and whale and alligators rolled out on the floor with the rushing and steaming water. The whale died easily, having been pretty well used up before. A few great gasps and a convulsive flap or two of his mighty flukes were his expiring spasm. One of the alligators was killed almost immediately by falling across a great fragment of shattered glass, which cut open his stomach and let out the greater part of his entrails to the light of day. The remaining alligator became involved in a controversy with an anaconda, and joined the melee in the center of the flaming apartment.

A number of birds which were caged in the upper part of the building were set free by some charitably inclined person at the first alarm of fire, and at intervals they flew out. There were many valuable tropical birds, parrots, cockatoos, mockingbirds, humming-birds, etc. as well as some vultures and eagles, and one condor. Great excitement existed among the swaying crowds in the streets below as they took wing. There were contained in the same room a few serpents, which also obtained their liberty; and soon after the rising and devouring flames began to enwrap the entire building, a splendid and emblematic sight was presented to the wondering and gazing throngs. Bursting through the central casement, with flap of wings and lashing coils, appeared an eagle and a serpent wreathed in fight. For a moment they hung poised in mid-air, presenting a novel and terrible conflict. It was the earth and air (or their respective representatives) at war for mastery: the base and the lofty, the groveiler and the soarer, were engaged in deadly battle. At length the fat head of the serpent sank; his writhing, sinuous form grew still; and wafted upward by the cheers of the gazing multitude, the eagle, with a scream of triumph, and bearing his prey in his iron talons, soared towards the sun. Several monkeys escaped from the burning building to the neighboring roofs and streets; and considerable excitement was caused by the attempts to secure them. One of the most amusing incidents in this respect, was in connection with Mr. James Gordon Bennett. The veteran editor of the *Herald* was sitting in his private office with his back to the open window, calmly discussing with a friend the chances that the *Herald* establishment would escape the conflagration, which at that time was threateningly advancing up Ann street, towards Nassau street. In the course of his conversation, Mr. Bennett observed: "Although I have usually had good luck in cases of fire, they say that the devil is ever at one's shoulder, and" — Here an exclamation from his friend interrupted him, and turning quickly he was considerably taken aback at seeing the devil himself, or something like him, at his very shoulder as he spoke. Recovering his equanimity, with the ease and suavity which is usual with him in all company. Mr. Bennett was about to address the intruder when he perceived that what he had taken for the gentleman in black was nothing more than a frightened orangutan. The poor creature, but recently released from captivity, and doubtless thinking that he might take some vacancy in the editorial corps of the paper in question, had descended by the water-pipe and instinctively taken refuge in the inner sanctum of the establishment. Although the editor— perhaps from the fact that he saw nothing peculiarly strange in the visitation—soon regained his composure, it was far otherwise with his friend, who immediately gave the alarm. Mr. Hudson rushed in and boldly attacked the monkey, grasping him by the throat. The book-editor next came in, obtaining a clutch upon the brute by the ears: the musical critic followed, and seized the tail with both hands, and a number of reporters, armed with inkstands and sharpened pencils, came next, followed by a dozen policemen with brandished clubs; at the same time, the engineer in the basement, received the preconcerted signal and got ready his hose, wherewith to pour boiling hot water upon the heads of those in the streets, in case it should prove a regular systematized attack by gorillas, Brazil apes, and chimpanzees. Opposed to this formidable combination, the rash intruder fared badly, and was soon in durance vile. Numerous other incidents of a similar kind occurred; but some of the most amusing were in connection with the wax figures.

Upon the same impulse which prompts men in time of tire to fling valuable looking-glasses out of three-story windows, and at the same time tenderly to lower down feather beds — soon after the Museum took fire, a number of sturdy firemen rushed into the building to carry out the wax figures. There were thousands of valuable articles which might have been saved, if there had been less of solicitude displayed for the miserable effigies which are usually exhibited under the appellation of "wax figures." As it was, a dozen fit firemen rushed into the apartment where the figures were kept, amid a multitude of crawl-in-snakes, chattering monkeys and escaped paroquets. The "Dining Brigand" was unceremoniously throttled and dragged toward the door; liberties were taken with the tearful "Senorita," who has so long knelt and so constantly wagged her doll's head at his side: the mules of the other bandits were upset, and they themselves roughly seized. The full-length statue of P. T. Barnum fell down of its own accord, as if disgusted with the whole affair. A red-shirted fireman seized with either hand Franklin Pierce and James Buchanan by their coat-collars, tucked the Prince Imperial of France, under one arm, and the Veiled Murderess under the other, and coolly departed for the street. Two ragged boys quarreled over the Tom Thumb, but at length settled the controversy by one taking the head, the other satisfying himself with the legs below the knees. They evidently had Tom under their thumbs, and intended to keep him down. While a curiosity-seeking policeman was garroting Benjamin Franklin, with the idea of abducting him. a small monkey, flung from the window-sill by the strong hand of an impatient fireman, made a straight dive, hitting Poor Richard just below the waist-coat, and passing through his stomach, as fairly as the Harlequin in the "Green Monster" pantomime ever pierced the picture with the slit in it, which always bangs so conveniently low and near. Patrick Henry had his teeth knocked out by a flying missile, and in carrying Daniel Lambert downstairs, he was found to be so large that they had to break off his head in order to get him through the door.

At length the heat became intense, the "figgers" began to perspire freely, and the swiftly approaching flames compelled all hands to desist from any further attempt at rescue. Throwing a parting glance behind as we passed down the stairs, we saw the remaining dignitaries in a strange plight. Someone had stuck a cigar in General Washington's mouth, and thus, with his chapeau crushed down over his eyes, and his head reclining upon the ample lap of Moll Pitcher, the Father of his Country led the van of as sorry a band of patriots as not often comes within one's experience to see. General Marion was playing a dummy game of poker with General Lafayette: Governor Morris was having a set-to with Nathan Lane, and James Madison was executing a Dutch polka with Madam Roland on one arm and Lucretia Borgia on the other. The next moment the advancing flames compelled us to retire.

We believe that all the living curiosities were saved; but the giant girl, Anna Swan, was only rescued with the utmost difficulty. There was not a door through which her bulky frame could obtain a passage. It was likewise feared that the stairs would break down, even if she should reach them. Her best friend, the living skeleton, stood by her as long as he dared, but then deserted her while, as the heat grew in intensity, the perspiration rolled from her face in little brooks and rivulets, which pattered musically upon the floor. At length, as a last resort, the employees of the place procured a lofty derrick which fortunately happened to be standing near, and erected it alongside the Museum. A portion of the wall was then broken off on each side of the window, the strong tackle was got in readiness, the tall woman was made fast to one end and swung over the heads of the people in the street, with eighteen men grasping the other extremity of the line, and lowered down from the third story, amid enthusiastic applause. A carriage of extraordinary capacity was in readiness, and, entering this, the young lady was driven away to a hotel.

When the surviving serpents, that were released by the partial burning of the box in which they were contained, crept along on the floor to the balcony of the Museum and dropped on the sidewalk, the crowd, seized with St. Patrick's aversion to the reptiles, fled with such precipitate haste that they knocked each other down and trampled on one another in the most reckless and damaging manner.

Hats were lost, coats torn, boots burst and pantaloons dropped with magnificent miscellaneous, and dozens of those who rose from the miry streets into which they had been thrown, looked like the disembodied spirits of a mud bank. The snakes crawled on the sidewalk and into Broadway, where some of them died from injuries received, and others were dispatched by the excited populace. Several of the serpents of the copper-head species, escaped the fury of the tumultuous masses, and, true to their instincts, sought shelter in the *World and News* offices. A large black bear escaped from the burning Museum into Ann street, and then made his way into Nassau, and down that thoroughfare into Wall, where his appearance caused a sensation. Some superstitious persons believed him the spirit of a departed Ursa Major, and others of his fraternity welcomed the animal as a favorable omen. The bear walked quietly along to the Custom House, ascended the steps of the building, and became bewildered, as many a biped bear has done before him. He seemed to lose his sense of vision, and no doubt, endeavoring to operate for a fall, walked over the side of the steps and broke his neck. He succeeded in his object, but it cost him dearly. The appearance of Bruin in the street sensibly affected the stock market, and shares fell rapidly; but when he lost his life in the careless manner we have described, shares advanced again, and the Bulls triumphed once more.

Broadway and its crossings have not witnessed a denser throng for months that assembled at the fire yesterday. Barnum's was always popular, but it never drew so vast a crowd before. There must have been forty thousand people on Broadway, between Maiden Lane and Chambers street, and a great portion stayed there until dusk. So great was the concourse of people that it was with difficulty pedestrians or vehicles could pass.

After the fire several high-art epicures grouping among the ruins, found choice morsels of boiled whale, roasted kangaroo and fricasseed crocodile, which, it is said, they relished; though the many would have failed to appreciate such rare edibles. Probably the recherche epicures will declare the only true way to prepare those meats is to cook them in a museum wrapped in flames, in the same manner that the Chinese, according to Charles Lamb, first discovered roast pig in a burning house, and ever afterward set a house on fire with a pig inside, when they wanted that particular food."

All the New York journals, and many more in other cities, editorially expressed their sympathy with my misfortune, and their sense of the loss the community had sustained in the destruction of the American Museum. The following editorial is from the *New York Tribune*, of July 14, 1865:

"The destruction of no building in this city could have caused so much excitement, and so much regret as that of Barnum's Museum. The collection of curiosities was very large, and though many of them may not have had much intrinsic or memorial value, a considerable portion was certainly of great worth for any Museum. But aside from this, pleasant memories clustered about the place, which for so many years has been the chief resort for amusement to the common people who cannot often afford to treat themselves to a night at the more expensive theaters, while to the children of the city, Barnum's has been a fountain of delight, ever offering new attractions as captivating and as implicitly believed in as the Arabian Nights, Entertainments: Theater, Menagerie and Museum, it amused, instructed, and astonished. If its thousands and tens of thousands of annual visitors were bewildered sometimes with a Woolly Horse, a What is It? or a Mermaid, they found repose and certainty in a Giraffe, a Whale or a Rhinoceros. If wax effigies of pirates and murderers made them shudder lest those dreadful figures should start out of their glass cases and repeat their horrid deeds, they were reassured by the presence of the mildest and most amiable of giants, and the fattest of mortal women, whose dead weight alone could crush all the wax figures into their original cakes. It was a source of unfailing interest to all country visitors, and New York to many of them was only the place that held Barnum's Museum. It was the first thing — often the only thing— they visited when they came among as, and nothing that could have been contrived, out of our present resources, could have offered so many attractions unless some more ingenious showman had undertaken to add to Barnum's collection of waxen criminals by patting in a cage the live Boards of the Common Council. We mourn its loss, but not as without consolation. Barnum's Museum is gone, but Barnum himself, happily, did not share the fate of his rattlesnakes and his, at least, most "unhappy Family." There are fishes in the seas and beasts in the forest; birds still fly in the air, and strange creatures still roam in the deserts; giants and pygmies still wander up and down the earth; the oldest man, the fattest woman, and the smallest baby are still living, and Barnum will find them.

Or, even if none of these things or creatures existed, we could trust to Barnum to make them out of hand. The Museum, then, is only a temporary loss, and much as we sympathize with the proprietor, the public may trust to his well-known ability and energy to soon renew a place of amusement which was a source of so much innocent pleasure, and had in it so many elements of solid excellence.

As already stated, my insurance was but $40,000, while the collection, at the lowest estimate, was worth $400,000, and as my premium was five percent., I had paid the insurance companies more than they returned to me. When the fire occurred, my summer pantomime season had just begun and the Museum was doing an immensely profitable business. My first impulse, after reckoning up my losses, was to retire from active life and from all business occupation beyond what my large real estate interests in Bridgeport, and my property in New York would compel. I felt that I had still a competence, and that after a most active and busy life, at fifty-five years, I was entitled to retirement, to comparative rest for the remainder of my days. I called on my old friend, the editor of the *Tribune*, for advice on the subject.

"Accept this fire as a notice to quit, and go a-fishing," said Mr. Greeley.

"A-fishing! " I exclaimed.

"Yes, a-fishing; I have been wanting to go a-fishing for thirty years, and have not yet found time to do so," replied Mr. Greeley.

I really felt that his advice was good and wise, and had I consulted only my own ease and interest I should have acted upon it. But two considerations moved me to pause: First, one hundred and fifty employees, many of whom depended upon their exertions for their daily bread, were thrown out of work at a season when it would be difficult for them to get engagements elsewhere. Second, I felt that a large city like New York needed a good Museum, and that my experience of a quarter of a century in that direction afforded extraordinary facilities for founding another establishment of the kind, and so I took a few days for reflection.

Meanwhile, the Museum employees were tendered a benefit at the Academy of Music, at which most of the dramatic artists in the city volunteered their services. I was called out, and made some off-hand remarks, in which I stated that nothing which I could utter in behalf of the recipients of that benefit, could plead for them half so eloquently as the smoking ruins of the building where they had so long earned their support by their efforts to gratify the public. At the same time, I announced that, moved by the considerations I have mentioned, I had concluded to establish another Museum, and that, in order to give present occupation to my employees, I had engaged the Winter Garden Theater for a few weeks, and I hoped to open a new establishment of my own in the ensuing fall.

The *New York Sun* commented upon the few remarks winch I was suddenly and quite unexpectedly called upon to make, in the following flattering manner:

One of the happiest impromptu oratorical efforts that we have heard for some time, was that made by Barnum at the benefit performance given for his employees on Friday afternoon, if a stranger wanted to satisfy himself how the man had managed so to monopolize the ear and eye of the public during; his long career, he could not have had a better opportunity of doing so than by listening to this address. Every word, though delivered with apparent carelessness, struck a key-note in the hearts of his listeners. Simple, forcible and touching, it showed how thoroughly this extraordinary man comprehends the character of his countrymen, and how easily he can play upon their feelings.

Those who look upon Barnum as a mere charlatan, have really no knowledge of him. It would be easy to demonstrate that the qualities that have placed him in his present position of notoriety and affluence would, in another pursuit, have raised him to far greater eminence. In his breadth of views, his profound knowledge of mankind, his courage under reverses, his indomitable perseverance, his ready eloquence and his admirable business tact, we recognize the elements that are conducive to success in most other pursuits. More than almost any other living man, Barnum may be said to be a representative type of the American mind.

I very soon secured by lease the premises, numbers 535, 537 and 539 Broadway, seventy-five feet front and rear, by two hundred feet deep, and known as the Chinese Museum buildings. In less than four months, I succeeded in converting this building into a commodious Museum and lecture-room, and meanwhile I sent agents through America and Europe to purchase curiosities. Besides hundreds of small collections, I bought up several entire museums, and with many living curiosities and my old company of actors and actresses, I opened to the public, November 13, 1865, "Barnum's New American Museum," thus beginning a new chapter in my career as a manager and showman.

CHAPTER X L.

MY WAR ON THE RAILROADS.

During my membership in the Connecticut Legislature of 1865, I made several new friends and agreeable acquaintances, and many things occurred, sometimes in the regular proceedings, and sometimes as episodes, which made the session memorable. On one occasion, a representative, who was a lawyer, introduced resolutions to reduce the number of Representatives, urging that the "House" was too large and ponderous a body to work smoothly; that a smaller number of persons could accomplish business more rapidly and completely; and, in fact, that the Connecticut Legislature was so large that the members did not have time to get acquainted with each other before the body adjourned *sine die*.

I replied, that the larger the number of representatives, the more difficult it would be to tamper with them; and if they all could not become personally acquainted, so much the better, for there would be fewer "rings," and less facilities for forcing improper legislation.

"As the house seems to be thin now, I will move to lay my resolutions on the table," remarked the member; "but I shall call them up when there is a full house."

"According to the gentleman's own theory," I replied, "the smaller the number, the surer are we to arrive at correct conclusions. Now, therefore, is just the time to decide; and I move that the gentleman's resolutions be considered." This proposition was seconded amid a roar of laughter; and the resolutions were almost unanimously voted down, before the member fairly comprehended what was going on. He afterwards acknowledged it as a pretty fair joke, and at any rate as an effective one.

The State House at Hartford was a disgrace to Connecticut; the Hall of Representatives was too small; there were no committee rooms, and the building was utterly unfit for the purposes to which it was devoted. The State House at New Haven was very little better, and I made a strong effort to secure the erection of new edifices in both cities. I was chairman of the committee on new State Houses, and during our investigations it was ascertained that Bridgeport, Middletown and Meriden would each be willing to erect a State House at its own cost, if the city should be selected as the new capital of the State. These movements aroused the jealousy of Hartford and New Haven, which at once appointed committees to wait upon us. The whole matter, however, finally went by default, and the question was never submitted to the people. Since that period, however, Hartford has been made the only capital city.

As the session drew near its close, the railroad controversy culminated by my introduction of a bill to amend the act for the regulation of railroads, by the interpolation of the following:

SECTION 508. No railroad company, which has had a system of commutation fares in force for more than four years, shall abolish, alter, or modify the same, except for the regulation of the price charged for such commutation; and such price shall, in no case, be raised to an extent that shall alter the ratio between such commutation and the rates then charged for way fare, on the railroad of such company.

The New York and New Haven Railroad Company seemed determined to move heaven and earth to prevent the passage of this law. The halls of legislation were thronged with railroad lobbyists, who button-holed nearly every member. My motives were attacked, and the most foolish slanders were circulated. Not only every legal man in the house was arrayed against me, but occasionally a "country member " who had promised to stick by and aid in checking the cupidity of railroad managers, would drop off, and be found voting on the other side. I devoted many hours, and even days, to explaining the state of things to the members from the rural regions, and, although the prospect of carrying this great reform looked rather dark, I felt that I had a majority of the honest and disinterested members of the house with me. Finally, Senator Ballard informed me that he had canvassed the Senate and was convinced that the bill could be carried through that body if I could be equally successful with the house. At last it was known that the final debate would take place and the vote be taken on the morning of July 13.

When the day arrived, the excitement was intense. The passages leading to the hall were crowded with railroad lobbyists: for nearly every railroad in the State had made common cause with the New York and New Haven Company, and every representative was in his seat, excepting the sick man, who had doctored the railroads till he needed doctoring himself. The debate was led off by skirmishers on each side and was finally closed on the part of the railroads by Mr. Harrison, of New Haven, who was chairman of the railroad committee. Mr. Henry B. Harrison was a close and forcible debater and a clear-headed lawyer. His speech exhibited considerable thought, and his earnestness and high character as a gentleman of honor, carried much weight. Besides, his position as chairman of the committee naturally influenced some votes. He claimed to understand thoroughly the merits of the question, from having, in his capacity as chairman, heard all the testimony and arguments which had come before that committee; and a majority of the committee, after due deliberation, had reported against the proposed bill.

On closing the debate, I endeavored to state briefly the gist of the case— that, only a few years before, the New York and New Haven Company had fixed their own price for commuters' tickets along the whole line of the road, and had thus induced hundreds of New York citizens to remove to Connecticut with their families, and build their houses on heretofore unimproved property, thus vastly increasing the value of the lands, and correspondingly helping our receipts for taxes. I urged that there was a tacit misunderstanding between the railroad and these commuters and the public generally, that such persons as chose thus to remove from a neighboring State, and bring their families and capital within our borders, should have the right to pass over the railroad on the terms fixed at the time, by the president and directors; that any claim that the railroad could not afford to commute at the prices they had themselves established was absurd, from the fact that, even now, if one thousand families who reside in New York, and had never been in our own State, should propose to the railroad to remove these families (embracing in the aggregate five thousand persons) to Connecticut, and build one thousand new houses on the line of the New York and New Haven Railroad, provided the railroad would carry the male head of the family at all times for nothing, the company could well afford to accept the proposition, because they would receive full prices for transporting all other members of these families, at all times, as well as full prices for all their visitors and servants.

And now, what are the facts? Do we desire the railroad to carry oven one-fifth of these new comers for nothing? Do we, indeed, desire to compel them to transport them for any definitely fixed price at all? On the contrary, we find that during the late rebellion, when gold was selling for two dollars and eighty cents per dollar, this company doubled its prices of commutation, and retains the same prices now, although gold is but one-half that amount ($1.40). We don't ask them to go back to their former prices; we don't compel them to rest even here; we simply say. increase your rates, pile up your demands juntas high as you desire, only yon shall not make fish of one and fowl of another. You have fixed and increased your prices to passengers of all classes just as you liked and established your own ratio between those who pay by the year, and those who pay by the single trip; and now. all we ask is, that you shall not change the ratio. Charge ten dollars per passenger from New York to New Haven, if you have the courage to risk the competition of the Steamboats; and whatever percentage you choose to increase the fare of transient passengers, we permit you to increase the rates of commuters in the same ratio.

The interests or the State, as well as communities, demand this law; for if is once fixed by statute that the prices of commutation are not to be increased, many persons will leave the localities where extortion is permitted on the railroads, and will settle in our State. But these railroad gentlemen say they have no intention to increase their rates of commutation, and they deprecate what they term "premature legislation," and an uncalled-for meddling with their affairs. Mr. Speaker, "an ounce of prevention is worth a pound of cure." Men engaged in plots against public interests always ask to be "let alone." Jeff Davis only asked to be "let alone,"' when the North was raising great armies to prevent the dissolution of the Union. The people cannot afford to let these railroads alone. This hall, crowded with railroad lobbyists, as the frogs thronged Egypt, is an admonition to all honest legislators, that it is unsafe to allow the monopolies the chance to rivet the chains which already fetter the limbs of those whom circumstances place in the power of these companies.

It was at this point in my remarks that I received the telegram from my son-in-law in New York, announcing the burning of the American Museum. Reading the dispatch, and laying it on my desk without further attention, I continued:

These railroad gentlemen absolutely deny any intention of raising the fares of commuters and profess to think it very hard that disinterested and conscientious gentlemen like them should be judged by the doings of the Hudson River and Harlem railroads. But now, Mr. Speaker, I am going to expose the duplicity of these men. I have had detectives on their track, for men who plot against public interests deserve to be watched. I have in my pocket positive proofs that they did, and do, intend to spring their trap upon the unprotected commuters on the New York and New Haven railroad.

I then drew from my pocket and read two telegrams received that morning, one from New York and the other from Bridgeport, announcing that the New York and New Haven Railroad Directory had held a secret meeting in New York, the day before, for the purpose of immediately raising the fares of commuters twenty per cent., so that in case my bill became a law they could get ahead of me. I continued:

Now, Mr. Speaker, I know that these dispatches are true; my information is from the inside of the camp. I see a director of the New York and New Haven railroad sitting in this hall; I know that he knows these dispatches are true; and if he will go before railroad committee and make oath that he don't know that such a meeting took place yesterday, for exactly this purpose. I will forfeit and pay one thousand dollars to the families of poor soldiers in this city. In consideration of this attempt to forestall the action of this legislature, I offer an amendment to the bill now under consideration by adding the word "ratio," the words "as it existed on the first day of July, 1865." In this way we shall cut off any action which these sleek gentlemen may have taken yesterday. I now evident that these railroad gentlemen have set a trap for this legislature; and I propose that we now spring the trap and see if we cannot catch these wily railroad directors in it. Mr. Speaker, I move the previous question.

The opposition were astounded at the revelation and the previous question was ordered. The bill as amended was carried almost with a "hurrah."' It is now an act in the statute book of the State, and it annually adds many dollars to the assessment roll of Connecticut, since the protection afforded to commuters against the extortions practiced by railway companies elsewhere is a strong inducement to permanent settlers along the lines of Connecticut railways. The New York and New Haven railroad company never forgave me for thus securing a righteous law for the protection of its commuters. Even as lately as 1871, the venders of books on the trains were prohibited from selling to passengers my autobiography which exposed their cupidity. A parallel railroad from New York to New Haven, would be good paying stock, and would materially disturb, if not destroy, the present railroad and express monopolies.

In the spring of 1866, I was again elected to represent the town of Fairfield in the Connecticut Legislature. I had not intended to accept a nomination for that office a second time, but one of the directors of the New York and New Haven Railroad, who was a citizen of Fairfield and had been a zealous lobby member of the preceding legislature, had declared that I should not represent the town again. As the voters of Fairfield seemed to think that the public interests were of more importance than the success of railroad conspiracies, combinations, and monopolies, I accepted their nomination.

Almost the only exciting question before that legislature was the election of an United States Senator. President Johnson had begun to show disaffection towards the Republican party which elected him, and the zealous members of that party were watching with anxious hearts the actions of those who offered themselves as candidates for offices of trust and responsibility. One of the Republican United States Senators had already abandoned the party and affiliated with Johnson. The other Senator was a candidate for re-election. He had been a favorite candidate with me, but when I became convinced that he sympathized with the recreant Senator and President Johnson, no importunities of political friends or any other inducement could change my determination to defeat him, if possible. I devoted days and nights to convincing some of my fellow-members that the interests of the State and the country demanded the election of Hon. O.S. Ferry to that important office.

Excitement ran high. Ex-Governor Wm. A. Buckingham was also a candidate. I knew he would make an excellent Senator, but he had filled the gubernatorial chair for eight years; and as the present Senator had held his office twelve years, and he was from the same city as Governor Buckingham, I urged that Norwich should not carry off all the honors; that Fairfield county was entitled to the office; and both before and at the Republican nominating caucus I set forth, so far as I was able, what I considered the merits and peculiar claims of Mr. Ferry. I suggested that Mr. Buckingham might rest on his laurels for a couple of years and be elected to fill the place of the next retiring Senator in 1868. Mr. Ferry started in the balloting with a very small vote indeed, and it required the most delicate management to secure a majority for him in that caucus. But it was done; and as the great strife was between the two other rival candidates, Mr. Ferry had scarcely a hope of the nomination and was much surprised the next morning to hear of his success. He was elected for the term beginning March 4, 1866, and one of his opposing candidates in the caucus, Ex-Governor William A. Buckingham, was elected, two years afterwards, for the senatorial term commencing March 4, 1869.

I was again chairman of the Committee on Agriculture, and on the whole the session at New Haven, in 1866, was very agreeable to me; there were many congenial spirits in the House and our severer labors were lightened by some very delightful episodes.

During the summer, Governor Hawley, Hon. David Gallup, Speaker of the House, Hon. O. S. Ferry, United States Senator, Mr. W. G. Coe, of Winsted, Mr. A. B. Mygatt, of New Milford, Mr. George Pratt, of Norwich, Mr. EL B Wales, of the *Scientific American*, Mr. David Clark, of Hartford, Mr. A. H. Byington, of Norwalk, and many other gentlemen of distinction, were occasionally guests at Lindencroft. Several lames we had delightful sails, dinners, and clambakes at Chiles Island, eight miles east of Bridgeport, a most cool and charming spot in the warm summer days. The health of my wife, which had been poor since 1855, prevented many occasions of festivity for which I had all other facilities; for Lindencroft was indeed a charming residence, and it afforded the requisite for the entertainment of large numbers of friends.

During the summer, Governor Hawley appointed me a commissioner to the Paris Exposition, but I was unable to attend.

In the spring of 1867, I received from the Republican Convention in the Fourth District in Connecticut, the nomination for Congress. As I have already re-marked, politics were always distasteful to me. I possessed, naturally, too much independence of mind, and too strong a determination to do what I believe I right, regardless of party expediency, to make a lithe and oily politician. To be called on to favor applications from office-seekers, without regard to their merits, and to do the dirty work too often demanded by political parties; to be "all things to all men" though not in the apostolic sense; to shake hands with those whom I despised, and to kiss the dirty babies of those whose votes were con; were political requirements which I felt I could never acceptably fulfill. Nevertheless, I had become, so far as business was concerned, almost a man of leisure: and some of my warmest, personal friends, insisted that a nomination to so high and honorable a position as a member of Congress, was not to be lightly rejected and so I consented to run. Fairfield and Litchfield counties composed the district, which, in the preceding Congressional election, in 1865, and just after the close of the war, was republican. In the year following, however, the district in State election went democratic. I had this democratic majority to contend against in 1867, and as the whole State turned over and elected the democratic ticket, I lost my election. In the next succeeding Congressional election, in 1869, the Fourth District also elected the only democratic congressman chosen from Connecticut that year.

I was neither disappointed nor cast down by my defeat. The political canvass served the purpose of giving me a new sensation and introducing me to new phases of human nature — a subject which I had always great delight in studying the filth and scandal, the slanders and vindictiveness, the plottings and fawnings, the fidelity, meanness and manliness, which by turns exhibited themselves in the exciting scenes preceding the election, were novel to me, and were so far interesting.

Shortly after my opponent was nominated, I sent him the following letter which was also published in the *Bridgeport Standard.*

Bridgeport, Conn., Feb. 8, 1867.
W. H. Barnum, Esq., Salisbury, Conn.

Dear Sir:

Observing that the Democratic party has nominated you for Congress from this district, I desire to make you a proposition.

The citizens of this portion of our State will be compiled, on the first Monday in April next, to decide whether you or myself shall represent their interests and their principles in the Fortieth Congress of the United States.

The theory of our government is, that the will of the people shall be the law of the land. It is important therefore, that the people shall vote understandingly, and especially at this important crisis in our national existence. In order, that the voters of this district shall fully comprehend the principles by which each of their congressional candidates is guided, I respectfully invite you to meet me in a serious and candid discussion of the important political issues of the day, at various towns in the Fourth Congressional District of Connecticut, on each weekday evening, from the fourth day of March until the thirtieth day of the same month, both inclusive.

If you will consent to thus meet me in a friendly discussion of those subjects, now so near and dear to every American heart, and, I may add, possessing at this time such momentous interest to all civilized nations in the world who are suffering from misrule, I pledge myself to conduct my portion of the debate with perfect fairness, and with all due respect for my opponent, and doubt not you will do the same.

Never, in my judgment, in our past history as a nation, have interests and questions more important appealed to the people for their wise and careful consideration. It is due to the voters of the Fourth Congressional District, that they have an early and full opportunity to examine their candidates in regard to these important problems, and I shall esteem it a great privilege if you will accept this proposition.

Please favor me with an early answer, and oblige,

Truly yours, P. T. BARNTTM.

To this letter Mr. William H. Barnum replied, declining to accept my proposition to go before the people of the district and discuss the political questions of the day.

When Congress met, I was surprised to see by the newspapers that the seat of my opponent was to be contested on account of alleged bribery, fraud and corruption in securing his election. This was the first intimation that I had ever received of such an intention, and I was never, at any time before or afterwards, consulted upon the subject. The movement proved to have originated with neighbors and townsmen of the successful candidate, who claimed to be able to prove that he had paid large sums of money to purchase votes. They also claimed that they had proof that men were brought from an adjoining State to vote, and that in the office of the successful candidate naturalization papers were forged to enabled foreigners to vote upon them. But, I repeat, I took no part nor lot in the matter, but concluded that if I had been defeated by fraud, mine was the real success.

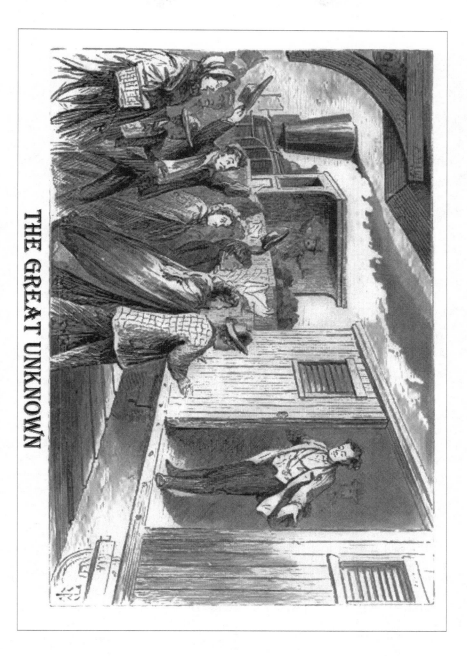

THE GREAT UNKNOWN

CHAPTER XLI.

BENNETT AND THE *HERALD*.

When the old American Museum burned down, and while the ruins were smoking, I had numerous applications for the purchase of the lease of the two lots, fifty-six by one hundred feet, which had still nearly eleven years to run. It will be remembered that in 1847 I came back from England, while my second lease of five years had yet three years more to run and renewed that lease for twenty-five years from 1851 at an annual rental of £10,000. It was also stipulated that in case the building was destroyed by fire the proprietor of the property should expend twenty-four thousand dollars towards the erection of a new edifice, and at the end of the term of lease he was to pay me the appraised value of the building, not to exceed $100,000. Rents and real estate values had tripled since I took this twenty-five years' lease, and hence the remaining term was very valuable. I engaged an experienced and competent real estate broker in Pine street to examine the terms of my lease, and in view of his knowledge of the cost of erecting buildings and the rentals they were commanding in Broadway, I enjoined him to take his time, and make a careful estimate of what the lease was worth to me, and what price I ought to receive if I sold it to another party. At the end of several days, he showed me his figures, which proved that the lease was fully worth $275,000. As I was inclined to have a museum higher up town, I did not wish to engage in erecting two buildings at once, so I concluded to offer my museum lease for sale. Accordingly, I put it into the hands of Mr. Homer Morgan, with directions to offer it for $225,000, which was $50,000 less than the value at which it had been estimated.

The next day I met Mr. James Gordon Bennett, who told me that he desired to buy my lease, and at the same time to purchase the fee of the museum property for the erection thereon of a publication building for the *New York Herald*. I said I thought it was very fitting the *Herald* should be the successor of the Museum, and Mr. Bennett asked my price.

"Please to go or send immediately to Homer Morgan's office," I replied, "and you will learn that Mr. Morgan has the lease for sale at $225,000. This is $50,000 less than its estimated value; but to you I will deduct $25,000 from my already reduced price, so you may have the lease for $200,000."

Bennett replied that he would look into the affair closely; and the next day his attorney sent for my lease. He kept it several days, and then appointed an hour for me to come to his office. I called according to appointment. Mr. Bennett and his attorney had thoroughly examined the lease. It was the property of my wife. Bennett concluded to accept my offer. My wife assigned the lease to him, and his attorney handed me Mr. Bennett's check on the Chemical Bank for $200,000. That same day I invested $50,000 in United States bonds; and the remaining $150,000 was similarly invested on the following day. I learned at that time that Bennett had agreed to purchase the fee of the property for he had been informed that the property was worth some $350,000 to $400,000, and he did not mind paying $100,000 extra for the purpose of carrying out his plans. But the parties who estimated for him the value of the land knew nothing of the fact that there was a lease upon the property, else of course they would in their estimate have deducted the $200,000, which the lease would cost. When, therefore, Mr. Bennett saw it stated in the newspapers that the sum which he had paid for a piece of land measuring only fifty-six by one hundred feet was more than was ever before paid in any city in the world for a tract of that size, he discovered the serious oversight which he had made; and the owner of the property was immediately informed that Bennett would not take it. But Bennett had already signed a bond to the owner, agreeing to pay $100,000 cash, and to mortgage the premises for the remaining $400,000.

Supposing that by this step he had shaken off the owner of the fee, Bennett was not long in seeing that, as he was not to own the land, he would have no possible use for the lease, for which he had paid the $200,000; and accordingly, his next step was to shake me off also, and get back the money he had paid me.

My business for many years, as manager of the Museum and other public entertainments, compelled me to court notoriety; and I always found Bennett's abuse far more remunerative than his praise, even if I could have had the praise at the same price, that is, for nothing. Especially was it profitable to me when I could be the subject of scores of lines of his scolding editorials free of charge, instead of paying him forty cents a line for advertisements, which would not attract a tenth part so much attention. Bennett had tried abusing me, off and on, for twenty years, on one occasion refusing my advertisement altogether for the space of about a year; but I always managed to be the gainer by his course. Now, however, when new difficulties threatened, all the leading managers in New York were members of the "Managers' Association," and as we all submitted to the arbitrary and extortionate demands of the *Herald,* Bennett thought he had but to crack his whip, in order to keep any and all of us within the traces.

Accordingly, one day, Bennett's attorney wrote me a letter, saying that he would like to have me call on him at his office the following morning. Not dreaming of the object, I called as desired, and after a few pleasant commonplace remarks about the weather, and other trifles, the attorney said:

"Mr. Barnum, I have sent for you to say that Mr. Bennett has concluded not to purchase the museum lots, and therefore that you had better take back the lease, and return the $200,000 paid for it."

"Are you in earnest?" I asked with surprise.

"Certainly, quite so," he answered.

"Really," I said, smiling, "I am sorry I can't accommodate Mr. Bennett; I have not got the little sum about me; in fact, I have spent the money."

"It will be better for you to take back the lease," said the attorney, seriously.

"Nonsense," I replied, "I shall do nothing of the sort, I don't make child's bargains. The lease was cheap enough, but I have other business to attend to, and shall have nothing to do with it."

The attorney said very little in reply; but I could see, by the almost benignant sorrow expressed upon his countenance, that he evidently pitied me for the temerity that would doubtless lead me into the jaws of the insatiable monster of the *Herald.* The next morning, I observed that the advertisement of my entertainments with my

Museum Company at Winter Garden was left out of the *Herald* columns. I went directly to the editorial rooms of the *Herald*; and learning that Bennett was not in, I said to Mr. Hudson, then managing editor:

"My advertisement is left out of the *Herald*; is there a screw loose?"

"I believe there is," was the reply.

"What is the matter?" I asked.

"You must ask the Emperor," said Mr. Hudson, meaning of course Bennett.

"When will the 'Emperor' be in?" I enquired

"Next Monday," was the answer.

"Well, I shall not see him," I replied; "but I wish to have this thing settled at once. Mr. Hudson, I now tender you the money for the insertion of my Museum advertisement on the same terms as are paid by other places of amusement; will you publish it?"

"I will not," Mr. Hudson peremptorily replied.

"That is all," I said. Mr. Hudson then smilingly and blandly remarked, "I have formally answered your formal demand, because I suppose you require it; but you know, Mr. Barnum, I can only obey orders." I assured him that I understood the matter perfectly, and attached no blame to him in the premises. I then proceeded to notify the secretary of the "Managers' Association" to call the managers together at twelve o'clock the following day; and there was a full meeting at the appointed time. I stated the facts in the case in the *Herald* affair, and simply remarked, that if we did not make common cause against any paper publisher who excluded an advertisement from his columns simply to gratify a private pique, it was evident that either and all of us were liable to imposition at any time.

One of the managers immediately made a motion that the entire Association should stop their advertising and bill printing at the *Herald* office and have no further connection with that establishment. Mr. Lester Wallack advised that this motion should not be adopted until a committee had waited upon Bennett and had reported the result of the interview to the Association. Accordingly, Messrs. Wallack, Wheatley and Stuart were delegated to go down to the office to call on Mr. Bennett.

The moment Bennett saw them, he evidently suspected the object of their mission, for he at once commenced to speak to Mr. Wallack in a patronizing manner; told him how long he had known, and how much he respected his late father, who was "a time English gentleman of the old school," with much in the same strain. Mr. Wallack replied to Bennett that the three managers were appointed a committee to wait upon him to ascertain if he insisted upon excluding from his columns the Museum advertisements — not on account of any objection to the contents of the advertisements, or to the Museum itself, but simply because he had a private business disagreement with the proprietor; intimating that such a proceeding, for such a reason, and no other, might lead to a rupture of business relations with other managers. In reply, Mr. Bennett had something to say about the fox that had suffered tail-wise from a trap, and thereupon advised all other foxes to cut their tails off; and he pointed the fable setting forth the impolicy of drawing down upon the Association the vengeance of the *Herald.* The committee, however, coolly insisted upon a direct answer to their question.

Bennett then answered: "I will not publish Barnum's advertisement; I do my business as I please, and in my own way."

"So do we," replied one of the managers, and the committee withdrew.

The next day the Managers' Association met, heard the report, and unanimously resolved to withdraw their advertisements from the *Herald*, and their patronage from the *Herald* job establishment, and it was done. Nevertheless, the *Herald* for several days continued to print gratuitously the advertisements of Wall Theater and Niblo's Garden, and inordinately puffed these establishments, evidently in order to ease the fall, and to convey the idea that some of the theaters patronized the *Herald*, and perhaps hoping by praising these managers to draw them back again, and so to nullify the agreement of the Association in regard to the *Herald*. Thereupon, the managers headed their advertisements in all the other New York papers with the line, "This establishment does not advertise in the *New York Herald*," and for many months this announcement was kept at the top of every theatrical advertisement and on the posters and playbills.

The *Herald* then began to abuse and vilify the theatrical and opera managers, their artists and their performances, and by way of contrast profusely praised Tony Pastor's Bowery show, and sundry entertainments of a similar character, which of course was well understood by the public and relished accordingly. Meanwhile, the first-class theaters prospered amazingly under the abuse of Bennett. Their receipts were never larger, and their houses never more thronged. The public took sides in the matter with the managers and against the *Herald*, and thousands of people went to the theaters merely to show their willingness to support the managers and to spite "Old Bennett." The editor was fairly caught in his own trap; other journals began to estimate the loss the *Herald* sustained by the action of the managers, and it was generally believed that this loss in advertising and job printing was not less than from $75,000 to $100,000 a year. The *Herald*'s circulation also suffered terribly, since hundreds of people, at the hotels and elsewhere, who were accustomed to buy the paper solely for the sake of seeing what amusements were announced for the evening, now bought other papers. This was the hardest blow of all, and it fully accounted for the abuse which the *Herald* daily poured out upon the theaters.

Bennett evidently felt ashamed of the whole transaction; he would never publish the facts in his columns, though he once stated in an editorial that it had been reported that he had been cheated in purchasing the Broadway property; that the case had gone to court, and the public would soon know all the particulars. Some persons supposed by this that Bennett had sued me; but this was far from being the case. The owner of the lots sued Bennett, to compel him to take the title and pay for the property as per agreement; and that was all the "law" there was about it. He held James Gordon Bennett's bond, that he would pay him half a million of dollars for the land, as follows: $100,000 cash, and a bond and mortgage upon the premises for the remaining §400,000. The day before the suit was to come to trial, Bennett came forward, took the deed, and paid $100,000 cash, and gave a bond and mortgage of the entire premises for $400,000.

Had I really taken back the lease as Bennett desired, he would have been in a worse scrape than ever; for having been compelled to take the property, he would have been obliged, as my landlord, to go on and assist in building a Museum for me, according to the terms of my lease, and a Museum I should certainly have built on Bennett's property, even if I had owned a dozen Museums up town.

In the autumn of 1868, the associated managers came to the conclusion that the punishment of Bennett for two years was sufficient, and they consented to restore their advertisements to the *Herald*. I was then carrying on my new Museum, and although I did not immediately resume advertising in the *Herald*, I have since done so.

Mr. Bennett died in 1872. In these pages I have not been sparing of criticism upon his business plans and schemes but cannot forbear acknowledgment of the extraordinary talent and tact of this great journalist. By enterprise and energy, he attained a world-wide reputation and a fortune of large proportions. Let personal conflicts be buried in forgiving forgetfulness.

CHAPTER XLII.

PUBLIC LECTURING.

During the summer of 1866, Mr. Edwin L. Brown, Corresponding Secretary of the "Associated Western Literary Societies," opened a correspondence with me relative to delivering, in the ensuing season, my lecture on "Success in Life," before some sixty lyceums, Young Men's Christian Associations, and literary Societies belonging to the union which Mr. Brown represented. The scheme embraced an extended tour through Pennsylvania, Ohio, Indiana, Illinois, Wisconsin, Missouri and Iowa, and I was to receive one hundred dollars for every repetition of my lecture, with all my traveling expenses on the route. Agreeing to these terms, I commenced the engagement at the appointed time, and, averaging five lectures a week, I finished the prescribed round just before New Year's. Before beginning this engagement, however, I gave the lecture for other associations at Wheeling, Virginia, Cincinnati, Ohio, and Louisville, Kentucky. I also delivered the lecture in Chicago, for Professor Eastman, who at that time had one of his Business Colleges in that city. He engaged the celebrated Crosby Opera House for the occasion, and I think, with perhaps two exceptions, I never spoke before so large and intelligent an audience as was there assembled. It was estimated that from five to six thousand ladies and gentlemen were gathered in that capacious building; and nearly as many more went away unable to obtain admission. I was glad to observe by the action of the audience, and by the journals of the following day, that my efforts on that occasion were satisfactory. Indeed, though it is necessarily egotistical, I may truly say that with this lecture I always succeeded in pleasing my hearers. I may add, that I have invariably, as a rule, devoted to charitable purposes every penny I ever received for lecturing, except while I was under the great Jerome Clock cloud in England, when I needed all I could earn.

My western tour was delightful; indeed, it was almost an ovation, I found, in fact, that when I had strayed so far from home, the curiosity exhibitor himself became quite a curiosity. On several occasions, in Iowa, I was introduced to ladies and gentlemen, who had driven thirty miles in carriages to hear me. I insisted, however, that it was more to see than to hear; and I asked them if that was not really the case. In several instances they answered in the affirmative. In fact, one quaint old lady said: "Why, to tell you the truth, Mr. Barnum. we have read so much about you, and your Museum and your queer carryings on that we were not quite sure but you had horns and cloven feet, and so we came to satisfy our curiosity; but, dear me! I don't see but what you look a good deal like other folks, after all"

On my tour, in attempting to make the connection from Cleveland, Ohio, to Fort Wayne, Indiana, via Toledo, I arrived at the latter city at one o'clock p. m., which was about two hours too late to catch the train in time for the hour announced for my lecture that evening. I went to Mr. Andrews, the superintendent of the Toledo, Wabash and Western Railway, and told him I wanted to hire a locomotive and car to run to Fort Wayne, as I must be there at eight o'clock at night.

"It is an impossibility," said Mr. Andrews; "the distance is ninety-four miles and no train leaves here till morning. The road is much occupied by freight trams, and we never run extra trains in this part of the country, unless the necessity is imperative."

I suppose I looked astonished, as well as chagrined. I knew that if I missed lecturing in Fort Wayne that evening, I could not appoint another time for that purpose, for every night was engaged during the next two months. I also felt that a large number of persons in Fort Wayne would be disappointed, and I grew desperate. Drawing my wallet from my pocket, I said:

"I will give two hundred dollars, and even more, if you say so, to be put into Fort Wayne before eight o'clock tonight; and, really, I hope you will accommodate me"

The superintendent looked me thoroughly over in half a minute, and I fancied he had come to the conclusion that I was a burglar, a counterfeiter, or something worse, fleeing from justice. My surmise was confirmed, when he slowly remarked:

"Your business must be very pressing, sir."

"It is indeed," I replied; "I am Barnum, the Museum man, and am engaged to speak in Fort Wayne tonight."

He evidently did not catch the whole of my response, for he immediately said. "Oh, it is a show, eh? Where is old Barnum himself?"

"I am Barnum," I replied, "and it is a lecture which I am advertised to give tonight; and I would not disappoint the people for anything."

"Is this P.T. Barnum?" said the superintendent, starting to his feet.

"I am sorry to say it is," I replied.

"Well, Mr. Barnum," said he, earnestly, "if you can stand it to ride to Fort Wayne in the caboose of a freight train, your well-established reputation for punctuality in keeping your engagements shall not suffer on account of the Toledo, Wabash and Western Railroad."

"Caboose!" said I, with a laugh, "I would ride to Fort Wayne astride of the engine, or boxed up and stowed away in a freight car, if necessary, in order to meet my engagement."

A freight train was on the point of starting for Fort Wayne; all the cars were at once ordered to be switched off, except two, which the superintendent said were necessary to balance the train; the freight trains on the road were telegraphed to clear the track, and the polite superintendent, pointing to the caboose, invited me to step in. I drew out my pocket-book to pay, but he smilingly shook his head, and said: "You have a through ticket from Cleveland to Fort Wayne; hand it to the freight agent on your arrival, and all will be right."

The excited state of mind which I had suffered while under the impression that the audience in Fort Wayne must be disappointed, now changed, and I felt as happy as a king. In fact, I enjoyed a new sensation of imperial superiority, in that I was "monarch of all I surveyed," emperor of my own train, switching all other trains from the main track, and making conductors all along the line wonder what grand mogul had thus taken complete possession and control of the road. Indeed, as we sped past each train, which stood quietly on a side track waiting for us to pass, I could not help smiling at the glances of excited curiosity which were thrown into our car by the agent and brakeman of the train which had been so peremptorily ordered to clear the track;

and always stepping at the caboose door, I raised my hat, always receiving in return an almost reverent salute, which the occupants of the waiting train thought due, no doubt, to the distinguished person for whom they were ordered by special telegram to make way.

I now began to reflect that the Fort Wayne lecture committee, upon realizing that I did not arrive by the regular passenger train, would not expect me at all, and that probably they might issue small bills announcing my failure to arrive. I therefore prepared the following telegram which I dispatched to them on our arrival at Napoleon, the first station at which we stopped:

Lecture Committee, Fort Wayne: Rest perfectly tranquil. I am to be delivered at Fort Wayne by contract by half-past seven o'clock— special train.

At the same station I received a telegram from Mr. Andrews, the superintendent, asking me how I liked the caboose. I replied:

The springs of the caboose are softer than down; I am as happy as a clam at high-water: I am being carried towards Fort Wayne in a style never surpassed by Caesar's triumphal march into Rome. Hurrah for the Toledo and Wabash Railroad!

At the invitation of the engineer, I took a ride of twenty miles upon the locomotive. It fairly made my head swim. I could not reconcile my mind to the idea that there was no danger; and intimating to the engineer that it would be a relief to get where I could not see ahead, I was permitted to crawl back again to the caboose.

I reached Fort Wayne in ample time for the lecture; and as the committee had discreetly kept to themselves the fact of my non-arrival by the regular train, probably not a dozen persons were aware of the trouble I had taken to fulfill my engagement, till in the course of my lecture, under the head of "perseverance," I recounted my day's adventures, as an illustration of exercising that quality when real necessity demanded. The Fort Wayne papers of the next day published accounts of "Barnum on a Locomotive," and " A Journey in a Caboose;" and, as I always had an eye to advertising, these articles were sent marked to newspapers in towns and cities where I was to lecture, and of course were copied — thus producing the desired effects, first, of informing the public that the "showman" was coming, and next, assuring the lecture committee that Barnum would be punctually on hand as advertised, unless prevented by "circumstances which he had no control."

The managers of railroads running west from Chicago, pretty rigidly enforce a rule excluding from certain reserved cars, all gentlemen traveling without ladies. As I do not smoke I avoided the smoking cars; and as the ladies' car was sometimes more select and always more comfortable than the other cars. I tried various expedients to smuggle myself in. If I saw a lady about to enter the alone, I followed closely, hoping thus to elude the vigilance of the brakeman, who generally acts as doorkeeper. But the car Cerberus is pretty well up to all such dodges, and I did not always succeed. On one occasion, seeing a young couple, evidently just married, and starting on a bridal tour, about to enter the car, I followed closely, but was stopped by the doorkeeper, who called out:

"How many gentlemen are with this lady."

I have always noticed that young, newly-married people, are very fond of saying "my husband" and "my wife;" they are new terms which sound pleasantly to the ears of those who utter them; so, in answer to the peremptory inquiry of the doorkeeper, the bridegroom promptly responded:

"I am this lady's husband."

"And I guess you can see by the resemblance between the lady and myself," said I to Cerberus, "that I am her father."

The astounded husband and the blushing bride were too much "taken aback" to deny their newly-discovered parent, but the brakeman said, as he permitted the young couple to pass into the car:

"We can't pass all creation with one lady."

"I hope you will not deprive me of the company of my child during the little time we can remain together," I said with a demure countenance. The brakeman evidently sympathized with the fond "parent" whose feelings were sufficiently lacerated at losing his daughter, through her finding a husband, and I was permitted to pass. I immediately apologized to the young bride and her husband, and told them who I was, and my reasons for the assumed paternity, and they enjoyed the joke so heartily that they called me "father" during our entire journey together. Indeed, the husband privately and slyly hinted to me that the first boy should be christened "P.T."

I fulfilled my entire engagement, which covered the lecturing season, and returned to New York greatly pleased with my western tour. Public lecturing was by no means a new experience with me; for, apart from my labors in that direction in England, and occasional addresses before literary and agricultural associations at home, I had been prominently in the field for many years, as a lecturer on temperance. My attention was turned to this subject in the following manner:

In the fall of 1847, while exhibiting General Tom Thumb at Saratoga Springs, where the New York State Fair was then being held, I saw so much intoxication among men of wealth and intellect, filling the highest positions in society, that I began to ask myself the question, What guarantee is there that *I* may not become a drunkard? and I forthwith pledged myself at that time never again to partake of any kind of spirituous liquors as a beverage. True, I continued to partake of wine, for I had been instructed, in my European tour, that this was one of the innocent and charming indispensables of Life. I, however, regarded myself as a good temperance man, and soon began to persuade my friends to refrain from the intoxicating cup. Seeing need of reform in Bridgeport, I invited my friend, the Reverend Doctor E. H. Chapin, to visit us, for the purpose of giving a public temperance lecture. I had never heard him on that subject, but I knew that on whatever topic he spoke, he was as logical as he was eloquent.

He lectured in the Baptist church in Bridgeport. His subject was presented in three divisions: The liquor-seller, the moderate drinker, and the indifferent man. It happened, therefore, that the second, if not the third clause of the subject, had a special bearing upon me and my position. The eloquent gentleman overwhelmingly proved that the so-called respectable liquor-seller, in his splendid saloon or hotel bar, and who sold only to "gentlemen," inflicted much greater injury upon the community than a dozen common groggeries — which he abundantly illustrated. He then took up the "moderate drinker," and urged that he was the great stumbling-block to the temperance reform. He it was, and not the drunkard in the ditch, that the young man looked at as an example when he took his first glass. That when the drunkard was asked to sign the pledge, he would reply, "Why should I do so? What harm can there be in drinking, when such men as respectable Mr. A and moral Mr. B drink wine under their own roof?" He urged that the higher a man stood in the community, the greater was his influence either for good or for evil. He said to the moderate drinker: "Sir, you either do or you do not consider it a privation and a sacrifice to give op drinking. Which is it? If you say that you can drink or let it alone, that you can quit it forever without considering it a self-denial, then I appeal to yon as a man, to do it for the sake of your suffering fellow-beings." He farther argued that if it was a self-denial to give up wine-drinking, then certainly the man should stop, for he was in danger of becoming a drunkard.

What Doctor Chapin said produced a deep impression upon my mind, and, a night of anxious thought, I rose in the morning, took my champagne bottles, knocked off their heads, and poured then contents upon the ground. I then called upon Doctor Chapin, asked him for the teetotal pledge, and signed it. He was greatly surprised in discovering that I was not already a teetotaler. He supposed such was the case, from the fact that I had invited him to lecture, and he little thought, at the time of his delivering it, that his argument to the moderate drinker was at all applicable to me. I felt that I had now a duty to perform save others, as I had been saved, and on the very morning when I signed the pledge, I obtained over twenty signatures in Bridgeport. I talked temperance to all whom I met, and very soon commenced lecturing upon the subject in the adjacent towns and villages. I spent the entire winter and spring of 1851-2 in lecturing free, through my native State, always traveling at my own expense, and I was glad to know that I aroused many hundreds, perhaps thousands, to the importance of the temperance reform. I also lectured frequently in the cities of New York and Philadelphia, as well as in other towns in the neighboring States.

While in Boston with Jenny Lind, I was earnestly solicited to deliver two temperance lectures in the Tremont Temple, where she gave her concerts. I did and though an admission fee was charged for the benefit of a benevolent society, the building on each occasion was crowded. In the course of my tour with Jenny Lind, I was frequently solicited to lecture on temperance on evenings when she did not sing. I always complied when it was in my power. In this way I lectured in Baltimore, Washington, Charleston, New Orleans, Cincinnati, St. Louis, and other cities, also in the ladies' saloon of the steamer Lexington, on Sunday morning. In August, 1853, I lectured in Cleveland, Ohio, and several other towns, and afterwards in Chicago, Illinois, and in Kenosha, cousin. An election was to be held in Wisconsin in October, and the friends of prohibition in that State solicited my services for the ensuing month, and I could not refuse them. I therefore hastened home to transact some bus which required my presence for a few days, and then returned, and lectured on my way in Toledo, Norwalk, Ohio, and Chicago, Illinois. I made the tour of the State of Wisconsin, delivering two free lectures per day, for four consecutive weeks, to crowded and attentive audiences.

My lecture in New Orleans, when I was in that city, was in the great Lyceum Hall, in St. Charles street, and I lectured by the invitation of Mayor Crossman, and several other influential gentlemen. The immense hall contained more than three thousand auditors, including the most respectable portion of the New Orleans public. I was in capital humor, and had warmed myself into state of excitement, feeling that the audience was with me. While in the midst of an argument illustrating the poisonous and destructive nature of alcohol to the animal economy, some opponent called out, "How does it affect us, externally or internally?"

"*E*-ternally," I replied.

I have scarcely ever heard more tremendous merriment than that which followed this reply, and the applause was so prolonged that it was some minutes before I could proceed.

On the first evening when I lectured in Cleveland, Ohio (it was in the Baptist church), I commenced in this wise: "If there are any ladies or gentlemen present who have never suffered in consequence of the use of intoxicating drinks as a beverage, either directly or in the person of a dear relative or friend, I will thank them to rise." A man with a tolerably glowing countenance arose. "Had you never a friend who was intemperate?" I asked.

"Never!" was the positive reply.

A giggle ran through the opposition portion of the audience. "Really, my friends," I said, " I feel constrained to make a proposition which I did not anticipate. I am, as you are all aware, a showman, and I am always on the look-out for curiosities. This gentleman is a stranger to me, but if he will satisfy me tomorrow morning that he is a man of credibility, and that no friend of his was ever intemperate, I will be glad to engage him for ten weeks at $200 per week, to exhibit him in my American Museum in New York, as the greatest curiosity in this country."

A laugh that was a laugh followed this announcement.

"They may laugh, but it is a fact," persisted my opponent, with a look of dogged tenacity.

"The gentleman still insists that it is a fact," I replied. " I would like, therefore, to make one simple qualification to my offer; I made it on the supposition that, at some period of his life, he had friends. Now, if he never had any friends, I withdraw my offer; otherwise, I will stick to it."

This, and the shout of laughter that ensued, was too much for the gentleman, and he sat down. I noticed throughout my speech that he paid strict attention, and frequently indulged in a hearty laugh. At the close of the lecture he approached me, and, extending his hand, which I readily accepted, he said, "I was particularly green in rising tonight. Having once stood up, I was determined not to be put down, but your last remark fixed me!" He then complimented me very highly on the reasonableness of my arguments, and declared that ever afterwards he would be found on the side of temperance.

I have lectured in Montreal, Canada, and many towns and cities in the United States, at my own expense. One of the greatest consolations I now enjoy is that of believing I have carried happiness to the bosom of many a family. In the course of my life I have written much for newspapers, on various subjects, and always with earnestness, but in none of these have I felt so deep an interest as in that of the temperance reform. Were it not for this fact, I should be reluctant to mention that, besides numerous articles for the daily and weekly press, I wrote a little tract on "The Liquor Business," which expresses my practical view of the use and traffic in intoxicating drinks. In every one of my temperance lectures since the beginning of the year 1869, I have regularly read the following report, made by Mr. T.T. Cortis, Overseer of the Poor in Vineland, New Jersey:

Though we have a population of 10,000 people, for the period of six months no settler or citizen of Vineland has required relief at my hands as overseer of the poor. Within seventy days, there has only been one case among what we call the floating population, at the expense of $4.00. During the entire year, there has only been but one indictment, and that a trifling case of assault and battery, among our colored population. So few are the fires in Vineland, that we have no need of a fire department. There has only been one house burnt down in a year, and two slight fires, which were soon put out. We practically have no debt, and our taxes are only one per cent on the valuation. The police expenses of Vineland amount to $75.00 per year, the sum paid to me; and our poor expenses a mere trifle. I ascribe this remarkable state of things, so nearly approaching the golden age, to the industry of our people, and the absence of King Alcohol. Let me give you, in contrast to this, the state of things in the town from which I came, in New England. The population of the town was 9,500— a little less than that of Vineland. It maintained forty liquor shops. These kept busy a police judge, city marshal, assistant marshal, four night watchmen, six policemen. Fires were almost continual. That small place maintained a paid Fire department, of four companies, of forty men each, at an expense of $3,000.00 per annum. I belonged to this department for six years, and the fires averaged about one every two weeks, and mostly incendiary. The support of the poor cost $2,500.00 per annum. The debt of the township was $120,000. 00. The condition of things in this New England town is as favorable in that country as that of many other places where liquor is sold.

It seems to me that there is an amount of overwhelming testimony and unanswerable argument in this one brief extract, that makes it in itself one of the most perfect and powerful temperance lectures ever written.

CHAPTER XLIII.

THE NEW MUSEUM.

My new Museum on Broadway was liberally patronized from the start, but I felt that still more attractions were necessary in order to insure constant success. I therefore made arrangements with the renowned Van Amburgh Menagerie Company to unite their entire collection of living wild animals with the Museum. The new company was known as the "Barnum and Van Amburgh Museum and Menagerie Company," and as such was chartered by the Connecticut Legislature, the New York Legislature having refused us a charter unless I would "see" the "ring" a thousand dollars' worth, which I declined. I owned forty per cent, and the Van Amburgh Company held the remaining sixty per cent in the new enterprise, which comprehended a large traveling menagerie through the country in summer, and the placing of the wild animals in the Museum in winter. The capital of the company was one million of dollars, with the privilege of doubling the amount. As one of the conditions of the new arrangement, it was stipulated that I should withdraw from all active personal attention to the Museum, but should permit my name to be announced as General Manager, and I was also elected President of the company.

Meanwhile, immense additions were made to the curiosity departments of the new Museum. Every penny of the profits of this Museum and of the two immense traveling menageries of wild animals was expended in procuring additional attractions for our patrons. Among other valuable novelties introduced in this establishment was the famous collection made by the renowned lion-slayer Gordon Cummings. This was purchased for me by my faithful friend, Mr. George A. Wells, who was then traveling in Great Britain with General Tom Thumb. The collection consisted of many hundreds of skins, tusks, heads and skeletons of nearly every species of African animal, including numerous rare specimens never before exhibited on this continent. It was a great Museum in itself, and as such had attracted much attention in London and elsewhere, but it was a mere addition to our Museum and Menagerie; and was exhibited without extra charge for admission.

The monthly returns made to the United States Collector of Internal Revenue for the district, showed that our receipts were larger than those of Wallack's Theater, Niblo's Garden, or any other theater or place of amusement in New York, or in America.

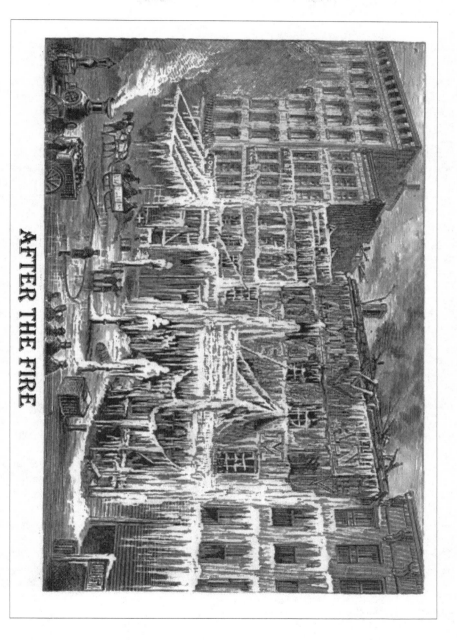

AFTER THE FIRE

Anxious to gather curiosities from every quarter of the globe, I sent Mr. John Greenwood, junior (who went for me to the isle of Cyprus and to Constantinople, in 1864), on the "Quaker City" excursion, which left New York, June 8, 1867, and returned in the following November. During his absence Mr. Greenwood traveled 17,735 miles and brought back several interesting relics from the Holy Land, which were duly deposited in the Museum.

Very soon after entering upon the premises, I built a new and larger lecture room, which was one of the most commodious and complete theaters in New York, and I largely increased the dramatic company. Our collection swelled so rapidly that we were obliged to extend our premises by the addition of another building, forty by one hundred feet, adjoining the Museum. This addition gave us several new halls, which were speedily filled with curiosities. The rapid expansion of the establishment, and the immense interest excited in the public mind led me to consider a plan I had long contemplated, of taking some decided steps towards the foundation of a great free institution, which should be similar to and in some respects superior to the British Museum in London. "The Barnum and Van Amburgh Museum and Menagerie Company," chartered with a capital of $2,000,000 had, in addition to the New York establishment, thirty acres of land in Bridgeport, whereon it was proposed to erect suitable buildings and glass and wire edifices for breeding and acclimating rare animals and birds, and training such of them as were fit for public performances. In time, a new building in New York, covering a whole square, and farther up town, would be needed for the mammoth exhibition, and I was not without hopes that I might be the means of establishing permanently in the city an extensive zoological garden.

It was also my intention ultimately to make my Museum the nucleus of a great free national institution. When the American Museum was burned, and I turned my attention to the collection of fresh curiosities, I felt that I needed other assistance than that of my own agents in America and Europe. It occurred to me that if our government representatives abroad would but use their influence to secure curiosities in the respective countries to which they were delegated, a free public Museum might at once be begun in New York, and I proposed to offer a part of my own establishment rent-free for the deposit and exhibition of such rarities as might be collected in this way. Accordingly, a week after the destruction of the American Museum, a memorial was addressed to the President of the United States, asking him to give his sanction to the new effort to furnish the means of useful information and wholesome amusement, and to give such instructions to public officers abroad as would enable them, without any conflict with their legitimate duties, to give efficiency to this truly national movement for the advancement of the public good, without cost to the government. This memorial was dated July 20, 1860, and was signed by Messrs. E. D. Morgan, Moses Taylor, Abram Wakeman, Simeon Draper, Moses H. Grinnell, Stephen Knapp, Benjamin R, Winthrop, Charles Gould, Wm. C. Bryant, James Wadsworth, Tunis W. Quick, John A. Pitkin, Willis Gaylord, Prosper M. Wetmore, Henry Ward Beecher, and Horace Greeley. This memorial was in due time presented, and was endorsed as follows:

"Executive Mansion, Washington, D. C, April 27, 1866.

The purpose set forth in this Memorial is highly approved and commended, and our Ministers, Consuls and commercial agents are requested to give whatever influence in carrying out the object within stated they may deem compatible with the duties of their respective positions, and not inconsistent with the public interests.

Andrew Johnson."

I went to Washington myself, and had interviews with the President, Secretaries Seward, McCulloch and Welles, and also with Assistant Secretary of the Navy, G.V. Fox, who gave me several muskets and other "rebel trophies." During my stay at the capital, I had a pleasant interview with General Grant, who told me he had lately visited my Museum with one of his sons and had been greatly gratified. Upon my mentioning, among other projects, that I had an idea of collecting the hats of distinguished individuals, he at once offered to send an orderly for the hat he had worn during his principal campaigns. All these gentlemen cordially approved of my plan for the establishment of a National Museum in New York.

But before this plan could be put into effective operation, an event occurred which is now to be narrated: The winter of 1867-68 was one of the coldest that had been known for years, and some thirty-severe snowstorms occurred during the season. On Tuesday morning, March 3rd, 1868, it was bitter cold. A heavy body of snow was on the ground, and, as I sat at the breakfast table with my wife and an esteemed lady guest, the wife of my excellent friend, Rev. A. C. Thomas, I read aloud the general news from the morning papers. Leisurely turning to the local columns, I said, "Hallo! Barnum's Museum is burned." "Yes, said my wife, with an incredulous smile, "I suspect it is." "It is a fact," said I, "just listen; 'Barnum's Museum totally destroyed by fire.' "

This was read so coolly, and I showed so little excitement, that both of the ladies supposed I was joking. My wife simply remarked:

"Yes, it was totally destroyed two years ago, but Barnum built another one."

"Yes, and that is burned," I replied; "now listen," and I proceeded very calmly to read the account of the fire. Mrs. Thomas, still believing from my manner that it was a joke, stole slyly behind my chair, and looking over my shoulder at the newspaper, she exclaimed:

"Why, Mrs. Barnum, the Museum is really burned. Here is the whole account of it in this morning's paper."

"Of course, it is," I remarked, with a smile, "how could you think I could joke on such a serious subject!"

The papers of the following morning contained full accounts of the fire; and editorial writers, while manifesting much sympathy for the proprietors, also expressed profound regret that so magnificent a collection, especially in the zoological department, should be lost to the city.

The cold was so intense that the water froze almost as soon as it left the hose of the fire engines; and when at last everything was destroyed, except the front granite wall of the Museum building, that and the ladder, signs, and lamp-posts in front, were covered in a gorgeous frame-work of transparent ice, which made it altogether one of the most picturesque scenes imaginable. Thousands of persons congregated daily in that locality in order to get a view of the magnificent ruins. By moonlight, the ice-coated ruins were still more sublime; and for many days and nights the old Museum was "the observed of all observers," and photographs were taken by several artists.

When the Museum was burnt, I was nearly ready to bring out a new spectacle, for which a very large, extra company had been engaged, and on which a considerable sum of money had been expended in scenery, properties, costumes, and especially in enlarging the stage. I had expended altogether, some $78,000 in building the new lecture-room, and in refitting the saloons. The curiosities were inventoried by the manager, Mr. Ferguson, at $288,000. I bought the real estate only a little while before the fire, for $460,000, and there was an insurance on the whole of $160,000; and in June, 1868, I sold the lots on which the building stood, for $432,000. The cause of the fire was a defective flue in the restaurant in the basement of the building.

Thus, by the destruction of *Iranistan* and two Museums, about a million of dollars' worth of my property had been destroyed by fire, and I was not now long in making up my mind to follow Mr. Greeley's advice on a former occasion, to "take this fire as a notice to quit, and go a-fishing/'

I dissolved with the Van Amburgh Company and sold out to them all my interest in the personal property of the concern. I was beset on every side to start another Museum, and men of capital offered to raise a million of dollars, if necessary, for that purpose, provided I would undertake its management; but I felt that I had enough to live on, and I earnestly believed the doctrine laid down in my lecture on "Money-Getting," in regard to the danger of leaving too much property to children.

As I now had something like real leisure at my disposal, in the summer of 1868 I made my third visit to the White Mountains. To me, the locality and scene are ever fresh and ever wonderful. From the top of Mount Washington, one can see, on every side within a radius of forty miles, peaks piled on peaks, with smiling valleys here and there between, and, on a very clear day, the Atlantic Ocean, off Portland, Maine, is distinctly visible — sixty miles away. Beauty, grandeur, sublimity, and the satisfaction of almost every sense combine to remind one of the ejaculation of that devout English soul who exclaims: "Look around with pleasure, and upward with gratitude."

At the Profile House, near the Notch, in the Franconia range, I met many acquaintances, some of whom had been there with their families for several weeks. When tired of scenery-hunting and hill-climbing, and thrown entirely upon their own resources, they had invented a "sell" which they perpetrated upon every newcomer. Naturally enough, as I was considered a capital subject for their fun, before I had been there half an hour they had made all the arrangements to take me in. The "sell " consisted in getting up a foot-race in which all were to join, and at the word "go" the contestants were to start and run across the open space in front of the hotel to a fence opposite, while the last man who should touch the rail must treat the crowd. Of course, no one touched the rail at all, except the victim. I suspected no trick, but tried to avoid the race, urging in excuse, that I was too old, too corpulent, and, besides, as they knew, I was a teetotaler and would not drink their liquor.

"Oh, drink lemonade, if you like," they said, "but no backing out; and as for corpulence, here is Stephen, our old stage-driver, who weighs three hundred, and he shall run with the rest."

And, in good truth, Stephen, in a warm day especially, would be likely to "run" with the best of them; but I did not know then that Stephen was the stool-pigeon whom they kept to entrap unwary and verdant youths like myself; so, looking at his portly form, I at once agreed that if Stephen ran I would, as I knew that, for a stout man, I was pretty quick on my feet. Accordingly, at the word "go," I started and ran as if the traditional enemy of mankind were in me or after me, but, before I had accomplished half the distance, I wondered why at least, one or two of the crowd had not outstripped me, for, in fact, Stephen was the only one whom I expected to beat. Looking back and at once comprehending the "sell," I decided not to be sold. A correspondent of the *New York Sun* told how I escaped the trick and the penalty, and how I subsequently paid off the tricksters, in a letter from which I quote the following:

"Barnum threw up his hands before arriving at the railing, and did not touch it at all! It was acknowledged on all sides that the 'biters were bit.' But you ran well, I said those who intended the 'sell.' 'Yes,' replied Barnaul, in high glee. 'I ran better than I did for Congress, but I was not green enough to touch the rail' Of course, a roar of laughter followed, and the 'sellers' resolved to try the game the next morning on some other newcomer; but their luck had evidently deserted them, for the next man also 'smelt a rat,' and, holding up his hands, refused to touch the rail. The two successive failures dampened the ardor of the "sellers", and they relinquished that trick as a bad job. But the way Barnum sold nearly the whole crowd of 'sellers' in detail, on the following afternoon, by the old 'sliver trick,' was a caution to sore sides. So much laughing in one day was probably never before done in that locality. One after another succeeded in extracting from the palm of Barnum's hand what each at first supposed was a tormenting 'sliver,' but which turned out to be a "broom splinter" a foot long which was hidden up B.'s sleeve, except the small point which appeared from under the end of his thumb, apparently protruding from under the skin of his palm. One 'weak brother ' nearly fainted as he saw come forth some twelve inches of what he first supposed was a 'sliver,' but which he was now thoroughly convinced was one of the nerves from Barnum's arm. Mr. O'Brien, the Wall street banker, was the first victim. When asked what he thought upon seeing such a long 'sliver' coming from Barnum's hand, he solemnly replied, 'I thought he was a dead man!' It was acknowledged by all that Barnum gave them a world of 'fun,' and that he and his friends left the Profile House with flying colors."

CHAPTER XLIV.

CURIOUS COINCIDENCES — NUMBER THIRTEEN.

Is the summer of 1868, a lady, who happened to be at that time an inmate of my family, upon hearing me say that I supposed we must remove into our summer residence on Thursday, because our servants might not like to go on Friday, remarked:

What nonsense that is! It is astonishing that some persons are so foolish as to think there is any difference in the days. I call it rank heathenism to be so superstitious as to think one day is lucky and another unlucky;" and then, in the most innocent manner possible, she added: "I would not like to remove on a Saturday, myself, for they say people who remove on the last day of the week don't stay long."

Of course, this was too refreshing a case of undoubted superstition to be permitted to pass without a hearty laugh from all who heard it.

I suppose most of us have certain superstitions, imbibed in our youth, and still lurking more or less faintly in our minds. Many would not like to acknowledge that they had any choice whether they commenced a new enterprise on a Friday or on a Monday, or whether they first saw the new moon over the right or left shoulder. And yet, perhaps, a large portion of these same persons will be apt to observe it when they happen to do anything which popular superstition calls "unlucky." It is a common occurrence with many to immediately make a secret "wish" if they happen to use the same expression at the same moment when a friend with whom they are conversing makes it; nevertheless, these persons would protest against being considered superstitious — indeed, probably they are not so in the full meaning of the word.

Several years ago, an old lady, who was a guest at my house, remarked on a rainy Sunday:

"This is the first Sunday in the month, and now it will rain every Sunday in the month; that is a sign which never fails, for I have noticed it many a time."

"Well," I remarked, smiling, "watch closely this time, and if it rains on the next three Sundays, I will give you a new silk dress."

She was in high glee, and replied:

"Well, you have lost that dress, as sure as you are born."

The following Sunday it did, indeed, rain.

"Ah, ha!" exclaimed the old lady, "what did I tell you? I knew it would rain."

I smiled, and said, " all right, watch for next Sunday."

And surely enough, the next Sunday it did rain, harder than on either of the preceding Sundays.

"Now, what do you think?" said the old lady, solemnly. "I tell you that sign never fails. It won't do to doubt the ways of Providence," she added with a sigh, "for His ways are mysterious and past finding out."

The following Sunday, the sun rose in a cloudless sky, and not the slightest appearance of rain was manifested through the day. The old lady was greatly disappointed, and did not like to hear any allusion to the subject: but two years afterwards, when she was once more my guest, it again happened to rain on the first Sunday in the month, and I heard her solemnly predict that it would, every succeeding Sunday in the month, "for," she remarked, "it is a sign that never fails." She had forgotten the failure of two years before; indeed, the continuance and prevalence of many popular superstitions is due to the fact that we notice the "sign" when it happens to be verified, and do not observe it, or we forget it, when it fails. Many persons are exceedingly superstitious in regard to the number "thirteen." This is particularly the case, I have noticed, in Catholic countries I have visited, and I have been told that superstition originated in the fact of a thirteenth apostle having been chosen, on account of the treachery of Judas. At any rate, I have known numbers of French persons who had quite a horror of this fatal number. Once I knew a French lady, who had taken passage in an ocean steamer, and who, on going aboard, and finding her assigned state-room to be "No. 13," insisted upon it that she would not sail in the ship at all; she had rather forfeit her passage money, though, finally, she was persuaded to take another room. And a great many people, French, English and American, will not undertake any important enterprise on the thirteenth day of the month, nor sit at table with a full complement of thirteen persons. With regard to this number, to which so many superstitions cling, I have some interesting experiences and curious coincidences, which are worth relating, as a part of my personal history.

When I was first in England with General Tom Thumb, I well remember dining one Christmas day with my friends, the Brettells, in St. James's Palace, in London. Just before the dinner was finished (it is a wonder it was not noticed before) it was discovered that the number at table was exactly thirteen.

"How very unfortunate," remarked one of the guests; "I would not have dined under such circumstances for any consideration, had I known it!"

"Nor I either," seriously remarked another guest.

"Do you really suppose there is any truth in the old superstition on that subject?" I asked.

"Truth!" solemnly replied an old lady. "Truth! Why I myself have known three instances, and have heard of scores of others, where thirteen persons have eaten at the same table, and in every case one of the number died before the year was out!"

This assertion, made with so much earnestness, evidently affected several of the guests, whose nerves were easily excited. I can truthfully state, however, that I dined at the Palace again the following Christmas, and although there were seventeen persons present, every one of the original thirteen who dined there the preceding Christmas, was among this number, and all in good health; although, of course, it would have been nothing very remarkable if one had happened to have died during the last twelve months.

While I was on my Western lecturing tour in 1866, long before I got out of Illinois, I began to observe that at the various hotels where I stopped my room very frequently was number thirteen. Indeed, it seemed as if this number turned up to me as often as four times per week, and so, before many days, I almost expected to have that number set down to my name wherever I signed it upon the register of the hotel. Still, I laughed to myself, at what I was convinced was simply a coincidence. On one occasion I was traveling from Clinton to Mount Vernon, Iowa, and was to lecture in the college of the latter place that evening. Ordinarily, I should have arrived at two o'clock pm; but owing to an accident which had occurred to the train from the West, the conductor informed me that our arrival in Mount Vernon would probably be delayed until after seven o'clock. I telegraphed that fact to the committee who were expecting me, and told them to be patient.

When we had arrived within ten miles of that town it was dark. I sat rather moodily in the car, wishing the train would "hurry up"; and happening, for some cause to look back over my left shoulder, I discovered the new moon through the window. This omen struck me as a coincident addition to my ill-luck, and with a pleasant chuckle I muttered to myself, "Well, I hope I won't get room number thirteen tonight, for that will be adding insult to injury."

I reached Mount Vernon a few minutes before eight, and was met at the depot by the committee, who took me in a carriage and hurried to the Ballard House. The committee told me the hall in the college was already crowded, and they hoped I would defer taking tea until after the lecture. I informed them that I would gladly do so, but simply wished to run to my room a moment for a wash. While wiping my face I happened to think about the new room, and at once stepped outside of my bed-room door to look at the number. It was "number thirteen."

After the lecture I took tea, and I confess that I began to think "number thirteen" looked a little ominous. There I was, many hundreds of miles from my family; I left my wife sick, and I began to ask myself, does "number thirteen" portend anything in particular? Without feeling willing even now to acknowledge that I felt much apprehension on the subject, I must say I began to take a serious view of things in general.

I mentioned the coincidence of my luck in so often having "number thirteen" assigned to me to Mr. Ballard, the proprietor of the hotel, giving him all the particulars to date.

"I will give you another room, if you prefer it," said Mr. Ballard.

"No, I thank you," I replied with a semi-serious smile; "if it is fate, I will take it as it comes; and if it means anything I shall probably find it out in time. That same night, before retiring to rest, I wrote a letter to a clerical friend, then residing in Bridgeport, telling him all my experiences in regard to "number thirteen." I said to him in closing: "Don't laugh at me for being superstitious, for I hardly feel so; I think it is simply a series of 'coincidences' which appear the more strange because I am sure to notice every one that occurs. "Ten days afterwards I received an answer from my reverend friend, in which he cheerfully said: "It's all right: go ahead and get 'number thirteen' as often as you can. It is a lucky number," and he added:

"Unbelieving and ungrateful man! What is thirteen but the traditional 'baker's dozen,' indicating 'good measure, pressed down, shaken together, and running over,' as illustrated in your triumphal lecturing tour? By all means insist upon having room number thirteen at every hotel; and if the guests at any meal be less than that charmed complement, send out and compel somebody to come in.

"What do you say respecting the Thirteen Colonies? Any ill-luck in the number? Was the patriarch Jacob afraid of it when he adopted Ephraim and Manasseh, the two sons of Joseph, so as to complete the magic circle of thirteen?

"Do you not know that chapter thirteen of First Corinthians is the grandest in the Bible, with verse thirteen as the culmination of all religious thought? And can

3 4 3 5 6

anyone read verse thirteen of the fifth chapter of Revelation without the highest rapture?"

But my clerical friend had not heard of a certain curious circumstance which occurred to me after I had mailed my letter to him and before I received his answer.

On leaving Mount Vernon for Cedar Rapids the next morning, the landlord, Mr. Ballard, drove me to the railroad depot. As I was stepping upon the cars, Mr. Ballard shook my hand, and with a laugh exclaimed: "Good-by, friend Barnum, I hope you won't get room number thirteen at Cedar Rapids today." "I hope not!" I replied earnestly, and yet with a smile. I reached Cedar Rapids in an hour. The lecture committee met and took me to the hotel. I entered my name, and the landlord immediately called out to the porter:

"Here, John, take Mr. Barnum's baggage, and show him to 'number thirteen?'"

I confess that when I heard this I was startled. I remarked to the landlord that it was certainly very singular, but was nevertheless true, that "number thirteen" seemed to be about the only room that I could get in a hotel.

"We have a large meeting of railroad directors here at present," he replied, "and 'number thirteen' is the only room unoccupied in my house."

I proceeded to the room, and immediately wrote to Mr. Ballard at Mount Vernon, assuring him that my letter was written in "number thirteen," and that this was the only room I could get in the hotel. During the remainder of my journey, I was put into "number thirteen" so often in the various hotels at which I stopped that it came to be quite a matter of course, though occasionally I was fortunate enough to secure some other number. Upon returning to New York, I related the foregoing adventures to my family, and told them I was really half afraid of "number thirteen." Soon afterwards, I telegraphed to my daughter who was boarding at the Atlantic House in Bridgeport, asking her to engage a room for me to lodge there the next night, on my way to Boston. "Mr. Hale," said she to the landlord, "father is coming up today; will you please reserve him a comfortable room?" "Certainly," replied Mr. Hale, and he instantly ordered a fire in "room thirteen!" I went to Boston and proceeded to Lewiston, Maine, and thence to Lawrence, Massachusetts, and the hotel register there has my name booked for "number thirteen."

My experience with this number has by no means been confined to apartments. In 1867, a church in Bridgeport wanted to raise several thousand dollars in order to get freed from debt. I subscribed one thousand dollars, by aid of which they assured me they would certainly raise enough to pay off the debt. A few weeks subsequently, however, one of the "brethren" wrote me that they were still six hundred dollars short, with but little prospect of getting it. I replied that I would pay one-half of the sum required. The brother soon afterwards wrote me that he had obtained the other half, and I might forward him my subscription of "thirteen" hundred dollars. During the same season I attended a fair in Franklin Hall Bridgeport, given by a temperance organization. Two of my little granddaughters accompanied me, and, telling them to select what articles they desired, I paid the bill twelve dollars and fifty cents. "Whereupon I said to the children, "I am glad you did not make it thirteen dollars, and I will expend no more here tonight." We sat awhile listening to the music, and finally started for home, and, as we were going, a lady at one of the stands near the door, called out: "Mr. Barnum, you have not patronized me. Please take a chance in my lottery." "Certainly," I replied; "give me a ticket." I paid her the price (fifty cents), and after I arrived home, I discovered that in spite of my expressed determination to the contrary, I had expended exactly "thirteen" dollars!

I invited a few friends to a "clam-bake" in the summer of 1868, and, being determined the party should not be thirteen, I invited fifteen, and they all agreed to go. Of course, one man and his wife were "disappointed," and could not go. and my party numbered thirteen. At Christmas, in the same year, my children and grandchildren dined with me, and finding, on "counting noses," that they would number the inevitable thirteen, I expressly arranged to have a high chair placed at the table, and my youngest grandchild, seventeen months old, was placed in it, so that we should number fourteen. After the dinner was over, we discovered that my son-in-law, Thompson, had been detained downtown, and the number at dinner table, notwithstanding my extra precautions, was exactly thirteen.

Thirteen was certainly an ominous number to me in 1865, for on the thirteenth day of July, the American Museum was burned to the ground, while the thirteenth day of November saw the opening of "Barnum's New American Museum," which was also subsequently destroyed by fire.

Having concluded this veritable history of superstitious coincidences in regard to thirteen, I read it to a clerical friend, who happened to be present; and after reading the manuscript, I paged it, when my friend and I were a little startled to find that the pages numbered exactly thirteen.

CHAPTER XLV.

SEASIDE PARK.

From the time when I first settled in Bridgeport, and turned my attention to opening and beautifying new avenues, and doing whatever lay in my power to extend and improve that charming city, I was exceedingly anxious that public parks should be established, especially one where good driveways, and an opportunity for the display of the many fine equipages for which Bridgeport is celebrated, could be afforded. Mr. Noble and I began the movement by presenting to the city the beautiful ground in East Bridgeport now known as Washington Park — a most attractive promenade and breathing-place, and a continual resort for citizens on both sides of the river, particularly in the summer evenings, when one of the city bands is an additional attraction to the pleasant spot. Thus, our city was far in advance of Bridgeport proper in providing a prime necessity for the health and amusement of the people.

Up to the year 1865, the shores of Bridgeport, west of the public wharves, and washed by the waters of Long Island Sound, was inaccessible to carriages, or even to horsemen, and almost impossible for pedestrianism. The shore edge, in fact, was strewn with rocks and boulders, which made it, like "Jordan" in the song, an exceedingly "hard road to travel." A narrow lane reaching down to the shore enabled parties to drive near to the water for the purpose of clamming, and occasionally bathing; but it was all claimed as private property by the land proprietors, whose farms extended down to the water's edge. On several occasions, at low tide, I endeavored to ride along the shore on horseback, for the purpose of examining "the lay of the land," in the hope of finding it feasible to get a public drive along the water's edge. On one occasion, in 1863, I succeeded in getting my horse around from the foot of Broad street, in Bridgeport, to a lane over the Fairfield line, a few rods west of "*Iranistan* Avenue*," a grand street which I have since opened at my own expense, and through my own land. From the observations I made that day, I was satisfied that a most lovely park and public drive might be, and ought to be opened along the whole waterfront as far as the western boundary fine of Bridgeport, and even extending over the Fairfield line.

Foreseeing that in a few years such an improvement would be too late and having in mind the failure of the attempt in 1850 to provide a park for the people of Bridgeport, I immediately began to agitate the subject in the Bridgeport papers, and also in daily conversations with such of my fellow-citizens as I thought would take an earnest and immediate interest in the enterprise. I urged that such an improvement would increase the taxable value of property in that vicinity many thousands of dollars, and thus enrich the city treasury; that it would improve the value of real estate generally, in the city; that it would be an additional attraction to strangers who came to spend the summer with us, and to those who might be induced from other considerations to mall the city their permanent residence; that the improvement would throw into market some of the most beautiful building sites that could be found anywhere in Connecticut; and I dwelt upon the absurdity, almost criminality, that a beautiful city like Bridgeport, lying on the shore of a broad expanse of salt water, should so cage itself in, that not an inhabitant could approach the beach. With these and like arguments and entreaties, I plied the people day in and day out, till some of them began to be familiarized with the idea that a public park close upon the shore of the Sound, was at least a possible if not probable thing.

But certain "conservatives," as they are called, said: "Barnum is a hair-brained fellow, who thinks he can open and people a New York Broadway through a Connecticut wilderness;" and the "old fogies" added: "Yes, he is trying to start another chestnut-wood fire for the city to blow forever; but the city or town of Bridgeport will not pay out money to lay out or to purchase public parks. If people want to see green grass and trees, they have only to walk or drive half a mile either way from the city limits, and they will come to farms where they can see either, or both, for nothing; and, if they are anxious to see salt water, and to get a breath of the Sound breeze, they can take boats at the wharves, and sail or row till they are entirely satisfied"

Thus, talked the conservatives and the "old fogies." who, unhappily, even if they are in a minority, are always a force in all communities. I soon saw that it was of no use to expect to get the city to pay for a park. The next thing was to see if the land could not be procured free of charge, or at a nominal cost, provided the city would improve and maintain it as a public park. I approached the farmers who owned the land lying immediately upon the shore, and tried to convince them that, if they would give the city, free, a deep slip next to the water, to be used as a public park, it would increase in value the rest of their land so much as to make it a profitable operation for them. But it was like beating against the wind. They were "not so stupid as to think that they could become gainers by giving away their property." Such trials of patience as I underwent in a twelvemonth, in the endeavor to carry this point, few persons who have not undertaken like almost hopeless labor, can comprehend.

At last, I enlisted the attention of Messrs. Nathaniel Wheeler, James Loomis, Francis Ives, Frederick Wood, and a few more gentlemen, and persuaded them to walk with me over the ground, which to me seemed in every way practicable for a park. These gentlemen, who were men of taste, as well as of enterprise and public spirit, very soon coincided in my ideas as to the feasibility of the plan and the advantages of the site; and some of them went with me to talk with the land-owners, adding their own pleas to the arguments I had already advanced. After much pressing and persuading, we got the terms upon which the proprietors would give a portion and sell another portion of their land, which fronted on the water, provided the land thus disposed of, should forever be appropriated to the purposes of a public park. But, unfortunately, a part of the land it was desirable to include, was the small Mallett farm, of some thirty acres, then belonging to an unsettled estate, and neither the administrator nor the heirs could or would give away a rod of it. But the whole farm was for sale — and, to overcome the difficulty in the way of its transfer for the public benefit, I bought it for about $12,000, and then presented the required front to the park. I did not want this land or any portion of it, for my own purposes or profit, and I offered a thousand dollars to anyone who would take my place in the transaction; but no one accepted, and I was quite willing to contribute so much of the land as was needed for so noble an object. Indeed, besides this, I gave $1,400 towards purchasing other land

and improving the park; and, after months of persistent and personal effort, I succeeded in raising, by private subscription, the sum necessary to secure the land needed. This was duly paid for, deeded to, and accepted by the city, and I had the pleasure of naming this new and great public improvement, "Seaside Park."

Public journals are generally exponents of public opinion; and how the people viewed the new purchase, now their own property, may be judged by the following extracts from the leading local newspapers, when the land for the new enterprise was finally secured:

[From the "*Bridgeport Standard*,'" August 21, 1865.]

Bridgeport has taken another broad stride of which she may well be proud. The Seaside Park is a fixed fact. Yesterday Messrs. P. T. Barnum, Captain John Brooks. Mr. George Bailey, Captain Burr Knapp, and Henry Wheeler generously donated to this city sufficient land for the Park, with the exception of seven or eight acres, which have been purchased by private subscriptions. Last night the Common Council appointed excellent Park Commissioners, and work on the sea wall and the avenues surrounding the Park will be commenced at once. Besides securing the most lovely location for a park to be found between New York and Boston, which for all time will be a source of pride to our city and State, there is no estimating the pecuniary advantage which this great improvement will eventually prove to our citizens. Plans are on foot and enterprises are agitated in regard to a park hotel, seaside cottages, horse railroad branch, and other features which, when consummated, will serve to amaze our citizens to think that such a delightful seaside frontage had been permitted to lie so long unimproved. To Mr. P.T. Barnum. we believe, is awarded the credit of originating this beautiful improvement, and certainly to his untiring, constant and persevering personal efforts are we indebted for its being finally consummated. Hon. James C. Loomis was the first man who heartily joined with Barnum in pressing the plan of the Seaside park upon the attention of our citizens, but it is due to our citizens themselves to say that, with an extraordinary unanimity, they have not only voted to appropriate $10,000 from the city treasury to making the avenues around the Park, and otherwise improving it, but they have also generously aided by private contributions in purchasing such land as was not freely given for the Park.

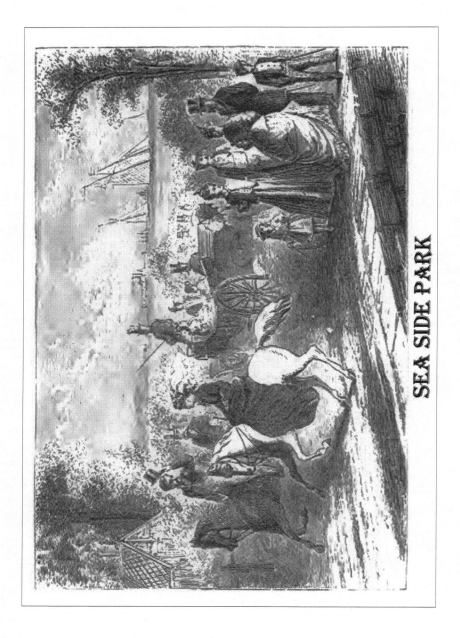

SEA SIDE PARK

Thus, was my long-cherished plan at length fulfilled; nor did my efforts end there, for I aided and advised in all important matters in the laying out and progress of the new park; and in July, 1869, I gave to the city several acres of land, worth, at the lowest valuation, $5,000, which were added to and included in this public pleasure-ground, and now make the west end of the park.

At the beginning, the park on paper and the park in reality, were two quite different things. The inaccessibility of the site was remedied by approaches which permitted the hundreds of workmen to begin to grade the grounds, and to lay out the walks and drives. The rocks and boulders over which I had more than once attempted to make my way on foot and on horseback, were devoted to the building of a substantial sea-wall under the able superintendence of Mr. David W. Sherwood. Paths were opened, shade-trees were planted; and fortunately, there was, in the very center of the ground, a beautiful grove of full growth, which is one of the most attractive features of this now charming spot; and a broad and magnificent drive follows the curves of the shore and encircles the entire park. A large covered music-stand has been erected; and on a rising piece of ground has been built a substantial Soldiers' Monument.

The branch horse railroad already reaches one of the main entrances and brings down crowds of people every day and evening, and especially on the evenings in which the band plays. At such times the avenues are not only thronged with superb equipages and crowds of people, but the whole harbor is alive with row-boats, sail-boats and yachts. The views on all sides are charming. In the rear is the city, with its roofs and spires; Black Rock and Stafford lights are in plain sight; to the eastward and southward stretches "Old Long Island's sea-girt shore;" and between lies the broad expanse of the salt water, with its ever-fresh breezes, and the perpetual panorama of sails and steamers. I do not believe that a million dollars, today, would compensate the city of Bridgeport for the loss of what is confessed to be the most delightful public pleasure-ground between New York and Boston.

CHAPTER XLVI

WALDEMERE.

When I first selected Bridgeport as a permanent residence for my family, its nearness to New York, and the facilities for daily transit to and from the metropolis were present and partial considerations only in the general advantages the location seemed to offer. Nowhere, in all my travels in America and abroad, had I seen a city whose very position presented so many and varied attractions. Situated on Long Island Sound, with that vast water view in front, and on every other side a beautiful and fertile country with every variety of inland scenery, and charming drives which led through valleys rich with well-cultivated farms, and over hills thick-wooded with far-stretching forests of primeval growth — all these natural attractions appeared to me only so many aids to the advancement the beautiful and busy city might attain, if public spirit, enterprise and money grasped and improved the opportunities the locality itself extended. I saw that what Nature had so freely lavished must be supplemented by yet more liberal Art.

Consequently, and quite naturally, when I projected and established my first residence in Bridgeport, I was exceedingly desirous that all the surroundings of *Iranistan* should accord with the beauty and completeness of that place. I was never a victim to that mania which possesses many men of even moderate means to "own everything that joins them," and I knew that *Iranistan* would so increase the value of surrounding property that none but first-class residences would be possible in the vicinity. But there was other work to do, which, while affording advantageous approaches to my property, would at the same time be a lasting benefit to the public; and so, I opened *Iranistan* Avenue, and other broad and beautiful streets, through land which I freely purchased, and as freely gave to the public, and these highways are now the most convenient as well as charming in the city.

To have opened all these new avenues, in their entire length, at my own cost, and through my own ground, would have required a confirmation of Miss Lavinia Warren's opinion, that what little of the city of Bridgeport and the adjacent town of Fairfield was not owned by General Tom Thumb, belonged to P.T. Barnum. Everywhere through my own lands I laid out and threw open public streets, and on both sides of every avenue I laid out and planted a profusion of elms and other trees. In this way, I have opened miles of new streets, and have planted thousands of shade-trees in Bridgeport; for I think there is much wisdom in the advice of the Laird of Dumbiedikes, in Scott's "Heart of Mid-Lothian," who sensibly says: "When ye hae naething else to do, ye may be aye sticking in a tree; it will be growing when ye're sleeping." But, in establishing new streets, too often, when I had gone through my own land, the project came literally to an end; some "old fogy" blocked the way— my way, his own way, and the highway — and all I could do would be to jump over his field, and continue my new street through land I might own on the other side, till I reached the desired terminus in the end or continuation of some other street; or till,

WALDEMERE

unhappily, I came to a dead stand-still at the ground of some other "old fogy," who, like the original owners of what is now the shore-front of Seaside Park, "did not believe there was money to be made by giving away their property."

Conservatism may be a good thing in the State, or in the church, but it is fatal to the growth of cities; and the conservative notions of old fogies make them indifferent to the requirements which a very few years in the future will compel, and blind to their own best interests. Such men never look beyond the length of their noses, and consider every investment a dead loss unless they can get the sixpence profit into their pockets before they go to bed. My own long training and experience as a manager impelled me to carry into such private enterprises as the purchase of real estate that best and most essential managerial quality of instantly deciding, not only whether a venture was worth undertaking, but what, all things considered, that venture would result in. Almost any man can see how a thing will begin, but not every man is gifted with the foresight to see how it will end, or how, with the proper effort, it may be made to end. In East Bridgeport, where we had no "conservatives" to contend with, we were only a few years in turning almost tenantless farms into a populous and prosperous city. On the other side of the river, while the opening of new avenues, the planting of shade-trees, and the building of many houses, have afforded me the highest pleasures of my life, I confess that not a few of my greatest annoyances have been occasioned by the opposition of those who seem to be content to simply vegetate through their existence, and who looked upon me as a restless, reckless innovator, because I was trying to remove the moss from everything around them, and even from their own eyes.

In the summer of 1867, the health of my wife continuing to decline, her physician directed that she should remove nearer to the sea-shore.

Lindencroft was sold July 1, 1867, and we immediately removed for a summer's sojourn to a small farm-house adjoining Seaside Park. During the hot days of the next three months we found the delightful sea-breeze so bracing and refreshing that the season passed like a happy dream, and we resolved that our future summers should be spent on the very shore of Long Island Sound. I did not, however, perfect my arrangements in time to prepare my own summer residence for the ensuing season; and during the hot months of 1868, we resided in a new and very pretty house I had just completed on State street, in Bridgeport, and which I subsequently sold, as I intended doing when I built it. But, towards the end of the summer, I added by purchase to the Mallett farm, adjoining Seaside Park, a large and beautiful hickory grove, which seemed to be all that was needed to make the site exactly what I desired for a summer residence.

But there was a vast deal to do in grading and preparing the ground, in opening new streets and avenues as approaches to the property, and in setting out trees near the proposed site of the house; so that ground was not broken for the foundation till October. I planned a house which should combine the greatest convenience with the highest comfort, keeping in mind always that houses are made to live in as well as to look at, and to be "homes" rather than mere residences. So, the house was made to include abundant room for guests, with dressing-rooms and baths to every chamber; water from the city throughout the premises; gas, manufactured on my own ground; and that greatest of all comforts, a semi-detached kitchen, so that the smell as well as the secrets of the cuisine might be confined to its own locality. The stables and gardens were located far from the mansion, on the opposite side of one of the newly opened avenues, so that in the immediate vicinity of the house, on either side and before both fronts stretched large lawns, broken only by the grove, single shade-trees, rock-work, walks, flower-beds and drives. The whole scheme as planned was faithfully carried out in less than eight months. The first foundation stone was laid in October, 1868; and we moved into the completed house in June following, in 1869.

It required a regiment of faithful laborers and mechanics, and a very considerable expenditure of money, to accomplish so much in so short a space of time. Those who saw a comparatively barren waste thus suddenly converted to a blooming garden, and, by the successful transplanting and judicious placing of very large and full-grown forest trees, made to seem like a long-settled place, considered the creation of my new summer home almost a work of magic, but there is no magic when determination and dollars combine to achieve a work. When we moved into this new residence, we formally christened the place "Waldemere," literally, but not so euphoniously, "*Waldammeer*," "Woods-by-the-Sea," f or I preferred to give this native child of my own conception an American name of my own creation.

On the same estate and fronting the new avenue I opened between my own property and the public park, I built at the same time two beautiful cottages, one of which is known as the "Petrel's Nest," and the other, occupied by my eldest daughter, Mrs. Thompson, and my youngest daughter, Mrs. Seeley, as a summer residence, is called "Wave wood." From the east front of Waldemere, across the sloping lawn, and through the reaches of the grove, these cottages are in sight, and before the three residences stretches the broad Sound, with nothing to cut off the view, and nothing intervening but the western portion of Seaside Park.

Having made up my mind to spend seven months of every year in the city, in the summer of 1867, I purchased the elegant and most eligibly situated mansion, No. 438, Fifth Avenue, corner of Thirty-ninth street, at the crowning point on Murray Hill, in New York, and moved into it in November.

CHAPTER XLVII.

REST ONLY FOUND IN ACTION.

After the destruction by fire of my Museum, March 3rd, 1868, I retired from business, not knowing how utterly fruitless it is to attempt to chain down energies peculiar to my nature. No man not similarly situated can imagine the *ennui* which seizes such a nature after it has lain dormant for a few months. Having "nothing to do," I thought at first was a very pleasant, as it was to me an entirely new sensation.

"I would like to call on you in the summer, if you have any leisure, in Bridgeport," said an old friend.

"I am a man of leisure and thankful that I have nothing to do; so you cannot call amiss," I replied with an immense degree of self-satisfaction.

"Where is your office downtown when you live in New York?" asked another friend.

"I have no office," I proudly replied. "I have done work enough, and shall play the rest of my life. I don't go downtown once a week; but I ride in the Park every day, and am at home much of my time."

I am afraid that I chuckled often, when I saw rich merchants and bankers driving to their offices on a stormy morning, while I, looking complacently from the window of my cozy library, said to myself, "Let it snow and blow, there's nothing to call me out today." But nature will assert herself. Reading is pleasant as a pastime; writing without any special purpose, soon tires; a game of chess will answer as a condiment; lectures, concerts, operas, and dinner parties are well enough in their way; but to a robust, healthy man of forty years' active business life, something else is needed to satisfy. Sometimes like the truant schoolboy I found all my friends engaged, and I had no playmate. I began to fill my house with visitors, and yet frequently we spent evenings quite alone. Without really perceiving what the matter was, time hung on my hands, and I was ready to lecture gratuitously for every charitable cause that I could benefit. At this juncture I hailed with delight a visit from my friend Fish (the enterprising Englishman of chapter thirty-two) and his daughter, who came to see the new world, and found me just in the humor to act as guide and exhibitor. I now resumed my old business and became a showman of "natural curiosities " on a most magnificent scale: and, having congenial and appreciative traveling companions, and no business distractions, I saw beauty and grandeur in scenes which I had before gazed on unimpressed. For the third time I visited Cuba, then New Orleans, Memphis, Louisville, Cincinnati, Baltimore and Washington, noting and enjoying the emotions of my English friends. The awe with which they gazed on the great cataract of Niagara; their horror at seeing slaves driven to work with whips in the plantations of Cuba, the tearful silence of the young English lady as she gazed down into the beautiful valley of the Yumurri, the disgust of my friend when he found Castle Thunder not a great fort as he had imagined, but a tobacco warehouse, all made scenes interesting that were old to me.

In April, we made up a small, congenial party of ladies and gentlemen, and visited California via the Union and Central Pacific Railroads.

We journeyed leisurely, and I lectured in Council Bluffs, Omaha and Salt Lake City, where amongst my audience were a dozen or so of Brigham Young's wives and scores of his children. By invitation, I called with my friends on President Young at the Bee-Hive. He received us very cordially, asked us many questions, and promptly answered ours

"Bamum," said he, "what will you give to exhibit me in New York and the eastern cities?"

"Well Mr. President," I replied, "I'll give you half the receipts, which I win guarantee shall be $200,000 per year, for I consider you the best show in America."

"Why did you not secure me some years ago when I was of no consequence?" he continued.

"Because, you would not have 'drawn' at that time," I answered.

Brigham smiled and said, "I would like right well to spend a few hours with you, if you could come when I am disengaged." I thanked him, and told him I guessed I should enjoy it; but visitors were crowding into his reception-room, and we withdrew.

During the week we spent in seeing San Francisco and its suburbs, I discovered a dwarf more diminutive than General Tom Thumb was when first I found him, and so handsome, well-formed and captivating that I could not resist the temptation to engage him. I gave him the soubriquet of Admiral Dot, dressed him in complete Admiral's uniform, and invited the editors of the San Francisco journals to visit him in the parlors of the Cosmopolitan Hotel.

Immediately there was an immense furor, and Woodward's Gardens, where "Dot" was exhibited for three weeks before going east, was daily thronged with crowds of his curious fellow citizens, under whose very eyes he had lived so long undiscovered.

Speaking of dwarfs, it may be mentioned here, that, notwithstanding my announced retirement from public life, I still retained business connections with my old friend, the well-known General Tom Thumb. In 1869, I joined that celebrated dwarf in a fresh enterprise which proposed an exhibition tour of him and a party of twelve, with a complete outfit, including a pair of ponies and a carriage, entirely around the world.

This party was made up of General Tom Thumb and his wife (formerly Lavinia Warren), Commodore Nutt and his brother Rodnia, Miss Minnie Warren, Mr. Sylvester Bleeker and his wife, and Mr. B.S. Kellogg, besides an advertising agent and musicians. Mr. Bleeker was the manager, and Mr. Kellogg acted as treasurer. In the Fall of 1869, this little company went by the Union Pacific Railway to San Francisco, stopping on the way to give exhibitions at Omaha, Denver, Salt Lake City, and other places on the route, with great success.

After a prolonged and most profitable series of exhibitions in San Francisco, the company visited several leading towns in California and then started for Australia. On the way they stopped at the Sandwich Islands and exhibited in Honolulu. From there they went to Japan, exhibiting in Yeddo, Yokohama and other principal places, and afterwards at Canton and elsewhere in China. They next made the entire tour of

Australia, drawing immense houses at Sydney, Melbourne, and in other towns, but they did not go to New Zealand. They then proceeded to the East Indies, giving exhibitions in the larger towns and cities, receiving marked attentions from Rajahs and other distinguished personages. Afterwards they went by the way of the Suez Canal to Egypt and gave then entertainments at Cairo; and thence to Italy, exhibiting at all available points, and arrived in Great Britain in the summer of 1871.

While I am about it, I may as well confess my connection, *sub rosa*, with another little speculation during my three years' "leisure." I hired the well-known Siamese Twins, the giantess, Anna Swan, and a Circassian lady, and, in connection with Judge Ingalls, I sent them to Great Britain where, in all the principal places, and for about a year, their levees were continually crowded. In all probability the great success attending this enterprise was much enhanced, if not actually caused, by extensive announcements in advance, that the main purpose of Chang-Eng's visit to Europe was to consult the most eminent medical and surgical talent with regard to the safety of separating the twins.

We spent some time in the Yosemite; stopping by the way at the Mariposa grove of big trees, whence I sent to New York a piece of bark thirty-one inches thick.

Concluding a most enjoyable trip, we returned to New York, and first of June my family removed to our summer home, Waldemere. There the good and gifted Alice Cary, then in feeble health, and her sister Phoebe, were our guests for several weeks.

In September, I made up a party of ten, including my English friend, and we started for Kansas on a grand buffalo hunt. General Custer, commandant at Fort Hayes, was apprized in advance of our anticipated visit, and he received us like princes. He fitted out a company of fifty cavalry, furnishing us with horses, arms and ammunition. We were taken to an immense herd of buffaloes, quietly browsing on the open plain. We charged on them, and, during an exciting chase of a couple of hours, we slew twenty immense bull buffaloes, and might have killed as many more had we not considered it wanton butchery.

Our ten-day's sport afforded me a "sensation," but sensations cannot be made to order every day, so, in the autumn of 1870, to open a safety-valve for my pent-up energies, I began to prepare a great show enterprise, comprising a Museum, Menagerie, Caravan, Hippodrome and Circus, of such proportions as to require five hundred men and horses to transport it through the country. On the tenth of April, 1871, the vast tents, covering nearly three acres of ground, were opened in Brooklyn, and filled with ten thousand delighted spectators, thousands more being unable to obtain entrance. The success which marked the inauguration of this, my greatest show, attended it the whole season, during which time it visited the Eastern, Middle and Western States from Maine to Kansas.

At the close of a brilliant season, I recalled the show to New York, secured the Empire Rink, and opened in that building November 13, 1871, being welcomed by an enthusiastic audience of ten thousand people. The exhibitions were continued daily, with unvarying popularity and patronage, until the close of the holidays, when necessary preparations for the spring campaign compelled me to close. One of the most interesting curiosities added at that time, was a gigantic section of a California "big tree," of such proportions that on one occasion, at the Empire Rink, it enclosed two hundred children of the Howard Mission. This section I afterwards presented to

Frank Leslie, who had it mounted and roofed to form a summer-house on his Saratoga estate, where it now stands, a unique ornament and attraction.

During the winter of 1871 and 1872, I worked unremittingly, re-organizing and re-enforcing my great traveling show. To the horror of my very able but too cautious manager, Mr. W. C. Coup, and my treasurer, Mr. Hurd, I so augmented the already innumerable attractions, that it was shown beyond doubt, that we could not travel at a less expense than five thousand dollars per day, but, undaunted, I still expended thousands of dollars, and ship after ship brought me rare and valuable animals and works of art. Two beautiful Giraffes or Camelopards, were dispatched to me (one died on the Atlantic), and a third was retained for me at the Zoological Gardens, London, ready to be shipped at a moment's notice. As no giraffe has ever lived two years in America, all other managers had given up any attempt to import them, but this only made me more determined to always have one on hand at whatever cost.

My agents in Alaska procured for me several immense sea-lions and barking-seals, which weighed a thousand pounds each, and consumed from sixty to a hundred pounds of fish daily.

My novelties comprised an Italian goat "Alexis," taught in Europe to ride on horseback, leap through hoops and over banners, alighting on his feet on the back of the horse while going at full speed. I had also many extraordinary musical and other automatons and moving tableaux, made expressly for me by expert European artists.

But perhaps the most striking additions to my show were four wild Fiji Cannibals, ransomed at great cost from the hands of a royal enemy, into whose hands they had fallen, and by whom they were about to be killed and perhaps eaten.

The following happy hit is from the pen of Rev. Henry Ward Beecher, as it appeared in that excellent paper of which he was editor, the New York *Christian Union* of February 28th, 1872:

"Should not a paternal government set some limit to the enterprise of Brother Barnum, with reference, at least, to the considerations of public safety? Here upon our desk, lies an indication of his last perilous venture. He invites us 'and one friend' — no conditions as to 'condition' specified— to a private exhibition of *four living cannibals*, which he has obtained from the Fiji Islands, for his traveling show. We have beaten up in this office, among the lean and tough, and those most easily spared in an emergency, for volunteers to visit the Anthropophagi, and report; but never has the retiring and self-distrustful disposition of our employees been more signally displayed. The establishment was not represented at that exposition. If Barnum had remembered to specify the 'feeding-time,' we might have dropped in, in a friendly way, at some other period of the day."

Perceiving that my great combination was assuming such proportions that it would be impossible to move it by horse power, I negotiated with all the railway companies between New York and Omaha, Nebraska, for the transportation by rail, of my whole show, requiring sixty to seventy freight cars, six passenger cars, and three engines. The result is well remembered. The great show visited the States of New Jersey, Delaware, Maryland, Pennsylvania, District of Columbia, Virginia, Ohio, Indiana, Kentucky, Illinois, Missouri, Kansas, Iowa, Minnesota, Wisconsin and Michigan, often traveling one hundred miles in a single night to hit good-sized towns every day, arriving in time to give three exhibitions, and the usual street pageant at eight o'clock, a.m. By means of cheap excursion trains, thousands of strangers attended daily, coming fifty, seventy-five and a hundred miles. Thousands more came in wagons and on horseback, frequently arriving in the night and "camping out." The tenting season closed at Detroit, October 30th, when we were patronized by the largest concourse of people ever assembled in the State of Michigan

With wonderful unanimity the public press acknowledged that I exhibited much more than I advertised, and that no combination of exhibitions that ever traveled had shown a tithe of the instructive and amusing novelties that I had gathered together. This universal commendation is, to me, the most gratifying feature of the campaign, for, not being compelled to do business merely for the sake of profit, my highest enjoyment is to delight my patrons. The entire six months' receipts of the Great Traveling World's Fair, amounted to nearly one million dollars.

When not with the company, I spent most of my time at my ideal home, Waldemere, which I enlarged and beautified at a cost of ninety thousand dollars, There I had the honor and pleasure of entertaining Horace Greeley, my life-long friend, and of arranging for him those simple, healthful country amusements, so grateful and refreshing to a care-worn politician.

In October, I visited Colorado, accompanied by my English friend, John Fish, and a Bridgeport gentleman who had an interest with me in a stock-raising ranch in the southern part of that Territory. We took the Kansas Pacific Railroad to Denver, seeing many thousands of wild buffalo — our train sometimes being stopped to let them pass. The weather was delightful. We spent several days in the new and flourishing town of Greeley. I gave a temperance lecture there also at Denver. At the latter city, in the course of my remarks, I told them I never saw so many disappointed people as at Denver. The large audience looked surprised, but were relieved when I added, "half the inhabitants came invalids from the east, expecting to die, and they find they cannot do it. Your charming climate will not permit it!" And it is a fact. I am charmed with Colorado, the scenery and delightful air, and particularly would I recommend as a place of residence to those who can afford it, the lively, thriving city of Denver. To those who have some capital and yet have their fortunes to make, I say, "go to Greeley."

We took the narrow-gauge road from Denver to Pueblo, stopping at Colorado Springs, and the "Garden of the gods." The novel scenery here amply paid us for our visit. From Pueblo I proceeded forty miles by carriage to our cattle ranch, and spent a couple of days there very pleasantly. We have several thousand head of cattle there, which thrive through the winter without hay or fodder of any kind. A railroad has just been opened from Pueblo to Trinidad which passes through a corner of my ranch.

At the close in Detroit of the great Western railroad tour, I equipped and started South a Museum, Menagerie and Circus, which, while it made no perceptible diminution in the main body, was still the largest and most complete traveling expedition ever seen in the Southern States. Louisville was designated as the rendezvous and point of consolidation of the various departments, and the new expedition gave its initial exhibition in the Falls City, November 4th. Much of the menagerie consisted of animals of which I owned the duplicate, and hence, could easily spare them without injuring the variety in my zoological collection. I was aware, also, that many of the rare specimens would thrive better in a warmer climate, and as the expense of procuring them had been enormous, I coupled my humanitarian feelings with my pecuniary interests, and sent them South.

In August, I purchased the building and lease on Fourteenth street, New York, known as the Hippotheatron, purposing to open a Museum, Menagerie, Hippodrome and Circus, that would furnish employment for two hundred of my people who would otherwise be idle during the winter. I enlarged and remodeled the building almost beyond recognition, at an expense of $60,000, installed in it my valuable collection of animals, automatons and living curiosities, and on Monday evening, November 18, the grand opening took place. It was a beautiful sight; the huge building, with a seating capacity of 2,800, filled from pit to dome with a brilliant audience, the dazzling new lights, the sweet music and gorgeous ornamentations completing the charm. The papers next morning contained long and eulogistic editorials.

Four weeks after this inauguration, I visited my Southern show at New Orleans. While seated at breakfast at the St. Louis Hotel and perusing an account of the flooding of my show-grounds in that city, the following telegram was handed me:

> New York
> December 24.

To P. T. Bamum, New Orleans:

About 4 a.m. fire discovered in boiler-room of circus building; everything destroyed except 2 elephants, 1 camel.

> S. H. HUED, Treasurer.

The smaller misfortune was instantly forgotten in the greater. Calling for writing material, I then and there cabled my European agents to send duplicates of all animals lost, with positive instructions to have everything shipped in time to reach New York by the middle of March. I directed them further to procure at any cost specimens never seen in America; and through sub-agents to purchase and forward curiosities — animate and inanimate — from all parts of the globe. I then dispatched the following to my son-in-law:

> New Orleans
> December 24.

To S. H. Hurd, New York:

Tell editors I have cabled European agents to expend half million dollars for extra attractions; will have new and more attractive show than ever early in April.

> P. T. BARNUM.

These details attended to, I resumed my breakfast, and took a calm view of the situation. Returning to New York, I learned that my loss on building and property amounted to nearly $300,000, to meet which I held insurance policies to the amount of $90,000. My equestrian company, in which I took great pride, was left idle until the opening of the summer season. The members lost their entire wardrobes, a loss which can only be appreciated by professionals. The Equestrian Benevolent Society kindly gave them a benefit at the Academy of Music, on the afternoon and evening of January

7, 1873. Many stars in the Equestrian, Dramatic and Musical firmament volunteered for the occasion, and the two entertainments were largely attended. Being called upon to "define my position," I stepped upon the stage and made a few off-hand remarks, which were reported in the morning papers as follows:

LADIES AND GENTLEMEN: I have catered for so many years for the amusement of the public that the beneficiaries on this occasion seem to have thought that the showman himself ought to be a part of the show: and, at their request, I come before you. I sincerely thank you, in their behalf, for your patronage on this occasion. How much they need your substantial sympathy, the ashes across the street can tell you more eloquently than human tongue could utter. "Those ashes are the remnants of all the worldly goods " of some who appeal to you today.

For myself, I have been burned out so often, I am like the singer who was hissed on the stage: "Hiss away," said he, "I am used to it." My pecuniary loss is very serious, and occurring, as it did just before the holidays, it is all the more disastrous.

It may, perhaps, gratify my friends to know, however, that I am still enabled to invest another half million of dollars without disturbing my bank account. The public will have amusements, and they ought to be those of an elevating and an unobjectionable character. For many years it has been my pleasure to provide a class of instructive and amusing entertainments, to which a refined Christian mother can take her children with satisfaction.

I believe that no other man in America possesses the desire and facilities which I have in this direction. I have, therefore, taken steps, through all my agents in Europe and this country, which will enable me to put upon the road, early in April, the most gigantic and complete traveling museum, menagerie and hippodrome ever organized.

It has been asked whether I will build up a large museum and menagerie in New York. Well, I am now nearly sixty-three years of age. I can buy plenty of building sites and get plenty of leased lots for a new museum; but I cannot get a new lease of life.

Younger members of my family desire me to erect in this city an establishment worthy of New York and of myself. It will be no small undertaking; for if I erect such an establishment, it will possess novel and costly features never before attempted. I have it under consideration, and within a month shall determine whether or not I shall make another attempt; of one thing, however, you may be assured, ladies and gentlemen, although conflagrations may, for the present, disconcert my plans, yet, while I have life and health, no tire can burn nor water quench my ambition to gratify my patrons at whatever cost of money or of effort. I shall never lend my name where my labors and heart do not go with it, and the public shall never fail to find at any of my exhibitions their money's worth ten times told.

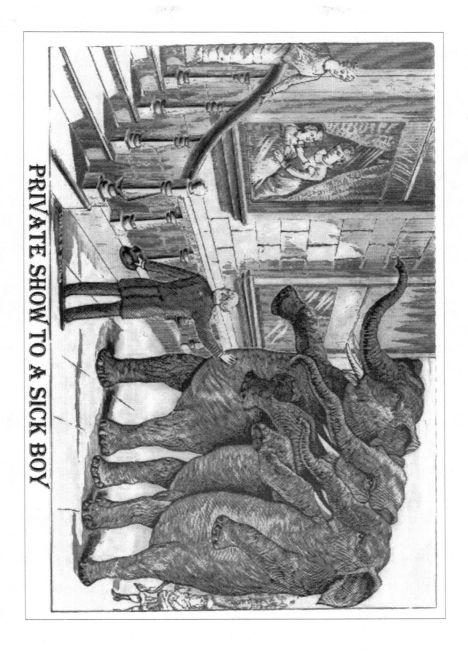

PRIVATE SHOW TO A SICK BOY

Before the new year dawned, I received tidings that my agents had purchased for me a full collection of animals and curiosities, and by the first week in April, 1873 — but three short months after the fire — I placed upon the road a combination of curiosities and marvelous performances that by far surpassed any attempt ever made with a traveling exhibition in any country. Indeed, so wonderfully immense was "Barnum's Traveling World's Fair" in 1873, that its expenses greatly exceeded five thousand dollars per day, and my friends almost unanimously declared that it would "break" me. I suppose there is a limit beyond which it would be fatal to go, in catering for public instruction and amusement, but I have never yet found that limit. My experience is that the more and the better a manager will provide for the public, the more liberally they will respond. The season of 1873 was far from being an exception to this experience. My tents covered double the space of ground that I had ever required before, and yet they were never so closely *crowded* with visitors. Where thousands attended my show in 1872, numbers of thousands came in 1873. It visited the largest cities in Connecticut, Massachusetts, Rhode Island, Maine, New Hampshire, Vermont, and the Middle and Western States, as far as St. Louis, Mo., taking Canada on the return route to New York.

While in Cleveland, Ohio, a little incident occurred which was described as follows by one of the Cleveland papers:

A PRIVATE SHOW TO A SICK BOY-A PLEASANT EPISODE.

Mr. P. T. Barnum's ambition to give the public a better show than anyone else can give them for the same money is well known, though very few are aware of the great pleasure he takes in providing amusement for little children. An incident happening in our city yesterday illustrated this characteristic very strikingly. There is a little five-year-old invalid up town who has become quite a favorite with the great showman, who never fails to visit him in passing through Cleveland. Yesterday morning the little fellow heard the doorbell ring, and his face lit up with joy as Mr. Barnum entered the sick-room. The usual pleasant greetings ensued, and the great manager threw his soul into the work of entertaining the child as completely as when surrounded by thousands he talks in his great show. The child was delighted, but the shadow which is always as near joy as the thorn is to the rose, stole over the little "Trot's" face on reflecting that he could not see the menagerie. "'Never mind." said Mr. Barnum, " if you cannot go to the show, we must bring the show to you." So saying, he departed, and a half hour later the child and the whole family were astonished to see a drove of elephants, camels and dromedaries marched into the yard, and come to a halt near the child's window. The little one was held up where he could see the animals, and their keeper made them go through a regular performance. "Trot " gave his orders to the unwieldy elephants, and, by a sign from the keeper, they were all obeyed. In half an hour the matinee terminated, and the detachment of the procession marched back to the show-grounds, leaving the child wild with delight. Mr. Barnum's love for the little ones has been frequently shown by the generous invitations he everywhere extends to orphans to attend his exhibitions free of charge; but this effort to please a little child is a unique illustration of that characteristic.

Notwithstanding my frequent visits to the "traveling show," I managed to spend much of the summer at my delightful "Waldemere."

In September, of 1873, as I had not visited Europe since 1869, I concluded to run over and see the International Exhibition at Vienna, and visit other parts of Europe, to rest my over-worked brain, and see what could be picked up to instruct and edify my amusement patrons.

On landing at Liverpool, I was met by my old friend, John Fish, Esq., the "enterprising Englishman." Mr. Fish was the last friend who shook my hand as I left Liverpool in 1859, and the first to grasp it as I landed in 1873. After spending a few days at his house, in Southport, the "Montpelier of England," a delightful watering-place eighteen miles from Liverpool, I proceeded to London. I met many of my old English friends here, including, of course, my esteemed friend and faithful agent, Robert Fillingham, Esq., and then hastened on to Cologne, Leipsic, Dresden, and Vienna, which latter city I reached ten days before the closing of the great World's Fair. Those ten days I devoted most assiduously to studying the marvels of this great World's Exhibition, and I witnessed the ceremonies which terminated what is generally conceded to be the largest and best International Exhibition that the world ever saw. I proceeded leisurely back to Dresden, stopping at Prague on the way. Thence I went to Berlin, and, at each city, I took time to see all that was interesting. While at Berlin, I received letters from my Manager, Coup, and Treasurer, Hurd, saying they would be able to secure a short lease of the Harlem Railroad property in New York, bounded by Fourth and Madison avenues and Twenty-sixth and Twenty-seventh streets, containing several acres, for the purpose of carrying out my long-cherished plan of exhibiting a Roman Hippodrome, Zoological Institute, Aquaria, and Museum of unsurpassable extent and magnificence. I immediately telegraphed them to take the lease, and within twenty-four hours from that time I was in telegraphic communication with seventeen European cities where I knew were the proper parties to aid me in carrying out a grand and novel enterprise.

I visited all the zoological gardens, circuses, and public exhibitions, wherever I went, and thus secured numerous novelties and obtained new and valuable ideas.

At Hamburg, I purchased nearly a shipload of valuable wild animals and rare birds, including elephants, giraffes, a dozen ostriches, etc., etc.

I had concluded all my purchases in Hamburg on the eighteenth of November, 1873, and was taking a few last looks around the city previous to starting for Italy, when, on the twentieth inst., I received from my son-in-law, Mr. Hurd, a telegraphic dispatch announcing the death of my wife on the day previous.

It is difficult for those who have not had the sad experience, to imagine the degree of anguish which overwhelms one, when called to part with a beloved companion with whom he has lived forty-four years. That anguish must be greatly enhanced when such a death comes sudden and unexpected. But when the intelligence is not only unlooked for, but as, in my case, it finds the sorrowing husband four thousand miles away from the bedside of his dead wife, alone, in a strange land, where his native tongue is not spoken: when he reflects that children, grandchildren and other kindred are mourning over the coffin where he is needed, and where his poor stricken heart is breaking to be, the utter loneliness of that mourner cannot be truly comprehended. Long accustomed as I have been to feel that God is good, and that His ways are always right, that He overcometh evil with good, and chastens us "for our profit," I confess the "cloud" seemed so utterly black that it was hard to realize it could have a silver "lining;" and my tongue ceased to move when I attempted to say, as surely we all ought unhesitatingly at all times to say, "Not my will, but Thine be done."

I remained in my room for several days, and on that Saturday, on which I felt confident my children and friends were accompanying her remains to our beautiful Mountain Grove Cemetery, my lonely head was bowed, and my tears flowed in unison with theirs, while I implored our dear Father to give them strength to bear their loss and to sanctify her death to the benefit of us all.

She died at our New York residence, surrounded by children and friends, who had the satisfaction of knowing that she passed away without pain. The Bridgeport Standard gave the following account of the funeral services:

The remains of Mrs. P.T. Barnum were brought to this city, upon the 10:12 express this morning, and were taken to Waldemere, where the funeral services were held this afternoon. The house was filled with the relatives and friends of the deceased, to render the last sad tribute of affection and respect, among whom were many of our must prominent citizens and their families, and a number of the clergy of the city. The remains, which had been embalmed in New York, in accordance with a request received by telegram from Mr. Barnum, who is at Hamburgh, were enclosed in an elegant rosewood casket, and placed in the east parlor at Waldemere. The casket was covered with crowns and crosses, and wreaths of white roses, beautifully arranged. At the head of the casket was a large cross of evergreens, with the word "Mother" in white roses, across the arms, and at the base, "Charity," also in white roses. The funeral services were conducted by Rev. Abel C. Thomas, of Philadelphia. He also made a few short remarks upon the past life of the deceased and addressed comforting words to the mourning friends. Alter a closing prayer the doxology — "Praise God from whom all blessings flow,"' was sung by all present, after which an opportunity was given to view the remains. The funeral procession then winded its sorrowful way "from Waldemere and the sound of many waters to the quiet of Mountain Grove." The remains were then placed in the public receiving vault until the return of Mr. Barnum from Europe.

After this sad blow I could not bear the thought of "sight-seeing," and I yearned to be where I could meet sympathizing friends and hear my native tongue. I therefore returned to London and spent several weeks in quiet.

P. T. BARNUM'S WIFE, CHARITY,
AT THE AGE OF 65.

CHAPTER XLVIII.

AMONG MY FRIENDS AND NEIGHBORS.

At length, the continual letters from my manager roused me to action, and I went at it with a will. What I did is shown in the following extract from the *London Era:*

BARNUM'S NEXT SENSATION.

The greatest showman of the day is once more in London, completing preparations for the opening of the immense Hippodrome which he is erecting in New York. Some idea of the means which are being taken to create a sensation may be derived from the following facts: Mr. Barnum has not only sent agents to Spain and Africa to secure attractions, but has himself visited the Hippodrome in Paris, the Circus Renzat Vienna, Myers' Circus at Dresden, Salamonski and Carre's Circus at Cologne, the Zoological Gardens at Hamburgh, Amsterdam and other Continental cities, selecting and purchasing the choicest animals procurable, and engaging the most talented artists. He has secured what may fairly be called an endless variety of attractions, ranging from a race-horse to a Roman chariot. With the Messrs. Sanger alone he has done business to "the tune" of £11,000. He has already shipped to New York elephants, camels and horses, trained for every species of Circus performance. On the 25th a further "batch" will be dispatched, including sixteen ostriches, ten elands, ten zebras, a team of reindeer, with Lapland drivers, a troupe of performing ponies, monkeys, dogs, goats, etc., etc. The armor and costume makers of London are to be set to work immediately the pantomines are off their minds and hands, and some portion of the paraphernalia which is to contribute to the gigantic whole will be shipped weekly. The Hippodrome will open in April next, and in the preliminary parade, we have no doubt, the citizens will find reason to say that their greatest and most popular showman has far outstripped all his former efforts. We may add that the New York enterprise will in no way interfere with the famous tent show everywhere known as "Barnum's Great Museum. Menagerie, Circus and Traveling World's Fair."

Ten days afterwards the *London Times*, whose editor had seen the original contract, published the following article:

A THEATRICAL CONTRACT.

Mr. P.T. Barnum. who is now in this country, has just entered into a contract with Messrs. Sanger, of Astley's Amphitheatre, for the purchase of the whole of the plant, wardrobe, and paraphernalia connected with the pageant of the "Congress of Monarchs" exhibited at the Agricultural Hall four or five years since. The contract is as follows:

"This agreement made at the City of London, January 2nd, 1874, between Messrs. John and George Sanger, of the said city of London, Eng., and P. T. Barnum, of New York, United States of America, witnesseth, that for the sum of £33,000 sterling (Independent of £11,000 worth before purchased of Messrs. Sanger.), the said Messrs. J. and G. Sanger agree to complete and deliver to the said P. T. Barnum, duplicates of all the chariots, costumes, trappings, flags, banners, and other paraphernalia used by the said J. and G. Sanger in the production of the great pageant representing the Congress of Monarchs. Every article thus furnished by the said Messrs. John and George Sanger shall be new, and of the same quality and style used by them aforesaid. This collection embraces 13 gorgeous carved and gilt emblazoned chariots, and appropriate harness for 162 horses; 1,136 elegant and appropriate suits of armor, court dresses, etc., to faithfully represent all the principal Monarchs and Courts in the world, and a facsimile of all the flags, banners, and everything else used in this pageant, except the horses, elephants, ostriches, giraffes, camels, and other living animals. These the said Mr. P.T. Barnum will provide for himself. The arms of all nations represented on that occasion shall also be delivered to the said P. T. Barnum. The whole to be completed and delivered to the said P.T. Barnum or his agent, in London by February 22nd, 1874. The said P.T. Barnum hereby agrees to pay the said £33,000 to the said Messrs. J. and G. Sanger for the make and perfect delivery of the articles hereby agreed upon— £13,000 to be paid upon the signing of the contract, and the remaining £20.000 on the 22nd day of February next, or upon the earlier completion of the contract by the said Messrs. John and George Sanger. Property to be delivered to Mr. Robert Fillingham, the said P. T. Barnum's agent, and to be approved by him."

This document was signed on Tuesday, and the £13,000 paid. Messrs. Sanger will have on view at their Royal National Amphitheatre the costumes they are about to provide Mr. Barnum.

Already had we leased from the Harlem Railroad Company a plot of land in the center of New York valued at over a million of dollars, and on that land, we were to erect buildings which would probably cost two hundred thousand dollars.

Curiosity impelled me to attend the Tichborne trial one day. I was told it would be useless to attempt it, as none were admitted without a court order. I, however, applied at the door of Westminster Hall, where a great crowd was waiting unable to get in. In reply to my request to be admitted, a policeman asked if I had an order from the court. Upon my answering in the negative he remarked: "Even if you had, you could not get in today, for every inch of room is occupied; but in no case can you ever get in without an order from the court."

I asked for the inspector who had charge of the police. Inspector Deming was pointed out to me, and I handed him my card.

"Are you the great American Museum man?" he asked.

"Yes," I replied; I am the Museum man, the Tom Thumb man, the Jenny Lind man, and the Showman."

"My dear sir," said the inspector, "I am glad to see you. Please write your name on the back of your card and I shall always prize it as a souvenir. I am very happy that I can show the celebrated showman something he never saw before."

He then led me into Westminster Hall, secured me a good seat, pointed out the "claimant," Lord Chief Justice Cockburn, Justices Weller and Lush, Dr. Kenealy, Mr. Hawkins, and other prominent personages.

I arrived in New York from Liverpool by the steamer Scotia, April 30, 1874, rejoiced to reach my native land again, and delighted to find my children and grandchildren in good health. The great Roman Hippodrome had been open about a week, and on the evening of my arrival I was called out by the audience and was driven in my carriage around the immense arena and saw what, to me, was indeed a great "show" — the largest assemblage of people ever gathered in one building in New York. I may be permitted to add, that my enthusiastic reception was at once a testimonial of the public appreciation of one of my greatest efforts in my managerial career, and a verdict that it was a complete and gratifying success.

This *"truly stupendous and superb spectacle"*, as the unanimous voice of the press pronounced it, opened every evening with an allegorical representation of a "Congress of Nations," in a grand procession of gilded chariots and triumphal cars, conveying the Kings, Queens, Emperors, and other potentates of the civilized world, costumed with historical correctness, royally surrounded, and accompanied and followed by their respective courts and splended retinues. The correctness and completeness of this historical representation required nearly one thousand persons and several hundred horses, besides elephants, camels, llamas, ostriches, etc. The rich and varied costumes, armor and trappings, the gorgeous banners and paraphernalia, and the appropriate music accompanying the entrance of each nation produced an effect at once brilliant and bewildering. The entire public, and the press, both secular and religious, declared unanimously what is unquestionably true — that never before since the days of the Caesars has there been so grand and so interesting a public spectacle.

Following this superb historical introduction were all kinds of races by high-bred horses imported by scores from Europe and ridden and driven by accomplished experts of both sexes. To these succeeded various first-class entertainments, including the wonderful performances of the Japanese athletes, thrilling wire-walking exploits, athletic sports by non-professionals for prizes awarded as encouragements to such enterprises, semi-weekly balloon ascensions by Prof. Donaldson, the whole interspersed with a plenty of genuine fun in the monkey and donkey races, and in "Twenty minutes of the Donny brook Fair and Lancashire Races "— and with all was "thrown in" my magnificent menagerie.

Although the Hippodrome could accommodate ten thousand spectators, for weeks in succession all the best seats were engaged days in advance, and it is literally true that at every evening performance thousands were turned away. My patrons included the President of the United States and his Cabinet, Governors and Judges, the Clergy of all denominations, and all the best people of our land, who expressed but one opinion, that the exhibition, as I intended it should be, far surpassed the most sanguine expectations of what managerial experience and endeavor could possibly accomplish. In the very midst of such success, the necessity of covering the central part of the Hippodrome with glass, putting in heating apparatus, and otherwise preparing the immense building for the winter campaign, compelled me to temporarily transfer the entire vast establishment to Boston for three weeks from August 3rd, thence to Philadelphia, returning and reopening in New York about September 20th.

After the exciting scenes and unremitting labor of several weeks in New York, I retired to Waldemere for rest. No sooner had I arrived at Bridgeport than a newspaper paragraph announced to me that my friends and neighbors had determined to tender to me a public dinner. Flattering as this testimonial was, my first impulse was to express my gratitude for the tendered compliment, but by no means to accept it. But my mere arrival had already been the occasion of a spontaneous and enthusiastic welcome, which a large number wished to make more formal and complete, so that the proposed tender of a dinner remained inevitable, and the following correspondence ensued:

Bridgeport, June 6, 1874.
To Hon. P. T. Barnum:

DEAR SIR: As a mark of our esteem for your liberality and energy in private enterprise and in promoting the industries and public improvements of our city, we cordially invite you to dine with us on some early and convenient occasion.

Yours, very truly,

R. T. CLARKE	F.W. PARROTT	HANFORD LYNON	F.G. FOWLER
G.B. WALLER	SAML. B. SUMNER	ALBERT EAMES	H.S. SANFORD
GIDEON THOMPSON	W.H. NOBLE	C. SPOONER	F. HURD
FRANCES IVES	F.A. BENHAM	ROBERT HUBBARD	JOHN BROOKS
ALFRED HOPKINS	SHELTON & LYON	N. WHEELER	CARLOS CURTIS
J.E. DUNHAM	A.W. WALLACE	JARRATT MORFORD	J.&G.A. STAPLES
IRA GREGORY	JOHN D. CANDEE	KNOWLES AND CO.	ELI THOMPSON
JAMES C. LOOMIS	G.W. BARKER	GEO. MALLORY	D.N. MORGAN
E.B. GOODSELL	WESSELLS BROS.	R. TOMLINSON	JAMES A. HOUSE
W.H. PERRY	A.R. LAMB	CHAS. B. HOTCHKISS	H.R. PARROTT
D.F. HOLLISTER	M.H. WILSON	G.H. HOLLISTER	E.C. WILMOT
JACOB KIEFFER	D.W. SHERWOOD	W.R. HIGEY	L.F. CURTIS
LEWIS W. BOOTH	T.M. PALMER	W.S. EDWARDS	S.C. NICKERSON
F. HUBBELL	SAMUEL C. KINGMAN	JOHN E. POND	Z. GOODSELL
T.R. CRUTTENDEN	JOHN D. WHITNEY	HUBBELL JONES & CO	WM. E. SEELEY
CHESTER RUSSELL	W.H. MALLORY	JH & JN BENHAM	J.W. SMITH
T. HAWLEY & CO	H. BUCKINGHAM	GEO. W. BACON	S.B. FERGUSON
E. BIRDSEY	D.M. READ	W.H. ADAMS	W.G. LINEBURGH
E.V. HAWES & SON	WILLIS & LANE, LYON, CURTIS & CO, AND OTHERS		

WALDEMERE, BRIDGEPORT. CONN.,
June 6, 1874. To His Honor, R. T. Clarke, Mayor, and Others

GENTLEMEN: It is always pleasant to receive the approval of one's neighbors. To be tendered a public dinner by the most prominent and substantial Inhabitants of a city where I have resided tor more than a quarter of a century, is a compliment as gratifying as it is unexpected.

Though conscious that to my recent return from abroad may be attributed your selection of myself at this time from among other citizens who have materially aided in "promoting the industries and public Improvements of our city," yet I cannot forego the pleasure that I always enjoy in social intercourse with friends, and therefore your invitation is gratefully accepted. Any date agreeable to yourselves, alter the sixteenth inst., will be convenient to me.

Respectfully yours,
P.T. BARNUM.

COMPLIMENTARY DINNER TO P.T. BARNUM.
[From the *Bridgeport Republican Standard*, July 3, 1874.]

The complimentary dinner given by the citizens of Bridgeport to P.T. Barnum, at the Atlantic House, Thursday evening, June 25. was in every respect a success, gratifying alike to the guest in honor of whose energy, thrift, public spirit and genuine philanthropy it was given, and to those who had conceived and carried it out so happily. The fine dining hall of the Atlantic House was set with four long tables, one across the head of the hall, and the other three running at right angles to it and lengthwise of the room. At the first were seated the presiding officer, Mayor Clarke; the guest of the evening, P.T. Barnum. Esq., and his immediate friends from abroad, with ex-Mayors of Bridgeport and other prominent citizens, while the men of all professions and callings, representing the wealth, respectability, enterprise and energy of our thriving town occupied the other tables, in all to the number of over two hundred. It is seldom that any public occasion calls out such a body of our townsmen, and the company was one of which any Bridgeporter might well feel proud. Among the most prominent of our older citizens present were Hanford Lyon, Esq., Capt. John Brooks. Philo Hurd and Eli Thompson, Esqs.; while amongst the prominent ex-city officials were ex-Mayors E. B. Goodsell and Jarratt Morford. Representatives from nearly all the prominent New York daily and weekly journals were also in attendance. The tables were profusely adorned with beautiful flowers, toward which nearly every large garden and greenhouse in town contributed, and these were tastily arranged in elegant vases, holders and stands, which displayed them to advantage and enhanced their beauty. Pyramids of fruit and delicate confections mingled with the flowers and added to the appropriate adornment. The bill of fare was an elaborate and exhaustive one, embracing all the luxuries of the season, cooked artistically, well served, and in profusion. The Wheeler &, Wilson Band, under leader Rosenburg, furnished music, and was, as usual, very fine. They played on the balcony in front of the hotel while the guests were assembling in the parlors, and subsequently enlivened the entertainment with judiciously selected and well-played airs. Thus music, flowers, fruits, a good dinner and a good company, all combined to make the occasion pleasant and memorable. The guests sat down at the tables at about eight o'clock, after grace by Rev. Dr. Hopper; but it was nearly ten before the inner man had been sufficiently satisfied with the constantly replenished supply of substantials and delicacies to admit of the "feast of reason and flow of soul" which was to follow. During the evening members of the committee were active in seems that the wants of the guests were supplied, and that nothing was left undone that would contribute to the success of the occasion. At ten o'clock, His Honor Mayor Clarke called for the reading of the letters from invited guests. Mr. G.C. Waldo, of the committee, read letters from several prominent gentlemen, who were prevented from attending, but who expressed their regard for the recipient of the compliment.

Mr. Charles A. Dana, of the *New York Sun*, wrote:

"I am not surprised that the people of Bridgeport should pay such a compliment to so public-spirited a fellow citizen."

Mr. George Jones, of the *New York Times*, wrote:

"I hope you will have a glorious time, and I desire to be considered in when Mr. Barnum's health is proposed, and further shall be glad to send the following: "P.T. Barnum, 'The Man who cannot grow old'"

Rev. Dr. Chapin's letter concludes:

"Nothing would have given me greater pleasure than to have met you and the good people of Bridgeport on the occasion referred to: but now, I ran only be with you in spirit — with the 'ardent spirit' which is perfectly consistent with a teetotal dinner, and wish you all a first-rate time."

Dr. Cuyler, of Brooklyn, wrote.

"Tell the good people of Bridgeport for me, that the pleasantest hours I have spent in their town have been passed under Mr. Barnum's hospitable roof, and that they deserve to have noble-hearted citizens when they appreciate them. They cannot do too much to honor the public-spirited man who has done so much for them. If I were present I should propose in clear crystal water this toast: A bright golden "Indian Summer" of life to our guest, who has made more children happy than any American of this generation. With a thousand good wishes, yours most cordially."

Gov. Dix wrote regretting that he was prevented from attending by his engagement to deliver an address to the graduating class of Union College, June 24.

The following is from Frank Leslie's letter:

"No man living more fully deserves the respect and confidence of all who know him. We have had business and friendly relations dating back twenty-five years, so I speak 'because I know the man.' Years ago, I was much impressed by the response of an old servant in answer to an inquiry as to what kind of person Mr. Barnum was: 'What manner of man is Mr. Barnum? Why, just one of the kindest-hearted, public-spirited men that lives. Money flows from him like water, in a just cause, and I haven't a good enough name to give him,' with a burst of enthusiasm. And so, sir, I can only echo the words of his old servant, and say of the man to whom you do honor, that I have not a good enough name to give him."

Mayor Clarke then announced the first regular sentiment of the evening, "Our Guest," and called upon Gen. William H. Noble to present it.

SPEECH OF GEN. NOBLE.
"The words of your invitation to our guest, while they are your just epitome of his deserts, are most fitting for my text.

"You offer him this banquet, and your goodly presence to mark your 'esteem for his liberality and energy in private enterprise and in promoting the industries and public improvements of our city.'

"This is no tribute, then, to mere wealth— your catalogue of merits gives no place to stocks, or bonds, or princely homes, or his broad acres of our city lots, stretching through every district of the corporation. Such things touch not the heart of our esteem. Why should they? Wealth is a mere implement to the soul that does with it. Besides, the bearing of our friend has never marked the sense of riches.

"Esteem is only due to wealth or talent when administered as a blessing held in trust, reaching beyond ourselves and yielding zest and opportunity to others. By this standard I ask the measurement of our friend.

"By private liberality and enterprise, you do not, of course, claim to mark its ingenious and versatile display in that old museum, store-house of curiosities, instruction, fun and moral drama, a kaleidoscope of shows and innocent amusements; nor that ceaseless throng of curious wonders drawn from every country, clime and race, to swell that 'innumerable caravan' of world's fairs and shows which circles through the land; nor will you claim, I think, as yours the newer spectacle of mammoth hippodrome which treats you to a congress of the nations, and a steeple-chase 'right up Broadway.' Nor do you intend to mark that enterprise of his which, as some return to China, and Japan, and the far-off islands of the sea, for contributions drawn from them to swell his curious inventory of wonders, he sent to them sweet singers, Tom Thumb and Nutt, and all that Lilliputian troop, to play, in their small way, the 'heathen Chinee' and hari-kari. But from all these we have had, indeed, through our imperial showman, substantial benefit and share, in concerts, songs and shows devoted to some charity or other goodly work in our midst, and from the vast returns of all his ventures put into the improvements, foundations and shapeliness of our city. The marks of some of these shall last through time, and perish only with the Republic and the waning of the solid earth.

"And first, our guest, in a life of thirty years amongst us, has, in his homes, so administered his trust, that we have shared their comely aspects and the grace and refinement of their surroundings. I speak not of the genial hospitality and courtesy which, within his threshold, have been the property of every guest — his latch-string was ever out to them — but of his open gates, whose posted words invited all to enter and enjoy his grounds.

"Most of us remember *Iranistan*, that aerial, oriental villa, whose domes and minarets were for every flitting train an attraction, a name and an advertisement for us and him.

"It was as original as our friend, and was said to duplicate the Brighton Palace of George the IV.; but, beside that squat thing, ours had wings and airy elevation, as unlike it as an eagle to a terrapin. Seen by moonlight, *Iranistan* was like some delicate tracery of arch and pinnacle, photographed on the air, from those fairy Moslem gardens across the Bosphorus. It was, by his permission and invitation, our showplace, and our little park of twenty acres, our flower garden and pleasure ground. His trees, and shrubs, and flowers were about as much ours as his. In fact, I believe that throng which circled through its drives and shades, in carriages and on foot, enjoyed its loveliness in larger measures than our friend. But he had the advantage of us in that

THE TRUE LIFE OF THE WORLD'S GREATEST SHOWMAN

return whichever comes to reward a pleasure granted others. The cost of our enjoyment, though a heavy footing in his books, was never counted a loss.

"Next came Lindencroft, a world too narrow for our friend— a kind of resting-place while prospecting round for his new home at Waldemere. That is a region discovered by himself and traversed by him and other Livingstones about 1865. What a fit and speaking name, this Waldemere, child of the woodland and the wave, how suited to its aspects and surroundings, so fragrant with woodland odors, so fresh with ocean breath. Here again our friend is but our steward and head gardener, dispensing liberality and elegance in keeping with his larger means. The statues, fountains, lakes, swans, walks, lawns and ribbon wreaths of leaf and flower, which girt its zone and area, and its woodland shades are as open to our enjoyment as to his. Yea, by his invitation, set down at its gates, that means 'Come, be welcome to breathe the balmy fragrance and that "ozone" which, all unconscious how, has brought to the three score years of our friend, the vigor and the pluck if not the 'flame of youth.' Had Hispania's knightly Leon, voyaging westward, but struck at Waldemere, instead of Florida's balmy shore and flowery glades, he would have had small need to seek in fruitless quest those fabled waters whose reviving lave were said to bring to all the vigor and the bloom of youth, to fire the currents of the blood, and stay the waning tides of life.

"Let no man look on such a use of wealth— the making of one's home and its surroundings to minister to the pleasure, taste and instruction of his townsmen and fellows — and tell me that down in the heart and purposes of him who so does and deals out his store, there is not gentle kindness, refinement and grace of thought and feeling. Verily, if our friend hath sins — and who of us has not — such doing covers a multitude thereof. There is a refinement in flowers, in love of art and nature, that follows the footsteps of their presence. He who ministers thereto fulfills a mission whose sermons are in the woodlands and the rocks, and its songs in breezes and the babbling brooks. Let no man sneer at the love of flowers and fronds, and tinge of leaf, which God has made and tinted, as too frivolous and feminine to become the toughness of manly, athlete, mental fiber. He who derides them knows not their meaning; such tastes mark culture and refinement, and diviner levels reached in the ascent of our race. From behind the flower that blooms and smiles in the wintry sunshine of some humble cottage window, there looks a woman's soul beyond the hard facts of life, toward that refinement and a higher civilization which comes with and follows that flower.

"But, as your invitation points out, the doings of our friend have been especially felt in the industries and public improvements of our city.

"One of his first works here was on our 'Greenwood.' Out on the border of our city, beside the little stream which girts a goodly spread of plateau, woodlands, dale, and shade and rolling hill, lies 'Mountain Grove.' Our friend discovered its fitness for our loved ones' last resting-place, secured its titles, and with that magnetic way of his inspired others to the purpose of its dedication to the sacred dead. After Greenwood and Mount Auburn, it was one of the first well-ordered and tastefully laid out cemeteries in the country. To this graceful public improvement our friend added, from the proceeds of a concert by Catherine Hayes, its comely gateway. I here, too, pay just tribute to those gentlemen to whose care and tasteful administration of its business and improvements our cemetery owes so much.

"Our guest was in full swing in his imperial campaign with Jenny Lind, when, somehow, he and I were brought to work together in that East Bridgeport, whose early, rapid growth and solid foundations are due to his liberal trust and out-pour of means for my administration. I could not have met another man so open-handed and confiding. He found me overloaded with some seventy acres, substantially projected and mapped as now— a foot-bridge built along the railroad into its heart had ensured success, with means. He brought these. The whole of our bargain and work together was an index of the man. Of course, he knew me, and of my doings— had seen my map and advertisement. He saw at once how we could work together. Not half an hour was spent in terms of purchase and in putting them on paper, before I was on the rail for Bridgeport with £20,000 in my pocket to buy more land and 'push things.' He took no deed, looked up no titles; I told him how things were, he found them so, and ever has. My receipt for money, and one little half page of terms were all our writings.

"From that day to the great clock disaster, it was one continuous rush of streets and grades, trees, factories, dwellings, churches, schools. Washington Park, now worth $200,000, was laid out and dedicated to the public. There was no stint of money. His means, drawn from concerts, museum, Tom Thumb, and all, were poured into East Bridgeport. Had Jerome, and those who abetted him, not crippled and tangled our friend in the wreck of clocks, no one can tell, with the powerful backings since come among us, what East Bridgeport might have become. Sometimes success and good come of disaster. That magnificent industry and its swarm of kindred works, so ably engineered and allied by our friend and senator before me, Nathaniel Wheeler, but for this clock disaster would hardly have found the opportunity so valuable for us and all.

"Throughout our work together, and since, my old associate, in other parts of the city, has kept up his tireless betterment of the situation. State street was started westward, but blocked by others, who would not consent to that extension which afterwards they craved. *Iranistan* avenue was laid down by him through a swamp and mud creek, where tides (dyked out by him) flowed and old scows floated over land today built on and bordered with trees and walks. By his push and enterprise, this avenue now stretches a mile of splendid thoroughfare, and is the western entrance to our park.

"The last conspicuous monument of our friend's enterprise is Seaside Park. Its fitness for such use was, by himself and other Livingstones, discovered about the same time as Waldemere. Through his exertions, and the enlisted aid of others, Seaside has been made a breathing place and pleasure ground for our people forever. The names and generous donations of those whose land formed a large part of the track have gone into history and should have a monument.

"In our friend's administration of the trust of wealth, you have an example of its wisest use for the good of his fellows. This is a day of unexampled charities and large handed benevolence donations by hundreds of thousands, and millions, are poured out of the trust which God has given in store, for various objects of public good. It is of some moment to judge rightly of that use of means which benefits the most and reaches most. I do not know that any one way or purpose should be set down for all; men, though divine in giving, are human in their judgment. Each acts according to his character, habits of thought, and life. Let all give for good purposes, as they are wont. He may rest well satisfied with his work who appeals thereby to the better instincts of the race; who, instead of devoting his wealth to the waifs and overburdened of life, makes opportunities tor self-help, homes and industry for others; who devotes his stores of wealth to such an improvement as East Bridgeport, where the chance of homes and industries, and all the strength and stamina of a people that gather around those homes are made possible to every willing toiler. Our townsman, Howe, made his millions out of the profits of his great invention. But not content with its possession and holding as an unproductive fund, he devoted it to that magnificent industry which bears his name and gives bread and comfort to thousands.

"But when men, like our friend and guest, have so administered the trust of their talents and means, as to bring prosperity, improvements, comfort and refinement to others, there becomes due to them a grateful recognition of duties well discharged, from their fellows and the community in which they live. Such testimony to merit inspires both giver and receiver with a kindly fellowship. We give ovations to soldiers; why not to duty-doing citizens as well? Peace hath her victories, her toils and struggles, and her triumphs, less costly and wasteful, to be sure, but ministering to happiness and wealth. There is power in those men who move the business of the world. I believe in Caesars and Napoleons— not those of conquest, who squander human life and stores of hard-earned wealth, whose path is desolation— but in Caesars and Napoleons who engineer and organize the industries of the world; who minister in the ten thousand channels where flow the busy throng of human workers, to swell the flood and direct its currents; who bridge our mighty rivers, swing high in air above the masts of ships aerial pathways; who tunnel mountains, unite oceans, band people and nations with iron nerves and arteries of intercourse and commerce; who girt the world with speaking fire.

"But Caesars want a following. No man alone, however great his means, can of himself accomplish much. Strength lies in union, in harmonious action, and in conspiracies for good as well as evil. If one can do so much, with centered energies and wealth, how much a whole community who join their peaceful Caesars in all works looking towards the good of the community in which they live. May this our guest and friend, one of our peaceful Caesars, live to do among us as in the past, but with a heavier following and more earnest help. Long may it be before that flag, which from the pinnacle at Waldemere marks his hospitable presence, shall descend to note an absence from which there is no return!"

The scholarly, elegant and able effort of General Noble received alike the attention and applause which were its due; and when he sat down Mr. Barnum arose amid a perfect tempest of cheers and such an enthusiastic greeting as visibly touched his heart. His speech was interrupted with frequent applause; and his allusions to prominent men, who had been his co-workers in building up Bridgeport — Nathaniel Wheeler, J. C. Loomis. Gen. Noble and others— were greeted with special and prolonged cheers; while the many happy hits should have been heard to be properly appreciated. The following is an outline of

MR. BARNUM'S SPEECH.

"Your Honor the Mayor, Neighbors and Friends: I offer you my most profound thanks for this spontaneous expression of your esteem. No words of mine can express the debt of gratitude which I owe you.

"Among all the toils and pleasures, the vicissitudes and successes of an active and eventful life, this day and this occasion will ever stand out a red-letter day on the calendar of my history. It will be cherished by myself, my children and my children's children, with feelings of joy and thankfulness.

"It is no trifling thing for a man of the world, of active temperament and positive ideas, to have so lived as to have won the esteem and confidence of the general public; but it is an honor inestimable to become an exception to the divine maxim, 'A prophet is not without honor save in his own country and his own house,' and to be thus honored by a multitude of my most prominent and substantial neighbors, among whom I have lived for more than thirty years. And during that period, I have received nothing but unvaried kindness from the citizens of Bridgeport. In my wanderings I have always left our beautiful city with regret, and ever returned to it with renewed pleasure, for in this my home I am always sure of meeting smiling faces and warm hearts.

"I only wish, gentlemen, that I better deserved your compliment. Others sitting at this table merit and receive your approbation. We have here gentlemen who have introduced manufactures and capital into Bridgeport, without which it would have still been a mere country village. These gentlemen, for their energy and liberality, command the gratitude of their neighbors, and I trust, at no distant day. they will receive tangible evidence thereof.

"East Bridgeport owes its existence, in a great measure, to Gen. Wm. H. Noble. It was his original conception, and all its streets were opened under his supervision.

"Our respected fellow citizen Captain John Brooks was the first president of Mountain Grove Cemetery, and he aided materially in its formation.

"Hon. James C. Loomis was one of the most ardent advocates for the establishment of Seaside Park, and my efforts in that direction were warmly sustained by Hon. Nathaniel Wheeler, Frederick Wood, Esq., Ron. Wm. D. Bishop, and others whom I have not time to name.

"When we speak of the material prosperity of Bridgeport, we remember with gratitude the name of Hon. Nathaniel Wheeler, to whom we are indebted for the establishment of the Wheeler & Wilson Co.'s manufactories here, and who was also instrumental in bringing hither the noble Elias Howe. Jr., and many other enterprising others might be mentioned who have contributed largely to the present position of the most thriving city in New England; and our citizens can never be too grateful for the liberality and energies of our principal capitalists and business men.

"I should have declined the honor of this dinner, and been content with the privilege of receiving your invitation, had I not felt that this occasion might perhaps encourage others in cultivating a spirit of liberality, a spirit of improvement, in fact, a public spirit, that should redound to the public good.

"I but came to Bridgeport as an experiment in 1842, and rented part of a house in State street, for ninety dollars per year. I had no predilections in favor of Bridgeport, but I discovered that most of the shore of Long Island bound, from Greenwich to New London, was healthy and delightful, and, all things considered, I preferred Bridgeport to any other place, and I have never changed my opinion.

"When I started for Europe last autumn, I said to my poor wife I did not expect to see a more pleasant locality than Waldemere — and I did not. Indeed, I fully believe it is one of the most delightful and healthy residences on the face of the earth.

"This shore around Bridgeport has long been celebrated for its fine and peculiarly invigorating air. It has been remarked that there has been during the last forty years as there is today, an unusual number of persons living here whose ages range from eighty-five to ninety-five and even one hundred years and upwards. I could recall the names of scores of such persons within my recollection, and many such are now living here. This is, in a degree, attributable to "OZONE," which scientific experiments have demonstrated exists in larger quantity in the air of Bridgeport than in that of any other locality on this continent.

"General Noble has put me in a reverse position to the man who received a scratch on the face, and when he heard his lawyer depict his terrible injuries to the jury, burst into tears and declared he had no conception how shockingly he had been injured.

"If I have done what the general has so generously stated, it is because I could not help it. Having taken Bridgeport as my lifelong residence, I could not help doing all in my power to add to its beauty and its prosperity. I had a pride in the place of my selection and had no desire to expend my money elsewhere; consequently, I felt a pleasure in laying out new streets, raising valleys and lowering hills, erecting houses and factories and Inducing capitalists and manufacturers to come among us.

"I felt like the old darkie who was sued by a man. Before the morning of the trial arrived, the plaintiff withdrew his suit and paid the cost. But the old darkie went to court and insisted upon having a trial. The judge told him the suit was withdrawn.

"Nebber mind dat." exclaimed the ancient African, 'call de case, call de case, I want to hear how 'em roar!'

"And so with me. If I conceived that a new street, a new building, or the planting of a few hundred trees would improve things, I was anxious to 'call de case and hear how 'em roar.'

"The advice of the Irishman in the scrimmage at Donnybrook Fair was: 'Wherever you see a head, hit it.'

"That is the way I feel; whenever I see a swamp-hole or a bit of salt meadow, I want to hit it.

"Some persons present will remember that when I built *Iranistan.* a large brook crossed Fairfield avenue between *Iranistan* and the homestead of Ira B. Wheeler. Travelers stopped to water their horses in that stream. A salt-meadow swamp set up close to the south side of Fairfield avenue and boats came up to the street. When I bought the swamp, filled it up, and turned the stream into a large stone sewer. Col. Hall sued, or threatened to sue me, for obstructing navigation! That entire swamp meadow is now solid ground.

"Now, some say that when I make improvements, I do it with an eye to future profit. I am glad to acknowledge that this is generally true. I have certainly made some expensive improvements, which I feel sure convince me, but I am glad to have it understood that mine is usually a *profitable philanthropy*. I have no desire to be considered much of a philanthropist in any other sense. If by helping those who try to help themselves, I do it without ultimate loss, the inducement is all the greater and if by improving and beautifying our city, and adding to the pleasure and prosperity of my neighbors at a profit, the incentive to 'good works' will be twice as strong as if it were otherwise.

"I don't believe much in the doctrine that teaches persons to sit still, suck their fingers and be fed, clothed and lodged by the charity of others; I believe in teaching people to be active, industrious, economical and temperate. Above all, I believe in teaching the doctrine of honesty as taught by Ralph Waldo Emerson, when he said that it is impossible for one man to rob or injure another without, at the same time, injuring himself more than anybody else. I believe in teaching that all wrongdoing and all violations of nature's laws cause us to lose our self-respect, our manhood and the confidence of mankind, so that it is impossible to gain anything thereby, hence that honesty is, as Franklin said, the best 'policy,' and that *right* in any shape is *always* the best 'policy.' And those who do right and try to help themselves do not generally need free gifts from others. King David truly said he had 'never seen the righteous forsaken, nor their seed begging bread.' Therefore, I want it to be understood, that when I make improvements I am benefiting the community by giving employment to working people.

"But there is a funny side to my improvements and experiences in Bridgeport. When I first settled here I knew nothing about making new streets, erecting buildings, laying out pleasure grounds, etc.

"I had traveled considerably, and picked up some knowledge of human nature, and that was all. Hence, in making 'improvements,' I made many ludicrous blunders. I had bought up during several years numerous parcels of land west of Fairfield avenue, and it so happened that a low piece of salt meadow lay between two pieces of my upland. Thinking that at some future time I might want that salt marsh filled up, I called on Deacon Silliman, the reputed owner, and told him he had a piece of salt meadow I wished to buy.

'I have no salt meadow to spare', said the deacon. 'Well, I'll let you have another piece in exchange. I only want yours so as to connect my two pieces of land,' I replied. 'I don't know which salt meadow you mean,' said the deacon. 'Jump into my wagon and I will show it to you in ten minutes,' I answered, and away we went. Arriving at the spot, I pointed out the coveted piece of marsh. 'Why, Mr. Barnum, you have owned that salt meadow these three years!' exclaimed the astonished deacon. I was always vexed that the deacon did not give me a quit-claim for twenty-five dollars; the joke would have been worth that.

"On another occasion I was in the Island of Cuba. I went to a nursery there, admired the young palms, bananas, India rubber plants, indigo and coffee trees, etc., and having no special knowledge of such things, but desiring to enrich the conservatories of *Iranistan* with every rare plant and flower, I purchased a lot of these shrubs and then gave the nurseryman an order for flower seeds, which were to include everything which he had that was rare. He made me up over a hundred packages of seeds, at an expense of some fifty dollars. When planted in the grounds of *Iranistan*, I found I had purchased seeds of catnip, pennyroyal, mullen, daisies, and lots of weeds common to us, but quite 'rare' to the Havana nurseryman.

"And so, on my late visit to Europe, with a desire to beautify the grounds of Waldemere, I engaged the best gardener in the Crystal Palace Gardens at Sydenham, and sent him to America. I looked over the various rare plants, with which these grounds abound, and made numerous selections for Waldemere. On placing them in my grounds, my neighbors discovered 'dusty miller,' and several other common plants among my supposed choice varieties.

"But, gentlemen, I will not detain you; I cannot tell you how glad I am to meet you, nor can I sit down without saying how grateful I am for the kindness and delicate forethought you have shown in deferring on this occasion to my public advocacy of teetotalism for thirty years. I trust our natural flow of spirits will keep us jolly, and hope that somehow or other you will manage to do what I always desire my patrons to do, viz.: 'Get the worth of your money.' "

Mr. Barnum sat down amid prolonged applause, and when that had subsided and the band had played an appropriate air, George Mallory, Esq., chairman of the Dinner Committee, announced the next regular toast, "The Municipal Government of our City; may Wisdom guide and govern the deliberations and acts of its council, and Ability and Honesty the execution of its laws.

MAYOR R.T. CLARKE'S SPEECH.
After responding directly to the toast, Mayor Clarke said:

"When I first came to Bridgeport, something more than twenty years ago, I used to take an occasional walk after bank hours into the country. I enjoyed the fields, the quiet, the almost complete solitude of the uninhabited regions through which I strolled. The scene would be enlivened now and then by the flight, part play and part fear, of some squirrel bounding along a stone wall. Next there would come a glimpse of civilization in some cow getting her living in a live-acre lot of daisies and sorrel, bounded by a moss-grown and venerable rail fence; and once in a while aboriginal scenes would reappear in an encampment of New Milford or Kent Indians, who had strayed for a few weeks away from home. Where did I go for these walks of mine? Not very far. That was East Bridgeport when I first came here. There were the houses of a few old residents on 'the Point.' The rest was mainly fields, and as much country as Tashua is today; and it is a fact that I have more than once seen Indians encamped in the woods which were in those days near the east end of the present railroad bridge.

"The change from that time to this is very much like a dream. I need not tell you to whose enterprise it is that we are mainly indebted for that change. We have him here with us as the guest of the evening. I will not enter into those particulars which have and will be, no doubt, thoroughly discussed by the eloquent speakers to whom we are to have the privilege of listening. I will but say, in a word, that no one can compare Bridgeport as it was with Bridgeport as it is, without an impulse of gratitude towards that genius of industry, sagacity and boldness in whose honor this meeting is given, and that there can be in the years to come no impartial history of Bridgeport written which shall leave out the name of P.T. Barnum."

Mayor Clarke was liberally applauded, and "when the tumult dwindled to a calm "he announced the next toast, "The Manufacturing and Commercial Interests of Bridgeport,"

And called upon Don. Nathaniel Wheeler to respond. He was received with a very flattering burst of applause, and after some pithy and appropriate remarks about the growth of the city and its manufactures, he continued:

"When manufacturers visited Bridgeport with a view to locating here, our distinguished guest met them in a cordial and generous manner, and would say to them, "If you wish to locate here, take my lands for a site." It was this generous and far-seeing policy that brought to our city numerous manufacturing establishments. Among them may be mentioned that of Elias Howe, that of Schuyler, Hartley & Graham, the Hotchkiss establishment, and many others, and thus our town grew up to be a city of shops, stores and residences. You have seen the stranger coming in from all directions as to a place inviting for business enterprise, because there was thrift, life and spirit in Bridgeport.

"And today our city oilers to business men the greatest inducements of any place in the land. (Applause.) It is near New York, and yet sufficiently in New England to command the best class of mechanics and artisans. And I am happy to note the effect of bringing this class of men to our town. And I will add that whenever strangers have come here, or mechanics have come here, they have always been met by open-handed encouragement from our guest. The products of Bridgeport go into every family on the continent, and to every continent on the earth, and are stamped with words indelibly, 'Manufactured at Bridgeport, Conn.' You cannot find a town or village but has Bridgeport represented in it by one of the most useful instruments ever devised by the skill of man. Go to Mexico, or South America, yes, even to the homes lining the remote tributaries of the La Platte, and you will find it doing its duty and saving labor to the poor female of the country. Go to Asia and you will find it; and even in China and Japan.

I wish to have it understood that our guest laid the foundation of all this business, and I am glad to be here to honor him and sound his praise. We did not come here to examine some wonderful specimen of human longevity, or with a curious eye to view some wonderful product of the sea— (Mr. Barnum—'Mermaid!' Laughter.) — we came here to honor the man who has honored Bridgeport and laid the foundation of her prosperity, and has always given to Bridgeport 'more than her money's worth.'" (Applause.)

Mayor Clarke then announced the next regular sentiment, "The Press," to which Mr. G. C. Waldo responded as follows:

"We have tonight heard how the great energy, perseverance, indomitable will and spirit of Mr. Barnum have contributed to his success; but one great element of that success has not been mentioned. No one knows better than P.T. Barnum the value of printer's ink. He values it and uses it, and without it he might today have still been a wandering showman, exhibiting from town to town, instead of the great chief and head he undoubtedly is, of all men in his business! (Applause.) Mr. Barnum himself will tell you that! (Mr. Barnum, interrupting, 'Yes, without printer's ink I should have been no bigger than Tom Thumb!') Mr. Barnum thoroughly understands the value of judicious advertising, and if you would succeed as he has, 'go and do likewise!' " (Applause.)

Mr. Morris, of the *New York Times*, then said:

"Mr. Barnum represented the energy and enterprise of the American race, and the better side of those qualities, too. He went abroad with his money to purchase what was valuable there, but more valuable here, and would bring him an increase on his investment in turn. He was the thrifty, enterprising and indomitable Yankee, and illustrated the characteristic and distinctive element of the American mind. He knew the value of printer's ink, and of the men who made printer's ink the vehicle of news and information. Mr. Barnum owed much to the editorial fraternity, and they in turn were indebted to him for liberality and courtesy. The editorial profession had always been ready to aid any honest enterprise, and herald whatever was worth heralding. The press of New York acknowledged Mr. Barnum the greatest showman of the world, and one of the most truly philanthropic. On behalf of the members of the New York press, he thanked Mr. Barnum for the kindness and courtesies extended to them, and expressed a wish that one so ready to assist his fellows might live long to enjoy many such occasions, at which he hoped to be present. (Applause.)

The next sentiment was "Our Homes," to which Dr. C.E. Sanford responded as follows:

"Our homes, models of refined taste, surrounded with nature's loveliest adornments; pleasant to behold, pleasanter to know, pleasantest to possess. I thank you. Mr. Chairman, for inviting me to respond to such a sentiment. Next to my profession, I love my home, and I love the many pleasant homes of Bridgeport. A very intelligent lady said to me, only a few days ago: 'I do believe your city has more charming homes than any other place of its size I was ever in. Every house has its bit of lawn, fine shrubbery and beautiful flowers.' It is just next to impossible to find a dwelling lacking in these thoroughly delightful elements, and the thought suggests itself that if something of all this is not due to Mr. Barnum, much of it may certainly be due to the partner of his early life, the creator of his many beautiful homes which have adorned our city, she whose memory will be ever green in the hearts of those who knew her best. No one who was acquainted with the late Mrs. B., but knew her almost idolizing love for all that is beautiful in the world of tree and flower, and *Iranistan*. Lindencroft and Waldemere have been and are fit embodiments of her taste for elegant adornment. And such an example has not been lost upon the inhabitants of Bridgeport. Many years ago, when we, then outsiders, first heard of Bridgeport, we learned to know it because Barnum lived here, and he lived here because 'Charity' built for him.

"*Iranistan*, built when he was abroad, and surrounded it with all the loveliness of nature and art. I can well imagine how other matrons and other households, stimulated by such au example, have built more wisely and spent more time and effort in beautifying and adorning their homes. After the trial by fire and by time came Lindencroft; less pretentious, but perhaps not less beautiful in its chaste simplicity, and last of all she fashioned Waldemere; and we shall never gaze upon its rounding slope of sun-kissed lawn with its rich borders of bright, fragrant flowers, upon its mounds of moss-grown stone and shell, its wooded park and its wave-washed shore (only the rim of our fair park between) without remembering her to whom I believe this community are indirectly so deeply indebted for so much that is beautiful about our homes. The contagion of example is intense and effective, and I can readily see how it spread from these houses which your wealth erected and her taste adorned, to others less pretentious— spread, because the loving heart and the fervent mind of woman is always ready for such an influence. And just here, Mr. Barnum, in the name of the citizens of Bridgeport and of strangers who may visit here, I desire to thank you for again throwing open to the public your beautiful grounds at Waldemere, your latest and perhaps your best model of a charming home. It has been well said 'that he who causes two blades of grass to grow where but one has grown before is a public benefactor.' If this is true, he who converts a New England cow pasture into an almost perfect paradise of loveliness, and then lets down the bars and says to all man and womankind, 'come in and enjoy this with me,' shall at least receive our warmest thanks.

"Mr. Barnum has always been a good feeder, but by no means a high liver, and herein is one great secret of his health. Good, plain, substantial food, and plenty of it; for the solid physique, with the constantly worked brain and nerve and muscle, must needs find plenty of good blood with which to replenish. I remember very well one summer when I was frequently at his house, Mr. Barnum's dessert, day after day, was cold boiled rice and milk. Very simple and very nutritious. No irritating stimulants; no dyspeptic pastry. Show him the reasonableness and healthfulness of taking a given food or drink, it would be tried; of denying it and it was 'passed.' And with all respect to Mr. Barnum's unselfishness (just here I imagine) lies the foundation of his anti-rum and anti-tobacco principles. He made up his mind, saw, felt and was convinced it was an injury to him, and, presto, he would have none of it. So, he has been the foe of rum and tobacco, and he believes they are his and the foes of all mankind. He says they break down, they weaken, they destroy. So, he fights them, especially the former, with lance well held in rest, and with his well-known vigor and zeal.

"But, sir, you have always shown your love for us by spending your money freely in our midst. Your open grounds at Waldemere 'so passing fair,' will prove a rapid education in the love of the beautiful."

Next in order came "The City of Hartford" responded to by David Clark, Esq., of that city. Mr. Clark said:

"To show you how he is appreciated in Hartford, I will tell you what a citizen said of him: 'If he had been a citizen of Hartford, it would have been the capital of the State twenty years ago, and a city of one hundred thousand inhabitants. (Applause.)

Instead of being at the head of sloop navigation, the ocean steamers would have arrived at her ports by some Suez Canal that he would have constructed.' I only have to say that I hope Mr. Barnum will send that man a ticket to his Roman Hippodrome. (Laughter and cheers.) Twenty-six years ago, I visited Bridgeport, but saw the elements of success were wanting, out since then her advancement has been excelled by no town in the State, which is in a treat degree owing to the energy and public spirit of your distinguished fellow-townsman. For this he is entitled to great credit, and this honor is justly due him, and his memory will always be cherished by those who know the story of his good deeds. Shakespeare made Mark Antony say that 'the evil men do, lives after them, while the good they do is often interred with their bones.' That might do for that generation, but henceforth it is the good men do that will live after them." (Applause.)

Mr. Clark sat down amid applause, and the Chairman announced the "Town of Danbury." responded to by the Hon. D.P. Nichols, of that place, who thanked the committee for the compliment to Danbury, and closed with the wish that Mr. Barnum might live long to benefit the city of his adoption, and honor the place of his nativity.

Mr. Nichols received hearty applause.

Next on the program was a poem by Judge S. B. Sumner. It was splendidly delivered, kept the company in a roar of laughter, and is one of the happiest efforts that Judge Sumner has ever produced. We are pleased to be able to lay it before our readers, and can assure them that it is simply "perfect of its kind," but needs the Judge's excellent delivery to be properly set out. Round after round of applause greeted every happy hit, and compelled a temporary suspension of the reading.

JUDGE S. B. SUMNER'S POEM

"I'm no pianist; ne'ertheless a paean I must sing, this night in honor of our guest, the famous Money-King; The man who keeps informing us that poverty's a blunder, and rolls up wealth before our eyes, while we look on and wonder.

"There's no such thing as ciphering the gauge of such a man; Today its business in New York—tomorrow in Japan; One day beneath the sea, to find some learned, lovely shark, The next, way off on Ararat, for pieces of the Ark!

"Sometimes he calls for quarter, with the giant Fe-Fo-Fum; And then again he captures us with General Tom Thumb; One day in Bridgeport, staking out new streets across his farm, The next, in Windsor Castle, with Victoria on his arm;

"One day upon the prairies, looking out for freaks of nature; The next, in Hartford, speech-making before the Legislature; One day the Bearded Woman; next, the Mermaid with her comb: And now the Hippopotamus, and now the Hippodrome.

BARNUM FIVE SECONDS AHEAD

"Today recalling from the deep, oblivious shades of death, and so rejuvenating and rejoicing old Joice Heth; Tomorrow, showing all at once, the wondrous Twins of Siam, And Julius Caesar's boxing-gloves, and fish-pole used by Priam.

"One day the fiery element his big Museum slashes, but next day, lo! it rises as a Phoenix from its ashes; And while the croakers shake their heads, and dubiously figure. The Crocodile gives broader smiles, the show keeps growing bigger!

"I never, never, saw his like; and so I might as well Give o'er at once the vain attempt all his exploits to tell; It's all recorded— read of all — on everybody's shelf; the biography of P.T. Barnum. written by himself.'

"There's not a journal round the world, whose columns haven't known 'im Nor board fence, on whose superfice bill-posters haven't shown him; No savage or philosopher, no Gentile, Greek or Roman. But knows of this ubiquitous, inevitable showman.

"But 'showman' though he style himself, we know the word but tells a vulgar fraction of what force within his manhood dwells; An orator of wide repute, a poet and a preacher. An author and an editor, a student and a teacher!

"A wit of ever-ready fund within his storehouse ample; Of Temperance, alike renowned Apostle and example: Philanthropist, with human kind not merely sympathetic, But generous and bountiful, and grandly energetic.

"And last — by no means least — of all; and that is why we come Thus heartily to welcome him— a lover of his home! A home that proudly crowns today a whilom barren waste, The triumph and the marvel now of fine aesthetic taste!

"But prouder monument for him: within the city's bound, Full many a score of happy habitations may be found. Whose owners will not soon forget the prudent head that planned the homes they ne'er had builded, but for Barnum's helping hand!

"Oh, when the leaf of human life is turning sere and yellow, One's best reflection can but be, that be bus served his fellow; How many a man had been a wreck, whose fate had quite undone him If Barnum hadn't raised, and put wheels under him, and 'run him.'

"Now, if our fellow citizen had been a sordid hunks. Who hoarded all his treasures in old stockings and in trunks, we simply should have set him down a flinty-hearted sinner, instead of voting him a 'brick' and complimentary dinner.

"And so, we wish it understood, and thoroughly inferred, These testimonials of esteem — we mean them, every word, We toast not wealth, nor simply brains, but, as we proudly can. The qualities that always make the hero and the man.

'Long life and health to him and his, to do and gather good, And when at last he shall be called to cross the Stygian Hood, Surviving friends, with tearful eyes. beholding him embark, Shall place his statue, I predict, within the Seaside Park;

"And every boy who looks thereon, the record shall review, And learn what steady Yankee pluck and industry can do; And as our city grows apace, au ever crescent fame, As halo, shall surround her pristine Benefactor's name.

"And meanwhile, he'll be ransacking the Universe for 'stars,' And lav a cable through the air from Jupiter to Mars, And institute a comet race, on some tremendous wager, And case up Taurus, Scorpio, the Whale, and Ursa Major!

"And mire the Twins— on Gemini! — to manage a balloon, And make an exhibition of the old man in the moon; And in the vast arena, pit the Sickle of the Lion. Against the vaunted sword and belt of arrogant Orion

"And, finally, discovering the brink of Hades' crater, Put out the conflagration with his Fire Annihilator; Exorcise from the neighborhood, the 'cussed' imps of evil, Nor rest, till he has raised, reformed, and then — engaged— the Devil!

When quiet had been restored, Mayor Clarke announced "The Bar and Bench," to which the Hon. J.C. Loomis eloquently replied. His remarks commanded marked attention and appreciative and hearty applause. "The Veterans of the Show Business" was then announced by the chairman, and was responded to by Mr. Fordyce Hitchcock, of New York, who alluded to his management for Mr. Barnum of the old Museum for many years, and who said:

"It has ever been the endeavor of my friend to avoid everything calculated to offend the most delicate taste or mislead the mind of the young (Applause.) But it is said Barnum is a grand humbug. I ask if any went into his Museum that did not get his money's worth. I have traveled over Europe and found no place that compared with Barnum's old Museum. And that institution saved many young men, who sought it instead of going into dens of vice. If that is being a humbug, let us all learn to be humbugs." (Applause.)

The chair then announced that the lateness of the evening compelled a shortening of the program, and that the Rev. Dr. Hopper would respond to the toast "The Clergy" as the last sentiment of the evening.

DR. HOPPER'S SPEECH.

"Mr. Mayor and Gentlemen: I am glad that I have the pleasure of being present on this occasion. I desire to add my little quota to the interest of the hour. I bring all of which my nature is susceptible, for I am in entire rapport with the object of the meeting. It seems to be highly befitting that the clergy should be represented at this banquet given in honor of our esteemed guest, and I am glad that the custom which once prevailed in old England of dismissing the clergy to an ante-room after the saying of grace, does not prevail in this country, but that with impunity they may sit through the entire feast, par taking of the choicest viands, sharing even in the offering of genial toasts. It is proper that we should be present at this time for many reasons. In the first place, our honored friend has always taken kindly to the clergy, ever ready to manifest a genuine and tangible sympathy for them in their sacred mission. Mr. Barnum, during his long and eventful life, has "fastened, as with hooks of steel, to his broad nature many of the clergy of every denomination, who are among his truest and most devoted friends. Among this number are the distinguished Drs. Chapin, Cuyler, Thomas, Emerson and others, who. had circumstances permitted, would have gladly been personally present, and brought floral wreaths as expressions of their sincere sympathy and affection for the man. And many of the profession, who have fallen upon sleep, resting from life's conflicts, could they leave their quiet graves, or celestial homes, would be here and vie with us in our offerings. Let us believe, as it is not inconsistent with our holy faith, that unseen they are bending over us.

"It is befitting that we should speak, because I think our friend may have been originally designed for the church. I don't know that he ever himself harbored such a thought, I only judge from his youthful reply, as a Sunday-school scholar, to the question implied in the words of Christ to Martha, 'One thing is needful.' I quote the closing paragraph: 'The one thing needful,' says the young preacher, 'is to believe on the Lord Jesus Christ, follow in his footsteps, love God, and obey his commandments, love our fellow-man. and embrace every opportunity of administering to his necessities. In short, the one thing needful is, to live a life that we can always look back upon with satisfaction, and be enabled ever to contemplate its termination with trust in Him who has so kindly vouchsafed it to us, surrounding us with innumerable blessings, if we have but the heart and wisdom to receive them in a proper manner.

"Noble sentiment for a youth! Surely, here is a minister in embryo. I could wish that with a sanctified life, he had elevated himself to this noble calling. No doubt but that he would have been greatly successful. With his fine mesmerism, how he would have electrified the people; what a spiritual showman he would have made; how he would have exhibited the menagerie of the heart, in which ferocious beasts, in the form of fiery passions, prey upon the soul. And with his genial love and trust in mankind, seeing ever the good in the midst of degrading vices, how lovingly he would have exhibited the true and the noble still lingering in man's nature, more beautiful than birds of tropical plumage, even the birds of Paradise. Indeed, in some departments of our work, we claim Mr. B. as a faithful, earnest laborer. We all know how devoted he has been for years to the cause of temperance. In all our churches, as well as in public halls, his manly, persuasive voice has been lifted up against the evil. What hard, stunning blows he has dealt upon the face of this modern Moloch, at whose fiery shrine thousands are yearly sacrificed. The cause of temperance is the cause of true religion. In the name of humanity, we thank him for these efforts.

"It is befitting that the clergy should here have a voice, because our friend, in addition to the great interest which he has always taken in the secular affairs of our city, has never failed to generously assist the churches in the days of their weakness and poverty.

"He doubtless saw that the growth and prosperity of his favorite city would largely depend upon the elevating influence of Christian sanctuaries. In almost every church book in the city is recorded at different limes a liberal subscription from Mr. B.

"And I here acknowledge the generous aid, pecuniarily, which he rendered to the church over which I have the honor to preside, in the days of her feebleness.

"So, then, I say again, most emphatically, it is highly befitting that the clergy have a voice at this festival.

"In closing, please, friend Barnum. accept our kind congratulations and offerings of sincere friendship. As the years with you roll on towards the deep sunset, may you find the evening of life serene and beautiful, and your faith in God and love for humanity increase as the shadows longer grow."

Mr. George Mallory begged leave to offer, as a final sentiment, the following, one in which any could join: "May the flag at Waldemere long continue to float over that dwelling, indicating, as it does, that its owner is 'at home.' " (Applause.)

Three cheers were then called for by Mayor Clarke in honor of P.T. Barnum, which were given with a rousing will, and the company dispersed at about one o'clock.

Among those present who would have been called upon to speak, had not the lateness of the hour prevented, were the Rev. E.W. Maxey, the Rev. Edwin Johnson, the Rev. D.O. Ferns, the Rev. Father Synott. the Rev. Dr. Richardson, the Rev. N.L. Briggs, and others.

It must be a matter of congratulation to Mr. Barnum that this entire movement was so spontaneous, and that no effort was needed to make it a grand success. There was a balance in the hands of the committee of fifty dollars, which was given to the Bridgeport Orphan Asylum.

[From the *Republican Standard* (Editorial), July 3, 1874.]

P. T. BARNUM.

The press and the people of Bridgeport united in an ovation to P.T. Barnum, Thursday evening, in acknowledgment of the honor due him for the public improvements he has inaugurated and pushed through in this city, with unceasing energy, for the past thirty years. To the press he acknowledges his obligations for success in life. It has given him fame, so far and wide that his name is familiar to every eye that can read and every ear that can hear, while almost every pocket has contributed to his store of wealth. Without the press, he says he would today "be a pigmy no bigger than Tom Thumb," instead of being at the head' of his profession. If the press is thus the father of P.T. Barnum, it follows that it is the grandfather of East Bridgeport and all other public improvements wrought out by his hand. It is to be hoped, therefore, that East Bridgeport will hold its grand* father in all due honor and reverence.

We have always admired the public spirit of P.T. Barnum. He is accustomed to work with herculean energy and enthusiasm to acquire his money, and then he shows the same zeal in spending it, and to this characteristic Bridgeport is indebted for all those public improvements inaugurated by him. We admire the way and manner in which he works out his plans. Instead of sending petitions to the Common Council, having committees appointed to examine and report, advertising for hearings, ordering the street commissioners to do the work, then make assessments, having appeals to the board of review, and all that, he merely tells "Dave Sherwood " to open a street here, fill up a swamp there, dig down this hill, blast out that rock, build houses, etc., and the work is done and he is ready for the next one, before he even could get a petition through the Common Council. It may be very true that he does all these things for the sake of making more money thereby, yet this fact by no means lessens the obligations of Bridgeporters to him, but they might well pray for a dozen more such men who have sufficient intelligence to perceive that their own personal interests can be best advanced in making public improvements.

As a specimen of his style of working for himself and the public combined, we may refer to his straightening and extending State street. Formerly State street beyond Park avenue, turned at an angle north-westerly, he caused a change in its direction, widening it, filled up a swamp in his own land and made a good firm road across it, moved one large block of houses, and spent some $12,000 in the operation, thus making a line public improvement which will be beneficial to the city as long as the city lasts. All this he did without calling for aid outside of his own pocket. But in doing this he saw that the street when extended beyond, would greatly enhance the value of his property and yield him a rich return, perhaps at no distant day. This is his usual mode of working, and though private interests may prompt his action, yet he so works in all his improvements that the public shares very largely in the accruing advantages. Any city is blessed which has such intelligent persons whose motto is "to do good and to make money" without being so selfish as to refrain from any work because they do not get all the good that comes from their venture. It is for such deeds that the citizens of Bridgeport have worthily honored Mr. Barnum.

The American Register, published in Paris, in its issue of July 11, 1874, speaking of this dinner, says:

The press, the pulpit, the bench and bar were all liberally represented. It may seem strange to Europeans that such distinguished men should accept invitations to a dinner in honor of a common showman, as Mr. Barnum is too often called; but their surprise will cease when we tell them what that gentleman really is. True, he is a showman, but he is also a man of considerable personal acquirements, of great public spirit, and a good citizen. He is an excellent representative of the indomitable strength and energy of our young nation. Moreover, he is a man of great generosity, and knows how to spend money as well as to make it. By this we mean that he spends it in a way which tends to the public good. There are very few men who have ever known Mr. Barnum who would not have been pleased to join in a dinner given to him, and since we were not able to be present on the occasion, we are happy to pay our tribute in another form to that liberal-minded and large-hearted man.

LINES

ATTESTED BY A DRIVE TO P.T. BARNUM'S PLACE (WALDEMERE) AT SEASIDE PARK, PORT, CONN., FIVE YEARS AFTER ITS COMPLETION.

Fair Waldemerel Thou gem of art and nature,
Glorified by breath of June like emerald
In diamond setting! With thy rich robe
Of verdure and sparkling waves
Of ocean dancing round thy
Borders— glancing and Hashing in the
Sunlight, meet setting for a spot
So fair! The stranger's eye
Resteth upon thee as some surprising
Scene of marvelous beauty, bursting
Upon the gaze with all thy ease
And grace of architecture,
Adorned with fountain, statuette and
Floral vase, each in its favorite niche
In favored *Waldemere*—
Well chosen spot!

By Seaside murmuring— and well
Combined its mansion of palatial
Structure, rearing its grand
Proportions with many varied
Turrets, in graceful dignity.
Floating aloft, its silken banner
Waves from crowning tower,
Bearing its owner's monogram
On its proud silken folds.

No need in statue bronze of stalwart
Indian, with springing wolf at feet
And tomahawk in hand.
To guard thy entrance, fair *Waldemere*,
For who would mar such scene
Of beauty, made for the eye to
Feast upon? Who could defile thy
Precincts, or with evil wish to
Harm thee, while with inviting
Aspect such harmony of art and
Nature greets the human vision?
Dark and unlighted be the
Heart, which ruthlessly would violate
Such type of Paradise.
Farewell, sweet *Waldemere*:

I ne'er may look upon thy face again.
But I will leave the token of a stranger's
Benediction, for the ray of happiness
And sunshine thou hast unconscious
Shed upon the traveler's heart.

H.E.B. Bridgeport, June, 1874.

CHAPTER XLIX.

HIPPODROMICAL, HYMENEAL AND MUNICIPAL.

In July, 1974, immense canvas tents were made of sufficient capacity to accommodate all my great Roman Hippodrome performances. These tents, with the expense of removing the whole Hippodrome establishment to Boston for a three weeks' exhibition, cost me nearly fifty thousand dollars. During the three weeks' exhibition in Boston, the tents were crowded each afternoon and evening with the most delighted audiences. Excursion trains on all the railroads leading to Boston brought thousands of visitors to the Hippodrome every day, and the Boston and New England papers, secular and religious, without exception, were loud in praise of what all acknowledged to be by far the most gorgeous, extensive, instructive and expensive traveling exhibition of which we have any record.

From Boston the entire Hippodrome was transported by railroad to Philadelphia, where a success was achieved fully equal to that in Boston. The Hippodrome afterwards visited Baltimore, Pittsburgh and Cincinnati, everywhere drawing immense crowds, and opened again in my great Hippodrome building in New York, in November, where, for several months, it afforded a treat to the American public that will probably not be witnessed again in this generation. I am confident that nothing less than my reputation for forty years as a liberal caterer for public instruction and amusement, would have brought a paying response to my efforts. The great religious community aided mostly in sustaining this hazardous enterprise.

In the autumn of 1874, I married again. My second wife is the daughter of my old English friend, John Fish, Esq., whom I have embalmed in the thirty-second chapter of this book, under the title of "An Enterprising Englishman." We were married in the Church of the Divine Paternity, Fifth Avenue, New York, by my old and esteemed friend, the Rev. Dr. Chapin, in the presence of members of my family and a large gathering of gratified friends. After a brief bridal tour, our wedding receptions were attended at Waldemere.

In December, 1874, His Majesty, David Kalakau, King of the Sandwich Islands, visited New York. I invited the king and his suite to attend the Hippodrome, which they did on the afternoon of December 26th. During the entire performance, I was seated by the side of the king, who kept up a pleasant conversation with me for a couple of hours. I took occasion to remind him that this was by no means the first time I had had the honor of "entertaining " royalty, as he would see from my book — a handsome presentation copy of which he had accepted from me on Christmas day. He expressed himself highly delighted with my entertainment, and said he was always fond of horses and racing. Some twelve thousand persons were present, and when the exhibitions were about half finished they called loudly "The King! The King!" Turning to me, His Majesty inquired the meaning of this, I replied: "Your Majesty, this vast audience undoubtedly wishes to give you an ovation. This building is so large that they cannot distinctly see Your Majesty from every part, and are anxious that you should ride around the circle in order that they may greet you."

The king looked surprised, and presently the audience commenced calling "The King! Barnum! Barnum! The King!" At that moment my open barouche was driven into the circle and approached where we were sitting.

"No doubt Your Majesty would greatly gratify my countrymen," I remarked, "if you would kindly step into this carriage with me and ride around the circle." The king immediately arose, and, amid tremendous cheering, he stepped into the carriage. I took a seat by his side, and he smilingly remarked, sotto voce: "We are all actors."

The audience rose to their feet, cheered and waved their handkerchiefs as the king rode around the circle, raising his hat and bowing. The excitement was indeed tremendous. The king remained till all the performances were finished, and expressed himself as greatly pleased with the whole entertainment. A prominent New York paper, in speaking of this event, said:

"Of course, Americans see no impropriety in King Kalakau's responding to the public call to show himself to the multitude by riding around the Hippodrome ring. Had an American President or other distinguished American gentleman thus responded, it would have been considered as quite the thing in this republican country. To Europeans, however, it will look very different. They will be astonished that any man on earth would have had the presumption to propose making a show of a living monarch, albeit his kingdom may not be the most extensive in the world, and we confess that, in our opinion, the only human being on the footstool who would have the temerity to show up a king is our worthy countryman, Phineas T. Barnum."

I trust that King Kalakau saw no "temerity" in my proposition. At all events, he seemed to enjoy his reception, and so did I, and, as they say in whist, "the honors are easy."

It is said that "It never rains, but it pours." and just at this time I was visited by a shower of royalty and nobility. The King of Hawaii had scarcely left New York before I received an invitation to breakfast with Lord Rosebery at the Brevoort House, Fifth Avenue. Lord Rosebery is a prominent member of the British Parliament, where he sits as Baron Rosebery. The invitation stated that his Lordship would sail for England on the twenty-seventh of January, and that having seen most of our country, and its "lions," he did not like to leave without having an interview with Barnum. I accepted the invitation. The breakfast came off at ten o'clock in the morning of January 26th, and I need scarcely say that it was a most dainty, delightful and *recherche* affair. Only one gentleman besides his Lordship was present. I found my host a very intelligent gentleman. He had been in America once before, and he seemed well "posted" in regard to our country and its institutions. He said he had read my autobiography, and had witnessed with amazement and delight the scenes at my Roman Hippodrome. These enhanced his desire to see "the man who was so celebrated throughout the world for the magnitude and perfection of his enterprises as a caterer for public gratification."

I accepted the compliment as gracefully as I could, and we were soon conversing socially without restraint on either side. Lord Rosebery is a good story-teller, and, what is still more pleasing to a loquacious old traveler like myself, he is a capital listener. While discussing the luxurious meal, we interchanged amusing anecdotes and personal experiences, some of mine so tickling his lordship's keen sense of humor that, more than once, he pushed back his chair from the table and gave vent to his hilarity in hearty, unrestrained laughter.

After a couple of hours we parted, exchanging photographs and autographs. His lordship expressed himself highly pleased with the interview, and politely added that he hoped to meet me in England, whenever I shall carry out my intention of taking a great show to that country.

In March, 1875, the nomination for Mayor of the city of Bridgeport was tendered me by a committee from the Republican party, but I declined until assured by prominent members of the opposition that my nomination was intended as a compliment, and that both parties would sustain it. Politically, the city is largely democratic, but I led the republican ticket, and was elected, April 5th, by several hundred majority. On the twelfth of April the newly elected Common Council held its first meeting, on which occasion I delivered the following Inaugural Address:

Gentlemen of the Common Council:

Entrusted as we are, by the votes of our fellow-citizens, with the care and management of their interests, it behooves us to endeavor to merit the confidence reposed in us. We are sometimes called the "fathers of the city." Certainly, our duty is, and our pleasure should be, to administer the municipal government as a good and wise father conducts his household, caring for all, partial to none. No personal feelings should dictate our official acts. "We are not placed here to gratify personal or party resentment, nor to extend personal or party favor in any manner that may in the remotest degree conflict with the best interests of our city. As citizens we enjoy a great common interest. Each individual is a member of the body corporate, and no member can be unduly favored or unjustly oppressed without injury to the entire community. No person or party can afford to be dishonest. Honesty is always the best policy, for "with what measure ye mete it shall be measured to you again."

A large portion of this honorable body are now serving officially for the first time, and therefore may not be fully acquainted with the details of its workings; but we are all acquainted with the great principles of Justice and Right. If we fail to work according to these eternal principles, we betray the confidence placed in us, and this our year of administration will be remembered with disapprobation and contempt.

Let us bring to our duties careful judgment and comprehensive views with regard to expenditure, so that we may be neither parsimonious nor extravagant, but, like a prudent householder, ever careful that expenses shall be less than the income.

Our city is peculiarly adapted for commercial purposes; it should be our care therefore to adopt such measures as tend to promote trade, manufactures and commerce. Its delightful and healthy locality makes it also a desirable place of residence. We should strive to enhance its natural beauty, to improve our streets and, with moderate expenditure, to embellish our parks, by which means we shall attract refined and wealthy residents.

As conservators of the public peace and morals it is our duty to prevent, so far as possible, acts which disturb one or the other, and to enforce the laws in an impartial and parental spirit.

The last report of our Chief of Police says: "'Tis a sad and painful duty, yet candor compels us to state that at least ninety per cent, of the causes of all the arrests during the year are directly traceable to the immoderate use of intoxicating liquors, not to speak of the poverty and misery it has caused families which almost daily come under our observation."

In the town of Vineland, N. J., where no intoxicating drinks are sold, the over- seer of the poor stated in his annual report that in a population of 10,000 there was but one indictment in six months, and that the entire police expenses were but seventy-five dollars: per year, the sum paid to him, and the poor expenses a mere trifle. He further says: "We practically have no debt, and our taxes are only one per cent, on the valuation." Similar results are reported in the town of Greeley, Colorado, where no liquors are sold.

Our laws license the sale of intoxicating drinks under certain restrictions on week days, but no man can claim the right under such license to cause mobs, riots, bloodshed or murder. Hence no man has, or can have, any right by license or otherwise to dispense liquors to intoxicated persons, nor to furnish sufficient liquor to cause intoxication. Our duty is therefore to see that the police aid in regulating to the extent of their legal power a traffic which our laws do not wholly prohibit. Spirituous liquors of the present day are so much adulterated and doubly poisoned that their use fires the brain and drives their victims to madness, violence and murder. The money annually expended for intoxicating drinks, and the cost of their evil results in Bridgeport or any other American city where liquor-selling is licensed, would pay the entire expenses of the city (if liquors were not drank), including the public schools, give a good suit of clothes to every poor person of both sexes, a barrel of flour to every poor family living within its municipal boundaries, and leave a handsome surplus on hand. Our enormous expenses for the trial and punishment of criminals, as well as for the support of the poor, are mainly caused by this traffic. Surely then it is our duty to do all we can, legally, to limit and mitigate its evil as no person ever became a drunkard who did not sincerely regret that he or she ever tasted intoxicating drinks, it is a work of mercy, as well as justice, to do all in our power to lessen this leprous hindrance to happiness. We should strive to exterminate gambling, prostitution and other crimes which have not *yet* attained to the dignity of a "license."

The public health demands that we should pay attention to necessary drainage, and prevent the sale of adulterated food. The invigorating breezes from Long Island Sound, and the absence of miasmatic marshes serve to make ours one of the most healthy cities in America. Scientific experiments made daily during the whole of last year have established the fact that our atmosphere is impregnated with ozone, or concentrated oxygen, to an extent not hitherto discovered on this continent. No city of the same size in America, is so extensively known throughout our own land and in Europe as Bridgeport. It should be our pleasure to strengthen all natural advantages which we possess as a city by maintaining a government of corresponding excellence.

A plentiful supply of pure water is necessary to the health of a city. Experience has proved that the city should own and control the Water Works, or require the Water Company to furnish a regular and reliable supply sufficient for the wants and necessities of the people. I invite your most serious and disinterested consideration of "the water question."

The custom of selling fruits and vegetables by measure tempts to fraud, and I earnestly recommend that the practice of selling these products by weight be adopted in this city.

Every employee of the city should be strictly held to perform the duty assigned and to earn the money paid him. We should support no drones.

All condemned prisoners should be kept continually employed, and thus made to contribute to their own support, and the expenses incurred by their wrong doing.

As cleanliness is conducive alike to health and morality, I recommend that we establish one or more floating baths, a portion of which might be free, and the rest subject to a small charge, which would nearly or quite cover the expense of the whole.

As the city at certain periods is obliged to borrow money on which it pays interest, I advise that at seasons when the city treasury has a surplus, we shall, as is customary in other cities, place this money where it will draw interest until needed.

It is painful to the industrious and moral portions of our people to see so many loungers about the streets, and such a multitude whose highest aspirations seem to be to waste their time in idleness or at baseball, billiards, etc.

No person needs to be unemployed who is not over fastidious about the kind of occupation. There are too many soft hands (and heads) waiting for light work and heavy pay. Better work for half a loaf than beg or steal a whole one. Mother earth is always nearby, and ready to respond to reasonable drafts on her never-failing treasury. A patch of potatoes raised "on shares" is preferable to a poulticed pate earned in a whisky scrimmage. Some modern Micawbers stand with folded hands waiting for the panic to pass, as the foolish man waited for the river to run dry and allow him to walk over.

The soil is the foundation of American prosperity. Then multitudes of our consumers become producers; when fashion teaches economy, instead of expending for a gaudy dress what would comfortably clothe the family; when people learn to walk until they can afford to ride; when the poor man ceases to spend more for tobacco than for bread; when those who complain of panics learn that "we cannot eat our cake and keep it," that a sieve will not hold water, that we must rely on our own exertions and earn before we expend, then will panics cease and prosperity return. "While we should by no means unreasonably restrict healthy recreation, we should remember that "time is money," that idleness leads to immoral habits, and that the peace, prosperity and character of a city depend on the intelligence, integrity, industry and frugality of its inhabitants.

Frank Leslie's Illustrated Newspaper of July 24th, contained a picture entitled "His Honor P.T. Barnum, Mayor of Bridgeport, Presiding at a Meeting of the Common Council of that City." The editor's remarks are as follows:

Mayor Barnum's message was a model of brevity and practical thought. Having at the beginning of his official career declared war against the whisky dealers, he next proceeded to open the struggle. For twenty years the saloons had been kept open on Sundays, and it was declared impossible to close them. Mr. Barnum has all his life acted upon the quaint French aphorism that "nothing is so possible as the impossible." He gave notice that the saloons must be closed. A select committee of citizens volunteered to aid in collecting testimony in case the sellers should disregard the proclamation, and leave the latch-string to their back doors displayed on the outside. Although the doors were open, the keepers refused to sell except to personal friends. The committee-men stood opposite the saloons, and took the names of a dozen or so who were admitted. The next morning the saloon-keepers were arrested, and when they found their "friends" had been subpoenaed to appear as witnesses, they pleaded guilty and immediately brought out their pocket-books to pay the judicial "shot." This plan effectually broke up Sunday traffic in liquor, thus insuring a quiet day for the citizens, and greatly accommodating the saloon-keepers, the best portion of whom really favor a general closing on Sunday.

The next reform was directed against a private gas corporation that had been lighting the streets at a figure that he deemed exorbitant. A contract was made with a Boston portable gas company, by which the cost of keeping the city bright at night was reduced one-half.

But the most striking of all was his action against the water-works corporation, of which he was, with one exception, the largest stockholder. He denounced the management severely for not keeping good faith with the city under the charter given it, and appointed a committee of investigation. A report was submitted with a recommendation that the corporation be sued and deprived of its local privilege if it did not immediately conform to the letter of its agreement, and Mr. Barnum promptly concurred in the recommendation. He also appointed a Retrenchment Committee, through the investigation of which he expects to affect a still further reduction of local expenses.

This is good work for two months, and the citizens have a grateful appreciation of this new phase of his joking propensities. Although now sixty-five years of age, the same patient industry that has made him the prince of entertainers, marks all his official actions. He is honest, impartial, laborious; far-seeing, judicious and sanguine. Care finds as firm a resting-place upon him as water does on a duck's back. By nature, an organizer of men and systems, he is his own best executive officer. No one knows so well as he how men may be best governed, and no one can so pleasantly polish oil the rough sides of mankind. Successful beyond the usual measure as an intelligent, courteous and considerate showman, he has already proved himself the most acceptable of mayors.

During my administration as Mayor, I had occasion three times to veto certain propositions of the Common Council.

At the dawn of the second century of our national existence I issued the following proclamation, and was glad to see that my suggestions were patriotically and enthusiastically carried out by my constituents:

Mayor's Office, Bridgeport, Ct., Dec. 30, 1875.

To the Citizens of Bridgeport:

The experiment of a people governing themselves has been tried on this continent for a hundred years. During this period, and under this rule, we have grown to such proportions, prosperity and power, as has never been attained in a century by any nation under monarchical government As a nation we owe unbounded gratitude to the Fathers of the Republic who by toil, sacrifice and blood, planted the seed of this great and free nation.

As citizens of one of the most prosperous, delightful and healthy cities in Puritan New England, I know you will rejoice to recognize in some befitting manner the beginning of the second century of our great and noble Republic.

I recommend, therefore, that a national salute be fired, the bells of our city be rung for half an hour, beginning at midnight of Friday, and that Saturday, the birthday of our centennial year, be celebrated with even greater demonstrations of joy and enthusiasm than marks our anniversary of American Independence. Especially do I request that the national emblem shall adorn our public buildings, and that all citizens shall display the American flag from their residences and places of business.

P. T. BARNUM, Mayor.

My Hippodrome, in 1875, was transported by rail throughout the United States, going as far east as Portland, Maine, and west to Kansas City, Missouri It proved a tolerably successful season, notwithstanding the depressed state of finances generally.

It gives me pain to record that our aeronaut, Professor Donaldson, having made his daily balloon ascension on Thursday, July 15, from our Hippodrome grounds at Chicago, was never heard from afterwards. He took with him Mr. N.S. Grimwood, a reporter of the *Chicago Journal*, whose body was found in Lake Michigan a few weeks afterwards. Prof. Donaldson was doubtless drowned during the terrible storm which occurred on the night of the ascension. He was a man of excellent habits, clear brain and steady nerve, fearless, but not reckless, and respected by all who knew him. His last was his 138th ascension.

A couple of newspaper extracts, which are but a fair specimen of hundreds, will give an inkling of the enthusiasm with which my latest amusement enterprise was greeted throughout the entire country:

[From the *Providence (P. I.) Journal*, May 13, 1875.]

Phineas Taylor Barnum's Great Roman Hippodrome arrived yesterday as per announcement, and after a parade through the streets, that awakened everybody to a sense of its magnitude, gave two exhibitions on the Federal Street Common, which not only called together the largest audience ever seen in this city, but furnished them with such amusement and excitement as are rarely offered, and gave the most thorough satisfaction.

[From the *Troy Daily Press*, June, 1875.]

P.T. Barnum is probably the only man in the world who can keep together such a monstrous show and make it pay, as visited Troy yesterday. There were two performances, afternoon and evening, and the mammoth tent was crammed to its utmost capacity on each occasion. Scarcely a family in Troy that was not represented. All classes went, from the highest to the lowest. The reserved seat side was filled long before the performances began, so that those who were late were obliged to stand or go away. Hundreds were turned away, because there was not even standing room. It is safe to say that twenty-five thousand people witnessed the pageant. People from the surrounding country for thirty miles came on the cars, on horseback, and in wagons. The blockade of vehicles of every description for a quarter of a mile around the tents was unprecedented in this city. Everybody was pleased. Thousands, we might say, were so well pleased with the afternoon performance that they stand on the ground until evening and went in again. Some had lunches with them, and spread themselves out on the grass and waited for night. The program is too long to mention in detail. But there are scores of Interesting and thrilling acts which should be seen by everybody. Those who did not see the great show here yesterday missed an important event in their lives.

About the middle of June, I visited Niagara Falls with Mrs. Barnum and several friends, including Misses Pattie and Julia Hutchinson, of Southport, England, former neighbors of my wife, who were our guests during the summer. Leaving our friends at Niagara, my wife accompanied me to Akron, Ohio, where my Traveling World's Fair was to exhibit. On our arrival, the night before the show was to come, the Mayor of Akron waited on us. We were invited to a concert (where, in response to loud calls, I gave a short speech), and were afterwards serenaded at the hotel. The next morning, I was escorted to Buchtel College by its noble-hearted founder, Mr. J.R. Buchtel, and an old friend, Rev. D. C. Tomlinson. The students would not let me off without a speech. I gave them a few off-hand remarks which I hope may prove beneficial to some of my auditors. Returning to Buffalo we rejoined our friends, whom we left at Niagara, and there, too, I met the Hippodrome, which remained a couple of days. Early on the morning of the second day I dispatched a special train to Niagara Falls with some hundreds of our Hippodrome company, to whom I was glad to give this first opportunity of seeing the great Cataract. Our band accompanied them, crossed the Suspension Bridge to Canada, playing "God Save the Queen" and "Yankee Doodle," and returned to Buffalo in time for the afternoon exhibition. In July, I visited the Hippodrome at Chicago and St. Louis, being ten days absent from home. I spent most of the summer at Waldemere, looking after the interests of the city, and enjoying the season heartily with my family and friends. Our clam-bakes, picnics, charming country rides, weekly concerts in Seaside Park by our two best city bands, and numerous other pleasures in this most healthy and delightful locality, were extremely enjoyable, and caused the time to fly much more rapidly than we wished.

[From, the *Baltimore Saturday Night*, March 6, 1875.]

BARNUM AND HIS BOOK.

On last Sunday night a rather novel lecture, both as to theme and handling, was delivered by Henry Hilgert, Esq., at the hall of the *Turn Verein Vorwaerts* on Fayette street. The large hall was crowded with ladies and gentlemen, belonging largely to the more educated and refined class of Germans, and the audience having acquaintance with the orator through the medium several lectures delivered last year anticipated an instructive and agreeable entertainment. We are pleased to agree with the German daily papers of our city in the statement that the expectations of all who were present were more than realized.

Mr. Hilgert took for his text "Barnum and his Book."

After an interesting introduction of his subject, in which he dwelt with caustic severity upon the weakness of those who run into hasty judgment of men and their works without really knowing anything about them, the lecturer said: "As I know of no book which is better adapted to become a thoroughly instructive and agreeable guide through life, for the youths of our country, than the record and experiences of the exemplarily industrious, intelligent, strictly honest and moral citizen, Phineas Taylor Barnum, I will devote my today's address to him and his book." Charity Barnum, the showman's first wife, was very highly spoken of, and recommended to the ladies as a wife, mother and companion worth imitating.

Mr. Hilgert, after giving some of Barnum's anecdotes, which, by the way, he rendered to perfection, gave a graphic description of Barnum's career as a merchant, editor, showman, legislator and public lecturer, and in all was his enthusiastic panegyrist. In the description of Barnum's seven years' hard work to pay off over half a million dollars indebtedness incurred by endorsements for the Jerome Clock Company, the speaker waxed warm and eloquent, and called forth applause that testified fully to his ability as an advocate.

After explaining Barnum's manly behavior in great pecuniary catastrophes, and after giving a graphic description of Barnum's suffering in Hamburg in 1873 upon the arrival of the news of the death of his beloved wife, Mr. Hilgert concluded his lecture with the following words:

"I have perhaps detained you longer than you anticipated, and certainly longer than I should have done if I had been able to compress the abundance of interesting material into a smaller compass, and, at the conclusion of my address, I give you my thanks for your very close attention, and I pray you to recommend the good citizen, Phineas Taylor Barnum, to your children as an exemplary man. When you give one of your daughters away in matrimony, advise her to imitate Charity Barnum; when your son leaves home to try his luck upon the ocean of life, give him Barnum for a guide; when you yourself are in trouble and misery and near desperation, take from Barnum's life and teachings consolation and new courage, and, after you all have received instructive enjoyment from Barnum's mind, heart, and actions, join me in the wish that the old gentleman in his new matrimony may find many joyful and happy days."

The applause, which during the lecture on several occasions was loud enough, was almost deafening at its conclusion.

During the autumn of 1875, under the auspices of "The Redpath Lyceum Bureau," in Boston, I delivered about thirty times a lecture on "The World and How to Live in It," going as far east as Thomaston, Maine, and west to Leavenworth, Kansas, and including the cities of Boston, Portland, Chicago, Kansas City, etc. When finished, the Bureau wrote me as follows: "In parting for a season, please allow us to say that none of our best lecturers have succeeded in delighting our audiences and lecture committees so well as yourself."

On November 28, and following days, I offered all my show property at auction. This included my Hippodrome and also my "World's Fair," consisting of museum, menagerie and circus property. My object was to get rid of all surplus stock, and henceforth to have but one traveling show, which, as ever, should be as good as money and experience could make it. To this end my agent bid in all such property as I could use, and now I am properly prepared for our Centennial year. My traveling show consisted of Museum, Menagerie and Circus of immense proportions, and I introduced patriotic features that gave the people a Fourth of July celebration every day. My establishment traveled in three trains of railway cars. We took along a battery of cannon, and every morning we fired a salute of thirteen guns. We introduced groups of persons costumed in the style of our Continental troops, and supplemented with the Goddess of Liberty, a live eagle and some first-class singers, who, with a chorus of several hundred voices, sang the "Star Spangled Banner" and other patriotic songs, accompanied with bands of music and also with cannon placed outside our tents, and fired by means of electricity. We closed our patriotic demonstration by singing "America" ("My Country, 'Tis of Thee "), the entire audience rising and joining in the chorus. At night we terminated our performances with fireworks, in which thrilling revolutionary scenes were brilliantly depicted. Our grand street procession was a gorgeous and novel feature. It began to move when the salute was fired, and I depended upon the patriotism of each town we visited to add to the effects of our National Jubilee by ringing of bells at the same time. My assistant managers were my son-in-law, Mr. Hurd, and Messrs. Smith Brothers June and Bailey, late proprietors of the European Menagerie and Circus, which I purchased entire and added to my other attractions. My official term as Mayor expired April 3, 1876. I peremptorily refused a re-nomination, preferring to travel a portion of the time with my grand Centennial show, and meet face to face the millions of friends who, during the last year, have been my generous and I trust gratified patrons.

The last meeting of the Common Council under my administration was held Friday evening, March 29. *The Bridgeport Farmer* of the next day said:

The desks of the members and reporters were each adorned with a beautiful bouquet, presented "with the compliments" of the Mayor, and this raising of municipal business to a higher level was evidently appreciated by all present. It was a novelty, but then Mayor Barnum made a name by the introduction of novelties.

The New York Daily Graphic of March 30 read:

Mr. P. T. Barnum, Mayor of Bridgeport, has uttered his valedictory message. The document is very much like the man. He disapproves of the reports of the Chief of Police and Clerk of the Police Commissioners because they declare that liquor saloons and brothels cannot be closed, and he even reproves the latter for his "flippant manner of dealing with the subject. Barnum must have his joke or two, withal, and he can no more subsist without his fun than could a former Mayor of this city. He ventures to allude in this solemn document to the management of the New York and New Haven Railroad Company as "the good bishop and his directors;" makes a first-rate pun on the names of two citizens; and says to the Aldermen, "And now we have, like the Arabs, only to 'fold our tents and silently steal away,' congratulating ourselves that this is the only stealing which has been performed by this honorable body." Mr. Barnum's administration in Bridgeport has been mild, but characterized by firmness and independence. His trouble with the Jews was of short duration, for he is most respectful towards all theologies. He has not been able to carry out his extreme temperance views; but he has made a very good Mayor of a city for whose prosperity he has labored for half a lifetime.

The following extract is from the *Bridgeport Leader* of April 5:

We do not know of anyone connected with the city government of last year who was more pleased in being relieved of the cares of office than our late Mayor, P.T. Barnum. That Mr. Barnum could have been re-elected Mayor this year, had he not, months ago, emphatically declared his intention to retire at the close of his official term, has always been our firm conviction, and, aside from this, that he was about the only one of the Republican party who could be.

He retires from office voluntarily, commanding the respect of his constituents, and far better appreciated for those sterling qualities of rigid independence and honest desire to serve the city, irrespective of all other considerations, than any Mayor we have had for years.

From the *Bridgeport Standard* of March 30:

Mayor Barnum's Message, printed on the first page of today's paper, will repay perusal, as he says many things and makes sundry suggestions which if heeded will be for the benefit of the city. There is no candid man who will not be pleased with more or less of his suggestions, since they are not the clap-trap of a politician, but the utterances of an old citizen of Bridgeport, who has the best interests of the city at heart, and sincerely desires its best prosperity in all things.

Gen. Noble, on moving the printing of the Mayor's Message, said:

"I think it due to the Mayor and to his office to say here that, however much members if this Council may have differed from the Mayor on the subject matter of his messages, no one who has read them will hesitate to accord to them very marked ability and thorough study of their topics. The message on the subject of the ordinance amendment, which proposed to subject the Police Commissioners to the resolves of the Council, I do not think could have been more clearly, tersely or exhaustively presented by any gentleman well learned in the law."

The usual congratulatory resolution, complimenting the Mayor on his faithfulness, and expressing the high opinion of the Council for him, was passed by a unanimous rising vote, and the meeting adjourned.

My successor, a Democrat, "as elected by a majority of six hundred votes.

-

Note. — During the forty years that I have been a manager of public amusements, the number of my patrons has been almost incredible. From a careful examination of my account books for the different exhibitions which I have owned and controlled, I find that more than eighty-two millions of tickets, in the aggregate, were disposed of. and numerous exhibitions which I have had at various times are not included in this statement.

The traveling exhibitions which I managed during the six years preceding my purchase of the New York American Museum, in 1841, were attended by 1,500,000 persons

The American Museum, which I managed from 1841-1865, when it was destroyed by fire, sold   37,560,000 tickets

My Broadway Museum, in 1865-6-7 and 8, sold   3,640,000 tickets

My Philadelphia Museum, in 1849, 1850 and 1S51. sold   1,800,000 tickets

My Baltimore Museum, sold   900,000 tickets

My traveling Asiatic Caravan, Museum and Menagerie in
851-2-3 and 4, sold   5,824,000 tickets

My great traveling World's Fair and Hippodrome, in
1871-2-3-4-5 and 6 sold   7,920,000 tickets

My other traveling exhibitions in America and Europe sold   2,200,000 tickets

General Tom Thumb has exhibited for 34 years and sold   20,400,000 tickets

Jenny Lind's Concerts, under my management, were
attended by   600,000 persons

Catherine Hayes' 60 Concerts in California, under
my contract, sold   120,000 tickets

Thus, my patrons amount to the enormous number of 82,464,000

Of course, eighty-two millions of different individuals have not visited my various exhibitions, for many persons visited my Museums, etc., scores and some undoubtedly hundreds of times. But, taken altogether, I think I can, without egotism, say that amused and instructed more persons than any other manager who has ever lived. In addition, to the eighty-two millions who have visited my public exhibitions, I may add that I have delivered over seven hundred public lectures, which were attended in the aggregate by 1,300,000 persons. My first autobiography, published in 1851, reached a circulation of 160,000 copies, besides which two separate editions were published in England, one in Germany and one in France. These, in the aggregate, had probably more than a million of readers. Of my autobiography, "Struggles and Triumphs," published in 1869 and written up to 1877, 240,000 copies have been printed in America, and a different edition in London, all of which I estimate have had two millions of readers. It will thus be seen that "Barnum" has occupied so much public attention for forty years, that the fact need not be wondered at (and it *is* a fact) that in 1870, a letter mailed to New Zealand, and addressed simply "Mr. Barnum, America.'" came as direct to me at Waldemere, in Bridgeport, Conn., as it could have done if my full address had been written on the envelope. P. T. B.

CHAPTER L.

FOREIGN AND DOMESTIC.

In December, 1876, I received a second invitation from Lord Rosebery to breakfast with him in New York. On parting with his lordship in 1874, his warm expressions of pleasure at having met me, and his assurances that he hoped and intended to renew our acquaintance, left no room for embarrassing misgivings on this occasion. Our meeting at the Brevoort House was very cordial. His lordship took me in his brougham to the New York Club, and there I first learned that our breakfast companions were Martin Farquhar Tupper and the chief editor of a prominent New York daily paper. Mr. Tupper and myself had held a correspondence previous to his leaving England, and the author of "Proverbial Philosophy" was apparently delighted at the unexpected meeting of his "dear friend Barnum." The occasion was an exceedingly enjoyable one, and if, as is said, laughter aids digestion, I am confident that three of the quartette were not troubled with dyspepsia after that delicious and *recherche* meal. Since his marriage with Miss Rothschild, I have received a letter from Lord Rosebery, in which he makes pleasant and witty allusion to that never-to-be-forgotten breakfast. The transatlantic friends of this brilliant nobleman are pleased to know that he has been recently chosen Lord Rector of the University of Aberdeen.

In 1876 I accompanied my Great Show as far East as Halifax, Nova Scotia, where we exhibited early in August. While in the Dominions of Her Majesty Queen Victoria, we changed our song and chorus of the Star-Spangled Banner to God Save the Queen, with decidedly good effect. The Show proceeded west to Illinois. The financial result of the traveling season (1876) was satisfactory.

In the autumn of 1876, I wrote a book of fiction, founded on fact, entitled "The Adventures of Lion Jack; or, How Menageries are Made." It was a real boys' book, and I dedicated it to the boys of America. It was published by Carleton, of New York. Sampson, Low & Co., of London, also published it. Many copies have been sold in both countries. *The London Times*, in its weekly edition, March 23, 1877, gave "Lion Jack" a favorable notice in a third of a column. It is sold in my traveling show, as well as by Carleton & Co.

Among many other valuable additions to my traveling show of 1877 were six beautiful and remarkably trained black Trakene Stallions from Germany. My agents, Bailey and June, after scouring Europe in search of novelties, purchased them at large figures from James Myers, proprietor of the Great American Circus in Paris. They formed a novel and pleasing feature, and, with other startling novelties, aided to secure to me a still more profitable season than that of 1876.

On the 11th of April, 1877, my family were stricken with a heavy sorrow in the sudden death of my daughter, Pauline T. Seeley, at the age of thirty-one years, leaving a husband and three children. This blow would have been insupportable to me did I not receive it as coming from our good Father in Heaven, who does all things right.

In July, 1877, I sailed for England, with my wife, in the Cunard steamer *Russia*, both of us arriving home eight weeks later in the *Scythia* of the same line. At the request of the captains and passengers, I gave a lecture on each steamer for the benefit of the Seamen's Orphan Institution in Liverpool. I also gave my lecture on "The World, and How to Live in It," several times in the Royal Aquarium Theatre, London, in Alexandra Palace, London, Southport Winter Gardens, and in Bolton. I likewise lectured on Temperance in Hawk Stone Hall, London, at which the celebrated Rev. Newman Hall presided; and I gave a similar lecture in Hengler's Circus building, Liverpool. The London *Entracte*, the *London Sporting and Dramatic News*, and several other metropolitan papers, published *illustrations* of my appearance in the forum, and numerous London journals gave favorable notices of my lectures. I was glad to meet many of my old friends in England after an absence of eighteen years. I have nearly as many personal friends in London as in the city of New York. In the latter city the boys often hail me in the streets and ask me questions about the show, and a similar occurrence took place on this last visit to London. As I was one day coming out from my hairdresser's, near Regent street, where it was known I went every day, a bevy of lads called me by name and inquired if it was time, as they had read in the papers, that I was going to bring over my Great Show from America.

The immense patronage which my own country bestows on my efforts is all that keeps me from taking my big show to Europe, where my name is as well-known as in America.

The *London (England) World*, a very popular weekly, of which Edmund Yates, the novelist, is editor and proprietor, has a specialty in each of its issues headed "Celebrities at Home." In this department have appeared sketches of Lord Beaconsfield, Gladstone, Tennyson, Carlyle, John Bright, Spurgeon, etc. General Grant is the only American who has been selected for portraiture besides myself. The editor obtained from some person in Bridgeport, probably an Englishman, the following sketch, which he published in March, 1877. My neighbors generally say it is a truthful representation of me and my surroundings "at home," but I think the writer has made the picture too flattering:

CELEBRITIES AT HOME
P.T. BARNUM

A stranger in America, happening to alight at Bridgeport, a thriving city of some twenty-five thousand inhabitants, beautifully situated on the shore of Long Island Sound, within sixty miles of New York city, might be surprised to find that it owes much of its prosperity to the business tact and energy of its most prominent citizen, Phineas Taylor Barnum. Ask any inhabitant of this third city of the State of Connecticut who built those rows of cottages, reminding an English traveler of those built by the more philanthropic manufacturers at home, and the answer comes, "Barnum." How is it that so many operatives possess homes of their own? Again, the answer. "Barnum helped them." Who planned your Mountain Grove — one of the most beautiful cemeteries in America? "Barnum started it, and thus did away with an old, neglected burying-ground, that used to be in the heart of the city. "And your lovely Seaside Park; who originated that? "Oh, Barnum, of course; he gave some of the land, begged and bought the remainder, and never rested until the park became what it is— the greatest ornament and blessing of our city." You may go on with the catechism, ad libitum, and will find that this "showman" has been a zealous worker in, and generally prime mover of every public improvement. That his fellow-citizens appreciate his efforts is apparent, for they elected him mayor, twice sent him to represent the town in the State Legislature, nominated him for the United States Congress, and, on one occasion, within the last few years, on his return from a visit to England, over two hundred of the most substantial citizens of Bridgeport gave him a complimentary dinner, "in honor of the liberality and energy in private enterprise; in promoting the industries and public improvements of Bridgeport, and the genuine philanthropy of their popular fellow-townsman.

Mr. Barnum, when at home, is in great request. Few temperance meetings are considered complete unless he is a prominent speaker; few church bazaars expected to succeed unless he opens them with a humorous speech, which seldom fails to open hearts and purses. The youngest urchin can point the way to Seaside Park, and there, standing on a slight eminence, looking down on the park and across its narrowest part to the waters of the sound, over whose surface steamers, yachts, and every variety of water craft are continually passing, stands Waldemere, from whose cupola floats a silken flag bearing the well-known monogram, P.T.B., whenever the king of showmen is at home. Waldemere — Woods by the Sea— so named by its owner's friend, Bayard Taylor, is a naturally beautiful estate beautified by art. Its well-kept lawns, broad and sweeping, are ornamented with fountains of bronze and marble; statues gleam against a background of grove and thicket; the house is girdled with a broad belt of flowers, and flower-beds of every English device border the drives from gateway to porch. The house itself is not easily described, being a curious but pleasant melange of Gothic, Italian and French architecture and decoration, presenting a front a hundred and sixty feet long to the water, whereby most of the rooms command a very charming view. On entering one is pleasantly struck by the spaciousness of hall and rooms. One can breathe as freely indoors as out. Nothing is small or contracted. The house is furnished luxuriously but not ostentatiously; taste as well as wealth being evident in the arrangement of every room. Pictures of high merit hang on tinted walls and stand on easels. Chinese vases of quaint and wonderful design guard the fireplaces; busts and statuettes fill nooks and corners; capacious bookcases fail to hold the latest works; while mantels and etagers hold costly *bric-a-brac* in artistic confusion. Many of these ornaments abound in interesting reminiscences for the "great showman" and for his friends. On a pedestal in a place of honor, stands a marble bust of Jenny Lind, whose original contract with P.T. Barnum hangs framed in one of the halls, the signatures of Jenny Lind, Sir Jules Benedict, Giovanni Belletti and P.T. Barnum, compelling us to pause for a moment before it. A corner bracket in a cozy sitting-room holds a small Parian Bacchus— a Christmas gift from the Swedish nightingale to Mr. Barnum, in good-natured ridicule of his firm temperance principles and practice. In an etagere in this same pleasant room lie dimpled marble models of Tom Thumb's hand and foot taken when his size was smallest and his fame greatest. One cannot spend half an hour inspecting Waldemere without discovering that Mr. Barnum is a firm believer in cleanliness either for its relation to godliness or for its own merits. The mansion is intersected with a very network of waterpipes— there being scarcely a room that has not its bath room and lavatory attached. There are rooms bearing the names of distinguished guests who have occupied them. A spacious bedroom, with hangings and furniture of pale green and white, is known as the "Greeley room." for here Horace Greeley had reposed. Two pleasant rooms are associated with the memory of the sister poetesses, Alice and Phoebe Cary. Doubtless there will sometime be a "Twain room" for the humorist is a frequent guest at Waldemere.

Mr. Barnum's second wife is a young English lady of culture, the daughter of an old friend of his in Lancashire. The good taste displayed in the ornamentation of Waldemere is due to Mrs. Barnum, who is highly appreciated by the best families of Bridgeport as a charming hostess, an intelligent and agreeable conversationalist, and a kind neighbor and friend. Mr. Barnum's daughters regard her as a treasure added to their enjoyment, and to their father's happiness and comfort. As for Mr. Barnum himself his round full-face beams with extra smiles when he is near her. He never seems quite so happy as when listening to her playing opera music on the grand piano, riding at her side in the family landeau to and from church, in Seaside Park, or on the numerous pleasant avenues in the vicinity of Bridgeport.

Mr. Barnum's library, or. as he calls it, "work-shop," is an imposing octagonal room furnished and paneled with cherry, birch and maple woods. Opening on one hand is a lavatory, and on another a room where his private secretary works within call. At a large and much littered desk, with papers strewn ankle-deep around his chair. Mr. Barnum spends nearly every morning of his life communicating with his agents in every land— often interrupted by some employees desiring orders, or by some friend or stranger asking advice or more substantial help, but never laying down his pen, which is traveling rapidly as ever ere the door has closed behind the visitor. He is economical of his time, never wasting or submitting to be robbed of a moment of the hours set apart for business. Woe to the adventurer or visionary who intrudes at this time. He is weighed, found wanting and dismissed in two minutes. These long mornings, and a short time devoted on the arrival of each mail to answering the letters they never fail to bring, these hours over— the keen but conscientious man of business, the head of so many undertakings — enjoys himself with as much apparent freedom from care as the workman who has just pocketed a good week's wages. If Mr. Barnum, when working, dislikes to be interrupted, Mr. Barnum, when enjoying himself, is even less tolerant of business intrusion. The intruder may desire to purchase valuable land and come with the money in his pocket; he is none the less decisively told to "come in the morning." The personal appearance of P.T. Barnum will interest those who may not have seen the man nor his portrait. Tall, portly, erect, in spite of his sixty-seven years of hard work and several fortunes earned and lost, and won again, with a high forehead, gray hair curling crisply around a bald head, with a firm, decided step and voice, he is very different from the popular conception of a showman— as indeed his social standing upsets the general idea of a showman's natural and proper status.

In the spring of 1877 I offered $10,000 for the return of the kidnapped Charley Ross to his afflicted parents. But though my offer was published far and wide on both sides of the Atlantic, all efforts for his restoration proved unavailing.

In August, 1877, I visited Des Moines, and proceeded west with my show as far as Council Bluffs, Iowa, and thence to my cattle ranch in Colorado. I gave temperance speeches in Denver and Greeley, and also gave my lecture on "The World, and How to Live in it," in the former city and at Colorado Springs.

In November, 1877, I was elected to represent Bridgeport in the General Assembly of Connecticut. My majority was 212, although the political party with which I am identified is usually 700 in the minority. It was a personal sacrifice to me to leave my home to help make our State laws at Hartford, but I did not feel at liberty to refuse the demand upon my services, and I endeavored to fulfill my duty as a citizen of the Commonwealth without undue exertions party-wise. The Speaker, Hon. Chas. H. Briscoe, offered me the choice of chairmanship of half a dozen standing committees. I told him that on the two former occasions when I was in the Legislature I was Chairman on Agriculture (having plowed with an elephant), but I should now prefer to be one of the Committee on Temperance. He appointed me chairman of that committee. We succeeded in getting several favorable changes in our liquor laws, yet, like Oliver Twist, we asked for more. During the winter I gave a number of lectures in the vicinity of Hartford. Among numerous social gatherings which I attended in that city, I remember none more pleasant than a dinner given to half a dozen of his friends by Governor Hubbard. The Republican party had a majority in both Houses, and of course carried such measures as they desired. There was, however, one exception. At our party caucus, when it was announced that a nomination was to be made for a Republican Superintendent of the Public School Fund to supersede the Democratic incumbent, who was acknowledged by all parties to be an honest, intelligent and capable person, I insisted that no change should be made. I reminded the members of the caucus that the position was a responsible and important one; that a large amount of the State's money, held as a sacred trust, was under the control of the present incumbent, Mr. Miles; that mortgages were being foreclosed, and several complicated law suits were before the courts, the details of which Mr. Miles thoroughly understood, and that, although I did not know that gentleman and never saw him, I should insist upon his re-appointment. But, as is usual in politics, ardent members were anxious to serve the party, and a new nomination was insisted on. I declined to vote, and when the name of the new nominee was subsequently presented in the House I opposed it, giving my reasons, and appealed to the honor of my brother Republicans to not let partisan feelings conflict with the general interests of our State. Of course, I was strongly opposed, but when the final vote was taken by yeas and nays I had the gratification of seeing over twenty Republicans stand up for "civil service," and Mr. Miles was again appointed. I have never seen that gentleman to this day, but I feel that the Commonwealth of Connecticut was a gainer by his re-appointment.

In April, 1878, my great traveling show opened for a fortnight at the American Institute building, in New York, and then proceeded to Philadelphia.

The show, as usual, was transported through the country on nearly a hundred railway cars of my own, preceded a fortnight in advance by my Magnificent Advertising Car, carrying press agents, the "paste brigade," numbering twenty, and tons of immense colored bills, programs, lithographs, photographs, electrotype cuts, etc., to arouse the entire country for fifty miles around each place of exhibition to the fact that "P.T. Barnum's New and Greatest Show on Earth," with its acres of tents and pavilions could be reached by cheap excursion trains on certain days specified in the bills and advertisements. The show went East to Bangor, Maine, and west to Illinois, reaching New York and opening at Gilmore's Garden in October, for seven weeks to crowded houses.

In the summer of 1878, I expended some twenty thousand dollars in the purchase and reclamation of a large tract of salt marsh adjoining Seaside Park and the grounds of Waldemere on the west. This marsh has been inaccessible from time immemorial, annually producing plentiful crops of mosquitoes. The times were hard, many laboring men in Bridgeport were suffering for want of employment, and although it was evident I should never be reimbursed for half my expenditures, I could see that the improvement would be a great public benefit, and remembering the dykes in Holland which I had so frequently seen with astonishment and admiration, I determined, as I told my neighbors, to "cheat my heirs," by expending a good sum *pro bono publico*. I built this dyke straight across a channel which let in the tide-water every twelve hours and covered an immense tract of low salt meadow. I made the dyke seventy feet wide at bottom, and of sufficient width on the top to form a fine street leading from one of our city avenues to the beach on Long Island Sound. This gives nearly a mile high and dry front on the salt water connecting with Seaside Park. I propose to make a present to the city of this "water" front, 150 feet in width, which will give them as an extension of their already beautiful Park, a delightful additional boulevard for carriages and promenade on the very edge of Long Island Sound, where the plashing salt waves may be seen, heard and enjoyed for all time. Mayor Morford (of opposite politics from myself) in his message to the Common Council of Bridgeport, characterized my proposition as a "liberal offer," and said, "the Barnum Boulevard, in connection with the Seaside Park, adding nearly a mile to the present park-drive, would be the finest improvement of the kind on the Atlantic Coast. "

The *Bridgeport Leader* of May 1, 1878, in referring to this enterprise, said:

It is one of the peculiarities of Mr. Barnum, that he is always undertaking some kind of a public improvement which no one else would think of, and besides this he does it at his own expense. When he takes hold of any great work which at the least will require years of waiting before any return can be hoped for to recompense for the original outlay, it is reasonable to believe that pecuniary gain is not the sole object of these undertaking. It is not too much to say that no six men. living or dead, have done more for Bridgeport than the "Great Showman," and, although we do not doubt that could the books be balanced, that he has virtually sunk at least more than a quarter of a million of dollars in improving the city, he is still as anxious as ever to leave the impress of his enterprise upon the most unpromising portions of the place. The building of the dyke from the western terminus of Short Beach northerly to the western end of South avenue, promises the least pecuniary return of the money invested of any of the enterprises Mr. Barnum has entered into. Yet we know of no work which promises in the end to add more to the attractiveness of the place than this.

It will be those who will people this section in the future who will recognize the wisdom and foresight of the man who had nothing to gain save the notable ambition of "tearing the world better for having lived in it," and did not hesitate to take upon himself the expense and the risk of beginning a work of which every year's delay is an irreparable damage to the city.

The road contemplated to be constructed from the west end of Seaside Park to Mr. Barnum's dyke, when completed, will give Bridgeport one of the handsomest drives by the sea shore on Long Island Sound. — *Bridgeport Leader*, Nov. 13, 1878.

Colonel O.B. Hall, a quaint old neighbor of mine, hitherto unsuspected of any poetic tendencies, thus expressed his admiration of my achievement:

TO P.T. BARNUM.

Had you but lived in days gone by,
When Captain Noah sailed above
The tops of trees, and mountains high,
With relatives, and beasts and dove.
You could have saved that great expense,
In building arks and catching beasts,
By making dams and dykes and fence,
And many millions saved at least
Of souls that found a watery grave
While swimming round the Ark, and plead
With Noah, to take them in and save

From being numbered with the dead.
He did not care a dam or dyke to make.
To stop that flood which spread so wide;
To Ark! to Ark! he said, betake,
We'll on the ocean gayly ride.
Well stored lockers in the Ark
With sweetmeats, wine and solid grub,
When he and kin did quick embark.'
With haste and speed, on board his tub.
One of each sex of beasts that roam,
Likewise, did board his pitchy boat,
All others left to their sad doom,
When that old craft did rise and float.
for could have dammed that rising tide,
And saved unnumbered human souls,
By stopping sea from spreading wide.
Which covered earth above the poles.
But as it was, no one could live
On earth, through that calamity,
When Heaven ope'd its riddling sieve,
Through which was pour'd a mighty sea.
The fish were pleased to hear it pour,
And see the angling lubbers strive
To find a floating plank or door.
On which to ride and keep alive.
But you, more wise, have done a deed
To stay the water's tide o'erflow,
Where crossed 'skeetera used to breed,
On those salt meadows down below.
Ozone, that pure and healthy air,
Will soon embalm that sea of grass,
And Heavenly zephyrs free and fair,
Will linger o'er it ere they pass.
It soon will be like Eden's land,
Where flowers bloom and fig trees grow,
And you, like Adam, have command,
Of this fair garden down below.
Those railroad ties will stand as guard,
To keep the flowing tide aback,
Protecting safely "boulevard"
As driveway for a carriage track,
Where "lads and lasses blithe and gay."
Can ride with pleasure o'er the pave.
And bless that man who, in his day,
Redeemed that place from under wave.

The Bridgeport Standard of Nov. 8, 1878, says:

> Hon. P. T. Barnum is known all the world over as a Bridgeport man, and he has done as much, or more for the place, regardless of party or sect, than any man living. The people of Bridgeport have honored him with their confidence and it has never been abused.

In November, 1878, I consented, much against my will, to accept another nomination to represent Bridgeport in the General Assembly of Connecticut. I was re-elected by a majority of several hundred votes. My opponents on the Democratic ticket were Hon. W. D. Bishop and Hon. Nathaniel Wheeler.

The Manchester (England) Examiner and Times published an editorial article coupling my name with those of the British Ministry, to which I replied as follows:

To the Editor of the *Examiner and Times*, Manchester, England:
Sir: In your issue of the 3rd \ instant you make mention of me as "the late Mr. Barnum." For the benefit of numerous friends in Great Britain, who have not before heard of my being classed among the "lates,'" I beg to say that my age is among the sixties and that, having been a teetotaler for thirty years, I am robust in health, and maintain the same vigor I possessed at forty. I am proprietor of the most extensive Museum. Menagerie, World's Fair and Hippodrome that ever traveled, being run at an expense of $3,000 (or £600 sterling) per day, and my highest ambition, professionally, now is to pay to the British Government one hundred thousand dollars (£20,000) for the privilege of exhibiting alive, for five years, its "white elephant," King Ketowayo, the captive Zulu. I shall be glad to receive, by an early mail, a note of acceptance from my friend Lord Beaconsfield. who so kindly mentioned me in his "Lothair."

Truly yours,
P. T. BARNUM.
Waldemere, Bridgeport, Conn., November, 1879.

CHAPTER LI.

THE GREAT ALLIANCE.

BERGH VANQUISHED — TRANSFORMATION SCENE— BABY ELEPHANT— THE GREAT ALLIANCE— WINTER QUARTERS OF THE GREAT BARNUM-LONDON SHOW — VALLEY OF THE SHADOW OF DEATH — FOUR PULLMAN CAR LOADS OF EDITORS — TORCH-LIGHT PROCESSION AND GRAND OPENING— TESTIMONIALS FROM GARFIELD AND ARTHUR— MY VOYAGE TO EUROPE — PRESENTATION OF FOUNTAIN TO BETHEL; ALSO, "THE BARNUM BOULEVARD" AND DYKE TO THE CITY OF BRIDGEPORT —ANOTHER BABY ELEPHANT— "JUMBO," THE GREATEST OF THE GREAT — VALEDICTORY.

In 1879 and 1880, the show under the same management was very successful. I introduced the firing of Zazel from a cannon. This has since been the principal feature of other shows, as has also the tattooed Greek whom I first introduced to the American public in 1876. While exhibiting in the Rink in 1880, I had a business encounter with Henry Bergh, Esq., which created much interest and excitement in the arena and in the newspapers. A New York daily paper gave the following faithful account of the affair:

The controversy between P.T. Barnum and Henry Bergh, which has occupied public attention for a few days, was ended yesterday in favor of the veteran showman. It will be remembered that Mr. Bergh compelled Mr. Barnum to discontinue the act of the fire-horse Salamander, on the grounds of cruelty to the animal and danger to the audience. Mr. Barnum, with an eye to a stupendous advertising scheme, and doubtless with a wish to assure his patrons that everything had been done to secure their safety, challenged Mr. Bergh to meet him in the circus ring on Monday afternoon and to reply to his explanations. Yesterday the vast American Institute Building was unable to accommodate the crowds who clamored for admission. Shortly after the opening of the show Superintendent Hartfield, of the Society for the Prevention of Cruelty to Animals, entered in command of seven of his officers. Police Captain Gunner, who originally made the report that caused Mr. Bergh's interference, was also on hand with a posse of twenty policemen, who were assigned positions around the ring. At the conclusion of the bareback horsemanship of Orrin Hollis. Mr. Barnum entered the arena amid an outburst of applause. When this had subsided, Mr. Barnum began his speech and said:

"Ladies and Gentlemen: I have been catering to the public for forty-eight years, yet I am here today expecting arrest by this large force of police, and imprisonment and trial by a jury of my countrymen. The patent fact is just this: Mr. Bergh or I must run this show. Mr. Bergh has published that I have endangered the lives of my audiences. Long before he was known to society, I was a subscriber to a society in London, similar to the one of which he is chief, and of which Queen Victoria was a patron. It was I who called the attention of the Mayor of the city to the necessity for such a society here, and I am, in Bridgeport, what Mr. Bergh is here. I know more about animals than he knows. They are taught and governed only by kindness. The fire-horse Salamander's performance has been witnessed by the Emperor of Germany. Prince Bismarck, Queen Victoria, and many of the most prominent people in Europe, and he, like other animals, being valuable, self-interest demands protection and proper treatment. In this performance, not a hair of the horse is singed.

'Years ago,' continued Mr. Barnum, 'Mr. Bergh demanded that I should furnish the rhinoceros with a tank of water to swim in, when such a proceeding would have killed it. I explained to Mr. Bergh the nature of the animal and its requirements, and he troubled me no further. In 1866, during my absence from New York, Mr. Bergh frightened my manager into sending the snakes to New Jersey to be fed, objecting to their being supplied with live toads and lizards, although it was explained to him that, while they were only attracted by living food, they crushed and killed it before swallowing. On my return I ordered them to be fed with live frogs in order to preserve their lives.

"I hold in my hand," said Mr. Barnum, "a letter from Mr. Bergh, dated "Rooms of Society, No. 826 Broadway, Dec. 11, 1866," from which I will read an extract:

"I am informed that several live animals were recently thrown into the cage with your boa constrictor to be devoured! I assert, without fear of contradiction, that any person who can commit an atrocity such as the one I complain of is semi-barbarian in his instincts. It may be urged that the reptiles will not eat dead food. In reply to this I have only to say— then let them starve; for it is contrary to the merciful providence of God that wrong should be committed in order to accomplish a supposed right. But I am satisfied that this assertion is false in theory and practice, for no living creature will allow itself to perish of hunger with food before it — be the aliment dead or alive. On the next occurrence of this cruel exhibition this society will take legal measures to punish the perpetrator of it.

(Signed)
Henry Bergh, President."

"I sent a copy of this letter to the elder Prof. Agassiz and received the following autograph letter in reply. It is too rich to keep longer from the public:

Cambridge, Feb. 28, 1867.

P. T. Barnum, Esq.:

Dear Sir: On my return to Cambridge I received your letter of the 15th January. I do not know of any way to induce snakes to eat their food otherwise than in their natural manner— that is alive. Your museum is intended to show the public the animals as nearly as possible in their natural state. The society of which you speak is, as I understand, for the prevention of unnecessary cruelty to animals. It is a most praiseworthy object, but I do not think the most active members of the society would object to eating lobster salad because the lobster was boiled alive, or refuse roasted oysters because they were cooked alive, or raw oysters because they must be swallowed alive. I am, dear sir, our obedient servant,   L. Agassiz.

"On March 4, 1867, I enclosed Prof. Agassiz's letter to Mr. Bergh, from whom I demanded an apology for his abuse, and an acknowledgment of his mistakes as to snakes eating dead food. Three days later Mr. Bergh replied, acknowledging the receipt of mine. He then wrote as follows:

"Your letter contains a threat to give my letter to the public unless I write you a letter for publication, stating that since reading Prof. Agassiz's letter to you I withdraw my objections, etc. In reply to this I have to say that the hastily written note to which you refer was not intended for publication."

"Hastily written, indeed," commented the great show king, 'calling my acts atrocities and me semi-barbarous in my instincts.' He then proceeded with the letter:

"I am convinced of the necessity of laboring more assiduously in the cause of protecting the brute creation in order to counteract the unhappy influence which the expressions of that distinguished savant (Prof. Agassiz) are calculated to occasion. I scarcely know which emotion is paramount in my mind, regret or astonishment, that so eminent a philosopher should have cast the weight of his commanding authority into the scale where cruelty points the index in its favor.

Henry Bergh, President."

"He detailed other obstacles which Mr. Bergh had thrown in his way. and intimated that if he (Bergh) would stick to his own business, that he (Barnum) would run his own show, and conform to the laws as decided by a jury of his countrymen. In conclusion Mr. Barnum said: 'I now expect to be arrested, but if I should be. I shall place a hoop of fire around Henry Bergh that will make him warmer than he has been in the past, and probably than he ever will experience in the future.'

"The effort was received with tremendous cheering. The horse Salamander was then brought into the ring by Prince Nagaard, its trainer, and the fire hoops were lighted. Mr. Barnum ran his hand through the blaze, and then stepped through the flaming circle, hat in hand. Ten clowns performed a number of ludicrous antics through the hoops, and then the horse parsed through without showing any signs of fear and without singeing a hair. Mr. Barnum had not yet finished the illustration, however, for he requested Superintendent Hartfield to walk through the still blazing hoops. Without hesitation he did so, and he got more applause than Madame. Dockrill in her four-horse act. Superintendent Hartfield then stated that his superior, Mr. Bergh, had evidently made a mistake in the matter; that there was neither cruelty nor danger in the performance, and that the society had no cause for action. Amid the wildest excitement and cheers for the plucky Barnum, Capt. Gunner, looking somewhat crestfallen, withdrew his officers, and the show went on. Salamander again went through his tricks last night without interruption.

Although I was forced to resent his ill-advised interference and mistaken accusation, this episode did not impair my personal regard for Mr. Bergh and my admiration of his noble works.

In the spring of the same year, 1880, I erected on the principal street of Bridgeport a fine building for business purposes. It was built behind a board screen or casing the full height of the structure. Its purpose was to protect the workmen and enable them (time being an object) to work regardless of inclement weather, but when, the work being finished, the screen was removed in the night-time, and early risers saw, instead of unsightly boards, a handsome building of brick, with granite and terra cotta ornaments, and a fine statue of America gazing benignly down, from her alcove in the second story, on the wondering and admiring crowd below, I was suspected of having planned a very effective transformation scene.

So late as 1880, no traveling show in the world bore any comparison with my justly-called "Greatest Show on Earth." Other show-managers boasted of owning shows equaling mine, and some bought of the printers large colored show bills pictorially representing my marvelous curiosities, although these managers had no performances or curiosities of the kinds which they represented. The cost of one of their shows was from twenty thousand to fifty thousand dollars, while mine cost millions of dollars. Their expenses were three hundred to seven hundred dollars per day, while mine were three thousand dollars per day. The public soon discovered the difference between the sham and the reality, the natural consequences of misrepresentation followed; the small showmen made little or nothing, some went into bankruptcy each season, while mine was always crowded, and each succeeding year showed a larger profit.

My strongest competitors were the so-called "Great London Circus, Sanger's Royal British Menagerie and Grand International Allied Shows." Its managers, Cooper, Bailey & Hutchinson, had adopted my manner of dealing with the public, and consequently their great show grew in popularity.

On the tenth of March, 1880, while in Philadelphia, one of their large elephants, Hebe, became a mother. This was the first elephant born in captivity, and the managers so effectively advertised the fact that the public became wild with excitement over the "Baby Elephant." Naturalists and men of science rushed in numbers to Philadelphia, examined the wonderful "little stranger" and gave glowing reports to the papers of this country and of Europe. Illustrated papers and magazines of this and foreign lands described the Baby Elephant with pen and pencil, and before it was two months old I offered the lucky proprietors one hundred thousand dollars cash for mother and baby. They gleefully rejected my offer, pleasantly told me to look to my laurels, and wisely held on to their treasure.

I found that I had at last met foemen "worthy of my steel," and pleased to find comparatively young men with a business talent and energy approximating to my own, I met them in friendly council, and after days of negotiation we decided to join our two shows "in one mammoth combination, and, sink or swim, to exhibit them for, at least, one season for one price of admission. The public were astonished at our audacity, and old showmen declared that we could never take in enough money to cover our expenses which would be fully forty-five hundred dollars per day. My new partners, James A. Bailey and James L. Hutchinson, sagacious and practical managers, agreed with me that the experiment involved great risk, but, from the time of the Jenny Lind Concerts, the Great Roman Hippodrome and other expensive enterprises, I have always found the great American public appreciative and ready to respond in proportion to the sums expended for their gratification and amusement.

This partnership entered into, we conceived the idea of building a monster emporium or winter quarters to accommodate all our wild animals, horses, chariots, railroad cars, and the immense paraphernalia of the united shows, instead of distributing the same in different localities. We enclosed a ten-acre lot in Bridgeport adjacent to the New York, New Haven and Hartford Railroad. In this enclosure we erected an elephant house one hundred feet square, kept heated to the temperature naturally required by these animals. Here thirty to forty elephants are luxuriously housed and trained to perform in a circus ring in the center.

In another large building the lions, tigers and leopards, which require a different temperature, are lodged and trained. Still another accommodates the camels and caged animals. The monkeys have roomy quarters all to themselves, where they can roam and work their mischievous will unrestrained. The amphibious animals, hippopotami, sea-lions, etc., have in their enclosure a huge pond heated by means of steam pipes, where the elephants are permitted their great enjoyment, a bath. A building three hundred feet long covers eight lines of tracks where the cars are stored, and these tracks are all connected by switches with the New York, New Haven and Hartford Railroad. In a circus ring exclusively for the purpose the riders, acrobats, etc., practice in the winter, so as not to lose their hard-won skill and suppleness. The chariots are all placed in one huge store-house, and are run into position by the larger elephants, which, standing behind the chariots, put their heads against them, and, with wonderful intelligence and docility, push them in place at the direction of their keeper. The elephants are always called into requisition when a car gets off the switches, and indeed they do all the heavy work of the winter quarters. A nursery department maintained for the reception and careful tending of new-born animals adjoins the office of the veterinary surgeon. The harness, paint and blacksmith shops are all immense and distinct. The accommodations include stabling for seven hundred of our best horses, and store-rooms for canvas, tent-poles and innumerable properties. Editors and artists flocked to see the quickly-famous winter quarters, and well-illustrated articles appeared in leading periodicals. The public also were anxious and curious to see the workings of this city of wonders, but were reluctantly denied admission, as visitors deranged the necessarily strict routine of the establishment, and were themselves in no little danger, many of the wild animals which are perfectly tractable when alone with their keepers, being permitted to leave their cages and frolic at large in their respective buildings. The signs which designate the different buildings are visible from all trains passing through Bridgeport.

In November of 1880, while in New York on business, I was suddenly attacked by an almost fatal illness, and laid for many weeks between life and death, unconscious of the tender solicitude shown me by countless good friends in this country, and the cable messages of inquiry that came thickly from others in foreign lands; the knowledge of all which will be ever a bright and grateful memory. Dr. Chapin, then on his death-bed, sent a messenger daily; reporters besieged the house at all hours, and contributed bulletins of my progress or relapse to all the principal New York papers; while the Associated Press kept the remoter public informed by telegraph of my condition. When strong enough I went to Florida, to recuperate in that delightful climate, returning in April to take up my old avocations with the old zest, and little less than the old strength.

The Barnum & London Circus opened in New York March 18, 1881, heralded by a torchlight procession through the city on Saturday night, March 16th, which was witnessed by more than half a million of people and pronounced the most brilliant display ever seen in America. A New York paper thus described it:

The street parade Saturday night was the grandest pageant ever witnessed in our streets, and fully met the anticipations of the thousands of spectators thronging the entire route. The whole equipment and display was magnificent, without a single weak feature to mar the general effect. The golden chariots, triumphal and tableau cars were more numerous, more ponderous, more elaborate and gorgeous in finish than any other establishment has brought here; the cages of wild animals were more numerous than usual, many of them were also open, and their trainers rode through the streets in the cages of lions, tigers, leopards, hyenas and monster serpents. There were cars drawn by teams of elephants, camels, dromedaries, zebras, elk, deer and ponies. And there appeared in the grand cavalcade three hundred and thirty-eight horses, twenty elephants, fourteen camels, jet black dromedaries, a large number of ponies, zebras, trained oxen, etc., also three hundred and seventy men and women. The cavalry of all nations was represented in the various uniforms worn, mounted upon superb chargers, and the costumes throughout were brilliant and beautiful. Music was furnished by four brass bands (one composed of genuine Indians), a calliope, a fine chime of bells, a steam organ, a squad of Scotch bag-pipers, and a company of genuine plantation negro jubilee singers.

Electric and calcium lights illuminated the whole. Windows were sold in New York, along Broadway, for five dollars, eight dollars and ten dollars, from which to view the pageant. So certain were we that this great street pageant and the marvelous combination of novelties to be produced throughout the season, would totally eclipse any former show enterprise, that on Saturday, March 26th, we brought, in drawing-room cars, from Washington, D.C., and Boston, and all the principal cities on those routes, the editors of all the leading papers. These gentlemen, nearly one hundred in number, witnessed the torchlight procession Saturday night, and our opening performance at the Madison Square Garden Monday night, March 28th. They were lodged at hotels at our expense, and by us returned to their homes on Tuesday; a very costly piece of advertising, which yet yielded us a magnificent return in the enthusiastic editorial endorsements of so many papers of good standing, whose representatives had seen our show and exclaimed as did the Queen of Sheba to King Solomon, "The half was not told me."

The following extract from the New York *Herald* of March 29th will give some idea of the variety and excellence of our attractions for 1881:

MADISON SQUARE GARDEN-BARNUM'S CIRCUS AND SHOW.

The management at Madison Square Garden have redeemed their promise to give the public one of the best arenic exhibitions in connection with a menagerie that ever has been witnessed in New York. Long before the doors were opened they were besieged by anxious hundreds, and at a quarter past eight o'clock there was scarcely a seat to be obtained in the vast edifice. It was stated by one of the proprietors that about nine thousand persons were present, and fully three thousand who could not be accommodated were refused admission. The spectacle can therefore be better imagined than described. Indeed, it was worth the price of admission alone to see the immense crowd and note the intense interest exhibited by all classes present, from the representatives of wealth and fashion, who were there in large numbers, to the little arabs to whom a circus is a paradise. The arrangements for the convenience of the audience were in every way complete. Each individual was provided with a chair, so that all crowding was avoided, while an ample supply of ushers promptly and without confusion conducted the holders of tickets to their respective places. Everything was new and clean, from the costumes to the sawdust. No bad flavors disturbed the nostrils; electric lights made the auditorium as bright as day; the ventilation was good and a strong force of police were present to preserve order had their services been required. The only drawback to the performance was that the spectator was compelled to receive more than his money's-worth; in other words, that while his head was turned in one direction he felt that he was losing something good in another. Three rings were provided, marked on the programs as Circle No. 1, No. 2 and No. 3; the equestrianism taking place in the two outer rings and the central space being reserved more especially for what are technically known as "ground acts." The display began with the usual pageant, in which a vast number of rich dresses and handsome animals were exhibited, after which there was a general introduction of the most notable curiosities, including General Tom Thumb and Lady Chang, the Chinese giant, the bearded woman, the American baby elephant, giant horse, ox, a pair of giraffes broken to harness, and other features. Six common plow oxen were next shown, after which followed extraordinary performances on horseback, gymnastic and athletic exercises, juggling, wire-rope walking, trapeze-flying and other attractions "too numerous to mention." Among the most interesting portions of the performance were the military drill and other feats by twenty trained elephants, the balancing by a Japanese family and the extraordinary jumping of the group of leapers who ended the program. The clowns were exceptionally good and one or two quite original. Altogether the show is well worth seeing.

Very early in the traveling season of 1881, we enlarged our already immense tents three different times, and yet so great was the multitude that attended our exhibitions — many coming on excursion trains twenty, thirty and even fifty miles — that at half the towns we visited we were unable to accommodate all who came, and we turned away thousands for want of room. In every town we were patronized by the elite, and frequently the public and private schools, as well as manufactories, were closed on "Barnum Day," school committees and teachers recognizing that children would learn more of natural history by one visit to our menagerie than they could acquire by months of reading.

In Washington, President Garfield told me he always attended my shows, and when Secretary Blaine said, ""Well, Barnum! all the children in America are anxious to see your show," the president smilingly added, "Yes! Mr. Barnum is the Kris Kringle of America."

Sir Edward Thornton, the British Ambassador, secured seventy-five seats at one of our exhibitions in Washington, and the next day wrote me a letter in which he said, "I certainly consider it the best organized and most complete establishment of that kind that I have ever visited, and that it is the most instructive and enjoyable." General Sherman wrote, "I say without hesitating that it surpasses anything of the kind I have seen in America or Europe." I received the autographic endorsements of President Garfield, Vice-president Arthur, Secretary Blaine, McVeagh, Roscoe Conkling, Hunt, Secretary of the Navy, Robert T. Lincoln, T. L. James, Senators Frye, Salisbury, Lamar and Platt of Connecticut, Gov. Hawley and most of the foreign ambassadors, cabinet ministers and United States senators. The furor which my show never fails to excite everywhere was tersely and wittily expressed in a notice posted up in a factory in a town which we visited last season. "Closed on account of the greatest interference on earth. "

The immense patronage which my own country bestows on my efforts is all that keeps me from taking my big show to Europe, where my name is as well-known as in America.

For years showmen have asserted that I did not own my show; others assumed to be my relatives and representatives. Determined to put down these false assertions and assumptions I sued the *Philadelphia Sun* for $100,000 damages in April, 1881, for saying that I merely hired out my name. The publisher, convinced of his error, retracted the statement and apologized. I withdrew the suit, having obtained all the redress I desired. In May, 1881, the desire to acquire, for my show-season of 1882, attractions which only my personal negotiations could secure, I revisited England, sailing in the *Scythia*. After four pleasant weeks I returned in the *Gallia*, successful in the object of my journey and invigorated by that finest of all tonics, a sea-voyage. Desiring to aid in beautifying the village of Bethel, it being my birthplace, from which a busy checkered life has never alienated my interest, I presented to my old companions a bronze fountain eighteen feet high, made in Germany; the design a Triton of heroic size, spouting water from an uplifted horn. It was a gala day for Bethel, the streets and residences were decorated with flags and bunting, a procession of police, fire companies with their engines, bands of music, citizens and invited guests in carriages, etc., paraded the town, and they formed in line around the square, newly adorned by the fountain. All of which was described, and the fountain illustrated in *Frank Leslie's Illustrated Newspaper* of Sept. 3, 1881. From a grandstand many speeches were made, and as my old friends would not permit me to be merely a listener and looker-on, and as reminiscences of the old days presented themselves thickly in my mind, in wide and often amusing contrasts to the customs and conditions of today, I addressed them.

"MY FRIENDS: Among all the varied scenes of an active and eventful life, crowded with strange incidents of struggle and excitement, of joy and sorrow, taking me often through foreign lands and bringing me face to face with the king in his palace and the peasant in his turf-covered hut, I have invariably cherished with the most affectionate remembrance the place of my birth, the old village meeting-house, without steeple or bell, where in its square family pew I sweltered in summer and shivered through my Sunday-school lessons in winter, and the old school-house where the ferule, the birchen rod and rattan did active duty, and which I deserved and received a liberal share. I am surprised to find that I can distinctly remember events which occurred before I was four years old.

"I can see as if but yesterday, our hardworking mothers hetcheling their flax, carding their tow and wool, spinning, reeling and weaving it into fabrics for bedding and clothing for all the family of both sexes. The same good mothers did the knitting, darning, mendings, washing, ironing, cooking, soap and candle making, picked the geese, milked the cows, made butter and cheese and did many other things for the support of the family.

"We babies of 1810, when at home, were dressed in tow frocks, and the garments of our elders were not much superior, except on Sunday, when they wore their "go-to-meeting clothes " of homespun and linsey-woolsey.

"Rain water was caught and used for washing, while that for drinking and cooking was drawn from wells with their "old oaken bucket" and long poles and well sweeps.

"Fire was kept overnight by banking up the brands in ashes in the fire-place, and if it went out one neighbor would visit another about daylight the next morning with a pair of tongs to borrow a coal of fire to kindle with. Our candles were tallow, home-made, with dark tow wicks. In summer nearly all retired to rest at early dark without lighting a candle except upon extraordinary occasions. Homemade soft-soap was used for washing hands, faces and everything else. The children of families in ordinary circumstances ate their meals on trenchers (wooden plates). As I grew older our family and others got an extravagant streak, discarded the trenchers and rose to the dignity of pewter plates and leaden spoons. Tin peddlers who traveled through the country with their wagons supplied these and other luxuries. Our food consisted chiefly of boiled and baked beans, bean porridge, coarse rye bread, apple sauce, hasty pudding eaten in milk, of which we all had plenty. The elder portion of the family ate meat twice a day— had plenty of vegetables, fish of their own catching, and occasionally big clams, which were cheap in those days, and shad in their season.

BRONZE FOUNTAIN PRESENTED TO MY NATIVE TOWN

These were brought from Norwalk and Bridgeport by fish and clam peddlers. Uncle Caleb Morgan of Wolfpits or Puppytown, was our only butcher. He peddled his meat through Bethel once a week. It consisted mostly of veal, lamb, mutton or fresh pork, seldom bringing more than one kind at a time. Probably he did not have beef oftener than once a month. Many families kept sheep, pigs and poultry, and one or more cows. They had plenty of plain substantial food. Droves of hogs ran at large in the streets of Bethel.

"When one of the neighbors wanted to feed his hogs, he went out in the street and called 'Pig,' which was pretty sure to bring in all the other hogs in the neighborhood. I remember one man, called 'Old Chambers,' who had no trouble in this respect, and he was the only one excepted from it. He had a peculiar way of getting his hogs from the general drove. When he wanted them he would go out into the street and shout Hoot! hoot! hoot! At this cry all the hogs but his own would run away, but they understood the cry and would stand still and take the meal.

"Our dinners several times each week consisted of "pot luck," which was corned beef, salt pork and vegetables, all boiled together in the same big iron pot hanging from the crane which was supplied with iron hooks and trammels and swung in and out of the huge fireplace. In the same pot with the salt pork, potatoes, turnips, parsnips, beets, carrots, cabbage and sometimes onions, was placed an Indian pudding, consisting of plain Indian meal mixed in water, pretty thick, salted and poured into a homemade brown linen bag which was tied at the top. When dinner was ready the Indian pudding was first taken from the pot, slipped out of the bag and eaten with molasses. Then followed the "pot-luck." I confess I like to this day the old-fashioned "boiled dinner," but doubt whether I should relish a sweetened dessert before my meat. Rows of sausages called "links " hung in the garret, were dried and lasted all winter.

"I remember them well, and the treat it was when a boy, to have one of these links to take to school to eat. At noon we children would gather about the great fireplace and having cut a long stick would push the sharpened end through the link, giving it a sort of cat-tail appearance. The link we would hold in the fire until it was cooked and would then devour it with a keen relish.

"There were but few wagons or carriages in Bethel when I was a boy. Our grists of grain were taken to the mill in bags on horseback, and the women rode to church on Sundays and around the country on week days on horseback, usually on a cushion called a pillion fastened behind the saddle, the husband, father, brother or lover riding in front on the saddle. The country doctor visited his patients on horseback, carrying his saddle-bags containing calomel, jalap, Epsom salts, lancet and a turnkey, those being the principal aids in relieving the sick. Nearly every person sick or well was bled every spring.

'Teeth were pulled with a turnkey, and a dreadful instrument it was in looks, and terrible in execution. I can remember that once I had a convenient toothache. Like many other boys I had occasions, when school was distasteful to me, and the hunting fur birch or berries, or going after fish were more of a delight than the struggle after knowledge. This toothache struck in on a Monday morning in ample time to cover the school hour. I was in great pain, and held on to my jaw with a severe grip. My mother's sympathetic nature permitted me to stay at home with the pain. My father was of rather sterner stuff. He didn't discover I was out of school until the second day. When he found out I had the teethache, he wanted to see the tooth. I pointed out one, and he examined it carefully. He said it was a perfectly sound tooth, but he didn't doubt but it pained very much, and must be dreadful to bear, but he would have something done for it. He gave me a note to Dr. Tyle Taylor. Dr. Tyle read the note, looked at the tooth, and then, getting down the dreadful turnkey, growled, "Sit down there, and I'll have that tooth out of there, or I'll yank your young head off." I did not wait for the remedy but left for home at the top of my speed— and have not had the toothache since.

"I remember seeing my father and our neighbors put through military drill every day by Capt. Noah Ferry in 1814, for the war with Great Britain of 1812-15.

"My uncles, aunts and others, when I was a child, often spoke about ravages of Indians from which their ancestors had suffered, and numbers of them remembered and described the burning of Danbury by the British in 1777.

"One season I attended the private school of Laurens P. Hickok (now Prof. Hickok), in which his sweetheart, Eliza Taylor, was also a scholar. One day he threw a ruler at my head. I dodged, and it struck Eliza in the face. He quietly apologized and said she might apply that to some other time when she might deserve it. He and his wife are still living in Andover, Mass., a happy grey-haired old couple of eighty or more.

"Eliza's father, Esquire Tom Taylor, sometimes wore white-topped boots. He was a large, majestic-looking man, of great will-force, and was considered the richest man in Bethel. Mr. Eli Judd was marked second in point of wealth. Every year I took twelve dollars to Esquire Tom Taylor to pay the interest on a two hundred dollar note which my father owed him. I also annually carried four dollars and fifty cents, to Eli Judd for interest on a seventy-five dollar note which he held against my father. As these wealthy men quietly turned over each note filed away in a small package till they found the note of my father, and then endorsed the interest thereon, I trembled with awe to think I stood in the presence of such wonderfully rich men. It was estimated that the richer of them was actually worth three thousand dollars!

"Esquire Tom made quite a revolution here by one act. He got two yards of figured carpet to put down in front of his bed in the winter, because the bare board floor was too cold for his feet, while he was dressing. This was a big event in the social life of that day, and Esquire Tom was thought to be putting on airs which his great wealth alone permitted.

"When I was but ten years old, newspapers came only once a week.

"The man who brought us the week's papers came up from Norwalk and drove through this section with newspapers for subscribers and pins and needles for customers. He was called Uncle Silliman. I can remember well his weekly visit through Bethel, and his queer cry. Oncoming to a house or village he would shout 'News! News! The Lord reigns!' One time he passed our schoolhouse when a snow storm was prevailing. He shouted: 'News! News! The Lord reigns — and snows a little.'

"It took two days, and sometimes more, to reach New York from Bethel or Danbury. My father drove a freight or market wagon from Bethel to Norwalk. Stage passengers for New York took sloop at Norwalk, sometimes arriving in New York the next morning, but were often detained by adverse winds several days.

"Everybody had barrels of cider in their cellars and drank cider — spirits called "gumption." Professors of religion and the clergy all drank liquor. They drank it in all the hat and comb shops, the farmers had it at hay and harvest times. Every sort of excuse was made for being treated. A new journeyman must give a pint or quart of rum to pay his footing. If a man had a new coat he must "sponge " it by treating. Even at funerals the clergy, mourners and friends drank liquor. At public venues the auctioneer held a bottle of liquor in his hand and when bidding lagged he would cry "a dram to the next bidder," the bid would be raised a cent and the bidder would take his dram boldly and be the envy of most of the others.

"The public whipping post and imprisonment for debt both flourished in Bethel in my youthful days. Suicides were buried at cross-roads. How blessed are we to live in a more charitable and enlightened age, to enjoy the comforts and conveniences of modern times and to realize that the world is continually growing wiser and better.

"I sincerely congratulate my native village on her character for temperance, industry and other good qualities.

"And now, my friends, I take very great pleasure in presenting this fountain to the town and borough of Bethel as a small evidence of the love which I bear them and the respect which I feel for my successors, the present and future citizens of my native village.

Our Great Barnum-London Show closed its season at Newport, Arkansas, November 12, 1881, from whence it came direct to its Winter Quarters, at Bridgeport, arriving on the morning of November nineteenth. The entire show traveled, during the season of thirty-three weeks, 12,266 miles. Bay City, Michigan, was the furthest point north which the Show visited. Bangor, Maine, the further east; Galveston, Texas, the furthest south, and Omaha, Nebraska, the furthest west.

CHAPTER LII.

TWO FAMOUS ELEPHANTS.

On February 2, 1882, "Queen," one of my twenty-two elephants gave birth to a young one at our "winter-quarters" in Bridgeport. The event had long been anticipated and thoroughly published throughout America and Europe. Scientists, all over the country, had been informed that the period of gestation being known to be about twenty months, a "Baby Elephant" might be expected early in February. The public press, naturalists, college professors and agents of zoological gardens in Europe were on the *qui vive*, and when the interesting event was imminent it was telegraphed through the associated press to all parts of the United States, and about sixty scientists, medical men and reporters arrived in time to be present at the birth. The next morning more than fifty columns of details of the birth, weight and name of the Baby Elephant appeared in the American papers, and notices cabled to London and Paris appeared in the morning papers. As this was the second elephant ever born in captivity, either in America or Europe, it created a great sensation. Its weight was only one hundred and forty-five pounds at birth. We named it "Bridgeport," after the place of its nativity and of my residence.

We opened our Great Show for the season of 1882 on Monday, March 13th, in Madison Square Garden, New York City, having given an illuminated street pageant the preceding Saturday evening, which eclipsed all similar exhibitions ever witnessed in America. The fame of the "Baby Elephant" had created quite a furor in the public mind, and from the very first night of opening, our efforts were crowned with success totally unprecedented in the show business. Day after day, and night after night, we turned away multitudes for want of room.

"Jumbo," the largest elephant ever seen, either wild or in captivity, had been for many years one of the chief attractions of the Royal Zoological Gardens, London. I had often looked wistfully on Jumbo, but with no hope of ever getting possession of him, as I knew him to be a great favorite of Queen Victoria, whose children and grandchildren are among the tens of thousands of British juveniles whom Jumbo has carried on his back. I did not suppose he would ever be sold. But one of my agents, who made the tour of Europe in the summer and autumn of 1881 in search of novelties for our big show, was so struck with the extraordinary size of the majestic Jumbo that he ventured to ask my friend, Mr. Bartlett, Superintendent of the Zoological Gardens, if he would sell Jumbo. The presumption of my agent startled Mr. Bartlett, and at first he replied rather sarcastically in the negative, but my agent pushed the question and said, "Mr. Barnum would pay a round price for him." Further conversation led my agent to think that possibly an offer of $10,000 might be entertained. He cabled me to that effect, to which I replied: "I will give ten thousand dollars for Jumbo, but the Zoo will never sell him." Two days afterwards my agent cabled me that my offer of $10,000 for Jumbo was accepted, I to take him in the Garden as he stood. The next day I dispatched Mr. Davis by steamer to London, with a bank draft for £2000 sterling,

WINTER QUARTERS OF THE GREAT BARNUM-LONDON SHOW

payable to the order of the Treasurer of the Royal Zoological Gardens, London.

From that time an excitement prevailed and increased throughout Great Britain which, for a cause so comparatively trivial, has never had a parallel in any civilized country. The council and directors of the Royal Zoo were denounced in strong terms for having sold Jumbo to the famous Yankee shopman, Barnum. The newspapers, from the *London Times* down, daily thundered anathemas against the sale, and their columns teemed with communications from statesmen, noblemen and persons of distinction advising that the bargain should be broken at all risk, and promising that the money would be contributed by the British public to pay any damages which might be awarded to Barnum by the courts. It is said that the Queen and the Prince of Wales both asked that this course should be adopted. I received scores of letters from ladies and children, beseeching me to let Jumbo remain, and to name what damages I required and they should be paid. Mr. Laird, the ship-builder, wrote me from Birkenhead that England was as able to pay "Jumbo claims" as she was to pay the "Alabama claims," and it would be done if I would only desist and name my terms. All England seemed to run mad about Jumbo; pictures of Jumbo, the life of Jumbo, a pamphlet headed "Jumbo-Barnum," and all sorts of Jumbo stories and poetry, Jumbo Hats, Jumbo Collars, Jumbo Cigars, Jumbo Neckties, Jumbo Fans, Jumbo Polkas, etc., were sold by the tens of thousands in the stores and streets of London and other British cities. Meanwhile the London correspondents of the leading American newspapers cabled columns upon the subject, describing the sentimental Jumbo craze which had seized upon Great Britain. These facts stirred up the excitement in the United States, and the American newspapers, and scores of letters sent to me daily, urged me not to give up Jumbo.

The editor of the *London Daily Telegraph* cabled me to name a price for which I would cancel the sale, and permit Jumbo to remain in London:

London, February 22.

P. T. Barnum, N. Y.:

Editor's compliments; all British children distressed at Elephant's departure; hundreds of correspondents beg us to inquire on what terms you will kindly return Jumbo. Answer, prepaid, unlimited.

LESARGE, *Daily Telegraph*.

I cabled back as follows:

New York, February 23, 1882.

To Lesarge, *Daily Telegraph*, London:

My compliments to Editor *Daily Telegraph* and British Nation. Fifty-one millions of American citizens anxiously awaiting Jumbo's arrival. My forty years' invariable practice of exhibiting the best that money could procure, makes Jumbo's presence here imperative. Hundred thousand pounds would be no inducement to cancel purchase. My largest tent seats 20.000 persons and is filled twice each day. It contains four rings, in three of which three full circus companies give different performances simultaneously.

In the large outer ring, or racing track, the Roman Hippodrome is exhibited. In two other immense connecting tents my colossal Zoological collection and museum are shown.

Wishing long life and prosperity to British Nation and *Telegraph* and Jumbo, I am the public's obedient servant,

P.T. BARNUM.

This dispatch was published in the *London Daily Telegraph* the next morning and was sent by the London Associated press to the principal newspapers throughout Great Britain, which republished it the following day, giving the excitement an immense impetus. Crowds of men, women and children rushed to the "Zoo" to see dear old Jumbo for the last time, and the receipts at the gates were augmented nearly two thousand dollars per day. A "fellow " or stockholder of the Royal Zoo sued out an injunction in the Chancery Court against the "councilors" of the Zoo and myself to quash the sale. After a hearing, which occupied two days, the sale was declared valid, and Jumbo was decided to be my property.

The fateful day arrived when Jumbo was to bid farewell to the Zoo, and then came the tug of war. The unfamiliar street waked in Jumbo's breast the timidity which is so marked a feature of elephant character. He trumpeted with alarm, turned to re-enter the Gardens, and, finding the gate closed, laid down on the pavement. His cries of fright sounded to the uninitiated like cries of grief, and quickly attracted a crowd of sympathizers. British hearts were touched, British tears flowed for the poor beast who was so unwilling to leave his old home. Persuasion had no effect in inducing him to rise, force was not permitted, and indeed it would have been a puzzle what force to apply to so huge a creature. My agent, dismayed, cabled me, "Jumbo has laid down in the street and won't get up. What shall we do?." I replied, "Let him lie there a week if he wants to. It is the best advertisement in the world." After twenty-four hours the gates of his paradise were reopened and Jumbo allowed to return to his old quarters, while my agents set to work to secure him by strategy. A huge iron-bound cage was constructed with a door at each end and mounted on broad wheels of enormous strength. This, with the doors open, was backed up against the door entrance to Jumbo's den, and the wheels sunk so that the floor of the cage was on a level with that of the elephant's. A passageway was thus formed through which Jumbo must pass to reach the outer air. After much hesitation, he was persuaded to follow his keeper, Scott; through this cage to take his daily airing. For several days this ruse was repeated, then, as he entered the cage, the door behind him was swiftly closed, then the door in front of him, and Jumbo was mine.

On account of the national interest manifested in "Jumbo," we presume the "British Lion" is for the time forgotten; and we therefore suggest the above as the most appropriate coat-of-arms for England. — London Fun.

Meanwhile Jumbo came up in Parliament, where the President of the Board of Trade was questioned in regard to precautions being taken to protect the passengers on shipboard. Mr. Lowell, our American Minister to the Court of St. James, in a speech given at a public banquet in London, playfully remarked, "the only burning question between England and America is Jumbo." *The London Graphic, Illustrated News, Punch*, and all the London papers published scores of pictures and descriptions of Jumbo, in prose and poetry, for several weeks in succession.

On the morning of his capture, March 25, 1882, the wheels of his cage were dug free of the ground, twenty horses attached, and in the comparative silence of the following night, Jumbo was dragged miles to the steamship, *Assyrian Monarch*, where quarters had been prepared for him by cutting away one of the decks. The Society for the Prevention of Cruelty to Animals hovered over Jumbo to the last, and titled ladies and little children brought to the ship baskets of dainties for Jumbo's consumption during the voyage.

After a rough passage he arrived in New York, in good condition, Sunday morning, April 9th, and next day was placed on exhibition in the menagerie department of our Great Show where he created such a sensation that in the next two weeks the receipts in excess of the usual amount more than repaid us the $30,000 his purchase and removal had cost us. Being a little wearied after the excitement of this achievement and knowing well that there is no rest and recuperative like a sea voyage, I sailed with my wife in the City of Rome, for Liverpool, the latter part of May. We spent most of our time at the home of my wife's parents in Lancashire, making brief trips to London, visits made pleasant by the social attentions of old friends. I was present at the dinner given by Mr. Henry Irving, the eminent actor, on the stage of his Lyceum Theatre, June 25th. About seventy gentlemen of note were present, including Lord Lytton, the Lord Mayor Sir Julius Benedict, Dion Boucicault, etc. The banquet was enlivened by speeches, and much humor and repartee. The Lord Mayor jocosely asked me what countryman I was. I replied, "A Yankee." Augustus Sala, whose ready wit is proverbial, immediately said, "I can prove that Barnum is more English than

American." "How is that?" asked Mr. Henry Irving. "Because his better-half is English," was the famous editor's reply.

I also attended, by special invitation, a grand Military Tournament at the Agricultural Hall, at which the Prince and Princess of Wales, the Duke of Cambridge, and other members of the Royal Family, were present. My seat was located within a few feet of the Royal box. During the entertainment, some sixty of the Royal Life Guards, mounted on their jet-black steeds, gave what is called the "Musical Ride," consisting of an ingenious and exciting series of marches, countermarches, evolutions and figures, not unlike those presented in the "grand entrees" of my circus rings. The large area of the Agricultural Hall gave space for elaboration. When I was pointed out to the Prince of Wales and the Duke of Cambridge, they rose and gave me a good stare, and then smilingly conversed. I fancy that, remembering my success in securing "Jumbo," these royal personages were wondering whether I contemplated coming down with a swoop and carrying the Royal Life Guards off to America!

The success of the Great Show during the season of 1883 is well and briefly chronicled in the following extract:

[From *Harper's Weekly*, November 4, 1882.]

Few persons, outside of those immediately engaged in its management, have any idea of the vast amount of labor and money required to run a first-class circus. Mr. Barnum, having recently fallen into the hands of the interviewers, has given to the public press some points concerning his "Greatest Show on Earth " that are of curious interest. For instance, a single item of expenditure amounts to a snug fortune, viz., that of wintering the animals and their keepers, trainers and attendants, and getting matters into shape for the spring opening. Last year, said the veteran showman, this cost nearly a quarter of a million dollars, and that during a time when not a dollar was being earned. But large as it is, the cost of wintering is a mere "flea-bite" to that of securing fresh novelties. For this purpose, scores of agents under large salaries are sent around the world every year to gather up the best of all that is new, regardless of expense. This year men have gone on these errands to far-away countries where no show agent ever before appeared. To meet the necessities of but one of these agents $70,000 were recently deposited with Messrs. Brown Brothers & Co. One of the most costly ventures was the Jumbo affair. The figures are not given, but the round outlay is said to have been enormous. Another important item this year was the printing, which cost $175,000 exclusive of newspaper advertising. The gross receipts of the season of thirty-one weeks were a million and three-quarters of dollars. The receipts in New York were nearly $60,000 per week. In Philadelphia, $69,115.85 were taken in six days, four of which were rainy, and in Boston a single week rolled in $74,051.03.

CHAPTER LIII.

THE WHITE ELEPHANT.

On the 9th of August, 1883, my wife and I made our usual summer trip to Europe, being met, as always, by my father-in-law, John Fish, who on this occasion, said, "Mr. Barnum, I am always glad to see you set your foot on English soil, for I really believe that every voyage you make across the Atlantic adds a year to your life."

"Then I will hereafter make two trips a year," I replied, which set my matter-of-fact English father-in-law to practicing arithmetic, in order to discover how long I should live if I became purser of a steamship and made a dozen trans-Atlantic trips a year!

Among the pleasantest of our fellow-passengers on the Adriatic, I count Sir Charles Lees, then Governor-General of the Bahamas, sometime prominent representative of the British government in Africa and Asia. I had with me several agents, on their way to these countries to secure natives for my Ethnological Congress. The knowledge of strange tribes and races which Sir Charles had acquired during long residence in foreign countries, he not only obligingly imparted to them, but gave them letters of introduction which were of much service to them in Siam, Burma, India, etc., and placed me under further indebtedness by introducing me to the Foreign Office in London. Though our busy hours may prevent our exchanging the visits we so faithfully promised each other, I shall always retain the pleasantest memory of this genial, cultured Englishman, and the conversations and stories with which we abbreviated the voyage. Touching Mackey, the California millionaire, he told a story that lost none of its point because of the deliberate, dryly humorous manner of narrating. Mackey, he said, was present on one occasion when Sir Charles, as the Queen's representative, opened the Parliament at Nassau, with much bravery of ermined robes, and due observance of ceremonies. In his speech, he spoke of the government debt as amounting to £60,000. Afterward, Mackey said, "Is that really all you owe?"

"That is all," replied Sir Charles.

"Well," said the money king, with a comical smile, "*I have a devilish good mind to give you a check for it!*"

In the summer of 1883, my little friend Tom Thumb died of apoplexy. He was at the time of his death a portly little man, of middle age, and in prosperous circumstances. His widow, the charming little Lavinia, of Chapter XXXVII, has since married again, and is now known as the Countess Magri.

In November I had the pleasure of entertaining at Waldemere Mr. Matthew Arnold, on the occasion of his lecturing in Bridgeport.

The official accounts of the show at the end of the traveling season gave much cause for congratulation. The expenses for the season amounted to $1,034,000, or more than $6,000 for each of the 176 exhibition days, out of which six performances were lost. A glance at some of these records of receipts will show where we get enough to pay $6,000 a day and still have sufficient to make a very satisfying division of profits at the end of the season. Take the six days in Philadelphia: April 30th, $8,416.75; May 1st, $12,000.15; May 2nd, $16,382.15; May 3rd, $17,187.25; May 4th, $16,064.80; May 5th, $10,053. 10-aggregating a grand total of $80,130.20 from that city alone. Out of Chicago, in the ten days, from June 4th to June 14th, both inclusive, the show took $119,172.30. Then take the single day's receipts into notice: Detroit, $15,538.10; Cleveland, $14,762.20; Pittsburgh, $14,376.20; Cincinnati, $14,133.65; Toronto, $13,864.80; Hamilton, $13,451.50; Toledo, $13,372.25; Baltimore, $13,352.05; Washington, $13,294.90; Louisville, $12,937.75, Montreal, $15,896.75; Brooklyn, $13,732.00.

I was the recipient of a very novel compliment at Christmas. Labouchere, M.P., the publisher of *London Truth*, dubbed his Christmas number "Barnum in Britishland," and every line was devoted to imaginary interviews of P.T. Barnum with the most prominent Britishers, beginning with a hobnobbing *tete-d-tete* with the Prince of Wales. It was a witty hit (done up in rhyme) at the foibles, follies, customs, fashions and sharp practices supposed to exist in Britishland. The sale reached a third edition and exceeded by many thousands that of any previous season. The gratuitous advertisement was highly appreciated by me.

The New York Sun, about the same time, published the following:

Under the moral influence of a great illuminated motto— "Whatsoever ye would that men should do to you, do ye even so to them" — in his luxuriously furnished parlor at Waldemere, his country seat near Bridgeport, the reporter found the venerable showman, P.T. Barnum. Plump, ruddy lively and active, the veteran looked as if he had juggled away a score, at least, of his seventy-four years. "But I'm getting pretty well on in years." he said, "for I was born on July 5, 1810."

"What is your actual present physical condition?" the reporter asked,

"I don't positively know, without trying, whether I could turn a somersault or not, but the chances are that I could, at least, as well as ever. At all events, I never was better in my life. I eat well, sleep well, and enjoy the most perfect health. Perhaps to maintain this condition I should walk more than I do, but I walk some, and go out riding every day twice. All the disease I have is old age. and my neighbors say I should not plead that, for I'm as young as most men of sixty. The sickness I had in New York three years ago, when the doctors gave me up, was the only one I had in many years, and seems to have renovated me— given me a new lease of life."

"What have been and are the personal habits that have conduced to such a good result?"

Primarily, regularity; secondarily, abstinence from things that tend to shorten life. Sometimes, when neighbors do not come to me I go out to them in the evenings and play a game of whist, and occasionally I go to the theatre, but as a rule I am in bed by 10 o'clock every night. All my work, directing my personal business, conducting my correspondence, and communicating with my partners, I do in the forenoons, getting through it in time for a drive before my dinner, which I take in the middle of the day. After dinner, I am accustomed to doze for three or five minutes. If I just lose consciousness that long I am as much refreshed as if I had slept for hours. After that I take another drive. In the evening an hour's reading, a few games of cribbage or whist, or a little music fills up the time until my hour for retiring I am always up by 7 o'clock in the morning."

"How long have you maintained such regular habits?"

"As far as practicable since 1847, when I became a teetotaler, although when I was a traveling showman my hours were necessarily not so good."

"Did you drink much prior to 1847?"

"Well, I wouldn't have allowed anybody to tell me so, but when I look back over that time I know now that I did. When I built my magnificent Oriental country seat *Iranistan*. I was proud of the house, but ten times prouder of my wine cellar than of anything else I had. I was not in the habit of drinking distilled liquors, but every day at dinner took my bottle of champagne, or its equivalent in other wines or malt liquors. I did no business after noon, and my mother-in-law used to say sometimes that I was 'heady' after dinner. I felt quite offended by the suggestion and threatened to go back to whisky if it was repeated, for I really considered myself quite a temperance man, since I drank only wine, and thought my after-dinner feelings were due to overeating rather than drinking. But I got the Rev. Dr. Chapin to come up to Bridgeport and deliver a temperance lecture, for the subject of which he took 'The Moderate Drinker,' and I saw myself in quite a new light. I realized for the first time the bad example I was setting, and when I went home that night was so worried that I could scarcely sleep. The next morning, I had my coachman knock the necks off all the champagne bottles I had in my cellar, some five or six dozen; the port and other medicinal wines I gave away in cases of sickness, and the liquors I returned to the dealers. That was the end of my drinking. As young bumblebees are biggest when they are first hatched, so I was, in the first heat of my conversion, an enthusiast on the subject of teetotalism. I went all over Connecticut and New York delivering free lectures on the subject, and even went out to Wisconsin, stumped the State at my own expense, and at least helped to carry it on a temperance platform." "You shut off on tobacco also?"

"Yes— or at least I stopped its use. I never chewed, but I was a great smoker. When I went over to England lecturing, in 1856, after the Jerome Clock Company disaster overwhelmed me, I was in such a situation that every pound was of importance to me, and as I was then using every week a sovereign's worth of cigars. I thought I would practice economy and stop it. One Sunday I chewed chamomile flowers all day instead of smoking, by a druggist's advice, and they almost killed me. The next day I went to smoking again and continued it up to 1860. I could give up liquor easily enough, but not tobacco, and I averaged ten cigars a day. One day in 1860, on my way down to the museum, I felt a strange choking sensation away down in my throat, and then a throbbing or palpitation of my heart. I had noticed it a little for a year before but paid no particular attention to it until then. I asked my manager, Greenwood, what it was, and he said it was heart disease, and the symptoms I described as mine meant death. That scared me pretty badly. I determined to give up business at once, retire to the country, and prepare to die. but before doing so consulted Dr. Willard Parker. He examined me and said: 'You may have a very hard heart, for all I know, but you have as strong a one as there is in New York. Nicotine is all that is the matter with you. Stop smoking.' I did so at once, I was so scared, and never smoked again. For a year, however, I used to carry bits of calamus in my pocket to chew when I wanted to smoke." "So, in your unregenerate state you used to drink and smoke. Did you gamble?" "No, never. I never even speculated in stocks, but once in my life. That was in the time of the great panic, ten years or more ago. I had some money lying idle in bank, and, seeing everything tumbled down to the lowest point apparently, I thought it would be a good time to buy and hold on for a raise. So, I took down $100,000 to Hatch & Foote and told them to put it in whatever they thought best. They invested it, and I thought I was sure of making $25,000 anyway, but on the whole, I lost. Some of my stocks went up eventually, but others went down, and I was a loser. With that exception I have owned no railroad stocks or other speculative securities. I have my legitimate business as a showman and want no other. In it I never made a mistake, but whenever I stepped outside I was pretty sure to."

"Why, when you made your will recently, did you take the trouble to call a conclave of physicians to certify to your condition?"

"Because of what I have seen of contests over wills, in the case of Frank Leslie and a dozen others. Why, we have had one right here, that over the will of Capt. John Brooks, who died in full possession of all his faculties, but pretty old, and left most of his money to the church, and now relations he scarcely ever heard of are contesting his will. They had me on the witness stand, and asked me what, in my opinion, was Capt. Brook's mental condition. I replied that I thought his mind was as sound as that of any rich man who has poor relations. They dropped me pretty quickly. I don't suppose that there is anything in my will that anybody will contest, but I don't propose to leave any ground for legal trouble over it. I provide that any legatee who makes a contest shall, as the penalty of so doing, forfeit whatever is bequeathed to him in the will, and I have left a fund of $100,000 in reserve in the hands of the executors until the will is probated, expressly to fight any contestant who may arise. And if that is not enough, they can then go and apply the estate to make the fight. As a measure of precaution, I called in my personal physician, who is an allopath, a prominent homoeopathic physician, and the Treasurer of the Bridgeport Hospital, who is a leading doctor, and had them not only witness my will, but make oath that they believed me to be of sound mind."

"Independent of the donations you have made to advance your own landed interests, you have given largely solely for the public good, have you not?"

For the first time in the course of the interview, Mr. Barnum spoke with manifest reluctance. "I think." he said, "that it is not a becoming thing in me to recapitulate what my good fortune has enabled me to do for my friends and neighbors, for so I deem all Bridgeport. There are doubtless many among them who, had they been equally successful in having the means to dispose of, would have been at least as liberal as I have been. I had been lucky, and naturally wished those about me to have some share in my luck. It will all be told when I am gone. In this matter I should, for once, prefer to drop the showman and not seem to be "blowing my own horn." "Let me speak for him," interpolated a friend who was present, "as I believe I can correctly, so far, at least, as the main things deserving of mention. Many years ago, he and his then associate, Gen. Noble, donated to the City of Bridgeport, Washington Park, a beautiful grove surrounded by churches and fine residences, which the city would not sell now for hundreds of thousands of dollars. Then he, individually, gave the city $70,000 worth more of land for park purposes, on condition that the city is bound to forever maintain it as a park, and always to have a free bathing ground on its front. In the City Cemetery, he gave several thousand dollars worth of lots for a burial plot for the Grand Army of the Republic: as much more for the Fire Department of Bridgeport; three thousand single graves for poor people, on condition that they should be scattered all over the cemetery, not located in any one place together, where the spot might come to be known by the opprobrious name of Potter's Field, and the further condition that the very poor shall be buried for nothing, and in no case shall more than $1 be charged, instead of the ordinary rate of $7. In addition to all that, he gave some $50,000 worth of land for the cemetery. In his native town of Bethel, a few miles from here, he erected a fountain that cost him $10,000 in Berlin, and with the fitting up and ground about it, represented $20,000 at least. He gave..."

"There! There! Stop!" interposed Mr. Barnum. "No more of that. To sit here and listen to you going on in that way makes me feel as if you were reading my obituary aloud."

"To add to the attractions of "The Great Combined Show " during the season of 1884, my agents in Africa and in India and other parts of Asia, among whom were Messrs. J. B. Gay lord, Charles White, and Thomas H. Davis, after many months residence in those lands, procured a number of additional ethnological specimens for exhibition in my "Grand Congress of the Nations." These novelties included specimens of the following tribes, namely: Nubian warriors, Zulu chiefs, Afghans, Hindus, Todas Indians, and Singing and Dancing Nautch Girls of India. A preliminary private exhibition of these ethnological rarities was given to members of the press and of the clergy in Madison Square Garden, New York, on the afternoon of March 15, 1884, which was attended with the customary success. In the evening of the same day they were introduced to the public as part of the Great Show.

The particular additional feature, however, by which the season of 1884 was made memorable, was the exhibition for the first time in any civilized country of that rare and beautiful animal, which for ages has been recognized in Siam, Burma, and other Buddhist countries as the "Royal Sacred White Elephant." This absolutely unique curiosity was accompanied by a Burmese orchestra and a retinue of Buddhist priests in full ecclesiastical costume, the sacred animal being surrounded by the same attendants and the like paraphernalia as during the performance of religious ceremonies in his native country. The priests were also supplied with documents, under the royal seal, attesting the sacred character of the beast, and with the royal bill of sale executed by King Theebaw's Master of Elephants, and also bearing the king's seal.

Until my agent first visited Bangkok, the capital of Siam, and there saw the king's "Sacred White Elephants", I had supposed that they were literally white, instead of technically so. Those who had not seen these animals, nor read authentic descriptions of them, had the same idea as myself. When, therefore, my Sacred Elephant arrived in London, a large portion of the public, having expected to see a milk-white elephant, were disappointed. The following article, which I clip from the *New York Tribune* of Feb. 17, gives the facts in the case:

P.T. Barnum and his partners have dispelled a wide-spread popular illusion, that the so-called sacred white elephants of the kings of Siam and Burma either are, or ever were, literally white. They say they have secured as perfect a specimen of this animal as exists anywhere, and they do not claim that it is "white" in the strict sense of that word, yet, it is the same species, and exact counterpart of those white sacred elephants worshiped for centuries by the Buddhists. Up to this time, no European monarch has ever been able to procure a sacred white elephant, or even get it into a Christian country, and in that Barnum has succeeded.

A rival showman, who labored under the "popular" illusion, had a common elephant painted milk-white, and so exhibited it for a time as a genuine specimen purchased in Siam. Two leading New York illustrated papers, early in 1882, were deceived into publishing pictures of this "pure white"-washed animal as a genuine Sacred White Elephant from Siam. The owner of this imposition soon announced that it had suddenly died. It was simply dyed! And thus, another proof added to millions which have preceded it, demonstrates that truth will always triumph over falsehood.

In his own land the white elephant is held in the utmost veneration; and as the people believe that if one of them leaves their country his departure will be the signal for dire calamities to them; and as, moreover, any person who is instrumental in sending one out of the country without the royal permission is liable to the penalty of death, the difficulty of procuring one for exportation has hitherto been so great as to have proved insurmountable. As, however, it has ever been my aim to bring together under our tents, utterly regardless of cost, the real marvels of this wonderful earth, I determined, if possible, even at the cost of half a million dollars, if necessary, to procure a curiosity which centuries of unsuccessful endeavor had seemed to prove utterly unattainable. Unfortunately, just as my agents seemed on the verge of success, they were doomed to disappointment. A white elephant purchased by them in Siam many months before Toung Taloung was obtained, was poisoned on the eve of its departure by its attendant priests rather than that it should fall into the hands of profane Christians. Finally, however, after three years of patient persistence, and the exercise, on the part of half a score of our shrewdest agents, of wonderful tact, diplomacy, and untiring energy, often at the peril of their lives, and the outlay of a quarter of a million dollars, our efforts were crowned with victory. We now possessed and regularly exhibited the first and only animal of the kind that ever had been seen or that probably ever will be seen in a Christian land. So enormous were the difficulties which had to be conquered in order to get this only genuine White Elephant out of Burma, that I am satisfied no other successful attempt to export one will ever again be made.

The Royal Sacred White Elephant, Toung Taloung, was purchased at Mandelay, in Burma; and having been brought away under the royal warrant of King Theebaw, was shipped from Rangoon, in British Burma, in the steamship Tenasserim, on December 8, 1883. After passing through the Suez Canal, and touching at Malta, it arrived safely at Liverpool, England, on January 14, 1884. Thence it was taken to London, where it was exhibited for several weeks at the Royal Zoological Gardens, Regent's Park, receiving the endorsement of many eminent scientists, prominent among whom was Professor W.H. Flower, President of the London Zoological Society and Curator of the Royal College of Surgeons. On March 13, 1884, it was shipped in the steamer *Lydian Monarch* for New York, and at that city it arrived on the 28th of the same month. On the 31st a special private exhibition of it was given to several hundred naturalists, scientists, Eastern travelers, scholars, leading physicians and clergymen, editors of New York and other papers, and other persons, whose closest scrutiny I invited, but who none of them doubted that the animal was what he was described to be, namely, a genuine white elephant from Burma. Many certificates of his genuineness, now in our possession, were given by such eminent authorities as Colonel Daniel B. Sickles, late Minister to Siam; Colonel Thomas W. Knox, the only American to whom the King of Siam has ever presented the Order of the White Elephant; Mr. Edward Greey, author of "The Golden Lotus;" Mr. David Ker, Siamese correspondent of the New York Times; Frank Vincent, Jr., author of "The Land of the White Elephant" and many others.

As might have been anticipated, as a consequence of the exhibition of so unique a curiosity, not to speak of the other novelties, the tour of the "Greatest Show on Earth," during the season of 1884, was quite as successful as any previous one. The Show visited the principal cities of the United States as far east as Lewiston, ME., and as far west as Kansas City and Omaha.

It is worthy of special remark that with regard to the genuineness of the Sacred White Elephant, which has been the subject of so much discussion, every claim made in behalf of Toung Taloung has been substantiated by subsequent events. The *Siamese Weekly Advertiser*, a paper printed partly in English and partly in Siamese, and published at Bangkok, the Siamese capital — where, the King and his Court reside— in its issue of March 7th, 1885, prints the following editorial:

> White Elephant. — It is stated that a White Elephant has been obtained at Pratabaung and will be sent to Bangkok as speedily as possible. There will doubtless be the usual pompous demonstrations in connection with bringing it to Bangkok, conferring on it a title and giving it a home in the vicinity of the p dace. Foreigners naturally are surprised that such eminent honors should be conferred upon an animal, by no means white, though perhaps a shade or two lighter than the ordinary elephant in some parts of the body.

The same paper, in its issue of April 18th, 1885, speaks as follows of the presentation of the elephant above referred to:

> On the 3rd instant. His Royal Highness Somdetch Chowfah Mahamalah Bararahp Parapako conducted a male elephant into the Palace for presentation to His Majesty the King of Siam. His Majesty graciously accepted the animal and presented a sum of money and sundry articles of clothing to be given to Tepan. the mother, and her son, Ayungtoh Karens, the owners of the elephant The Siamese officials who brought the elephant to Bangkok were honored with an audience of His Majesty and were the recipients of suitable presents also.

Certainly, the King of Siam ought to be accepted as good authority on the subject of white elephants, and here we have an account of his receiving with highest honors and rewards a "White Elephant," which in sacred attributes and required peculiarities of marking would have no comparison with ours. And this is supplemented by more recent proof from Burma, which in the Autumn of 1885 was conquered by Great Britain. The correspondent of the *London Daily Standard*, who entered Mandelay, the Capital, with General Prendergast's army, says:

I saw King Theebaw's Sacred White Elephant close by in a magnificent palace of his own. The only white about him is two small dirty spots, almost imperceptible.

The Manchester (Eng.) Mail says:

Barnum's Sacred White Elephant, exhibited in London last year, appears to have been whiter than King Theebaw's.

King Theebaw's White Elephant died soon after his royal master's overthrow, and the *New York Commercial Advertiser*, commenting on the fact, says:

Mr. Barnum's White Elephant was, after all, whiter than him of Mandelay.

The tour of the Great Show during the summer of 1884 was marked by an incident which is worthy of note here. The authorities of a thriving New England town, at which we were advertised to appear, demanded an exceptionally exorbitant sum as a license fee. Though our advance agent demurred to the imposition, the authorities, thinking no doubt that we would submit to it rather than pass by a town where the receipts for a day had averaged $10,000, were immovable. They reckoned without their host, however. We at once changed our plans, cancelled the date for their town, and announced instead that we would give the intended exhibition at 'a smaller town twelve miles off.' The merchants, hotel-keepers and other business men of the larger town offered us four times the amount of the license-fee demanded if we would adhere to our original purpose and exhibit there. We, however, were immovable in our turn, and declined to change our plans a second time. On the day of the exhibition we ran a large number of excursion trains to the smaller town; the other town was nearly deserted; and the day's receipts for the exhibition were not $10,000, but $12,760.

Another incident, of a widely different character, by which the year 1884 was marked as a bright spot in my calendar, was the opening of the Natural History Museum of Tuft's College, near Boston, of which admirable educational institution I was a trustee at its foundation. The want of a natural history museum had long been felt, and some time ago my friend, President E.H. Capen, made an appeal to me to supply the need. To this appeal I responded; and the outcome has been the erection of a large and handsome stone structure, partially furnished with a fine collection of natural history specimens and other curiosities interesting and useful to students. The building was completed in the spring of 1884, and it was formally inaugurated at the Commencement exercises of the college, held on the 10th of June in the same year. The name of the founder had been kept a secret, but it was then publicly announced by President Capen in the course of his address.

The event was described by the *Christian Leader* of June 26th as follows:

There had been great curiosity in regard to the donor whose great heart had added to the group of buildings on College Hill the elegant structure in stone to be known as the Natural History Museum. When, as the tone of the President's address eliminated one after another till it was clear that Phineas Taylor Barnum was the man, the applause became a shout, and for what seemed many minutes the throng testified their gratitude for the magnificent gift— of a character so exactly accordant with the spirit of the donor— in every articulate and muscular form In which an enthusiastic people know how to manifest their joy. It will hereafter be our great pleasure to put Mr. Barnum into the category of Tufts, Packard, Walker and the Goddards. It was the feature of the day, and it made the day most memorable in the history of Tuft's College.

President Capen's address on the occasion was as follows:

LADIES AND GENTLEMEN: I had hoped to have the supreme felicity of Introducing to you here and now the founder of the Natural History Museum. He made some weeks ago an engagement to be present, but within a few days has been obliged to cancel it. There has been a great deal of curiosity during the past year to know the name of our generous benefactor. A good many guesses have been ventured, but very few of them, so far as I know, have come near the mark. Our friend is one who has taken a deep interest in this college from the start. His name is on the original list of its trustees with Charles Tuft and Silvanus Packard and Oliver Dean and Thomas A. Goddard. He begun life in poverty, but by an energy and a spirit of enterprise almost unequaled, even in this country, and in the face of difficulties that would have appalled most men, he has conquered poverty and secured for himself a place among the men of princely fortune. He had no such educational advantages as the young men of this college enjoy. Even the lads in our primary schools get better training than he received. But by diligent use of his opportunities, by studious habits and an active brain he has not only stored his mind with varied and useful knowledge, but, as you shall presently see, has become the master of a vigorous and idiomatic style of English which would put many a college man to shame. Through all his life he has been a man of unbounded public spirit. In the city of his adoption be is, by unanimous consent, the foremost citizen, pouring out his money like water for every species of public improvement. I doubt if a single New England city has his superior in this respect. He is a man of pure life, who has taught temperance by precept and example to young and old alike. He is a man of positive religious convictions and deep religious life, the friend for many years of the venerable Dean of Tuft's Divinity School, the Kev. Dr. Sawyer, and the parishioner and life-long friend of the lamented Chapin. He has been prominently identified with the Church to which his laith has allied him and promoted its enterprises by generous contributions. In his business he has sought to combine popular amusement with popular education. He has searched all climates, from the frozen polar regions to the blazing tropics, regardless of pecuniary cost, that he might secure specimens of the rarest of living creatures for exhibition. Years ago, he built up in the city of New York a museum, which the late Professor Henry, of the Smithsonian Institution, characterized as one of the most important educational institutions in this country. And now, in the latter end of his varied and useful lite, he has chosen this college in which to create an instrumentality in which his name may be perpetuated, and the work to which his best energies have been devoted may be carried forward on authentic basis forever. Five years ago, I took occasion to call his attention to this subject, and again some fourteen months since I renewed the suggestion. The response was almost instantaneous. From that moment until now the work has been pushed forward with an energy that is electric. The sum of $55,000 has been set apart for this object, which is ample for the erection of the building, for partially furnishing it with specimens, leaving a fund for its care and maintenance. I have received the following letter, which I am sure you will be glad to hear, an in which, in the absence of our friend, I will venture to read;

My dear Mr. President, it is with unfeigned regret that I find it impossible to attend the commencement exercises at Tuft's, as promised. Often have I wished to be with you on these occasions, if for no other reason than to mark by my presence the deep interest I take and have always taken in an institution the prosperity of which I have watched with no small degree of satisfaction and pride. But a busy life has invariably brought with it duties which have deprived, from time to time, the realization of my desire to visit College Hill in June. Planning with more than usual foresight (as I had imagined) to be with you this year and believing that the time had come when I could in person extend my congratulations to the faculty and students. I find I must forego even this visit. But if absent in the flesh, I am with you in spirit, and my thoughts will wander to you in your rejoicings of commencement on the 18th instant. Deprived in my own youth of rare educational advantage, I have learned to appreciate their worth and to take solid delight in every evidence of greater enlightenment; and progress. I never see an urchin plotting his way unwillingly to school but I contrast the meagre facilities of sixty years ago with the present wealth of instrumentalities within the reach of every American boy and girl. And so, when I hear the common school-bell ring, I bless the day which no longer sees any valid reason for ignorance in this country. I have always declared that I took more pleasure in paying my school-taxes than any other; for education often tends to lessen vice and crime, as wed as to secure its recipients reputation, honor and success. I may be pardoned, Mr. President, if on this occasion I assert that my interest in the higher education if the day has ever been constant and profound. Had my earlier advantages been greater I might have achieved more; but looking back on a long and eventful career, I confess, in no boasting given, that I have conscientiously labored to elevate and enable public amusements which pay no small part among the educational agencies of the times. How successful I have been in blending healthful and moral instruction with retraction it is not for me to state. But the satisfaction experienced in my life-work has been in itself a reward altogether apart from and superior to any golden harvest I may have reaped. Not that I am insensible to the latter, for it is because of it that I am able, under the providence of a Good Father, who has blessed me all my life, to do somewhat for Tufts in the foundation of the Barnum Museum of Natural History. I am happy in the thought that this museum will be another factor in the work of the college. Helping it on its high career of usefulness. I have for many years past decided to do something for an institution the growing excellence and thoroughness of which must commend it to the lovers of knowledge everywhere. And now that the decision has been made, and the Museum Building erected, I hope the college may possess for many decades to come, facilities sufficient to inspire its students to investigations in a branch of science which so wonderfully reveals in varied form the infinite wisdom and power of the Creator. But I am afraid this letter exceeds all bounds, and should it be read on Commencement Day it would be considered irksome. And yet I cannot close without assuring you. Mr. President, the officers, teachers, patrons and students of the college, of my strong faith in the brilliant future of Tufts. I believe, from what I know of sacrificing spirit and intellectual standing of its faculty, that possibilities within its reach will be attained, and that it will become an educational center fostered and nourished not only by men of brains, but also by men of fortune. It augurs well for the future of any cause when people of medians are ready to give generously in its behalf. The history of most denominations today reveals the fact that there is more giving than formerly, and with it corresponding prosperity. Whilst feeding the churches, let us not neglect to foster the colleges, but endeavor to give them such prestige and position as shall enable them to exercise the most salutary influence and do the very best work. Hoping that others may do much more than I have, and all will feel a pleasure in contributing according to their means, I am, my dear Mr. President,

Respectfully yours,
P. T. Barnum.

After reading the letter, President Capen said: "I give you the health of the Founder of the Barnum Museum of Natural History. May his life be prolonged. May he have prosperity and success. May his declining days be crowned by domestic happiness and inward peace." The audience arose and greeted the sentiment with heart and voice. It was an ovation. When General Grant became financially embarrassed in 1884 he was specially anxious to secure Mr. W.H. Vanderbilt in the sum of $150,000, loaned to him under peculiar circumstances – the noble-hearted General and his wife made over to him all their personal property, including the valuable trophies and mementos presented to him not only in America but by monarchs, princes and other admirers during his celebrated trip around the world. Recognizing the fact that people everywhere would feel interested in seeing these trophies, and that I could by exhibiting them in a most elegant and suitable manner throughout the civilized world gratify millions of persons of taste and appreciation, while I could afford to compensate General Grant so liberally for the privilege as to assure him a fine income, I wrote to him the following letter and sent it by special messenger:

New York, January 12, 1885.
To General U. S. Grant, twice President of the United States, etc.:

Honored sir: The whole world honors and respects yon. All are anxious that you should live happy and free from care. While they admire your manliness in declining the large sum recently tendered you by friends, they still desire to see you achieve financial independence in an honorable manner. Of the unique and valuable trophies with which you have been honored, we all have read, and all have a landable desire to see these evidences of love and respect bestowed upon you by monarchs, primes and people throughout the globe. While you would confer a great and enduring favor on your fellow men and women by permitting them to see these trophies you could also remove existing embarrassments in a most satisfactory and honorable manner. I will give you one hundred thousand dollars cash, besides a proportion of the profits, if I may be permitted to exhibit these relics to a grateful and appreciative public, and I will give satisfactory bonds of half a million dollars for their safe-keeping and return.

These precious trophies of which all your friends are so proud, would be placed before the eyes of your millions of admirers in a manner and style at once pleasing to yourself and satisfactory to the best elements of the entire community. Remembering that the mementoes of Washington, Wellington, Napoleon, Frederick The Great and many other distinguished men have given immense pleasure to millions who have been permitted to see them. I trust yon will in the honorable manner proposed, gratify the public and thus inculcate the lesson of honesty, perseverance and true patriotism so admirably illustrated in your career.

I have the honor to be truly your friend and admirer,

P. T. BARNUM.

I called at General Grant's residence soon afterwards, and was politely received by him, his wife, and son, Colonel Frederick Grant. I said to the General, after our greeting. "General, since your journey around the world you are the best-known man on the globe."

"No, sir," replied the General, "your name is familiar to multitudes who never heard of me. Wherever I went, among the most distant nations, the fact that I was an American led to constant inquiries whether I knew Barnum."

Proceeding to the business on which I had called, the General informed me that the trophies were no longer under his control, as Mr. Vanderbilt, after refusing to take them, out of respect to the General, had finally accepted them on condition that after General Grant's decease they should be lodged in some safe public place in Washington, where all could see them.

"After all, Mr. Barnum," said General Grant, "under the present arrangements, everybody who visits Washington can see them."

"Yes, General," I replied, "but millions of persons who will never visit Washington will regret that I had never brought these historical relics where they would see them."

I shall always believe, regardless of any profit (or loss) which might have accrued to me, that my plan was one creditable to all concerned, and that it is to be regretted that it was not carried out.

I was reminded of General Grant's assurance of my name being known to the ends of the earth, when a few weeks later I received a letter addressed to "Mr. Barnum, America," and posted in Noulmein, British Burma, on January 15th. It had been stamped seven times on its face and back and bore the marks of the Post Office of Bombay, Brandisi, the "Sea Post Office," and the Post Office in New York, whence it was transmitted to Bridgeport. The envelope contained two letters in the Burmese language, to the attendants on the White Elephant. *The Daily Standard* remarked:

The fact that the address was simply "Mr. Barnum. America." goes to show that our fellow-townsman is *the* Mr. Barnum, not only of the United States, or North America but of the world.

CHAPTER LIV.

ALICE.

Our Great Barnum-London Show opened its season at Madison Square Garden, New York City, Monday, March 16th, 1885, and closed at Newburg, NY., Saturday, October 24th, whence it was shipped directly to Winter Headquarters, Bridgeport, Conn. In the course of 192 days, exclusive of Sundays, it traveled 8,471 miles and exhibited in New York, Pennsylvania, New Jersey, Connecticut, Massachusetts, Rhode Island, Maine, New Brunswick, New Hampshire, Vermont, and the Provinces of Quebec and Ontario, Canada. The net profits were larger than those of the previous year.

The first event of note during the season— and a most lamentable one — occurred at Nashua, N. H., on Saturday afternoon, July 18th, when "Albert," a very large and treacherous Asiatic elephant, attacked James McCormick, one of the keepers, inflicting internal injuries, which resulted in death the next day. For this, and to present further possible loss of life, Albert was sentenced to death, and executed in a ravine in the suburbs of Keene, N. H., on Monday, July 20. After he had been chained to four large trees, and the location of his heart and brain marked with chalk, thirty-three members of the Keene Light Guard were marshalled in line at sixteen paces, and, at the word of command, discharged a volley into the huge culprit with such accuracy of aim that he fell dead, without a struggle. Albert was worth 810,000. His remains were presented to the Smithsonian Institute, Washington, D. C.

On Tuesday, Sept. 10th, at St. Thomas, Ontario, Canada, occurred a universally announced and regretted tragedy, by which the Show suffered a great and irreparable loss. At about 9 o'clock on the evening of that day, Jumbo, the biggest, noblest, most famous, popular, and valuable of beasts, was killed. "While being led along the main line of the Grand Trunk Railway to his car, an unexpected special freight train rushed upon him. There was no time for escape, and the locomotive struck Jumbo with terrific force. The engine was badly broken and derailed, and Jumbo's skull fractured and internal injuries inflicted by his huge body being crushed between the freight train and a train of show cars standing on an adjacent track. He died in a few moments. The dwarf clown elephant, "Tom Thumb," had a leg broken, but has since recovered, retaining only an interesting little limp as a souvenir of his narrow escape. The death of Jumbo was cabled all over the world, and, for the time, almost monopolized public attention, both at home and abroad. I received hundreds of telegrams and letters of sympathy. The *London Pall-Mall Gazette*, one of the leading English newspapers, referred editorially to the event as follows:

Mr. Barnum has, of course, been interviewed respecting the death of Jumbo, and the great showman, with that peculiar repose in faith which is one of his strongest characteristics, keeps on believing that Jumbo's death may prove a trump card yet. "The loss is tremendous," says Mr. Barnum, "but such a trifle never disturbs my nerves. Have I not lost \ million dollars by fires, and half as much by other financial misfortunes? but long ago I learned that to those who mean right and try to do right, there are no such 'things as real misfortunes. On the other hand, to such persons, all apparent evils are blessings in disguise."

My first thought was of the many thousands who were counting on seeing the giant beast, the largest living creature in the world.

Fortunately, in the case of Jumbo, science achieved a substantial victory over death. Professor Henry A. Ward, the distinguished head of Ward's Natural Science Establishment at Rochester, N.Y. was for many months engaged in the labor of preserving Jumbo's form, and also preparing his skeleton for exhibition. This great work has been successfully concluded, and the public can now look upon Jumbo as majestic and natural as life, while beside him stands the prodigious framework of massive bones which sustained the vast weight of his 'flesh.

So many letters have been received by me from all parts of the world, asking the exact size of the lamented Jumbo, that I am impelled to print the measurements made by Professor H. A. Ward.

Jumbo's Size.

Neck— Smallest circumference	11 feet, 6 inches.
Body— Circumference at shoulders	16 feet, 4 inches.
Circumference at middle	18 feet.
Circumference at hind legs	17 feet.
Fore legs—	
Circumference of leg 3 feet above sole of foot	3 feet, 10 inches.
Circumference of leg 5½ feet above sole of foot	5 feet, 7 inches.
Hind legs—	
Circumference of leg 2 feet above sole of foot	3 feet.
Circumference of leg 4 feet above sole of foot	4 feet, 8 inches.
Length of tail	4 feet, 6 inches.
Length in all	14 feet.
Height to shoulder	12 feet.
Weight	7 tons.

Soon after Jumbo's death, I succeeded in purchasing from the Directors of the Zoological Society's Garden, London, the great African Elephant "Alice," for sixteen years the companion and so-called "wife" of the great Jumbo. Alice, it will be remembered, was so sorrowfully excited when my agent attempted to remove Jumbo, February, 1882, that her groans and trumpetings frightened the wild beasts in the great "Zoo" into such howlings and roarings as were heard a mile away. When Jumbo was killed the English newspapers called Alice "Jumbo's widow," and several of the illustrated weeklies gave pictures of her wearing her "widow's cap."

Alice joined the Greatest Show on Earth in the early days of her widowhood and was exhibited side by side with the skeleton and stuffed hide of Jumbo. This pathetic juxtaposition did not apparently affect her spirits. The dead Jumbo and the living Alice were among the most interesting features of the show season of 1886, both at the Madison Square Garden, from April 1st to April 24th, and in New York,

Pennsylvania, Maryland, District of Columbia, Virginia. Ohio, Kentucky, Indiana, Tennessee, Michigan, Illinois, Iowa, Wisconsin, Minnesota, Nebraska, Missouri, Kansas, Georgia, South Carolina and North Carolina. The show, as usual, was larger and better than ever before, and its financial success proportionate. This was the first visit of the great show to the Southern States, where it was received with the greatest enthusiasm. It visited, during its season of 1886, 21 States and 144 cities, traveled 10,447 miles, and gave 344 performances. Its longest single run was from Springfield, Mo., to Memphis, Tenn., 285 miles.

In pursuance of my custom of visiting my Great Show at such places as are railroad centers, where I know thousands will come in by excursion trains, I last year met the show at Erie, Pa. I did not make myself known (for I like to mingle with the crowd incognito, and get information and pleasure listening to the various remarks, and especially criticisms, about the different details of the show) but seated myself among the audience, surrounded by the country people. It was a great satisfaction to witness their delight at the various exhibitions brought into the arena. One old farmer and his wife, who sat on the seat in front of me, attracted my attention.

"I declare, Sally," says the man, "I ain't seen a circus since I was twenty-one. I never did think it possible to do such wonderful things as I have seen here today."

"I have never," replied Sally, "seen a circus since I was a gal. But I was determined to see Barnum's, I had heard so much about it. It certainly beats all I had ever dreamt of."

"After all," said the husband, "'there is one thing I would give more to see than the whole show, and that is Barnum himself."

, "Well, perhaps you may see him," replied the wife, "they say he sometimes goes with his show." "I hope I will get a look at him," said the husband. After a while, a young rider about three-and-twenty years of age, a perfect athlete and equestrian, came into the ring, riding four bare-backed horses. They were very spirited animals, and they went through their various evolutions with such perfection and celerity as to bring repeated thunders of applause. Presently the youthful rider turned a somersault, alighted upon his head, and in that position, with his heels in the air, rode several times around the ring. All were wondering at this extraordinary feat, when my old farmer friend jumped to his feet, wild with excitement, swung his hat in the air and exclaimed, "I'll bet five dollars that's Barnum. There ain't another man in America who can do that but Barnum." I did not disabuse his mind. He felt that he had gotten his money's worth, and I was satisfied.

During the six weeks of the exhibition in New York, I was a constant visitor in the afternoons and an occasional one in the evenings, at which latter times I renewed many old acquaintanceships. When it was not possible to attend both, I always gave the preference to the afternoon performances, so as to meet as many as possible of my little friends and patrons, to whose amusement and happiness it is such a pleasure to minister. To me there is no picture so beautiful as ten thousand smiling, bright-eyed, happy children; no music so sweet as their clear ringing laughter. That I have had power, year after year, by providing innocent amusement for the little ones, to create such pictures, to evoke such music, is my proudest and happiest reflection. Often, as I walked through the Madison Square Garden, I was the recipient of spontaneous bursts of applause and clapping of little hands from the multitude of children present. These incidents are among the pleasantest of my life and never to be forgotten. The show left the city for its annual traveling season and traveled through the following states, first going to Brooklyn, New Jersey, Pennsylvania, Delaware, New York, Connecticut, Massachusetts, Maine, New Hampshire, Vermont, Rhode Island, back to New York State, through Canada, then into New York State again, Pennsylvania, and lastly New Jersey, closing the season in Hoboken, on October 22, 1887. It was a most satisfactory season financially, although not quite as extensive as formerly. In its travels the show visited 175 cities, covering over 10,500 miles of territory and meeting with but few accidents, and none of any consequence. From Hoboken all the animals and material were safely transported to the winter quarters at Bridgeport.

At the close of the season, Messrs. Hutchinson, Cole and Cooper, feeling a desire for more leisurely lives than the terms of our partnership permitted, and being possessed of fortunes large enough to gratify all reasonable tastes, withdrew from the firm, with my free consent, and the show property was housed for the winter with myself and Mr. James A. Bailey as equal partners and proprietors, and under the name of the Barnum & Bailey Show.

The sad news of Jenny Lind's death in London November 2, 1887, news which flashed across the world awakening universal sorrow and regret, appealed peculiarly to me. It was not only that the dead songstress was associated with one of the most successful business enterprises of my life, and one of which I am particularly pleased, but from the time of our first association I conceived for the woman and the artist a warm regard which was not impaired by any subsequent events. Her impulses were always good, and if the somewhat abrupt termination of her engagement with me was not in keeping with the fine sense of justice which ordinarily regulated her actions, the blame must rest on her interested advisers, not on Jenny Lind.

In the years that have passed since then we have each held ourselves ready to do the other any friendly service possible and have taken a mutual pleasure in recalling the many humorous and pathetic incidents of our concert season. I remember the glorious voice of the Nightingale, not alone in the raptures of unrivalled singing, but low and soft, with pitying tender words, as she sought to comfort one in trouble; or ringing out in the hearty laughter of blithe and vigorous young womanhood. From my very heart came the words of sympathy I sent to her devoted husband, and from his, I am sure, came the message he cabled from Malvern, England, where he had just laid the body of his worshipped wife:

P. T. Barnum, New York:

Fully appreciate your condolences, coming from one who well knew my beloved wife, and was always remembered by her with sincere regard.

Otto Goldschmidt.

So dies away the last echo of the most glorious voice the world has ever heard.

CHAPTER LV.

THE CHURCH AND CIRCUS.

Years ago, no two institutions were more actively antagonistic than the Church and Circus. The former waged fierce and uncompromising war against the latter, the Methodist Church going so far as to make it a part of their discipline that attendance at a circus entailed forfeiture of membership. That the Church should ever tolerate, patronize or even recognize as an educator the circus was a possibility that probably entered into the dreams of no man but myself, and perhaps no man but myself believed it possible to organize a circus which should respect the Church and all pertaining to it.

In those days the circus was very justly the object of the Church's adversions. Its spectacular attractions consisted principally of six to ten entree horses, with riders; two fairly good equestrians, whose standing feats on horseback were made on a broad pad saddle; half a dozen apprentice boys, who rode more or less (and rather less than more) and joined in flip-flaps, hand-springs and, in the afterpiece, "The Tailor of Tarn worth " or "Pete Jenkins," in which drunken characters were represented and broad jokes, suited to the groundlings, were given. Its fun consisted of the clown's vulgar jests, emphasized with still more vulgar and suggestive gestures, lest providentially the point might be lost. Educational features the circus of that day had done. Its employees were mostly of the 'rowdy element, and it had a following of card-sharpers, pick- pockets and swindlers generally, who Mere countenanced by some of the circus proprietors, with whom they shared their ill-gotten gains. Its advent was dreaded by all law-abiding people, who knew that with it would inevitably cause disorder, drunkenness and riot. It will scarcely be believed that it was the custom of most of such circuses to engage in advance the firemen of the town they proposed to visit to help to protect the circus company against possible attacks of the rabble, who were apt to be belligerently indignant when too outrageously victimized. Some circus proprietors paid no salary to their ticket-sellers, but let them cheat it out of their customers by giving them short change in the rush and excitement which usually prevailed around the ticket wagon.

THE MISSION OF THE CIRCUS.

Everyone in these enlightened days concedes that human nature imperatively demands amusement and recreation. The childish mind to which all the world is yet fresh and interesting and the jaded brain of the adult call with equal insistence for "something new and strange." Granted the necessity of amusements and the desirability of their being morally clean and healthful and instructive, the provider of such entertainments is a public benefactor and may reasonably ask for his wares the countenance of the Church.

The so-called circus of today, with, I regret to say, some exceptions, is a widely different affair from that of the past. When under proper management it is decorous and orderly in operation and composed of features which appeal to all ages, classes and conditions. While modestly submitting to bear the generic title of circus, a genuine tent exhibition under tint name must comprise a menagerie and museum, the accumulating of which necessitated a diligent searching of the whole earth at an incredible pecuniary outlay. In the proper circus of today the athlete demonstrates the perfection of training of which the human body is capable. His feats of strength and graceful agility pleases the understanding as well as the eye, and if the average small boy does stand on his head and practice turning "hand-springs " and "flip-flaps" with exasperating persistence for three weeks running after going to the circus his physique will be all the better for it. The juggler shows the marvelous precision and nicety of touch which can be acquired by patient practice. In the real circus of today the intelligent lover of horse-flesh will find the finest specimens of the equine race trained to do almost anything but talk. There the scientific mind is attracted by such strange examples of mechanism as the talking machine, an ingenious duplicate of the structure of the human throat, giving forth under manipulation a very human, if not very sweet, voice. The ethnologist finds gathered together for his leisurely inspection representatives of notable and peculiar tribes, civilized and savage, from far distant lands— types which otherwise he would never see, as they can only be sought in their native countries at the risk of life, and at an expenditure of time and money possible to very few. The menagerie of wild beasts, birds and reptiles — comprising every curious specimen of animal life from the denizens of the torrid African jungle to those of the Polar-regions— form a study that will impart more valuable information in two hours than can be obtained from reading books on zoology in a year.

THE MORALITY OF THE EMPLOYEES.

The morality of a genuine circus troupe compares favorably with that of any equal number of any other profession or trade. Many of them are educated and intelligent; most are loyal to strong family affections and to such domesticity as is attainable while traveling, For the rest, they are obliged to behave well. The circus proprietor has a more complete jurisdiction over his employees than any pastor over his congregation. "Would any clergyman dare to punish profanity by fine and drunkenness by expulsion? which is exactly what the best type of circus proprietor can do and does. He has the whip hand and retains during the season a proportion of the employee's salary, which he receives at the end of the season if his record is good, not otherwise. Business interests compel strict discipline, and who shall say that the employee who is compelled to behave well is not, at the end of the season, somewhat the better for eight months of compulsory sobriety, civility and orderly living?

The best circus of today is not a fair mark for the Church's hostility, and while the circus has advanced in merit, the Church has no less grown in tolerance. In my capacity of circus proprietor, I have been the recipient of many flattering and amusing amenities on the part of the Church. As, for instance, when on Sunday evening, May 21, 1882, I entered the Church of the Messiah, New York City, Rev. Robert Collyer, pastor, and quietly took a back seat only to find the keen clear eyes of the preacher fixed upon me, and to hear his resonant voice announce, "I see P.T. Barnum in a back pew of this church, and I invite him to come forward and take a seat in my family pew. Mr. Barnum always gives me a good seat in his circus and I want to give him as good in my church." I thought the reverend gentleman had the courage of his convictions to a most unusual degree, and I was grateful to his congregation for the gravity with which they listened to this very remarkable "pulpit notice" and made way for me, with some embarrassment, as I took the prominent seat so peremptorily indicated.

Again, last summer, a few days before my great show was to visit St. Albans, Va, I received a letter signed by the clergy of that town reminding me that my organization was to arrive among them on Sunday morning early, and asking that I would give orders that none of the paraphernalia, wagons, etc. should be in transit between the railroad depot and the show grounds during the hours of divine service. I was punctilious in seeing that their very reasonable request was respected. Being in St. Albans myself that Sunday, I received, with my company, printed invitations to attend a prominent church. I, at least, went, and heard a very good sermon, and the preacher did not take the occasion to decry the calling I represented, as happened to Miss Emma Abbot recently.

The Methodist said:

Barnum's Greatest Show on Earth, which we have visited at the American Institute in this city, is entirely worthy of public patronage. It is amusing, interesting and instructive.

The Christian Union said:
The delighted public has once more an opportunity of enjoying that Great Moral and Instructive Exhibition which Mr. P. T. Barnum has for a generation or two, and for a very moderate money consideration, innocently pleased and educated amusement-loving America.

The Independent said:

Barnum claims that his show is the Great Moral and Instructive Exhibition— and Barnum tells the truth. All the world says so.

Perhaps my experience has been exceptionally fortunate, but I am convinced that the Church and my circus, at least, are today on very good terms.

A secular recognition of my Great Show as an educator — a recognition of which I am very proud— is contained in the following letter:

UNITED STATES NATIONAL MUSEUM.
under the direction of The Smithsonian Institution,

Washington, May 1, 1882.
Dear Mr. Barnum: Will you do us the favor to allow Mr. Clark Mills to make a face- mask of your countenance from which to prepare a bust for the National Museum, to be placed in our series of representations of men who have distinguished themselves for what they have done as promoters of the natural sciences.

Very truly yours,
SPENCER BAIRD.

And my generous foe, Mr. Henry Bergh, the well-known and respected president of "The Society for the Prevention of Cruelty to Animals" with whom I have had several tilts, as recorded in these pages), said in a letter to a New York paper in the summer of 1885, I regard Mr. Barnum as one of the most humane and kind-hearted men living. He manages an exhibition which, in view of its vast magnitude and amazing excellence of details, has no equal in the world."

CHAPTER LVI.

MY FIFTH GREAT FIRE.

On November 20, 1887, I was again, and for the fifth time, a heavy loser by fire. About ten o'clock on that night fire broke out in the great animal building of the winter quarters at Bridgeport, Conn., and in spite of strenuous efforts to subdue the flames it was entirely consumed, and so rapidly that there was not time to rescue the animals. Of the herd of thirty-four elephants thirty escaped. One lion, Nimrod, a fine specimen and great favorite, was led out by his keeper. With these exceptions, the entire menagerie perished in the flames. An immense quantity of properties, canvas tents, poles, seats, harness, etc., stored in the second story was also destroyed.

Many thrilling incidents of that night will long remain vividly in the memory of those who witnessed them. A terrified spectator, who did not realize that the released lion would obey the restraining hand of his keeper, tangled in his mane, shot at the beast, which, startled, broke away, outstripped his pursuers and entered a barn some distance from the scene of the conflagration. There he attacked a cow and calf, whose cries brought their owner, a Mrs. Gilligan. Mistaking the lion in the dim light for a huge dog, she stoutly belabored him with a broom-stick, saying, "Shoo! shoo! " The lion kept on making a meal of the cow and calf, but growled such a vigorous objection to being interrupted that the widow retreated precipitately, crying, "A bear! a bear!" A neighbor caught up his gun and ran to her assistance, and, little reckoning what noble game he was slaughtering, through the window of the barn he shot the trapped king of the forest dead.

The elephant, "Grade," rushed into the Sound, where she was found next morning swimming exhaustedly. She died of cold and exposure while being towed to shore. The white elephant determinedly committed suicide. Liberated with the rest of the elephants, he rushed back into the flames. Driven out again and again, each time he returned until the keepers were forced to abandon him to his fate. In the fiercest of the flames he was seen wildly thrashing his trunk in the air, then with one loud cry fell and was seen no more. The fire approached in a weird and picturesque way a very large portrait of myself painted on the end of the building overlooking the N.Y., N. H. & H. Railroad. For many minutes the picture glowed intact in an unbroken frame of flame.

As a strong force of water was suddenly turned into the fire hose, the great coils swelled and writhed and leaped along the ground, and many of the excited on-lookers fled in horror, and told honest stories of the huge boa constrictors that were wandering about seeking whom they might devour. At two o'clock in the morning the telegraphic dispatch telling the dire news reached my rooms at the Murray Hill Hotel, New York, and was received by my wife, who is authority for the following story:

"I roused Mr. Barnum, who turned on his pillow just enough to focus one eye at me as I stood shivering in the chill morning air.

"'What is it?' said he.

"A telegram," said I. "What about it?" said he." "I'll read it to you," said I.

Bridgeport, Nov. 21, 1887.

To P. T. Barnum, Murray Hill Hotel:
    Large animal building entirely consumed. Six horses in ring barn burned, together with entire menagerie except thirty elephants and one lion.

C. R. Brothwell.

"I am very sorry, my dear," said he calmly, "but apparent evils are often blessings in disguise. It is all right."

"With that he rolled back into his original comfortable position and, I give you my word for it, in three minutes was fast asleep."

The loss by this fire was $250,000. Insurance, only $31,000. Many people thought I would be deterred by this disaster from ever collecting another menagerie. Some even surmised that I would give up the show business altogether. But I am not in the show business alone to make money. I feel it my mission, as long as I live, to provide clean, moral and healthful recreation for the public to which I have so long catered, and which has never failed to recognize most generously my efforts. Mr. Bailey was as little dismayed as myself. From all parts of the world dealers in wild animals and our own hunters telegraphed, cabled and wrote what they had to offer us. Eleven days after the fire I found Mr. Bailey intently reading a pile of telegrams and letters and making memoranda. To my inquiry as to what he was doing, he coolly remarked, "I am ordering a menagerie." "What! all in one day?" I ejaculated, somewhat surprised. "Certainly," he replied, "I know from these telegrams just where we can get every animal we want, and in six hours we shall own a much finer menagerie than the one we have lost. "

Apropos of this fire it is a strange coincidence that four of the most famous elephants the world ever saw, elephants which contributed very largely to the reputation and prosperity of my show, have all come to untimely ends. The baby elephant, a most amiable and popular little creature, died April 12, 1886, at the tender age of four years, in the very spot where he was born. Jumbo was killed by a locomotive, and the white elephant and Alice perished tragically in the burning of the Winter Quarters.

The following petition, started without my knowledge, was signed by the mayor, three ex- mayors, bank presidents and cashiers, and more than one thousand of our principal citizens, including all our chief merchants and prominent business men, and I have not heard a dissenting voice:

To Messrs. Barnum & Bailey:
    Gentlemen— The undersigned citizens and business houses of Bridgeport learn with regret that a proposal has been made to remove the Winter Quarters from this city. We respectfully request that such proposal be not entertained by you, but that the Winter Quarters will still remain in this city.

We should consider it a great injury to our city to have you remove, and trust that you will favorably consider our request to remain.

Bridgeport, Conn., Nov. 23, 1887.

BURNING OF WINTER QUARTERS, BRIDGEPORT, CT.

Nearly every newspaper in the world will probably publish an account of my last fire. The hundreds of copies already received from every part of the United States and Canada express sympathy for my losses and admiration for the determination on my part to "die in harness," and hand down to future generations "The Greatest Show on Earth," unimpaired in magnitude and merit. I am proud to say that the most powerful and influential newspaper in the world, *The London Times*, of November 22, 1887, devotes an editorial of more than a column to a complimentary sketch of my career, in which it recognizes mine as an institution of "definite educational value." The *Times* describes me as "the genial showman, favorably known in both hemispheres," and among other pleasant things also says:

"It would not be easy to forget the promptitude and energy with which one disaster after another was repaired as soon as sustained, with which the loss of some central object of interest was made good by the discovery of another, and the way, in short, in which many of the qualities which adorn a general or a statesman were displayed, in no insignificant degree, in an undertaking so humble as the conducting of a show. Madame Jenny Lind, who probably, notwithstanding her magnificent voice, owed a large measure of her popularity in America to Mr. Barnum's management, always bore testimony to the absolute integrity and honor of his dealings with her.

We confess to a very friendly feeling for Mr. Barnum, and trust that his menagerie will soon rise from its ashes, and that the catastrophe by which it has been dispersed may furnish the means of rendering the successor still more attractive than the original."

My well-beloved City of Bridgeport, at this writing the second in the state, bids fair soon to become the first in population, as it has long been in enterprise. Important factors in its almost unprecedented growth and prosperity are its beautiful position on the shore of Long Island Sound and its desirable location with respect to the railroads. On the direct line of the Consolidated R. R. from New York to Boston, via Hartford (tapping the Boston & Albany R. R. at Springfield, Mass.), also via New London & Providence; it is also the terminus of the Housatonic and Naugatuck Railroads, both of which lines pass through fertile valleys, whose inexhaustible water-power feeds innumerable manufactories. Eighty-two passenger trains and thirty-five freight trains arrive in the Bridgeport depot every twenty-four hours, and three steamboats ply daily between New York and Bridgeport, besides freight steam propellers. There is also daily steamboat communication with Port Jefferson, L. I.

From the time I first settled in Bridgeport, forty years ago, when its inhabitants numbered only six thousand, I have been, by public and private enterprises, closely identified with its growth. For nearly forty years I have been opening streets, planting trees, filling swamps, making docks, and erecting houses and factories in Bridgeport. As those persons who own the houses they live in are generally the best citizens, since they feel the responsibilities of householders and taxpayers, I sell them lots on credit, and build them small, convenient houses, my condition being that they shall furnish one-third of the cost of the houses alone, repaying the rest in easy installments, covering a period of ten or a dozen years, if they desire it.

The Bridgeport Hospital was inaugurated November 11, 1884. His Excellency William B. Harrison, Governor of the State, and the Mayors of all the cities in Connecticut were among the numerous distinguished guests, including prominent physicians from New York and elsewhere. A banquet, music and speeches occupied four hours. As president of this noble institution I made the opening speech and congratulated the audience on being present at this dedication of a Church, the M Church of Good Works/' where the Good Samaritan stood far above priest or levite, and where persons of all creeds could worship in harmony and love.

On the 16th of December, 1884, the Mayor and Common Council of Bridge- port passed a vote of thanks for one thousand dollars placed by me in the City Treasury for the purchase annually of two gold medals to be presented to the two students in the "Bridgeport High School" who shall write and pronounce the best two English orations.

The corporation known as the "Bridgeport Hydraulic Company," of which I was president, was unable, in consequence of the rapid growth of the city, to furnish that "abundant supply of pure water" which its charter required, without obtaining it from some other source than the Pequonnock River. By acquiring the rights of Mill River, a stream of great volume and purity, and bringing it through very large pipes some eight miles into the city, Bridge- port has now a water-power whose natural force throws a stream over the tops of its highest buildings, and thus renders the use of fire engines unnecessary. This great blessing will largely enhance the growth and prosperity of our beautiful and thrifty city. Prominent among our finest buildings is the Sea Side Institute, erected by Drs. Oliver and Lucian Warner, as a club-house for the fifteen hundred women employed in their corset factory. Perfectly appointed, with parlors, music-rooms (two Steinway pianos), sewing-rooms, bathrooms, restaurant, class-rooms, library, a great hall accommodating six hundred people (with stage, etc.), this Institute is as unique in elegance as it is in purpose. Mrs. Cleveland, wife of the President of the United States, paid to the Warner Brothers' generous gift the fitting and graceful tribute of signifying her willingness to open the Institute in person. The occasion was a most enjoyable one for the working women, every one of whom Mrs. Cleveland took by the hand, and for the few guests invited, among whom were my wife and myself. Excellent speeches were made by the Rev. Drs. Collyer and Taylor, of New York, and the formal opening of the Institute was greeted with an appreciative enthusiasm well merited by the founders. The beautiful Sea-sid9 Park in Bridgeport, whose beginning twenty years ago I described in Chapter XLV., has now become the most lovely Park which lies on Long Island Sound. On several occasions it has been enlarged by valuable land fronting the Sound presented by me. My last gift of thirty acres at the West end, on which, including the Dyke and original purchase money, I had expended more than fifty thousand dollars, extends the Park boundary to a creek, which in the near future the City of Bridgeport will bridge, thus extending the shore drive to Fairfield, Southport, Westport and Norwalk, a distance of fourteen miles. At an expense of $90,000 I filled up forty-five acres of low, marshy land, owned by me, adjoining the Park, raising it six feet. This expensive improvement has materially enhanced the beauty of the Park and will be a great public benefit

As I close this volume I am more thankful than words can express that my health is preserved, and that I am blessed with a vigor and buoyancy of spirits vouchsafed to but few; but I am by no means insensible to the fact that I have reached the evening of life (which is well lighted, however), and I am glad to know that though this is indeed a beautiful, delightful world to those who have the temperament, the resolution, and the judgment to make it so, yet it happily is not our abiding-place; and that he is unwise who sets his heart so firmly upon its transitory pleasures as to feel a reluctance to obey the call when his Father makes it, to leave all behind and to come up higher, in that Great Future when all that we now prize so highly (except our love to God and man) shall dwindle into insignificance. Waldemere, Bridgeport, Conn., 1888.

POSTSCRIPT.

Appended is the first proclamation of the new firm of Barnum & Bailey:

An Open Letter.

"Waldemere, Bridgeport, Conn., Dec. 1, 1887. Rising, Phoenix-like, from the ashes of my fifth great fire, which only served to illuminate my path of duty as the American people's champion amusement provider, I have taken into equal partnership my energetic and experienced friend and former associate, James A. Bailey. We have enlarged and vastly improved The Greatest Show on Earth, which we propose to establish as a permanence, with a reserve capital of several millions of dollars. We also intend at an early date to establish in all our principal cities great museums of natural and artificial curiosities, to which will be added a spacious lecture room for scientific experiments and historical lectures, panoramas, pantomimes and light entertainments of a pleasing and general nature. The Barnum & Bailey Show will present to this and future generations a World's Fair and a moral School of Object Teaching, of unexampled variety and superior excellence, more amusing, instructive, comprehensive and vast than was ever before seen or dreamed of. It is the pride of my declining years that I am able to give, as the result of my long life of experience and determined effort, that innocent and educational diversion which everyone concedes that human nature imperatively demands.

The public's obedient servant,
PHINEAS T. BARNUM.

MR. BAILEY'S POLICY.

In re-entering the amusement field by becoming Mr. P.T. Barnum's equal and sole partner, and assuming the personal management of the great combined exhibitions bearing our names, I respectfully avail myself of the opportunity afforded to briefly and plainly state the basis upon which they are organized, the principles upon which they will be conducted, and the policy that will, under all circumstances, be rigidly enforced and adhered to.

I have returned to the show business to stay, so long as my health and life are spared, and to do my full share, in not only placing and maintaining the Great Barnum & Bailey World's Fair of Wonders upon a far higher, broader and more liberal plane than was ever attained by any similar enterprise, but to continually enlarge its possessions and strengthen its popularity.

The partnership is not a temporary, but a permanent one, equally binding upon both partners, their heirs, administrators, executors, or assigns; and the death of either of them will in no wise affect the existence and continuation of the show.

It is not an experiment, but a solid, established business enterprise, whose name and character are continuous and permanent.

It will never, under any circumstances, or at any time or place, be divided, and the malicious circulators of libels or slanders to the contrary will be prosecuted and punished to the full extent of the law.

It will be honestly advertised.

The whole of it will always be exhibited in every place, large or small, wherever it is advertised to appear, and in no place will a single feature or act be omitted.

The magnificent free street pageant will never be anywhere curtailed by the omission of a single attraction.

Its menagerie and museum tent will never be taken down at night, until after the conclusion of both the circus and hippodrome performances.

The afternoon and evening performances will invariably be equally complete, perfect and satisfactory, and, under no circumstances, will the evening performance be, in the slightest degree, abbreviated, cut, or neglected; but each and every act thereof will be presented according to the printed program.

The convenience and pleasure of its patrons will be specially considered.

It will be a place which an unattended child can visit with perfect safety.

Its employees will be required to deal fairly and courteously with all, and to answer all proper questions intelligently and politely.

No peddling will be permitted under its tents.

No camp followers, street fakirs, gamblers, or disreputable or intoxicated persons will be tolerated on its grounds.

Everything in the slightest degree calculated to offend or annoy its patrons will be absolutely prohibited. Morality, purity and refinement will be the rule without exception.

I shall always be present to investigate any complaints and to strictly enforce the above regulations, and all others that may be necessary to protect both the public and our own good name.

JAMES A. BAILEY.

Made in the USA
San Bernardino, CA
25 November 2018

THANK YOU FOR READING!

If you enjoyed this book, we would appreciate your customer review on your book seller's website or on Goodreads.

Also, we would like for you to know that you can find more great books like this one at www.CreativeTexts.com

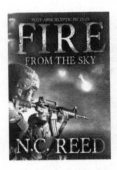

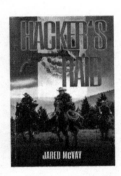

CREATIVE TEXTS PUBLISHERS
CT PUBLISHERS
www.creativetexts.com
PO BOX 50, BARTO, PA 19504